Eighth Edition

INTERNATIONAL ECONOMICS

A Policy Approach

Euro Update

Eighth Edition

INTERNATIONAL ECONOMICS

A Policy Approach

Euro Update

Mordechai E. Kreinin

Michigan State University

University Distinguished Professor

The Dryden Press

Harcourt Brace College Publishers

Fort Worth   Philadelphia   San Diego   New York   Austin   San Antonio
Toronto   Montreal   London   Sydney   Tokyo

Publisher	George Provol
Acquisitions Editor	Gary Nelson
Product Manager	Kathleen Sharp
Developmental Editor	Stacey Sims
Project Editor	Elaine Richards
Art Director	Bill Brammer
Production Manager	Darryl King

Cover image by Bob Asbille Design

ISBN: 0-03-045242-2
Library of Congress Catalog Card Number: 97-66070

Address for orders:
The Dryden Press, 6277 Sea Harbor Drive, Orlando, FL 32887-6777
1-800-782-4479

Address for editorial correspondence:
The Dryden Press, 301 Commerce Street, Suite 3700, Fort Worth, TX 76102

Website address:
http://www.hbcollege.com

THE DRYDEN PRESS, DRYDEN, and the DP logo are registered trademarks of Harcourt Brace & Company.

Printed in the United States of America

9 0 1 2 3 4 5 6 039 9 8 7 6 5 4 3 2 1

The Dryden Press
Harcourt Brace College Publishers

To my daughters
Tamara
Elana
Miriam

The Dryden Press Series in Economics

Baldani, Bradfield, and Turner
Mathematical Economics

Baumol and Blinder
Economics: Principles and Policy
Seventh Edition (also available in micro and macro paperbacks)

Baumol, Panzar, and Willig
Contestable Markets and the Theory of Industry Structure
Revised Edition

Breit and Elzinga
The Antitrust Casebook: Milestones in Economic Regulation
Third Edition

Brue
The Evolution of Economic Thought
Fifth Edition

Edgmand, Moomaw, and Olson
Economics and Contemporary Issues
Fourth Edition

Gardner
Comparative Economic Systems
Second Edition

Gwartney and Stroup
Economics: Private and Public Choice
Eighth Edition (also available in micro and macro paperbacks)

Gwartney and Stroup
Introduction to Economics: The Wealth and Poverty of Nations

Heilbroner and Singer
The Economic Transformation of America: 1600 to the Present
Third Edition

Hess and Ross
Economic Development: Theories, Evidence, and Policies

Hirschey and Pappas
Fundamentals of Managerial Economics: Theories, Evidence, and Policies
Sixth Edition

Hirschey and Pappas
Managerial Economics
Eighth Edition

Hyman
Public Finance: A Contemporary Application of Theory to Policy
Fifth Edition

Kahn
The Economic Approach to Environmental and Natural Resources
Second Edition

Kaserman and Mayo
Government and Business: The Economics of Antitrust and Regulation

Kaufman
The Economics of Labor Markets
Fourth Edition

Kennett and Lieberman
The Road to Capitalism: The Economic Transformation of Eastern Europe and the Former Soviet Union

Kreinin
International Economics: A Policy Approach
Eighth Edition

Lott and Ray
Applied Econometrics with Data Sets

Mankiw
Principles of Economics
(also available in micro and macro paperbacks)

Marlow
Public Finance: Theory and Practice

Nicholson
Intermediate Microeconomics and Its Application
Seventh Edition

Nicholson
Microeconomic Theory: Basic Principles and Extensions
Seventh Edition

Puth
American Economic History
Third Edition

Ragan and Thomas
Principles of Economics
Second Edition (also available in micro and macro paperbacks)

Ranamathan
Introductory Econometrics with Applications
Fourth Edition

Rukstad
Corporate Decision Making in the World Economy: Company Case Studies

Rukstad
Macroeconomic Decision Making in the World Economy: Text and Cases
Third Edition

Samuelson and Marks
Managerial Economics
Second Edition

Scarth
Macroeconomics: An Introduction to Advanced Methods
Third Edition

Stockman
Introduction to Economics
(also available in micro and macro paperbacks)

Walton and Rockoff
History of the American Economy
Eighth Edition

Welch and Welch
Economics: Theory and Practice
Sixth Edition

Yarbrough and Yarbrough
The World Economy: Trade and Finance
Fourth Edition

PREFACE

Although Americans have gained a better understanding of their domestic economy since World War II, knowledge of international economics has remained limited. In recent years, however, international economic matters so frequently occupied the financial headlines that attention has been forced beyond domestic concerns to those of the world market.

Through its eight editions, this book has provided a simplified yet comprehensive analysis of international economic relations, with the fundamental objective of extracting maximum policy insight from a minimum number of theoretical constructs. Written for students with only one or two previous courses in the principles of economics, it is designed primarily as a basic text for a one- or two-term undergraduate sequence in international economics. Although the volume contains analytical tools, the material is arranged so that the theoretical sections may be omitted and the main text used also in policy-oriented noneconomics courses. Finally, the book is useful as supplementary reading for students of international relations and business administration, as well as for economics students in money and banking courses.

The method of presentation has remained unchanged through all editions. Each subject is expounded verbally before any use is made of analytical tools beyond simple supply and demand curves. Whenever technical terms and tools are needed, they are carefully explained. Although the focus is on policy, the necessary theoretical underpinnings are fully presented.

THE EIGHTH EDITION

Part One of the book addresses international trade and commercial policy, while Part Two is devoted to international financial relations. As in previous editions, the two parts are *interchangeable and may be studied in either order.* Each chapter concludes with a chapter *Summary,* a list of *Important Concepts,* and review questions. The appendices, which contain *more complex formulas and theoretical material,* appear at the end of each relevant chapter.

- All topics have been thoroughly updated, and many examples come from the mid-1990s.
- The original arrangement that enabled uninitiated readers to skip over the technical sections without loss of continuity has been retained. These technical sections are now featured as *Additional Insights* boxes and are clearly set apart from the text, allowing instructors to cover important concepts in more detail. However, they may also be skipped without any loss of continuity.

- Relevant bibliographical material is contained in footnotes rather than end-of-chapter notes. This arrangement relates additional readings to specific subsections and makes them useful for instructors who wish to assign term papers.
- Most of the references are selected at a level accessible to undergraduate students. Instructors wishing to assign book reviews will find sources of books dealing with policy matters in the bibliography at the end of this book.
- Sources of widely used statistical information and reviews of current developments are also offered at the end of the book, along with a list of readers for supplementary reading.

New to this Edition

- The Euro update incorporates up-to-date material in an appendix at the end of the book.
  - Chapter 16 is now presented with a detailed discussion of the Euro, the hurdles European countries had to cross, and the international implications of the common currency.
  - Chapter 17 is updated with new material covering the causes and effects of the "Global Financial Crisis of 1997-99."
- Tables, graphs, data, and in-text examples throughout the textbook have been updated to reflect current developments in international trade and finance.
- Chapter 2 now includes a brief discussion of Adam Smith's explanation of trade based on absolute advantage and a simplified version of the "Additional Insights" box on complete specialization.
- In chapter 3, the discussion of the factor proportions model has been simplified and a brief discussion of wage disparity has been added to the coverage of human skills.
- A new Additional Insights box in chapter 4 addresses the case for protection for a single factor of production. Coverage of customs unions includes a 1996 study by the World Bank indicating the danger of trade-diverting in their effects.
- In chapter 6, coverage of older treaties has been reduced to accommodate extended coverage of regional and bilateral relations including economic reforms in eastern Europe and other countries undergoing trade liberalization.
- Chapter 12 expands its coverage on currency boards in light of their growing international importance.
- At the request of reviewers, the discussion of fiscal and monetary policies under alternative exchange-rate regimes in chapter 14 has been converted to an Additional Insights box for greater instructor flexibility.

New topics include:
- The uproar over U.S. efforts to sanction foreign companies with investments in Cuba, Libya, and Iran. p. 231
- Recent tensions between the U.S. and China over intellectual property rights. p. 201
- The Mexican currency crisis of December 1994. p. 472
- The European Union's efforts to reduce its budgetary deficits as a preliminary to adopting the Euro as a single currency and moving to fixed exchange rates by 1999. p. 442
- Japan's challenge of Brazil's content requirement on cars before the World Trade Organization. p. 148
- Recent efforts to establish requirements for a minimum level of European-produced programming on European television. p. 148

Instructor's Manual and Test Bank

This edition of *International Economics* is accompanied by an Instructor's Manual with a test bank. This manual, written by Don Clark of the University of Tennessee-Knoxville, should prove a useful supplement as it summarizes and highlights the key features of the text. The following items are provided for each of the seventeen chapters:

- A brief overview or summary
- An outline of the distinguishing features
- References for outside reading
- Answers to the end-of-chapter questions
- Multiple-choice questions (10–15)

The Dryden Press will provide complimentary supplements or supplement packages to those adoptors qualified under our adoption policy. Please contact your sales representative to learn how you may qualify. If as an adoptor or potential user you receive supplements you do not need, please return them to your sales representative or send them to:

ATTN: Returns Department
Troy Warehouse
465 South Lincoln Drive
Troy, MO 63379

ACKNOWLEDGMENTS

My deep gratitude is due the many professors who took the trouble to write words of encouragement, suggestions, and constructive criticism of previous editions. Special thanks for their many helpful comments go to:

A.K. Barakeh, *University of South Alabama*
W. Max Corden, *Australian National University*
Gerald M. Meier, *Stanford University*
Robert E. Baldwin, *University of Wisconsin*
Franklyn D. Holzman, *Tufts University*
Don Clark, *University of Tennessee-Knoxville*
Philip S. Thomas, *Kalamazoo College*
Lawrence H. Officer, *University of Illinois at Chicago*
Elias Dinopoulos, *University of Florida*
Matthew Martin, *University of Delaware*
Steven Matusz, *Michigan State University*
Sergio Mendez, *Concordia College*
Henry Thompson, *University of Tennessee, Knoxville*
Richard L. Lucier, *Denison University*
Sohrab Behdad, *Denison University*
Gerald V. Egerer, *Sonoma State University*
William J. Baumol, *Princeton University and New York University*
Robert W. Gillespie, *University of Illinois*
Norman N. Mintz, *Columbia University*
Milledge Weathers, *Adrian College*
Alexander Zampieron, *Bentley College*
Louis Green, *San Diego State University*
Michael Connolly, *University of Miami*
Oscar Flores, *Moorhead State University*
Kenneth Louie, *Penn State, Erie*
Thomas Lowinger, *Washington State University*
Robert Gillespie, *University of Illinois*
Abdul Turay, *Radford University*

Special thanks go to the entire book team at The Dryden Press for all their extraordinary help with this edition: Gary Nelson, Stacey Sims, Kathleen Sharp, Elaine Richards, Darryl King, Bill Brammer, and Annette Coolidge. I would also like to thank Erica Lazerow for copyediting this edition.

Last, but not least, I wish to thank Lisa Harmon for her masterful typing of the extensive revisions of this edition.

Mordechai E. Kreinin

Contents

World Trade and the National Economy

T his chapter describes the field of international economics, distinguishing between international and domestic transactions. It then offers a quantitative overview of the importance of international trade to the global and the national economy.

DEFINITION

International economics concerns the flow of commodities, services, and productive factors (capital and labor) across national boundaries. Trade in commodities refers to imports and exports of merchandise. Service transactions involve such activities as shipping, travel, insurance, or tourist services performed by companies of one country for the residents of another. Capital flows represent the establishment of manufacturing plants in foreign countries, or the acquisition of foreign bonds, stocks, and bank accounts. Labor flows describe the international migration of workers.

WHAT IS UNIQUE ABOUT INTERNATIONAL ECONOMICS?

International transactions constitute an extension of domestic transactions. In both cases, trade offers the benefits of **specialization**. Exchanges of goods and services among individuals enable them to specialize in what they do best. Likewise, domestic exchange enables regions of the country to specialize in the same manner. Thus, the exchange of Idaho potatoes, Florida oranges, Washington-produced aircraft, and Michigan-made cars enhances efficiency of production and improves living standards for each of these states. Internationally, U.S. import of German cameras, Japanese cars, and Brazilian coffee, and U.S. export of grains, jet aircraft, and sophisticated computers fosters specialization in the participating countries, thereby producing more than they could without trade and increasing the living standards of all.

The reasons for and the benefits from international transactions are no different from the reasons for and the benefits from domestic transactions: to reap the fruits of increased output from a given amount of resources attendant upon greater specialization.

Why then is it necessary to distinguish between domestic and international economic relations? Why study international economics as a separate field? Because the existence of national boundaries has profound implications for the *conduct* of trade. The following are a few of the differences between domestic and foreign trade that emanate from this fact.

Exchange Rates   Transactions within a country are financed by that country's own currency, usually through the writing of checks. But a universal currency does not exist. Instead, each country issues its own currency. An **exchange rate**—the price of one currency in terms of another—is used to translate values from one currency to another. For example, if the dollar is worth 2 German marks ($1 = 2 D.M.), then a 200 D.M. German camera would cost $100 in the United States, and a $10 million American jet aircraft would be valued at 20 million D.M.s in Germany. Many exchange rates vary from day to day in response to changes in supply and demand conditions in the foreign exchange markets. International transactions require payments or receipts in foreign currencies, and these must be converted to the domestic currency through the exchange rates, which themselves are subject to change. This process introduces risks and complications that are unknown in domestic trade.

Commercial Policies   A national government can introduce a variety of restrictions upon international transactions that cannot be imposed on domestic transactions. These could include

(a) a **tariff**, which is a tax on an imported commodity.
(b) an **import quota,** which places a maximum limitation on the *amount* of the commodity that may enter the country (for example, one million tons of sugar).
(c) a **voluntary export restraint (VER),** where the governments of an importing country and an exporting country (say, the United States and Japan) negotiate a quantitative limitation on the export of a certain commodity. The Japanese government limited automobile shipments to the United States during the years 1981–1986 under such an agreement.

(d) an **export subsidy,** where a government pays exporters a sum of money for each unit of the product they export in order to make them more competitive abroad.

(e) **exchange control,** where a country, such as India, restricts the ability of its citizens to convert their money (rupees) to foreign currencies, such as the U.S. dollar.

Such measures may have profound effects on the economy. Yet they only concern international, not domestic, transactions.

Different Domestic Policies Each country has its own central bank and finance ministry, and hence its own monetary and fiscal policies. These in turn determine its rates of inflation, economic growth, and unemployment. While these policies apply to all regions or states within a country, they vary from one country to another. Consequently, while the rate of inflation is the same throughout the regions of France, it differs between France and Germany. This differential rate not only affects the competitive position between the two countries, but their competition with third countries as well.

Statistical Data We know more about the composition, size, and direction of international trade than we do about the same features of domestic transactions. Since there are no "border checkpoints" along state lines to compile such information, it is uncertain what particular commodities and their quantities are being traded between New York and California. But when a shipment of merchandise leaves or enters the country, the exporter or importer must fill out an export or import declaration describing the shipment in terms of its weight, value, destination or source, and other characteristics. From these trade declarations, which are required by all countries, detailed statistics can be compiled on international trade that are not available for domestic trade.

Relative Immobility of Productive Factors Factors of production are much more mobile domestically than they are internationally. No one can prevent workers from moving between Virginia and Texas. But immigration restrictions, language barriers, and different social customs constitute formidable barriers to people's mobility between countries. While capital can move between countries much more easily than labor, it is also more mobile domestically than internationally.

Marketing Considerations Differences in demand patterns, sales techniques, market requirements, and the like make international transactions more difficult than domestic ones. Many Japanese sleep in futon beds and have little use for American sheets and pillowcases. American exports of electrical appliances to Europe must be adjusted for the different electric current. And automobiles exported to the United Kingdom or Japan require steering wheels on the right side of the vehicle, as the British and Japanese drive on the left side of the road.

In sum, exporters often need to make special adjustments in their product design in order to penetrate a foreign market.

Summary   The preceding six areas of significant difference between domestic and foreign transaction refer to the conduct of trade, rather than its rationale and benefits. They highlight important and unique features that require their own special field of international economics.

INTERNATIONAL TRANSACTIONS—AN EMPIRICAL GLIMPSE

International economics is the oldest branch of economic study, dating back to David Hume (1752), Adam Smith (1778), and David Ricardo (1817). Interest in this field has expanded in recent years, partly as a result of the vast growth of international transactions.

A case in point is the phenomenal and uninterrupted expansion of international merchandise trade. The value of world exports grew from $108 billion in 1958 to $5 trillion in 1995. The greatest increase was in the trade of manufactured products, followed by minerals and agricultural products. In 1995 the United States was the world leader in merchandise transactions, accounting for 11.6 percent of world exports and 15.0 percent of world imports. Germany and Japan followed as the second and third largest traders (table 1.1.A). Table 1.1.B shows the network of total exports by major areas in 1995. Nearly a third of world trade is conducted among European countries. While most of the exports of manufactured products originate in the industrial countries, the manufacturing exports of certain developing countries (especially Asia) have grown rapidly in recent years.

The figures in the previous paragraph are expressed in current dollars. Thus the increases in trade value over time consist of price increases as well as expansions in the real volume of trade. The real volume of world exports grew at an annual rate of 6 percent between 1950 and 1994, while global output rose at an annual rate of 4 percent. Thus during these 45 years, real world output was multiplied 5 1/2 times, while real world trade was multiplied 14 times, showing increased openness of many economies to trade. The process continued in 1995 when the global volume of export increased by 8 percent while output grew by 3 percent.

Commodity trade is not the only component of international transactions that has expanded rapidly. As the share of services in GDP (services make up two-thirds of GDP in the industrial countries) rises, so do international service transactions. The United States is the leading exporter and importer of commercial services—shipping, tourism, travel, banking and insurance, communications, professional services, and so forth—in the world (table 1.1.C);

TABLE 1.1.A

Leading Exporters and Importers in World Merchandise Trade, 1995 (Billion Dollars and Percentage Share)

Exporters	Value	Share of World Export	Importers	Value	Share of World Import
United States	583.9	11.6%	United States	771.3	14.9%
Germany	508.5	10.1%	Germany	443.2	8.6%
Japan	443.1	8.8%	Japan	336.0	6.5%
France	286.2	5.7%	France	274.5	5.3%
United Kingdom	242.1	4.8%	United Kingdom	265.3	5.1%
Total World	**5,033**	**100%**	**Total World**	**5,170**	**100%**

TABLE 1.1.B

Network of World Trade, 1995 (Billion Dollars)

Origin	North America	Latin America	Western Europe	Asia	Other
North America	279	100	148	211	36
Latin America	108	47	39	22	7
Western Europe	162	53	1510	211	215
Asia	310	29	214	662	63
Other	39	7	176	101	63

TABLE 1.1.C

Leading Exporters and Importers in World Trade in Commercial Services, 1995 (Billion Dollars and Percentage Share)

Exporters	Value (f.o.b.)	Share of World Export	Importers	Value (c.i.f.)	Share of World Import
United States	188.2	16.1%	United States	131.6	11.2%
France	95.1	8.1%	Japan	121.6	10.3%
Italy	70.2	6.0%	Germany	119.2	10.1%
Germany	68.8	5.9%	France	76.4	6.5%
United Kingdom	66.4	5.7%	Italy	69.0	5.8%
Japan	63.9	5.5%	United Kingdom	55.3	4.7%
Total World	**1,170**	**100%**	**Total World**	**1,180**	**100%**

Source: WTO *Annual Report*, 1996

global trade in these services approached $1.2 trillion in 1955. Finally, there has been a massive increase in private capital flows, with transfers of capital between countries amounting to many trillions of dollars each year. Direct foreign investment, involving the establishment of manufacturing plants in foreign countries, is also growing rapidly. The global "stock" of direct foreign investment has been estimated at about $2.6 trillion, with the United States being the leading "host" country, followed by the U.K., France, and China in that order. A truly global marketplace is emerging for the production and distribution of most goods and services, a process often referred to as globalization.

These trading relationships are experiencing profound changes with the transformation of the global economy. Changes in Eastern Europe include the division of the Soviet Union into 15 constituent countries; the emergence of Eastern European countries independent from the former U.S.S.R.; the replacement of communist dictatorships by democratic rule; and the gradual replacement (in former socialist states) of central planning by capitalist market economies. These countries are labeled *transitional economies*, in reference to their transition from central planning to market economies. As Eastern Europe becomes integrated into the world trading and financial system, its share in world trade (under 3 percent in 1995) is likely to rise.

Far outstripping the growth rate of the industrial countries, the Asian Pacific Rim countries are developing rapidly with annual GDP growth of 6 to 10 percent. They include China (particularly its coastal regions) where the government of the population numbering 1.2 billion has adopted a market economic system along with political dictatorship; the Newly Industrial Economies (NIEs) of South Korea, Taiwan, Hong Kong, and Singapore, which are on the threshold of a fully developed status; and the remaining Asian countries, such as the ASEAN[1] bloc, in which government regulations are being stripped away and replaced by market forces. Even the Indian economy is beginning to stir, with its relaxation of government controls.

Many Latin American countries have adopted democratic governments, and are pursuing sensible macroeconomic policies while allowing market forces to replace government regulations—thus accelerating their growth rates. Only the African continent appears to be languishing. But in general, it is quite likely that in the next century the distinction between developed and underdeveloped countries will become blurred—significantly affecting global trade and investment flows.

FOREIGN TRADE IN THE NATIONAL ECONOMY

Aggregate Measures   The analysis of international economic relations in subsequent chapters will demonstrate that the United States is a pivotal

---

[1]Including the Philippines, Thailand, Indonesia, and Malaysia.

TABLE 1.2	Gross Domestic Product of the United States (Billion Dollars)			
		1981	1997	
Personal Consumption Expenditures		1,843	5,494	
Gross Private Domestic Investment		472	1,256	
Government Purchases of Goods and Services		597	1,454	
Net Exports of Goods and Services		26	-93	
Exports		367		965
Imports		341		1,059
Total GDP		2,938	8,111	

Source: *Survey of Current Business*

member in the world trading and financial community. Two features of its economy make this country ideally suited for such a central role: It is simultaneously a giant among nations, and a **relatively closed economy.** The first feature refers to the fact that the U.S. gross domestic product (GDP) makes up a fifth of global output and it is the leading trading nation. As a consequence, whatever occurs in the United States may have profound implications for the rest of the world. For example, a recession in the United States lowers its demand for imported materials and other goods, which may cause problems for exporting countries that rely on the U.S. market. Thus, American economic policies that affect the country's trade position also impact its trading partners.

On the other hand, the term "closed economy" refers to the fact that the United States is **relatively** independent of foreign trade. Because of its size and the diversity of its resources, the American economy can satisfy most consumer wants and national needs with minimum reliance on foreign trade. This contrasts with other industrial economies in which foreign trade plays a significant, if not a dominant, role. Thus, merchandise exports constitute 11 percent of GDP in the United States (up from about 4 percent in the 1960s), 15 percent of GDP in Japan, between a quarter and a third of GDP in the large European countries, and around one half of GDP in the small European countries. The United States is therefore more immune than other countries to disturbances originating abroad.

In 1997, U.S. gross domestic product amounted to $8,111 billion, while exports of *goods and services* measured 12 percent of GDP (table 1.2).

Disaggregation Yet this should not be construed to mean that the American economy is independent of foreign trade in either a quantitative or qualitative sense. The quantitative importance of foreign trade cannot be judged solely on broad aggregative measures, because its impact is not

TABLE 1.3	*Merchandise Trade by Sectors, 1995 (Billion Dollars)*					
	Exports			**Imports**		
Sector	U.S.	Japan	Germany	U.S.	Japan	Germany
Food	59	2	25	37	54	43
Raw materials	22	2	6	16	21	12
Mining products	25	7	18	84	76	46
Ores and other materials	7	1	3	6	11	6
Fuels	10	2	4	62	54	28
Nonferrous metals	7	4	9	15	11	12
Manufactures						
Iron and steel	8	18	17	15	6	15
Chemicals	62	30	69	42	24	42
Semi-manufactures	33	20	43	53	16	37
Office and telecommunications equipment	98	107	31	140	38	43
Automotive products	52	81	85	108	12	45
Other machinery and transport equipment	130	124	68	110	25	64
Textiles and clothing	14	8	21	52	25	36
Other consumer goods	54	34	43	87	31	42
Total manufactures	450	422	446	608	178	324
Total trade	**583**	**443**	**509**	**771**	**336**	**443**

Source: WTO *Annual Report*, 1996, Vol. III, Appendix tables

spread evenly over all sectors of the economy. A substantial portion of GDP is made up of such items as construction activities and personal services—many of which never enter international trade and are therefore termed **nontraded goods**—that are not directly affected by changes in trade policies. Most of the direct effects of such changes are concentrated in the commodity-producing sectors.

But even sectoral figures are too aggregative. Foreign trade among industrial nations is extremely specialized, and the manufacturing sector in particular contains variations that are not reflected in the sectoral average. In assessing the role of foreign trade in individual industries, it is customary to examine the ratio of exports to output and the ratio of imports to consumption. There are numerous industries in which one or the other of these ratios is very high, at times upward of 15 to 20 percent. Such industries are often termed, respectively, **export-** and **import-competing** industries. In the United States, steel and motor vehicles are examples of import-competing industries with imports exceeding a quarter of U.S. consumption in recent years; whereas aircraft, chemicals, and office equipment are examples of export industries. Thus, there are industries in which foreign trade plays an important role.

TABLE 1.4	U.S. Merchandise Trade with Major Trading Areas, 1995 (Billion Dollars)			
	Primary Products		Manufactures	
Trading Partner	U.S. Exports	U.S. Imports	U.S. Exports	U.S. Imports
Canada	19	48	107	100
Japan	23	3	41	124
Western Europe	30	25	104	125
Mexico	9	15	38	48
China	3	2	8	46
World	134	163	450	608

Source: WTO *Annual Report*, 1996, Vol. II

Table 1.3 shows foreign trade by main sectors. In 1995 U.S. merchandise exports and imports amounted to $583 billion and $771 billion respectively. The United States is a net exporter of farm products, chemicals, certain types of machinery, and aircraft (its biggest single exporter is the Boeing Corporation); and a net importer of fuels, iron and steel, motor vehicles, and certain consumer goods. Its main trading partner is Canada, followed by Japan (table 1.4).

Similar tabulations can be constructed for each trading nation. Consider Japan: Devoid of natural resources, Japan imports most of the raw materials and other primary products it requires (table 1.3). On the other hand, Japan imported only $178 billion of manufactured goods and exported $422 billion in 1995. Within the manufacturing sector, Japan had sizable trade surpluses (exports greater than imports) in motor vehicles, and certain types of machinery and office equipment. Canada, well endowed with land and natural resources, had a sizable trade surplus in primary products but a deficit in manufactured goods. Finally, all the European countries have a combined deficit in primary products and a surplus in manufactured goods, but much of their trade is among themselves. Table 1.3 shows the relevant German statistics.

Qualitative Considerations   Nor can the United States be considered independent of foreign trade in the qualitative sense. To say that imports of goods and services amount to 12 percent of the gross domestic product is to understate their importance in several respects. American imports contain important primary commodities that cannot be produced domestically but are crucial for numerous productive processes. Their absence would considerably curtail domestic production, lower consumer satisfaction, and interfere with the nation's ability to meet its goals. Over 70 percent of U.S.

agricultural imports are "complementary commodities"—commodities such as tropical products that cannot easily be grown in the United States. Likewise, the absence of imported fuel could have severe adverse effects on the nation's output and environment. In the future, the same may apply to other basic materials. Although most manufactured imports compete directly with domestically produced substitutes, foreign trade widens consumer choice through diversification of available products, and expands producers' horizons in marketing their products and investing their capital. Opening the economy to the fresh winds of foreign competition also adds to its viability by curbing domestic monopoly power and spurring technological progress as well as product improvement. And foreign imports can also be used to curtail inflationary pressures at home. Countries often relax import restrictions to cope with domestic inflation by increasing supply. Moreover, the external trade position of the country influences aggregate output and income, because exports add to aggregate demand and many imports replace domestic production. Finally, American imports amounting to 3/4 trillion dollars constitute an important source of dollar earnings for many countries whose stability is vital to the United States. Similar considerations can be articulated with respect to exports. Thus, it would be misleading to suggest that the diminution of foreign trade would work no hardship on the American economy.

Summary   These are important qualifications, but they do not change the position of the United States *relative* to that of other countries. Comparatively speaking, this country is indeed a giant among nations, and although the United States has become increasingly open to foreign trade, it is still a closed economy compared to other countries. Whatever happens in the American economy has more important repercussions abroad than foreign developments have upon the United States. And this dual characteristic qualifies the United States to play a pivotal role in the world economy. However, the rapid growth of other economies is causing a gradual shift in economic power from a single hegemony (the United States) to a tripolar system driven by Japan, Europe, and the United States.

FORUMS FOR TRADE AND MONETARY ISSUES

Following are the principal organizations and groups of countries that deal with the world's trade and financial problems.

The World Trade Organization (WTO)   Made up of 120 countries that account for most of world trade, this multilateral trade organization provides a framework for trade negotiations and lays down ground rules for the conduct of international trade. It superseded the General Agreement on Tariffs and Trade (GATT) in 1995.

International Monetary Fund (IMF) With 181 member countries, the IMF focuses primarily upon international monetary matters. It makes financial resources available to members, and supervises the international currency system as well as the behavior of countries with respect to their exchange rates and related matters.

World Bank This international financial institution offers loans for development to LDCs from subscription capital as well as from funds raised on the world's capital markets.

The European Union (EU) is a cohesive regional grouping that includes 15 West European countries. Headquartered in Brussels, Belgium, it used to be called the Economic Community (EC) or Common Market.

Group of Ten This group, consisting of the ten major industrial countries, pursues consultations on economic matters, and attempts to coordinate economic policies. Its members include the United States, the United Kingdom, Japan, Germany, and France—known as the Group of Five (G-5)—Italy and Canada—forming the Group of Seven (G-7)—and Belgium, the Netherlands, and Sweden.

The United Nations Conference on Trade and Development (UNCTAD) This U.N. organization concerns international matters of trade and development.

Organization for Economic Cooperation and Development (OECD) Consisting of 26 developed countries in North America, Western Europe, Japan, Oceania, and Mexico, this consultative group addresses a wide variety of economic matters.

NAFTA A regional free-trade agreement between the United States, Canada, and Mexico.

Summary

The field of international economics concerns the movement across national boundaries of goods, services, and productive factors. It is the conduct of trade, rather than the reasons for its being or the benefits derived from it, that distinguishes international from domestic transactions. But that distinction is important, as manifested in exchange rates, various commercial policies, different domestic policies, statistical data, the relative immobility of productive factors, and marketing considerations.

International transactions have grown rapidly over the years, at a faster rate than the global output. In 1995 total world merchandise exports totaled $5 trillion, and global transactions in commercial services amounted to $1.2 trillion. The United States is the largest single trading nation.

Although foreign trade occupies a smaller share of the U.S. economy than that of other countries, there are certain industries (export- and import-competing industries) in which it plays a significant role.

International and regional forums for trade and financial negotiation include the WTO, the IMF, the World Bank, the European Union, the Group of Ten, the UNCTAD, the OECD, and NAFTA.

Important Concepts

Specialization

Exchange rate

Export subsidy

Tariff

Import quota

Voluntary Export Restraint (VER)

Relatively closed economy

Nontraded goods

Export industries

Import-competing industries

Exchange control

Review Questions

1.   What features distinguish international from domestic transactions?

2.   What can you say about the growth of world trade in both nominal and real terms? Was it faster than the growth of output?

3.   Evaluate the statement, "The United States is a closed economy, hence foreign trade is of no consequence to it."

4.   Distinguish between (a) export industries, (b) import-competing industries, and (c) nontraded goods. Give examples of each.

5.   Using the figures in table 1.3, what can you say about the trade structure of the United States and Japan?

ORGANIZATION OF THIS BOOK

Following the traditional approach, this textbook is divided into two parts. Part One is devoted to international trade relations. It outlines the principles that govern world trade and investment and discusses the factors that determine the direction of that trade. It then analyzes the effect of various policies that obstruct the free flow of trade and deals extensively with regional and international organizations that are designed to promote the orderly functioning of the trading system and to increase the welfare of developed and developing countries.

Part Two focuses on international financial relations. It explains the present currency arrangements (known as the International Currency System), dwells at length on the policies of individual countries within the framework established by the community of nations, and concludes with a discussion of alternative currency arrangements and international financial history. The analysis is accompanied by examples of financial episodes of the 1980s and 1990s. The book concludes with a list of the most widely used sources of statistics about individual countries and the world economy.

International Trade Relations

INTRODUCTION

P art One of this book is concerned with the advantages of unobstructed trade in goods and services, and with public policies that affect the flow of trade. This part of international trade theory is known as the pure theory of international trade to distinguish it from exchange rate and related monetary matters. The word *pure* carries no moral connotation. It underscores the fact that the theory deals with trade in its barter essentials and that monetary phenomena do not occupy a central role in it.

DATA ON INTERNATIONAL COMMODITY TRADE

Because this Part begins by explaining the pattern of international trade, or which country exports what commodity, it is useful to indicate how and where the student may develop an empirical content to accompany analysis. Statistical compilations exist to show the sources and destinations of each product involved in international trade. The United Nations and other international organizations classify all commodities according to the Standard International Trade classification (SITC). The SITC comprises one-, two-, three-, and four-digit classes. Commodity groups in the one-digit class are fewest in number and least detailed; those in the other classes are greater in number and more detailed, up to the four-digit class, which has the most commodities and is the most refined in detail. Items 5 through 8 of the one-digit class are manufactures: Item 5 is chemicals, 7 denotes machinery and transport equipment, and 6 and 8 are other manufactures. Each of these items is further subdivided into its components and subcomponents. For example SITC 7 is divided into categories 71, nonelectrical machinery; 72, electrical machinery; and 73, transport equipment. Category 71 is subdivided into 711, nonelectrical power machinery; 712, agricultural machinery; 714, office machines; and so on. And 714 is further subdivided into 714.1, typewriters; 714.2, accounting machines; and so forth.

The original sources of these data are import and export declarations filed by traders as goods enter or leave a country. Each country uses that information to compile its own statistics, usually under a very detailed classification. It then converts the information to the SITC, and sends it to the U.N.

The most comprehensive quarterly and annual statistics for all countries, using four-digit SITC, are published by the United Nations in *Commodity Trade Statistics*.[1] Information on trade flows as well as on domestic economic variables for the industrialized countries is contained in the OECD's publication, Main Economic Indicators. For the United States, a very detailed (ten-digit) classification of traded commodities is published quarterly in the U.S. Census Bureau report of exports and imports. U.S. trade may be compared with domestic production of a given commodity by means of the Census Bureau publication, *United States Commodity Imports and Exports as Related to Output.* For other countries, such a comparison may be found in the United Nations publications.

Part One begins by considering why nations trade and what determines the types of commodities that are imported and exported—that is, the commodity composition of trade. In the process, it sheds additional light on the relation between national economic conditions and trade and exchange relations. The discussion then turns to government policies that obstruct the free flow of goods across national boundaries when protection of domestic industry is the foremost objective. Subsequent chapters discuss regional and international organizations designed to promote free trade or to advance the interests of a certain group of countries. It concludes with a chapter on international factor movement.

Review Question

■ How would you go about comparing the export/output ratio of commercial aircraft between the United States and France?

---

[1]"Partner country" statistics contain many sizable discrepancies: a country's export of a given commodity does not always match the importing country's reported import of that commodity. This is true of both volume and value figures. Some of the reasons for the discrepancies are that different countries often categorize the same product differently; there is a time lapse between departure and arrival of goods; and traders may under- or over-invoice exports or imports to take advantage of government policies (subsidies, exchange controls, and so on).

Why Nations Trade

N ations trade with each other for fundamentally the same reasons that individuals or regions engage in exchange of goods and services: to obtain the benefits of specialization. Since nations, like individuals, are not equally suited to produce all goods, all would benefit if each specialized in what it could do best and obtained its other needs through exchange. The point is self-evident, for in a free society communities would not engage in trade if it did not benefit them. This chapter focuses on the gains to individual nations from international exchange of goods, it demonstrates the conditions under which trading countries benefit from trade, and in the process it develops a method of determining which goods are exported and which are imported by each country.

THE PRINCIPLE OF COMPARATIVE ADVANTAGE

The Gains from Trade

Asked why she engages in foreign trade, any businessperson can promptly offer a superficial, yet correct answer: She purchases a commodity abroad if and when it is cheaper abroad than at home, and she sells a commodity abroad when it fetches a higher price abroad than it does domestically. She buys where it is cheapest and sells where it is dearest in order to maximize her profit. In other words, relative prices at home and abroad determine which goods are exported and which are imported by any given country—the commodity composition of trade.

But what makes some goods cheaper in one country and others cheaper in another? To the businessperson this is of no consequence; she simply converts one currency into another at the prevailing exchange rate and compares prices. But to the economist this is the crux of the matter, for it is only by answering this question that she can determine whether such profit-maximizing behavior on the part of individual traders is beneficial to the country. And, equally important, saying that a commodity is cheaper in one country than in another implies the use of an exchange rate. But the exchange rate itself must in some way be determined by relative costs and prices in the two trading countries. Thus, by simply falling back on the businessperson's statement, we are, at least in part, explaining relative prices by relative prices. In order to break out of the circular reasoning, it is necessary to investigate what determines the relative cost–price positions of the two countries.

To do this we go to a principle originally enunciated early in the nineteenth century by the English economist David Ricardo: the principle of **comparative advantage** or, stated inversely, comparative cost. It is most easily explained by a simplified example similar to the one Ricardo used. Assume that the world consists of two countries, say the United States and the United Kingdom, which produce two commodities, wheat and textiles. Suppose further that the only factor of production employed in producing the two goods is labor in a homogeneous form. This means that the value of each product is determined exclusively by its labor content (yielding the so-called labor theory of value). Goods move freely between the two countries but labor is mobile only domestically, not internationally. Transport costs are also assumed not to exist. Technology is presumed to remain constant, unaffected by trade. Although this is a highly simplified case, it yields considerable insight of general application, as we shall see.

Suppose that the production conditions prevailing in the two countries are those of Scheme 1.

Scheme 1 Production Conditions

Country	One Person-Day of Labor Produces
United States	60 bushels of wheat *or* 20 yards of textiles
United Kingdom	20 bushels of wheat *or* 10 yards of textiles

Clearly, labor is more productive absolutely in the United States than in the United Kingdom in both the textile and the wheat industries: One day of labor produces more of everything in the United States than it does in the United Kingdom. The United States has **absolute advantage** over the United Kingdom in the production of both goods.[1] But it should not be concluded that because the United States is more efficient in the production of both commodities, it would produce both of them when trade opens up, or that the United Kingdom would produce none. To suggest this is to deny the mutual advantage to be derived from international trade. The condition postulated here, that one country is absolutely more productive than another in most of their mutual pursuits, is not uncommon. Yet mutually beneficial trade does take place, even between countries as extremely different in productive efficiency as the United States and India.

What is important in the problem at hand is *comparative*, not absolute, advantage. A vertical comparison of the figures in Scheme 1 shows that the *degree* of American advantage over the United Kingdom is not the same in both industries. The United States has a 3 to 1 advantage in wheat, but only a 2 to 1 advantage in textiles. Comparatively speaking, therefore, the United States has a greater advantage in wheat and a lesser advantage in textiles. The United Kingdom is in the reverse position; it has an absolute disadvantage in both goods, but the extent of disadvantage is greater in wheat and lesser in textiles, because labor can produce only one-third as much wheat as in the United States, but it can produce fully one-half as much textiles. Since we are merely comparing the degree of advantage and disadvantage in producing the two goods, the analysis can be expressed by asserting that the United States has a *comparative advantage* in wheat while the United Kingdom has a *comparative advantage* in textiles.

This situation is analogous to that of a doctor who is absolutely more efficient than his nurse in the performance of both medical and paramedical duties. But the degree of his advantage is much larger in the first type of duty than in the second. And just as it pays the doctor to concentrate on the former and hire a nurse to do the latter, so it is to America's advantage to specialize in wheat and purchase British textiles.

But this is running somewhat ahead of our story. The productivity comparison between the two countries is possible only because of the existence of an international common denominator—a given quantity of homogeneous labor. Had this been absent, the vertical comparison in Scheme 1 would have been impossible. Consequently, it is more general and meaningful to focus on the horizontal, *within-country*, comparison, although the conclusion is the same in both cases.

---

[1]Forty years before Ricardo, Adam Smith offered an explanation of trade based on **absolute advantage**. Suppose that one person-day of labor was capable of producing the following quantities of output in each of the two countries:

Country	One Person-Day of Labor Produces
United States	60 bushels of wheat *or* 20 yards of textile
United Kingdom	20 bushels of wheat *or* 40 yards of textile

Then it is self-evident that the United States has an (absolute) productivity advantage over the U.K. in wheat production and the U.K. has a productivity advantage in textile production. The U.S. will export wheat to the U.K. and import textile from the U.K. But the Ricardian conditions postulated in the text are rather common, and offer a more comprehensive explanation of trade.

What do we see from that vantage point? Domestically, the United States must give up 3 bushels of wheat to obtain 1 yard of textiles. Obviously, wheat is not convertible into textiles in any mechanical sense; but by forgoing 3 bushels of wheat, enough labor (and other resources if present) is released to be put into textile production to produce 1 yard of textiles. This is what the internal cost ratio of 3 to 1 (or 60 bushels of wheat for 20 yards of textiles) means: The resource cost, sometimes called the "opportunity cost," of 1 yard of textiles in the United States is 3 bushels of wheat. Conversely, the cost of 1 bushel of wheat is 1/3 yard of textiles. What is the situation from the British point of view? Domestically, the resource cost of 2 bushels of wheat is 1 yard of textiles, because by giving up 1 yard of textiles enough labor is released to produce 2 bushels of wheat. And conversely, 1 bushel of wheat costs 1/2 yard of textiles. The relative cost of producing the two commodities in the two countries can be summarized as follows:

> One unit of textiles costs 3 units of wheat in the United States and 2 units of wheat in the United Kingdom. *Textiles are cheaper* (in terms of wheat) *in the United Kingdom.*

> One unit of wheat costs one-third of a unit of textiles in the United States and one-half of a unit of textiles in the United Kingdom. *Wheat is cheaper* (in terms of textiles) *in the United States.*

Each country specializes in the product that it can produce more cheaply, and obtains the other commodity through trade. The United States would produce and export wheat, and the United Kingdom would produce and export textiles.

Having established each country's specialization, we need to determine the limits to mutually beneficial exchange. The United States would be unwilling to trade 3 bushels of wheat for anything less than 1 yard of textiles, for it can do better at home. But it would be willing to trade 3 bushels of wheat for more than 1 yard of textiles, or to purchase 1 yard abroad for less than 3 bushels. Similarly, if the United Kingdom were able to obtain through trade more than 2 bushels of wheat per yard of textiles, it would trade, for the resource cost of obtaining wheat by trading away textiles is less than that of giving up textile production to produce wheat at home. But the United Kingdom would be unwilling to trade 1 yard for less than 2 bushels, for it can do better at home.

In sum, the appropriate comparison for each country is between the resource cost of the commodity produced at home and the cost when it is acquired from abroad in exchange for the export good. The figures of Scheme 1 can be transformed into the limits to mutually beneficial trade, as given in Scheme 2.

Scheme 2   Limits to Mutually Beneficial Trade

1 yard of textiles $\begin{cases} = \text{maximum of 3 bushels of wheat for the United States} \\ = \text{minimum of 2 bushels of wheat for the United Kingdom} \end{cases}$

The United States is willing to purchase 1 yard of textiles for anything less than 3 bushels of wheat, while the United Kingdom is willing to sell 1 yard of textiles for anything more than 2 bushels of wheat. Trade can take place anywhere between these limits. Stated differently, the domestic cost ratios of the two commodities in the two countries constitute the limits to mutually beneficial trade. Within these limits, it is to the advantage of each country to concentrate on the production of the good in which it has a comparative advantage and to obtain the other product through trade.

To see that trade is indeed beneficial to both nations, select any international price ratio within the specified limits, such as 1 yard of textiles = $2\frac{1}{2}$ bushels of wheat. Trading at this ratio enables each country to consume more than is possible without trade. Let us say that the United States, employing its entire labor force, produces 600 bushels of wheat, of which it consumes 400 and exchanges 200 for textiles. The United Kingdom at full production manufactures 200 yards of textiles, of which it consumes 120 and exchanges 80 for wheat. With international trade, the 200 bushels of wheat are exchanged for 80 yards of textiles, permitting the United States to consume 400 bushels and 80 yards and the United Kingdom to consume 200 bushels and 120 yards. Without trade, the United States can transform (in terms of resource conversion) the 200 bushels into only $66\frac{2}{3}$ yards of textiles, making available a total of 400 bushels and $66\frac{2}{3}$ yards. The United Kingdom, without trade, can transform the 80 yards of textiles into only 160 bushels of wheat, making available 120 yards and 160 bushels. All this is summarized in table 2.1, which demonstrates how both countries benefit from the exchange.

Demand Considerations

Referring back to Scheme 2, it will be observed that the internal cost ratios (namely, supply conditions) provide the limits to mutually beneficial trade. Within these limits, the actual exchange ratio is determined by the relative strength, or intensity, of each country's demand for the other country's product.

Since the demand for the imported good is expressed in terms of units of the country's own export product—the entire exchange being in barter terms—it is known as *reciprocal demand*. In other words, production costs determine the limits, while reciprocal demand determines what the actual exchange ratio will be within these limits. The further apart the two domestic cost ratios, the more room there is for mutually advantageous trade, and the

TABLE 2.1	**Production and Consumption with and without Trade, Where the International Exchange Ratio Is 1 Yard = $2\frac{1}{2}$ Bushels**	
	United States	**United Kingdom**
Production at full capacity	600 bushels of wheat	200 yards of textiles
Consumption with trade (80 yards for 200 bushels)	400 bushels of wheat 80 yards of textiles	200 bushels of wheat 120 yards of textile
Consumption without trade	400 bushels of wheat $66\frac{2}{3}$ yards of textiles	160 bushels of wheat 120 yards of textiles

larger the benefits that can be derived from trade by both countries—in the sense that the net increase in available goods over the no-trade position is larger. At the other extreme, when the two domestic cost *ratios* are identical, there are no advantages to trade. Each country is as well off **in isolation** (without trade) as with trade, so there is no inducement to engage in trade. In the real world, before trade can commence, the difference between the two cost ratios must be large enough to compensate for transport costs[2] and artificial barriers to trade.

Finally, in our simple example, the distribution of the benefits between the two countries depends on where the exchange ratio settles. If it ends up near the British cost ratio of 1 yard of textiles = 2 bushels of wheat, the United States derives most of the gain; if it is close to the American cost ratio of 1 yard of textiles = 3 bushels of wheat, the United Kingdom reaps most of the benefits. The commodity exchange ratio is often referred to as the "commodity terms of trade," for it shows the price of one product in terms of the other. In a multiproduct world, these prices must be expressed in terms of composite indexes, and the **terms of trade** of each country become *the export-price index divided by the import-price index.*

Now the link between the commodity terms of trade and the distribution of the benefits from trade among the trading countries occupies a central role in policy debates involving the developing countries. However, the exchange ratio is a rather superficial barometer of the division of the gains from trade. If the ratio ends up near the British domestic ratio (say 1 yard = $2\frac{1}{10}$ bushels), this is a result of the high intensity of British desire for wheat compared to the relatively low level of American eagerness for textiles. It is true that this trade ratio is more beneficial to Americans in the sense that it increases their available textiles per unit of wheat given up by more than it increases the wheat available to the United Kingdom per unit of textile given up. *But* the Americans are much less eager for textiles than the British

[2]Put differently, the cost or price differential would have to be greater than the transport costs per unit of the product before trade can commence. Goods for which the price differential falls short of the transport costs would not be traded. Such costs give rise to *nontraded goods.*

are for wheat. Consequently, in terms of satisfaction, or utility, reflected in the eagerness of demand, the Americans may not gain more than the British. Once the "commodity gain ratio" is translated into "utility ratio," the gain appears rather equally divided.

On the other hand, if a country or group of countries can "artificially" increase the price of exports by exercising monopoly power on world markets, they gain and the rest of the world loses. This is what the oil producing countries succeeded in doing in the mid-1970s and again in 1979–1980.

In reality, demand factors often occupy a more important role than the one ascribed to them here. In the example of Scheme 1, both goods are homogeneous commodities: There is only one universal type of wheat and only one kind of textile. But much of the trade that takes place in the world is in differentiated products: Each commodity has various gradations of quality, size, flavor, and so on, and even differences in packaging and brand names are important. In such circumstances it is no longer true that identical cost ratios would result in no trade. For example, it is reasonable to assume that automobile production has approximately the same rank of comparative advantage in Italy, France, and West Germany. And consequently it would be difficult to explain the intercountry exchange of Fiats, Renaults, and Volkswagens on the grounds of cost differentials. A large part of the explanation must lie in consumer preferences for the foreign brand, even when the price equals that of its domestic counterpart. Since these cars are of roughly similar quality and size, the benefit from such trade is a psychic gain in the mind of the consumer, derived from having a variety of brands. The fact that there are such psychic benefits is self-evident; otherwise there would be no exchange of cars. But the size of the gain cannot always be measured.

This example can be generalized to many industrial products. They are traded even when cost ratios are identical in the countries involved, because consumers may prefer the foreign brands for reasons that have nothing to do with production costs. Since much of world trade is in differentiated products, demand considerations play an important role in determining its composition. They are abstracted from in this chapter only for the sake of simplicity. Hence we now return to the analysis of a world in which all products are homogeneous.

Why Complete Specialization?

A feature of the Ricardian example that may have puzzled the reader is that trade leads each country to specialize completely in the production of the commodity in which it has a comparative advantage. *In isolation*, every country must produce both goods if it wishes to consume both. Production and consumption are necessarily identical. International trade makes it possible for the production mix to be different from the consumption mix, with the differences being made up by trade. But must the

United States get completely out of textile production and devote itself exclusively to wheat? Likewise, must the United Kingdom abandon wheat production altogether and specialize in textiles? Certainly this is not true in the real world, where even the most casual observation shows that countries produce some of the same types of goods as those they import.

The answer is that **complete specialization** is unique to this type of example and arises from the assumption that production costs per unit of output remain constant as output expands or contracts. When trade opens up, the United States expands its wheat production and contracts its textile production while the reverse happens in the United Kingdom. If the unit cost rises with output (known as *increasing cost* situations), then the American wheat price rises as production expands and the British wheat price declines as production contracts. Precisely the reverse happens to textile prices. Thus, increasing cost conditions constitute a mechanism that forces prices in the two countries to *converge.* And once prices of the last (marginal) unit traded are the same in the two countries, there is no inducement for trade to expand further. Prices can easily become equal *before* complete specialization is reached.

But this mechanism is absent under constant cost. Then production costs remain unchanged as output expands and contracts, and there is no tendency toward price convergence. Because the cost curves are horizontal, prices do not converge as output expands in one country and contracts in the other (fig. 2.1). Therefore, the process does not stop until complete specialization is reached—until the United Kingdom discontinues wheat production and the United States gets out of textile production. Production under constant cost conditions results in complete specialization.[3]

COMPARATIVE OPPORTUNITY COST

Who Exports What?

Next suppose that labor is not the only factor of production but one of several. Hence, the common denominator that made it possible to compare productivity between countries is no longer available, for when several productive factors enter into the production process, the productivity of each of them separately is of little consequence. Instead, it is necessary to measure their joint productivity.

For convenience we concentrate on the inverse of productivity, or unit production cost, by aggregating the resources that go into the production of one unit of output. But resources or factors are diverse. The only way to aggregate labor, land, and capital is to add up their money value. Thus, instead of a Ricardian labor productivity scheme, we end up with a production cost scheme (Scheme 3), where costs in each country are mea-

[3]The only exception occurs if one of the countries is too small to supply its trading partner with all the partner's needs of the commodity. Then the small country would be completely specialized in its export good, while the large country would produce both goods, but it would still export its export good and import the other.

FIGURE 2.1 *Supply Curves of Wheat and Textiles under Constant Cost Conditions*

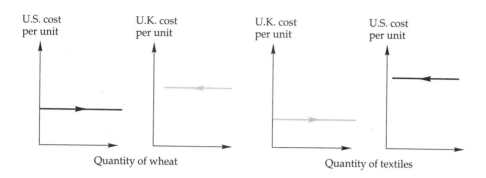

sured in terms of its currency.[4] Although the same two commodities are retained, Scheme 3 differs from Schemes 1 and 2, for it deals with cost of production per unit of output (the inverse of labor productivity[5]). But the principle of comparative advantage (or cost) remains inviolate.

Scheme 3   Production Costs per Unit of Output

	Wheat per Bushel	Textiles per Yard
United States	$1	$3
United Kingdom	£1	£1

Since we do not know the exchange rate (for there is no exchange rate before trade opens up), there is no way of comparing costs in absolute terms

[4]Note that the ratios of Scheme 3 need not be the inverse of those in Scheme 1 because Scheme 3 includes all production costs and is not restricted to labor costs. It would, however, be instructive for the interested reader to work through an example where the production cost ratios are exactly the inverse of the labor productivity ratios postulated in Scheme 1. Scheme 3 would then read

	Wheat	Textiles
United States	$1	$3
United Kingdom	£1	£2

[5]To see that production costs are the inverse of productivity, assume that a worker earns $10 per hour producing widgets. If the worker produces 10 widgets per hour, the cost per widget is $1. If the worker's productivity rises to 20 widgets per hour, the cost per widget declines to $10/20, or 50 cents.

between the two countries. But the intracountry (horizontal) comparison is still possible as before. In the United States, the resource or factor cost of 1 yard of textiles is 3 bushels of wheat. The dollar signs represent composite factor cost—it takes three times as big a resource basket to make 1 yard of textiles as to grow 1 bushel of wheat. It is in this sense that the two goods are interchangeable, but this is the only relevant sense for the economy as a whole.

To restate, the opportunity (or resource) cost of 1 yard of textiles in the United States is 3 bushels of wheat. In the United Kingdom, on the other hand, the resource cost of 1 yard of textiles is 1 bushel of wheat. Comparatively speaking, therefore, textiles are three times as expensive (in terms of wheat) in the United States as in the United Kingdom. In the same sense, wheat is relatively cheaper in the United States than in the United Kingdom: One bushel costs $\frac{1}{3}$ of a yard in the United States and a full yard in the United Kingdom. This establishes the fact that the United States has a comparative advantage in wheat while the United Kingdom's is in textiles; they will specialize and trade accordingly.

The Limits to Mutually Beneficial Exchange

Having ascertained the direction of trade should it open up, we next establish the limits to mutually beneficial exchange. Domestically, the United States can obtain 1 yard of textiles for 3 bushels of wheat, for by forgoing 3 bushels of wheat, enough resources are released to produce 1 yard of textiles. It will trade only if it can obtain 1 yard of textiles for less than 3 bushels of wheat. Domestically, the United Kingdom can obtain 1 bushel of wheat per yard of textiles. It would trade only if 1 yard of textiles yielded more than 1 bushel of wheat. As before, the domestic cost ratios set the limits within which the exchange ratio must fall (Scheme 4). If the cost ratios are identical in the two countries, no trade takes place (the limits simply collapse into one point) unless motivated by demand factors as in the case of differentiated products.

Scheme 4   Limits to Mutually Beneficial Trade

---

1 yard of textiles $\begin{cases} = \text{maximum of 3 bushels of wheat for the United States} \\ \\ = \text{minimum of 1 bushel of wheat for the United Kingdom} \end{cases}$

Scheme 4 can be transformed into a simple diagrammatic form. In figure 2.2, yards of textiles are plotted against bushels of wheat. The U.S. cost ratio of 3 bushels of wheat per yard of textile is represented by a straight line from the origin with a slope of 3. A similar line, but showing a 1 to 1 cost

FIGURE 2.2   *Region of Mutually Beneficial Trade*

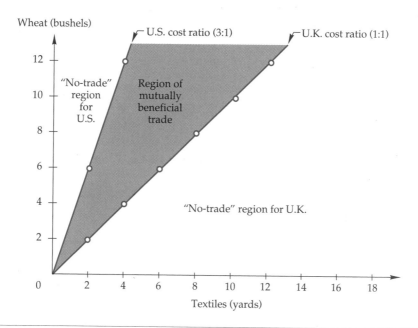

The region of mutually beneficial trade lies between the cost ratios of the two countries. Outside that region one of the two countries will not trade.

ratio, is drawn for the United Kingdom. The two cost ratios are shown in colored rays from the origin, while the area between them is shaded. All exchange ratios falling between the two lines constitute the region of mutually beneficial trade, where for each country the opportunity cost of acquiring the imported good in exchange for exports is less than that of producing it domestically. Outside this region, one or the other of the two countries will not want to trade, for it can do better at home. The trade region is bounded by the cost or supply ratios of the two countries. Thus, cost conditions determine the limits to mutually beneficial trade.

Precisely where within these limits trade will occur depends on **demand considerations,** or on the relative intensity of each country's demand for the other country's product. If the British are far more eager for U.S. wheat than Americans are for British textiles, the exchange ratio (terms of trade) would fall close to the U.K. domestic cost ratio of 1 to 1. Conversely, if Americans are more eager for British textiles than Britons are for American wheat, the exchange ratio would end up close to the U.S. domestic ratio of 3 to 1.

The Limits to a Sustainable Exchange Rate[6]

This analysis can be carried further. We know from our example that the United States produces and exports wheat and that the United Kingdom produces and exports textiles. Therefore, the limits to the exchange ratio of Scheme 4 can be translated from commodities into money by *assigning to each commodity the price it commands in the country in which it is produced, in terms of the currency of that country.* In other words, 1 yard of textiles costs £1, while 1 bushel of wheat costs $1. The limits of Scheme 4 are thereby converted into the respective currency values illustrated by Scheme 5.

Scheme 5   *The Limits to the Dollar–Pound Exchange Rate*

$$1 \text{ yard of textiles } = £1 = \begin{cases} \$3 \text{ (3 bushels of wheat)} \\ \\ \$1 \text{ (1 bushel of wheat)} \end{cases}$$

Given the production costs of Scheme 3, the values in Scheme 5 must be the limits to the pound–dollar exchange rate.[7] Suppose we arbitrarily select the midpoint of £1 = $2 and apply it to the production cost example on which this is based (Scheme 3). By converting the pounds sterling cost to dollar cost at this exchange rate, we obtain Scheme 6.

Scheme 6
Production Costs of Scheme 3 in Terms of Dollars Where £1 = $2

	Wheat per Bushel	Textiles per Yard
United States	$1	$3
United Kingdom	$2	$2

Clearly, the United States undersells the United Kingdom in wheat, and the United Kingdom undersells the United States in textiles. This is precisely the answer attributed to the businessperson at the beginning of this chapter. But now it is clear that comparative advantage lies behind the statement that one buys where it is cheapest and sells where it is dearest after converting foreign prices to domestic currency at the going exchange rate. It is also clear that the limits to the exchange rate are determined by the cost ratios.

[6]Note: This section and the next require some familiarity with exchange rates.

[7]The example of footnote 4 yields the following limits to the exchange rate:

$$£2 = \begin{cases} \$3 \\ \$2 \end{cases} \text{ or } £1 = \begin{cases} \$1.50 \\ \$1 \end{cases}$$

At any exchange rate selected from *outside* the limits of Scheme 5 one country undersells the other in both commodities, as the reader can verify for herself.

More Than Two Commodities

In reality, each country produces many commodities, but the principle of comparative advantage holds nevertheless. All goods produced by each country must be **ranked internally** in the order of their domestic costs. Suppose the United States and the United Kingdom produce five commodities, A, B, C, D, and E with the production costs as given by Scheme 7 *(ranked* in order of magnitude within each country).

Scheme 7   Production Costs in Two Countries with Five Goods

	\multicolumn{5}{c}{Commodity}				
	A	**B**	**C**	**D**	**E**
United States	$1	$4	$9	$15	$20
United Kingdom	£1	£2	£3	£4	£5

At an exchange rate of £1 = $3, the British costs converted into dollars become:

	A	**B**	**C**	**D**	**E**
U.K. cost (£1 = $3)	$3	$6	$9	$12	$15

The United States exports commodities A and B, while the United Kingdom undersells the United States in commodities D and E and therefore exports them. Commodity C is not traded, for its cost is the same in both countries. It is important, when considering the position of any country, to rank all commodities by degree of comparative advantage. Once ranked in that order, the exchange rate determines which commodities are exported and which are imported.

Examples from U.S. Trade[8]

In the 1970s and early 1980s, much public attention was focused on the decline in U.S. exports—and the increase in imports—of autos and steel. In part, this was widely attributed to wrong managerial decisions: delays in the introduction of new technology in the case of steel and the "wrong" product mix and inferior quality in the case of automobiles. However, much of the deterioration can be analyzed in terms of production costs. To do that, it is necessary to *rank* all industries *within each* country by order of their production cost: from the lowest to the highest cost industries. This is equivalent to

[8]This section is based on M. E. Kreinin, "Wage Competitiveness in the U.S. Auto and Steel Industries," *Economic Inquiry,* January 1984; and "U.S. Trade in High-Technology Products," *Journal of Policy Modeling,* Winter 1985.

| TABLE 2.2 | |

Indices of Unit Labor Cost in Iron and Steel and All Manufacturing for 1980 (1964 = 100) in Five Countries

Country	Hourly Compensation		Output per Hour		Unit Labor Cost	
	Iron and Steel	All Mfg.	Iron and Steel	All Mfg.	Iron and Steel	All Mfg.
United States	382	316	119	141	321	224
Japan	725	807	352	394	206	205
Germany	448	461	227	217	197	212
United Kingdom	827	898	119	167	689	538
France	754	632	221	233	341	271

Source: Complete source information is available in footnote 8 reference.

ranking them by comparative advantage. A variant of this approach calls for comparing—*within* each country—the behavior of production cost in motor vehicles and in iron and steel *relative* to their counterpart in the entire manufacturing sector. Such a comparison is made here for labor production costs, which is labor compensations (wages and salaries plus fringe benefits) divided by productivity.

However, labor productivity within each country is available in the form of an index; it shows performance relative to some base period. Consequently, labor costs must also be calculated in the same manner. Should the data reveal that a consistent rise in the labor cost in one of the industries (or both) was far in excess of the national manufacturing average, it can be inferred that the industry moved down in the ranking by comparative advantage.

Table 2.2 shows the 1980 indices of labor compensation, labor productivity, and unit labor cost in the steel industry; and for all manufacturing in five countries. The United States, along with the United Kingdom and France, lost comparative advantage in steel as unit labor cost advanced much more than its counterpart in all manufacturing. No such loss occurred in Japan and Germany. The sharp rise of U.S. labor cost in this industry relative to all manufacturing is a result of a long-standing trend, where compensation advanced at a rate far ahead of its counterpart in all manufacturing whereas productivity rose at a much slower rate.

A similar tabulation for the automobile industry shows that within the United States, unit labor cost for motor vehicles edged considerably ahead of that for all manufacturing, primarily due to a faster rise in labor compensation, which more than offset the small differential in productivity. Within Japan unit labor cost in autos moved in tandem with that of all manufacturing.

Table 2.3 shows the unit labor cost (compensation divided by productivity) for each of the three industries *relative* to all manufacturing *within* the

TABLE 2.3	Ratio of Unit Labor Cost within Three Countries, 1980/81		
Industry Ratio	**United States**	**Japan**	**Germany**
Iron and Steel/			
All Manufactures	1.57	0.93	1.02
Motor Vehicles/			
All Manufactures	1.42	1.07	1.18
High Technology/			
All Manufactures	0.90	0.95	1.08

Source: Complete source information is available in footnote 8 reference.

United States, Japan, and Germany at a point in time (1980). U.S. production cost in the iron and steel and the motor vehicle industries exceeds that for all manufacturing by 57 and 42 percent, respectively. That excess is far smaller, or nonexistent, in Japan and Germany. It is these ratios that indicate the loss of U.S. comparative advantage in iron and steel, and an incipient loss in motor vehicles.

What has happened since the 1980s? By the early 1990s the U.S. steel industry increased productivity and slashed production costs: The man-hours required to produce a ton of steel were down to 3 from 10 in the 1980s. Steel exports were up, and requests for import protection were down. But in the mid-1990s the situation changed again, with imports rising and exports falling in 1995-97. Substantial strides were made by the auto industry: GM requires 3.64 workers per day to assemble a vehicle, down from 4.88 in 1989. But the industry still trails its Japanese competitors: Nissan, Japan's most efficient automaker, requires only 2.09 man-days. Of course many Japanese models are now produced in the United States.

In contrast to the steel and automobile industries, the United States always had a comparative advantage in an array of high-technology industries, such as chemicals, computers, aircraft, medical instruments, and certain specialized machinery. Unit labor cost in this sector was *below* its counterpart in all manufacturing—which cannot be said for our European trading partners (table 2.3). That advantage has increased in the 1990s. For example, the U.S. software industry holds 75 percent of the world market, and its employment grew at 9.6% per year between 1987 and 1994.

ABSOLUTE ADVANTAGE AND WAGE RATES

We now return to the Ricardian example of labor productivity used in the first part of this chapter. While comparative advantage held the center of the discussion, absolute advantage in the Ricardian model cannot be disregarded, for it determines the **relative wage rates** in the two countries.

Given the labor-productivity figures of Scheme 1, assume that the wage rate in the United States is $30 per day. Free mobility of labor between industries ensures that wage rates within the country are the same in both industries—for, if they were not, labor would move from the low-wage to the high-wage industry until wage rates were equalized. The question is: What must the British wage rate be?

Under the productivity conditions postulated in Scheme 1, the answer can be obtained by determining which wage rate, relative to the one assumed for the United States ($30 a day), would enable the United Kingdom to undersell America in textiles and be undersold in wheat. In other words, the relative wage rate must conform to the configuration of comparative advantage developed before, to make possible mutually beneficial trade.

Since an American worker produces 60 bushels of wheat per day, the cost of wheat is $30/60, or $0.50 per bushel. And because the United States undersells the United Kingdom in wheat, the British price must be *above* $0.50 per bushel. A British worker produces 20 bushels per day, so his *minimum* wage must be $10, for any rate below that level would yield a price lower than the American price. Similarly, an American worker can produce 20 yards of textiles a day, and at a daily wage of $30 this yields a cost of $1.50 per yard. Because the U.K. undersells the U.S. in textiles, the British price must be $1.50 per yard or less, implying that a British laborer who produces 10 yards a day must earn less than $15 a day. At any higher wage rate the U.K. would not remain competitive in textiles. Thus if the established pattern of trade is to prevail, the British wage rate must be somewhere between $10 and $15 a day, or between one-half and one-third of the American wage rate. These limits are equal to, and are determined by, the productivity ratios in the two industries.

That the wage ratio cannot depart from these limits is illustrated by the events following the reunification of Germany in 1990. For political reasons, the German government established a wage level in East Germany of 80 percent of West German wage rates. But East German productivity measured only 30–50 percent—depending on the industry—of West German productivity. Since the wage ratio between the two countries did not lie within the productivity ratios, most East German firms could not compete, resulting in mass unemployment. The German government has been pouring $100 billion in investments per year into East Germany in an attempt to raise their productivity levels to 70–80 percent of those of West Germany. That way East Germany will be able to compete globally in the industries in which it has a comparative advantage—but the process takes years to complete.

It is also possible to evaluate the frequent complaints of protectionist forces in the United States that they cannot withstand foreign competition because foreign wages are lower than American wages. Time and again, in hearings before congressional committees, representatives of import-competing industries demand the imposition of a "scientific tariff": a tariff that would equalize wage rates here and abroad. Alternatively stated, their claim is that the tariff level should equal the difference between American wage rates and wage rates prevailing in competing countries. Now we see that this is an untenable position, for if the British wage rate were equal to the American one, the United States would undersell the United Kingdom in all commodities. There could be no two-way trade under such conditions. The relative wage rate in two countries is determined by the differences in productive efficiency. And American wages are among the highest in the world because this economy is among the most productive. (We defer to the next chapter the question of *why* it is more productive.) It is true that in our example American textiles cannot compete. But that is because, in the example, the United States does not possess a comparative advantage in that commodity. The same applies to a 1982 complaint of U.S. mushroom growers, that they cannot compete with Chinese mushrooms because of low wage rates in China. Similarly, fears that the United States cannot compete with Mexico because of low wage rates[9] there, overlook the fact that in industries in which the United States has a comparative advantage, the American productivity advantage is large enough to offset the lower wages in Mexico.

On the other hand, as productivity in other countries rises (labor production costs decline) relative to that in the United States, their standard of living catches up with that of America, and may even surpass it.

SUMMARY OF POLICY IMPLICATIONS

To recapitulate, international trade raises the real income of the community by improving the efficiency of resource utilization. The ranking of industries in the order of their comparative advantage, combined with the exchange rate, determines which commodities are to be exported and which are to be imported. The country's resources are most efficiently utilized if they are distributed and employed along this order. Consequently, policies that distort this ranking, such as tariffs and quotas imposed on specific commodities, result in inefficient resource allocation and loss of income to the community.

Demands of import-competing industries for protection—under one guise or another—are often unwarranted. What they are asking for is selective protection or, essentially, tariff protection for themselves. That would distort the industrial ranking and lead to inefficient resource utilization. The claim that they cannot compete may be correct from their own points of view. But satisfaction of their demand for protection would be injurious to

---

[9]This argument was prevalent in the 1993 debate over the North American Free Trade Agreement (NAFTA) discussed in a later chapter.

the economy as a whole. The reason they are not competitive is that they rank low in the order of comparative advantage. Allocative efficiency requires that they contract in size and their resources be transferred to the growing industries. Government help in this transfer process—in the form of direct loans, retraining programs, and the like—would contribute to efficiency all around and help alleviate human suffering.

Indeed, the introduction of trade causes redistribution of income in society. The gainers are those people associated with industries in which the country has a comparative advantage, while the losers are those associated with industries in which the country lacks a comparative advantage. Much of the debate over trade policy is a dispute between gainers and losers. In evaluating it, we should keep in mind that the gains to society are much larger than the losses, and that government needs to introduce mechanisms, such as direct financial assistance or occupational retraining, to help the losers adjust to free trade. In that respect, the introduction of trade is similar to technological advances, which raise the living standards of society at large, but cause some people to lose their jobs.

Far from contributing to inflation—as is sometimes alleged by the popular media—international trade is **anti-inflationary.** Suppose that bad weather conditions cause a poor harvest in Russia, making it necessary for that country to purchase huge quantities of grain from the United States. The price of grain (as well as of meat and other products derived from grain) will rise in the United States. This always happens to the price of an exported commodity. However, this does not mean that the conduct of trade is inflationary, because it overlooks what happens to the price of imports.

At a simplified level, assume that the United States barters its wheat for Russian crude oil. The United States can obtain the oil it needs either by producing it at home (say, at the Alaskan North slope) or by bartering it for wheat. Given the immensely efficient American agriculture, it is cheaper to obtain oil by bartering it for wheat. Conversely, Russia is a low-cost producer of gas and oil and a high-cost producer of grain. By the law of comparative advantage, it pays the Russians to import part of the grain they need for domestic consumption in exchange for gas and oil. Each country *compares the cost of producing the commodity at home with what it would cost to barter it on the international market for its export good.* It follows the cheaper option. And as a result the price of oil in the United States declines.

When imports as well as exports are considered, the effect of foreign trade is to lower rather than to raise the average price level of all goods. Additionally, competitive pressure from foreign producers often constitutes a *barrier to price increases* by domestic producers. It spurs local producers to introduce technological innovations and greater efficiency. In the case of the auto industry, it is often suggested that foreign competition induced the U.S.

manufacturers to introduce small cars in the late 1970s, thereby conforming to consumer preferences. Japanese competition also forced U.S. automakers to improve the quality of their products while containing prices—all to the benefit of American consumers.

It is in the interest of a country to engage in balanced, mutually beneficial, and market-directed trade. It is contrary to its interest to pursue policies that distort its comparative advantage by providing protection to inefficient industries. There is no particular advantage in the ability to undersell other countries in everything only to encourage huge trade surpluses.

Dynamic Gains from International Trade

The foregoing analysis of the benefits from international trade followed the traditional line of emphasizing specialization and reallocation of *existing* resources. In fact, these gains can be outweighed by the impact of trade on the country's growth rate and therefore on the volume of *additional* resources made available to, or employed by, the trading country. These are termed **dynamic** benefits, in contrast to the **static** effects of reallocating an unchanged quantity of resources. The reason for the disproportionately little space devoted to these factors is that they are difficult to measure as well as to theorize upon. But their importance should not be underestimated. The short discourse that follows is intended to be indicative rather than exhaustive.

Consider first a fully employed economy. Its income and output are equal and may be considered two sides of the same coin. For what does it imply to state that the price of a desk is $100? First, this is its value as a unit of output. Next, the price reflects the fact that a total of $100 in income was generated and paid to productive factors used in the production of the desk in the following forms: wages and salaries for labor, rental income for the use of natural resources, interest paid on capital, and *profit* return for entrepreneurial ability. This example can be generalized to all goods and services produced in a given year. Their final value, the gross domestic product, equals the income generated in the production process. In turn, the economy's growth rate is determined by (among other things) the degree to which the population is willing to abstain from current consumption (their propensity to save), so that resources can be released from production of consumer goods and used for investment purposes.

For, if in a fully employed economy all income is spent on consumer goods—meaning that the saving rate is nil—then all resources must be occupied in the production of these goods and no investment is possible. On the other hand, should consumers abstain from consuming part of their income, or save, resources would be freed to produce investment goods, making possible economic growth and the attainment of larger streams of output in future years. It is this saving–investment process that generates growth and development.

It is an integral part of economic theory, demonstrated time and again in empirical studies, that the level of saving in the community, or abstinence from consumption, is positively related to the community's income. The higher the income is, the higher the saving is, too, because it is easier to save out of higher levels of earnings. Therefore, any positive increment to the community's income necessarily results in added saving: When income is higher the possible rate of growth is higher.

But this is precisely what international trade was shown to do. Income rises because of more efficient utilization of fully employed resources. This raises savings and makes additional resources available for investment purposes. Furthermore, since the opening up of the economy to foreign trade changes relative prices, the tendency toward higher investment is accentuated if investment goods are imported or are made out of imported materials, for the price of imports goes down relative to that of exports and other goods as a result of trade.

An extreme example of this case is that of developing countries in which capital equipment cannot be produced, for technical or other reasons. In such a case, it is not just a matter of forcing resources toward more efficient uses when the country moves to specialize in "simple" products and import capital goods. The resources could not possibly have manufactured the latter goods because they are unsuitable for that purpose. In that case the country must worry not only about the saving rate and the release of resources from current consumption, but also about how to convert these resources into investment goods. Because such transformation is not possible at home, it can be accomplished only by exchange of exportables for imported capital equipment. International trade is the only vehicle by means of which the conversion can be carried out, thereby becoming a main instrument of growth. Indeed, when development is inhibited by insufficient imports of capital goods, underutilization of other factors may occur. Trade (and aid) can break this bottleneck, and place the economy on a higher growth path.

This point underscores the fact that international trade does not comprise only flows of finished products intended for the final consumer. Rather, much of it consists of exchanges of factors of production in the form of plants and equipment and semiprocessed or raw materials. And since many developing countries do not possess the know-how and ability to produce them at home—even if they were willing, however inefficiently, to devote resources to their production—their importation amounts to much more than specialization in production. It enables the country to reach otherwise unattainable horizons in technology and efficiency. A technological gap of centuries may thus be bridged within a generation. *A country that is integrated into the global economy is likely to enjoy the benefits of technological spillover from inventions developed in other countries.* Trade and investment is an important channel through which knowledge is conveyed throughout the world.

This is not all. There are important benefits to developed and developing countries alike that arise from the fact that foreign trade increases the size of the national market. Exports enable small and moderately sized countries to establish and operate many plants of efficient size, which would be impossible if production were confined to the domestic market. Not only can firms enjoy *economies of scale,* but the economy as a whole benefits from the salutary impact of competitive pressure on prices, product improvement, and technological advancement. Innovation is often held back when competition is lacking. Furthermore, expansion of an industry ensures the availability of such things as a pool of skilled labor on which individual firms can draw (these benefits are known as economies external to the firm but internal to the industry). And overall industrial expansion usually brings with it the creation and development of the necessary infrastructure, such as transportation and power facilities, on which whole industries can draw (economies external to the industry). In turn, imports assure the existence of competitive pressure on domestic import-competing industries, even those that are internally monopolized. They also dampen inflation in the importing country.

This discussion indicates the immense potential of dynamic benefits that can flow from international trade. That the effect of these benefits is not the same in all countries is due to many causes, not the least of which is the willingness of government to avail itself of such "blessings" as free-trade policies.

Appendix 2–1 (following) offers an advanced analysis of the gains from trade.

Summary

This chapter establishes the conceptual basis for international trade. Comparative advantage, or industry differential in the *degree* of advantage, determines the existence of trade, the pattern of trade, and the limits to mutually beneficial exchange. Within these limits, the actual exchange ratio (or terms of trade) is determined by the relative intensity of demand of each country for the other country's product. In fact, demand considerations often assume far greater importance in determining trade flows. Both countries are shown to benefit from trade, as resources are reconfigured in line with comparative advantage, thereby increasing their efficiency.

By assigning each commodity a price according to its producing country's currency, the limits to mutually beneficial trade convert to the limits to a sustainable exchange rate. The principle of comparative advantage extends to multicommodity cases, whereby all goods produced by each country are ranked internally in the order of their domestic costs. The automobile and steel industries illustrated this principle when they declined in the U.S. ranking between 1960 and 1980 and hence lost their competitive positions.

While comparative advantage determines the direction of trade, absolute advantage determines relative wage rates and hence the relative living standards of the two countries. The wage ratio between two countries must fall within the productivity ratios of its industries to facilitate the comparative advantage configuration of production. Otherwise one of the countries could not compete even in the products in which it has a comparative advantage. Indeed "excessive" wage rates caused East Germany to be noncompetitive and resulted in mass unemployment.

There are other advantages to trade in addition to the more efficient allocation of resources. First of all, trade helps a country to contain its inflation—in fact, trading is actually anti-inflationary in that it allows imports to be bought more cheaply than it would cost to produce them at home. Second, the dynamic gains from trade place the country's real GDP on a higher growth path, because trade encourages savings and investment. Third, trade introduces new goods, inputs, and technology to the country. Finally, trade increases the size of the market, enabling a country's firms to enjoy economies of scale.

Important Concepts

Comparative advantage	Anti-inflationary trade
Country "in isolation"	Absolute advantage
Terms of trade	Industry ranking
Demand considerations	Static gains from trade
Relative wage rates	Dynamic gains from trade

Review Questions

1.   a. In what sense are the cost data of footnote 4 related to the figures of Scheme 1?

   b. Based on the figures of footnote 4, determine the

   - Direction of trade once it develops
   - Limits to mutually beneficial trade
   - Limits to a sustainable exchange rate.

2. Evaluate the following statements:
   a. In international trade, domestic cost ratios determine the limits of mutually beneficial trade, whereas demand considerations show where, within these limits, the actual exchange ratio will lie.
   b. Comparative advantage is a theoretical concept. It cannot be used to explain any real-world phenomena.
   c. The opening up of trade raises the price of export goods; hence trade is inflationary.
   d. The concept of absolute advantage offers explanations for East Germany's high unemployment rates in the 1990s.

3. Using the figures of Scheme 1, determine the limits to the U.K.–U.S. wage ratio.

4. What can you say about the following relationships?
   a. Absolute advantage and the relative standard of living
   b. Absolute advantage and the direction of international trade
   c. Comparative advantage and the direction of trade
   d. Comparative advantage and the relative standard of living

5. Demonstrate the benefits of trade to two trading countries.

6. a. Use the theory of comparative advantage to explain why it pays for:

   - The United States to export grains and import oil
   - Russia to export oil and import grains.

   b. Why does the popular press believe that grain exports are inflationary to the United States? What is wrong with this proposition?

7. (*For the well-initiated student*) Demonstrate, with the use of transformation and indifference curves, that trade is beneficial to both trading countries in the case of constant cost.
   Hint: Use (and explain) the following charts and the information contained in them.

| **FIGURE 2.A** | *International Trade under Constant Opportunity Costs* |

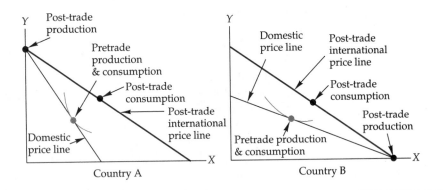

Note that constant cost is represented by straight line pretrade transformation curves. The two straight, colored lines, with their slopes equal in the two countries, represent the post-trade international price. In this case the domestic price ratio is independent of the position of the indifference curves.

8. Suppose that between 1960 and 1980 U.S. steel industry wage rates tripled while general manufacturing wage rates doubled, and that productivity in the steel industry advanced equally with that in all manufacturing. Also suppose that in Japan during the same period, both wage rates and productivity in the steel industry rose in tandem with that of all manufacturing.

   What happened to U.S. comparative advantage in steel over this period?

9. Discuss the U.S. comparative advantage in:
   a. Motor vehicles and steel
   b. High-technology products.

Chapter 2 Appendix 2–1

MORE ADVANCED ANALYSIS OF THE STATIC GAINS FROM TRADE

Chapter 2 showed that a differential price *ratio* between two countries gives rise to mutually beneficial trade. The static gains from trade were demonstrated in the case of constant opportunity cost, usually leading to complete specialization. This appendix shows the static gains in the context of increasing opportunity cost, where specialization may be incomplete.

The Consumer Indifference Map

According to the theory of consumer demand, the indifference curve represents various combinations of two goods, say wheat (*W*) and textiles (*T*), among which the consumer is indifferent. In figure A2–1.1 the consumer, presented with a large number of alternative combinations, finds herself indifferent to the choice among the following combinations of *W* and *T*:

Point	Textile (Quantity)	Wheat	MRS: ΔTextile/ΔWheat
a	8	1	
b	4	2	–4
c	2	3	–2
d	1	4	–1

These, as well as all the other combinations lying on the curve, yield equal amounts of satisfaction to the consumer. Each of the goods

is subject to diminishing marginal utility, meaning that the more of it that there is in the consumer's possession the less intensely she wants additional units. Thus when she has 8 units of *T* and only 1 of *W* (point *a*), she is willing to give up 4 of *T* to get an extra unit of *W*. But once the *T* in her possession declines to 4 and the *W* rises to 2 (point *b*), she is only willing to part with 2 *T* to obtain an extra unit of *W*. And beyond that point, an extra unit of *W* is worth to her only 1 unit of *T*.

These substitutions that leave the consumer equally well off are summarized in the last column of the table. Using the Greek delta symbol Δ to denote change or increment (negative for decrement), the ratio $\Delta T/\Delta W$ stands for what economists call the marginal rate of substitution (MRS) of *W* for *T*. The fact that it is declining is merely a reflection of the law of diminishing marginal utility of each good. And it is this feature that makes the indifference curve convex to the origin. The MRS between any two points along the curve is the slope of the line that connects the two points, such as $\overline{bc}$. And that slope (MRS) declines as we move down from *a* to *d*.

Each consumer has a whole map of such indifference curves (figure A2–1.2), with the higher ones (further away from the origin) indicating higher levels of satisfaction. Because utility cannot be measured, all we can say is that combinations represented by indifference curve III are more satisfactory[1] than those depicted by II, but we cannot say by how much. It is an essential feature of the map that the curves composing it do not intersect. For if curve I intersects

[1] It is only with the help of the indifference map of the consumer that we can say whether the consumer prefers combination *a* (with more *T* but less *W*) to combination *b*.

FIGURE A2–1.1	*Consumer Indifference Curve*

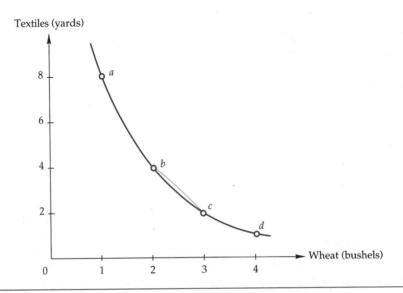

The consumer indifference curve represents combinations of textile and wheat that yield equal satisfaction to the consumer.

curve II, then at the point of intersection the two curves yield equal satisfaction, which is clearly inconsistent with the fact that at all preintersection points, curve II represents a higher level of satisfaction than curve I. Ordinary demand curves can be derived from the indifference map.

The Community Indifference Map

Can indifference curves of many individuals be aggregated to form the locus of points yielding equal satisfaction to the community or country? In other words, can we scale the axes in millions of units and have indifference curve I show all the combinations of the two goods providing a given level of satisfaction to all citizens combined, and so on for curves II and III? Strictly

speaking, the answer is no. For one thing, individual ranking of commodity combinations requires the use of majority rule unless the preferences of all are identical. And this need not result in a harmonious or transitive ranking, making it impossible to draw a community indifference curve.[2]

Even if this were not the case, we must remember that the ranking of situations is done by majority rule, with no "protection" offered to the minority. Indeed, if majority rule prevails, no one knows how strongly members of the "losing" minority feel about the outcome. Translated into real-world situations, any change (such as free trade or technological advance) that improves the position of society as a whole (and should therefore place it on a higher community indifference curve) is also likely to change

| FIGURE A2–1.2 | *Consumer Indifference Map* |

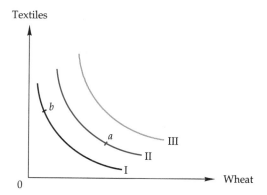

Higher indifference curves represent higher levels of satisfaction.

income distribution, so that even if we increase the total amount of goods available to society, it does not necessarily follow that the amount bestowed upon each member of the community would rise. As long as we are unable to compare the intensity of feelings of the gaining majority with that of the losing minority, we must adhere to the rule that the community as a whole is better off (and should be placed on a higher indifference curve) if and only if some of its members are better off, and *none* is worse off, than before the change. This can occur only when the income distribution remains unaf-

fected by the change in total income, or when the losers are compensated to a point at which they are as well off as before.

In sum, the community indifference curve is not a neat concept. It requires some heroic assumptions, such as permitting one dictator to make decisions (and rank combinations) for the entire community. Alternatively we must assume transitivity in ranking, coupled with unchanged income distribution or compensation of losers. Only then can we generalize from an individual to a country and employ the concept of community indifference curves. For

[2] To see what is meant by this possible (though not necessary) outcome, assume that three individuals X, Y, and Z are asked to rank commodity combinations A, B, and C in order of their preferences, and the ranking comes out as follows:

	X	Y	Z
1	A	B	C
2	B	C	A
3	C	A	B

Two of three persons (X and Z) prefer A to B, two of three persons (X and Y) prefer B to C, and two of three persons (Y and Z) prefer C to A. This violates the logical rule that if A is preferred to B and B is preferred to C then A ought to be preferred to C. It is known as lack of transitivity in preference ordering.

FIGURE A2–1.3   *Constant Opportunity Cost (in Millions of Units)*

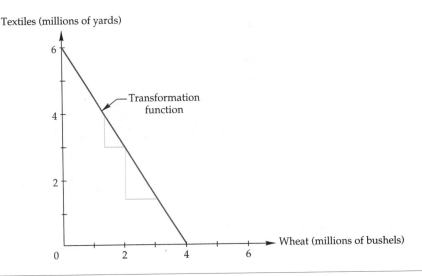

A linear transformation curve represents constant opportunity cost between the two goods.

pragmatic reasons economists do make these assumptions and use the concept, as we shall do here. Thus, the country will be thought of as having a map of nonintersecting community indifference curves, with the higher curves indicating higher levels of satisfaction.

Transformation Curves

Each country also has a given amount of resources that can be employed to produce two goods: wheat (W) and textile (T). As figure A2–1.3 shows, if all resources are devoted to the production of T, then 6 million yards can be produced. Alternatively, if all resources are employed in producing W, 4 million bushels can be grown. In between these two extremes lie all the possible combinations of the two goods that these resources can produce. The locus of these combinations is known as the *transformation function* or curve, because movement along this

curve indicates the transformation of one commodity into the other in the sense that resources are transferred from one industry to the other.

If the resources are *identically suited* for the production of the two goods, they can be shifted back and forth from one industry to another without any loss of efficiency. Certainly this would be the case if there was only one homogeneous factor (such as labor) or if two or more factors were used in a fixed and identical proportion in the production of both goods and were equally suited for the two industries. This is the constant-opportunity-cost case, and it is depicted by a straight-line transformation function. The cost of extra units of W in terms of T given up (when the resources are transferred from T to W) does not vary along the function and is equal to the constant slope of the curve. It is shown by the vertical to horizontal ratios of the gray-shaded lines. This is the Ricardian case, which leads to complete

FIGURE A2–1.4   *Increasing Opportunity Cost (in Millions of Units)*

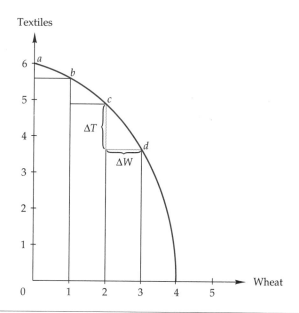

A concave transformation curve represents increasing opportunity cost between the two goods.

specialization once trade opens up: The country would produce either 6 million yards or 4 million bushels, depending on its comparative advantage relative to its trading partner (see fig. 2–A, p. 40).

Commonly, the country's resources are not equally suited for the production of both goods; some are more efficient in textile (T) production, others in wheat (W). In that case the two extreme points of producing only one commodity will exist as before, each point (on one of the two axes) showing how much of a good can be produced if all resources are devoted to its production. But the transformation of one good into the other (in the sense of resource transfer) will be different.

Starting, say, from 6 million yards of T, the transformation of T to W will not be at a fixed ratio yielding a straight line. Instead we encoun-

ter a (colored) line concave to the origin, depicting increasing opportunity cost (figure A2–1.4). At point a all the country's resources, presumably including some resources better suited for the production of W, are employed in production of T. As we move from a to b to obtain the first million bushels of W, the resources first transferred from T to W are better equipped to manufacture W to begin with. Thus, the cost of 1 million W is only 0.5 million yards of T; the ratio of 1 to 2 is depicted by the slope of the straight line connecting a to b. Moving from b to c we begin to transfer from industry T to W some resources that are better suited to produce T. Thus, it costs nearly 0.75 million of T to obtain the second million W. By the same token, a move from c to d shows that the third million units of W is obtainable at an opportunity cost of over 1 million yards of T. Finally, to obtain the fourth million

FIGURE A2–1.5   *Equilibrium in Isolation*

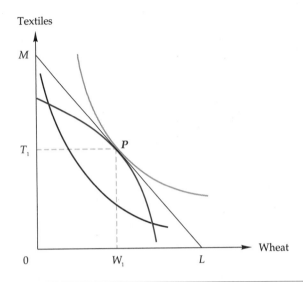

Equilibrium without trade occurs where the transformation curve is tangent to the highest possible indifference curve (point P).

bushels of W implies transferring all resources to industry W, including those that are ideally suited for T. Thus, the cost rises to 3.5 million yards of T.

What the concave opportunity-cost curve depicts is a rising ratio of $\Delta T/\Delta W$. This ratio is known as the marginal rate of transformation (MRT). At any point on the curve, it is equal to the slope of the curve. This is the case of increasing opportunity cost with which we are presently concerned.

Equilibrium in Isolation (without Trade)

The transformation function shows all the combinations of the two commodities that the country can produce given its resources. Points inside the curve represent unused resources (for

example, unemployment), while points outside the curve represent commodity combinations that cannot be attained. Thus, the country will strive to produce somewhere along the curve. But where? That is determined by the pattern of demand, or the community preference scheme for the two goods, as reflected in the community indifference map.

Given its resources, the country attempts to maximize satisfaction—namely, consume on the highest possible community indifference curve. And that indifference curve is one tangent to the transformation function. In figure A2–1.5, P is the equilibrium point of consumption and production, with $\overline{0T_1}$ and $\overline{0W_1}$ produced and consumed. Without international trade, domestic production and consumption are equal. The slope of ML (the common tangent to the indifference curve and the transformation function) is the commodity price ratio prevailing on the domestic market: $\overline{OM}$ of T is exchangeable for $\overline{OL}$ of W (note that in the constant-cost case depicted in figure A2–1.3, the domestic price ratio equals the slope of the transformation function and is independent of demand conditions).

International Trade: Similar Tastes

In order to introduce international trade, we must consider two countries: the United States and the United Kingdom. We first assume that the tastes of the two populations, as reflected in the shape of their indifference maps, are identical. On the other hand, their transformation curves are different: The United Kingdom is better suited to produce textiles, and the United States is better suited to produce wheat. The colored curves in figure A2–1.6 depict the two countries in isolation. Given its resource endowment, as represented by its transformation curve, each country reaches the highest possible indifference curve. Equilibrium production and consumption are obtained from the tangency solution at points E and F for the United Kingdom and the United States, respectively. Given equal demand patterns, the supply conditions determine relative market prices.

Relative prices of T and W are different in the two countries, as indicated by the different slopes of price lines MN for the United Kingdom and PR for the United States (shown in black). This establishes the fact that there is room for mutually beneficial trade. In particular, textiles are relatively cheaper in the United Kingdom, with $\overline{OM}$ of T exchangeable for $\overline{ON}$ of W, while wheat is relatively cheaper in the United States, where $\overline{OP}$ of T are exchangeable for $\overline{OR}$ of W.[3] These relative price ratios establish the fact that the United Kingdom has a compar-

ative advantage in T, the United States in W. They would move to specialize accordingly.

Each country would move along its transformation curve toward more specialization in production: the United Kingdom from point E upward, the United States from F downward. The slopes of the tangents to the two curves (the respective price lines) change as they move; indeed, the two slopes converge. Post-trade equilibrium is reached when the two price lines become parallel, meaning that the price ratios in the two countries are equal. In other words, after trade opens up, it will proceed to the point at which commodity prices are equalized. The gray-shaded price lines that are tangents to indifference curves II at C_A and C_B meet this requirement. But so do an infinite number of other "pairable" points along the two transformation functions.

To pinpoint the unique equilibrium solution, another condition must be satisfied. In the two-country world depicted here, what one country exports the other must import. The quantity traded by each country is the difference between what is produced and what is consumed domestically. As the production point travels along the transformation curve toward its equilibrium point, the price line tangent to it becomes flatter in the United Kingdom and steeper in the United States. Given the (preexisting) community indifference map of each country, the price lines become tangent to higher and higher indifference curves as this process proceeds. And it is this tangency position that determines the consumption points.

Suppose that consumption points C_A and C_B in the two countries are such that both equilibrium conditions are met. Thus the United Kingdom produces at P_A and consumes at C_A, while the United States produces at P_B and consumes at C_B; each pair of points is measured

---

[3] Ratios of quantities exchanged are employed to indicate relative prices.

FIGURE A2–1.6

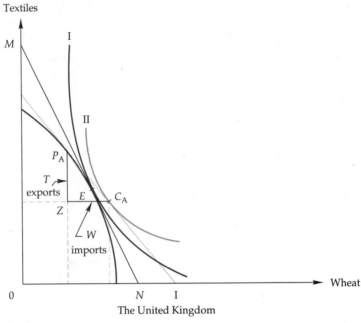

The United Kingdom

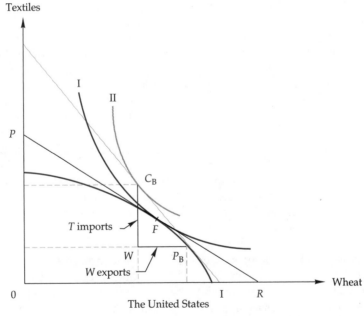

The United States

When the shape of the transformation curve differs between the two countries, their price ratios (when in isolation) also differ. Both countries benefit from trading at the international price ratio. Specialization may be incomplete under increasing cost conditions.

with respect to the axes of the country concerned. The difference between production and consumption is made up by trade. The United Kingdom produces more T than it consumes, and the excess $\overline{P_A Z}$ is exported. It consumes more W than it produces, and the difference $\overline{ZC_A}$ is imported. By similar reasoning, the United States imports $\overline{C_B W}$ (=$\overline{P_A Z}$) of T and exports $\overline{WP_B}$ (=$\overline{C_A Z}$) of W. The "trade triangles" of the two countries are thus identical.

Both countries land on a higher indifference curve (II) than they were able to attain in isolation (I), thereby demonstrating that both gain from trade. In this case, trade enables each country to specialize in production according to the suitability of its resources and to remain unspecialized in consumption. This divergence between production and consumption mixes is not possible without trade. How much the gain is to each country cannot be determined, because there is no way to measure satisfaction. The indifference curves merely tell us the ranking of utility levels in ascending order, as we proceed upward away from the origin. Readers who are uneasy about using community indifference curves may simply note that trade enables each country to consume outside the region of possible production.

While each country moves to produce more of the commodity in which it has a comparative advantage, specialization in this case is not complete. Commodity prices were equalized before either country got completely out of the production of the other product. Thus, the post-trade equilibrium situation finds each country producing some of both products. This is a possible, but not necessary, result of increasing opportunity cost.[4]

What accounts for the difference between the transformation curves of the two countries?

The answers can be many and varied. It could be that the United Kingdom has developed a more efficient technique for producing T, and the United States employs more efficient means for manufacturing W. Or the two countries may have become equipped by tradition or the skill of their labor forces in the production of their respective products. A third possible explanation, rooted in the differences between resource endowments of the two countries, will be explored in the next chapter.

Differences in Demand

Differences in demand are illustrated in figure A2–1.7. The colored lines represent the pretrade positions; they depict identical transformation functions but different indifference curves. The resulting price lines $\overline{MN}$ and $\overline{PR}$ (in black) show that textiles are relatively cheaper in the United Kingdom (where consumers prefer wheat), and wheat is relatively cheaper in the United States (where consumers prefer textiles). This establishes the pattern of comparative advantage and the lines of specialization once trade opens up. As before, the post-trade equilibrium position must satisfy the conditions of equal prices in the two countries (parallel price lines) and equal quantities of each commodity imported and exported. The gray-shaded price lines meet these conditions.[5] Given the indifference maps, the two countries will consume at C_A and C_B and produce at P_A and P_B. In this case, they move toward less specialization in production and greater specialization in consumption. In other words, trade makes it possible to satisfy divergent wants from identical production conditions. Consequently, both countries experience a rise in welfare, as indicated by the fact that they find themselves on higher indifference

---

[4] To see that it is not a necessary result, note that not all points along each transformation are "pairable" with points on the other function, in the sense that they have identical slopes.

[5] The international price line may be thought of as an alternative transformation curve available to the country, along which it might exchange one product for the other.

FIGURE A2–1.7 *Equilibrium with Trade: Different Indifference Curves*

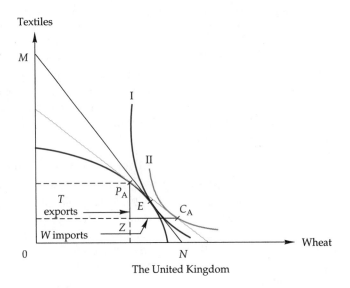

The United Kingdom

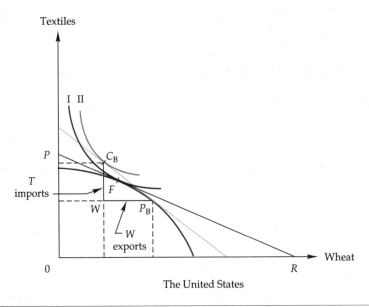

The United States

When the shape of the indifference curve differs between the two countries, their price ratios (when in isolation) also differ. Both countries benefit from trading at the international price ratio. Specialization may be incomplete under increasing cost conditions.

curves. The United Kingdom exports $\overline{P_A Z}$ of T and imports $\overline{C_A Z}$ of W, while the United States exports $\overline{P_B W}$ ($=\overline{C_A Z}$) of W and imports $\overline{C_B W}$ ($=\overline{P_A Z}$) of T.

The General Case

In the general case, both the transformation curves and the indifference maps may differ. If the resulting pretrade price lines are not parallel, there is room for mutually beneficial trade. The relative prices established before trade determine the pattern of comparative advantage and the direction of trade. Only when the two pretrade price lines are parallel is there no room for trade. This can come about if both the transformation curves and the indifference maps of the two countries are identical. Alternatively, it can happen when the two sets of curves differ in such a way as to precisely offset each other—in other words, if each country prefers to consume the commodity that it can produce best and if that preference exactly compensates for the degree of production advantage so as to produce identical prices.

CHAPTER 3

The Commodity Composition of Trade

s long as economists were interested merely in demonstrating the gain from international trade, the analysis presented in the previous chapter was adequate. In a nutshell, it demonstrates the self-evident proposition that whenever the domestic price (or cost) ratio is different in two countries, there is room for mutually beneficial trade, and the *greater the difference is in the price ratios, the greater the static gain will be.*

But during the present century the attention of international trade theorists turned from the gain from trade to the determinants of the commodity composition of trade. In other words, they have attempted to unravel the factors that determine which country exports what commodity. To be sure, this question was not ignored in the last chapter. Rather, the answer was given on two levels. In the context of the opportunity cost discussion, it is stated that each country exports the commodity that is relatively cheaper in that country, without exploring the reason for its lower cost. The Ricardian model with one factor of production (labor) probes a little deeper and hypothesizes that each country exports the commodity that it can produce at lower average labor cost (or higher average labor productivity). In other words, differential labor productivity is said to be the cause of the price differences. (Appendix A3–1 offers a formal presentation of the Ricardian model.)

This answer requires no further amplification as long as we are only concerned with the gains from trade. But if we wish to focus on the commodity composition of trade, the propositions articulated above may be inaccurate, and even if they are accurate, they are inadequate, because they beg further questions.

With respect to accuracy, the answer centering on labor productivity is more specific and therefore more meaningful than the one postulating differential opportunity cost ratios, even though it is based on a simple assumption. It attributes the price differential to only one factor: differences in average labor productivity. As applied to the real world, this is a testable hypothesis that can be confirmed or rejected by empirical observations. Labor is not the only cost involved in producing a commodity. Although it is the most important single element, its effect can be swamped by other cost components. Moreover, the flow of manufactured products is not determined by cost and supply considerations alone. Manufactures are characterized by what economists call product differentiation or lack of homogeneity. What is essentially the same product appears on the market in a great variety of forms that differ from one another in quality, dimensions, packaging, brand name, and so on. The buyer is swayed by many factors other than price. And because industrial goods make up most of world trade, it cannot be concluded *a priori* that costs of production determine the direction of trade flows. The demand side of the equation cannot be ignored.

Even if labor productivity were the determining factor of who exports what, it still demands an answer to *what determines labor productivity?* A widely studied and rather specific explanation of the commodity composition of trade is the **factor proportions** (or **endowment**) **theory.** First introduced by the Swedish economists E. F. Heckscher and B. Ohlin, the theory was refined after World War II by Paul Samuelson and made into a very elegant, though restrictive, construct. Stripped to its bare essentials, this theory is a marriage between the resource endowment of the country, on the one hand, and the economic characteristics of the commodities traded, on the other.

THE FACTOR PROPORTIONS THEORY

Consider a world of two countries, the United States and the United Kingdom, producing two commodities: textiles and wheat; with two factors of production: labor and capital.[1] All production is carried on by purely competitive firms; there are many firms in each industry, none large enough to influence by its own actions the conditions prevailing in the market. Prices of the two products and of the two factors are determined by supply and demand; each firm accepts these prices and adjusts its activities to them. In other words, firms are price takers on both the commodity and factor markets. Also, free internal mobility of labor and capital between industries ensures that the price of each factor is the same in the two industries within each country. On the other hand, factors are not free to move

[1] This is sometimes referred to as a *2 by 2 by 2 model*. See R. Jones, "Two-ness in Trade Theory," Princeton, *Special Papers in International Trade*, no. 12, 1976. Most conclusions generalize to higher dimensional models, such as 3 by 3 by 3.

between countries, so that pretrade compensations of each factor can differ internationally.

Each producer of a commodity has a range of available production methods from which one is selected. The basic economic feature that distinguishes various production techniques is the labor/capital ratio. The producer adjusts the factor use ratio to the ratio of factor prices in the marketplace. The more expensive labor is relative to capital, the less labor and the more capital the producer would use. Each commodity is assumed to be produced under identical production conditions in the two countries,[2] in the sense that *if faced with the same factor prices, producers in both countries would use the two factors in the same ratio.* In other words, the processes available in the two countries for the production of a given commodity are the same and, if factor prices were the same, the two countries would select the identical process—or factor use ratio—to produce the product. Economists summarize this by saying that each commodity has identical production functions, or isoquants, in the two countries.

On the other hand, the production processes required differ from one commodity to the other within each country in a definite, unique, and consistent manner: For any given pair of factor prices, the production of wheat utilizes a higher capital/labor ratio than the production of textiles.[3] This is expressed technically by saying that wheat is **capital intensive** relative to textiles or, equivalently, that textiles are **labor intensive** relative to wheat. The extension of this relationship to a world of more than two commodities involves the *ranking* of all goods by their capital/labor ratio. A fundamental assumption of the model is that this ranking (not necessarily the ratios themselves) is the same in the two trading nations. In other words, wheat is the relatively capital-intensive commodity, textiles the relatively labor-intensive product, in both the United States *and* the United Kingdom.

In the simplest case, where the ratio of factor inputs is fixed, the above statement may be illustrated by the example shown in table 3.1.

In both countries, the capital to labor ratio is 5 to 2 in the case of wheat and 2 to 4 in the case of textiles. Wheat, (like automobiles and steel), is a capital-intensive good, while textiles (like footwear and lumber) are labor-intensive commodities. Highly sophisticated products, such as jet aircraft or

---

[2] An additional assumption is that if a producer increases the use of both factors by a given proportion, output will rise by that same proportion. This is known in economics as *constant returns to scale.* It is to be sharply distinguished from the law of diminishing returns in that it allows both factors to vary, while the concept of diminishing returns operates when one factor is variable and the other remains fixed. Consequently, it is possible for a firm to function under constant returns to scale and at the same time be subject to diminishing returns.

[3] Remember that, within each country, factor prices are the same in both industries. This is guaranteed by the free and unobstructed mobility of factors within each country as assumed in the model. Thus, if the price of labor (wage rates) were higher in the wheat than in the textile industry, labor would move from the latter to the former until wage rates were equal in both.

TABLE 3.1	*Production Conditions in the U.S. and U.K.*

| | Input Requirement in the Production of: | |
	100 Bushels of Wheat	**10 Yards of Textiles**
United States	5 units of capital + 2 days of labor	2 units of capital + 4 days of labor
United Kingdom	5 units of capital + 2 days of labor	2 units of capital + 4 days of labor

supercomputers, are considered technology intensive because they require significant expenditures on research and development along with large numbers of scientists and engineers.

How are countries distinguished from one another? They differ in their *resource endowment:* The United States possesses a higher capital to labor ratio than the United Kingdom. We say it is the relatively **capital-abundant** country, while the United Kingdom is the relatively **labor-abundant** country. For example, assume that the United States has 100 million workers and $4,000 billion of capital, whereas the United Kingdom has 30 million workers and $600 billion of capital. This works out to $40,000 of capital per worker in the United States and $20,000 of capital per worker in the United Kingdom. It also explains why labor is more efficient in the United States: Each worker has more capital available than a comparable worker in Great Britain.

Note that it is the endowment *ratio,* rather than the absolute amount of each factor available, that is important. If we assume (as this model does) that demand conditions are similar in the two nations, then relative factor prices are determined by their supply as reflected in the resource endowment. Thus, capital becomes relatively cheaper in the United States and labor relatively cheaper in the United Kingdom. More precisely, the capital to labor *price* ratio is lower in the United States than in the United Kingdom. Combine this result with the earlier postulates concerning manufacture in the two countries and the following conclusions emerge: The United States specializes in the production of wheat, the commodity that uses much of its relatively cheap factor (capital)—it exports wheat and imports textiles; the United Kingdom specializes in textiles, the commodity that uses much of the relatively cheap factor (labor) there—it exports textiles and imports wheat. Wheat is relatively cheaper in the United States because it is capital intensive, while textiles are relatively cheaper in the United Kingdom because they are labor intensive.

This result can be translated into the example of the previous chapter. It was shown there that the United States had a comparative advantage in wheat, the United Kingdom in textiles, with comparative labor cost or productivity determining this outcome. Now we can add that U.S. labor is relatively more productive in wheat production because wheat is a relatively capital-intensive commodity and American labor has more capital to work with than does British labor, since the United States is the relatively capital-abundant country. On the other hand, the United Kingdom, being the relatively labor-abundant country, acquires *comparative* advantage in textiles, a commodity that requires relatively less capital in its production. In general, *each country exports the commodities that are relatively intensive in the factor with which it is relatively well endowed.* In an indirect sense, each country exports the services of its abundant factor and imports the services of its scarce factor— as embodied in the two bundles of traded goods. Appendix 3–2 offers a sketchy graphical explanation of the factor proportions model.

For over twenty years economists have been practically wedded to this explanation of the pattern of international trade, for several reasons. In the first place, it is a logically tight structure, where the conclusions follow uniquely and neatly from the assumptions. It is a very simple explanation (perhaps much too simple) that lends itself readily to geometric and mathematical manipulations—a quality that fascinates modern economists. Second, despite its limitations and the problems discovered in attempts to test it empirically, it is *highly useful in explaining a wide range of observed phenomena.* For example, in trade between industrial countries and under-developed countries (LDCs), industrial nations are relatively capital abundant and tend to export capital-intensive products, while LDCs are relatively labor abundant and tend to export labor-intensive products.

Additionally, the model implies that each country exports the *services* of its abundant factor, embodied in the bundle of its exported goods, and imports the *services* of its scarce factor, embodied in the bundle of its imported goods. It follows that commodity trade and international factor movement are substitutes for each other. If Canada or Europe erects protective barriers to keep out American (capital-intensive) goods, U.S. corporations can send capital to these countries, establishing factories and producing within them, thereby bypassing the tariff wall. Such branch plants or subsidiary corporations abroad are known as **direct foreign investment.** Conversely, to the extent that the United States keeps out Mexican (labor-intensive) products, Mexican workers will migrate to the United States—legally or illegally. The most effective way to curtail immigration from Mexico is to open up the U.S. market to their products. Workers would then produce in Mexico and ship their labor-intensive commodities to the United States. This may be one of the outcomes of the North American Free Trade Agreement (NAFTA).

The model may also be attractive because it concentrates solely upon the most elementary properties of the trading countries. Any other explanatory factor that could conceivably be advanced—such as labor productivity or production cost—raises the question of what determines that factor itself. By embedding the explanation in the bare essentials of the country's economic structure we minimize the need for such questions. The natural resources of the country are determined by nature and not by any economic factors. Immigration policies and sociological factors affecting birthrates, rather than economic variables, are the main determinants of labor supply, although an important qualification is introduced by the fact that the size of the labor force and its level of participation are at least partly related to economic conditions. The point is probably least valid in the case of capital, where it is certainly legitimate to inquire into the economic causes of past investment that led to today's capital stock. These certainly include the saving behavior of past generations that made resources available for investment, natural resources, entrepreneurial ability of the population, and a degree of destruction through wars and other causes. To the extent that technological developments control investment, we can still ask what (besides human genius) motivates new technology. But all these are causes of past behavior. Today's capital stock can be taken for granted. Consequently, despite these qualifications, the model reduces to the bare essentials of the economic structure, at least when considered as of the period under study.

Finally, because the model employs the country's economic structure to explain trade, the process can be reversed to inquire into the effect of international trade on the economic structure, especially on the remuneration of factors of production and the distribution of income among those factors.[4] Since the model implies that each country exports the *services* of its abundant factor and imports the *services* of its scarce factor, it follows that the introduction of international trade into an otherwise isolated economy raises the demand for the abundant factor—and therefore its remuneration—while lowering returns to the scarce factor. (The opposite result follows from the imposition of a tariff.) With incomplete specialization, and under the assumption of this model, international trade would lead to the equalization of factor prices between the trading nations.[5]

Additional Insights

More specifically, the process of **factor price equalization** is based on changes in the factor-use ratios in the production of the two commodities. In the example used earlier, and under conditions of incomplete specialization, trade causes the United Kingdom to produce more textiles and less wheat, thereby shifting resources from wheat to textiles. But because of the difference in the factor-use ratio in the two industries, resources are released from the wheat industry at a relatively high capital to labor ratio and can be absorbed into the textile industry only at a relatively low capital to labor ratio. Thus the process involves freeing relatively more capital and less labor than can be absorbed. In the market scrambling that ensues, the price of capital falls and that of labor rises. This must be the outcome if (as the model

---

[4] The distribution of income among factors of production (the total return to labor, to capital, to natural resources, and to entrepreneurial ability) is known as the *functional distribution of income*. It is to be distinguished from the size distribution, designed to assess the degree of income inequality in the population.

[5] These results do not follow the Ricardian model, which leads to complete specialization.

FIGURE 3.1   *Effect of Trade on Factor Prices*

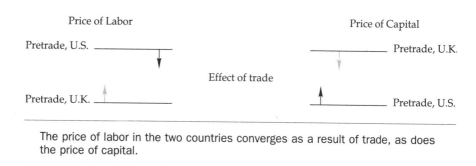

The price of labor in the two countries converges as a result of trade, as does the price of capital.

assumes) all factors are fully employed before and after trade. Precisely the reverse holds true in the United States, where resources are released from textiles at a relatively low capital to labor ratio and are absorbed into producing wheat at a relatively high capital to labor ratio. This process entails a rise in the price of capital and a fall in the price of labor.

Two consequences of this transformation are among the topics explored by economists since World War II. First, the internal distribution of income in each country has changed, with the relatively abundant factor (capital in the United States and labor in England) gaining and the relatively scarce factor losing from the introduction of trade. (This is known as the Stolper-Samuelson theory, named after the scholars who developed it.) These effects occur in both industries as long as specialization is incomplete and both goods are produced in the two countries. But in each country the loss to the scarce factor is less than the gain to the abundant factor, so that the community as a whole benefits from the introduction of trade.[6] Conversely, restrictions on trade would benefit the relatively scarce factor. Australia, for example, has in the past imposed tariffs in order to affect the internal distribution of income in favor of labor, which is scarce there relative to land. This may also explain why vast segments of the American labor movement favor various forms of protection from imports, labor being scarce relative to capital in the United States. However, there are superior means at the disposal of government to change income distribution, such as taxes and subsidies.

Second, in comparing factor remunerations between countries, we notice that the introduction of trade lowers the price of capital in the United Kingdom and raises it in the United States. Since capital is the relatively scarce factor in the United Kingdom and was more highly priced there than in the United States before the advent of trade, this constitutes a convergence of the two prices. Similar convergence occurs in the price of labor as it rises in England and declines in America. Schematically, these movements can be illustrated as in figure 3.1. This convergence takes place in both

[6] While trade has income-distribution consequences, so does every change in the economy—such as technological progress or shifts in consumer preferences. But it is always possible to compensate the losers out of the increase in total income of the community, or at least cushion the losses by providing support programs for the losers.

industries as long as specialization is incomplete. Under the assumptions of incomplete specialization in both countries, identical technologies, constant returns to scale,[7] and absence of transport cost and barriers to trade so goods prices converge completely, there would be complete factor–price equalization between countries. But because these assumptions do not obtain in the real world, there is only a tendency in this direction.

Empirical Testing

Considering its virtues, one may ask whether there is anything wrong with the model. The answer is that empirical tests yielded mixed results. For a long time it was impossible to test the factor proportions theory because commodities entering international trade could not be decomposed into their labor and capital components. The production processes in an industrial economy are rather complex. Each final good, such as automobiles, can be decomposed into its labor, capital, and material inputs. And the last item (such as steel and other metals) also must be decomposed in the same procedure, and so on down the line. Only by working backward through the production processes to the crude material stage, which itself is found in natural form, can one sum up the total labor and capital inputs embodied in each final product. Indeed, for most traded commodities, the labor and capital content in the final stage of fabrication is only about half the total.

This impasse was broken in the late 1930s, when mobilization required precise knowledge of the production processes in the economy. If the government decides to increase the production of airplanes by one thousand units, to avoid bottlenecks it must also know what inputs from other industries would be required. In fact, any massive shifts in the commodity composition of production, for demobilization or for any other reason, necessitates such knowledge. Smooth transition of the economy is impossible without it. Nobel laureate Wassily Leontief was the first to develop a method that provided this information for the United States in the form of input–output tables. These show the interindustry flows of goods and services as they work their way through the production processes into final form. This work has since been taken over by the U.S. Department of Commerce, and similar studies are available for numerous other countries.

Once input–output statistics became available, it was possible to decompose American exports and imports into their labor and capital components, which Leontief did in the mid-1950s. He discovered that a

---

[7] This implies that the marginal product of each factor depends only on the factor-use ratio and is completely independent of the scale of operations.

representative basket of American exports embodied more labor and less capital than one of American imports. Certainly the capital to labor ratio was higher for imports than exports. Since the United States was by far the most capital-abundant country in the world, this result contradicted the factor proportions theory. His finding caused great consternation among theorists and came to be known as the **Leontief scarce-factor paradox.**

Since that time, similar data from other countries have been subject to the same analysis, but in many cases they failed to verify the theory. It should be pointed out that in the 1950s the United States occupied an extreme position in the spectrum of countries ranked by the capital to labor endowment ratio and therefore could be considered the relatively capital-abundant country in relation to the rest of the world. This is not true of other nations that may trade with some countries that are capital abundant and others that are labor abundant relative to themselves.[8] For them, the proper test requires examination of bilateral trade relationships. Many tests, however, failed to confirm the accepted doctrine.

These results touched off a heated debate among economists that lasted two decades. Most writers attempted to salvage the factor proportions theory by reconciling it with the empirical findings. Leontief himself pointed to the great effectiveness of American labor, resulting from superior management, better training, and stronger motivation. He concluded that since American labor is three times as effective as its foreign counterpart (even when using the same capital equipment), when labor is measured in efficiency units the United States comes out as the relatively labor-abundant country, and the theory is thus vindicated.

In a more general way, data show that the U.S. exports products that are more skill intensive, as well as technology intensive, than those it imports. Since new goods made with innovative technology are less capital intensive than goods with mature technologies suitable for mass production, they show up as labor intensive on a simple capital-labor scale.

Other economists claimed instead that U.S. import restrictions so heavily protect labor-intensive industries that the observed import basket is artificially biased toward capital-intensive products. Still others maintained that the trouble lies in confining the model to two factors of production and ignoring natural resources. In fact, what the United States imports is natural-resource-intensive products. Because these necessitate much capital in their

---

[8] A study of the composition of Soviet trade in 1955–1968 shows conformity with the factor proportions hypothesis. The study concludes, "When the Soviets trade with relatively developed countries they import capital intensive commodities and export labor intensive goods. When they trade with nations at similar development level, imports and exports embody factors in approximately equal proportions, and when they trade with underdeveloped regions, they export capital intensive and import labor intensive products." Steven Rosefielde, "Factor Proportions and Economic Rationality in Soviet International Trade, 1955–68," *American Economic Review*, September 1974: 674–675.

production, they show up as capital intensive on a capital-labor scale. Other theoretical as well as statistical reconciliations were advanced, and the data were modified and manipulated in various directions.

ALTERNATIVE THEORIES

Although the factor proportions theory cannot explain all international trade, and indeed should not have been expected to do so in the first place, it still has considerable explanatory power. But it is unreasonable to expect one simple theory to account fully for such a complex phenomenon as trade in all goods among one hundred nations. In particular this theory cannot adequately explain the vast expansion of trade among the industrial countries whose factor endowment ratios are rather similar. Much of this exchange is **intra-industry trade,** namely, trade in similar products that are differentiated (or distinguished) from each other by some feature(s). It is not surprising, therefore, that during the 1970s and 1980s several alternative explanations appeared in the professional literature,[9] some of which are reviewed next.

Sector-Specific Factors   The **sector-specific model** is a widely used variant of the factor proportion theory. It assumes a two-sector economy, with agriculture (A) using land and labor, and manufacturing (M) employing capital and labor. Labor is perfectly mobile between the two sectors, whereas capital and land are specific to manufacturing and agriculture respectively. In each sector labor is combined with a fixed quantity of the other factor (capital in M or land in A), to produce the product. Hence labor is subject to diminishing returns, and the value of the marginal product of labor (VMP_L)[10] declines in each sector. Labor mobility ensures that the wage rate, which equals the VMP_L, will be equalized across the two sectors. Indeed, this equality condition determines the distribution of labor between the two sectors.[11]

Suppose the country is land abundant so that it has a comparative advantage in A. When free trade is introduced to an otherwise isolated economy, the domestic price of A rises. Labor is drawn from M to A, so that more labor is combined with (specific factor) land, while less labor is combined with capital. The value of the marginal product of land rises and that of

---

[9] See, for example, R. Baldwin, "Determinants of the Commodity Structure of U.S. Trade," *American Economic Review,* May 1971.

[10] The value of the marginal product of labor is the price of the product times the marginal physical product of labor.

[11] See R. W. Jones, "A Three-Factor Model in Theory, Trade and History," in J. Bhagwati et al. (eds.), *Trade, Balance of Payments, and Growth: Essays in Honor of C. Kindleberger,* Amsterdam, North Holland, 1971.

capital declines: Owners of land gain and capital-owners lose. Hence there is a potential conflict between the owners of factors specific to the expanding and contracting industries (the gainers and losers).[12] The effect of trade on the mobile factor is ambiguous, as shown in Appendix 3–3 at the end of this chapter.

While trade benefits the entire country, it may leave some groups worse off: Owners of factors specific to the export industries gain from trade; owners of factors specific to the import-competing industries lose from trade. The mobile factor can either gain or lose. These redistributional effects are highlighted by this model. In fact, much of the debate over trade policy is an argument between the losers and the gainers.

Human Skills In industrial economies, the training and sophistication of the labor force is the most important characteristic distinguishing one country from another. Therefore, countries that are relatively well endowed with professional personnel and highly trained labor will specialize in and export skill-intensive goods. Conversely, relative abundance of unskilled labor promotes the export of commodities embodying mostly untrained labor. A test of this hypothesis requires information on the skill content of products entering international trade and the matching of this information with the relative abundance (or scarcity) of skill in the trading nations.[13]

An extension of this hypothesis can be used to explain comparative advantage in high-technology products. Because they are produced by knowledge-intensive industries, these products tend to be developed in countries with both a high proportion of research scientists and engineers in the labor force and a willingness to spend a relative large share of their GDP on research and development.

International trade is sometimes invoked to explain the rise in income inequality in the United States (and to a lesser extent in Europe) over the past 20 years.[14] That phenomenon includes increased earnings disparity between college and high school graduates. One possible reason is the large influx from the Far East of products intensive in unskilled labor, in exchange for U.S. exports of skill-intensive products. In the United States that reduces

---

[12] Income distribution effects that arise because some factors are immobile represent a temporary, transitional problem. In contrast the distributional effects in the factor proportions model are permanent. Thus a possible interpretation of the sector-specific model is that it corresponds to the short-run version of the Heckscher-Ohlin theory. Because capital is not mobile across sectors in the short run, there is a direct conflict of interest among capitalists in the export and import-competing industries. See J. P. Neary, "Short-run Capital Specificity and the Pure Theory of International Trade," *Economic Journal*, 86, 1987.

[13] See D. Keesing, "Labor Skills and Comparative Advantage," *American Economic Review*, May 1966.

[14] See J. Cole and C. Towe, "Income Distribution and Macroeconomic Performance," IMF Working Paper no. 96/9t, November 1996. There has also been an increase in income inequality between rich and poor countries. See L. Pritchett, "Forget Convergence: Divergence Past, Present, and Future." *Finance and Development*, June 1996.

demand for unskilled workers and increases demand for skilled workers. A rival explanation for the rise in income disparity is technological advance: more advanced technologies require ever rising skills, thereby raising demand for skilled workers and lowering demand for unskilled workers. Although both these explanations may be valid, most economists subscribe to the second one (technology) as the main cause of increased income inequality.

Product Cycle   The **product cycle** hypothesis stresses the *standardization* process of products.[15] Early manufacture of a new good involves experimentation with both the feature of the product and the manufacturing process. Therefore, in its beginning stages, the good is nonstandardized. As markets grow and the various techniques become common knowledge, both the product and the process become standardized and perhaps even subject to international standards and specifications. At that time, production can begin in less sophisticated nations. According to this hypothesis, highly sophisticated economies are expected to export nonstandardized goods, while less sophisticated countries specialize in more standardized goods.

Monopolistic Competition and Intra-Industry Trade   All the explanations mentioned above, along with the factor-endowment theory, have one thing in common: They maintain that international trade is based on *differences* between countries, either in technology or in factor endowments (or variants thereof). Namely, trade is based on comparative advantage and it *compensates for national deficiencies*, whether in capital, labor skill, management, or technological sophistication. The gain from trade derives from the fact that it enables countries to specialize and to reallocate resources among different activities. The result is that countries import and export *dissimilar* goods. In the absence of scale economies, and with perfect competition in all markets, this is the only possible basis for trade. But once we allow for economies of scale, trade can arise even if both technology and resource endowment are identical between countries. Economies of scale means that if all inputs are increased by a given percentage, output rises by a *greater* percentage. It implies that production cost per unit of output *declines* as the scale of operations expands.

Consider first economies of scale that are *external* to the firm. All individual firms are perfectly competitive, yielding no economic profits, but the productivity of the firm depends on how large an industry it is a part of

---

[15] R. Vernon, "International Investment and Trade in the Product Cycle," *Quarterly Journal of Economics*, May 1966; and L. Wells, "A Product Cycle for International Trade?," *Journal of Marketing*, July 1968. Note that rapid technological diffusion shortens the product cycle.

(not on the size of the firm itself). This would be the case when the size of the industry determines the availability of specialized labor skills to all firms, the development and diffusion of inventions, and the like. The fashion, watch, or high-technology industries are possible cases in point. This feature may explain why firms in such industries tend to cluster in one geographical area, such as the Silicon Valley in California, where many high-tech firms are concentrated. In such an industry labor productivity would increase, and unit labor cost would decline, as the industry expands in size.

Suppose the watch industry is subject to such scale economies while the pen industry is not. Assume also that Switzerland and France have identical technology in each of the two industries. Yet despite the identical technologies in the watch industry, the unit labor cost would be lower in the country where that industry is larger (this is not the case in the pen industry). If Switzerland started out with a larger-sized watch industry, it would have lower production costs (based solely on the size of the industry) and become an exporter of watches. Correspondingly, France would become a watch importer. As trade causes the industry to expand in Switzerland and to contract in France, the Swiss cost advantage would gradually increase. This process may go on until (a) the French watch industry disappears altogether and France specializes completely in pens, while Switzerland produces both commodities; or (b) the Swiss watch industry absorbs all the labor in that country, so that Switzerland produces only watches, while France continues to produce both goods. In either case Switzerland would export watches and import pens.

But what is it that made the Swiss watch industry larger than that of France to begin with? We cannot tell! It may simply be a historical accident. However, the advantage gained from that accident accumulates over time. Thus we *cannot predict* the pattern of trade. If the watch industry was initially of the same size in the two countries, neither one would have a cost advantage. But as soon as something happens to tilt the size advantage in favor of one country, it would acquire a cost advantage, which would be self-reinforcing over time.

Such trade, based on scale economies, is unambiguously beneficial to both countries. As the production of watches becomes increasingly concentrated in one country (no matter which one), the industry size in that country expands and production costs (which are inversely related to the size of the industry) decline. But there is no corresponding increase in production cost in the pen industry, regardless of how it is rearranged between countries, for that industry is not subject to scale economies. Hence with a given amount of resources, more of the two goods can be produced after trade than before.

In sum, scale economies lead to international specialization and trade even in the absence of different technologies and resource endowment.

Although its pattern is unpredictable, this trade is additional to that generated by comparative advantage, and it benefits both countries.

Once we leave the world of perfectly competitive firms, it is possible to have scale economies within the firm and to combine the roles of economies of scale and comparative advantage in generating trade. Suppose the watch industry is monopolistically competitive while the pen industry is perfectly competitive.

Monopolistic competition is a market structure in which there are many firms, and entry into the industry is easy and unrestricted, ensuring that economic profits will be competed away and be zero in the long run. In these aspects the market structure is similar to perfect competition. But unlike perfect competition, consumers do not view the good produced by the various firms as perfect substitutes. Rather, the good produced by each firm is differentiated in some way—such as the service associated with it, packaging, or even brand name—from those produced by other firms in the industry. Such firms can operate under increasing returns to scale: If the firm increases all inputs by a given proportion, its output rises by a *greater* proportion. Put differently, the firm's unit production cost declines as output expands.

Expansion of the market has two beneficial effects for consumers: It produces a larger number of firms producing a wider range of varieties of the (differentiated) product; and because each firm would *produce a larger output, at a lower average cost,* each variety would be available at a lower price.

Assume that Switzerland is a relatively capital abundant country while France is relatively labor abundant, and that the watch industry is relatively capital intensive while the pen industry is relatively labor intensive. If watches were a homogeneous product (a perfectly competitive industry) then, when trade opens up, Switzerland would export watches to France and import pens.

But the watch industry is monopolistically competitive, with each firm manufacturing a different *variety* of watches. Because of economies of scale in producing each variety, neither of the two countries would produce all the varieties. Switzerland will become a net exporter of watches. But there will be consumers in Switzerland who prefer varieties produced by French firms, and those watches will be imported. So there will be an exchange of watches between the two countries, or *intra-industry trade.*

The overall trade pattern that would emerge in these circumstances would have both interindustry (between industries) and intra-industry components.[16]

---

[16] For discussion, see S. Linder, *An Essay on Trade and Transformation,* New York: Wiley, 1961; E. Helpman, "International Trade in the Presence of Product Differentiation Economies of Scale and Monopolistic Competition," *Journal of International Economics,* August 1981; and P. Krugman, "New Theories of Trade among Industrial Countries," *American Economic Review,* May 1983.

(a) Interindustry trade would reflect comparative advantage. Switzerland would export watches to France and would import pens.

(b) In addition there would develop intra-industry trade that has nothing to do with comparative advantage. Because economies of scale in watchmaking prevent one country from producing all the varieties, Switzerland and France would export to each other different varieties of watches. The pattern of intra-industry trade is unpredictable.

Switzerland would export only watches (and no pens) under both types of trade, thus becoming a net exporter of watches. France would export pens under interindustry trade and watches under intra-industry trade. It would be a net exporter of pens and a net importer of watches. The more similar the countries are in their technologies and factor endowments, the less would be their interindustry and the greater would be their intra-industry trade. Indeed much of the trade among the industrial countries is of the intra-industry variety, while most North–South trade tends to be of the interindustry variety.

However, intra-industry examples can be found in North–South trade. For instance, General Electric has realized that because American consumers prefer refrigerators with two doors, it is unprofitable to manufacture single-door refrigerators within the United States. In contrast, the Mexican preference lies with single-door refrigerators. Therefore, G.E. supplies the low-volume, double-door segment of the Mexican market from its U.S. plants, and the low-volume, single-door segment of the U.S. market out of Mexico.[17]

Intra-industry trade introduces an additional gain from international trade. Because trade creates a larger market, a country can reduce the number of varieties it produces, thereby lowering production costs of each variety (economies of scale effect), and at the same time increase the number of varieties available to consumers (via imports). There is a gain from lower prices and a gain from a wider choice. This benefit accrues to all, and no redistributional effects occur. It calls for very little economic adjustment to trade. Indeed European economic integration proceeded with minimal internal disruption in the participating countries because it generated mainly intra-industry trade from which all benefit. Likewise the U.S.–Canada auto agreement (1965), which set up free trade in automobiles and parts between the two countries, enabled Canada to reduce the number of models (varieties) it produces and lower per-unit production costs.

---

[17] See J. Gannon, "NAFTA Creates Jobs for Joe and José," *Wall Street Journal*, March 29, 1993, editorial page.

At the same time, it increased the number of models available to Canadian consumers.

AN EMERGING CONSENSUS?

The contemporary view treats separately two components of international trade: (a) **Interindustry trade** is the exchange between countries of totally different commodities, such as trading textiles and shoes for aircraft and computers; or the exchange of primary materials for finished manufactures. Much of this trade is between nations of vastly different factor endowments, such as the LDCs and the industrial countries, and can be explained by the traditional factor endowment model, or its extension into skills and technology.

(b) **Intra-industry trade** refers to a two-way trade in a similar commodity such as the exchange of automotive products between the United States and Canada or among some of the European countries. A growing proportion of international trade falls in this category. Much of it is conducted among the industrial countries, whose factor endowments have become increasingly similar.

Two features of the producing firms involved in intra-industry trade are important: (a) They tend to be oligopolies[18] or monopolistically competitive, mainly with differentiated products; and (b) economies of scale in production and distribution play an important role in their behavior.

Under these circumstances, factor endowments determine whether a country will be a net exporter or a net importer within broad commodity classes, but the advantages of long production runs lead each country to produce only a limited range of products within each class. The result is that countries with similar capital–labor ratios and skill levels will still have an incentive to specialize in producing different goods within each industry and to engage in trade—hence the emergence of vast intra-industry trade.

The benefits from such trade are not confined to reallocation of resources. They include the rationalization of industries to take advantage of economies of scale, greater competition among large firms (across national boundaries), and a larger **product variety** available to consumers. The effects on income distribution and on returns to factors, so prominent in comparative advantage models, are vastly outweighed by these benefits. All productive factors gain from trade.

One reason the United States and Europe find it difficult to adjust to increased imports from the LDCs, even when accompanied by increased

---

[18] A few large firms make up each industry.

exports to them, is that these imports represent interindustry rather than intra-industry trade. Resources within the importing country must shift from one industry to another rather than within segments of the same industry.

ECONOMIC ADJUSTMENT TO CHANGING CIRCUMSTANCES

For a true understanding of the manifold factors that generate international trade, it must be remembered that these influences are never stationary. They change over time, both within and between countries. Technological advance, capital accumulation, acquisition of new skills, and invention of new products are commonplace in all dynamic economies. They occur practically every year and in turn change the ranking of industries in terms of comparative advantage. Industries that could easily meet price competition on world markets at one time may suddenly find themselves shrinking in size because of their inability to compete. Such **dynamic changes in comparative advantage** require resources in the economy to be mobile enough to shift from sluggish to competitive sectors. The economy itself must be in a process of continuing transformation to meet new circumstances. This requirement applies particularly to interindustry trade.

Consider the attempts of the developing countries to industrialize. What new industries can they establish? Apart from production based on locally available materials, their comparative advantage lies in industries that are both technologically unsophisticated and labor intensive. Textiles, footwear, and lumber products all offer concrete possibilities. More advanced developing countries (where hourly compensation is one-tenth that of the United States, and the labor is well-trained) have moved to develop steel, automobile, and consumer electronic industries. Thus, while India and Pakistan establish textile mills, it is necessary for some European countries to contract their textile industries and shift to the production of more advanced products. In terms of their comparative advantage, it pays them to specialize in the latter type of commodities and import the cheaper textiles from abroad.

A reverse change in the structure of comparative advantage may occur if and when developed countries introduce and enforce high antipollution standards. For these standards may raise the production cost of many synthetic materials above that of their natural substitutes, which are produced mainly in the developing countries. These countries would then regain the competitive advantage that they had previously lost to synthetics.

Japan's postwar development offers a dramatic illustration of the changing nature of comparative advantage. Directly after World War II,

Japan was an underdeveloped and relatively labor abundant country, exporting labor-intensive goods such as textiles. In fact, American textile mills felt threatened and sought protection from Japanese competition. During this time, however, the Japanese slowly increased their capital stock through very high levels of savings and investment. Thus, by the 1970s, Japan had become relatively capital abundant, and began to export capital-intensive goods such as steel and automobiles. Wages in Japan rose, and the Japanese textile industry found it hard to compete against the cheap textiles imported from other, less developed, Asian countries. At the same time, Japan was advancing its technological capability by training research scientists and engineers and spending 2.7 percent of its GDP on research and development (R&D)—a similar proportion to that of the United States and Germany. In 1963, 61 percent of all R&D scientists in the world worked in the United States, but by 1984 that number dwindled to 49 percent, while Japan's share rose from 15 to 23 percent. As a result, by the 1980s and 1990s Japan was competing with the United States in high-technology products, including sophisticated instruments and machinery, computers, and microchips.[19] This direct competition in an array of high-technology products, as well as in automobiles, is one reason for the continuous trade friction between the United States and Japan.

Korea, following in Japan's footsteps, is now entering the capital-abundance stage—for example, it now exports steel to Japan. Other Asian countries, such as China and Thailand, are still labor abundant but are gradually increasing their capital stock.

In such a dynamic world it is incumbent upon advanced countries to shift resources to more sophisticated industries rather than impose restrictions on imports of simple products from the LDCs. But here comes the hitch: What on paper is a one-paragraph description of economic transformation is in reality a severe problem of human adjustment. Production equipment must be scrapped and new machinery installed. Workers must be retrained in new skills and sometimes relocated. At times, even entire communities are disbanded, and ghost towns appear where once there were thriving cities. In other words, the shift that benefits the entire nation occurs at the expense of considerable hardship to a minority of dislocated people. This problem is common to any type of economic change—such as the introduction of new technology—not only to change brought about by foreign trade. Public assistance in the adjustment process can help smooth over and speed up the transformation, but hardships remain nonetheless.

Consequently, it is not surprising that the industries directly affected by new import competition strive to protect their interests by demanding

---

[19] Other examples of such industries are jet aircraft, robotics, fiber optics, office automation, genetic engineering, and certain chemicals.

tariff or quota protection, with the labor unions joining in. The eventual benefit to all, after the transformation has been completed and workers moved to higher paying jobs, is lost sight of. The vested interest of the minority often prevails; certainly little attention is paid to the consuming public that stands to benefit from cheaper imports. The resulting protection of textiles industries such as in the United States and Europe has become a major grievance of many developing nations.

Another contemporary illustration is the insistence of the (politically powerful) Japanese farmers on import protection for farm products, which thereby perpetuates their very inefficient agricultural practices. American food exports are not allowed to penetrate that market, much to the chagrin of U.S. policymakers. Within Japan, the policy of protecting agriculture incurs the wrath of the large industrial exporters, who fear American retaliation in curbing imports of Japanese manufactured products.

To all countries, developed and developing alike, the inability to transform may spell economic stagnation and continuing challenges. Difficulties in making the adjustment to new patterns of production as dictated by shifting world demand is one of the problems that has plagued the British economy. Despite the hardships involved, an economy must maintain the dynamism necessary for continuous change as it adapts to shifts in comparative advantage. The government can help by maintaining a high level of aggregate production and employment so that labor and capital released from declining industries will find alternative employment. It can also provide direct assistance to alleviate the burden of interindustry transfers.

Additional Insights

ECONOMIC GROWTH

Economic growth is represented by an outward shift in the production-possibilities curve. But the shift is usually *not symmetrical*. Rather, growth tends to have a bias toward the production of one of the goods. It is represented in figure 3.2 by an outward shift in the transformation function from the bold to the shaded color, and is shown to be biased toward either wheat (part a) or textiles (part b). That bias may arise either because technological progress occurs in one sector of the economy (Ricardian model); or, if motivated by expansion of factor supplies, the growth is biased toward the product that is intensive in the factor whose supply has increased.

The following conclusions apply to a large country: If the growth is disproportionately large in the direction of the country's exports (figure 3.2a, **export-biased growth** in the United States), the country's terms of trade would deteriorate. Conversely, if the production possibilities curve expands disproportionately in the direction of the country's imports (figure 3.2b, **import-biased growth** in the United States), the country's terms of trade would improve.

FIGURE 3.2	*Two Patterns of U.S. Economic Growth*

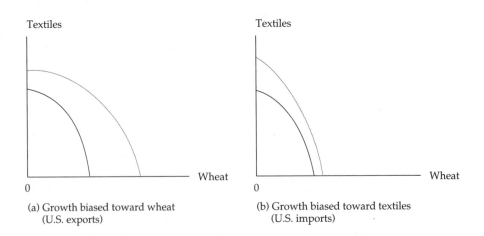

(a) Growth biased toward wheat
   (U.S. exports)

(b) Growth biased toward textiles
   (U.S. imports)

Economic growth is represented by an outward and nonsymmetrical shift in the transformation curve. It is usually biased toward one of the two commodities.

Summary

This chapter analyzes the explanation of the commodity composition of trade by asking: What causes a country to have a comparative advantage in one type of commodity and a disadvantage in another? Under the factor proportions theory, the pattern of trade is presented as a marriage between the relative factor endowment of the country and the relative factor intensity of the commodity. Each country exports the commodities that are intensive in its relatively abundant factor and imports the commodities that are intensive in its relatively scarce factor. Indirectly, the country exports the services of its abundant factor (thereby raising its price), and imports the services of its scarce factor (thereby lowering its price). That theory does indeed explain a wide range of observed phenomena, including some of the U.S. investment in Canada and Europe, and aspects of the Mexican migration into the United States. It also demonstrates the effect of trade on factor prices and the distribution of income.

But because empirical tests (the Leontief paradox) failed to support the factor proportion theory in full, alternative explanations were developed to supplement it. One suggests the extension of the model to three factors, with one factor mobile between two industries while two others are each specific to its industry and hence immobile. Other explanations rely on human skills and technological developments. But the most recent theory, which explains much of the trade among industrial nations, abandons some of the assumptions of the factor endowments model. Instead, this theory introduces monopolistic competition and economies of scale, conditions that can give rise to both interindustry and intra-industry trade. It suggests gains from trade beyond the mere efficient allocation of resources, including consumer benefits from a larger variety of products and increased production efficiency.

Far from being a static concept, comparative advantage is very dynamic. It changes as the factors underlying it change. This is perhaps most vividly illustrated by Japan's postwar development, when its comparative advantage was altered from labor-intensive to capital-intensive goods, and more recently to technology-intensive products.

Economic growth, while represented by an outward shift in the production-possibilities curve, usually is not depicted symmetrically. In fact, growth is most often either export-biased or import-biased.

Important Concepts

Factor proportions (or endowment) theory

Capital-intensive products

Capital-abundant country

Direct foreign investment

Product cycle

Monopolistic competition

Factor price equalization

Leontief scarce-factor paradox

Sector-specific model

Labor-intensive products

Labor-abundant country

Interindustry trade

Intra-industry trade

Product variety

Dynamic changes in comparative advantage

Export-biased growth

Import-biased growth

Review Questions

1. What is meant by "Relative factor intensity of a commodity" and "Relative factor abundance of a country"? How are these concepts used to explain the commodity composition of trade? Demonstrate that under this analysis commodity movement and factor movement are substitutes for each other. Was the Leontief paradox a verification of that explanation? If not, what was it?

2.   Does the factor proportions theory provide a good explanation of intra-industry trade? If not, can you outline an alternative explanation for this growing phenomenon?

3.   Does the factor proportions theory shed any light on Mexican migration to the United States? How does it account for U.S. direct investment in Canada?

4.   Explain the dynamic nature of comparative advantage using Japan's experience as an example.

5.   Once the United States acquires a comparative advantage in jet aircraft production it can be sure of a dominant position in the global market forever. Do you agree with this statement? Explain.

6.   Distinguish between interindustry and intra-industry trade, providing examples of each. Offer possible explanations for interindustry and intra-industry trade.

7.   Explain and elaborate on the following statement: Under the factor endowment model, the main gain from trade is found in resource reallocation. Under the "monopolistic competition, economies of scale," theory, there are other gains as well. What are these other gains?

8.   Present four alternative explanations of the commodity composition of international trade.

9.   Why is economic growth usually represented by a nonsymmetrical shift in the transformation curve?

Chapter 3 Appendix 3–1

FORMAL PRESENTATION OF THE RICARDIAN MODEL—THE CASE OF A ONE-FACTOR ECONOMY

Equilibrium in Isolation (without Trade)

It was seen in Chapter 2 that an economy consisting of one factor of production, homoge-neous labor, would be represented by a linear transformation curve, showing constant opportunity cost between goods X (say textiles) and Y (say wheat). This curve can be derived formally as follows:

Labor productivity in each industry, which summarizes the technology of the economy, is

Constant Cost Transformation, or Production Possibilities, Curve

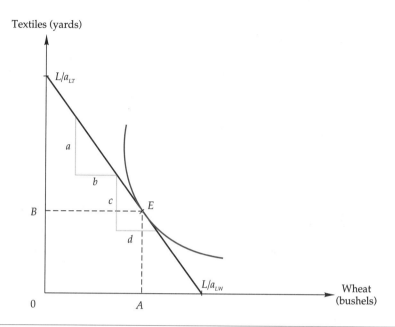

For a country in isolation, equilibrium is represented by the tangency of the transformation curve to the highest possible indifference curve, point *E*.

measured by the number of hours of labor required to produce a unit of each good. (Higher productivity means that fewer hours are required to produce a unit of the good.) This measure is known as unit labor requirement. Define

a_{LT} as the number of hours of labor needed to produce a yard of textiles

a_{LW} as the number of hours of labor needed to produce a bushel of wheat

L as the total labor resources available to the economy, which can be divided between the textile and wheat industries.

If Q_T and Q_W are, respectively, total output of textiles and wheat, then labor used in the production of textiles is $a_{LT}Q_T$, and labor used in

the production of wheat is $a_{LW}Q_W$. Since total labor supply in the economy is *L*, the limits of production cannot exceed labor availability; hence they are defined by the inequality:

$$a_{LT}Q_T + a_{LW}Q_W \leq L$$

Figure A3–1.1 shows the economy's transformation or production-possibilities curve. If the entire labor force were engaged in the production of textiles (vertical axis), then L/a_{LT} yards and no wheat would be produced. If the entire labor force were devoted to the production of wheat (horizontal axis) then L/a_{LW} bushels and no textiles would be produced. This determines the two end points. Connecting them with a straight line yields the constant-opportunity-cost curve shown in black in figure A3–1.1. The opportunity cost of wheat in terms of textiles is the number of yards of textiles the economy must give up to obtain an extra bushel of wheat. It is constant throughout the line (segment $a/b = c/d$ and so on) and is equal to minus the slope of the line. Specifically, the opportunity cost is

$$\frac{L/a_{LT}}{L/a_{LW}} = \frac{a_{LW}}{a_{LT}} \qquad (1)$$

or the unit labor requirement in wheat relative to the unit labor requirement in textiles.

Points along the transformation curve represent different output mixes that *can* be produced. Where along the curve will the economy actually settle? Given its transformation curve, the economy will try to get onto the highest (one of the many preexisting) community indifference curves (CIC). This is the CIC tangent to the transformation curve (shown in color), yielding equilibrium at point E, and product mix: $0A$ bushels of wheat and $0B$ yards of textile. The slope of the CIC equals the price ratio of the two goods P_W/P_T. At equilibrium the slope of the transformation curve equals that of the CIC. Hence at E

$$P_W / P_T = a_{LW} / a_{LT} \qquad (2)$$

Since no profit can exist in a one-factor economy, the hourly wage equals the value of what a worker can produce in one hour. Because a_{LT} hours are required to produce a yard of textiles, the hourly wage in the textile industry is P_T/a_{LT}. And as a_{LW} hours are needed to pro-

duce a bushel of wheat, the hourly wage in the wheat industry must be P_W/a_{LW}. By transposing equation (2) we see that at equilibrium hourly wages are the same in the two industries: $P_W/a_{LW} = P_T/a_{LT}$. That outcome is guaranteed by the free mobility of labor between industries.

Introduction of Trade

Suppose there are two countries, the United States and the United Kingdom (shown in superscripts in the following notations), and that the above equilibrium conditions exist within each country. However, U.S. labor is *relatively* less productive than that of the United Kingdom in the manufacture of textiles and relatively more productive in wheat production.[1] Stated differently, U.S. labor requirement in textile production is relatively greater than the United Kingdom's, and U.S. labor requirement in wheat production is relatively *smaller* than the United Kingdom's:

$$a_{LT}^{U.S.} / a_{LW}^{U.S.} > a_{LT}^{U.K.} / a_{LW}^{U.K.} \text{ or} \qquad (3)$$
$$a_{LT}^{U.S.} / a_{LT}^{U.K.} > a_{LW}^{U.S.} / a_{LW}^{U.K.}$$

U.S. relative productivity is higher in wheat than in textiles, so the United States has a comparative advantage in wheat. U.K. relative productivity is greater in textiles than in wheat, conferring upon it a comparative advantage in textiles. The condition outlined in equation (3) is translated into the transformation curves of the two countries shown by the black lines in figure A3–1.2. The U.S. transformation curve is flatter than the United Kingdom's. In isolation wheat is cheaper (in terms of textiles) in the United States, while textiles are cheaper (in terms of wheat) in the United Kingdom.[2] The actual pro-

---

[1] The analysis does not specify what gives rise to these productivity differentials.

[2] We infer relative prices from the quantities exchanged. In the United States it takes a lot of wheat to buy few textiles, and in the United Kingdom it requires a great deal of textiles to obtain a little wheat.

FIGURE A3–1.2 **U.K. and U.S. Transformation Curves Based on Equation 3**

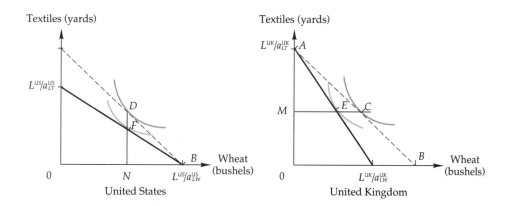

The international price ratio, represented by the blue line, enables each of the two countries to reach a higher indifference curve than in isolation.

duction and consumption mix is determined in each country at the point of tangency of the transformation curve to the highest CIC, (shaded gray), as in figure A3–1.1. It is at points E and F for the United Kingdom and the United States respectively. In isolation, a country produces and consumes the same mix of the two products.

When trade opens up under constant cost conditions, each country moves to specialize in the good in which it has a comparative advantage. If the two countries are of equal size, both would specialize completely. However, if the United Kingdom were too small to supply the entire U.S. demand for textiles (at the prevailing price), only the United Kingdom would specialize in textiles, while the United States would produce both commodities. But the United States would still export wheat and import textiles. In what follows, we assume that both countries become *completely* specialized: The United States would produce only wheat, at point B, and import all its textiles from the

United Kingdom; and the United Kingdom would produce only textiles, at point A, and import all its wheat from the United States.

At what price ratio will the international exchange take place? That depends on supply and demand conditions in each country. Because free trade (assuming no transport cost) would equalize the price of each commodity in the two countries, it would certainly equalize the price ratio, P_W/P_T, so that the international trade line (colored), common to both countries, would have the same slope on the two panels. Additionally, the international price ratio would be *between* the price ratios prevailing in isolation in the United States and the United Kingdom, so the slope of the international price line would be between the slopes of the two transformation lines: $P_T^{U.S}/P_W^{U.S} > P_T^{I}/P_W^{I} > P_T^{U.K}/P_W^{U.K}$ where the superscript I stands for international.

But there are many such possible lines of common slopes. To be uniquely determined, the international price line must meet another condition: The quantity of wheat exported by the United States must equal the quantity of wheat imported by the United Kingdom, and the quantity of textiles exported by the United Kingdom must equal the quantity of textiles imported by the United States. The dashed line on each panel in figure A3–1.2 meets both conditions.

Next, we determine the consumption mixes for the two countries along the (colored) international trade line by locating its point of tangency to the highest possible CIC (shaded with color). This occurs at points C and D for the United Kingdom and the United States respectively. The difference between the production mix and the consumption mix in each country is made up by trade.

Thus the United States exports BN of wheat and imports ND of textiles, and the United Kingdom exports AM (= DN) of textiles and imports MC (= BN) of wheat. The two trade triangles △AMC and △BND are identical. Both countries gain from trade, as each ends up on a higher CIC than it does without trade.

Another way of interpreting the gain from trade is to view the (colored) international trade line as an alternative transformation curve. Starting from point B (all wheat and no textile) the United States can acquire textile in two ways: by diverting its own resources from the wheat to the textile industry, thus moving up along its domestic (solid) transformation curve; or by trading its wheat for textiles on the international market, moving up along the (dashed) international trade line. The United States clearly acquires more textiles for each unit of wheat it gives up by following the second route. Likewise, starting from point A (all textiles and no wheat) the United Kingdom can acquire wheat in two ways: diverting its own resources from textile to wheat production, thus moving down its domestic (solid) transformation curve; or trading its textiles for wheat on the international market, moving down along the (dashed) international trade line. It clearly acquires more wheat per unit of tex-

tile given up by using the second route. *Trade benefits both countries.*

Still another way of demonstrating precisely the same point is to consider alternative ways of using an hour of labor. The United States can use it directly to produce $1/a_{LT}^{U.S.}$ yards of textiles. Alternatively, it can employ it to produce $1/a_{LW}$ bushels of wheat, and then trade the wheat for textile at the international price P_W^I/P_T^I. An hour of labor would then yield: $(1/a_{LW}^{U.S.})(P_W^I/P_T^I)$ yards of textiles. It obtains more textiles in the second route *if:*

$$(1/a_{LW}^{U.S.})(P_W^I/P_T^I) > 1/a_{LT}^{U.S.} \qquad (3a)$$

or if

$$P_W^I/P_T^I > a_{LW}^{U.S.}/a_{LT}^{U.S.} \qquad (3b)$$

or if

$$P_T^I/P_W^I < a_{LT}^{U.S.}/a_{LW}^{U.S.} \qquad (3c)$$

To see that this condition necessarily obtains in international trade, recall from equation (2) that along the domestic transformation curve $P_T^{U.S.}/P_W^{U.S.} = a_{LT}^{U.S.}/a_{LW}^{U.S.}$. And under the steeper (dashed) international price line P_T^I/P_W^I is smaller than the U.S. price ratio $(P_T^{U.S.}/P_W^{U.S.})$. Clearly equation (3c) holds. By similar reasoning, the United Kingdom would acquire more wheat per unit of labor by devoting its labor to textile production and trading the textiles for wheat on the international market. Trade is beneficial to both countries.

As a numerical illustration, suppose the unit labor requirements were as follows:

	Textiles	Wheat
United States	$a_{LT}^{U.S.} = 3$	$a_{LW}^{U.S.} = 1$
United Kingdom	$a_{LT}^{U.K.} = 4$	$a_{LW}^{U.K.} = 4$

Namely:

One hour of labor in the United States produces $\frac{1}{3}$ yard of textiles

One hour of labor in the United States produces 1 bushel of wheat

One hour of labor in the United Kingdom produces $\frac{1}{4}$ yard of textiles

One hour of labor in the United Kingdom produces $\frac{1}{4}$ bushel of wheat

The United States has an absolute advantage in both commodities but a comparative advantage in wheat. The United Kingdom has an absolute disadvantage in both commodities but a comparative advantage in textiles.

Suppose the international price ratio is 1 yard = 2 bushels.

In direct production, an hour of U.S. labor produces $\frac{1}{3}$ yard of textiles. Indirectly an hour of U.S. labor produces 1 bushel of wheat, which it can trade on the international market for $\frac{1}{2}$ yard ($> \frac{1}{3}$ yard) of textiles.

In direct production, an hour of U.K. labor produces $\frac{1}{4}$ bushel of wheat. Indirectly an hour of U.K. labor produces $\frac{1}{4}$ a yard of textiles, which it can trade on the international market for $\frac{1}{2}$ ($> \frac{1}{4}$) bushel of wheat.

Both countries benefit from trade.

Chapter 3 Appendix 3–2

THE FACTOR PROPORTIONS THEORY

Students thoroughly familiar with advanced price theory will recognize that the transformation curve of a country can be derived from its contract curve, which in turn is the locus of points of tangency between two sets of isoquants, each set pertaining to one of the country's two industries. The Edgeworth-Bowley box diagram is used to delineate the country's fixed amount of resources, made up of two productive factors (for example, labor and capital), and the contract curve is drawn inside the box. That curve is the locus of points of efficient allocation of the two productive factors between the two industries; from any point off the contract curve one can move to *certain points* on that curve and increase the output produced by the given quantity of the two factors. We can show the contract curve for each country (in the factor space) from which the transformation curves (in the commodity space) can be derived.

The assumptions of the factor proportions model, outlined in Chapter 3, are built into the two diagrams (figure A3–2.1). The size of each country's box shows its resource endowment: Country A is relatively capital abundant, and B is relatively labor abundant. Within each box, the locus of points of tangency between industry X isoquants and industry Y isoquants is called the *contract curve*. It is shown in shaded color and bold color for countries A and B respectively. Besides pure competition and perfect internal factor mobility, the model's assumptions are as follows:

(a) The isoquants of industry X are identical in both countries; so are the isoquants of industry Y.

FIGURE A3–2.1   *The Edgworth-Bowley Box Diagrams*

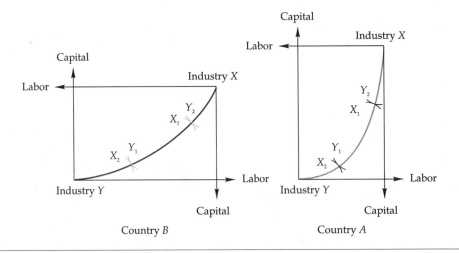

Two box diagrams show country *A* to be labor abundant and country *B* to be capital abundant. The isoquants of good *X* are identical in the two countries, as are the isoquants of good *Y*. The contract curve for each country is the locus of points of tangency between the *X* and *Y* isoquants.

(b) Industry *Y* is labor intensive relative to industry *X* and *X* is capital intensive relative to industry *Y*, and this relationship holds for both countries. Translated into a multicommodity world, this assumption means that the *ranking* of industries by the labor/capital ratio required for production (that is, the factor use ratio) would be the same in both countries even if the factor price ratio varied. This assumption is known as the nonreversibility of factor intensities.

(c) Both commodities are produced under diminishing returns but constant returns to scale. The latter assumption implies that any straight ray from each origin (say of industry *Y*) will intersect the isoquants of the industry depicted on the origin (for example, the *Y* isoquants) at points of equal slopes. The economic meaning of this is that all such points of intersection show equal ratios between the marginal physical productivities of the two factors in the given industry. In other words, under constant returns to scale, the marginal productivity of a factor in a given industry is independent of the scale of operations and depends only on its ratio to the

FIGURE A3–2.2   *Post-trade Production Equilibrium*

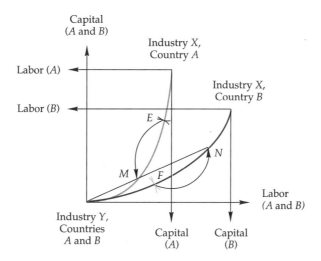

Possible post-trade equilibrium is established where a ray from the origin intersects the contract curves of the two countries, such as at points *M* and *N*.

other factor in use (that is, on the factor use ratio). And the factor use ratio is identical along a straight ray from the origin; it is equal to the constant slope of that ray.

(d) Country *A* is capital abundant relative to country *B*, while *B* is labor abundant relative to country *A*. This is indicated by the relative size of the two boxes.

As a next step, place the box diagram of country *A* on top of the one of country *B*, in such a way that their origins for industry *Y* will coincide. This is shown in figure A3–2.2, where the isoquants are deleted for the sake of clarity, and the contract curves are shown in the same colors

as in figure A3–2.1. The identical *Y* isoquants for both countries coincide exactly, while the identical *X* isoquants start at two different points of origin. Any ray from the (joint) origin of *Y*, such as $\overline{YMN}$, intersects the contract curves of the two countries at points *M* and *N*, where the *Y* isoquants common to the two countries have equal slopes. In other words, the ratio of the marginal products of the two factors in industry *Y* is the same in both countries. Since within each country, factor mobility ensures that the ratio of the marginal products of the two factors is the same in industries *Y* and *X*, that ratio must also be the same in industry *X* of the two countries. Geometrically this means that the straight line connecting *M* with the origin of industry *X* in country *A* is parallel to the straight line connecting *N* with the origin of industry *X* in country *B* (not drawn).

Equality of the marginal products ensures that the output mixes at point M for country A and at point N for country B would result in identical product prices (or price ratios) in the two countries. And this is the requirement for post-trade equilibrium. Depending on demand patterns (depicted by CICs in the commodities space but cannot be shown on a box diagram), the pretrade output mix was E in country A and F in country B. The opening of trade moved that mix to points M and N, respectively. The relatively capital-abundant country A moved to specialize more in the relatively capital-intensive product X; and the relatively labor-abundant country B moved to specialize more in the relatively labor-intensive product Y. Specialization is incomplete in both countries as is the case in figure A2–1.6. Thus there is one-to-one correspondence between the output mix in the factor "space" and in the commodity "space." *As long as specialization is incomplete* (that is, each country produces some of both products), not only would commodity prices be equalized between the two countries at the post-trade production equilibrium points such as M and N, but factor prices would also be equalized.

But the number of such post-trade production equilibrium points is unlimited, as there are unlimited rays from the joint origin Y that would intersect the two contract curves. Which one would prevail depends on the relative international prices of the two products. If Y's price rises relative to X, the ray shifts counterclockwise and more Y is produced in both countries, while if the price of X rises relative to Y, the ray shifts clockwise, and more X is produced in both countries. Thus the "relevant" ray must depend on conditions of demand as well as supply; it must be derived in a way that ensures the identity of the two trade triangles. Only then is the final equilibrium uniquely determined.

Not all points on the two contract curves are "pairable" in the sense of intersecting a straight ray from origin Y, in much the same way that not all points along the two transformation curves are pairable in the sense of having equal slopes. Thus the price of Y relative to that of X can rise to a point where the *ray from the joint origin Y becomes the diagonal of country B's box diagram.* Here country B completely specializes in industry Y, and further increases in the relative price of Y can lead only country A to move upward along its contract curve to produce more Y and less X. Conversely, if the price of X relative to that of Y rises to a point where the *ray from the joint origin Y becomes tangent to country A's contract curve*, then country A is completely specialized in X and produces no Y. Further increases in the relative price of X would lead only country B to move downward along its contract curve toward greater specialization in X.

Thus the two rays whose descriptions are italicized in the previous paragraph delineate the limits to incomplete specialization. All rays falling within these limits indicate incomplete specialization and correspond to points of equal slopes of the two transformation functions in the commodity space. The size of *the range of incomplete specialization* depends on two features:

(a) It varies directly with the similarity of relative factor endowments of the two countries. The more the factor endowment ratios differ, the more the shapes of the two box diagrams differ (this can be readily seen by adding labor to country B, leaving all else unchanged) and the smaller the range of pairable points along a ray from joint origin Y.

(b) It varies inversely with the similarity of the production isoquants of X and Y. The more alike they are, the less the "belly"

FIGURE A3–3.1   *Wage Rate Determination*

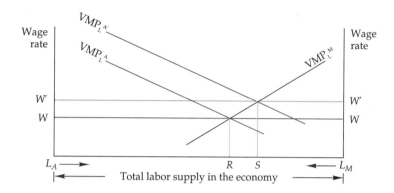

Equilibrium wage rate occurs where the VMP of the two industries is equalized.

of the two contract curves and the smaller the range of "pairable" points along a ray from origin *Y*. The extreme case, which corresponds to the Ricardian model of constant opportunity costs, is the one of identical isoquants of the two commodities. The contract curve of each country becomes the diagonal of its box diagram, and there is no range of incomplete specialization. Once trade opens up, country *A* moves to specialize completely in product *X*, and country *B* in product *Y*.

Chapter 3 Appendix 3–3

THE MOBILE FACTOR IN A SECTOR-SPECIFIC MODEL

In the sector-specific model described in Chapter 3, labor is the mobile factor; it is combined with capital in sector *M*, and with land in sector *A*. How is the fixed quantity of labor in a (fully employed) economy distributed between the two sectors?

In figure A3–3.1, the total labor supply is shown along the horizontal axis. Labor in sector *A* is measured rightward from origin L_A, while labor in sector *M* is measured leftward from origin L_M. Since labor is subject to diminishing returns in each sector, the value of the marginal product of labor in manufacturing[1] (VMP_L^M) schedule (drawn in black) slopes negatively, measured leftward from origin L_M. Likewise the VMP_L^A (shown in bold color) is measured rightward from origin L_A. They intersect at height W, the equilibrium wage rate in the economy: $W = VMP_L^M = VMP_L^A$. The allocation of labor between the two sectors is at point R: $L_A R$ in agriculture, and $L_M R$ in manufacturing. When trade opens up, food prices rise, so that the VMP_L^A shifts upward to $VMP_L^{A'}$. The labor allocation point moves from R to S as more labor is employed in sector A and less in M. The wage rate rises (to W'), *but less than proportionately to the increase in food prices.* So the wage rate falls relative to the price of food but rises relative to the price of manufactures. Workers may gain or lose from free trade depending on whether they consume mostly manufactured goods or mostly food.[2]

---

[1] The price of manufacturing times labor's marginal physical product.

[2] For further elaboration see R. Ruffin and R. Jones, "Protection and Real Wages: A Neoclassical Ambiguity," *Journal of Economic Theory*, April 1977.

Protection of Domestic Industries: The Tariff

In light of the gains from international trade, one would expect free trade to be the prevailing rule and artificial barriers to trade the exception. Yet even casual observation may convince the reader that we live in a protection-ridden world, where government interference with the free flow of goods and services is anything but an exception. As in other areas of national concern, commercial policies do not represent the reasoned opinions of a single decision maker. They are a product of pressure groups vying for the attention of legislators and policymakers. The result hardly squares with the dictates of economic analysis.

Traditionally, the most common instrument of protection, though by no means the only one, has been the import tariff. It is a highly charged political issue, with import-competing industries clamoring for protection, export industries often favoring free trade, and the consumer who pays the cost of protection being neither vocal nor adequately represented.

As a general rule, nations accord heaviest protection (in various forms) to industries in which they have a comparative disadvantage. In countries with a comparative advantage in manufacturing, such as Europe and Japan, agriculture receives the most protection. In countries with a comparative advantage in agriculture or natural resources, such as Australia or the LDCs, manufacturing receives the highest protection. In the United States heavy protection is spread over several industries such as textiles and sugar; there is no typical protected industry.

This chapter analyzes the various effects of the tariff on the economy, considers arguments for protection, and explores measures taken by the community of nations to reduce protection and liberalize international trade.

SOME INSTITUTIONAL CONSIDERATIONS

Export versus Import Duty

The tariff is a tax levied upon a commodity when it crosses a national boundary. The most common tariff is the import duty, although some countries, primarily exporters of agricultural commodities and raw materials, also employ export taxes. Export taxes may be used to produce government revenue, or to curtail exports in order to prop up world prices of a primary commodity, as when Saudi Arabia discourages the export of oil.

In the United States, the Constitution prohibits the imposition of a tax on exports. Consequently, whenever the U.S. government wishes to restrict exports in order to control domestic prices (as in the case of soybeans in 1972), it resorts to direct quota restrictions or complete bans on overseas shipments.

Additional Insights

Import and export taxes are symmetrical in their effect on a country's resource allocation. A tax on imports raises their prices in the taxing country relative to the prices of other commodities and draws resources from export industries to import-competing industries. A tax on exports discourages overseas shipment of the taxed commodities and lowers their prices in the taxing country relative to other prices. Consequently, resources are pushed out of the export industries into the import-competing industries. (This insight is attributed to a 1936 article by professor Abba Lerner.) Since export taxes are relatively rare, we shall focus mainly on import duties.

Protection versus Revenue

Historically, tariffs were imposed mainly as a source of government revenue. The **revenue tariff** is the easiest tax to administer, because collection can be executed by officers stationed at official points of entry along the border. Many developing nations still rely on tariffs for financing government operations because of this ease of collection. Among industrial countries today, however, tariffs are levied for the protection of domestic industries. The small revenue generated by a **protective tariff** is a pleasant by-product, but is not its major objective. A duty is purely revenue-driven if it does not cause resources to move into industries that produce domestic substitutes for the imported commodities. A tariff levied on a commodity that is not produced at home, such as an import tax on coffee, or on a commodity whose domestic substitutes bear the same taxation, may serve to illustrate such a duty. At the other extreme, a *prohibitive* tariff—one high enough to keep out all imports—yields only protection and no revenue. For most taxed commodities, both the protection and the revenue are present. In 1995, U.S. customs duties generated about $19 billion in revenue, or 1.3 percent of government receipts.

Types of Tariff

We distinguish between *ad valorem* duty, specific duty, and compound duty. The **ad valorem** tax is a fixed percentage of the value of the commodity, as when imported cars are taxed at 5 percent of value. A **specific** duty is a fixed sum of money per physical unit of the commodity, say $100 per imported automobile. A **compound** duty is a combination of the two, as when a car is taxed at $50 per unit plus 2 percent of value. The United States uses both specific and *ad valorem* duties in roughly equal proportion; European countries rely mainly on *ad valorem* taxes.

What are the advantages and disadvantages of each kind of tax? The *ad valorem* tax is more equitable than the others because it distinguishes among fine gradations of the commodity as they are reflected in its price. The person importing a Rolls Royce pays more than a counterpart importing a Volkswagen. On the other hand, under a specific duty each person would pay the same amount, resulting in a higher percentage tax on the cheaper import.

In addition, the *ad valorem* tax provides a more constant level of protection to domestic industry in times of inflation than the specific duty does. Since world prices have been rising in recent decades, the level of protection accorded by a fixed sum of money declines as the tax becomes a smaller fraction of value, while the *ad valorem* duty, given as a fixed percentage, is not subject to the same decline.

On the other side of the ledger, a specific duty is easy to apply and administer, while an *ad valorem* tariff requires evaluation of the price of the commodity by the tax official before the tax can be calculated. There are two bases for such valuation: the **F.O.B. price** and the **C.I.F. price.** The first stands for *free on board* and indicates the price of the commodity on board ship at the port of embarkation (if shiploading costs are excluded, we obtain the F.A.S. or *free alongside* price). The second designation stands for *cost, insurance, and freight* and covers the cost of the commodity up to the port of entry. It includes ocean freight and other intercountry transportation costs, which the F.O.B. price excludes. The United States uses the F.O.B. price for computing the tariff, while most European countries employ the C.I.F. value.

Since there are advantages and disadvantages to both specific and *ad valorem* duties, a sensible compromise may be to use the specific duty for standardized products and the *ad valorem* duty for goods with a wide range of grade variations.

Because tariff-setting in the United States is a congressional prerogative, the American tariff reflects the influence of a great variety of political pressure groups. This is one reason the tariff classification has traditionally been rather long and complex, compounding the difficulty of administering the tariff. The customs officer must determine the classification within which each imported product falls. Since various categories are subject to different tax rates, this determination is very important to the importer. Indeed, much tariff litigation revolves around the classification of imported commodities, as well as their valuation (in the cases of *ad valorem* duties). The uncertainty that results from the complexity of the list is in itself a hindrance to international trade. To complicate matters further, a given product may be subject to different rates depending on its source of supply. This reflects the fact that an importing country may accord preferential treatment to certain exporting countries in the form of lower rates. In the case of the United States, the statutory tariff, set by Congress in the 1930s, is much higher than the rates charged on imports from most countries after a long succession of reciprocal tariff reductions. The latter duties, in turn, are higher than those charged on manufacturing imports from many LDCs that are accorded special preferential status in the United States.[1]

U.S. tariff rates are generally low, usually averaging between 5 and 10 percent. However, certain commodities, including various textile items, are subject to much higher rates, and thus cause "spikes" in the U.S. tariff schedule. This situation is not uncommon in the tariff schedules of Europe and Japan as well.

Economic Effects of the Tariff

Who Pays the Tariff?

It is customary to think that the cost of the tariff is paid by the importer when the commodity enters the country and is then passed on to the consumer as a price increase. Because this is the administrative procedure, there is a natural tendency to conclude that the tariff is paid by the citizens of the country imposing it. Often, however, this is not true.

Consider the United States as a coffee importer and Brazil as an exporter. Suppose that the free-trade price of coffee is $50 per ton, and the United States imposes a specific duty of $10 per ton. The immediate effect would be to raise the U.S. domestic price to $60. In response, Americans would consume less; they would either switch to substitute products such as

---

[1] Tariff rates are published by individual countries, in their respective languages, but translations of all tariff schedules into the five major languages are printed in the *International Customs Journal,* published by the International Customs Tariff Bureau in Belgium. Tariff systems of foreign countries are also described in various issues of *Overseas Business Reports* published by the U.S. Department of Commerce. The American tariff is reported in *The Tariff Schedule of the United States, Annotated.* Many countries adhere to a standardized classification of commodities known as the Brussels Tariff Nomenclature (BTN) in levying their tariffs. Where an item falls within the tariff classification can be very important. In 1994 Nissan won a court battle in the United States that classified its multipurpose vehicles as cars, paying 2.5 percent duty, rather than trucks, subject to 25 percent duty.

tea, or cut down on their consumption of hot beverages altogether. The United States is a large enough consumer of coffee so that a reduction in its imports would have a marked effect on its global price. Suppose that this forces the free-trade price to decline from $50 to $45. Then the $10 duty would raise the U.S. domestic price to $55. Now the U.S. consumer pays $55 per ton (up from $50 under free trade), while the Brazilian producer receives $45 per ton (down from $50 under free trade). The difference of $10 per ton is the import duty collected by the U.S. government.

While under free trade the price paid by the consumer equals that received by the producer, the tariff drives a wedge between the two. After the tariff, American consumers pay $5 *more* per ton, but the country as a whole (consumers plus the government combined) pay $5 *less* per ton. That latter price, $45 per ton, is what Brazilian coffee exporters receive, down from $50 under free trade. As Brazil's export price declines, the coffee exporters are, in effect, forced to absorb part of the duty. The burden or *incidence* of the duty is divided between the Americans and the Brazilians. The U.S. domestic price rises and the Brazilian export price declines, the two changes adding up to the amount of the tariff.

A country's **terms of trade** is defined as its export price divided by its import price (P_x/P_m). For the United States (the country as a whole), the import price declines from $50 to $45. If we assume that nothing happens to its export price (another commodity), the U.S. terms of trade rise or improve. Brazil's export price declines from $50 to $45. If we assume that nothing happens to its import price (another commodity), its terms of trade decline or deteriorate. What one country (the United States) gains in the terms of trade, the other country (Brazil) loses. This contrasts to expansion in the **volume of trade,** which benefits both countries.

On the other hand, now assume that a small country, such as Belgium, imposes a $10 per ton import duty on coffee. The price in Belgium would rise from $50 to $60, and Belgian coffee consumption would decline. But Belgium is a small country, and therefore is not a major buyer on the global market. Hence, the decline in its consumption *would have no effect on the world coffee price.* It would remain unchanged, and Brazil's export price would remain at $50. Thus, the entire effect of the tariff would occur inside Belgium, and there would be *no change* in its—or Brazil's—terms of trade. Indeed a **small country** is defined as a country that cannot, by its own action, affect world market prices and hence its terms of trade. The United States is one of only a handful of nations that would be classified as **large countries** according to this definition.

Graphic Exposition

Using graphs, we can visually demonstrate the preceding discussion and point out its essential features.

Whether a commodity is exported or imported by a country depends on the relationship between its domestic price (intersection of the domestic demand and supply curves) and the prevailing international price. If the two prices are equal, the product would not be traded. Should the international price exceed the domestic price, the commodity would be exported. And if the international price is below the domestic price, the good would be imported. The following graphs focus on such an importing country and distinguish between both a small and a large importing country.

The Small Country Case In figure 4.1, curves D and S (drawn in black and color) represent the domestic demand and supply in the Belgian coffee market. Without any international trade, equilibrium would settle at point E, where the domestic price is $70 per ton. But world market price, denoted by P_w, is $50 per ton. As a small country, Belgium can purchase all it wants at that price without affecting it. At $50 per ton there is excess demand in the amount $\overline{ab}$, the quantity imported. A $10 per ton tariff raises the domestic price to $60 ($P_w^t$), while the world market price remains unchanged. The quantity imported (excess demand at the price of $60) then declines to $\overline{cd}$ (= ef). But this reduction in the quantity of Belgian imports does not affect the world coffee price, because it is a small country. Belgium's terms of trade (P_x/P_m) remain unchanged.[2] Its consumers pay the entire tariff. While the consumers pay $10 per ton more, the country as a whole (consumers plus government combined) pay the same price ($50) as before. The entire government revenue from the tariff—$10 per unit times the quantity imported, cd, or the rectangular area G—is paid by domestic consumers.

The Large Country Case Now contrast this outcome with a large coffee importer, such as the United States. When an import duty is imposed and the price rises in the American market, consumers also curtail consumption. But in this case, the decline in imports occurs in a country that is a major coffee buyer on the global market—thus depressing world prices and forcing the exporting countries to absorb part of the tariff.

Figure 4.2 describes the U.S. coffee market, where D and S again represent the domestic supply and demand, with equilibrium at point E. Without trade, the domestic price would be $70 per ton. At the world price (P_w) of $50 per ton, imports under free trade total quantity ab. The $10 per ton tariff curtails domestic consumption. But since the United States is a major coffee buyer, the world coffee price declines by $5 per ton (from $50 to $45). The tariff raises the domestic price to $55. Tariff revenue equals $10 times imports cd, or the rectangular area G.[3] *Thus, only one-half of the tariff is paid by the domestic consumers, with the foreign exporters financing the other half.*

---

[2] P_x represents the price for Belgium's exportable goods (not shown here, and assumed to remain unchanged), while P_m stands for the import price paid by the Belgian economy as a whole (consumers and government combined).

[3] Technically, the line connecting the vertical axis with points e and f should have a positive (upward) slope. It is shown here to be horizontal for the sake of simplicity.

FIGURE 4.1   *The Belgian Market for Coffee*

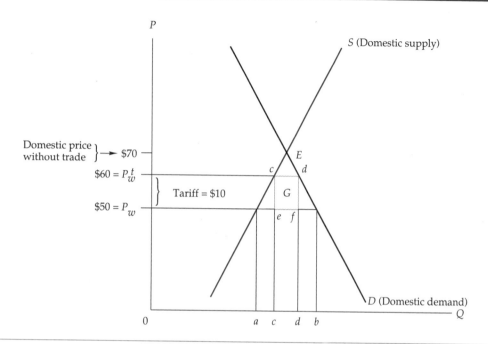

In a small importing country, the domestic price rises by the full amount of the tariff.

In this case the price of coffee to the American consumer rises by $5—from $50 under free trade to $55 under the tariff. But out of the $55 the U.S. government receives $10. So the price paid by the country as a whole (consumers and government combined) declines by $5—from $50 under free trade to $45 under the tariff. While the consumer pays $5 more than under free trade ($55 per ton), the country as a whole pays $5 less ($45 per ton). In other words, the tariff reduces the price of imported coffee by $5, and the country's terms of trade (P_x/P_m) improve. Brazil's terms of trade thus deteriorate.

Only a large importing country can improve its terms of trade by levying a tariff. But a small country can do so by imposing an *export tax* or by otherwise withholding its exports from world markets, *if* it is a major world supplier of a certain commodity. The African country of Ghana is a large exporter of cocoa; it accounts for one-third of the global supply. If it withholds some of its exports from the global market, the world price of cocoa would rise, and Ghana's terms of trade (P_x/P_m) would improve. Saudi Arabia has the same power to manipulate its oil exports.

FIGURE 4.2 *The U.S. Market for Coffee*

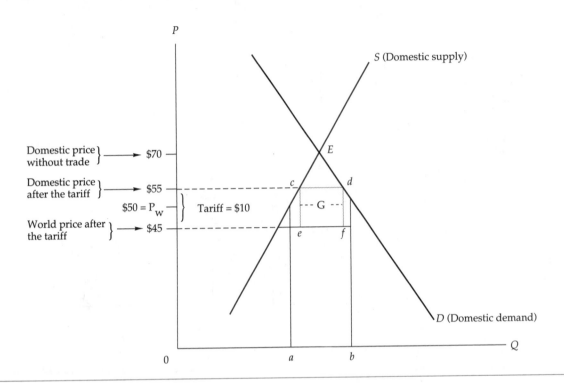

In a large importing country, the price rises by a portion (one-half in this diagram) of the tariff, while the exporting country absorbs the other portion.

A more complete graphical analysis of this case involving a large importing country is offered in the first part of Appendix 4–1.

Domestic Effects

In order to focus attention on the domestic effects in a tariff-imposing country, we assume it to be a *small* one. The internal price of imports rises by the full amount of the duty, an increase that has several consequences. In the first place, it forces some consumers to curtail consumption of imports and to switch to domestically produced substitutes. The latter are presumably less desirable; otherwise, they would have been purchased even in the absence of the tariff. Consequently, this change constitutes a welfare loss to the consumer. In other words, the tariff distorts relative market prices by "artificially" raising the prices of imports, thereby inducing the consumer to purchase less desirable domestic products.

Second, production expands in the industries producing substitutes for the tariff-ridden imports. Under conditions of full employment, this is accomplished by drawing resources away from other industries,[4] which presumably rank higher in the order of comparative advantage (otherwise, the resources would have been employed in the tariff-ridden industries even before the tariff). This is a loss in production efficiency for the economy as a whole and is often called production cost. It is worth emphasizing that the producers of the protected commodity gain from this transformation; the loss occurs in the efficiency of the economy as a whole as these producers are able to attract resources from other sectors. These two losses are partly offset by an increase in government revenue, which under our present assumption is collected only from domestic sources. Concentrating strictly on what happens within the importing country, we see a net loss in real income coupled with a redistribution of income from the consuming public to the producers of the protected commodities and to the government. Because the tariff raises the price to the consumer and gives protection to the domestic producer, its *domestic effects are comparable to those of a combined tax on the consumers and a subsidy to the producers.*

These changes can be seen in figure 4.3. It depicts the internal supply and demand conditions for a tariff-ridden commodity (such as automobiles). In the absence of any international trade, the domestic price is set at P_1—the intersection of domestic supply (colored) and demand (black) curves. Under free trade and in the absence of transport cost, the domestic price cannot differ from the world price, assumed here to be P_2. Remember that our discussion involves a small country that has no effect on world price. At P_2 domestic consumption is $0b$, production is $0a$, and imports—the difference between the two—equal ab.

A tariff in the amount of P_2P_3 raises the domestic price to P_3 and produces the following effects: Internal consumption of automobiles declines by $\overline{hb}$ as consumers move up along the demand curve from d to f. Thus, the tariff forces consumers to curtail consumption of the taxed commodity and switch to less desirable substitutes (the consumption effect of the tariff). Domestic automobile production rises by $\overline{ag}$ as producers move up along the supply curve from c to e (the production effect of the tariff). In a general equilibrium context $\overline{ag}$ represents the resources that the protected auto industry was able to bid away from the other, more efficient, industries. Imports decline by $ag + hb$. Finally, the shaded rectangle, import volume $\overline{ef}$ $(= \overline{gh})$ times tariff per unit P_2P_3, represents government revenue from the tariff.

---

[4] For this reason economists would prefer a general tariff of equal rate applicable to all imports over the now common differential tariffs on different goods.

FIGURE 4.3   *Domestic Effects of the Tariff*

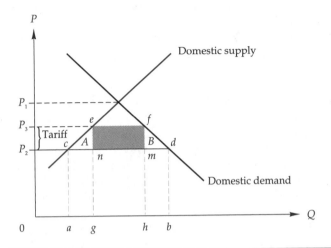

A small country necessarily loses from a tariff. Its deadweight net loss is triangles *A* + *B*.

Additional Insights

The Economic Cost of the Tariff—Further Considerations   The economic cost of the tariff can be examined in greater detail with the tools of welfare economics. These tools will be developed first.

Consider the demand curve *D* in figure 4.4. Points on it show the prices that consumers would be willing to pay for various quantities. In conjunction with a supply curve (not shown), a market price is established at OP_1. Once determined, all buyers pay this uniform price. But in fact it is the price that only the marginal buyer was willing to pay. Other (intramarginal) purchasers, more eager for the product, would have been willing to pay higher prices, as indicated by points on the demand curve above *A*. (Less eager buyers, whose preferences lead to points below *A* on the demand curve, do not purchase the product.) Yet despite this differential eagerness, they all pay the same price. The difference between what consumers would have been willing to pay and the market price that they actually pay is known as **consumers' surplus.** In the diagram it is measured by the area of the triangle P_1AB.[5] If the market price rises to OP_2, then the consumers' surplus becomes P_2CB. It *declines* by the shaded area P_1P_2CA. Note that the demand curve need not be extended to intersect the price axis in order to determine the *change* in consumers' surplus.

Next consider the supply curve *S* in figure 4.5. Points on it show the quantities sellers are willing to supply at varying prices. In conjunction with a demand curve (not

---

[5] The perfect price-discriminating monopolist would charge each consumer what she is willing to pay, instead of one market price for all. She would thereby appropriate the area of the triangle for herself.

FIGURE 4.4	*Consumers' Surplus*

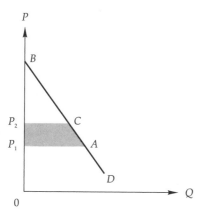

Consumers' surplus declines by the shaded area as price rises from P_1 and P_2.

FIGURE 4.5	*Producers' Surplus*

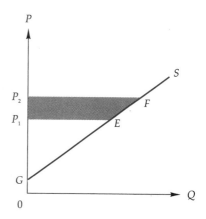

Producers' surplus rises by the shaded area as price rises from P_1 and P_2.

shown), a market price is determined at OP_1. Once it is established, all sellers receive this uniform price. But in fact only the marginal seller required this price to effect a sale. More efficient (intramarginal) sellers would have been willing to sell for less, as indicated by points on the supply curve below E. (Less eager sellers, requiring prices above OP_1, do not sell). Yet despite this differential eagerness (perhaps reflecting productive efficiency), all sellers obtain the same price. The difference between the price that the sellers would have required to part with the product, and the market price they all actually receive, is known as **producers' surplus.** In figure 4.5, it is measured by triangle P_1GE. If the market price rises to OP_2, then the producers' surplus becomes P_2GF. It *increases* by the shaded area P_1P_2FE. Note that the supply curve need not be extended all the way to the price axis to determine the *change* in producers' surplus.

We are now in a position to analyze the welfare effect of the tariff, using figure 4.3. Tariff P_2P_3 raises the post-trade domestic price from OP_2 to OP_3. As a result of this increase, the consumers' surplus *declines* by area P_3P_2df, the producers' surplus *rises* by area P_3P_2ce, while government revenue *rises* by the shaded rectangle *efmn*. The net welfare loss from the tariff is therefore equal to the sum of the areas of the two **welfare triangles** A and B.[6] It is known as the **deadweight loss.** Apart from this net loss, the tariff results in income redistribution away from the consumers and to the government and the producers of the protected commodity.

---

[6] The size of the two welfare triangles can be measured as the height (the tariff t) times the base divided by 2.

$$\text{Triangle } A = \frac{t}{2} \times \overline{cn}$$

and

$$\text{Triangle } B = \frac{t}{2} \times \overline{md}$$

(continued on p. 96)

An important consequence of these effects is that the tariff produces a gain to the factors of production that are heavily utilized in the import-competing industries. The textile workers of America, for example, stand to benefit from a high tariff on imported textiles, in much the same way as resources employed in the export industries gain from free trade. Countries have at times levied tariffs with the objective of helping a certain productive factor at the expense of others in the economy. The total loss to the country enacting such policies far outweighs the gain to the particular resources. Also, domestic taxes and subsidies are better ways to redistribute income in the economy, should such a course be deemed desirable.

Finally, a tariff may have such important indirect consequences as increasing the degree of monopoly in the country, thereby lowering productive efficiency, penalizing consumers, and retarding economic growth. If the country imposing the duty is so small that its internal market can support only one or two firms, foreign competition provides a stimulus to innovation and growth and a necessary check on pricing policies. The tariff reduces or bars such stimuli. Even in a large country, imports may provide the major competitive spirit when the industry is monopolized. This may partly explain the clamor for protection by the U.S. steel industry, where oligopolistic practices prevail. It also points out why such protection is contrary to the public interest. This is particularly true in times of inflation, when removal of import restrictions can help contain price increases. Indeed, countries often liberalize import restrictions as an anti-inflationary device.

We turn next to the internal repercussions in the exporting country. Nothing happens there if the importing nation is small. But if it is large, the price of the export good is depressed, because less of it is now purchased by the country levying the tariff. This leads to a curtailment of production and an increase in domestic consumption of the commodity. Introduction of trade has the opposite effect on the exporting nation; it raises the domestic price of the exported commodity. Thus, it should have surprised nobody that the price of wheat in Canada went up in the mid-1960s when the government concluded an agreement to sell a billion bushels to China, or that the price declined when the agreement expired. It merely reflected the increase and subsequent decline in the demand for Canadian wheat.

---

[6]*(Footnote 6 continued)*

Combining the two triangles results in

$$\frac{t}{2}\,(\overline{cn}) + \frac{t}{2}\,(\overline{md})$$

or

$$\frac{t}{2}\,(\overline{cn} + \overline{md})$$

But $(\overline{cn} + \overline{md})$ constitute the decline in imports resulting from the tariff. Hence the size of the triangle equals $t/2$ times ΔM. Countries expend considerable efforts to measure this area, the main difficulty of which is estimating ΔM. Imports are subject to many influences, and it is necessary to isolate the effect of one factor: the tariff.

Likewise, the price of wheat in the United States doubled in 1972 after large sales to Russia.

In the exporting country, the producers of goods subject to foreign import taxes lose, while the consumers gain. The exporting country as a whole loses, not only because resources are now less efficiently allocated, but because its terms of trade deteriorate. This latter effect reflects the fact that the exporting country pays part of the tax collected by the importing country.

Effect of Real Income

The tariff inevitably causes a reduction in the real income of the world as a whole. The effects on the terms of trade in the importing and exporting countries cancel each other out; all that remains is a reduction in the volume of trade compared to what it would have been under free-trade conditions. This constitutes a reduction in the world's real income, both because the production patterns are distorted and no longer conform to comparative advantage configurations and because consumers are induced to shift from their ideal consumption mix to less desirable substitutes.

This does not mean that every country must lose from the tariff, however. The exporting nation loses because of both the reduction in the volume of trade and the deterioration in the terms of trade. But the importing country is subjected to two conflicting forces: a loss of real income caused by the reduction in the volume of trade and a gain due to improvement in the terms of trade. If the country is large enough to affect the terms at which it trades, and if the tariff is not high, the latter effect may be stronger than the first, resulting in a net gain in real income. Economists call the tariff rate that maximizes this net gain the **optimum tariff.**[7] Its size depends on the very factors that determine the terms of trade effect. (The section on the "Economic Cost of the Tariff" in Appendix 4–2 offers a graphic exposition of the two-country case.)

Developing countries sometimes attempt to justify their complex and cumbersome systems of protection on the grounds that they provide an optimum tariff. But this is not a defensible position. These countries are too small relative to total world trade in whatever they import to affect the terms at which they trade—to "force" the exporters to pay part of the tariff. Their optimum import tariff is necessarily zero. In their export trade, however, such countries may be able to exploit monopoly power and pass on a tax to outside interests. But only in the case of primary exports can a single developing country be important enough as a supplier to affect world prices. For example, a tax levied by Brazil on coffee exports, or by Saudi Arabia on oil

---

[7] Corresponding to the *optimum tariff* on imports, there is an *optimum tax* on capital inflow that could be imposed by a country if it is a large enough borrower to improve the terms of borrowing abroad (interest rates).

exports, may restrict world supply of the commodity and raise its price, so that foreign consumers pay part of the tax. As a major exporter of the product it taxes, a country may in this manner improve its terms of trade.

In the case of developing countries, the taxed export good is usually an agricultural product or a raw material. Such export taxes are sometimes hidden in the activities of marketing boards set up by the government to stabilize prices and thereby stabilize the income received by the growers. Ostensibly designed to iron out excessive price fluctuations, the board can also push export prices above long-run equilibrium levels by withholding supplies or by paying farmers a lower price than it receives abroad, inducing them to produce less. And this action improves the terms of trade of the exporting country.

Some industrial nations are large enough to benefit from an import levy, and there is little doubt that the United States is one of them. Available evidence suggests that the incidence of the American tariff is about equally divided between the foreign exporters and the domestic consumers. But in many products the height of the American tariff exceeds its "optimum" level in the technical sense of the word. Furthermore, a leading nation like the United States should think twice before using its tariff as a vehicle for taxing other poorer nations. It makes little sense to engage in foreign-aid programs and then proceed to nullify part of the aid by imposing import duties. Whatever minor economic gain may accrue could be more than offset by political losses. This is one reason for the removal of import duties on tropical food products by the industrial countries. Because commodities such as coffee and cocoa are not produced in temperate-zone areas (the United States and Europe), the tariff on them offers no protection to a domestic industry. Its removal would improve the terms of trade of the producing LDCs.

Other Effects

Although not purposely designed to deal with balance-of-trade problems, a tariff does have balance-of-trade implications. Because it restricts imports of the products on which it is levied, the duty is generally thought to improve the country's external trade (exports minus imports) position. This result need not hold if the economy is operating near full employment. Under these circumstances, the shift of consumer demand from imports to domestically produced substitutes requires that labor and machines be shifted from somewhere else in the economy to the import-competing industries. If the factors of production come from the export industries, then exports *may* decline by as much as imports, and there will be no improvement in the trade position. Similarly, if the resources come from other import-competing industries, the net effect on imports will be nil. Furthermore, any bidding away of resources through the price mechanism usually contributes to a general increase in the price level, which in turn impairs the country's competitive standing and may nullify the initial gain of reduced imports. These considerations are less important when the economy is initially at unemployment; then the resources required to produce the import substitutes are abundantly available and need not be attracted from alternative uses.

An immediate implication of the preceding paragraph is that a tariff increases employment if it is imposed during a recession. It is true that unemployed workers and machines are put to work to meet the new demand. It does not follow, however, that the tariff should be used for that purpose; not only can the effect be negated by foreign retaliation (which would cause a reduction in exports), but domestic fiscal and monetary measures are far more effective instruments of domestic stabilization. They can increase employment without the loss in economic efficiency caused by the tariff.

Finally, because a tariff restricts competitive imports, it contributes to whatever monopoly power exists in the domestic economy. This further impairs allocative efficiency, technological progress, and economic growth.

Some Empirical Estimates

With the help of theoretical constructs and statistical tools, we can estimate the various economic effects of the tariff. Most studies of the subject are based on the *reductions* in tariff rates that have taken place multilaterally since World War II. The measurements are restricted to the "static" or allocative effect of the tariff.

A possible framework for the analysis of the effect of tariff reductions on the importing country is presented in figure 4.6. Taking these linkages one at a time, empirical evidence suggests that between one-third and one-half of any reduction in the American tariff accrues to the foreign exporters in the form of increased export prices. The United States is large enough to affect the terms at which it trades. Thus, foreign exporters pay part of its tariff by lowering their export prices. Conversely, when the U.S. tariff is reduced, these exporters reap part of the benefit by raising export prices. Small countries experience no terms of trade change.

For the world as a whole the terms of trade effects (on various countries) cancel out. But the volume of world trade rises: the increase estimated to result from the last round of global trade negotiations (called the Uruguay Round, concluded at the end of 1993) is over $500 billion per year, and world income is estimated to rise by $200 billion per year (relative to global GDP of about $35 trillion).

Still, the effect on U.S. employment is likely to be small.[8] The same may be said of the effect of trade liberalization among the United States, Canada, and Mexico, known as NAFTA.

---

[8] See D. Tarr and M. Morkre, *Aggregate Costs to the United States Tariffs and Quotas on Imports,* Washington, D.C.; Federal Trade Commission, 1984. For much higher estimates see D. Trefler, "Trade Liberalization and the Theory of Endogenous Protection," *Journal of Political Economy,* February 1993.

FIGURE 4.6	*Schematic Effects of Tariff Reduction*

Tariff reduction →(Various elasticities)→ Cut in import prices →(Import demand elasticities)→ Increase in import volume →→ Changes in domestic production, money income, real income (welfare), employment, balance of payments

Additional Insights[9]

Thus far, the discussion of the distortions caused by tariffs has related strictly to consumption and production misallocations of goods and services that *already exist*. But we live in an age of advanced technology, where discovery and development of *new goods* is commonplace. Many goods used daily today did not even exist 20 years ago. The word *good* in this context is not limited to consumer products. Rather, it should be interpreted broadly to include inputs, production processes and organization (such as *just-in-time* inventory management), new technologies, and other modern ways of conducting business. Technological and managerial improvement in anything related to production and distribution is included under the rubric of a new good.

More often than not, new goods, as defined above, are invented in the industrial countries and imported into the developing countries. One effect of tariffs and nontariff barriers or NTBs (such as import quotas) is to *keep out such new goods,* thereby depriving consumers of newly developed merchandise, producers of new material inputs and technological improvements, and the economy as a whole of new means of organizing production and distribution.

These costs are far higher than the cost of the tariff measured by holding constant the set of goods in use. A recent paper shows that the traditional measure of the economic cost of the tariff, as a percent of GDP, can be approximated by the square of the tariff rate. Thus a 10 percent tariff, equivalent to 0.1, would cost the economy $0.1^2 = 0.01$, or 1 percent of GDP in production and consumption misallocation of existing goods. The cost of NTBs can be calculated in the same fashion by converting each NTB into its tariff equivalent. If the tariff equivalent of tariffs and NTBs combined is 25 percent or 0.25, then the cost to the economy, by the traditional measure, is $0.25^2 = 0.0625$, or 6.25 percent of GDP. By contrast, if the exclusion of new goods is included in the cost calculations, the reduction in GDP caused by trade restrictions is *almost twice* the size of the restrictions. Thus a 10 percent tariff lowers GDP by 19.8 percent, and a 25 percent tariff and NTBs (not uncommon in LDCs) implies a fall in GDP of 47 percent. The gains to LDCs from eliminating trade restrictions can be enormous. And indeed many developing countries have removed or lowered such restrictions unilaterally, to good advantage.

[9] Based on P. Romer, "New Goods, Old Theory, and the Welfare Costs of Trade Restrictions," *Journal of Development Economics*, 1994.

HOW PROTECTIVE IS THE TARIFF?

Public discussions of the tariff issue often involve intercountry comparisons of the level of protection, on which policy decisions frequently are based. But protection cannot be measured or compared simply. What the measure of protection purports to convey is *the amount of potential imports kept out of the country by the tariff.* This is a very difficult figure to derive, and the problems of estimating it are often overlooked or sidestepped in public pronouncements. These problems will now be sorted out.

Ad Valorem and Specific Duty

Whenever specific duties are employed, they must be converted into their *ad valorem* equivalent to facilitate international or intercommodity comparisons. Only when it is expressed as a percent of price is the tariff rate independent of the unit of the commodity on which it is levied, thus making duties on diverse commodities comparable. The conversion is made by dividing the duty by the average price of the transactions undertaken over the preceding year.

Nominal versus Effective Tariff Rates

Even when expressed as a percent of price, the tariff rate published in the country's tariff schedule (known as the **nominal tariff rate**) does not convey the level of protection accorded to the domestic producers. While nominal tariffs apply to the total value of imports, they protect only the portion of that value produced at home. For example, assume that country *A* levies a 20 percent import tariff on desks, but imported lumber and other materials that go into the domestic production of desks enter duty-free. Assume further that these imported materials constitute one-half of the final value of the desk, so that the value added in domestic manufacturing is one-half. In other words, if the desk sells for $100, then the manufacturer spends $50 on imported inputs, and home production adds another $50 to its value. The 20 percent tax levied on imported desks yields $20 per desk. But this sum protects only that component of the desk's value produced at home, namely half its total value. To that component it accords an **effective protective rate** of 40 percent ($20 as a percentage of $50). If the imported raw materials were taxed at 10 percent, then the effective rate of protection given the desk manufacturer would be 30 percent. It is evident that if the final product entered duty-free, while imported raw materials used in domestic production were taxed, then the domestic producer of the final good would be taxed rather than protected. For example, a tariff on steel raises its domestic price, and constitutes a tax on auto producers and other industries that use steel as an input. Likewise, a tariff on computer chips constitutes a tax on the computer industry. A tariff on the final product protects domestic import-competing activities; duty on imported materials taxes the users of these materials by raising their cost. Effective protection nets out these two effects.

In essence, the effective protective rate measures the degree of protection given to domestic production activities. It is defined as *the percentage increase in domestic value added per unit of output made possible by the tariff structure* (that is, tariffs on both the final product *and* on imported inputs) compared to a situation under free trade. The effective protection for a final product *increases* as the nominal rate imposed on it *increases*, and as the nominal rate imposed on imported materials used in the production process *decreases*. It also varies with the proportion of imported inputs that constitute the final value of the product (a proportion that may itself change as the situation changes from free trade to tariff). These relationships can be derived from a mathematical formula.[10] Alternatively, in what follows they are shown in a series of examples.

Consider a leather wallet whose C.I.F. import price in Belgium *under free trade* is 1,000 Belgian francs. The cost of the leather of which the wallet is made is 500 francs on the world market, so that a wallet made in Belgium out of imported leather would have a domestic value added of 500 francs at free-trade prices.[11]

---

[10]A simplified formula for the effective protective rate derived from the above definition is:

$$g_j = \frac{t_j - a_{ij}t_i}{1 - a_{ij}}$$

where g_j is the effective protective rate on final product j, t_j is the nominal tariff rate on final product j, t_i is the nominal tariff rate on imported input i, and a_{ij} is the share of i in the total value of j in the absence of tariffs.

The formula is derived as follows: Value added in industry j (per unit of output), without any tariff, is

$$v_j = p_j(1 - a_{ij})$$

Value added in industry j, with tariffs on both the input and the output, is

$$v'_j = p_j(1 + t_j) - p_j a_{ij}(1 + t_i) = p_j[(1 + t_j) - a_{ij}(1 + t_i)]$$

where p_j and p_i are the prices of the output and input, respectively.

$$g_j = \frac{v'_j - v_j}{v_j} = \frac{p_j[(1 + t_j) - a_{ij}(1 + t_i)] - p_j(1 - a_{ij})}{p_j(1 - a_{ij})}$$

$$= \frac{(1 + t_j) - a_{ij}(1 + t_i) - (1 - a_{ij})}{1 - a_{ij}} = \frac{1 + t_j - a_{ij} - a_{ij}t_i - 1 + a_{ij}}{1 - a_{ij}}$$

$$= \frac{t_j - a_{ij}t_i}{1 - a_{ij}}$$

When there are many inputs the formula is:

$$g_j = \frac{t_j - \Sigma(a_{ij}t_j)}{1 - \Sigma a_{ij}}$$

[11] A problem that arises in obtaining these figures is that the free-trade prices of outputs and inputs, and therefore the value added under free trade, cannot be observed directly in a country under a tariff regime. There are two ways of circumventing this problem. The tariff-ridden prices can be deflated by the tariff rates to obtain the implied free-trade prices, or the ratio of the value added to the final product price can be inferred from that of another country where tariff rates are close to zero.

Case 1 A 40 percent tariff on wallets would raise their domestic price to 1,400 francs, and a tariff on leather of 20 percent would raise its domestic price to 600 francs. The domestic value added under protection is 1,400 − 600 = 800 francs, compared with 500 francs at free-trade prices. The difference of 300 francs constitutes 300/500 = 60 percent effective protection on leather wallets compared with a 40 percent nominal tariff rate. *When the tariff rate on the final output exceeds the rate levied on the input, the effective protection on the output exceeds the nominal rate imposed on it.*

Case 2 Next, consider a case in which the tariff on leather wallets is 30 percent, raising their domestic price to 1,300 francs, and the tariff on leather is 40 percent, raising its domestic price to 700 francs. The domestic value added under protection is 600 francs, compared with 500 francs at free-trade prices. The difference of 100 francs constitutes a 100/500 = 20 percent effective protection on wallets compared with 30 percent nominal rate. *When the tariff rate on the input exceeds that on the final output, the effective protection accorded the final output falls short of the nominal rate imposed on it.*

Thus, the effective protective rate on a product will exceed, be equal to, or fall short of the nominal rate on the product, depending on whether the nominal tariff is higher than, equal to, or lower than the nominal tariffs on material inputs. Negative effective protection results when tariffs raise the cost of inputs by a larger absolute amount than they raise the price of the product.[12]

Case 3 In addition to the tariff rates on the output and input, the effective rate of protection depends also on the share of domestic value added in the product price. This share was assumed to be 0.5 in the above examples. In contrast, assume now that the free-trade C.I.F. import price of a leather wallet in Belgium is 1,000 francs as before, but the imported inputs are 800 francs and the domestic value added under free trade is only 200 francs. Now reconsider case 1 above. The 40 percent tariff on wallets raises their domestic price to 1,400 francs, while the 20 percent tariff on imported leather raises its price to 960 francs. The domestic value added under protection becomes 1,400 − 960 = 440 francs, compared with only 200 francs under free trade. This constitutes an effective protective rate on wallets of 240/200 = 120 percent. This result underscores an important fact. If a country establishes a

---

[12] In terms of the notation of footnote 10, where g_j is the effective protection on project j,

If $t_j > t_i$ then $g_j > t_j$

If $t_j = t_i$ then $g_j = t_j$

If $t_j < t_i$ then $g_j < t_j$

If $t_j < a_{ij}t_i$ then $g_j < 0$ (negative protection)

plant for the final processing of a product, importing most inputs at a semi-final stage of fabrication at zero or very low duties, then even moderate nominal protection on the final product translates into a very high effective protection.

Several important implications follow from the concept of effective protection. First, although the consumer reacts to changes in the final price that reflect the nominal tariff rates, *the producer reacts to changes in the cost of the production processes, and these are affected by the effective rate.* Thus, it is the effective rate of protection that indicates the degree of resource misallocation caused by the tariff structure. The distortionary effect of protection *rises with the degree of dispersion* or differential levels of effective tariffs between commodities, because that distorts the ranking of industries by comparative advantage. *The fact that the tariff is a sectoral measure is what makes it most harmful.*

A second corollary to this analysis concerns the tariff structure of most industrial countries. They admit raw materials virtually duty free, semi-processed goods at low duties, and finished manufactures (especially of the labor-intensive variety) at moderately high duty rates. This structure means that the effective protection on finished manufactures is much higher than the nominal rates indicate (see case 1 above). Recent calculations suggest that *the effective rates on many finished products are double their nominal counterparts.* This is illustrated by the following example[13] of the cascading tariff structure by degree of processing in the textile industry:

	United States		EU	
	Nominal tariff	**Effective tariff**	**Nominal tariff**	**Effective tariff**
Raw cotton	6%	6%	0%	0%
Cotton yarn	8	12	7	23
Cotton fabrics	16	31	14	29

Developing countries maintain that the sharp **escalation** of effective protection by degree of processing encourages the importation of goods into the developed nations in raw or semiprocessed form and therefore discourages industrialization (in the form of final processing) in the developing world.

A third conclusion, applicable to developed and developing countries alike, is that changes in tariff rates on imported inputs have an inverse effect on the level of protection accorded to final products. For example, protection of steel in the United States raises its prices and increases production costs in all industries (such as the automobile industry) that use steel as an input.

---

[13] From A. Yeats, "Effective Tariff Protection in the U.S., EC and Japan," the *Quarterly Review of Economics and Business,* summer 1974.

Protection on wool fabric raises the prices of suits made of wool. The significance of this point is underscored when we consider a developing country pursuing an import substitution policy as a road to industrialization. Often in such cases, the country begins by building up a final assembly plant under a high protective tariff and using untaxed imported inputs. As a second stage, the country begins to **deepen** domestic production by manufacturing the inputs at home and according them high protection. And so it proceeds backward through the production process adding new layers of inputs. What the government often does not realize is the fact that by imposing tariffs on imported inputs, it actually lowers the level of effective protection accorded the final product (see case 2 above). By that very action it may render the final assembly plant unprofitable.

Fourth, this analysis has implications for a country's export position as well. Although export industries must sell at world market prices, they often use imported inputs for which they must pay domestic prices augmented by a tariff. In case 1 above, if the Belgian producers had to export their wallets at the world market price of 1,000 francs apiece, but pay a 20 percent tariff on leather, then the tariff would raise the cost of their input from 500 to 600 francs and lower value added from 500 to 400 francs. The producers would thus sustain a negative protection—a tax—of 20 percent. To retain the free-trade value added of 500 francs (that is, to compensate the producers for the increased cost of input caused by the tariff) would require that the producers receive an export subsidy of 100 francs, 10 percent of the price of the product. Such subsidies (that is, **rebates** of the tariff paid on imported materials) are often practiced in developing countries to protect their export position, because in the absence of the subsidy firms may not have any inducement to export.

Finally, rates of effective protection can be used indirectly as a rough guide to determine comparative advantage. The analysis of Chapter 2 revealed that economic efficiency requires the ranking of industries by degree of comparative advantage. A country would then export the commodities ranked high and import those ranked low on its scale of industries. Under free-market competitive conditions, the price mechanism would generate such a ranking, thus establishing efficient allocation of resources.

But in many developing countries, free-market conditions are rare. Instead, trade is restricted by a variety of policy instruments such as high tariffs, import quotas, exchange controls, and so on. Moreover, these restrictions are applied selectively by the government to encourage activities that it perceives to be in the best interest of the country and to discourage others. For example, the government may encourage cheap imports of investment goods (such as machinery) and discourage imports of consumer goods. These restrictions are often coupled with a variety of domestic market distortions such as artificially high wage rates in certain industries obtained through powerful labor unions. In such cases, not only is the free-market ranking distorted beyond recognition, but producers proceed to use capital-intensive processes relative to the country's factor endowments, because factor remunerations are distorted to such a point that they no longer reflect the factor endowments. (That is, the prices of imported capital equipment are artificially low and the price of labor artificially high.)

Suppose now that, faced with such distorted conditions, the government wishes to embark on a new development plan and decide more rationally which industries or projects it should promote; or, alternatively, an international aid organization must determine what projects to support. How can such new resources be allocated optimally? One possible guide is the effective rate of protection. Because that rate measures the inducement to the protected producers to expand their activities, it also reflects the degree of protection that the industry requires to operate on its present scale. The ranking of industries by the level of effective protection indicates their relative incentive to expand output under the existing structure of protection; it would produce a roughly inverse order to the ranking by comparative advantage. The industries at the low end of the scale in terms of effective protection are the ones that should be expanded.

A closely related guide to project selection is the **domestic resource cost (DRC)** of foreign exchange earned by exports or saved by import substitution. Every dollar so earned (or saved) by a developing country costs a certain amount in domestic currency (representing a bundle of domestic resources) expended on processing and other activities. The activities that should be supported are those in which the cost of a dollar earned or saved is least. The ranking of industries from the high to the low domestic currency cost per dollar earned would produce an ordering roughly similar to the ranking from high to low effective protection. In both cases, it is the low-ranking industries that deserve support and encouragement to expand.

This completes the discussion of effective protection. We turn next to other problems encountered in assessing the degree of the tariff's protection.

Aggregation Problems

It is a common objective of scholars and policymakers alike to aggregate tariff rates from the highly detailed and divergent commodity classifications by which they are reported into, say, the three-digit SITC. Some people may wish further to aggregate them into one average figure for each country, so as to have a ready-made intercountry comparison of the levels of protection.

But the aggregation of tariff rates is a thorny issue; there is no satisfactory way to average out the rates imposed on diverse commodities. The use of simple unweighted averages of tariff rates implicitly assumes that each commodity is of equal importance in the country's import trade. This, of course, is not realistic. An alternative aggregation procedure is to compute weighted averages, but here the problem is what weights to use. Ideally, one should weigh each rate by what imports would have been in the absence of the tariff. But because this is not known, many investigators employ the country's own tariff-ridden imports as weights. Such a procedure invariably biases the results downward, because the very high tariffs permit fewer imports and therefore receive little weight. At the extreme, a prohibitive tariff excludes all imports and therefore receives no weight and will not be represented at all in the calculation. A better solution is to weigh each tariff by the domestic consumption of the product. But because the two magnitudes are often not available on the same commodity classification basis, a possible compromise is to weigh each tariff by total world (or OECD) trade in the commodity to which the rate applies. Even this procedure incorporates some downward bias because of the similarity in the tariff structures of industrial countries.

Additional Insights

The Response to Price Change

Even in dealing with disaggregative figures, the nominal and effective tariffs do not, in and of themselves, provide a precise indication of the level of protection. In the final analysis, that level refers to the quantity of the imported commodity excluded from the domestic market. That exclusion operates through the price mechanism, and it comes about because the tariff raises the price of imports relative to that of domestic substitutes. But the extent to which the import price rises and the foreign export price falls depends on various elasticities. More important, the amount of imports excluded by a given percentage increase in import price depends on the response of the public to the price increase (the elasticity of demand for imports). The higher the response, the larger will be the exclusion caused by a given percentage rise in price and the more protective a given tariff will be.

This degree of response depends on a variety of factors, not the least of which is the availability of domestic substitutes. But one important variable determining the import-demand elasticity for any commodity is the share of imports in domestic production and consumption. It can be shown that the larger the share of imports, the smaller will be the elasticity. This relation is important because it permits us to make *a priori* judgments in some cases. Suppose one is comparing the degree of protection afforded by the American tariff with that of Italy. Because imports occupy a much smaller share of the U.S. market than of the Italian, the import-demand elasticity is higher in America and so is the degree of protection embodied in a given percentage price rise. Conversely, when we talk of multilateral tariff reduction, a given percentage reduction in the U.S. import price is translated into a larger increase in the volume of imports than in virtually any other country.

ARGUMENTS FOR PROTECTION

Against the background developed thus far, we can briefly evaluate some of the arguments heard in political and economic circles on behalf of the tariff. From the viewpoint of the welfare of the world as a whole, the most popular claim made for tariff protection is the so-called **infant-industry** argument. It asserts that industries that may benefit from large-scale operations because of the existence of external economies (such as good transport facilities, a well-trained labor force, or the "learning by doing" effect) should be allowed to grow to optimum size under a protective tariff. Validity of the argument depends on some form of "market failure";[14] otherwise, why would private investors not develop the industry under free-market conditions? Even if valid, it is an argument for *temporary* protection. Once the industry attains a desired size, the tariff can be removed. Japan's development is replete with illustrations of how an industry can be developed and fostered under tariff protection until it reaches an optimum size. In its development policy, Japan made effective use of both tariff protection and imported technology in the form of licensing agreements. Today it is one of the world's largest exporters.

Often there are difficulties with the practical application of this theory. First, the argument can be abused, as it has been at times by declining industries that attempt to protect their position in the market and thereby perpetuate inefficiency. Even the American steel industry advanced the argument once in an effort to convince Congress to impose import quotas on steel. Second, once it has been imposed, a tariff is rather difficult to eliminate, regardless of the industry's competitive standing. Finally, even in cases where the infant-industry position applies, it is more efficient to offer a production subsidy as a means of helping the industry to expand. While the tariff imposes both production and consumption costs on the economy, a subsidy embodies only production costs, not consumption costs. More generally, a tariff is equivalent to a tax on the consumer *plus* a (disguised) subsidy to the producer. By contrast, a direct subsidy does not contain the tax element, and the subsidy component is provided in an overt fashion. It is then open for all interested parties to inspect and evaluate. And, when the time comes, it is somewhat easier to discontinue.

From the point of view of an individual nation taken as a whole, the only rational argument for the tariff is improvement in the terms of trade (the optimum tariff). However, this applies only to the major importers that are large enough to affect the terms at which they trade, and assumes that other countries would not retaliate. The gain to the importing country is matched by a terms-of-trade loss to the exporting country.

Tariffs may at times be used to increase employment or improve the balance of payments. But both objectives can be met more effectively and

---

[14] Two types of market failure are suggested in this context: (a) Imperfect capital markets—absence of financial institutions that would channel savings to finance new investment. The first-best solution is to create a better capital market; but protection can be justified as a second-best solution. (b) Appropriability—firms in the industry generate social benefits, such as improved technology for the economy as a whole, for which they are not compensated. Therefore they produce less than an optimum amount, and the industry should be protected so as to induce an expansion in its output. In general, market failure should be remedied by policies aimed *at its source*, because indirect policy responses (such as tariff protection) lead to distortions elsewhere in the economy. Domestic policies should be used to correct domestic distortion and such externality is better corrected by a production subsidy.

more efficiently by fiscal, monetary, or exchange-rate policies. Protection is an expensive way to create jobs. On the other hand, a period of unemployment in the domestic economy is not a good time to reduce tariffs. After all, the main objective of such a reduction is to increase efficiency by transferring resources to industries in which the country has a comparative advantage, and the existence of widespread unemployment would make such a transfer very difficult. In recent years, the U.S. labor movement has generally favored protectionism for fear of job losses in such import-competing industries as steel, footwear, and textiles. However, foreign retaliation can create equally severe unemployment in the export industries.

Perusal of testimonies before Congressional committees on foreign trade reveals a wide array of arguments for protection, the most common of which states that the United States cannot compete with countries in which wage rates are a fraction of its own. The demand is for a tariff that would be equal to the wage differential—also known as a **scientific tariff.**

But wage rates are only one component of production cost; productivity is another important element. If, for example, U.S. wage rates are seven times those of their Mexican counterparts, but the productivity of an American worker is more than seven times greater than that of the average Mexican worker, U.S. production costs would be lower—not higher—than those prevailing in Mexico. This was discovered by some American companies that moved to Mexico in search of lower wages, only to find that their production costs increased instead. Indeed, it was shown in Chapter 2 that U.S. wages are higher *because* U.S. productivity is higher. America's major competitors in global markets are not the low-wage nations of the developing world, but rather Germany and Japan—both high-wage countries. The fact is that the U.S. competitive position in manufacturing is strong. If anything, it has improved greatly in recent years, as production costs in Europe and Japan have risen far more than those in the United States.[15]

However, certain nations, including Mexico, have a competitive advantage over the United States in labor-intensive industries such as textiles, brooms, and footwear. These are low-wage industries in which the United States lacks a comparative advantage. The perpetual demand by these *low-wage* industries in the United States for tariffs to equalize wage rates with foreign competitors makes no sense, because these are goods that the United States should be importing. Resources should instead be transferred to the high-technology industries (such as chemicals, robotics, and computers) in which the United States has a comparative advantage. Despite the fact that these latter industries pay much higher wages, they compete effectively in global markets.

---

[15] See M. N. Baily, "Productivity and Competitiveness in American Manufacturing" *The Brookings Review,* winter 1993. The issue of relative wage rates and the extent to which it is offset by productivity differentials was prominent in the debate over NAFTA.

Demands to keep out cheap foreign imports—simply because they undersell local products—go back many years. A famous reply to this argument is contained in a short satire by Fredric Bastiat. Titled "The Petition of the Candlemakers," it is an imaginary petition presented to the French Chamber of Deputies in the early nineteenth century:

> We are subjected to the intolerable competition of a foreign rival whose superior facilities for producing light enable him to flood the French market at so low a price as to take away all our customers the moment he appears, suddenly reducing an important branch of French industry to stagnation. This rival is the sun.
>
> We request a law to shut up all windows, dormers, skylights, openings, holes, chinks, and fissures through which sunlight penetrates. Our industry provides such valuable manufactures that our country cannot, without ingratitude, leave us now to struggle unprotected through so unequal a contest. . . . In short, granting our petition will greatly develop every branch of agriculture. Navigation will equally profit. Thousands of vessels will soon be employed in whaling, and thence will arise a navy capable of upholding the honor of France. . . .
>
> Do you object that the consumer must pay the price of protecting us? You have yourselves already answered the objection. When told that the consumer is interested in free importation of iron, coal, corn, wheat, cloth, etc., you have answered that the producer is interested in their exclusion. You have always acted to *encourage labor,* to *increase the demand for labor.*
>
> Will you say that sunlight is a free gift, and that to repulse free gifts is to repulse riches under pretense of encouraging the means of obtaining them? Take care—you deal a death-blow to your own policy. Remember: hitherto you have always repulsed foreign produce because it was an approach to a free gift; and the closer this approach, the more you have repulsed the good. . . .
>
> When we buy a Portuguese orange at half the price of a French orange, we in effect get it half as a gift. If you protect national labor against the competition of a *half-gift,* what principle justifies allowing the importation of something just because it is *entirely a gift?* . . . The difference in price between an imported article and the corresponding French article is a *free gift* to us. The bigger the difference, the bigger the gift. . . . The question is whether you wish for France the benefit of free consumption or the supposed advantages of laborious production. Choose, but be consistent.[16]

---

[16] A condensation of Bastiat's petition quoted from Yeager and Tuerck, Trade Policy and the Price System, Scranton, Pa.: International Textbook Company, 1966. Ironically, in August 1986 candle imports from China were found to injure the U.S. candle industry.

That the demand for protection is not restricted to commodities is illustrated by a *Wall Street Journal* (Sept. 4, 1996, p. A–2) story about American mathematicians seeking immigration curbs on foreign scholars because of high unemployment in the profession. Recent math Ph.D.s face a jobless rate of 10.7 percent, and immigrants tend to win 40 percent of the math jobs that become available every year. Thus, while U.S. society benefits from foreign talent, individual American mathematicians pay the price. (Similarly, Japanese wrestlers attempt to keep foreign wrestlers out of Japan.)

Economically, immigration is like free trade in that its costs can be concentrated but its benefits dispersed. Imported Chinese textiles may displace South Carolina factory workers, but consumers across the United States pay less to clothe their families. Imported Chinese mathematicians may force American Ph.D.s to resort to teaching high school, but workers nationwide may find their productivity and wages rising because of the innovations those foreign scholars produce.

Industries often claim that their products and the labor skills they utilize are essential to national security and should therefore be preserved by import protection. For example, in the United States the machine-tools industry received protection on national security grounds. Whether true or not, this is not a subject on which the economist can pass judgment, except to indicate that if it is true, the industry should be directly and overtly subsidized out of the defense budget.

Similarly, the argument that a nation needs the tariff in order to have something to bargain down in tariff negotiations overlooks the fact that the country is better off without the tariff, regardless of the level of protection it encounters in the markets of its trading partners. If the argument is modified to suggest that the "bargaining tariff" is used to secure the best of all worlds in which no nation employs a protective tariff, then its validity depends on the effectiveness of the tariff in securing such a situation.

Additional Insights

A case for protection is sometimes made from the point of view of a single factor of production. Through its domestic effects, the tariff can be used to redistribute income among factors (in favor of the relatively scarce factors and away from the relatively abundant ones) or income groups. But whether desirable or not, there are other, more efficient, means of redistributing income in society (namely domestic taxes and subsidies).

Finally, many arguments for protection have been advanced in recent years with respect to developing economies. They suggest that the tariff and other means of commercial policy be used to rectify market imperfections existing in the domestic economies of these countries. For example, it has been demonstrated that labor mobility between sectors of the economy is low in many developing countries.

This phenomenon is particularly apparent with respect to movement from subsistence agriculture to manufacturing and has its origin in the traditional attachment of the indigenous population to its place of birth and the extended family. But suppose that economic efficiency requires such a move and that the wage differential is not large enough to overcome the inherent obstacles to mobility. The proposed remedy is to impose a protective tariff on manufactured imports. That would enable industrialists to charge higher prices for their products and thus pay higher wages, inducing labor to move to manufacturing. In other words, where the allocative mechanism in the economy is not sufficiently lubricated in the sense that resources do not respond swiftly or in sufficient quantities to market price differentials, there is a need to artificially augment the differential in order to bring about the necessary mobility. The tool suggested for accomplishing this is the protective tariff.

The argument makes sense as far as it goes. It suffers from ignoring the fact that there are far better instruments than tariffs to produce wage differentials and promote mobility. The best solution is to offer a direct subsidy to workers to help them move. Next comes a general production subsidy to manufacturing firms. But that is an inferior solution because it attracts capital as well as labor to the expanding industries. Import protection is still worse because it also distorts demand. It is a "third-best" option. The same may be said about the use of tariff policy to eliminate all sorts of domestic distortions,[17] to achieve a desired investment pattern, or to promote rapid growth of certain industries. There is a whole array of instruments at the disposal of the government, and it is usually suboptimal to use international *commercial* policy to influence the *domestic* economy. Distortions should be dealt with by measures that come as close as possible to the source of the trouble; otherwise undesirable side-effects would be created. Hence it is misguided to call upon tariff protection to correct a variety of economic and social ills. But the point is purely academic if the country is so underdeveloped that no policy instruments other than the tariff are available.

Additional arguments for protection, which apply to industries dominated by oligopoly firms, will be considered at the end of the next chapter.

In sum, while tariff protection is very common in the present-day world, rational justifications for its use are scarce. The world as a whole, as well as most individual countries, would be better off if it were dispensed with as an instrument of national policy. The question examined next is whether there has been any progress toward this end.

---

[17]In developed and developing countries alike, if factors of production are not mobile between industries, then the introduction of trade into an isolated economy will not produce the expected shift in resource allocation and production mix. The resources that remain "stuck" in the import-competing industries will suffer a reduction in remunerations. But because the consumers will still enjoy the more favorable international prices, society as a whole benefits from the introduction of trade. However, if in addition to factor immobility there is wage rigidity, so that factors refuse to accept a reduction in remunerations, unemployment will result. Under these conditions the economy may be better off without trade than with it. But domestic measures designed to promote factor mobility and wage flexibility are superior to commercial policy for dealing with this situation.

APPROACHES TO FREE TRADE

In the 1980s and 1990s it has become widely recognized that import protection is harmful, and several developed and underdeveloped countries as well as transitional economies have unilaterally liberalized their import regimes. Often such liberalization is the centerpiece of general economic reform. Yet many nations still appear reluctant to reduce tariffs. For them tariff reduction has come to be regarded as a concession to others and is offered only reciprocally. To deal with tariffs and other trade barriers the community of nations is engaged in a process of trade liberalization. It is carried out on both the multinational and regional levels.

The International Approach

The first approach is associated with the **World Trade Organization (WTO)**, an international organization with a membership of 120 countries devoted to the promotion of international trade in general and the reduction of trade barriers in particular. The WTO superseded the General Agreement on Tariffs and Trade (GATT) in 1995. Its member countries hold periodic negotiating conferences in which tariff "concessions" are exchanged. The reductions agreed upon by any two or more partners are then extended to all member nations. This rule is known as the **Unconditional Most Favored Nation Principle (MFN);** it guards against discrimination in international trade. The result is successive rounds of tariff reductions, each applying to all sources of supply on a nondiscriminatory basis. The last completed set of tariff reductions (the eighth), known as the Uruguay Round, began in 1986 and was completed on December 15, 1993. The negotiating process and the rules under which the WTO operates will be described in Chapter 7.

The nondiscriminatory approach invariably leads to a worldwide increase in productive efficiency—as the world moves to specialize along lines dictated by comparative advantage—and to more desirable consumption patterns. Although the gains are not equally distributed, and some countries may even lose, there is a gain to the world as a whole (see Appendix 4–2). Additionally, small countries may experience important dynamic benefits flowing from the increased size of their markets and curtailed monopoly power at home.

The Regional Approach

The regional approach is exemplified by customs unions and free-trade areas. A **customs union** involves two or more countries that abolish all, or nearly all, trade restrictions among themselves and set up a common and uniform tariff against outsiders. **The European Union (EU),**[18] is a customs

[18]Originally called the European Economic Community (EEC), the name was changed in the mid-1970s to the European Community (EC). Consequently, we shall retain the name EEC in any references pertaining to years prior to 1976. As of 1994 it is commonly referred to as the European Union (EU).

union that originally encompassed West Germany, France, Italy, Belgium, the Netherlands, and Luxembourg. It was enlarged, as of July 1, 1973, to include Great Britain, Denmark, and Ireland. The 1981 accession of Greece, the 1986 accession of Spain and Portugal, and the 1995 accession of Sweden, Austria, and Finland increased the Union's size to 15 countries. Trade among members is free of restrictions; nonmembers must pay the common external tariff. An American producer shipping to France is discriminated against in favor of a German competitor to the extent of the duty.

In a **free-trade area (FTA),** trade among the member countries is also completely liberalized, or nearly so. But there is no common tariff against nonmember countries; each country is free to impose its own duty. For example, an FTA agreement encompassing the United States, Canada, and Mexico, known as the **North American Free Trade Agreement (NAFTA),** came into force in 1994. Under it Mexican exports to the United States would enter duty free, while similar exports from Asia would pay the U.S. tariff. There are numerous regional groupings in Latin America, Africa, and Asia.

A free-trade area differs from a customs union in that it does not have a common external tariff, and that difference presents a difficult problem of administration. Because the duty levied on imports from nonmember countries is not the same in all member countries, and because trade is free within the area, there is nothing to prevent a nonmember's exports from entering the high-duty member nation through a low-duty member. In order to avoid it, the free-trade area must retain border checkpoints between its members to investigate the origin of every commodity as it crosses the national boundary. Only if produced within the free-trade area is it accorded a duty-free status. Even this approach can be circumvented. The outside producer can set up a final finishing plant for the product in the member country that has the lowest tariff, with value added accounting for not more than 10 percent of the final product, and ship from there to the entire free-trade area.[19] Thus, the integrating nations must decide what portion of the value of each product must be produced within the region in order for it to be accorded duty-free status. Often the figure is 50 percent, and the rules (known as *rules of origin*) are enforced through the use of certificates of origin presented at border checkpoints. These rules themselves promote discriminatory behavior, because they force each member to source inputs from within the FTA, to meet the rules of origin criteria.

Customs unions and free-trade areas are exempt from GATT's Most Favored Nation rule. These organizations will be discussed in detail in Chapter 7. It is the approach to trade liberalization that concerns us here.

---

[19] Here is an example: Because there are no restrictions on U.S. imports from the Caribbean countries (under the so-called Caribbean initiative), Asian apparel firms have set up final assembly plants in these islands with the idea of exporting to the United States.

Unlike the international approach, it may or may not lead to an improvement in world allocative efficiency, because it contains an important element of discrimination against nonmember countries.

Indeed, the theory of customs unions, developed since World War II, deals mainly with the effect of regional integration on world allocative efficiency. It demonstrates that not every partial movement toward the optimal world of free trade is necessarily beneficial. Each case must be examined on its merits.

Static Effects   Consider a three-country world in which countries A and B form a customs union to the exclusion of C. In other words, A and B abolish all trade restrictions between themselves, while their imports from C remain subject to a tariff. The action has two effects. With respect to products in which A and B are competitive, the elimination of tariffs between them causes the replacement of some high-cost production by imports from the partner country. This effect, known as **trade creation,** is favorable to world welfare because it rationally reorganizes production within the union. Second, for products in which country C is competitive with one of the integrating countries, A or B begins to import from the other member what it earlier imported from C. If C is the most efficient producer, it would be the major supplier as long as its products receive the same tariff treatment as those of its competitor. But the tariff discrimination induces diversion of trade away from C toward a member country. This effect, known as **trade diversion,** is unfavorable, because it reorganizes world production less efficiently. Production shifts from the most efficient locations in C to less efficient ones inside the union. Finally, there is a favorable consumption effect, as consumers in each member state benefit from price reduction on imports from the partner country when intraunion tariffs are removed.

These three effects can be illustrated with the help of a partial equilibrium diagram pertaining to one commodity imported into country A. For simplicity, we assume that A is a small country, facing infinitely elastic (horizontal) supply curves from countries B and C (for a more elaborate presentation, see Appendix 4–2). For example, country A may be New Zealand, forming an FTA agreement with country B (Australia) to the exclusion of country C (the United States). Figure 4.7 shows the domestic demand and supply in country A for the imported product; it also shows the horizontal supply curves $\overline{P_1C}$ of country C and $\overline{P_2B}$ of country B (drawn in black). Country C is the least-cost producer.

Under free trade, price $\overline{0P_1}$ will prevail and quantity $\overline{Q_1Q_2}$ will be imported from country C. Next, if A imposes a nondiscriminatory tariff $\overline{P_1P_3}$, the domestic price rises to $0P_3$. Imports decline to $\overline{tT}$, but they come only from the most efficient supplier, country C, because suppliers from B will not be competitive. Finally, when A forms a customs union with B, to the exclusion of C, the tariff $\overline{P_1P_3}$ (assumed for simplicity to remain unchanged) is charged only on imports from C, not on those from B. The domestic price

FIGURE 4.7   *Static Effects of a Customs Union*

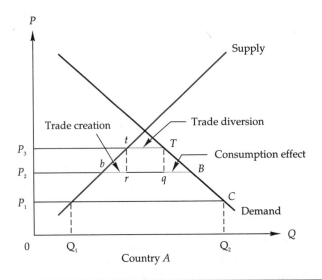

Under a customs union, price in the importing country declines from P_3 (world price plus nondiscriminatory tariff) to P_2 (price in the partner country). This results in an unfavorable trade diversion, Tt; favorable trade creation, *br;* and consumption, *qB* effects.

declines to $\overline{0P_2}$ and imports rise to $\overline{bB}$, but they will now come exclusively from B (because supply curves are infinitely elastic).

Our concern is in comparing the last two situations. Imports into A increase from $\overline{tT}$ to $\overline{bB}$. Trade diversion is represented by $\overline{tT}$, the decline in imports from the most efficient producer, country C. On the other hand, $\overline{br}$, the decrease in domestic output in A and its replacement by imports from B, represents trade creation, while $\overline{qB}$ is the favorable **consumption effect** representing the increase in domestic consumption.

These constitute the major static influences. The relative magnitude of the favorable trade creation plus consumption effects and the unfavorable trade diversion effect determine whether the customs union is, on balance, favorable to worldwide allocative efficiency. The tools of economic and statistical analysis make it possible to measure or at least to approximate these magnitudes. But the estimation is complex. It is not just a matter of looking at the increase in intra-area trade volume: first, because this volume is influenced by factors other than the formation of the customs union and, second, because even if the "integration effect" were isolated, the observed increase in intra-union trade comprises the trade creation and diversion combined.

But even without measurement, we can identify some factors that have *a priori* bearing on the relative size of the two effects. The larger the customs union, the smaller is the scope for trade diversion and the better is the chance that the customs union will have a favorable effect. At the extreme lies a "customs union" encompassing the entire world, where only trade creation and no trade diversion can occur, yielding the optimal situation of universal free trade. Second, the more similar the production patterns are within the integrating countries and the larger the differences are in production costs between them, the greater the scope is for trade creation. One proxy for the differences in production costs is the pre-integration tariff rates levied by the individual countries to protect their high-cost producers. Considerable variation in pre-integration rates on the same product among the countries might be taken as an indication of large differences in production costs. In general, the higher the pre-union tariff rates, the better the chances are for large trade creation as these rates are dismantled. Finally, the lower the common external tariff of the customs union, the less will be the degree of discrimination against outsiders and the smaller will be the scope for trade diversion.

Estimated annual trade creation in manufactures of the original EEC of six countries is $10 billion for 1969–1970, and trade diversion is less than $2 billion. Enlargement of the EC from six to nine countries is estimated to have resulted in $28 billion and $5 billion of annual trade creation and diversion respectively for 1977–1978.[20] (Note, however, that these estimates are in current dollars; between 1970 and 1978 EC prices doubled.) Accession of Greece, Spain, and Portugal is estimated to have caused net trade diversion.[21] It may be noted here that the creation of the EEC has not led to large-scale contraction of entire industries in any one country and their replacement by imports from another member. The tendency toward inter-industry specialization has been very limited. Instead, the main trend is toward intra-industry specialization: The same industry in various member countries moves toward specialization in specific types of subproducts (see Chapter 3). This eases adjustment to trade liberalization.

---

[20] A common measure of trade creation is the change in the ratio of total (external plus intracommunity) imports to consumption in the EEC between two years before and after integration, allowing for the effect on that ratio of factors other than integration. This is so because with constant consumption, the rise in imports equals the decline in domestic output. Trade diversion is measured by the change of external imports to consumption over the same period, and with similar allowance for nonintegration effects. See M. E. Kreinin, "Effects of the EEC on Imports of Manufactures," *Economic Journal*, September 1972, and "The Static Effect of EC Enlargement on Trade in Manufactured Products," *Kyklos*, 1981: 60–71. For a study relating to another area of the world, see M. E. Kreinin, "North American Economic Integration," *Law and Contemporary Problems*, summer 1981: 7–31.

[21] See M. Plummer, *Economic Effects of the Second Enlargement of the Communities*, Ph.D. Dissertation, Michigan State University, 1989.

But not all customs unions are net "trade creating." A 1996 study by the World Bank estimates that Mercursor (an FTA between Brazil, Argentina, Uruguay, and Paraguay) had a net trade-diverting effect. In particular, the phenomenal rise in intra-area trade was in industries, such as cars and machinery, which the four countries produce inefficiently relative to the outside world. They are made in Latin America only under heavy tariff protection. This finding points to a danger that many other regional groupings are trade-diverting in nature.

Dynamic Effects   Returning now to the theory of customs unions, there is more to their effect on world welfare than allocative efficiency. At least as important are the dynamic or growth considerations. A customs union expands the size of the market because of both the creation and diversion of trade. This makes possible production on a larger scale and infuses competition into markets from which it might have been absent. Indeed, the United States can be viewed as a large customs union in which the huge size of the market has made possible the establishment of many competitive firms, each with large-scale production. This fact is partly responsible for the tremendous productivity of the American economy.   ·

In the case of a new customs union, the scale effect is likely to be more powerful in the smaller integrating countries, because large countries enjoy these benefits even in the absence of integration. The favorable growth effect also stimulates imports from nonmember countries, partly offsetting static trade diversion. However, nonmember countries may on balance experience a reduction in their exports to the customs union, and this in turn contracts the size of their market and adversely affects their growth rates. The smaller they are to begin with, the more important this factor is likely to be. Again, favorable and adverse influences must be weighed against each other to assess the net impact on worldwide growth. The immense difficulties in doing this arise from the fact that a multitude of factors influence the growth rate, and it is not easy to isolate the effect of integration.

Finally, since the elimination of tariffs in the case of a customs union is not reversible, the expansion of the market is certain to last. This stimulates investment, both domestic and foreign, and thereby increases the growth rate. Such "investment creation" can be partly offset by what might be called "investment diversion," when investments are diverted from the most rational location in the world to the integrating region because of the tariff discrimination. Thus, if an American-based company shifts the location of a projected plant from the United States or Canada to the EC in order to circumvent the tariff wall and gain access to a large market, the outcome is unfavorable to worldwide growth. The same may be said of potential foreign-investment projects in nonmember countries (such as a developing country) that never materialize because they depend too much on exports to the customs union; the possibility of such exports comes into question because they would be discriminated against in the customs union.

In sum, the regional approach has a large number of effects that require individual study. The industrial countries have proceeded along both avenues of trade liberalization since World War II. Under the auspices of the GATT, tariffs have been reduced gradually to low levels. At the same time, small groups of countries have proceeded to eliminate tariffs altogether, and those in the EC have taken some further measures to form a cohesive group.

Summary

This chapter addresses the traditional instrument of import protection: the tariff. A tariff is a tax levied on an imported commodity. It yields government revenue, but its main purpose is to protect a domestic industry. It can be *ad valorem* (a percentage of the price) or specific (dollars per unit of the product).

A large country improves its terms of trade by imposing a tariff. By reducing the quantity of the product it buys on the world market, it depresses the global price—and hence pays less for its imports. This forces the foreign exporters to pay part of the duty. The domestic price of imports therefore rises only by a portion of the tariff. By contrast, a small country cannot improve its terms of trade by imposing a tariff; regardless of the country's actions, world prices remain unchanged. The domestic price then rises by the full amount of the duty (but a small country can sometimes improve its terms of trade by levying an export tax).

A tariff increases the domestic price in the importing country. That increase causes a decline in consumers' surplus, which is partly offset by a rise in producers' surplus and in government revenue. There is a *net* loss of two welfare triangles, known as the deadweight loss. Its measure is $t/2$ times ΔM. In a large country this loss *can* be more than offset by the gain in its terms of trade, yielding a net gain. The tariff rate that maximizes that net gain is called the *optimum tariff*. For a small country the optimum tariff is zero, because there is no terms of trade gain. For the United States the welfare cost of the tariff is far smaller than that caused by import quotas and other restraints on trade.

While the published tariff rate is referred to as the nominal tariff, the effective tariff is the protection accorded by the tariff structure to the domestic value added. It is positively related to the nominal protection on the final output, and negatively related to the nominal protection on imported inputs. It highlights the fact that protection of an imported input imposes a tax on the industries using that input. Development of the concept of effective protection was policy driven, and indeed the concept has several policy implications. Among them is the unfavorable effect of tariff escalation in industrial countries on the industrialization prospects of LDCs; the wasteful approach to development by the LDCs themselves when they deepen domestic production under protection in an import-substitution policy; the ranking of industries by comparative advantage in LDCs; and the rebates sometimes offered to exporters for the tariffs they pay on imported inputs.

From a world welfare point of view, the only valid argument for protection is the infant-industry argument, although it has been much abused. From a single-country point of view the only valid argument is the optimum tariff, but it applies only to a handful of large countries. The common arguments heard in political circles, such as the need for a tariff to equalize wage rates with those in foreign countries, are generally invalid.

Approaches to free trade include first the international approach under the WTO, where tariffs are reduced gradually on a nondiscriminatory basis. In this case there is an unambiguous gain to world welfare. Second, they include regional groupings, where trade restrictions are removed within the integrating group, and imports from nonmember countries are subject to tariff. Both a customs union (CU) and a free-trade area (FTA) eliminate restrictions on trade within that region. But while a CU sets up a common and uniform tariff against outsiders, each member country in an FTA maintains its own restrictions against nonmembers.

Because of their discriminatory nature, the effect of a CU or an FTA on welfare is ambiguous, and must be determined on a case-by-case basis. To do so we distinguish between the favorable trade creation effect and the unfavorable trade diversion effect. Trade creation occurs when the elimination of restrictions within the CU or an FTA causes a member country to increase imports from another member, *at the expense* of its own inefficient production. Trade diversion occurs when the discrimination against outsiders causes a member to replace imports from a most efficient nonmember country with imports from a less efficient supplier inside the CU or FTA. The relative magnitude of these two effects thus determines whether the regional grouping is favorable to welfare.

Important Concepts	Tariff protection	Large country
	Revenue tariff	Consumers' surplus
	Ad valorem tariff	Volume of trade
	Specific tariff	Producers' surplus
	Compound tariff	Welfare triangles
	F.O.B. price	Deadweight loss
	C.I.F. price	Optimum tariff

Terms of trade

Small country

Effective tariff

Tariff escalation

Deepening of production

Export rebate

Domestic resource cost (DRC)

"Scientific" tariff

"The Petition of the
   Candlemakers"

"Petition of the Mathematicians"

World Trade Organization (WTO)

Customs union

Nominal tariff rate

Free-trade area (FTA)

European Union (EU) or European
   Community (EC)

North American Free Trade
   Agreement (NAFTA)

Trade creation

Trade diversion

Consumption effect

Infant industry

Unconditional Most Favored
   Nation Principle (MFN)

"New" products

---

*Review
Questions*

1. Distinguish between the following:
   a. *Ad valorem* and specific tariff
   b. Nominal and effective protection
   c. Customs union and free-trade area
   d. GATT and the European Community
   e. Discriminatory and nondiscriminatory tariff reduction
   f. Trade creation and trade diversion (of a customs union)
   g. An import and export tax
   h. C.I.F. and F.O.B. price
   i. Large and small countries
   j. Consumers' and producers' surplus
   k. Optimum tariff and effective tariff

2. Explain the concept of "effective rate of protection."
   a. What does the effective rate on final goods depend upon
      and how?
   b. In what way does the effective rate analysis help to illuminate
      these policy issues:

      • Deepening of production in LDCs
      • Escalation of tariff rates by degree of processing in industrial
        countries

3. (*For the well-initiated student*) Assume that we have a two-country, tariff-ridden world and that the countries decide to remove the tariff in two *successive steps* of equal tariff cuts. Using a partial equilibrium diagram, demonstrate that the welfare benefits to the world as a whole are greater from the first than from the second tariff reduction. (Consult Appendix 4–2.) What empirical information do you have about the effects of tariff reductions?

4. Explain the concept of the optimum tariff. How can a tariff improve the welfare of one country and lower that of the world as a whole?

5. "A *customs union* constitutes a partial movement toward free trade and *must* therefore lead to an improvement in world welfare." Do you agree? Explain this statement, using a diagram to show the three effects of a customs union. Does the increase in intra-union trade measure trade creation?

6. Suppose the United States levied a 20 percent tariff on imported cars. Explain the effects on the
   a. U.S. terms of trade
   b. distribution of income within the United States
   c. U.S. welfare (or real income)
   Use graphs as needed.

7. Review and evaluate three common arguments for protection.

8. *Evaluate* each of the following statements:
   a. A tariff on textiles is equivalent to a tax on consumers and a subsidy to the textile producers and workers.
      (Use a diagram.)
   b. A tariff lowers the real income of the country, while at the same time it distributes income from the consumers to the governments and to the import-competing industry.
      (Use a diagram.)
   c. The best way to reduce the $200 billion U.S. budget deficit is to impose a 50 percent tariff surcharge to collect revenue.
   d. Chinese mushrooms undersell American mushrooms because Chinese labor is cheaper than American labor. We should impose a high tariff on mushrooms until China agrees to raise wage rates to the level prevailing in the United States.

9. Assess the possible effects of NAFTA. Is such an FTA likely to lead to an expansion of interindustry or intra-industry trade? How would such an FTA conform to the MFN provision of the WTO?

Chapter 4 Appendix 4–1

EFFECT OF THE TARIFF IN THE
LARGE COUNTRY CASE

A visual demonstration of this analysis requires
a simple but useful extension of the tools of
demand and supply. What follows pertains to a
one-commodity, two-country world in which
one country is the importer and the other the
exporter.

We begin with the importing country B.
Figure A4–1.1a shows supply and demand
curves for a single commodity in which country
B has a comparative disadvantage compared to
country A. P_1 is the equilibrium domestic price in
country B; the price that equates domestic supply
and demand and thereby clears the market. If the
world price is also P_1, country B will not trade in
that commodity. But at any price below P_1, country B will import the commodity in question.

Figure A4–1.1b describes country B's demand for imports. At price P_1 the demand for
imports is zero. As the price declines to P_2, two
things happen on the domestic market: The
quantity demanded rises as we move down
the (negatively sloped) demand curve, and the
quantity supplied declines as we move down
the (positively sloped) supply curve. The difference, or horizontal distance, between the
domestic quantities demanded and supplied at
P_2 (distance a) is what the country imports at
that price. That distance is plotted in A4–1.1b to
obtain another point of the import-demand
curve. Likewise, when price drops to P_3, the
quantity demanded increases and the quantity
supplied domestically declines further, so that
the quantity imported rises to b. Again it is
plotted in panel (b). By connecting all points in
figure A4–1.1b, we obtain the import-demand
schedule drawn in black.

In sum, the import-demand curve shows
the quantities that the country stands ready
to import at various prices. In all cases except
when one of the domestic schedules is of zero
elasticity (vertical), import demand is flatter
and more elastic than domestic demand. This
is so because its slope equals the combined
slopes of the domestic demand and supply
schedules. Therefore, both the demand and
supply schedules affect the shape of the import-
demand schedule. (A precise formulation of
the relationship is given later in this appendix.)
At prices above P_1, domestic quantities supplied
exceed those demanded, and import demand
becomes negative. This simply means that at
these higher prices the country becomes an
exporter of the commodity—and it is a useful
reminder of the fact that whether a commodity
is exported or imported depends on its domestic price relative to the international price.

Next we turn to the exporting country in
our configuration, country A. Figure A4–1.2a
shows domestic demand and supply, with equilibrium price P_1 established in isolation. At that
price, the country will not trade, and therefore
zero quantity is shown for export supply in
panel (b). When the price rises to P_2, the quantity supplied domestically increases as we move
up along the (positively sloped) supply curve,
while the quantity demanded internally declines as we move up along the (negatively
sloped) demand curve. The difference, or horizontal distance, between the quantities supplied
and demanded domestically at price P_2 is a units
of the commodity, the quantity that the country
will export at that price. We thus obtain another
point on the export-supply curve. By the same
token, as price rises to P_3, the quantity exported
increases to b. Connecting all the points in panel

FIGURE A4–1.1   *Importing Country B*

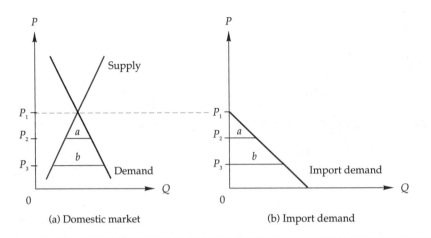

(a) Domestic market   (b) Import demand

The quantity of import demanded at each price is the excess of the quantity demanded over the quantity supplied domestically at that price.

(b) yields the export-supply curve drawn in color.

In sum, the export-supply schedule shows the quantities that the country stands ready to export at various prices. In all cases, except when one of the domestic schedules is of zero elasticity (vertical), export supply is flatter and more elastic than domestic supply, for its slope is made up of the combined slopes of the demand and supply functions. Both domestic supply and demand affect the shape of the export-supply schedule. (A rigorous formulation of this relationship is given later in this appendix.) An infinitely elastic (horizontal) export-supply schedule is generated when either domestic demand or domestic supply is infinitely elastic. At prices below P_1 export supply is negative, and the country becomes an importer of the commodity.

We are now prepared to illustrate world trade in one commodity. In Figure A4–1.3, the

fact that country A has a lower domestic equilibrium price than B establishes A as the exporter and B as the importer. Indeed, pretrade price in A is P_1 ($20), while that of B is P_2 ($60). From the exporting country we derive the export-supply curve, and from the importing country the import-demand curve, plotted in figure A4–1.3b in color and black respectively.

Now suppose that trade opens up. Post-trade equilibrium in the absence of transport cost and artificial barriers to trade requires that there be a common price in the two countries and that the quantity exported by one country be equal to the quantity imported by the other. Both conditions are met at price P_3, which is established by the intersection of the export-supply and import-demand curves. Note that the price in the exporting country rises while that in the importing country declines following the opening of trade. Production expands in the exporting country and contracts in the im-

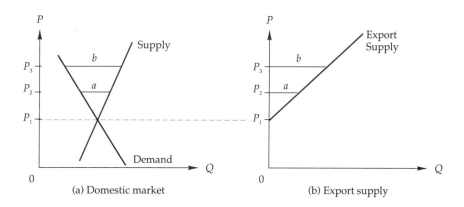

(a) Domestic market   (b) Export supply

The quantity of exports supplied at each price is the excess of the quantity supplied over the quantity demanded domestically at that price.

porting country, but the contraction stops short of complete specialization. The importing country continues to produce some of the product.

This free-trade position is now modified by the introduction of a tariff. For simplicity, we deal with a specific duty of $20 per unit of the product. Since the vertical axis denotes price, the duty can be measured as a $20 segment on that scale. Starting from the intersection of the export-supply and import-demand curves, we proceed left to where the vertical divergence between the curves equals $20. This occurs at $\overline{cd}$[1] (shaded gray in (b). The tariff is a wedge that causes the good's price in the exporting and importing country to differ by the amount of the tariff.

As a result of the tariff, the volume of trade declines to $\overline{ef}$ in the exporting country, which equals $\overline{gh}$ in the importing country and $\overline{id}$ (= $\overline{cj}$)

in the center panel. Second, the export price declines to P_5 ($30 per unit) in country A, and the import price rises to P_4 ($50) in country B. The difference between the two is the tax per unit levied by the government of B. Government revenue from the duty equals $\overline{gh}$ units of import times $\overline{cd}$ ($20 per unit). Half of it is paid by the exporters in A and half by the consumers in B. In this example, the incidence of the tariff is divided equally between the two countries—a result of the equal but opposite slopes of the import-demand and export-supply curves. The terms of trade of the importing country have improved, because it now obtains imports from A for $10 per unit less than before. While B's private consumers pay a higher price (P_4) for the commodity than under free trade, the country as a whole (the government and private sectors combined) pays a lower price, P_5. Thus, it is the

---

[1] Strictly speaking, the imposition of a tariff involves shifts in the demand or supply schedules. For simplicity, all such shifts are omitted here. Only the post-tariff equilibrium points are shown.

FIGURE A4–1.3   *Equilibrium with Trade*

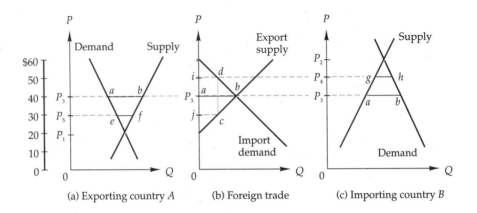

(a) Exporting country *A*   (b) Foreign trade   (c) Importing country *B*

Intersection of the import-demand and export-supply schedules determines the post-trade equilibrium. The tariff is divided between the exporting and importing countries.

---

behavior of *A*'s export price that indicates the changes in *B*'s terms of trade.

If the slopes of the import-demand and export-supply curves were not equal, the distribution of the tax burden between the two countries would also be unequal (see the algebraic demonstration later in this appendix). But in all large country cases the terms of trade of the importing country improve, as part of the tariff is paid by the exporters. In contrast, a small importing country faces an infinitely elastic export-supply curve, and its domestic price rises by the full amount of the tariff. The entire tariff is thus paid by domestic consumers.

ELASTICITY OF IMPORT DEMAND AND THE DOMESTIC DEMAND AND SUPPLY ELASTICITIES

The elasticity of import demand for a given product is positively (and uniquely) related to

the domestic demand and supply elasticities, and negatively related to the share of imports in domestic consumption and production.

Remembering that the volume of imports (Q_m) is the difference between the quantities demanded (Q_d) and supplied (Q_s) at home, we can derive the import-demand elasticity (Σ_D) from the definition of elasticity, as follows:

$$\Sigma_D = \frac{-P}{Q_m} \times \frac{\Delta Q_m}{\Delta P} = \frac{-P}{Q_m} \times \frac{\Delta (Q_d - Q_s)}{\Delta P}$$

$$= \frac{-P}{Q_m} \times \frac{\Delta Q_d}{\Delta P} + \frac{P}{Q_m} \times \frac{\Delta Q}{\Delta P}$$

Next, we multiply and divide the first term of the last expression by Q_d and the second term by Q_s:

$$\Sigma_D = \frac{\dfrac{-P}{Q_d} \times \dfrac{\Delta Q_d}{\Delta P} \times Q_d}{Q_m} + \frac{\dfrac{P}{Q_s} \times \dfrac{\Delta Q_s}{\Delta P} \times Q_s}{Q_m}$$

$$= \frac{\varepsilon_d \times Q_d}{Q_m} + \frac{\varepsilon_s \times Q_s}{Q_m}$$

where ε_d and ε_s represent domestic demand and supply elasticities, respectively. Thus,

$$\Sigma_D = \frac{Q_d}{Q_m} \times \varepsilon_d + \frac{Q_s}{Q_m} \times \varepsilon_s$$

ELASTICITY OF EXPORT SUPPLY AND THE DOMESTIC DEMAND AND SUPPLY ELASTICITIES

The export-supply elasticity of a given product is positively related to the domestic demand and supply elasticities and negatively related to the share of exports in domestic production and consumption. Remembering that the volume of exports (Q_e) is the difference between the quantities supplied and demanded domestically (Q_s and Q_d), we can derive the export-supply elasticity (Σ_x) from the definition of elasticity, as follows:

$$\Sigma_x = \frac{P}{Q_e} \times \frac{\Delta Q_e}{\Delta P} = \frac{P}{Q_e} \times \frac{\Delta(Q_s - Q_d)}{\Delta P}$$

$$= \frac{P}{Q_e} \times \frac{\Delta Q_s}{\Delta P} - \frac{P}{Q_e} \times \frac{\Delta Q_d}{\Delta P}$$

Next, we multiply and divide the first term by Q_s and the second term by Q_d:

$$\Sigma_x = \frac{\dfrac{P}{Q_s} \times \dfrac{\Delta Q_s}{\Delta P} \times Q_s}{Q_e} - \frac{\dfrac{P}{Q_d} \times \dfrac{\Delta Q_d}{\Delta P} \times Q_d}{Q_e}$$

$$= \frac{\varepsilon_s \times Q_s}{Q_e} + \frac{\varepsilon_d \times Q_d}{Q_e}$$

where ε_s and ε_d represent domestic supply and demand elasticities, recalling that the demand elasticity is negative. Thus,

$$\Sigma_x = \frac{Q_s}{Q_e} \times \varepsilon_s + \frac{Q_d}{Q_e} \times \varepsilon_d$$

A COUNTRY'S SHARE IN WORLD EXPORT MARKETS AND THE ELASTICITY OF DEMAND FOR ITS EXPORTS

The elasticity of demand for a country's exports of a given product is inversely related to its share in the world market.

If W is the world demand for imports of a given product and C is the quantity exported by competing sources (other countries), then $W - C$ is the quantity exported by the country in question. Let η_x be the elasticity of demand for the country's exports of the product; then

$$\eta_x = \frac{-P}{W - C} \times \frac{\Delta(W - C)}{\Delta P} = -\frac{P}{W - C}\left(\frac{\Delta W}{\Delta P}\right)$$

$$\frac{P}{W - C}\left(-\frac{\Delta C}{\Delta P}\right)$$

$$= \frac{-P(\Delta W / \Delta P)}{W - C} + \frac{P(\Delta C / \Delta P)}{W - C}$$

Multiply and divide the first term by W and the second term by C:

$$\eta_x = \frac{W(-P/W)(\Delta W / \Delta P)}{W - C} + \frac{C(P/C)(\Delta C / \Delta P)}{W - C}$$

$$= \frac{W}{W - C}\eta_w + \frac{C}{W - C}e_c$$

where η_w is the world demand elasticity for the product and e_c is the supply elasticity from competing sources.

One important implication of this relation is that even if the demand for a certain product is relatively inelastic, the demand for a particular country's exports of the product can be highly elastic if it has only a small share in total world markets. Applying this to the domestic market we can see how the demand for wheat can be inelastic but the demand for a single farmer's wheat infinitely elastic, when that farmer accounts for a very small share in the total supply.

IMPORT-DEMAND AND EXPORT-SUPPLY ELASTICITIES AND THE INCIDENCE OF A TARIFF

In figure A4–1.4 the pretariff international price is $\overline{OP}$ and the quantity traded is $\overline{OQ}$, as determined by the intersection of the import-demand and export-supply curves. A specific tariff of size t is then imposed, shifting export supply leftward to the broken line. Domestic price in the importing country rises by fraction s of the tariff, while its terms of trade improve by a fraction $(1 - s)$. The quantity traded declines by ΔQ. Our objective is to find an expression for s.

The elasticity of the import-demand curve at point E is

$$\left|\Sigma_D\right| = \frac{\Delta Q}{Q} \times \frac{P}{\Delta P} = \frac{\Delta Q}{\overline{OQ}} \times \frac{\overline{OP}}{st} \qquad (1)$$

From that we obtain

$$\frac{\Delta Q}{\overline{OQ}} = \left|\Sigma_D\right| \frac{st}{\overline{OP}} \qquad (2)$$

The elasticity of the export-supply curve at point E is

$$\Sigma_s = \frac{\Delta Q}{\overline{OQ}} \times \frac{\overline{OP}}{\Delta P} = \frac{\Delta Q}{\overline{OQ}} \times \frac{\overline{OP}}{(1-s)t}$$

Substituting (2) into (3) gives

$$\Sigma_s = \left|\Sigma_D\right| \frac{st}{\overline{OP}} \times \frac{\overline{OP}}{(1-s)t} = \left|\Sigma_D\right| \frac{s}{1-s}$$

Therefore,

$$\frac{s}{1-s} = \frac{\Sigma_s}{\left|\Sigma_D\right|}$$

and

$$\Sigma_s - s\Sigma_s = s \times \left|\Sigma_D\right|$$

$$s\left(\left|\Sigma_D\right| + \Sigma_s\right) = \Sigma_s$$

$$s = \frac{\Sigma_s}{\left|\Sigma_D\right| + \Sigma_s}$$

Dividing through by Σ_s, we obtain

$$s = \frac{1}{\left|\Sigma_D\right|/\Sigma_s + 1}$$

$$(1-s) = \frac{\left|\Sigma_D\right| + \Sigma_s - \Sigma_s}{\left|\Sigma_D\right| + \Sigma_s}$$

$$= \frac{\left|\Sigma_D\right|}{\left|\Sigma_D\right| + \Sigma_s}$$

$$= \frac{1}{1 + \Sigma_s/\left|\Sigma_D\right|}$$

Clearly it is the *relative* size of the import-demand and export-supply elasticities that determines the incidence of the tariff. In turn,

FIGURE A4–1.4 **Incidence of a Tariff**

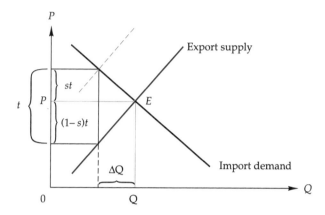

The ratio of the elasticities of import-demand and export-supply determines how the tariff is divided between the importing and exporting countries.

these elasticities are related to the domestic supply and demand elasticities in the respective countries.

The expressions above assume that the government does nothing with the tariff revenue. If, however, we assume that these funds are distributed to the population in the form of a general income subsidy, the expressions must be modified to take into account the added demand for imports arising from the added income (the marginal propensity to import). Also, this is a partial equilibrium formula, which refers only to a tax on a single product. A different, full-equilibrium formula would apply when analyzing the incidence of a tariff levied across the board on all products.

Similar formulas apply to the incidence of domestic indirect taxes, except that domestic rather than international elasticities are involved.

Chapter 4 Appendix 4–2

ECONOMIC COST OF THE TARIFF

In Chapter 4 the economic cost of the tariff was analyzed with the use of producers' and consumers' surpluses and changes in government revenue. But the analysis was restricted to a small country whose terms of trade remain unaffected, so that all the effects of the tariff are

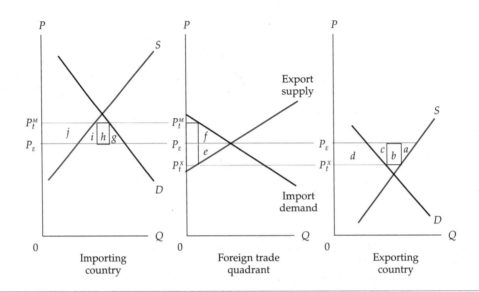

The tariff causes a welfare loss to the world as a whole that is measured by triangles *e* + *f* in the center quadrant.

visible inside the importing country. This can be extended to the more general case of a two-country world, where the terms of trade are affected by the tariff.

Figure A4–2.1 is similar to figure A4–1.3. The free-trade price is P_E, while the tariff-ridden price in the importing country is P_t^M and that in the exporting country is P_t^X. The following changes occur in the importing country:

Consumers' surplus declines by the area $g + h + i + j$.

Producers' surplus increases by area j.

Government revenue collected from domestic residents increases by area h.

The net deadweight loss equals the sum of the triangular areas $i + g$. The following changes take place in the exporting country:

Producers' surplus declines by area $a + b + c + d$.

Consumers' surplus increases by area d.

Government revenue accruing to the *importing* country increases by area b. (Area b is a transfer from the exporting to the importing country. It does not affect worldwide welfare because whereas it is a loss to the exporting country, it is an equal gain to the importing country.)

The net deadweight loss equals the areas of triangles $a + c$.

The net loss to the importing country is triangles i and g, while the net gain is rectangle b. Its *optimum tariff* is the tariff rate that would maximize the net gain, the area $[b - (g + i)]$. The exporting country sustains a net loss measured by the area $a + b + c$, of which b is a transfer to the importing country. To the world taken as a whole, the *net* deadweight *loss* from the tariff is triangles $a + c + i + g$. Geometrically, we have $i + g = f$, because their height is the same, and the base of f equals the combined bases of i and g,

both the difference between the free-trade imports and the tariff-ridden imports. By identical reasoning, areas $a + c = e$. Thus, in the foreign trade quadrant, the net welfare cost of the tariff to the world taken as a whole (that is, disregarding distributional effects) is area $e + f$. Without further marking of the diagram, it can be seen that if the tariff is removed in two successive steps of equal size, the first 50 percent reduction would improve world welfare by a far greater amount (trapezoid area) than the second and final reduction (remaining triangle).

Chapter 4 Appendix 4–3

STATIC EFFECTS OF A CUSTOMS UNION ON WORLD'S WELFARE

In figure A4–3.1 assume that S_a and D_a are the internal supply and demand curves in country A for a given product. S_b and S_c are the export-supply curves of countries B and C to country A, with C being a more efficient producer than B. S_b^t and S_c^t are the same two supply curves subject to a 100 percent tariff imposed by country A. Curve S^t indicates total supply of the commodity in country A ($S_a + S_b^t + S_c^t$). Price P_1 is established. Country A produces Q_a domestically and imports Q_b and Q_c from countries B and C, respectively.

When countries A and B form a customs union to the exclusion of C, the relevant supply curve in country B becomes S_b, while S_c^t remains in effect in country C.[2] Total supply in

country A's market becomes S_{CU}, consisting of $S_a + S_b + S_c^t$. The price in country A drops to P_2; domestic supply declines to Q_{a1}; imports from country B rise to Q_{b1}; and imports from country C diminish to Q_{c1}. These changes can be quantified in terms of their effect on producers' surpluses in all three countries, and on consumers' surpluses and government tariff revenue of country A. The following observations relate to each panel of the diagram:

(a) Country A enjoys an increase of consumers' surpluses of BAP_1P_2 and suffers a reduction of producers' surpluses amounting to $BAYZ$. There is a gain of ZYP_1P_2.

(b) Country B enjoys a gain in producers' surplus of $HGCD$.
Country A faces a loss in government

FIGURE A4-3.1   *Welfare Effects of a Customs Union*

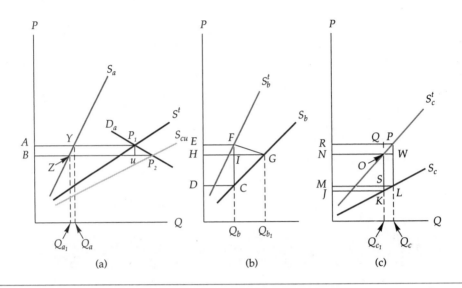

The gain to world welfare from a customs union is a triangle *CGF* (in panel b) and the loss is area *OPLK* (in panel c).

tariff revenue of *CDEF*. Since area *DCHI* is common to both, we obtain in part (b) a *loss of EHIF and a gain of ICG*.

(c) Tariff revenue of country *A* declines from *RPLM* to *NOKJ*. Subtracting the area *NOSM*, common to both, we get a loss of *RNOP + POSL* and a gain of *MJKS*. At the same time, producers' surpluses of country *C* decline by *MJKL*. Thus figure A4–3.1c yields the *following loss*:

$RNOP + POSL - MJKS + MJKL = RNOP$
$+ POSL + LSK = RNOP + POKL.$

Area *ZYP₁P₂* [the net gain in (a)] is equal by construction to areas *EFGH* in (b) plus *RNOP* in (c). Subtracting from this net gain in (a) the losses *EHIF* in (b) and *RNOP* in (c), we are left with a net gain of *FIG* in (b). Adding it to the earlier gain *CIG*, we obtain a *net gain of CFG* in part (b), to be weighed against the *net loss of POKL* in part (c). The net effect on world welfare depends on the relative size of the two areas.

CHAPTER
5

Nontariff Barriers (NTBs) to Trade

Although the tariff is a widely used instrument of protection, it is by no means the only one, nor is it the most harmful. Indeed, as tariff rates have been reduced under programs of multilateral trade liberalization, the **nontariff barriers (NTBs)** loom increasingly important. They will be considered in this chapter. Although most such policies restrict the flow of trade, the last two measures we will consider (export subsidies and VIEs) are designed to expand trade by artificial means. What they all have in common is their interference with competitive market forces.

IMPORT QUOTAS

Instead of imposing a tax on an imported commodity, as under the tariff, the government may directly restrict the volume of permissible imports to a certain maximum level. The absolute limit is known as the **import quota**. For example, the number of cars imported may be limited to 2 million. The limits are presumably below what would be imported under free-market conditions, for otherwise there would be no need for the quota. Indeed, if free-market demand for imports falls below the quota, the quota becomes ineffective or *nonbinding*. Thus a government-imposed quota of 2 million cars is nonbinding if only 1 million cars would be imported in the absence of restrictions. To administer the quota the government distributes *import licenses* to importers, allowing each one to import the commodity up to a prescribed limit. The importer is not free to import any quantity above that limit, regardless of market demand.

How Common Are Import Quotas?

Designed to protect domestic industries by restricting imports, quotas were very common in Western Europe immediately after World War II. Today, international trade in manufactured goods is virtually free of such restrictions in the developed nations. Import quotas are prohibited by the WTO.

Trade in agricultural products is subject to a variety of quantitative restrictions in virtually all the industrial countries, including the United States. They all protect their agricultural sectors because the farmers are politically powerful. In the European Union, aid to farmers often takes the form of price-support programs—the government sets prices somewhere above the free-market level and purchases the food surpluses that result from that fixed price. If imports were allowed in freely, the government would be supporting the prices (and income) of both foreign and domestic farmers. In order to maintain domestic prices above the international level, the EU imposes import quotas; at the same time, it employs export subsidies to dispose of the accumulated surpluses overseas. EU's quantitative restrictions on farm imports are equivalent to a 43 percent subsidy to EU agricultural production. Tight Japanese import quotas on food products incur the wrath of American farmers and the U.S. government, but their relaxation is furiously resisted by the inefficient Japanese farm industry. On the other hand, the United States and other countries have on occasion liberalized or lifted quota restrictions to combat specific shortages or general inflation.

In developing countries, quotas are used in all sectors for a mixture of reasons. Often, these countries attempt to develop new industries to produce substitutes for imported goods and believe that this can be accomplished only under a protective shield of import quotas. Tariffs, even high ones, do not provide the local manufacturer with the same degree of certainty. No one knows the level of supply and demand response to price change nor, therefore, how much of a foreign commodity would be excluded from the domestic market by a given tariff level. Consumers may prefer imported, internationally known brands even at higher prices. And foreign producers may choose to absorb part of the duty in order to avoid losing sales. None of these uncertainties exists in the case of quotas, where the volume of imports is limited by administrative action.

Economic Effects of Quotas

Because it restricts the volume of imports, the import quota raises the domestic price of the imported commodity in much the same way as does the tariff. Indeed the excess of domestic over foreign price can be regarded as the *implicit tariff equivalent* of the nontariff barrier. And that tariff equivalent can be calculated in percentage form by subtracting the foreign from the domestic price and dividing the result by the foreign price:

$$\frac{P_{\text{Domestic}} - P_{\text{Foreign}}}{P_{\text{Foreign}}}$$

For example, if the international price of a widget is $100, and an import quota raises its domestic price by $20 (to $120), then the tariff equivalent of that quota is 20/100, or 20 percent. Similar calculations can be made for any combination of nontariff barriers.

As a result of the quota-induced price hike, consumption of the imported product declines and consumers switch to less desirable domestic substitutes. Local production of substitute products then expands under the protection accorded to their producers, with resources drawn from other (presumably more efficient) industries. In contrast to the tariff, however, there is no revenue to the government. In this case it accrues to the holders of import licenses, who are able to charge a higher price for each unit of the restricted supply. This revenue is called **quota rents.** Only by **auctioning the import licenses** can the government recoup the rents.[1]

But the revenue aspect is not the only important difference between a tariff and a quota. While the tariff interferes with the market mechanism, a quota replaces it altogether with arbitrary government decisions. With tariffs, domestic price cannot differ from world price by more than the duty, and unlimited quantities of a product may be imported by anyone eager enough for the good to pay the tax. Thus, starting from a given tariff-ridden situation, with its attendant level of consumption and production costs, any rise in domestic demand can be satisfied from increased imports at the same price. Domestic production does not rise nor does the cost of protection in terms of misallocated resources and reduced desirability of the consumption mix. This is not so in the case of a quota. Here there is no limit to the differential between domestic and world prices. Since an upward quantity adjustment is not possible, any rise in domestic demand will simply raise the domestic price, leaving admissible imports unaltered. Such an increase raises the production and consumption costs of protection by forcing further misallocation of resources and less desirable consumption patterns.

Figure 5.1 describes the domestic situation in the car market of a small car-importing nation that faces infinitely elastic export supply on world markets. The initial demand and supply curves are shown in black and color respectively. In the absence of international trade, domestic price is P_1, while under free trade the price (world price) is P_2 and $\overline{ab}$ ($= \overline{cd}$) units are imported. A tariff t raises the domestic price to P_3, and imports are reduced

[1] See K. Hallberg and W. Takacs, "Columbia's Experience with Import License Auctions," Chap. 20 in M. E. Kreinin (ed.), *International Commercial Policy,* Taylor & Francis, 1993. It has in fact been proposed that the United States auction off quota rights; see F. Bergsten et al., *Auction Quotas and U.S. Trade Policy,* Washington, D.C.: Institute for International Economics, September 1987.

| FIGURE 5.1 | *Domestic Market for Cars in a Small Importing Country* |

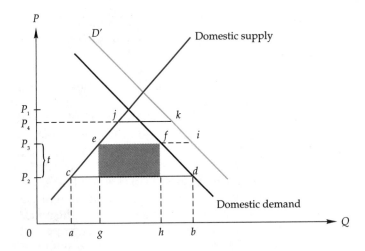

With constant demand and supply curves, the only difference between a tariff $P_2 P_3$ and a quota gh, is that the shaded area accrues to the government in case of a tariff and to the importers under a quota. However, as demand rises to D', the price under a tariff remains at P_3 while the quantity imported rises from ef to ei. In case of a quota, price rises to P_4 while the quantity remains constant at $jk(=ef=gh)$.

to $\overline{gh} (= \overline{ef})$. The same effect on the domestic price and the volume of imports would be produced if the government imposed an import quota of $\overline{gh}$. The only difference is the shaded area: It represents government revenue in the case of a tariff and quota rents, accruing to the holders of import licenses, in the case of a quota. If conditions were perfectly competitive in all markets, if the demand and supply curves were stationary, and import licenses were auctioned to produce the same government revenue as under the tariff, the effects of a tariff and a quota would be identical. This is referred to as the **equivalence of a tariff and a quota.** Such "equivalence" holds if three conditions are met: The import licenses are auctioned off by the government; the demand and supply curves are stationary; and perfect competition prevails in all markets.

Suppose there is an upward shift in domestic demand to D'. Under a tariff t, the domestic price can never exceed world price (P_2) plus the tariff. It therefore remains at P_3, and the volume of imports rises from $\overline{ef}$ to $\overline{ei}$. In other words, the increase in demand is accommodated by an increase in imports. On the other hand, in the case of an import quota, quantity adjustment is not possible; the volume of imports is fixed at $\overline{ef}$. Consequently, the upward shift in demand will produce a price adjustment. Domestic price rises to P_4, where the quantity imported remains unchanged at $\overline{jk}$ ($= \overline{ef}$). Similarly, if domestic producers become less efficient and the supply curve shifts toward the left, a quota would protect them from increased imports, while a tariff would not. In case of a decrease in domestic demand or an increase in domestic supply, the domestic price would decline under a quota, with the quantity imported remaining unchanged; while the volume of imports would decline under a tariff with the price remaining unchanged. The general conclusion is that as long as the quota remains "binding" (the controlled allocation falls short of what would be imported under free-market conditions), the adjustment to any shift in demand or supply occurs in the quantity of imports in the case of a tariff and in the domestic price in the case of a quota.

Additional Insights

Before any change in demand or supply, a tariff rate t or import quota gh cause the same deadweight welfare loss. In figure 5.2 it is shown as triangles cem and nfd. Starting from this position of equivalence, consider first a rise in domestic demand for the commodity. This is portrayed in figure 5.2 as a rightward shift to D' (shaded gray). With a tariff t, the price remains at P_3, the quantity imported rises to ei ($= gb$), and the welfare loss becomes triangles cem and dil; it remains roughly unchanged. With import quota gh, the price rises to P_4, where the quantity imported remains unchanged at jk ($= gh$). The welfare loss from a quota is greater, for it consists of the larger triangles, cjq and rkl. The equivalence of a tariff and a quota is broken: A quota is more harmful to welfare.

A reduction in domestic supply (caused by a drought, a rise in production costs, or other reasons) would be shown by a leftward shift in the supply schedule (holding demand constant). Following the same procedure, the results are similar: A quota is more harmful to welfare than a tariff, as it produces more sizable deadweight loss triangles.

A reduction in domestic demand or an increase in domestic supply produces the opposite result: A tariff is more harmful to welfare than its originally equivalent quota. Indeed, the downward shift can be so large as to render the import quota in-effective: Free market imports become smaller than the maximum mandated by the quota.

In all four cases, the equivalence of tariff t and quota gh breaks down. What they all have in common is that in the case of a tariff the price is constant and the quantity adjusts, while in the case of a quota the quantity is constant and the price adjusts. The case of an upward shift in demand is the most common in a growing economy, when a rise in income produces an increase in demand for the specific commodity.

Another possible difference between a tariff and a quota is suggested by the theory of effective protection. When a quota is imposed on an imported

| FIGURE 5.2 | *A Tariff and a Quota When Domestic Demand Rises* |

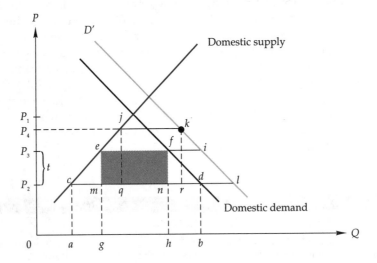

When demand rises to *D'*, the deadweight welfare loss remains roughly unchanged in case of a tariff (triangles *cem* and *idl*), but under a quota it rises to triangles *cjq* and *klr.*

raw material, it raises the production costs of the final output of which the material is a part. This is the same effect as that of a tariff on inputs. But whereas import duties on raw materials are sometimes rebated when the final product is exported, no such rebate occurs in the case of quotas.

A third important difference between a tariff and a quota concerns the case where the domestic producer of the import substitute is a monopolist. International trade, even with a tariff, imposes severe limitations on this producer's monopoly power. In particular, he cannot charge more than the world price plus the tariff, for consumers can switch to foreign imports in unlimited quantities. The tariff, therefore, poses a potential (if not actual) threat to his position. In the case of an import quota, all he needs to do is accommodate a certain fixed amount of imports; beyond that, he is the king of the marketplace. He may certainly charge more than he could with the tariff; he faces less competitive pressure than he would under the tariff; and in general he can cause greater damage to economic efficiency and growth. (Appendix 5–1 demonstrates that a profit-maximizing monopolist would indeed charge more under a quota than under a tariff.) He also is easily assured of any increase in sales resulting from a rise in domestic demand, because the volume of imports is fixed by decree.

Furthermore, for the competitor and monopolist alike, a tariff does not provide protection with certainty. The foreign exporter may choose to absorb all or most of the duty by reducing the export price and leaving the import price virtually unchanged. In that case, the volume of imports would decline very little, much to the dismay of the protection-seeking producers. Such an outcome is not possible in the case of a quota, where the volume of admissible imports is prescribed by the government. More generally, domestic producers, lacking precise knowledge of the supply and demand elasticities for their product, can never be sure how much imports would be excluded from the country by a given level of tariff protection. Certainty is guaranteed in the case of a quota.

In addition, import quotas require a cumbersome administrative apparatus. The administering government agency must decide how to allocate import licenses among importers as well as among sources of supply (exporting countries[2]) and how to distribute the yearly allocation over time. These decisions can be arbitrary and may bear no relation to consumer choice and producer cost. Furthermore, since sales of the restricted commodity yield quota rents to the importer, the import license itself assumes considerable value. If there is a free market for such licenses, the license to import a unit of the product would be worth the difference between its domestic and international price. For example, when the United States enforced a quota on imported oil in the 1950s, the free-market price of a permit to import a barrel of oil (known as a *ticket*) was exactly the difference between the domestic and foreign prices. An importer may be willing to bribe government officials to obtain a license. Thus, the system contains seeds of corruption.

Usually the import permits are given to domestic importers, so they collect the rents. But if foreigners receive the licenses, then the rents may be captured by them. For example, in the case of the U.S. sugar quota, the U.S. government distributes licenses to 24 foreign governments, who in turn allocate them to their own nationals. The annual welfare loss to the United States has been estimated at nearly $0.5 billion—half of which is the result of consumption and production distortions, and the other half from a transfer to foreigners who received the quota rents.

A final source of inefficiency arises from the fact that the import licenses are usually distributed among the importers who were functioning at the time the control was imposed. The system tends to freeze the situation as it existed at a certain base period. Total sales and profits cease to depend on the efficiency of the importing firms. A tax such as a tariff, while distorting relative prices, still permits competitive-market forces to serve as an allocation mechanism. The importers who are efficient enough to pay the tax get the business. Import quotas displace the market mechanism altogether,

[2] Often this is done by historical (free-market) shares, as in the case of the U.S. dairy quota.

and a powerful incentive for business efficiency on the part of importing firms is lost. Despite its high economic costs, it is the LDCs—which can least afford to tolerate inefficiency—that insist on using quotas.[3]

For all these reasons the member countries of the WTO decided to phase out import quotas and replace them with tariffs—a process known as *tariffication.*

VOLUNTARY EXPORT RESTRAINTS (VERs)

Partly because import quotas are not permissible under the WTO, and partly to avoid retaliation, countries frequently resort to **voluntary export restraints (VERs).** A VER is a bilateral agreement between two governments, under which the exporting country limits its export of a certain product (or products) to the importing country. Typically, it is the import-competing industries that pressure their government to negotiate a VER with the exporting country in order to lessen import competition. The exporters are forced to accept such quantitative limitations when they are threatened with more restrictive action by the importing country if they fail to agree. Because they are agreed to in advance, VERs pose no threat of retaliation. The agreement is administered by the government of the exporting country or by the exporters themselves.

VERs have become a widely used instrument for restricting trade. About 10 percent of world trade is covered by VERs; the most affected product categories include steel and steel products, textiles, agriculture and food products, automobiles and transport equipment, electronic products, footwear, and machine tools. In a specific example the United States attempted to convince the Soviet Union to curtail its exports of aluminum. Markets protected by VERs include the United States, the EU, and Canada, while exporters limited by these arrangements include Japan, Korea, Taiwan, and other LDCs.

Often VERs are negotiated with one or more major exporting countries, leaving other exporting countries unrestrained. For example, during 1981–1985 Japanese auto exports to the United States were subject to VER limitations, while European models were exempt.[4] Currently, the EU restricts imports of Japanese cars under a VER—which even limits sales of Japanese models produced in Europe by Japanese transplants. Another illustration is a VER limiting machine-tool exports to the United States from Japan and Taiwan (initiated in 1986) but not from European sources. A third example, the United States-Japan 1989 agreement on computer chips (since expired),

---

[3] A boycott, however, leads to a much more serious disruption of trade than a quota. It is usually imposed for political reasons. Under a **primary boycott** country *A* declares that it would not buy anything from (or, for that matter, sell to) country *B*. Under a **secondary boycott** country *A* declares that it would not buy anything from (or deal with) companies in third countries that deal with country *B*.

[4] One effect of the U.S. auto VER was to encourage Japanese investment in automobile production in the United States.

illustrates a different kind of VER. Under American pressure, Japanese producers of semiconductors cut overall *production* in order to raise their prices and become less competitive in the U.S. market. But by doing so they raised their prices in Europe as well, thereby incurring the wrath of the EU.

Herein lies an important difference between import quotas and VERs. While quotas may be global, VERs usually discriminate between sources of supply.[5] This is a violation of the nondiscriminatory rule embodied in the WTO's MFN principle, and consequently this measure bypasses the WTO mechanism. Exporters not covered by a VER agreement invariably benefit from it, as they can raise either the volume or the price of their exports to the importing market. Thus, European auto producers raised their export prices to the United States by substantial amounts as a result of the U.S.-Japan auto VER. In turn, the "restrained" exporters are induced to expand shipments to unrestricted destinations.

Since the VERs restrict supply and therefore raise import prices in the importing country, their welfare effects are similar to those of import quotas. However, because VERs are often administered by the exporting countries, exporters tend to raise their export price and capture much of the quota rents (shaded area in figure 5.1). It has been estimated that rent transfers resulting from VERs worldwide exceed $25 billion per year. In contrast, under quota restrictions, that revenue usually accrues to the importers.[6] It is thus possible to rank trade barriers in terms of the damage they cause to national welfare: *least harmful is the tariff, followed by import quotas, while the VER is the most harmful.*

A phenomenon common to both import quotas and VERs, when imposed on differentiated commodities, is known as **quality upgrading.** If Japanese auto exporters to the United States were restricted to 1.6 million units, without regard to the type of car, they would tend to ship the more elaborate models, loaded with optional equipment, to enhance the profit on each car sold. From the consumer viewpoint a quota or a VER, which raises the absolute dollar price by the same amount regardless of quality or grade, translates into a proportionately larger price hike on low- than on high-cost models. Consequently both supply and demand factors induce a shift toward more expensive Japanese models. Such product upgrading occurs in all cases of quotas and VERs imposed on manufactured goods.[7]

[5]See E. Dinopoulos and M. Kreinin, "Import Quotas and VERs," *Journal of International Economics,* February 1989.

[6]W. Takacs, "The Equivalence of Tariffs, Quotas and VERs," *Journal of International Economics,* 1978: 565–573; and T. Murray, W. Schmidt, and I. Walter, "On the Equivalence of Quotas and VERs," *Journal of International Economics,* 1983: 191–194.

[7]Falvey, Rodney E., "The Composition of Trade within Import Restricted Product Categories," *Journal of Political Economy,* 1979: 1105–1114; R. Feenstra, "Automobile Prices and Protection: The U.S.–Japan Trade Restraint," *Journal of Policy Modeling* (spring 1985); R. Feenstra, "VER in U.S. Autos 1980–81: Quality, Employment and Welfare Effects," chap. 2 in R. Baldwin and A. Krueger, *The Structure and Evolution of Recent U.S. Trade Policy* (Chicago: University of Chicago Press, 1984; C. Rodriguez, "The Quality of Imports and the Differential Welfare Effects of Tariffs, Quotas, and Quality Controls as Protective Devices," *Canadian Journal of Economics,* 1979: 439–449; and C. Boonekamp, "Voluntary Export Restraints," *Finance and Development,* December 1987.

One reason for the increased use of VERs and other NTBs is the desire of politicians to save domestic jobs that would otherwise be destroyed by imports. But apart from the fact that macroeconomic policies are superior instruments to expand employment, protectionism does not usually save many jobs. It often invites retaliation by other nations, hurting employment in the exporting industries, so that the net number of jobs saved is very small at best.

Beyond that, protectionism is an expensive and inefficient way to expand employment. Consider the case of the auto VERs. It has been estimated[8] that in 1982 the U.S. auto VER cost the United States $4 billion (rising to $5.8 billion in 1984) in higher prices charged by Japanese and European producers. This is a net transfer from the United States to Japan and Europe; and it is apart from the induced increase in automobile prices by U.S. manufacturers, which constitutes an internal transfer from consumers to producers. The VER is estimated to have saved about 22,000 American jobs in 1982. Thus a conservative estimate of the annual cost to the country of each job saved is $180,000, six times the average wage in the automobile industry.

Similarly, the annual cost per job saved by protection in the steel industry is set at about $175,000; in textiles, $43,000; and in tuna, $240,000. In Sweden, for every $20,000-a-year job in shipyards, Swedish taxpayers pay a $50,000 annual subsidy. And in Canada, protection of the clothing industry costs consumers $500 million per year to provide $135 million of wages to Canadian workers. Protection in any form is an expensive way to create jobs.

Under the Uruguay Round pact, VERs will be phased out by the year 2000.

INTERNATIONAL COMMODITY AGREEMENTS

International trade in certain primary commodities (namely raw materials or agricultural products) is governed by **International Commodity Agreements (ICAs),** allegedly designed to stabilize the world price of the commodity in question or dispose of surpluses. It is usually the producing nations that press for such agreements, claiming that when the response to price change on the part of consumers and producers is low, the market mechanism is too sluggish and cumbersome and needs to be modified by some central direction. After all, the performance of the price system as an allocation mechanism is contingent upon reasonably strong and prompt responses to price change. When the response is weak and tardy, violent

---

[8] See E. Dinopoulos and M. Kreinin, "Effects of the U.S.–Japan Auto VER on European Prices and U.S. Welfare," *Review of Economics and Statistics,* September 1988; and D. Tarr, *A General Equilibrium Analysis of the Welfare and Employment Effects of U.S. Quotas in Textiles, Autos and Steel,* Washington, D.C.: Federal Trade Commission, 1989.

price fluctuations frequently occur. If a bumper crop raises the supply of the commodity, it takes a huge decline in price to induce consumers to take even part of that increase. Likewise, a shift in consumer demand, for any reason, produces a large price change because producers cannot respond with sufficient speed and vigor to the new situation. Such circumstances may imply large fluctuations in the earnings of growers and in the terms of trade of the countries that produce the primary materials. If a country's economy is largely devoted to the production and exportation of one or two primary products, as economies in many developing countries are, then the entire level of economic activity tends to fluctuate along with these prices.

ICAs involve *both the producing and the consuming countries* (in contrast to cartels, which are strictly producers' organizations). They take one of three forms.

Export restriction schemes call for control over the quantity marketed internationally by means of national quotas for the production or export of the supplying countries. The 1993 cocoa agreement is of that form.

Buffer stocks set a minimum and a maximum price for the commodity to be maintained respectively by purchases or by sales from central stocks of the commodity in question. In this case, the objective is to maintain the price within a predetermined range.

Operation of a buffer stock is illustrated in figure 5.3. On both panels (a) and (b), P_E is perceived as the long-run equilibrium price (with S and D representing the original supply and demand schedules). The buffer stock management decides to limit price fluctuations to a range $P_F - P_C$ where P_F is the floor price and P_C is the ceiling price. Should supply rise to S_1 in panel (a) (for example, because of a bumper crop), price P_F is maintained by the buffer stock buying quantity $\overline{ab}$ (shaded color)—the excess supply at that price. Conversely, should supply decline to S_2 (for example, because of a drought), the buffer stock maintains the ceiling price P_C by selling out of stocks quantity $\overline{cd}$ (shaded color) of the commodity—the excess demand at that price. Likewise, upward and downward shifts in demand, with a stable supply schedule, can bring about selling and buying operations, respectively, by the buffer stock management. On panel (b), when demand rises from D to D_1, P_C is maintained by the sale of quantity $\overline{cd}$ out of central stocks. When demand declines from D to D_2, P_F is maintained by purchase of quantity $\overline{ab}$. All this can be accomplished by the buffer stock management standing ready to buy whatever quantities are offered to it at price P_F, and to sell whatever quantities are requested at price P_C.

Over time, the stabilization operations are expected to narrow the range of price fluctuations.

Multilateral contracts specify a maximum price at which producing countries are obliged to sell stipulated quantities to consuming countries and a minimum price at which consuming countries are obliged to purchase stipulated quantities from producing countries.

FIGURE 5.3   *Commodity Price Stabilization under a Buffer Stock ICA*

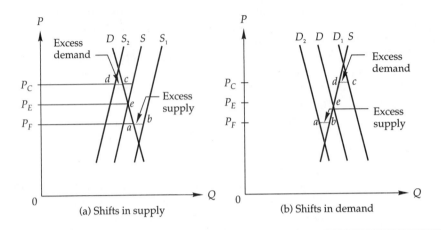

(a) Shifts in supply   (b) Shifts in demand

A buffer stock limits price fluctuations to the range $P_F P_C$ by buying the excess supply *ab* that arises when supply rises or demand declines, and selling excess demand *cd* that arises if supply declines or demand rises.

All three mechanisms interfere with the allocative functions of the market, preventing shifts of resources between industries and thereby causing inefficiencies. The buffer stock arrangement requires vast expenditures of money to maintain commodity stocks.

There is an inherent asymmetry in buffer stock agreements involving primary agricultural commodities. Price support at the low level depends on the availability of financial resources, and those can be expanded *if* the participating countries agree to do so. But maintenance of the price ceiling depends on the availability of the commodity in stock. Once the stock is exhausted, nothing can prevent the price from rising above the ceiling, at least until the next harvest comes in, rendering the agreement unoperational.

All past and present international commodity agreements suffer from attempts to fix and maintain a price different from the long-run equilibrium level. In most cases, it is difficult to determine that price. Even if it were possible to start at the correct level, that level changes over time in response to market forces. While these changes can go in all directions, the continuous pressure of the producing countries is only upward; in other words, they campaign for higher prices, which in turn lead to more production and larger surpluses (except in years of unusually high demand). Thus, agreements become a thinly disguised form of subsidy paid by the consuming nations (whose consumers pay the above-equilibrium prices) to the producing nations. And it is an inefficient method of subsidizing at that, for not only are consumers charged artificially high prices, but above-equilibrium prices stimulate excessive output. Moreover, the discrepancy between the equilibrium and the support prices usually leads to an accumulation of large stocks that are costly to store and maintain.

Besides the problem of financing and storing surpluses, many of the past and present agreements are threatened by noncompliance of small producers with the regulations—with each small country considering its own actions as not affecting the world price—and by the incentive offered by high prices to the production of synthetic substitutes.

Because most agreements have not been particularly successful and are difficult to negotiate to begin with, their use has declined in recent years. On the other hand, attempts are being made to find other ways to combat the effects of violent price fluctuations on developing countries. A coordinated international effort is presently under way to diversify production of materials, and direct international financial support is available from the IMF to countries that experience a particularly severe decline in export earnings in any given year. Since it does not interfere with the workings of the market mechanism, such **compensatory financing** is a more efficient method of offsetting fluctuations in commodity prices or export earnings.

Not all international commodity agreements involve primary commodities, and not all are called forth by developing countries. The major exception is textiles. If any sector of the industrial countries should have contracted to make room for imports from developing countries, it is textiles. By reason of simple technology and relative labor intensity of the production process, this industry is the first candidate for introduction into a developing economy attempting to industrialize. Resources in the industrial nations can almost invariably be put to better use elsewhere. Yet well known economic and political pressures prevail and keep the industry from contracting and imports from expanding. Administered by the WTO, the so-called **Multifibre Arrangement (MFA)** is an ICA among over 50 producing and consuming countries. It specifies a maximum amount of cotton, wool, and synthetic fibers that each exporting country may ship to each importing country. In addition, the United States and the EU have bilateral agreements with many supplying countries in which the latter undertake to *further* limit their textile exports to each of the two markets. In particular, strict limitations apply to the annual growth rate of imports. Consumers in the industrial countries and producers in the LDCs are the main losers from these restrictions. The Uruguay Round pact calls for phasing out the MFA over a ten-year period.

INTERNATIONAL CARTELS

Cartels are extensions of domestic monopolistic behavior into the international arena. When a group of business organizations of the same industry located in different countries, or a group of governments, agrees to limit competition and to regulate markets and restrict trade in some way, it is known as an **international cartel.** Unlike an ICA, a cartel agreement is limited to the suppliers, and does not include the consuming countries. For example, freight rates along the major shipping routes are set by conferences that include all the major lines serving a particular route.

The **Organization of Petroleum Exporting Countries (OPEC)** is a cartel that in 1973–1974 succeeded in quadrupling the price of crude oil (and doubling it again in 1979–1980). The Arab members of that cartel also used an oil embargo as a political weapon. In the long run, the power of the cartel to raise prices may be restricted by increases in supplies from outside the cartel, such as in the continental United States, Alaska, and the North Sea; by the development of alternative sources of energy, such as coal, gas, atomic power, and solar energy; and by reduced consumption as a result of higher prices.

Indeed in the 1980s a global oil glut developed. Crude oil prices plummeted from $36 a barrel in the late 1970s to $15–20 a barrel by the late 1980s and early 1990s, reducing the external trade surpluses of the major exporters. Countries like Nigeria and Mexico encountered balance-of-payments problems. The Soviet Union, which relied on oil and gold exports to finance imports from the West, faced major difficulties as the price of these two commodities dropped sharply.

Overt or illicit agreements often exist among major companies in the manufacturing and extractive industries. Their goals are many and varied, but in most cases they seek to fix prices, allocate world markets among the member firms to avoid competition, control technological research and development, and in other ways limit or alleviate competitive pressure. They may or may not tolerate smaller firms that are not members of the cartel and do not abide by its rules, depending on whether the firm's activities really disrupt the agreement or are merely a nuisance. When a major participant decides to opt out of the agreement, the entire operation of the cartel may be disrupted, much to the dismay of other members but to the joy of the consumers. Attempts by the U.S. Civil Aeronautics Board to introduce more competition in airline traffic reduced transatlantic fares substantially.

It is easy to see that cartel agreements are as harmful to the international economy as monopolies are to the domestic economy. They restrict output, misallocate resources, and extract higher prices from the public compared with conditions prevailing under competition. But international cartel action may even work counter to government policies. For example, an agreement among the large French, British, German, and Italian automakers to allocate markets among themselves and fix prices can easily remove the salutary effects that the European Community hoped to achieve by eliminating official barriers to trade. The same applies to other major industries on the European continent. It does no good to eliminate tariffs and quotas if firms agree among themselves not to invade each other's territory or to avoid competition in other ways. For this reason, the European Community found it necessary to adopt rules of competition in industry.

ADMINISTRATIVE, TECHNICAL, AND OTHER REGULATIONS

A myriad of government rules restrict the free flow of trade, although they may be ostensibly unrelated to protectionism. It is often difficult to determine whether these are bona fide technical regulations that happen to discriminate against imports or are regulations designed primarily to keep out imports.

For example, the French domestic tax on automobiles is graduated on the basis of a car's horsepower; as such, it raises the prices of American cars relative to domestic cars and can be regarded as discriminatory. In many countries importers must deposit at the government treasury, for six months and at no interest, a sum equal to half the value of their imports. Known as **minimum deposit requirement,** it is certainly a strong barrier to trade. Many Europeans regard the U.S. laws requiring automotive safety equipment as a protective device. And restrictions of minimum size on certain tomatoes sold in the United States discriminate against Mexican imports.

Other examples include complex customs procedures: a French requirement that all imported videotape recorders enter France through the tiny and inaccessible customs port of Poitiers with a staff of only four, and preferences given to local firms in purchases by the government (practiced by many countries, including the United States).

Health requirements are often regarded as trade restrictions. For example, in 1989 the EC banned imports of hormone-treated American beef. Regarding the action as a trade measure that would keep out $100 million of American exports, the U.S. government retaliated by imposing 100 percent duty on $100 million of assorted products exported by Europe to the United States. Japan's domestic distribution system and other "invisible barriers" are seen by some countries as limiting market access, as is the strong preference of Japanese companies for Japanese machinery and other goods.

Restrictions on *service* trade (banking, insurance, transportation, communication, etc.) have also multiplied in recent years. For example, Asian governments limit the number of flights of U.S. airlines to Asia. And finally, some countries fail to provide protection for such intellectual property rights of foreign citizens as copyrights, trademarks, and patents.

LOCAL CONTENT REQUIREMENT

A rather pervasive form of trade control is a regulation, known as a **local content requirement,** that specifies that a minimum fraction of a final good be produced domestically.[9] It offers protection to local factors of production and to the domestic producers of parts, and raises the price of inputs to the producer of the final good. Some governments may exempt firms from the regulation to the extent that they export the final product.

For example, to sell cars, tractors, and other capital goods in Brazil, Argentina, Mexico, or South Korea, a foreign manufacturer must set up domestic assembly operations and guarantee that a minimum specified portion of the value of the final product is made locally. In mid-1996 Japan brought Brazil's local content requirement on cars to international review at the WTO. A proposed regulation, requiring European TV stations to air a minimum amount of European-produced programs would be an example from the service sector.

Content laws often affect trade between second and third parties. For example, Japanese cars assembled in the United States are treated by France as American made (and therefore exempt from the quantitative limitation on Japanese cars) only if they have 80 percent American content.

BORDER TAX ADJUSTMENTS

A major form of nontariff barriers concerns rebates of domestic taxes to exporters. As a general rule, the WTO forbids export subsidies, including rebates of domestic taxes. The sole exception to this regulation is the rebate of indirect taxes to exporters, or **export rebates. Indirect taxes** are those levied on the product at some stage of its manufacture or sale, such as the excise or sales taxes in the United States and the value-added taxes[10] in Europe. They are all borne eventually either by the final buyer or by the producer, depending on whether the price of the product goes up by the full amount of the tax or by less than that. In other words, the tax is levied directly on products, and only in an indirect manner is it shifted to individuals.

---

[9] See G. Grossman, "The Theory of Domestic Content Protection and Content Preference," *Quarterly Journal of Economics*, November 1981: 583–604; and K. Krishna and M. Itoh, "Content Protection and Oligopolistic Interaction," mimeographed, National Bureau of Economic Research, 1985.

[10] The usual **value-added tax (VAT)** is an indirect tax imposed on each sale beginning at the start of the production and distribution cycle and culminating with the sale to the consumer. All the sellers in the chain collect the VAT from the purchasers at the time of sale, deduct from this amount any VAT they themselves have paid on their purchases, and remit the balance to the government. The net effect of offsetting purchases and sales is to impose the tax at each stage of production on the sum of wages, interest, rents, profits, and other factors of production not furnished by suppliers subject to the tax at the previous stage of production—hence, a tax on "value added."

If and when the product is exported, the WTO rule permits the government to rebate the tax to the exporter. Similarly, a country is permitted to levy a special import fee that equals the indirect tax. The export rebate and import fee combined are known as a **border tax adjustment** for internal taxes, and are designed to "level the playing field" relative to producers in countries that do not levy such taxes.

This permission does not apply to direct taxes—that is, taxes that are levied directly on people or on factors of production, such as the income tax or the corporate profits tax. The implicit rationale for this distinction is based on the poorly founded theory that indirect taxes are "shifted forward" and added in their entirety to the final price charged to the consumer, whereas direct taxes are paid at the source, either out of wages and salaries or out of profit, and do not affect the final price of the product. Consequently, only indirect taxes raise the domestic price and place local producers on an unfavorable competitive footing compared with their peers in other countries where such taxes may not exist or may not be as high; and only these taxes need an adjustment. But in fact direct taxes may be shifted to the consumer in precisely the same degree as the indirect taxes, depending on market conditions.

Be that as it may, the distinction has implications for trade between Europe and the United States. The United States relies mainly on direct taxes on income and profits to produce *federal* government revenue, and these are nonrebatable to exporters. This is not the case in most European countries. A major component of their public revenue comes from the value-added tax, which is a tax levied at each stage of the productive process on the value added at that stage. Because it is indirect, it is subject to border tax adjustment.

DUMPING

Dumping occurs when a commodity is sold to foreign purchasers at a price lower than the price charged for the identical product on the domestic market. (An alternative definition is the sale of a good in foreign markets below production cost.) The word *identical* makes it difficult to establish the existence of dumping, because in making international price comparisons full allowance must be made for differences in specifications, including packaging and other superficial features. International standards exist for judging whether a commodity has been dumped.

Government export subsidies are a form of dumping to be discussed in the next section. Our concern here is with dumping by private companies unrelated to government subsidies. It is customary to distinguish among three types of dumping: **Sporadic dumping** is disposal on foreign markets of an occasional surplus or overstock; it is tantamount to a domestic sale, and its effects are negligible. **Predatory dumping** occurs when a large home-based firm sells abroad at a reduced price in order to drive out competitors and gain control over the market, at which time it intends to reintroduce higher prices and use its newly acquired monopoly power to exploit that market. Potential rivals may then be discouraged from entering the field by the fear of a repeat performance on the part of the monopolist. This is the most harmful form of dumping.

Persistent dumping is a direct outgrowth of profit-maximizing behavior by monopolists. Consider a manufacturer who holds a monopoly position on the domestic market, where he is also protected from import competition by transport cost or government restrictions. In foreign markets, on the other hand, he faces the competition of producers from the host country as well as from third countries. Translated into economic terms, this situation implies that the demand elasticity is lower on the home market, where the consumer cannot turn to competing brands, than on foreign markets, where he can. The availability of close substitutes on foreign markets makes consumers highly responsive to price change in either direction. In other words, in terms of lost sales, the cost to the producer of charging a high price is lower at home than abroad. To maximize his overall net return, he would be led to charge a lower price abroad where he must meet competition than that charged at home where competitive pressure is lacking. Such dumping is harmful to the producers in the country receiving the dumped product, but this damage may be more than offset by the benefit to its consumers from the lower price.

A geometric representation of dumping is shown in figure 5.4, comprising three panels: demand on both the home and foreign markets, and a panel showing marginal cost and revenue. From the demand schedule on the home market we obtain the marginal revenue curve (MR_H). The demand on foreign markets yields the attendant marginal revenue (MR_F). Foreign demand is more elastic than home demand because of the availability of competing brands, which are regarded as close substitutes. The two marginal revenue curves (MR_H and MR_F) are added *horizontally* at each price to obtain the total marginal revenue (MR_T) shown in the right-hand panel (all MR curves are shown in color). The firm also has a marginal cost (MC) curve (drawn in black in the right-hand panel), and its intersection with MR_T determines the total quantity (Q_T) to be produced under profit-maximizing conditions.

How is Q_T divided between the two separate markets? Profit-maximizing behavior requires the division to be such that the marginal revenue in the two markets is equalized. Marginal revenue is the addition to total revenue derived from an increment of one unit of sales (or subtraction from a unit decrement). If MR_F is greater than MR_H, it would be profitable to shift sales from the home to the foreign market, since the addition to total revenue from the incremental foreign sales is larger than the loss of revenue from the reduced domestic sales. The opposite occurs if MR_H is greater than MR_F. Only equality of the two marginal revenues signals profit-maximizing equilibrium.[11]

FIGURE 5.4   *A Monopolist Facing Separate Markets*

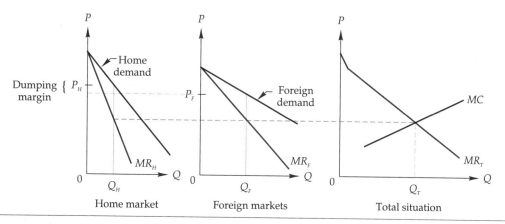

A monopolist facing two separate markets with different demand elasticities will charge a higher price in the market with less elastic demand, where buyers would be less induced to withdraw from the market as the price rises. The difference between the home and foreign price is called the **dumping margin.**

This position is shown in figure 5.4. Quantities Q_H and Q_F are sold on the domestic and foreign markets, respectively; by construction they add up to the total quantity Q_T. Given the two quantities, the demand curves (not the marginal revenue) determine the prices prevailing on the two markets P_H and P_F, the domestic price being higher than its foreign counterpart. The two prices are inversely related to the two price elasticities.[12]

---

[11]Following is a step-by-step procedure for drawing figure 5.4:

(a) Draw two separate demand curves in each of the two markets: home market (left-hand panel) and foreign markets (center panel). Make the foreign demand curve flatter (more elastic) than the domestic demand schedule.

(b) From each demand schedule, obtain the marginal revenue curve. Graphically this can be done by extending the demand curve to the quantity axis, bisecting the resulting $\overline{0Q}$ distance, and connecting the midpoint with the beginning of the demand curve on the price axis.

(c) For each price, add horizontally the two marginal revenues in the two markets to obtain total marginal revenue, plotted as MR_T in the right-hand panel. Its intersection with the marginal cost curve (in the same panel) yields the total quantity produced.

(d) From the intersection of MC and MR_T draw a straight horizontal dashed line to meet the two marginal revenue curves. The points are those at which the marginal revenues in the two markets are equal. They determine the equilibrium division of the output between the two markets: Q_H and Q_F. They determine the equilibrium division of the output between the two markets: Q_H and Q_F.

(e) Given these quantities, the price in each market is obtained by extending a vertical line from points Q_H and Q_F to the respective demand curves.

[12]An alternative definition of dumping is the sale of a commodity in a foreign market at a price below *production cost* (rather than home price). This can occur when the industry suffers excess capacity, so that the price charged *both* on the home and the foreign markets is below its full cost. Under this version, dumping can be inferred even when the home and foreign prices are the same. See W. Ethier, "Dumping," *Journal of Political Economy*, June 1982.

One condition necessary for all forms of dumping is a separation of the domestic and foreign markets; otherwise, it is always possible for a foreign purchaser to resell the product on the home market and cut into the monopolist's profit. Thus, dumping is essentially price discrimination applied to the international arena. Indeed, it is easier to practice price discrimination internationally than nationally, because the domestic market cannot be fragmented into separate markets, while both transport costs and government restrictions often form an effective barrier between the domestic and foreign markets. On occasion the pressure of domestic monopolists for import quotas and other restrictions can be traced to their desire to effect such a separation in order to practice price discrimination.

In actual practice it is difficult to distinguish the various types of dumping. Although predatory dumping is demonstrably harmful to the importing country, the same cannot be said of long-run dumping, which lowers the price to consumers. Yet government policy, often formulated under pressure from import-competing industries, applies to all of them. The most common measure to counteract dumping in the importing country is the imposition of an **antidumping import duty.** Such a duty, sanctioned by the WTO, is allowed for in the American tariff legislation, but its imposition requires elaborate proceedings to prove the existence of dumping.

Specifically, antidumping cases involve a two-step investigative procedure. First, the U.S. Commerce Department determines whether an imported product is being sold in the United States at a price below that prevailing in the exporting country ("sales at less than fair value"). In cases of positive findings, the International Trade Commission (ITC) institutes an investigation to determine whether the American industry "is being or is likely to be materially injured or is prevented from being established" by reason of such imports. In cases of affirmative determination, an antidumping duty is imposed. Such duties are assessed in addition to the normal tariff, and their size can vary with each shipment; it equals the price differential between the two markets. In other words, exporters can avoid these duties by raising their export price. As of June 10, 1995 there were 805 antidumping measures in force, of which 305 were imposed by the United States, 178 by the EU, 91 by Canada, and 86 by Australia.[13] These numbers are likely to grow when other means of protection, such as VERs, are phased out. While Japan has not traditionally used antidumping duties, in 1993 it imposed such duties on Chinese steel products—a first for Japan. For a recent U.S. example, in February 1990 the United States imposed a 15 percent antidumping duty on metal-stamping presses imported from three Japanese companies. But requests for antidumping duties are not always honored by the government. In 1992 the ITC rejected

---

[13] WTO, *Focus* Geneva, December 1995.

a request for an antidumping duty on Japanese minivans. While in the past most dumping complaints came from traditional industries such as shoes, textiles, and steel, today they come from the high-technology arena as well.

How complex dumping cases can become is illustrated by a dispute between two typewriter manufacturers: Smith Corona (United States) and Brother (Japan). For years Smith Corona (S-C) had been accusing Brother (B) of dumping, but B had been able to "dodge the bullet." After the U.S. Commerce Department imposed a 48.7 percent antidumping duty on B in 1980, the company added a computer memory to its typewriter and claimed, successfully, that the "new" product was not subject to the duty. In 1991 the Commerce Department again found in favor of a new petition by S-C and imposed a 60 percent antidumping duty on B. But again the triumph proved hollow, because by then B was assembling its word processors in Tennessee and the duty applied only to equipment made in Japan. Smith Corona countered by invoking a provision in the 1988 Trade Act that prohibits circumvention of antidumping orders by importing parts and assembling them in the United States. But B argued successfully that the law applies only to cases in which the parts are shipped from the home country (Japan), whereas its parts were shipped from third countries. Then in 1992 B turned the entire battle on its head by taking the offensive and filing an antidumping suit against S-C. Brother noted that it now supplied the U.S. market out of its Tennessee plant, while S-C (now 47 percent British owned) had a plant in Singapore. So the Japanese company claimed to be the real U.S. producer. Both companies are incorporated in the United States and conduct their manufacturing operations in several countries (including the United States), the main difference being that S-C does most of its research in the United States and B does it in Japan.

A form of dumping called *diversionary input dumping* occurs when imports are made out of materials that were dumped in the country where the finished goods were manufactured. In 1988 the U.S. Trade Act mandated the administration to negotiate the banning of such dumping.

EXPORT SUBSIDIES

In the previous sections we examined ways in which governments restrict imports or otherwise limit trade. But governments also use subsidies to stimulate exports. An *export subsidy* is a payment by the government to a firm for each unit of a product shipped abroad. Despite the WTO's prohibition, export subsidies abound, even though they cause a deadweight loss to the subsidizing country. Often such subsidies are a point of contention between the United States and its trading partners.

To capture the economic effects of an export subsidy, consider a small-country exporter whose action has no impact on the importing countries. Figure 5.5 describes the market for a single product in such a country. With the world price (P^w) above the domestic market-clearing price (e), the country exports quantity ab. To encourage an expansion of exports, the government offers a subsidy S for each unit exported. This raises the domestic price to P^s, and exports expand to cd. World price remains at P^w, so the subsidy (S) compensates exporters for the difference between P^s and P^w.

Three components make up the welfare effect of the subsidy:

		Areas in Figure 5.5
Gain in Producers' Surplus	[+]	$A + B + C$
Loss in Consumers' Surplus	[−]	$A + B$
Cost of Subsidy to the Government (S times the quantity exported cd)	[−]	$B + C + D$
Net Welfare Loss to the Country		$B + D$

Triangles B and D, the net loss, represent consumption and production distortions respectively.

If the subsidizing country is large, it incurs an added cost from the subsidy. For the increase in its exports reduces the world price, and hence its terms of trade deteriorate. Unlike a tariff, the volume and the terms of trade effects operate in the same direction in case of a subsidy, both worsening the country's welfare.[14] An export subsidy leads to an unambiguous welfare loss for the subsidizing country. Yet subsidies usually have their roots in the mercantilist desire to promote exports and protect employment, although there are better ways of attaining these goals.

What about the effect on the foreign, importing, country? In a two-country world that country enjoys a gain as its terms of trade improve. So if a large country subsidizes its exports to the United States, the United States benefits. But in a multicountry world these matters are not clear cut. A foreign government may subsidize the export of a good that competes with U.S. exports in a third market, thus worsening the U.S. terms of trade. European subsidies of agricultural exports have that effect.

Although foreign subsidies are beneficial to the importing country, they also affect its income distribution. While lowering the price to all consumers, they harm labor and capital in the industries competing with the

---

[14] Both a tariff and a subsidy support domestic producers, but they have opposite effects on the terms of trade.

FIGURE 5.5   *Effect of an Export Subsidy by a Small-Country Exporter*

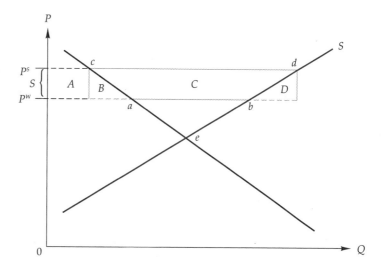

An export subsidy in the amount of *S* per unit of the product enables exporters to increase exports from *ab* to *cd*. Net welfare loss to the country are triangles *B* and *D*.

subsidized imports. For that reason they are considered an unfair trading practice, and the importing country is allowed—following an investigation—to assess **countervailing duties.** As of June 30, 1995 there were 128 countervailing measures in force, 103 of which were imposed by the United States. The increased use of countervailing duties by the United States in recent years reflects both the greater ease with which they can be applied under U.S. legislation, and the efforts by the United States to reduce other countries' use of subsidies. But the global increase in antidumping and countervailing investigations has led to a number of disputes as countries charge that the investigations and the imposition of duties are being used as a form of administered protection to restrict trade unreasonably.

We now return to a survey of overt and disguised export subsidies. In the field of agriculture both the United States and Europe employ domestic support prices, and then export some of their accumulated surpluses at low, subsidized prices. Under a 1985 plan, augmented in 1989, the United States subsidizes farm exports by offering the buying country a bonus in the form of grains from government-owned surpluses—which violates WTO rules. At times a U.S.–EU rivalry appears, as when the United States attempted to recapture certain markets lost to subsidized EU grain exports. In the early 1990s, a subsidy war between these two "giants," designed to capture the Chinese market, has hurt Australia, the traditional supplier of grains to China. Thus a small-country supplier can easily get caught in the export-subsidy crossfire.

In the manufacturing sector, a popular way of subsidizing exports is by giving the foreign buyer a loan at below-market interest rates to finance the purchase. The subsidy measure is the difference between the market interest rate and the rate actually charged. Such loans, targeted for specific purchases, are important in the case of "big ticket" export items such as aircraft or machinery. These are made through a special agency of the government involved, which in the United States is the Export-Import Bank. A significant portion of European exports (such as the A300 airbus) are so financed. Subsidized credits have two effects: They direct resources to the export industries that are favored by the subsidized loans; and they transfer income from the exporting to the importing country. Since about two-thirds of these loans are made by the industrial countries to LDCs, the income transfers are from rich to poor countries.

To avoid "subsidy wars" the OECD countries agreed on a minimum interest rate that may be charged on export credit. The rates, adjusted periodically, vary according to the duration of the loan and the level of development of the loan-receiving country. Relatively poor countries are eligible for lower rates.

But there is no limit to the ingenuity of nations in circumventing agreed-upon rules. In sales to LDCs, some industrial countries often mix development grants with export credits, thus enabling them to conceal very attractive credit terms under a guise of development assistance. A case in point occurred in April 1985 when a Japanese-led consortium won a Turkish contract to build a bridge over the Bosporus with a financial package that included more than $200 million in Japanese-government loans carrying a 5 percent interest rate. By calling the loans foreign aid rather than an export subsidy, Tokyo did not technically violate the OECD credit agreement. Such mixed credits reached $15 billion in 1987. And in May 1990 the Bush administration decided to adopt such a program.

Apart from direct subsidies to promote exports, many governments offer their nationals various production subsidies or aid in research and development. Although it is designed for domestic purposes, it has important trade effects as the subsidized industries compete on the international market. Indeed there is a long-standing dispute between the United States and Europe over the subsidies granted by European governments for the development of their A300 airbus jet aircraft. The Uruguay Round pact imposed limits on such subsidies, if they affect international competitiveness. Because many subsidies are often disguised in form, the WTO's subsidies code has proven ineffective in checking them.

"VOLUNTARY" IMPORT EXPANSION (VIE)

On several occasions the United States has insisted that Japan "voluntarily" expand its import of certain American products, including auto parts, semiconductors, or beef. In some cases the Japanese have responded by increasing the imported share of their domestic market, while in other instances they have agreed to import a certain minimum amount. Such a measure has become known as a **"voluntary" import expansion (VIE),** and has the same effect as a U.S. export subsidy in expanding the export of the commodity to which it applies. However, whereas an export subsidy worsens the U.S. terms of trade, a Japanese VIE (designed to expand U.S. exports to Japan) improves them.[15] Also, a Japanese VIE may favor U.S. exports to Japan at the expense of other exporting countries.

A VIE thus causes a departure from free-trade equilibrium. However, it is sometimes argued that the VIEs are designed to offset Japanese business practices that exclude imports, and in so doing they merely restore what would have been free market conditions.

NTBs VERSUS TARIFFS

VERs, import quotas, ICAs, antidumping duties, and other nontariff barriers are viewed as forms of managed trade. They have become increasingly widespread as protectionist pressure intensifies in many countries.[16] As tariff rates come down under WTO negotiations—to an average of 5 percent—countries turn increasingly to NTBs to protect local industries.

Yet tariffs have several advantages over NTBs. First, they only distort the market mechanism, while many NTBs displace it altogether. Second, tariffs are *transparent* in a sense that they are visible to all, and their magnitude is known (especially the *ad valorem* variety). In contrast NTBs are often hidden devices, in a sense that their protective level, effects on domestic prices, and sometimes even their very existence, are hidden. Few people in the United States realize that they pay a multiple of the world price for sugar because of the sugar quota.[17]

A correct way to measure the height of an NTB is to subtract the international from the domestic price, and divide the difference by the international price, thereby obtaining the tariff equivalent of the NTB. But with so many NTBs administered by virtually all countries this is an impractical task. Therefore a fully satisfactory measure of NTBs does not exist.

[15] See E. Dinopoulos and M. E. Kreinin, "An Analysis of Import Expansion Policies," *Economic Inquiry,* January 1990.

[16] For a survey see J. Bhagwati, *Protectionism,* Cambridge: MIT Press, 1990.

[17] For general discussion, see papers by R. Lawrence, W. Cline, and R. Baldwin on "U.S. Trade Policy" in the *American Economic Review,* May 1989: 118–133.

Lacking an ideal measure, international organizations developed a widely used substitute: *the percent of a country's imports covered by NTBs*. But this is a measure of the NTBs' coverage ratio, and not of their protective effect. To see why this is so, assume that automobile imports are subject to VER restrictions in both the United States and France. But the United States limits imports to 20 percent of the domestic market while France limits imports to 3 percent of the market. The measure would show the United States as much more restrictive than France, because a greater proportion of its imports is subject to VERs, while in fact precisely the reverse is true. In the extreme case where a country prohibits all imports of a commodity, no restricted imports would show up in the above measure.

Despite this problem, the measure is widely used because no better alternative is readily available. There now exists an inventory of NTBs for most developed and 80 developing countries. It shows that 17 percent of U.S. imports, 30 percent of EU imports, and 37 percent of Japan's imports were covered by NTBs in 1986.[18] The steady growth of NTBs in recent years offset some of the gains from tariff reductions achieved in multilateral negotiations.

Not only are NTBs more pervasive than tariffs, but they are very difficult to negotiate away. For that reason certain NTBs will be replaced by tariffs (a process known as *tariffication*) which will then be negotiated down.

STRATEGIC TRADE POLICY?

In a perfectly competitive environment, the only possible justifications for trade intervention by the government are the following:

1. Imposition of an optimum tariff on imported goods designed to improve the terms of trade;
2. Infant industry protection, but only if a direct subsidy is not feasible;
3. Possible offset to a domestic distortion, but only when domestic measures are not available.

These reasons have not been considered important enough to justify a departure from the traditional stance favoring free trade.

But recent analysis of trade in *oligopolistic* markets[19] has led to new arguments for trade intervention, known as **strategic trade policy**.[20] The

---

[18] S. Laird and A. Yeats, "Nontariff Barriers of Developed Countries 1966–86," *Finance and Development*, March 1989.

[19] Only a few firms exist in each industry, and barriers to the entry of new firms are formidable.

[20] See P. Krugman, "Is Free Trade Passé?" *Economic Perspectives*, fall 1987: 131–144; R. Baldwin, "Are Economists Traditional Trade Policy Views Still Valid?" *Journal of Economic Literature*, June 1992: 804–820; M. Kreinin, "U.S. Trade and Possible Restrictions in High Technology Products," *Journal of Modeling*, spring 1985: 69–105; R. Baldwin and H. Flam, "Strategic Trade Policy in the Market for 30–40 Seat Commuter Aircraft," *Weltwirtschaftliches Archive*, no. 3, 1989. G. Grossman and D. Richardson, "Strategic Trade Policy: A Survey of Issues and Early Analysis," in *Special Papers in International Economics*, Princeton: 1985; A. Dixit, "In Honor of Paul Krugman," *Journal of Economic Perspectives*, spring 1993: 176–183.

distinguishing characteristic of oligopolies is the existence and persistence of *oligopoly profits.* A strategic trade policy consists of government measures that would increase the global market share of "our" firms at the expense of "foreign" firms, and thereby raise the proportion of global oligopoly profits captured by "our" firms. This is particularly true in industries such as aircraft production, where only two or three firms can be sustained by the world market. When large initial outlays on plant and equipment or research and development (R&D) are required, then marginal cost declines as output expands and the initial outlay is spread over larger output. That limits the number of firms in the industry. A strong learning-by-doing effect could lead to the same result. In such cases, the government can offer support to "our" firms, say in the form of an export subsidy, so as to drive foreign competitors out of business, and leave the global market in the hands of "our" firm. Conversely, in dealing with an imported product, tariff protection offered to "our" import-competing oligopolies can increase their share in the global markets. In such situations trade intervention can increase national welfare. We will consider each of these cases in turn.

Subsidy Case Assume that two companies, Boeing (United States) and Airbus (Europe), are in the process of deciding whether to build a new aircraft. If either one of the firms goes ahead *alone,* it would realize a profit of $100 million. But if *both* firms proceed, each would lose $5 million. Now suppose that the U.S. government announces a credible commitment to subsidize Boeing to the tune of $10 million. Then Boeing is assured of a profit of $5 million even if Airbus goes ahead; it will proceed. But Airbus will *not* go ahead under these circumstances because it is certain that Boeing will build the aircraft, and hence it is sure to lose. Boeing's profit would then be $110 million ($100 plus the subsidy of $10), and it can easily repay the subsidy. Under a simplified assumption that each company produces entirely for export, a subsidy of $10 million enables Boeing to transfer $100 million of **monopoly rents** from Europe to the United States.

This illustration explains why nations pursue subsidies, even though traditional theory shows subsidies to be harmful under perfect competition.

Protection Case In another example consider an industry with two firms, one American and one Japanese. Assume that learning-by-doing and increasing returns to scale reduce production costs as output expands. Japan employs protective measures to close its domestic market, while the American market remains open. This enables the Japanese firm to expand output, lower production costs, and drive the American company out of business. The monopoly rents that the American company extracted from the U.S. consumers now pass to the Japanese firm.

Problems Although the above policies may appear attractive in theory, their execution is riddled with the following practical problems:

1. Governments lack information on which to base policy decisions. In the above subsidy case, the government needs to know how much profit would be earned from the new aircraft with and without competition from abroad. Such data are usually unavailable.
2. Subsidizing Boeing would lead to an expansion of aircraft output in the United States, thus removing specialized factors (such as engineers) from another industry—for instance, computers. Rents gained by the aircraft industry could then be lost by the computer industry.
3. In reality, the global market often can sustain more than two producers in a given industry. In that case, competition would eliminate the rents that the policy is designed to capture. In general, it is not clear how much oligopoly rents exist and persist in the global marketplace. The cost of the subsidy to the government, or the cost of protection to the consumers, may exceed the gain in rents.
4. An export subsidy may induce more domestic firms to enter the industry, and that can result in lower efficiency and higher average cost. Thus the benefits from rent shifting may be offset by increased production costs.
5. Foreign retaliation may nullify any gain from either protection or subsidies.

For these reasons economists shy away from recommending a strategic trade policy. Free trade remains the preferred option. Indeed, *trade liberalization in imperfectly competitive markets is often shown to be more welfare-enhancing than liberalization under perfect competition,* because it reduces the monopoly power of the firms and lowers prices (by reducing the markup of prices over marginal cost). For the same reason there is a stronger presumption that a customs union would be more welfare-enhancing under imperfectly competitive markets than under perfect competition.

Summary

This chapter examines a number of nontariff barriers (NTBs) to trade. Some of them, such as voluntary export restraints (VERs), have become common in recent years, but have proven to be more harmful than tariffs.

Import quotas and VERs, which are also known as quantitative restrictions, set an absolute limit on the quantity of a commodity that may enter the country. Because they limit the quantity of a good available on the domestic market, they raise its domestic price above the foreign price in much the same way as a tariff. With stationary demand and supply, and under perfect competition, the main difference between a quota and a tariff are the recipients of the quota rents: the government in the case of a tariff and the importers in the case of a quota. But when demand for the commodity rises, as is common in a growing economy, a quota is more harmful, since the welfare loss triangles that it generates are larger than those of a tariff. Similarly, when the domestic producer is a monopolist, a quota inflicts greater damage, because it does not limit his monopoly power nearly as much as a tariff.

Quotas are administered by the issuing of import licenses. Because these licenses are relatively scarce, they command a market value that is the difference between the domestic and the foreign price. The tariff equivalent of quantitative restrictions is measured as the percentage increase in the domestic over the foreign price.

Partly because quotas are illegal under the WTO, and partly to avoid retaliation, countries resort to using voluntary export restraints (VERs). Under a VER, an exporting country undertakes to limit exports of a commodity to an importing country, and the exporters tend to collect the rents. VERs tend to be discriminatory, because some supplying countries invariably remain unrestrained. All VERs are negotiated outside the framework of the WTO and are scheduled to be phased out.

While a main reason for imposing quotas or VERs is to save jobs in importing-competing industries, estimates show that the cost per job saved is usually a multiple of the average wages in the industry.

An international commodity agreement (ICA) is an organization of producing and consuming countries of a certain commodity, designed to restrict trade or limit price fluctuations. With the exception of textiles, ICAs apply to primary commodities (raw materials and agricultural goods). A common type of an ICA is a buffer stock, which keeps price fluctuations within prescribed limits by purchases or sales from central stocks for a particular commodity. This is done when there is either respectively, excess supply at the floor price or excess demand at the ceiling price. In general, ICAs are beset with problems and tend to break down.

There is an ICA in cotton, woolen, and synthetic textiles, known as the Multifibre Arrangement (MFA). This sets limits on the quantity that each exporting country may ship to each importing country. It is expected to be phased out by the year 2005.

An international cartel is an organization of producers in different countries or a group of governments that is designed to restrict supply of a commodity, raise its price, allocate markets, or in other ways interfere with competitive market forces. OPEC, which attempts to control the global price of oil, is the most widely known cartel. The ability of the cartel to raise prices is usually restrained by the availability of substitute products, and by the divergent interests of its members.

Several countries require foreign manufacturers to meet minimum local content standards in order to sell in its domestic market. A myriad of other rules and regulations are imposed by national governments that restrict the free flow of trade.

A bone of contention between the United States and Europe is the WTO-sanctioned border tax adjustment for domestic indirect taxes. A country levying a national sales tax or a value-added tax (VAT) may rebate these taxes to exporters and impose an import levy equivalent to the domestic tax. Such a border tax adjustment does not apply to direct taxes, such as the personal income tax or the corporate profit tax. VATs are common in Europe, while direct taxes are the mainstay of U.S. government revenue.

The sale of a product in a foreign market at a lower price than that charged in the country's home market is known as *dumping*. While consumers in the "dumped" country benefit, producers complain of unfair competition. If they can prove dumping as well as injury to the domestic industry, the country can levy an antidumping duty that equals the price differential. Predatory dumping, designed to drive foreign competition out of business and then raise the price in that country, is the most harmful type of dumping. Long-run dumping often arises when a monopolist faces competition only in the foreign market, resulting in a more elastic demand curve than in the home market. The monopolist therefore counters by charging a lower price in the foreign—more competitive—market. Antidumping duties are often a form of protection.

Two policies designed to expand exports are export subsidies and "voluntary" import expansion (VIEs). Under an export subsidy, the exporter receives a grant from the government for each unit exported. It results in a deadweight welfare loss plus a decline in the terms of trade of the subsidizing country. Such subsidies are outlawed by the WTO, and the country receiving the subsidized goods may impose countervailing duties on them. But countries can circumvent the WTO prohibition by subsidizing research and development and other activities that are reflected in the export price only indirectly. The Uruguay Round pact set limits on such subsidies. In other instances, governments mix the export subsidy with foreign aid.

"Voluntary" import expansion is an instrument practiced by the United States to induce Japan to increase imports of American products. If successful, it would raise the volume of American exports to Japan without a deterioration in the U.S. terms of trade. However, it can discriminate against third-country suppliers.

Although they are more harmful than tariffs, nontariff barriers are widespread. Short of calculating their tariff equivalent (a difficult task), there is no good way of measuring their effects. All that can be done is to assess their frequency.

While under perfect competition there are few valid reasons for government intervention in trade, oligopolistic markets offer a theoretical argument that revolves around the capture of global monopoly rents. Strategic trade policy suggests cases in which export subsidies or import protection may be useful in increasing "our" firms' share of the global market, and hence "our" share in global profits. But since the implementation of such policies is riddled with immense difficulties, free trade remains the recommended policy.

Important Concepts

Nontariff barriers (NTBs)

Import quotas

Quota rents

Auctioning import licenses

Equivalence of a tariff and a quota

Primary and secondary boycotts (FN3)

Voluntary export restraints (VERs)

Quality upgrading

Cost per job saved

International Commodity Agreements (ICAs)

Export restriction schemes

Buffer stocks

Multilateral contracts

Compensatory financing

Multifibre Agreement

International cartel

Organization of Petroleum Exporting Countries (OPEC)

Minimum deposit requirement

Local content requirement

Indirect taxes

Border tax adjustment

Value-added tax (VAT)

Export rebates

Dumping

Sporadic dumping

Predatory dumping

Persistent dumping

Antidumping import duty

Export subsidy

Countervailing duties

Voluntary Import Expansion (VIE)

Strategic trade policy

Monopoly rents

Tariff Equivalent of NTBs

Review Questions

1. Evaluate the following statements:
   a. As instruments of protection go, a tariff is less harmful to a country than a quota, and a quota is less harmful than a VER.
   b. Protection is an expensive and inefficient way to create jobs.
   c. International commodity agreements constitute the best way of helping LDCs combat the effect of violent price fluctuations (of their exports) on their economies.
   d. The Multifibre Agreement represents an excellent way to organize international trade. We should apply it to steel and other industries.

2. Suppose the U.S. steel industry is seeking protection from foreign imports. Compare and contrast (in terms of equivalence and related topics) the following measures of restricting steel imports: (a) a tariff, (b) a quota, and (c) voluntary export restraints. Use graphs as needed.

3. Explain how the tin buffer stock (ICA) functioned. What are some possible reasons for its collapse in 1986?

4. Explain these terms:
   a. Border tax adjustments
   b. Quality upgrading
   c. International cartel
   d. OPEC
   e. Export-credit subsidy

5. a. Define dumping and explain the three types of dumping.
   b. Show diagrammatically how persistent dumping may arise. Is this analysis equivalent to that of domestic price discrimination?
   c. What conditions are required for dumping to exist?
   d. What would an industry have to demonstrate in order to obtain protection from dumping? What form of protection is available? Give examples of industries that have sought protection from dumping.

6. What were the main effects of the U.S.–Japan Auto VER on the American economy?

7. Is import protection a good way to save jobs? Why or why not?

8. What are local content requirements?

9. Distinguish between antidumping and countervailing duties. What is diversionary import dumping?

10. a. Analyze the welfare effect of an export subsidy on the subsidizing country. What are its effects on the importing country?
    b. Contrast the effects of a subsidy and a tariff on the terms of trade.
    c. How can a subsidy be hidden behind economic aid?

11. What is the coverage ratio of NTBs? Is it a good measure of their protective effects? Why or why not? What is "tariffication" of NTBs?

12. Define voluntary import expansion (VIE).

13. What is meant by strategic trade policy? What are its limitations? How can export subsidies bring about an increase in the share of global profits obtained by "our" firms?

Chapter 5 Appendix

A DOMESTIC MONOPOLIST UNDER A TARIFF AND A QUOTA

This appendix formally demonstrates the proposition that when domestic production is carried on by a monopolist, a tariff would curtail the monopoly power by more than an "equivalent" quota—a quota that allows the same volume of imports as under the tariff. In Figure A5.1.1, assume that domestic demand is represented by the colored average revenue curve *AR*, yielding marginal revenue *MR* (drawn in shaded color) and that the monopolist's marginal cost is represented by *MC* (drawn in black). In the absence of international trade, the quantity produced and sold domestically is shown by the intersection of *MR* and *MC*, with the resulting price $\overline{0P}_D$.

Assume now that the international price of the commodity is $\overline{0P}$. If the economy is opened up to international trade, with a tariff $\overline{PP}_t$ imposed on the commodity, then the domestic price cannot rise above $\overline{0Pt}$. In fact, the demand curve would then become kinked: $\overline{P_tTT'D}$. Along its flat portion it coincides with the marginal revenue, MR_t. Domestic output would then be $\overline{P_tT}$, where T is the intersection of the *MC* and the MR_t curves, while imports would equal $\overline{TT'}$, *all sold at price* $\overline{0P_t}$.

If the import volume under the tariff regime, $\overline{TT'}$, is converted into a quota, then we have a dominant supplier model, under which the monopolist need only accommodate to a fixed amount of imports. Graphically, the market demand curve remains unaffected, but the demand curve facing the monopolist is the colored

FIGURE A5–1.1   *A Monopolist under a Tariff and a Quota*

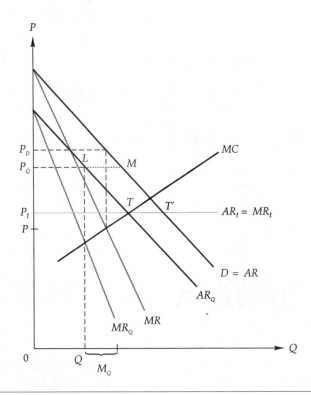

A monopolist protected by a tariff will charge price P_t, the world market price plus the tariff, and the quantity imported will be TT'. In case of an import quota TT', the monopolist's demand curve shifts leftward by that amount, and under profit maximization he would charge price P_Q, higher than P_t.

AR_Q, obtained by shifting the market AR leftward (horizontally) by the amount of the quota. The corresponding marginal revenue curve, MR_Q, is then generated. Domestic output is determined by the intersection of MC and MR_Q,

yielding price $\overline{OP_Q}$. The quantity imported, LM (shown as M_Q on the horizontal axis) is the same as that under a tariff regime ($LM = TT'$), but the price charged, and therefore monopoly profit accruing to the importers, is higher.

U.S. Commercial Policy

A country's commercial policies are measures designed to affect its trade relations with the rest of the world. Historically, the main commercial policy instrument employed by the United States has been the tariff, but in recent years greater reliance has been placed on nontariff barriers. Although in America's early years the tariff was used primarily for raising government revenue, it was later modified to serve the exclusive purpose of protecting domestic industry. Income and profit taxes became the major sources of revenue for the federal government. Because tariff rates have always been determined by Congress, they have reflected a host of political and economic pressures from diverse groups. The result was that the level of the American tariff in the first quarter of this century was high, reaching a peak in 1932 owing to the Smoot-Hawley Act of 1930. Indeed, the Smoot-Hawley tariff caused retaliation by other countries, and contributed to the spread of the Great Depression. The U.S. tariff schedule was a long, complicated, and cumbersome document. However, in the mid-1930s the administration sought and obtained legislation for a gradual reduction in tariff rates subject to limits prescribed by Congress. And in the period following World War II this legislation enabled the United States to be the moving force behind a 40-year trend of international trade liberalization under the General Agreement on Tariffs and Trade (GATT). The policies embodied in the trade legislation are reviewed in this chapter.

THE RECIPROCAL TRADE AGREEMENTS LEGISLATION

Since 1934 the cornerstone of American commercial policy has been the **Reciprocal Trade Agreements Act,** and it has been continued through a dozen periodic extensions. American participation in the GATT's (now the WTO) tariff negotiations is sanctioned by this legislation, as is the extent of duty reduction permissible at any one round of bargaining.

Two main lines of thought thread through the successive extensions of the reciprocal trade legislation, although their relative importance has varied from one extension to the next. On the one hand, the legislation has permitted continual, though limited, tariff reductions on U.S. imports. Since 1945, such reductions have been negotiated within the multilateral framework of the GATT, subject to the Unconditional Most Favored Nation Principle (nondiscrimination). On the other hand, most extensions of the law embody measures to "safeguard" the interest of domestic industry. This no-injury philosophy has found expression in the escape clause and national security provisions of the act.

To economists, the no-injury approach is clearly inconsistent with the general spirit of the reciprocal trade legislation. They regard tariff reduction first and foremost as a means to improve economic efficiency through increased international specialization. A larger volume of trade is expected to drive domestic resources away from relatively inefficient import-competing industries into industries that have competitive advantage. A similar process would take place abroad with the obvious result of increased efficiency all around. The safeguard provisions constitute a mechanism for preventing such shifts of resources. By protecting industries from import competition, they perpetuate allocative inefficiency and are therefore in direct conflict with what the act first set out to accomplish. We reduce tariffs and admit larger imports, but the instant such imports begin to have the beneficial effect of driving resources out of inefficient uses, we reverse course. This view of the main purpose of the tariff-reduction program is not shared by many legislators and public officials. In these circles the program has been historically regarded as primarily a means of expanding American exports and strengthening the Western Alliance.

The Trade Agreements Act was first proposed by the Roosevelt administration in 1934 as an antidepression measure designed to open up new export markets for American products. The offer of reciprocal tariff concessions was not an end in itself; it was meant to induce foreign countries to open their markets to American products. This view was superseded in the postwar period by a political objective. The program has come to be regarded as a means of strengthening the economies of friendly nations by opening the American market to some of their products. The dollar shortage after 1945 contributed considerably to this objective. Under these objectives, there exists no real inconsistency between extensive tariff reduction on the one hand and the prevention of injury to domestic interests on the other. If the U.S. goals are to open new export markets and cement the Western Alliance, why not attain them at the least cost in terms of displacement of domestic production?

The 1958 Extension and the Safeguard Provisions

This dual objective of tariff reduction and the prevention of injury has been the major trend in reciprocal trade legislation since 1954. The extensions of the act in 1955 and 1958 contain liberal provisions for tariff reduction. In 1958 Congress authorized the president to offer tariff concessions of up to 20 percent, to be spread evenly over four years. It was under this authority that the so-called Dillon Round was negotiated in the GATT in 1961. Because the United States is the only major country that requires legislative approval prior to entering into trade negotiations, the legislative mandate for tariff reduction becomes the framework for such negotiations. No country would offer greater concessions than the American delegation is authorized to offer.

At the same time Congress strengthened the protection to domestic interests against import competition. If, after a concession is granted, a domestic industry feels injured by import competition, it can apply for relief under the **escape clause.** A determination by the International Trade Commission of positive injury may lead to withdrawal of the concession if the president concurs with the Commission's recommendation. The escape clause is recognized in the WTO as a legitimate method of protecting domestic interests, and most trading nations find recourse to it when a domestic industry is threatened by severe import competition. Import restrictions can be reintroduced in such cases. But the country must then compensate its trading partners with liberalization of imports on some other products. In recent years, industries seeking relief from import competition have relied on the antidumping and countervailing duty provisions, rather than the escape clause.

A second avenue of relief is the **national security clause,** which permits withdrawal of concessions in cases where the affected domestic industry is essential to national security. In 1986 the administration negotiated, with Japan and Taiwan, a VER on machine tool exports to the United States, because such high-technology tools are used in manufacturing weapons.

It is reasonable to assume that in the early postwar period many concessions merely constituted reductions in **excess protection,** or protection over and above the prohibitive tariff rate (the rate necessary to keep out all imports). This is also known as "water in the tariff." But toward the end of the 1950s the no-injury provisions were becoming increasingly incompatible with the main objective of the legislation, even for those who viewed the program strictly as a tool of foreign policy. The concessions granted by the United States during the previous generation had more than halved the level of the tariff, a reduction that practically eliminated all the excess protection in the tariff structure. It was no longer possible to grant many concessions without inflicting injury on domestic industries by simply curtailing the amount of **"water" in the tariff.** From then on, any significant amount of further trade liberalization was likely to be injurious to domestic interests. To deal with this problem, economists have long advocated special provisions for adjustment assistance.

Trade-Adjustment Assistance

Given an adequate growth rate, the resources displaced by increased imports can shift to industries in which the United States enjoys comparative advantage. But this process takes time. In the short run, a number of workers, firms, and communities might be hurt. In a society that assumes responsibility for the economic well-being of its members, such an impact of public policy cannot be overlooked.

Legislators and public officials interested in continuing the program began to recognize the need for finding an acceptable substitute for tariff relief under the escape clause. If most Americans stood to benefit from the increased efficiency resulting from trade liberalization, a way had to be found to compensate those who would incur the short-run losses caused by displaced domestic production. Thus, support gathered behind a program for **trade-adjustment assistance (TAA).**

Instead of protecting import-competing industries by the escape clause and thus perpetuating inefficiency, why not promote their transfer to lines of production in which they can compete effectively? The government could facilitate such movements of resources by means of a program designed to aid those who are injured by import competition. Under this program, whenever Trade Commission investigations revealed that an industry had been injured by import competition generated by a previous tariff concession, its recommendation would not have to be limited to tariff relief. Instead, it could recommend direct assistance.

THE 1962 TRADE EXPANSION ACT

A trade-adjustment program was legislated for the first time by the Trade Expansion Act of 1962. Indeed, this was one of several drastic departures from the earlier reciprocal trade legislation. Under this program, workers unemployed as a result of tariff concessions could obtain extended unemployment compensation and retraining allowances. Eligible firms could obtain technical and managerial assistance to help find new market outlets or develop new products; long-term, low-interest loans; and some minor tax relief.

Under the act, the president was permitted to cut duties by up to 50 percent of their July 1962 level and to remove altogether duties that did not exceed 5 percent on that date. Also subject to removal were duties on agricultural commodities from the temperate and tropical zones. Tariff negotiations were to be conducted *on broad categories rather than on a product-by-product basis.*

It was under the authority of this legislation that the United States participated in the Kennedy Round of the GATT negotiations (1962–1967). What finally emerged from the five years of laborious bargaining was an average reduction of 35 percent in industrial tariff rates. These reductions took effect gradually over the 1967–1972 period.

THE TRADE REFORM ACT OF 1974

In 1974 Congress passed the Trade Reform Act, giving the administration new authority to reduce tariffs by 60 percent of their post–Kennedy-Round level and to eliminate tariffs of 5 percent or less as a part of trade agreements with other countries. In addition, the president was granted authority to negotiate away nontariff barriers. The Tokyo Round of GATT trade negotiations (1975–1979) was conducted under this authority, leading to tariff cuts averaging 35 percent, staged over 1980–1988.

Escape-clause relief continued to be available to domestic industries, in which import relief can take several forms: an increase in duty; imposition of a tariff on a duty-free item; suspension of the special treatment under the offshore assembly provisions[1] of the tariff schedule; negotiation of orderly marketing arrangements with foreign countries (that is, VERs); quantitative restrictions (which, however, must allow imports of no less than the quantity imported in a recent representative period); or any combination of the above. In the case where import restrictions are imposed, the president is authorized to negotiate compensatory concessions with foreign countries.

An alternative avenue of relief is available to groups of *workers* hurt by import competition—they may apply to the secretary of labor for adjustment assistance. Qualifying workers are eligible for supplementary unemployment compensation, retraining services, job search allowance, and relocation allowance. Adjustment assistance to eligible *firms* may take the form of loans or loan guarantees. Finally, adjustment assistance is also available to trade-impacted communities.

Until the mid-1970s the Trade Adjustment Assistance (TAA) program was hardly utilized. But the eased eligibility criteria in the 1974 act, coupled with the increased responsibility of the Labor Department in administering the program, has changed that. In the second half of the 1970s decade, one-half million workers received TAA funds. But only a small proportion of these workers participated in retraining, relocation, and related programs. Most of the money was spent on income maintenance as a supplement to the unemployment benefits. Instead of being retrained for new jobs, many laid-off workers in industries such as autos, apparel, and steel merely waited to be recalled to their old jobs while receiving generous TAA benefits. This use of the funds constitutes a disincentive to retraining and relocation. It is certainly

---

[1] These provisions in the U.S. tariff code allow the reimportation to the United States of semifinished products manufactured abroad out of parts exported from the United States, with duty charged only on that part of the value of the imported product that has been added abroad. As a result, thousands of processing plants have been set up by American corporations in such countries as Mexico and Taiwan; thus, suspension of these provisions could harm certain developing countries.

inconsistent with the intent of the TAA legislation. This is one reason the TAA program was sharply curtailed in the Reagan budget cuts of the 1980s. From a 1980 peak of $1.6 billion disbursed to 532,000 affected workers, the program shrunk by 1984 to $52 million, benefiting merely 16,000 workers. The Clinton administration subsequently restored funds for the TAA program.

The antidumping regulations were changed by the 1974 act to conform to the GATT's rule, which requires in addition to a finding of price discrimination, a determination of injury to domestic producers before countervailing duties can be imposed. On the other hand, the act gave the president authority to impose any type of import restrictions against countries employing unfair import restrictions on American products or those paying export subsidies, including subsidies of foreign supplies to third markets that displace American exports. Articles that infringe a U.S. patent would be excluded from entry into the United States. Since the 1980s the main type of protection sought by the American firms was antidumping and countervailing duties rather than the escape clause.

Finally, the act offers a **Generalized System of Preferences (GSP)** to the developing countries. It granted duty-free entry to the exports of manufactures, semimanufactures, and selected other products from developing countries and territories. The purpose of this program, which is similar to one introduced by other industrial nations, is to help promote the exports and economic development of developing countries (see Chapter 8).

There followed two pieces of legislation, in 1982 and 1984. The first encouraged the establishment of export-trading companies, common in other countries. It allows groups of companies and banks to join forces for the purpose of selling abroad, without fear of antitrust action. The second act authorized the president to negotiate reduction or elimination of barriers to trade in services, trade in high-technology products, and direct foreign investment and enhanced protection of intellectual property rights. It also extended the U.S. GSP, but with explicit provisions for "graduation," namely removal of GSP benefits of products in which beneficiary countries have achieved a sufficient degree of competitiveness.

It was under the provisions of this legislation that the U.S. administration entered a new round of GATT trade negotiations, known as the Uruguay Round, in 1986.

THE OMNIBUS TRADE AND COMPETITIVENESS ACT OF 1988

After three years of laborious work, a rather complex bill was enacted and signed into law. It includes both liberalizing and restrictive provisions.

On the liberal side the act grants authority to the administration to participate in the Uruguay Round where it may slash tariff rates by 50 percent. More directly, the act reduces or eliminates U.S. duties on dozens of products for which there is no U.S. source of supply. The act also authorizes a $980 million new program for retraining displaced workers and expands existing programs to help workers adjust to imports. Finally, industries that can currently qualify for import relief merely by showing serious injury from imports would be required to demonstrate that they are prepared to make "positive adjustment" to import competition to win import relief.

On the restrictive side, the most controversial item is the so-called **301 provision.** It requires the administration to list publicly countries that trade unfairly with the United States, negotiate removal of such practices within three years, and take retaliatory action if the negotiations fail. The first such listing was published in May 1989, designating Japan, India, and Brazil for unfair trading practices in specific industries. The ensuing negotiations with Japan covered a wide range of structural impediments to trade, such as wholesale and retail distribution systems in Japan (that tend to keep out imports), savings and investment patterns, pricing mechanisms, business behavior,[2] and bid-rigging. Japan was dropped from the list of unfair traders in May 1990, following an agreement with the United States concerning satellites, supercomputers, and lumber products. In 1996 China was cited for failing to protect intellectual property rights.

In the case of dumping, the act establishes as a U.S. negotiating goal in trade talks the banning of "diversionary input dumping"—cases in which finished products imported into the United States include materials that were dumped in the country where the finished goods were made.

Thirdly, the president is directed to act against countries that permit piracy of U.S. intellectual property. The administration must identify countries that do not protect copyrights and patents and initiate expedited unfair trade investigations. Also, holders of patents on processes by which products are made (as in the biotechnology and pharmaceutical industries) will be allowed to sue U.S. importers on any products that use their patented processes in a foreign country where the patents are not protected. Holders of patents need not prove injury in order to obtain government orders banning imports of products that infringe their patents.

Next, the president is required to negotiate with foreign countries to win greater access to their markets for U.S. makers of telecommunications equipment. The provision directs the president to use the threat of denying foreign companies access to the U.S. telecommunications market as leverage if their respective governments do not reduce barriers to U.S. companies. A lingering dispute between the United States and the EU relates to the impaired access of American companies to the European market for telecommunication equipment.

Finally, the act allows actions against unfair multinational subsidies to international consortia such as Airbus Industrie, a major competitor of Boeing Company, in commercial aircraft. Previously, U.S. companies could seek relief

---

[2] It is often suggested that Japanese companies tend to rely on old-time business contacts in awarding contracts, rather than opening their purchases to international competitive bids according to the custom of the United States and Europe.

from unfair trade practices when their competition was subsidized by just one country, but not when the subsidies were coming from several foreign nations.

Apart from the above provisions, the act allocates $2.5 billion for boosting exports of farm products (aimed mainly to counter EU agricultural subsidies); permits the president, in certain circumstances, to block foreign takeovers if there is evidence that they would impair national security; and gives a legal mandate for the U.S. policy of coordinating economic policies and exchange-rate strategies with other major nations.

REGIONAL AND BILATERAL RELATIONS

For most of the postwar period, U.S. policy relied on the multilateral approach, subject to the MFN rule. Apart from an FTA with Israel and the Caribbean initiative, the U.S. rejected regional arrangements for itself (although it supported them in Europe and elsewhere) and adhered to a nondiscriminatory policy. But by the 1980s this framework evolved into what might be called a tri-foci approach: multilateralism, regionalism, and bilateral relations. The WTO remains an important focus. But it is no longer an exclusive focus, and sometimes it is even overridden by the two alternative foci.

Regionalism The United States no longer eschews the regional approach. Partly as a response to the proliferation of regional arrangements around the globe (45 percent of world trade is now conducted within 33 regional groupings), and partly because of its own perceived commercial interests, the United States has entered upon a free trade agreement with Canada, established NAFTA, and is contemplating its possible extension to other countries. Overlapping proposals (for the next century) are being bandied about for an FTA of the Americas, for an FTA in Asia, and for an FTA with Europe. Of course if a legion of FTAs are linked together, a multilateral trading system may yet emerge.

Bilateral Relations Disputes, negotiations, and dispute settlements with individual countries or regions, such as the EU, Japan, China, Korea, Mexico, and even Canada, abound. They will be discussed in the next chapter.

THE POLITICAL ECONOMY OF PROTECTIONISM

In their 1985 summit communique, the heads of state of the seven largest industrial countries[3] stated: "Protection does not solve problems, it only creates problems." Why then is protectionism so widespread? As in other areas of national concern, commercial policies represent neither a majority

---

[3] The U.S., U.K., Germany, France, Japan, Canada, and Italy.

vote nor the reasoned opinions of a single decision maker. They are a product of pressure groups vying for the attention of legislators and policymakers.

The **political economy of protectionism** explains why protection from foreign competition is so common. First of all, there is a strong lobbying incentive for groups that gain from protection, and a lack of such incentive for groups that stand to lose from protection. Any specific trade restriction inflicts damage on the community as a whole, and confers benefits on a few small groups. But although the total loss to society exceeds the benefits to the gaining groups (and thus there is a net loss), the losses from protection are diffused, whereas the gains are concentrated. A restriction on the entry of a foreign product, such as textiles, reduces the quantity supplied and hence raises the product's price. The main loser from such action is the consumer, who must pay the higher price. Thus the loss is diffused over 250 million consumers, each paying a slightly higher price. Similarly, the U.S. sugar quota raises sugar prices (as well as the prices of goods made with sugar) by a few cents per pound, barely noticeable to the average buyer. Furthermore, in many cases consumers are not even aware of the relation between the price hike and protection. Consequently, they have little incentive to oppose the protective measure.

But the gains from protection are not diffused. Producers and workers in the protected industry, partly freed from the pressure of foreign competition, are able to charge a higher price for their product (such as domestic textiles). The benefits are heavily concentrated in the domestic manufacturers and labor unions of the particular industry, and the gains realized by each individual are sizable and visible. Hence the gainers, as a group, have an intense interest in the outcome. They are willing to engage in intense lobbying efforts and to expend large sums of money to assure a legislative outcome favorable to them.

This distribution of losses and benefits, and hence the interest of various political constituencies, explains why the pressure for protectionism is so great. There is a fundamental imbalance in the process of making trade policy; the advocates of protectionism start with a built-in advantage.

In recent years economists have developed models designed to study the *structure* of protection; namely to explain why some industries are accorded high and others low protection.[4] Several partly conflicting hypotheses

---

[4] For a sample of this literature, see R. E. Baldwin, "The Political Economy of Trade Policy," *Journal of Economic Perspectives,* fall 1989; R. E. Baldwin, *The Political Economy of U.S. Import Policy,* Cambridge: MIT Press, 1985; R. Stern, *U.S. Trade Policies in a Changing World,* Cambridge: MIT Press, 1987; W. A. Brock and S. P. Magee, "The Economics of Special Interest Politics: The Case of the Tariff," *American Economic Review,* Papers and Proceedings, 1978: 246–250; R. E. Caves, "Economic Models of Political Choice: Canada's Tariff Structure," *Canadian Journal of Economics,* 1976: 278–300; R. Findlay and S. Wellisz, "Endogenous Tariffs, The Political Economy of Trade Restrictions and Welfare," in J. N. Bhagwati, ed., *Import Competition and Response,* Chicago: University of Chicago Press, 1982, 223–243; J. M. Finger, K. H. Hall, and D. P. Nelson, "The Political Economy of Administered Protection," *American Economic Review,* 1982: 452–466; G. K. Helleiner, "The Political Economy of Canada's Tariff Structure: An Alternative Model," *Canadian Journal of Economics,* 1977: 318–326; H. Marvel and E. J. Ray, "The Kennedy Round: Evidence on the Regulation of International Trade in the U.S.," *American Economic Review,* March 1983: 190–197; J. Pincus, "Pressure Groups and the Pattern of Tariffs," *Journal of Political Economy,* August 1975: 752–778.

have emerged. The first one suggests that industries that are economically powerful and that find it easy to organize for a variety of purposes (for example, few firms in the industry), are able to secure high-level protection relative to industries that are not well organized. Conversely, if the product is used as an intermediate input by other industries (not by the final consumer), the ability and willingness of the using industries to exercise countervailing power may diminish the level of protection accorded to the product.

A second approach emphasizes the voting strength of those employed by the industry. It suggests that labor-intensive and geographically decentralized industries are able to secure higher protection than industries employing relatively few workers and much capital. A related hypothesis maintains that the aim of government in negotiating tariff cuts is to minimize labor adjustment costs. Hence protection is high in those industries where many workers are likely to be dismissed as a result of tariff cuts. A third approach claims that the objective of government is to ensure that low-income workers are not hurt by reduction in the level of protection.

Another view holds that protection is relatively high in those industries in which the country has a comparative cost disadvantage. Yet another interpretation centers on international bargaining and suggests that in its trade policy a government attempts to influence the policies of other governments. Hence protection is high on products exported by countries (such as LDCs) that are unwilling to liberalize their own imports. Finally, there exists a view that governments attempt to maintain the *status quo*, so that the protective structure mirrors the situation that existed at some historical period before the advent of large-scale trade liberalization.

Empirical tests undertaken thus far show that industries receiving the greatest protection are those characterized by a large number of workers, a high labor-output ratio, a small number of firms, and a historically high level of protection. Their workers tend to be unskilled and low paid. Because the empirical results are consistent with several of the hypotheses, the tests to date fail to discriminate between the conflicting theories.

INDUSTRIAL POLICY?

Missing from the sequence of legislative actions are provisions for **industrial policy** for the United States. Such a policy is defined as government attempts to encourage resources to move into industries that the government views as important to growth.[5] It is hoped that they would become internationally competitive, and capture world markets. While certain trade policies such as export subsidies and countervailing duties have an effect on resource move-

---

[5] See C. Boonekamp, "Industrial Policies of Industrial Countries," *Finance and Development*, March 1989; and "Industrial Policy," *Business Week*, April 6, 1992.

ment within the country, they do not amount to a policy of targeting potential winners (namely growth industries) and encouraging their development by direct production subsidies, tax preferences, and other means. Japan is alleged to have pursued such a strategy. But the consensus of professional opinion is that while the government may have played the role of catalyst in the development of certain industries, Japan's phenomenal growth was due more to a stable environment, a well-trained and educated labor force, and a high rate of savings and investment, than to targeting of industries.[6]

Of the various arguments heard in the industrial policy debate, the most rational one is the existence of externalities. If firms in the high-technology sector[7] generate new knowledge through research and development but are unable to capture for themselves all the benefit from that knowledge (it spills over to other firms), they would spend less than an optimal amount on R&D. The government should subsidize these firms to encourage and promote R&D expenditures.[8] An example of U.S. government-industry collaboration in high-technology development is *Sematech*. Established in 1988 to develop advanced manufacturing processes for the semiconductor industry, Sematech was financed equally by the government and industry.

But many observers maintain that it is not possible to determine which sectors will grow rapidly in *future* years and thereby identify potential winners; the marketplace does this far better than the government. Japan (as well as Europe) is known to have made costly mistakes in such targeting efforts. Suffice it to mention the European Supersonic Aircraft (the Concorde), which cost over $10 billion in government funds to develop but is now considered to be a commercial failure. Beyond that, governments do not necessarily act in the national interest, especially when making detailed microeconomic interventions. Instead, they are influenced by interest-group pressures. A policy of targeting winners will typically raise the welfare of small, fortunate groups by large amounts, while imposing costs on larger, more diffuse groups, such as the taxpayers. Excessive or misguided intervention may result because the beneficiaries have more knowledge and influence than the losers.

While the Reagan and Bush administrations steered away from industrial policy because it conflicted with their free-market philosophy, the

---

[6] See, for example, P. Trezise, "Industrial Policy Is Not the Major Reason for Japan's Success," *The Brookings Review,* spring 1983.

[7] This sector is usually defined in terms of factor inputs rather than the nature of its output. Thus the U.S. Department of Commerce identifies high-technology industries by the simultaneous presence of two characteristics: (1) above-average level of scientific and engineering skills or, alternatively, high R&D efforts relative to value added, and (2) a rapid rate of technological development. These criteria yield the following list of industries: aircraft and parts, computers and office equipment, electrical equipment and components, optical and medical instruments, drugs and medicines, plastic and synthetic materials, engines and turbines, agricultural chemicals, professional and scientific instruments, and industrial chemicals.

[8] However, part of the benefits from R&D spills over to other countries.

Clinton administration appears to be taking a more pragmatic approach. For example, upon taking office, the administration announced its intention to cooperate with a consortium of the big three U.S. auto companies in developing "a car of the future." Other initiatives might include increased expenditures on technological R&D and infrastructure; funding technological development of private firms; retraining workers and upgrading the quality of the labor force; and linking foreign aid to purchases in the United States.

Summary

U.S. trade policy is codified in the Reciprocal Trade Agreements Act. Its various extensions in the postwar period contain authorizations for the administration to liberalize trade within prescribed limits as well as provisions to safeguard the American industry from increased foreign competition, such as the escape clause and the 301 provision. These extensions of the act mandate American participation in successive rounds of GATT trade negotiations. Indeed, because the United States is the only major participant that requires prior enabling legislation, the authority contained in the act serves as the framework for the negotiations.

Ever since the 1962 Trade Expansion Act, legislation has contained provisions for trade adjustment assistance, although the program was not used extensively during the Reagan and Bush administrations. The 1974 extension offers a Generalized System of Preferences (GSP) to the developing countries. The last extension of the act was in 1988.

The political economy of protectionism helps to explain the prevalence of protectionism and why differential protection is accorded to different industries. The fact that the losses from protection are diffused while the gains are concentrated in the protected industries explains why protectionism is widespread.

Industrial policy, defined as government attempts to encourage resources to move into certain industries, was not practiced extensively in the United States during the 1980s. The Clinton administration, however, is more inclined toward such legislative actions in order to help U.S. industries become internationally competitive and capture world markets.

Important
Concepts

Reciprocal Trade Agreements Act

Safeguard provisions

Escape clause

National security clause

Excess protection ("water" in the tariff)

Trade-adjustment assistance

Offshore assembly provision (see footnote 1)

Generalized System of Preferences (GSP)

301 provision

Political economy of protectionism

Industrial policy

Review
Questions

1. Identify the main provisions of the following legislations:
   a. The Trade Expansion Act of 1962
   b. The Trade Reform Act of 1974
   c. The Omnibus Trade and Competitiveness Act of 1988

2. If protection is inferior to free trade, why do we live in a protection-ridden world? What factors determine the structure of protection?

3. What is industrial policy? Assess its usefulness for the United States.
4. Compare and contrast:
   a. The Offshore Assembly provisions of the U.S. trade legislation (see footnote 1).
   b. The safeguard provisions and trade adjustment assistance.

CHAPTER 7

International and Regional Trade Organizations among Developed Countries

The last fifty years witnessed a gradual liberalization of international trade in industrial products. The United States, through the trade-agreements legislation, has become a driving force behind this process by inducing other countries to offer reciprocal tariff concessions, liberalizing quotas, and removing other restrictions. But the institutional framework for multilateral negotiations has been provided by several international organizations that also have established and policed rules of conduct in trade matters, and provided a strong impetus to the liberalization process. Internationally, they include the General Agreement on Tariffs and Trade (GATT), now the World Trade Organization (WTO), and the United Nations Conference on Trade and Development (UNCTAD). Regionally, they consist of several customs unions and free-trade areas. The main regional organizations of industrial nations are the European Union (EU)[1], and a North American free-trade area encompassing the United States, Canada, and Mexico.

Institutions such as the WTO and EU are concerned primarily with trade matters, in contrast to the IMF and the European Monetary System (EMS), which are, respectively, international and regional organizations dealing with monetary exchange. It is important to recognize, however, that trade and payment restrictions are partly interchangeable in terms of their *effect* on trade flows if not in their intent. For example, a tariff restricts imports by

---

[1]Originally called the European Economic Community (EEC) (also known as the Common Market), its official name has been changed to the European Communities (EC), and in 1993/94 the name European Union (EU) came into use. When discussing its earlier days we refer to it as the EEC, while in current affairs it is called the EC or EU.

raising their prices, while exchange control lowers imports by limiting the amount of foreign currencies available to finance them. Consequently, it is of little value to remove one type of restriction while leaving the other intact. Policymakers, generally recognize that a simultaneous attack on both fronts is necessary. Thus, members of the WTO must belong also to the IMF and must abide by its international currency rules.

This chapter is concerned with the regional and international organizations dealing with trade liberalization. Because proper organization of the material requires certain departures from chronological order, it begins with the regional trade groups and continues with the WTO. Issues of trade and development will be taken up in the next chapter, while international financial organizations will be described in Part Two of the book.

REGIONALISM

At last count there were about 33 regional groupings in the world, involving over 120 countries. These consist of customs unions, free-trade areas, or preferential trading arrangements in Latin America (6), Africa (8), Asia,[2] the Middle East, Oceania,[3] and Eastern Europe.[4] Nearly half of world trade is conducted with regional groupings. The motives for the formation of regional blocks are many and varied, and include the producers' anticipation of trade diversion benefits (with little resistance from consumers); the expectation that a larger market, which facilitates scale economies, will contribute to greater productivity and thus enhance their competitive position; a frustration with the slow progress of global trade liberalization, and perception by some countries that they fail to benefit from the WTO process; the desire to enhance the nations' bargaining power in the WTO, and for LDCs to reduce dependence on the markets of industrial countries; a response to the formation of other trading blocs (domino effect); and the possible hope of moving toward greater political cohesion.

Economists are currently debating the merits of this regional movement. On the one hand, it is argued that many of the groupings divert trade and thus will only frustrate the goal of achieving a truly multilateral trading system in the world. But those who favor the regional approach maintain that it is easier to achieve "deep" liberalization among a small number of

---

[2] The ASEAN group, which includes the Philippines, Malaysia, Indonesia, Singapore, and Thailand, is a preferential trading arrangement and may perhaps lead to an FTA. The Asian-Pacific Economic Cooperation forum (APEC) consists of all the Pacific Rim countries, developed and developing alike. These include the United States, Canada, Japan, China, Australia, Korea, the ASEAN group, and others. They contemplate the possibility of liberalizing trade within this immense region.

[3] Australia–New Zealand free-trade area.

[4] The Central European Free-Trade Area consists of the Czech Republic, Hungary, Poland, and Slovakia. Some of the CIS countries of the former Soviet Union may also form an economic grouping.

countries than multilaterally, and that regional blocs can serve as stepping stones (rather than stumbling blocks) toward reaching multilateral agreements. In any event, it appears that the regional movement is here to stay. Therefore, the WTO will need to ensure that these groupings do not become "inward" looking[5] fortresses.

In what follows we will consider the regional groups in Western Europe and North America.

THE EUROPEAN UNION (EU)

Perhaps the most significant development in international trade matters after World War II was the establishment in 1958 of the European Economic Community (EEC), sometimes referred to as the European Common Market. Founded by the Treaty of Rome (signed in March 1957), it originally included six countries: West Germany, France, Italy, Belgium, the Netherlands, and Luxembourg. On July 1, 1977, the United Kingdom, Denmark, and Ireland acceded to the Community; Greece joined in 1981; Spain and Portugal acceded on January 1, 1986, while Sweden, Finland, and Austria joined in 1995, thereby raising the membership to 15 countries. Certain East European countries may accede in the future. In what follows the name Economic Community (EC) will be used for any pre-1993 reference to the European Union.

The founders of the EEC were motivated by desire for political integration and considered economic union only a vehicle, albeit an important one, to attain that goal. But so far the most meaningful progress there has occurred in the economic sphere.

Forerunners

Several organizations formed for the purpose of promoting economic cooperation in Europe preceded the EEC and in a sense can be considered its forerunners. First, the Organization of European Economic Cooperation (OEEC), encompassing practically all the countries of Western Europe, was established after World War II to coordinate reconstruction plans and channel American aid (under the Marshall Plan) to individual European countries.[6] Headquartered in Paris, this organization was also instrumental in bringing about liberalization of intra-European trade by gradually lifting import quotas. Today, with the United States, Canada, Japan, and Australia added to its

---

[5] For further reading, see N. S. Fieleke, "One Trading World or Many: The Issue of Regional Trading Blocs," *The New England Economic Review*, May/June 1992; and J. D. Melo and A. Panagariya, "The New Regionalism," *Finance and Development*, December 1992.

[6] The American counterpart organization was the Economic Cooperation Administration. After several metamorphoses, it is now the Agency for International Development (AID) and is engaged in economic aid to developing countries.

membership roster, the organization is called the **Organization for Economic Cooperation and Development (OECD)** and is essentially a coordinative and consultative agency of the industrial nations.

A more direct forerunner of the EEC, and one that eventually merged with it, is the European Coal and Steel Community, established in 1951. Encompassing the original six EEC countries, it abolished trade restrictions and set up a common market for coal and steel products. In addition, an organization called Euratom provided for cooperation among the same countries in the development of atomic energy for peaceful uses. Finally, mention may be made of the three-nation customs union made up of the Benelux countries,[7] which became part of the EEC.

Perhaps the final push toward integration was given by the realities of international politics, which dictated the need for bigness in international affairs if a country was not to become a second-rate power compared to Russia and the United States. To many Europeans, this meant regional integration.

Trade Restrictions

The EU is first of all a customs union; the member countries abolished all tariffs and other trade restrictions among themselves and set up a common and uniform tariff against outsiders. Thus, West German producers have free access to the French market (and vice versa), whereas Japanese and American producers must pay the common external tariff (CET) and in this sense are discriminated against. It is a requirement of the WTO that the CET not be more restrictive than the pre-union average tariff of the constituent countries. In the case of most industrial products, the CET is the unweighted average of the tariff rates that existed in the constituent countries before integration. An incidental result of this averaging process is that EU tariff rates tend to concentrate around their overall average, with little dispersion among commodities. The EU has agreements for a free-trade area with other European countries so that free trade in manufactures prevails throughout Western Europe. This arrangement is known as the **European Economic Area (EEA).** However, the EU also imposes a variety of nontariff barriers (such as VERs) on selective imports from Japan and other East Asian countries.

An important feature of the European Union is that a special fund was set up with the contributions of member countries to help accelerate development in the more backward areas of the EU. This aspect of the organization is known as *regional policy*. In addition, a whole array of rules was promulgated to assure competitive behavior in enterprises within the Communities and to prevent the development of cartels. And the EU is becoming increasingly assertive in the areas of industrial policy and investment regulations.

[7] Belgium, the Netherlands, and Luxembourg.

Agricultural Policy

Internal free trade was established for all products, industrial and agricultural alike. But because all the member countries support their agricultural sectors, they needed to develop common farm policies and impose tight and rather unusual import restrictions on many farm products. Not only are the governments directly involved in supporting agriculture, but the farm interests in each country are both deeply entrenched and politically powerful.

This political influence resulted in the **Common Agricultural Policy (CAP) of the EU** that consumes over one-half of the $115 billion Union's budget.[8] It has three interrelated components: price support, import control, and export subsidies. (a) The price support program ensures that the prices prevailing in the EU are well above market equilibrium, thereby raising the income of farmers to much higher levels than free markets would generate. Each year members of the Union agree on the price that they aim to maintain in the major consuming areas (main population centers), known as the *target price*. The EU maintains the price above market equilibrium by buying and storing the generated surpluses. (b) Severe import restrictions are imposed, designed to ensure that imports do not enter at a price lower than the target price, thereby preventing the EU from having to support the global prices. (c) Export subsidies enable the EU to unload the surpluses, accumulated by the price support, on world markets.

Although the EU may impose countervailing duties to prevent the importation of subsidized farm products, it subsidizes its own farm exports. For example, high support prices for meat, cheese, milk, and butter encourage production and discourage consumption of these products. The resulting surpluses—referred to as "milk lakes" in the case of milk—are often exported at world market prices that are far lower than the EU prices, much to the dismay of American farmers who lose foreign markets as a result. This is a clear export subsidy, consisting of the difference between the domestic support price and the world market (or export) price. The U.S. government often counters this practice with a subsidy to American farm exports or by other means.[9] The level of European subsidies was reduced as a result of the Uruguay Round.

In sum, the CAP has turned Europe from a net importer to a net exporter of food, at a great cost to European consumers and to the Union's budget. The EU lost an average of 1 percent of its GDP annually because of the CAP. And the policy brings the EU into direct conflict with other food

[8] EU revenues come from the customs duties on imports, and, by far the most important, a share of the domestic value-added tax (VAT) collected by EU member states.

[9] The 1985 "pasta war" is an example of U.S.–EU farm tensions. In response to preferential treatment given by the EU to Mediterranean (over American) citrus, the U.S. government imposed a prohibitive duty on European pasta. The EU then retaliated by increasing tariffs on imported U.S. lemons and walnuts. Other cases of mutual retaliation were in evidence in 1986 and 1989.

exporters, such as the United States, Australia, and Canada, because it artificially reduces their farm exports to Europe as well as to third markets. In the early 1990s Australia was caught in the crossfire of a subsidy war between the United States and the EU that was originally designed to capture China's market for grains. Traditionally this was an Australian market, and parts of it were lost to the United States because of subsidized shipments.

EU 1992—A Unified Market

On January 1, 1993, the EU moved further toward integration by adopting rules to ensure complete freedom of movement for goods, services, capital, and labor within the Communities.[10] Some of its provisions are considered below.

All *border checkpoints* for goods moving within the EU would be eliminated in the 1990s, shortening the time that loaded trucks take to move across national boundaries. One by-product of this change is that national quotas restricting imports from nonmember countries have to be replaced by EU-wide quotas. In the important case of Japanese cars, where pre-1992 regulations varied greatly between member countries, the Japanese have now agreed to limit shipments from Japan to 1.23 million cars per year, and to restrict sales out of their European transplants to 1.2 million cars annually. This VER is supposed to be phased out by the year 2000.

Technical standards with respect to health, safety, consumer protection, and the environment became common throughout the EU. *Rules of competition* within the Communities were strengthened, and airline regulations liberalized. *Public procurement* contracts of member governments, which amount to 10 percent of the Communities' GDP, were made open for bidding by firms throughout the EU. *University degrees* and professional diplomas acquired in each member state are recognized throughout the EU. National *insurance* regulations were reduced and unified, and large firms can now insure "big risks" with any insurance company throughout the EU.

Licensed *banks* within an EU country can now open branches and offer banking services in all member states. This last provision originally contained a **reciprocity** clause regarding non-EU banks: Before a non-EU bank is granted a license to operate across the Communities, the Commission will check to see whether all EU countries have equal access to the home-country market of the bank in question. Although this principle seems "fair,"

---

[10] For discussion, see the EC Commission, *The European Economy*, no. 35, March 1988 (issue devoted to "The Economics of 1992"); S. J. Key, "Financial Integration in the European Community," Federal Reserve Board *discussion paper* no. 349, April 1989; U.S. International Trade Commission, "The Effects of Greater Economic Integration within the EC on the U.S.," July 1989; M. E. Kreinin, "EC–1992 and World Trade and the Trading System," in proceedings of a 1989 Colloquium: *1992, Europe and America*, G. N. Yannopoulos (ed.), Manchester University Press, 1990; H. Flam, "Product Markets and 1992: Full Integration, Large Gains," *Journal of Economic Perspectives*, fall 1992; and papers on European Integration in *American Economic Review*, Papers and Proceedings, May 1992, 88–108.

it is difficult to apply in practice. Many countries have significantly different financial structures and different laws separating banking and securities' trade (such as the United States and Japan), and regional limitations on banking (such as the United States). For these reasons, a more acceptable alternative to reciprocity is **national treatment**. *Reciprocity would require non-EU countries, such as the United States, to treat EU firms in the same manner as the EU treats American firms. National treatment would require the United States to treat EU firms in the same manner as it treats its own firms, and in return the EU would treat American firms in the same manner as it treats European firms.* Under U.S. pressure, the EU Commission accepted the national treatment principle in the case of banks.

A **unified EU market** offers a wide range of important benefits. Both domestic and foreign producers can trade in a vast market where scale economies can be fully realized. Instead of meeting different requirements for each national market, industries can have their new products certified for sale throughout the Communities. Transportation costs have been reduced by eliminating delays at national frontiers. Finally, the unification infuses far greater competition in public procurement and other areas, while encouraging domestic and foreign investment in plants that can now produce for a much larger market. These factors were expected to increase the EU growth rate, and reduce consumer prices.

Although some of the provisions benefit both European and non-European firms, there are also provisions that discriminate against non-members.

Political Institutions

A set of political institutions, including a court of justice and a European parliament, were established to address EU matters and to move the EU members closer to political integration.

In the administrative branch of government, there are the Council of Ministers and the Commission. The council represents the 15 constituent governments, while the commission is the supranational decision-making body that presides over the vast bureaucracy at its Brussels headquarters. Regulations and directives issued by the Commission are legally binding, but major policies must be approved by the Council of Ministers. They include, but are not limited to, technical standards relating to pharmaceutical products, emission controls on passenger cars and commercial vehicles, food regulations (for example, rules for food additives and packaging), safety requirements and standards for industrial machines, and liberalization of air and road transport markets. In less essential matters there are no uniform standards; instead the EU adopted the principle of **mutual recognition:** Each EU member accepts the standards prevailing in other member countries. A member state cannot prohibit the importation and sale of a product lawfully produced and sold in another member state even if it does not comply with its domestic standards. For example, Germany cannot prohibit the import of French liqueur solely because its alcohol content is too low for it to be deemed a liqueur under German law. New products (such as pharmaceuticals) become eligible for sale in the entire EU *after one set of tests and certification* instead of the separate sets in each of the member countries.

Special Trading Arrangements between the EU and Developing Countries

Under the **Lomé Convention,** signed originally in 1975 and extended every five years, the EU established special trading arrangements with the 68 former British, French, and Belgian colonies in Africa, the Caribbean, and the Pacific. The latter are known as the **Associated States (AS).**

Under the Lomé Convention, the Associated States receive economic assistance from the EU exceeding $3 billion per year and are also granted technical assistance in a variety of forms. Also, the AS are granted free access to EU markets for manufactured exports, as well as for agricultural products not subject to the Common Agricultural Policy (CAP) of the Union; and they have preferential access for their agricultural products subject to CAP. EU rules of origin, which govern the preferential or free access to EU markets, were liberalized by considering the 68 countries as a single exporting unit. This means that successive working and processing operations can be carried out in a number of different countries and still qualify for duty-free entry to the EU.

Additionally, the Convention includes provisions for the stabilization of AS export earnings, known as STABEX. It assures monetary transfers to AS exporters of primary products when their effective earnings from one-year exports to the EU fall below the average earnings of the previous four years. Special arrangements were made to ensure a stable market for beef, rice, sugar, rum, and bananas—items of extraordinary importance for several AS countries.

In addition to Africa, the EU has contracted either association treaties or preferential trading agreements with Turkey and most countries in the Mediterranean Basin. Trade agreements have also been concluded with Argentina, Uruguay, and Brazil, but these are of a nonpreferential nature. Finally, the EU concluded trade and cooperation agreements with several East European countries.

THE EUROPEAN FREE TRADE AREA ASSOCIATION (EFTA)

At the time of the signing of the Treaty of Rome in 1957, an open invitation was issued to Western European countries to join the prospective organization, but for various reasons none except the Six was ready to sign. In particular, Great Britain did not wish to join for three main reasons. The British were generally dubious about the viability of any far-reaching agreement involving both Germany and France. They also did not wish to replace their form of agricultural support with that used on the Continent. Finally, joining the EEC would subject Great Britain to the common external tariff, making it impossible to maintain the imperial tariff preference system within the Commonwealth. Other countries did not join for reasons of international politics (neutrality in East–West relations).

As the EEC moved forward on the integration road, the British began to view with dismay the prospect of remaining outside. Consequently, they launched negotiations for membership in the late 1950s. But as successive negotiations failed, the British initiated the formation of a smaller trading group, the **European Free Trade Area Association (EFTA).** Originally consisting of Great Britain, Austria, Switzerland, Portugal, Sweden, Norway, and Denmark (with Finland as an associate member) and headquartered in Geneva, EFTA is in essence a free-trade area for industrial goods, with some special provisions for trade in farm products.

EFTA is a much looser organization than the EU. It does not have many of the union's institutional features; it has no common external tariff and no common economic policies; and unlike the EU, it does not bargain as one unit in the WTO. As the EU expanded and absorbed most members of the EFTA, the EFTA was reduced in size and today it consists only of Iceland, Norway, and Switzerland. They have concluded free-trade pacts with 12 countries, of which ten are in Eastern Europe.

Economic integration in Europe is now undergoing new changes. First, the EU is contemplating steps toward monetary unification (which we will discuss in Part Two). Second, under the European Economic Area, goods, services, capital, and workers can move freely within the entire 18-country region, and professional diplomas are recognized throughout. Third, the EU is contemplating, or has signed, association treaties with several countries in Eastern Europe and perhaps even with some of the former Soviet republics. The relationship with Poland, Hungary, and the Czech and Slovak republics (which formed an FTA among themselves) is the most advanced, and they are possible candidates for membership.

THE U.S.-CANADA FREE TRADE AREA (FTA)

Formation of an FTA between the two largest trading partners in the world—the U.S. and Canada—was an idea bandied about for many years. The two countries share the longest unprotected border in the world. About three-fourths of Canada's exports are destined for the United States, and two-thirds of its imports originate in the United States; in turn Canada accounts for about one-fifth of U.S. exports and imports. The capital markets of the two countries are closely knit. About 70 percent of U.S. imports from Canada were free of duty prior to 1989. Furthermore, since 1965 the two countries had a free trade agreement in automobiles and parts. It allows Canadian subsidiaries of the big-three U.S. automakers to rationalize production by specializing in a few models produced for the vast North-American market, thereby exploiting economies of scale in production and distribution.

Yet there were continuous trade frictions between the two countries, providing an impetus on both sides of the border to form an FTA. Such an FTA went into effect on January 1, 1989,[11] with tariff reductions to be spread over a 10-year period. This agreement eliminates all tariffs and quota restrictions on trade between the two countries, including agricultural quotas and export subsidies, as well as the restrictions placed on energy trade. Both countries accord national treatment to cross-border investment and to service transactions (each treats partner-country firms in the same manner as its own firms). And both countries will eliminate national preferences on federal government contracts in excess of $25,000, and provide copyright and patent protections to nationals of the partner country. Although the two countries maintain their existing antidumping and antisubsidy laws, sanction under those laws may be appealed to a new *bilateral* dispute settlement *tribunal*, whose decisions are binding.

Despite the agreement, there remains considerable trade friction. For example, the United States has complained that Canada subsidizes its lumber exports, and that its Honda exports to the United States fail to meet the minimum of 50 percent North American content stipulated by the agreement. These, as well as numerous other cases, were submitted to the binational review panel.

Even so, both countries enjoy static welfare gains from the elimination of the deadweight losses of protection; gains from economies of scale; improvement in efficiency forced by increased competition; and reduction in inefficiencies caused by uncertainty over the introduction of new protective measures. The benefits to Canada are estimated to be larger than those to the United States.

Apart from the FTA agreement with Canada, the United States has an FTA with Israel that was signed in 1985. Also, under the Caribbean initiative, countries in the Caribbean basin receive preferential trade status in the United States.

[11] The literature on the FTA includes Wannacott, *The United States and Canada: The Quest for Free Trade*, Washington D.C.: Institute for International Economics, March 1987; E. Fried, F. Stone, and P. Trezise (eds.), *Building a Canadian American Free Trade Area*, Washington D.C.: The Brookings Institution, 1987; R. Stern, P. Trezise, J. Whalley (eds.), *Perspectives on a U.S.–Canadian Free Trade Agreement*, Washington, D.C.: The Brookings Institution, 1987; and M. Kreinin, "North American Economic Integration," *Law and Contemporary Problems* (Duke University Law School) 44, no. 3, summer 1981. For a short report on the first two years of operations, see International Trade Commission, *International Economic Review*, April 1991.

NAFTA

An FTA encompassing the United States, Canada, and Mexico entitled the **North American Free Trade Agreement (NAFTA)** went into effect in January 1994.[12] All tariffs and quotas on manufactured and agricultural products will be eliminated by the end of the transitional period, set to last from five to 15 years (depending on the products). Tariffs could be reimposed temporarily on any product in case its imports *surge* in any given year. To qualify for duty-free entry, goods must meet rules of origin requirements: For automobiles, 62.5 percent of the value of the car must represent North American labor and materials; textiles must be made of North American fibers; and if imported materials are used in the fabrication of all other products, such materials must undergo substantial transformation within one of the three member countries.

With some exceptions, restrictions on direct foreign investment between the three countries will be lifted, with national treatment accorded to foreign investors. Similarly, Mexico will open its market to U.S. banks, insurance companies, securities firms, telephone companies, and land transportation companies. Intellectual property rights will be protected in all three countries. Disputes under the agreement are to be adjudicated by five-member panels, especially appointed for that purpose. But despite the agreement, several trade restrictions prevail within NAFTA, such as a U.S. import quota on Canadian lumber, and trade disputes between the three countries crop up often. These are adjudicated by the dispute settlement mechanism. For example, in mid-1996 a panel upheld Canada's very high tariff on dairy, poultry, and egg products, against a complaint by the United States. In the Fall of 1996 Mexico agreed (under U.S. pressure) not to market tomatoes in the U.S. below a certain price.

Because NAFTA includes two developed countries and one developing country (Mexico), its creation gave rise to a heated political debate; in particular, fears were expressed that a large number of U.S. jobs would be lost to low-wage Mexico and that the FTA would lead to environmental degradation in the border areas. Most economists viewed NAFTA favorably, expecting specialization along lines of comparative advantage; and indeed the net effect of NAFTA on the American employment has been small. But NAFTA had effects on other parts of the world as well. For example, considerable Asian investment poured into Mexico with the idea of selling their products in the U.S. market. Also, the Caribbean countries lost their preferred status over Mexico in the U.S. market. To deal with the internal political objections to NAFTA in the early 1990s two *side agreements* on labor

---

[12] See R. A. Pastor, "NAFTA as the Center of an Integration Process," *The Brookings Review,* winter 1993; ITC, *International Economic Review,* October 1992 and January 1993; and ISITC *The Year in Trade 1994* pp. 41–52.

standards and the environment were negotiated, committing each country to enforce its own laws in these matters.

Chile was considered a candidate for NAFTA, but because of resistance in the U.S. Congress its accession could not materialize. Instead in 1996 Chile became an associate member of the Mercusor FTA, consisting of Brazil, Argentina, Uruguay, and Paraguay; it also signed a free trade pact with Canada.

THE WORLD TRADE ORGANIZATION (WTO)

Following World War II, the trading nations convened in Havana and agreed to form an International Trade Organization (ITO) based on the charter negotiated there. But because the U.S. Senate failed to ratify the ITO, it was never established. As a substitute, the countries decided to set up an informal association, known as the General Agreement on Tariffs and Trade (GATT), to serve as a framework for multilateral tariff negotiations. Because Congress had already ratified the Trade Agreements Legislation, and the new organization could be regarded as merely an instrument to carry out that legislation, the administration did not consider it necessary to seek special ratification. On January 1, 1995 GATT was expanded and made into a formal World Trade Organization (WTO).[13]

The WTO sets and regulates a code of international trade conduct, which contains three fundamental principles: the principle of nondiscrimination embodied in the most-favored-nation clause (to be discussed next); a general prohibition of export subsidies (except for agriculture[14]) and import quotas, from which developing countries are exempt; and a requirement that any new tariff be offset by a reduction in other tariffs. Special clauses deal with the position and needs of the developing countries. The WTO provides an institutional framework for multilateral negotiations for reciprocal tariff reduction among the member nations. It also provides a setting for consultation between countries and a mechanism for resolving trade disputes. WTO's membership of 120 nations encompasses all the industrial countries, most East European countries, and many developing countries. Russia and China are not yet members. Member nations completed eight major confer-

---

[13] For a review of the first year of activities see WTO, *Focus*, December 1995.

[14] Interestingly, agricultural subsidies sometimes help rather than hinder economic welfare. In a world with neither agricultural support programs nor other governmental interventions, the United States would be a major exporter of grains. If, under present conditions, the United States removed its export subsidies but retained its price support, it would cease to be an exporter of grains—clearly a move away from the optimal situation. This proposition has general application. In any *piecemeal* removal of the existing maze of governmental interventions, we should be careful that the move is toward rather than away from the best allocation of world resources. A *partial* movement toward the optimal use of resources is not necessarily an improvement over the existing situation. Each case must be judged on its own merit. This rule also applies to a customs union.

ences and several minor ones to negotiate tariff concessions, the most recent of which was the **Uruguay Round** (1986–1993).

Because the WTO was set up as a result of the Uruguay Round, its functions are much broader than those of GATT which it replaced. In addition to overseeing rules pertaining to international commodity trade, it deals with transaction in commercial services, intellectual property rights, foreign investments, and related matters.[15] The international agreements in these areas are spelled out below, in discussion of the Uruguay Round.

The Unconditional Most Favored Nation Principle

All members of the WTO are expected to abide by a principle of nondiscrimination in levying tariffs known as the **Unconditional Most Favored Nation**[16] **(MFN) Principle:** The tariff rate levied on a given commodity by country A must be the same for all supplying countries, and tariff concessions exchanged between any two countries must be extended to all members of the WTO.

There are two main exceptions to this rule under the WTO. First is a customs union, which involves free trade among members and a common and uniform tariff against outsiders: Nonmember countries must pay the common external tariff, while member nations pay nothing when crossing into one another's markets, discriminating in favor of the members. The EU was established under this exception. The only proviso attached is that most intra-area trade be liberalized and that the post-union common tariff not be more restrictive than the pre-union average tariff of the constituent countries. Alleged violations of this rule can lead to trade disputes. For example, upon joining the EU, Spain increased its levies on certain farm imports. Under American pressure the EU agreed to compensate the United States by lowering duties elsewhere.

The second exception is a free-trade area that calls for free trade among members but permits each to levy its own tariff against outsiders. Here the degree of discrimination against nonmember states depends on the tariff levels of the constituent nations, because no common external tariff is introduced. NAFTA was set up under this exception.

In all cases of deviation from the most-favored-nation clause, the countries involved must seek a WTO waiver to the rule, and a waiver can also be granted under special circumstances not covered by the exception above. Outright violations of the principle do occur, however. Thus, the 1965 United States-Canada automobile agreement that liberalized trade in automobiles

[15] For details see *The World Trade Organizations,* Geneva, WTO, 1996.

[16] Each country must treat all its suppliers in the same manner that it treats its most favored supplier. Every year the U.S. Congress extends China's MFN status by one year. That means that Chinese goods enter the United States at the same tariff as that on goods from WTO members. In 1996 the Congress decided to change the somewhat misleading name "MFN," and state simply that it grants China "normal trading status."

and their parts between the two nations discriminates against third countries and violates the WTO. In recent years the frequent adoption of VERs and other discriminatory practices led to many violations of the MFN principle. And in many cases customs unions and FTA failed to meet WTO standards.

Developing countries are treated differently in three respects. First, they receive preferences in the markets of the industrial countries—a modification of the MFN rule. Second, the rule of reciprocity in the WTO negotiations does not apply to them. They obtain all concessions exchanged among the developed countries without having to reciprocate themselves. Third, they are exempt from the prohibition on quotas and export subsidies.

At this point it is useful to summarize four terms used in international trade law and that are often encountered in conjunction with the WTO or the EU:

1. *MFN Principle:* A WTO rule of nondiscrimination among supplying countries in a country's import regime. The MFN tariff is applied by a country to imports from other members of the WTO. It reflects the massive tariff reductions undertaken in the postwar period within the framework of GATT, now WTO.
2. *National Treatment:* Each country must treat foreign firms operating within its borders no less favorably than it treats its own firms. This is a principle of nondiscrimination between foreign and domestic firms. Since service transactions often require the establishment of foreign subsidiaries, this rule applies to them as well.
3. *Reciprocity:* "Our" country will treat "your" country's firms in the same way that "your" country will treat "our" country's firms.
4. *Mutual Recognition:* Each EU member recognizes the product standards applied by other member countries. It cannot bar a product from its market just because these standards are different from its own.

A major function of the WTO is to facilitate periodic multilateral negotiations for tariff reduction, subject to the MFN principle. The last three sessions were the "Kennedy Round," the "Tokyo Round," and the "Uruguay Round." Following are the main provisions of the Uruguay Round.

The Uruguay Round

After seven years of arduous bargaining, members of GATT concluded the Uruguay Round on December 15, 1993. It was the eighth and most ambitious round of multilateral trade negotiations. The outcome contained several important breakthroughs, and extended the rule of the WTO to new areas such as service transactions, intellectual property rights, and trade-related investment measures.[17] Also, for the first time countries agreed to lower and simplify the protection of agriculture.

One of the key results of the negotiations were *tariff reductions* averaging nearly 40 percent. Tariffs would be eliminated on pharmaceuticals; construction, agricultural, and medical equipment; paper; furniture; toys; and beer; and significantly reduced on chemicals and certain electronic items such as semiconductors, semiconductor manufacturing equipment, and electronic parts. Tariffs on most other items would be lowered by smaller amounts. Average post-UR tariff rates will be 4.0, 5.9, and 6.6 percent for the U.S., Japan, and the EU respectively. All cuts will be spread over a 5–10-year period, depending on the product.

The Uruguay Round agreed to reduce *subsidies on agricultural exports* by 21 percent. The ban on rice imports into Japan and South Korea was lifted and replaced by an import quota of 4 percent of domestic consumption, scheduled to rise to 8 percent over six years. *Nontariff barriers*, including VERs and import quotas (such as the U.S. quotas on sugar, dairy, and peanuts) will all be *replaced by tariffs*, subject to certain safeguards, with the tariffs to be gradually reduced over time. Certain agricultural tariffs (such as those on cut flowers) will also be reduced. These commitments will be phased in over 6 years for developed countries, and 10 years for developing countries.

The *Multifibre Arrangement*, which limits trade in textiles and clothing, will be phased out over a 10-year period. Many countries also agreed to a comprehensive binding of reasonable tariff rates. *All VERs will be phased out* over a 6-year period, and no new VERs will be allowed. The agreement provides incentive to use WTO safeguard rules, such as the escape clause, when imports cause a serious injury by suspending the rights to retaliate against such measures for the first three years of their existence. This would lessen the incentive to negotiate VERs. There will be an expedited WTO procedure to resolve disputes over the use of *antidumping laws*.

Export subsidies are prohibited by the agreement. Although certain domestic subsidies (such as regional assistance, or subsidies to help in

---

[17] Only the initial session was held in Uruguay. The bulk of the negotiation was carried on in Geneva, Switzerland. The literature on the Uruguay Round includes Congressional Budget Office, *The GATT Negotiations and U.S. Trade Policy*, Washington D.C.: U.S. Government Printing Office, 1987; J. Bhagwati, A. Kreuger, and R. Snape (eds.), "A Symposium on the Multilateral Trade Negotiations and Developing Country Interests," *The World Bank Economic Review* 1, no. 4, September 1987; R. Baldwin and D. Richardson (eds.), *Issues in the Uruguay Round*, Cambridge, Mass.: National Bureau of Economic Research, 1988; B. Balassa (ed.), "Subsidies and Countervailing Measures: Critical Issues for the Uruguay Round," Washington D.C., World Bank Discussion Papers, April 1989; Aho and J. Aronson, *Trade Talks: America Better Listen*, New York, Council on Foreign Relations, 1985; H. Stalson, *U.S. Service Exports and Foreign Barriers: An Agenda for Negotiations*, Washington, D.C.: National Planning Association, 1985; S. Anjara, "A New Round of Global Trade Negotiations," *Finance and Development*, June 1986; M. E. Kreinin, "The Uruguay Round—Phase II," in M. E. Kreinin (ed.), *International Commercial Policy*, Washington D.C., Taylor Francis, 1993; GATT, *Focus*, December 1993, no. 104; and International Trade Commission, *International Economic Review*, February 1992.

environmental cleanups) are allowed, subsidies for the development of high-technology products—considered "precompetitive" development activities—will be limited to 50 percent of applied research and 75 percent of basic research. In general, the agreement attempts to restrict subsidies that distort international competitiveness.

Many host countries impose *trade-related measures on direct foreign investment.* In particular, they include requirements that subsidiaries or branches of foreign companies use a minimum proportion of local productive factors (domestic content requirement), and/or export a minimum portion of their output. These measures, known as foreign investment performance standards, will be *phased out* over a 10-year period.

A framework agreement has been reached in the area of *service transactions,* which includes MFN treatment, national treatment, and market access (the avoidance of restrictions on the number of firms allowed in a market). Included under services are professional (such as accounting, legal, and engineering) services, computer services, communications, construction, distribution (wholesale and retail trade), educational services, financial (such as banking and securities) services, and health services. Countries are expected to accede to the service agreement gradually, as they submit their schedules of commitments to the WTO. However, thus far several countries have refused to provide liberal access to foreign financial services. Consequently, the United States (which has a comparative advantage in this area) restricts market access to firms from countries that do not reciprocate. For similar reasons the United States refused (in mid-1996) to join the agreement on telecommunications. Finally, thus far the EU has not accepted the U.S. proposal for "open skies," that would allow European and American airlines to compete freely on the two continents.

For *intellectual property rights,* the pact provides a 20-year protection of patents, trademarks, and copyrights for books, computer software, films, and pharmaceuticals. But it allows LDCs 10 years to phase in patent protection.

Procedures will be streamlined, harmonized, and made more transparent in import licensing, customs valuation, rules of origin, technical barriers to trade, sanitary measures, and dispute settlement.

Because the pact contains new areas that have not been covered in the past under GATT rules, it was decided to establish the *World Trade Organization* (WTO). It encompasses the GATT structure, but extends it to include trade in agricultural products, services, textiles, and intellectual property, as well as trade-related investment measures. It is expected that the dispute settlement mechanism will function better than under GATT, and that countries will bring disputes to the WTO for adjudication rather than try to resolve them bilaterally. Over 30 disputes were being adjudicated in the first year of operation.[18] For example, in 1996 the United States (later joined by

---

[18] See the WTO's *Focus,* June-July 1996.

the EU) brought to the WTO a complaint, on behalf of Kodak, that Japan's film market is closed and monopolized by Fuji. Also in 1996 the EU threatened to lodge a complaint at the WTO against a new U.S. policy that imposes sanctions against foreign companies that do substantial business with Cuba, Libya, or Iran. Note that only governments can bring complaints to the WTO, while in the case of NAFTA the dispute settlement mechanism is open also to private companies. The WTO's stature is commensurate to the IMF and the World Bank, but decisions are usually made by consensus. Among other things, the WTO will develop a work program on trade and the environment.

Although the agreement represents important progress, and extends the rule of the WTO to areas that have never before been tackled in negotiations, certain controversial issues remained unresolved. Not much was done on government procurement and the important market for financial services remains closed or restricted in many countries (although in 1994 China agreed to grant expanded rights to foreign banks).

It is estimated that the Uruguay Round will raise world income by over $200 billion annually. But as usual there will be winners and losers, both internationally and within countries. For example, for the first time the developing world is a clear beneficiary of a GATT round, as the MFA will be phased out and agricultural liberalization is accepted by the global pact. Within the United States, agricultural and high-tech interests would gain, while textiles, apparel, and other labor-intensive industries are likely losers. The outcome for certain service sectors is yet undetermined. Yet the world as a whole would benefit.

In a post-UR agreement, signed in March 1997, WTO members agreed to remove all tariffs on information-technology products by year 2000. Included are computers, semiconductors, software, fax machines, fibre optics and other items, with total world trade of $500 billion.

THE WTO AND THE ENVIRONMENT[19]

In 1991, after Mexico challenged a U.S. law banning the import of tuna caught in dolphin-killing nets, a GATT panel upheld the Mexican challenge. One reason for this is that the GATT/WTO provisions are concerned with products, and not with the methods or processes by which they are produced. In another example, Venezuela has protested against a gasoline regulation adopted by the U.S. Environmental Protection Agency (EPA).

---

[19] For further readings see GATT *International Trade* 1990/91, vol. I and the literature cited therein; P. Vimonen, "Trade Policies and the Environment," *Finance and Development*, June 1992; the *Economist*, May 30, 1992; U.S. International Trade Commission, *International Economic Review*, May 1992; and J. Whally and P. Vimonen, *Trade and the Environment: Setting and Rules*, Washington, D.C.: Institute for International Economics, 1993.

Indeed, there were several instances in which environmental laws and regulations were found to contradict WTO's rules. This triggered an assault on the WTO by environmental groups.

While the WTO does not interfere with purely domestic measures to protect the environment, such as domestic taxes and subsidies, its rules may conflict with **international environmental agreements,** or otherwise prevent the enforcement of environmental measures when trade is involved. Three ways in which environmental issues become internationalized include the impact of environmental policies on international competitiveness; the assertion of jurisdiction over other nations' environmental policies; and the transborder spillover of pollution into another country or the global commons.[20]

Competitiveness Countries vary greatly in the environmental standards they enact and enforce domestically. Differences are apparent in pollution absorptive capabilities, levels of industrialization, population densities, social choices about acceptable levels of pollution, costs in controlling pollution, and so on. Due to unawareness and the costs involved, pollution standards in LDCs are considerably lower than those of developed countries. But even among the industrial countries, standards vary both generally and with respect to particular environmental hazards.

It is claimed that lower standards "abroad" regarding industrial pollution place the "home" industry at an unfair competitive disadvantage—sometimes referred to as *ecological dumping.* One of the United States's primary objections to NAFTA concerned the lower environmental standards that reduce production costs in Mexico, and thus allegedly attract direct foreign investment there. To "level the playing field" it has been variably proposed that:

1. The environmental standards throughout the world be harmonized—clearly an impossible task.
2. Countries be allowed to impose special import duties on foreign products of environmentally unsound methods of production. This would violate the MFN principle, and in many cases would require raising tariffs above the levels established by earlier treaties.
3. Domestic industries competing against such environmentally harmful imports be offered subsidies to offset the lower production costs abroad. This could create domestic budgetary problems.

---

[20] This is apart from the issue of "sustainable development," which mandates development policies that are least damaging to the environment. See the *World Development Report 1992* of the World Bank; A. Steer, "The Environment for Development," *Finance and Development,* June 1992; and a series of articles in *Finance and Development,* December 1993, 6–23.

It is not known to what extent differential pollution standards affect a country's competitive position and its attractiveness to direct foreign investment. Nor is it clear where to draw the line between differences in environmental standards and other government policies that affect a country's competitive position.

Signatories to the Tokyo Round Agreement on Technical Barriers are required to notify the WTO secretariat of products to be covered by proposed technical regulations. Environmental considerations have become widely used as a rationale for applying such regulations. Indeed, between 1980 and 1990, 211 notifications were made on environmental grounds and 168 on grounds of public health and safety.

Jurisdiction over Other Nations' Environmental Policies Environmental groups often demand import bans against, or suspension of trading rights of, other nations that do not comply with expected environmental behavior. The proposed ban on U.S. imports of tuna caught in nets that kill dolphins falls under this category. Such actions would violate WTO's rules.

Transborder Spillover of Pollution Air and water pollution often do not remain within a country's borders, but instead spill over into neighboring countries. Moreover, cases of deforestation or global warming concern all nations, since forests, for example, provide carbon absorption services to the world. Such issues are best handled by multilateral agreements.[21] But there are several reasons why a country may not wish to join such an agreement. For instance, it may find the scientific evidence concerning an environmental problem unconvincing and its risk exaggerated; consider the proposed remedies ineffective; assign a low priority to solving the problem; disagree with the allocation of responsibility among countries; or try to obtain a free ride from the efforts of other countries.

Several of the international agreements concerning the environment contain trade provisions. For example, the Montreal protocol to phase out production and consumption of substances that deplete the ozone layer bans trade with nonsignatories. The Convention of International Trade in Endangered Species of World Fauna and Flora (CITES) lists species threatened with extinction and obligates parties to an almost complete trade ban against countries endangering these species. And the Basel convention aims to control trade in hazardous waste.

Such trade-related provisions may contradict WTO rules. All that countries are entitled to do under WTO is ban imports of hazardous or toxic substances on health and safety grounds. The situation therefore may call upon the WTO to amend its rules, or it may be handled by the granting of waivers. In either case it would be necessary to define "inadequate

---

[21] It has even been proposed to establish an international market for pollution rights. Countries would be allocated emission entitlements, and those can be either used or sold to other countries at a market price.

environmental standards," and to develop criteria to prevent abuse. The WTO is mandated to develop a work program on trade and the environment.

THE U.S.-JAPAN TRADE CONFLICT

Practically all countries employ trade restrictions, which results in strains in the international trading system. Retaliations and counterretaliation often add up to trade wars. In addition, the products or services around which the disputes revolve change constantly.[22]

While trade disputes come and go, the U.S. trade friction with Japan is a regular feature of the international scene. Two possible reasons for the strained relationship are the annual bilateral U.S. trade deficits with Japan that often exceed $50 billion, and the fact that the two countries compete head-on in high-technology products. American manufacturers complain about Japanese "unfair trading practices" and Japan's relatively closed market to imports and foreign investment. Agricultural imports to Japan are tightly limited by quotas and other governmental controls. In services, a variety of regulations restrict access to the Japanese market. For example, American construction companies cannot bid on public construction projects in Japan. In the manufacturing sector, where overt governmental restrictions are absent, business practices,[23] social pressures, taste, and perhaps administrative guidance are alleged to restrict imports. In particular, much of Japan's industry is organized in clusters of companies with interlocking directorates known as **Keiretsu.** Members of a Keiretsu buy from one another and exclude other companies—including foreign ones—from selling to their members. This and other exclusionary practices raise prices in Japan above world market prices, and cost Japanese consumers $110 billion per year. They are also a constant source of international irritation. There is fear that the Japanese "model" may be followed elsewhere in Asia. All this led experts to suggest extending international trade rules to cover competition policy within members of the WTO.

Over the years, the United States has engaged in steady negotiations with Japan over structural impediments to trade. These include such exclusionary practices as wholesale and retail distribution systems in Japan that exclude imports, pricing mechanisms, business practices, bid rigging, market allocation, group boycotts, the Keiretsu system, land use, and savings and investment patterns thought to cause trade imbalances. The fact

---

[22] A good source that describes these evolving trade relationships is the monthly *International Economic Review,* published by the U.S. International Trade Commission (ITC).

[23] See M. Kreinin, "How Closed Is the Japanese Market?" *The World Economy,* December 1988, and the literature cited therein; F. Bergsten and M. Noland, *Reconcilable Differences? U.S.–Japan Economic Conflict,* Institute for International Economics, 1993; and papers by R. Lawrence and G. Saxonhouse, "Is Japan's Trade Regime Different?" *Journal of Economic Perspectives,* summer 1993.

that in numerous products American producers control a large share of the market in all countries except Japan is often cited as a proof of Japanese exclusionary practices. So is the fact that imports satisfy a much smaller portion of domestic consumption in Japan than in all other industrial countries. Although Japan was dropped from the list of unfair traders in May 1990, these **structural impediments initiative (SII)** discussions continue. In the mid-1990s, after market-opening agreements were reached in such areas as auto parts, flat glass, medical equipment, telecommunications, and insurance services, much of the bilateral dispute shifted to areas such as aviation treaties, including landing rights for airlines and air cargo and the right of U.S. airlines to fly from Japan to Asian cities beyond Japan.

Also in the 1990s, serious bilateral disputes erupted between the United States and China, mainly over the issue of intellectual property rights. The United States threatened to impose trade sanctions on China if it did not enforce these rights with respect to discs and other intellectual property, and close factories that pirate U.S. products.

ECONOMIC REFORMS IN EASTERN EUROPE (TRANSITION ECONOMIES)

Eastern Europe and the 15 countries of the former Soviet Union are undergoing a process of dramatic economic restructuring.[24] This consists first of **privatization,** where government enterprises are sold to private interests—requiring a new legal framework to accommodate private property. Second, the government must relinquish control over resource allocation in the domestic economy, and permit market forces to determine prices and guide economic activity. As the "command economy" gives way to a market economy, the government must concentrate on providing macroeconomic stability through fiscal and monetary policies. This includes limiting government deficits and slowing down the expansion of money supply to lower inflation. In all cases it is a painful process, causing transitory unemployment and a reduction in living standards. As seen in figure 7.1, GDP in transition economies declines sharply after reforms are introduced, before it begins rising again.

Two types of strategy were employed by transition economies. The first, exemplified by Poland, the Czech Republic, and Estonia, is "shock therapy." Prices and trade were liberalized fast, inflation was choked by tight monetary policy, and the privatization and demonopolization of industry was started

[24] See World Bank, *World Development Report,* 1966 (issue devoted to transition economies); papers by O. Blanchard, J. Svejnar, and J. Sachs, in AEA Papers and Proceedings, May 1996; *IMF Survey,* July 26, 1993, August 9, 1993, November 25, 1996, and August 23, 1993; *Finance and Development,* March 1993 and December 1996; papers by J. Kornai, Fischer and Frankel, J. Sachs, and P. Desai in the *AER Papers and Proceedings,* May 1992: 1–21; 37–54; and R. Frydman et al., *The Privatization Process in Central Europe,* Budapest, London, NY: Central European University Press, 1993.

FIGURE 7.1	*The Evolution of GDP in Five Central European Countries*

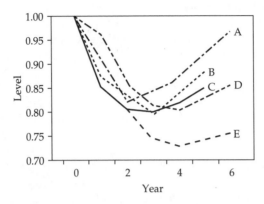

Note: Year before transition = 1. A = Poland, B = Slovakia, C = Czech Republic, D = Hungary, E = Bulgaria.

Source: O. Blanchard, "Theoretical Aspects of Transition," AEA *Papers and Proceedings,* May 1996, p. 188.

(if not finished) quickly. The second is the gradual approach to liberalization adopted by Russia and China, among others. China is a special case because 70 percent of its workers were in agriculture, a sector long crippled by low prices and poor productivity. Reform boosted productivity incomes and growth. But within Europe it appears that countries following the shock therapy approach suffered smaller falls in output and returned to growth more quickly than the "gradualists." Economic aid from the West to assist in this transformation is provided both directly and through the 41-member European Bank for Reconstruction and Development. Finally, the former socialist states, long isolated from the rest of the world, are integrating themselves into the global market economy. They are in the process of joining international organizations such as the WTO and the IMF, abolishing exchange control so as to introduce free convertibility of their currency to other currencies, and following the same trading practices as other market-economy countries. Indeed, the countries mentioned in figure 7.1 have redirected some of their exports away from Eastern Europe and toward the EU.[25] Even China, which retains dictatorial controls in the political sphere, is converting gradually to a market economy in the economic sphere. The result is a booming economy in southeast China.

[25] N. Sheets and S. Boata, "Eastern European Export Performance During the Transition," International Finance Discussion Papers/Federal Reserve Board, no. 562, September 1996.

Summary

This chapter addresses the process of trade liberalization that takes place both regionally and multilaterally. Within regions, trade is freed inside customs unions and free-trade areas (FTAs). While these have proliferated in recent years, the most cohesive regional grouping is the European Union (EU). It affords freedom of movement for goods, services, capital, and labor within its 15 member countries; has common external barriers against outsiders; and operates a common agricultural policy that consists of price supports, import controls, and export subsidies. A high degree of cohesion resulted from the Unified Market Program of 1992. The EU has special relationships with the Associated States (former colonies) in Africa and the Caribbean, and has established a free-trading relationship with the rest of Western Europe.

Examples of FTAs include the North American Free Trade Agreement (NAFTA); and Australia-New Zealand.

On a global level, trade is liberalized within negotiating sessions of the WTO/GATT, known as "rounds." The last (eighth) completed session was the Uruguay Round, which succeeded in lowering tariffs and liberalizing nontariff barriers to trade and in branching out to new areas such as services, trade-related investment standards, and intellectual property rights. The WTO also oversees several ground rules in international trade, including the outlawing of import quotas and export subsidies, the MFN and national treatment rules, and the like. In recent years several WTO rules have conflicted with environmental movements in the United States and elsewhere.

Because all countries commit trading violations, trade disputes have become a permanent feature of the global economic scene. In particular, Japan is considered by many observers to be a country that tends to exclude imports, and the U.S.-Japan trade friction has proved to be an ongoing phenomenon.

East European countries are undergoing transition to market economies after many years of socialism. As part of their transition they are intent on integrating themselves into the global trading system.

Important Concepts

Trade liberalization

Regionalism

Organization for Economic Cooperation and Development (OECD)

European Economic Area (EEA)

Common Agricultural Policy (CAP) of the EU

Unified EC market

Mutual recognition

Lomé convention

Associated States (AS)

The North American Free Trade Agreement (NAFTA)

Unconditional Most Favored Nation (MFN) Principle

Target price

Transition economics

Shock therapy vs. gradualism

WTO and the environment

Reciprocity

International environmental
agreements

World Trade Organization (WTO)

Keiretsu

Structural impediments initiative
(SII)

Privatization

National treatment

Uruguay Round

---

*Review
Questions*

1. a. Explain the following terms:
    - Trade creation of a customs union
    - Trade diversion of a customs union
      (Consult Chapter 4 as well.)

    b. How would you go about estimating the trade creation and trade
        diversion of the European Union? (What is the EU?)
    c. What special arrangements does the EU have with developing
        countries?
    d. What is the significance of 1992 in EU development?

2. a. What is the difference between a customs union and a free-trade
        area? Give examples of each.
    b. How do the EU and NAFTA differ from the WTO?
    c. How consistent are a CU and FTA with the MFN principle?
    d. Explain the U.S.–Canada FTA.
    e. What is NAFTA?

3. Outline the agreement reached in the Uruguay Round of trade
    negotiations.

4. Compare and contrast:
    a. Reciprocity and national treatment
    b. Reciprocity and mutual recognition
    c. The Unconditional MFN Principle and national treatment

5. What are the current conflicts between the WTO and the
    environmental movement?

6. Describe the nature and causes of the U.S.–Japan trade conflict.

7. What economic changes are taking place in the former socialist states?

CHAPTER 8

Selected Trade Problems of Developing Countries

We now turn to the interests of the developing countries in international trade. It should be emphasized at the outset that foreign trade is not the central issue in the development process. Economic development requires the generation of an internal saving–investment process of sizable magnitude within an economic, social, and political environment conducive to growth. Failure to develop usually has deep-seated domestic causes, such as inadequate supply of savings, skilled labor, entrepreneurship, managerial talent, and infrastructure and improper macroeconomic policies. These cannot be remedied by trade policy. However, because of the open nature of their economies, foreign trade is much more important to developing countries than it is to most developed nations. Exposure to foreign trade does spur economic development in a variety of ways, but the main impetus must come from within. A general discussion of development is beyond the scope of this book; this chapter is concerned merely with selected aspects of trade between the developed and developing countries.

ALTERNATIVE TRADE APPROACHES TO DEVELOPMENT

Two alternative trade approaches to economic development can be distinguished: import-substitution and export-promotion strategies.[1] Under the

[1] For a comprehensive review of alternative strategies see S. Edwards, "Openness, Trade Liberalization, and Growth in Developing Countries," *Journal of Economic Literature* 31, no. 3 (September 1993), and "Trade Policy, Exchange Rate, and Growth," working paper no. 4511, NBER, October 1993. Import-substitution policies were discussed by the World Bank in its *1986 World Development Report*. See also *IMF Survey*, July 14, 1986.

policy of **import substitution,** a country imposes high tariffs and nontariff barriers to imports, and behind this shelter it expands domestic production to replace imports. Usually the country starts by producing nondurable consumer goods, which require labor-intensive and unsophisticated techniques. Once this easy stage is completed, further import substitution becomes increasingly difficult. Usually, the next step is to turn to the final processing of assembly-type commodities, generating a shift in the composition of imports away from these final products and toward intermediate and capital goods. To this end, the protective structure is escalated by the degree of processing, with final goods more highly protected than intermediate ones. The effective protection of final goods can at times reach 1,000 percent, and the level of protection is very uneven between industries.

This protection policy can have several results. First, much capital was invested in industries that could not have survived without protection. The waste that arises when LDCs attempt to "deepen" their production of manufactured products was discussed in Chapter 4. Second, this policy raises the prices of import-competing goods, and draws resources away from the export industries into the import-competing industries. In turn, that makes it more difficult to export primary or manufactured products. Thus, *the policy discriminates in favor of import-competing industries and against export industries.* Production for domestic consumption is encouraged while production for exports is discouraged. Indeed, many LDCs pursue policies that are biased against their farm sectors, thereby lowering agricultural output, depressing rural income, and reducing exports. But a unit of foreign exchange saved by import substitution costs more in terms of domestic resources than a unit of foreign exchange earned by exports.

Third, because the domestic market is usually too small to support an optimal-size plant, excess capacity tends to develop. While costs per unit in textile and shoe production decline only 10 percent when plant output doubles, in industries such as steel, pulp and paper, and chemicals, optimal-size plants can operate at almost half the per-unit cost of plants of the size that can be sustained by the internal markets of most developing countries. Thus, the widening of the internal market is one main benefit that accrues from regional integration among the developing countries. However, such steps are usually insufficient and must be supplemented by orienting exports toward the developed world. In sum, the fact that specialization and economies of scale cannot be fully exploited raises costs and prices well above the world market level.

Fourth, because the system of protection and other policies subsidize the importation of capital goods (at times coupled with artificially high wage rates brought about by union pressure), there is a strong incentive to use capital-intensive techniques regardless of the country's factor endowments. This is one reason why the rapid growth in industrial production in many developing countries is often not accompanied by a rapid growth in industrial employment. Finally, foreign capital that flows into the protected industries often does not generate export earnings but instead aggravates the debt-servicing problem.

LDCs often justify their import-substitution strategies by the global environment in which they operate. They argue, for example, that competition from industrial countries inhibits development. Yet the evidence contradicts this proposition: Heavily protected industries in LDCs fail to attain efficiency, while unprotected industries often thrive. Another argument is that the multinational corporations (MNCs) transfer to LDCs technology that is appropriate only to industrial countries. But in fact MNCs transfer inappropriate technology only when they receive inappropriate market signals. In northern Mexico, where there are no powerful unions and wage rates are low, U.S. firms (producing for export) are far less capital intensive than in Mexican import-substituting industries.

Because of the shortcomings of import-substitution, several developing countries—for example, Taiwan and South Korea—have opted for an **export-promotion** strategy. This involves a change in the system of incentives in favor of exports, minimizing or eliminating the discrimination against them. Countries may even introduce a variety of fiscal incentives to increase exporters' earnings (such as export subsidies) or to reduce exporters' costs (such as reducing or removing duties on imported inputs or reducing the exporters' income taxes). Some countries (such as Mexico and Taiwan) established duty-free processing zones[2] into which inputs are imported duty free and from which final goods are exported after processing. Indeed, it is this measure, coupled with the offshore provision[3] in the American tariff law, that explains the existence in northern Mexico of 2,000 American plants, most of them just south of the California border. Similar extensive operations have been set up in Taiwan. In other cases, tariff rates have been reduced and harmonized, or the currency has been devalued (frequent minidevaluations in the case of Brazil). The major effect has been to expand the export of labor-intensive manufactured products and to avoid the establishment of insulated, highly inefficient, domestic industries.

Although import substitution up to a certain point can be beneficial, the development experience of countries following the export-promotion

---

[2] Duty-free zones are not limited to LDCs. Most countries (including the United States) have such zones, usually located around port areas, where imports are checked before paying the duty and entering the country officially.

[3] When a product made abroad out of U.S. components is reimported into the United States for further fabrication, only the value added abroad is subject to duty. Given the low wages in Mexico, the value added there is also low. Similar provisions exist in the tariff laws of Western European countries. They have proven highly beneficial in promoting LDCs' exports.

strategy has tended to be more favorable, in terms of growth rate and expansion of employment,[4] than that of countries developing strictly via import substitution. Analysis by the World Bank of 41 economies over the 1963–1985 period indicates that outward-oriented economies have performed better than inward-oriented ones. In fact, an Asian Development Bank study attributes the success of Asian economies to reliance on market forces, including an emphasis on exports, removal of tariffs, an adherence to appropriate exchange rates, and, in the area of industrial policy, the deregulation of private industry and the decontrol of public enterprises.[5]

Because of these favorable experiences, a process of economic restructuring is spreading among the LDCs in Asia and Latin America. Internally the reforms usually include a reduction of government budgetary deficits and control over money supply to lower the rate of inflation and otherwise provide a stable macroeconomic environment; privatization of public enterprises; a reduction of government interference in decisions that impinge upon resource allocation; and greater reliance on market forces. Externally the reforms include liberalization of imports; elimination of exchange control; and a shift from an import-substitution to an export-promotion strategy. Both *internal and external reforms must accompany each other.*[6] As a result, many developing countries are growing at a rate of more than double that of the industrial countries; their manufacturing exports are up; and they are competing effectively in global markets.

One example is India, long considered a laggard in the development enterprise. In mid-1991 it eliminated import licensing; cut tariffs; eased restrictions on foreign investment; liberalized the rupee; and restored fiscal order. By mid-1993 annual inflation was contained below 6 percent; foreign currency reserves were up; exports and foreign investment were increasing; and the fiscal deficit was declining.

India and China, with a combined population of 2 billion, are attempting to integrate themselves into the global economy. The same is true of the ASEAN group (Indonesia, Thailand, Malaysia, and the Philippines) that

[4] See D. Nayyar, "Transnational Corporations and Manufactured Exports from Poor Countries," *Economic Journal,* March 1978; Anne Krueger, "Alternative Trade Strategies and Employment in LDCs," *American Economic Review,* May 1978: 270–274; "Trade Policies in Developing Countries," in R. Jones and P. Kenen (eds.) *Handbook of International Economics,* vol. I, North-Holland, 1984; and "Import Substitution Versus Export Promotion," *Finance and Development,* June 1985; and B. Balassa, *Change and Challenge in the World Economy,* N.Y.: St. Martin's Press, 1985. For a different view see P. Streeten, "A Cool Look at Outward-Looking Strategies for Development," *The World Economy,* September 1982.

[5] See *Finance and Development,* September 1987; and *IMF Survey,* August 7, 1989. For additional analysis see C. Mann, "Towards the Next Generation of Newly Industrializing Economies: The Role for Macroeconomic Policies and the Manufacturing Sector," Federal Reserve Board, International Finance *Discussion Paper,* no. 376, March 1990. For a contrary view see A, Singh, "How Did East Asia Grow So Fast," *UNCTA Bulletin,* May–June 1995.

[6] See A. Alam and S. Rajapatirana, "Trade Reform in Latin America and the Caribbean," *Finance and Development,* September 1993; *Finance and Development,* March 1994, 2–5; and P. Low and J. Nash, "The Long and Winding Road Towards Freer World Trade," *Finance and Development,* Sept. 1994.

is following in the footsteps of the Asian NICs[7] (Korea, Taiwan, Hong Kong, and Singapore) and of many Latin American countries such as Mexico and Argentina. In October 1993, the voters in Peru approved a constitution that mandates liberalization policies. In general, Latin American countries are reported to have experienced the largest reduction in the degree of protectionism. But continued export-oriented growth requires adequate access to the markets of the developed countries. And there is evidence that nontariff barriers form a serious obstacle to LDCs' exports to the industrial countries, reducing them by about 18 percent.[8] It is mainly their demands for freer access to the developed countries' markets that have thrust the LDCs' trade problems into the international arena. The focus for this confrontation has been provided by the United Nations Conference of Trade and Development.

The U.N. Conference on Trade and Development

Most members of the United Nations are developing countries, yet international economic relations have been largely dominated by the score or so of industrial member nations. On several important grounds the developing countries feel that these relations serve exclusively the interest of the developed nations. In 1964, to provide a platform for their demands, the developing countries initiated an international conference known as the **United Nations Conference on Trade and Development (UNCTAD).** A permanent secretariat of the organization, under United Nations auspices, is headquartered in Geneva. A Trade and Development Board of 55 members meets twice a year, while plenary sessions of the entire membership (165 countries) are convened once every four years. LDCs' concerns relate mainly to price stabilization of primary products and improved access for their manufacturing exports to the markets of the industrial countries.

Demands Concerning Primary Products

Many of the complaints of the developing nations result from their dependence on the exportation of raw materials and agricultural products, commonly referred to under the heading "primary products." Most of their nonpetroleum export earnings are made up of such commodities. Furthermore, in 30 of these countries, over 80 percent of the export earnings are derived from only three leading commodities. As a consequence, the price movements of primary commodities are of prime concern to them.

A long-standing complaint of these nations is that their commodity terms of trade—the ratio of the export price index to the import price index—has been declining or deteriorating over the long run. In other

[7] Newly industrialized countries.

[8] UNCTAD *Bulletin*, May–June 1991.

words, they can buy fewer imports for a given quantity of their exports. A 1994 IMF study[9] finds support for that view. The theories behind the alleged decline in their export prices relative to import prices are many and varied. Much of their trade is an exchange of primary products for manufactured goods. It has been variably claimed that

1. As world income grows, the demand for manufactured goods expands faster than the demand for primary products, so that the relative price of the latter declines.
2. Because primary products are marketed competitively, their prices are flexible, and any improvement in productivity is partly passed on to the foreign consumers in the form of reduced prices. On the other hand, monopolistic practices in manufacturing make prices rigid in a downward direction, so that the benefits of productivity increases are reaped in the form of high earnings in the producing countries and not in the form of lower prices.
3. The development of synthetic substitutes lowers the demand for many primary materials and thereby depresses their prices.[10]

These and other theoretical arguments were marshaled to support the claim of a **secular deterioration in the terms of trade** of the developing countries. But these arguments can be countered by equally convincing propositions on the other side. And, more importantly, the vast number of empirical studies undertaken since the claim was first advanced in the 1950s are far from conclusive. The evidence on the problem is mixed and fails to substantiate the deterioration thesis.[11]

Moreover, even a deterioration in the commodity terms of trade is not in itself an indication of decline in economic welfare. It all depends on the cause of the deterioration. To see this, imagine that Brazil achieves a 15 percent productivity improvement in coffee production, thereby increasing the world supply of coffee. If, as a result, world coffee prices decline by

---

[9] See IMF Survey, October 31, 1994, pp. 350–352.

[10] Conversely, environmental cleanup requirements in the industrial countries may prove beneficial to LDC exports, for they raise the prices of competitive products produced in the developed countries. Thus, a rise in price of synthetic rubber, attendant upon environmental regulations, would make natural rubber from Southeast Asia more competitive.

[11] A recent study shows that the price of nonoil primary commodities relative to that of manufactures declined slightly between 1900 and 1986. But that decline was more than offset by an increase in quantity, so that the purchasing power of total exports of these products increased considerably. See E. Grilli and M. Yang, "Primary Commodity Prices, Manufactured Goods Prices, and the Terms of Trade of Developing Countries," *World Bank Economic Review,* January 1988: 1–48.

5 percent, Brazil's commodity terms of trade also deteriorate and to the same extent. But the economic lot of Brazilians still improves by 10 percent: the 15 percent rise in productivity minus the 5 percent decline in the terms of trade. That 5 percent represents the benefit derived by the rest of the world from Brazil's productivity improvement.[12]

This alternative concept, the volume of imports obtainable per unit of input employed in the export industries, is known as the *single factoral terms of trade.* It is measured by multiplying the commodity terms of trade by the productivity index in the export industries. In the present example, it is a better indicator of the effect of trade on economic welfare than are the commodity terms of trade. On the other hand, if the price of Brazilian coffee declined because of a shift in world taste from coffee to tea, then the commodity terms of trade would be an adequate indicator.

Demands to remedy the alleged "secular deterioration" by such methods as **indexing** (or pegging) the prices of primary commodities to those of manufactured goods[13] disappeared from the scene in the late 1970s.

Additional claims advanced by the developing nations in the area of primary products have to do with agricultural protectionism in the industrial world. Direct quantitative barriers of all sorts are imposed on temperate-zone products (and on sugar), while tropical products are subject to excise taxes in Europe. Both the prices and volume of exports are artificially depressed by such measures. This lowers foreign exchange earnings of the developing countries and seriously handicaps their development efforts, which depend on imported equipment. A partial liberalization of trade in tropical products was achieved in the Uruguay Round.

A third complaint of the developing countries concerns violent **short-run price fluctuations** in their exports, which in turn generate wide swings in export earnings and in domestic economic activity. Again, economic growth is said to be the casualty. Schematically, the two links in the argument are as follows:

Price fluctuations $\longrightarrow$ Fluctuations in foreign currency earnings $\longrightarrow$ Retardation of real growth and of investment

Because supply of, and demand for, primary products are price inelastic, large price fluctuations can be expected on *a priori* grounds and are verified in empirical studies.

---

[12] On the other hand, "immiserizing growth" occurs when technological advance in the export industry increases output and consequently depresses prices by more than the rise in productivity, resulting in a net loss to society. (See J. Bhagwati, "Immiserizing Growth," *Review of Economic Studies,* June 1958.) But this is a very unusual outcome.

[13] Under such an arrangement, prices of primary commodities would move up and down with the prices of manufactured goods, and in the same proportion.

However, the link from price fluctuations to variations in foreign currency earnings depends on whether the price changes are caused by shifts in the demand or the supply curve. Perhaps because the supply of agricultural commodities is dominated by weather conditions, supply shifts cause most of their price fluctuations (see chapter 5, figure 5.3, panel a). Here price and quantity move in opposite directions, so that foreign exchange earnings (price × quantity) need not fluctuate excessively. In the case of raw materials, most price fluctuations are caused by shifts in demand (figure 5.3, panel b), perhaps because demand is dominated by economic conditions in the industrial countries. In this case, price and quantity move in the same direction, and sizable fluctuations in foreign currency earnings may be expected. This can be verified by observing what happens to the rectangular area under equilibrium point e (which represents foreign currency earnings) when supply shifts (panel a) and when demand shifts (panel b).

With respect to the second link, a host of cross-sectional empirical studies failed to establish a negative correlation between a degree of price or foreign currency fluctuations on the one hand and growth rate in real GDP or in investment on the other. Although fluctuations may make planning more difficult, they do not appear harmful to the development enterprise itself. However, policymakers in the developing countries are often more concerned with their ability to *plan* than with the growth performance in the private sector. And, economic planning is handicapped by violent fluctuations in foreign exchange earnings.

To cope with this alleged problem UNCTAD developed a proposal for an **Integrated Commodity Program.** It envisaged international commodity agreements of the buffer stock variety for each of 10 to 18 primary commodities. The individual ICAs would be linked to a "common fund," made up of contributions from producing and consuming countries. But the reaction of the major industrial countries toward this program was negative. They suggested that past experiences with commodity agreements were far from encouraging and certainly not positive enough to warrant such a far-reaching enterprise. Second, the necessary financial commitment, when realistically appraised, could not be justified. Such large sums, if used to *diversify* the economies of the developing countries, would be likely to yield greater dividends in terms of the stabilization of export earnings.

What emerged was a modest proposal for a Common Fund of moderate proportions: $470 million to finance the buffer stock operations for 18 commodities and $350 million of voluntary contributions for market research and export promotion. The United States did not ratify the agreement.

There exists a direct method of stabilizing foreign currency earnings: the compensatory finance facility of the IMF. It enables a member to borrow (at low interest) when its export earnings and financial reserves are low and to make repayments when they are high. The drawings, for up to 3–5 years, can occur when a country's export earnings over a 12-month period fall considerably short of the 5-year average. This facility, along with STABEX of the EU, represents a more direct way of stabilizing foreign currency earnings than the roundabout means of price stabilization.[14]

Manufactured Products

As for manufactured goods, the main complaint of the developing nations is that the tariff structure of the developed countries discriminates against them.[15] First, rates are high on the labor-intensive simple-technology products in which they are interested. And, while multilateral concessions granted in GATT negotiations are extended to them without reciprocity, these concessions usually apply to commodities that are too sophisticated for them to manufacture. Indeed, while tariff rates on goods produced in the industrial world were lowered considerably, labor-intensive goods, such as textiles, were placed under direct quantitative restrictions. In part, this was due to the passive position that LDCs have taken in GATT negotiations. Historically, they offered no concessions of their own, preferring simply to receive the concessions that were exchanged among the industrial countries. These were granted to the LDCs under the MFN rule without the LDCs having to reciprocate. But as a consequence, the negotiations between the United States, Europe, and Japan centered on commodities that were of export interest only to the industrial countries. Indeed, it is in the interest of the developing countries to participate actively in WTO negotiations. Offering concessions would rationalize their import regimes,[16] and at the same time enable them to demand meaningful concessions from the industrial nations. This has been recognized by the developing countries during the Uruguay Round, in which they abandoned their passive stance and participated fully in the negotiations. Indeed, the Uruguay Round resulted in an agreement to phase out the textile quotas and to lower the protection of agriculture—both of abiding interest to the LDCs.

In the second place, the tariff structure of the industrial countries discourages industrialization elsewhere. In many cases, rates are low or non-existent on raw materials and rise gradually with the degree of processing or fabrication to which the product has been subjected. This means that effective rates of protection on the finished products are much higher than

---

[14] A comparison between the EU STABEX and IMF Compensatory Finance Facility can be found in World Bank, *World Development Report* 1986: 137–142. See also B. Suart and R. Pownall "The IMF Compensatory and Contingency Financing Facility," *Finance and Development*, December 1988.

[15] See D. Clark, "Nontariff Measures and Developing Country Exports," *The Journal of Developing Areas*, January 1993.

[16] An examination of possible LDC strategy in GATT negotiations can be found in "Developing Countries and the Global Trading System," reported on in the *IMF Survey*, August 7, 1989. See also "Trade Policy Issues and Developments," IMF *Occasional Paper* no. 38, 1985. A 1986 UNCTAD study estimates that complete elimination of the post Tokyo-Round trade restrictions (on an MFN basis) would increase LDCs' exports by nearly 12 percent, or $30 billion. See UNCTAD *Bulletin*, February 1986.

the nominal rates (often more than double), which further accentuates the tariff *escalation* and reinforces the incentives of the nonindustrial countries to export goods in their raw form. Certainly, the tariff structure that LDCs face discourages local processing of the products they export.

To offset and reverse this structure, the developing countries demanded tariff preferences for their manufactured exports in the markets of the industrial countries; they wished to be charged lower rates in the markets of each developed country than other industrial countries were charged for similar products.

Analytically, preferences are analogous to customs unions, because they give rise to two static effects on trade flows:

1. *The trade-creation effect:* Tariffs are reduced on imports from the **beneficiary countries,** which then displace some inefficient domestic production in the **donor**[17] **country.**
2. *The trade-diversion effect:* The tariff discrimination embodied in the preferences results in imports from third countries being displaced by those from the beneficiary countries in the markets of the donor countries.

One study[18] suggests that the structure of effective tariff protection of manufacturing industries in the developed countries is *positively* correlated with the comparative advantage of the developing countries. Therefore, an across-the-board, duty-free access (without exceptions or limitations) granted to the developing countries' exports could provide them with an incentive to expand industries in which they have a comparative advantage. Conversely, effective protection in the developed countries was shown to be negatively correlated with their comparative advantage. Consequently, a truly generalized, limitation-free preference scheme would improve allocative efficiency in the developed countries as well. Insofar as the output displaced is that of labor-intensive, technologically unsophisticated industries, the resources in the developed countries would be forced to move to industries in which they possess a comparative advantage. But internal political pressures in the donor countries invariably work to limit this effect. As will be seen in what follows, most preferential schemes include restrictions designed to limit the trade-creation effect. Yet UNCTAD studies indicate that the GSP did contribute to expansion of exports from LDCs.[19]

---

[17] The preference giving and receiving countries are known as "donor" and "beneficiary" countries respectively.

[18] Z. Iqubal, "The Generalized System of Preferences and the Comparative Advantage of Less Developed Countries in Manufactures," (mimeographed), *International Monetary Fund*, April 1974.

[19] UNCTAD *Bulletin*, May–June 1991.

Since the trade-diversion effect requires that a preferential margin be maintained, once preferences exist, the developing countries hold a vested interest in opposing general tariff reduction among the developed countries under the WTO because it reduces the margin of preferences.

When preferences were considered in the councils of nations during the 1960s, a host of substantive and administrative problems were raised. Yet sustained pressure from the developing nations, coupled with East–West politics and the vying for influence in the uncommitted world, kept the issue not only alive but in the forefront of international deliberations. These efforts came to fruition in the 1970s, when many industrial nations implemented preferential schemes in favor of the developing countries.

THE GENERALIZED SYSTEM OF PREFERENCES (GSP)[20]

Between 1971 and 1972, Japan and the Western European countries introduced **the Generalized System of Preferences** in favor of the developing countries under UNCTAD sponsorship; the United States and Canada did so on January 1, 1976. While the GSP offers LDCs tariff preferences, import of GSP-covered products also face a wide variey of nontariff measures in the markets of the industrial countries.[21] The schemes vary greatly in product coverage, lists of beneficiary countries, and measures to safeguard domestic output and employment in the donor countries. Because of their importance as major markets, we describe the schemes of the United States, the EU, and Japan.

The U.S. Scheme

Over 100 developing countries, 32 of which are classified as least developed,[22] are granted GSP status by the United States. About 4,100 products, mostly manufactures and semimanufactures, but also selected agricultural products, exported by these beneficiary countries may enter the United States duty free. However, various "sensitive" items are excluded from the scheme.

To qualify for preferential treatment, the product must be shipped directly from the beneficiary country to the United States without passing through the territory of another country, as well as meeting the **rules of origin** criteria. These mandate that the product be wholly manufactured

---

[20] For a study of the GSP, see T. Murray, *Trade Preferences for Developing Countries*, London: The Macmillan Press, 1977. A summary of recent UNCTAD studies of GSP schemes can be found in UNCTAD *Bulletin*, April 1988: 7–9; and C. MacPhee, "A Synthesis of the GSP Study Program," UNCTAD *Report*, no. IPT/19, December 1989.

[21] Clark and Zarilli, "Nontariff Measures and Industrial Nation Imports of GSP-Covered Products," *Southern Economic Journal*, October 1992.

[22] In total there are 42 countries classified as least developed among the developing countries, with a combined population of 390 million and an average annual per capita income of only $215.

within the beneficiary country; or, if imported materials and components are used, these must undergo "substantial transformation" in that country—a requirement that the value added there must account for at least 35 percent of the value of the finished product. The combined members of three regional associations[23] are each treated as single countries for the purpose of meeting the rules of origin criteria.

Preferential treatment does not apply to imports of an article from a particular beneficiary country if it accounts for more than 50 percent of total U.S. imports of this product, or if its shipments from the country during a calendar year exceed a given dollar amount. That dollar value is adjusted upward annually. These two ceilings, known jointly as the *competitive-need limitation*, can be waived under certain conditions. But they constitute an incentive to any developing country to avoid exporting to the United States even $1 beyond the limit, because that would subject its entire exports to the MFN duty.

A feature known as *graduation* was added to the program in 1985. A product can be graduated—removed—from the GSP list of particular beneficiaries if it is assessed that they can be competitive without the duty-free status. Or a country may be graduated from the program altogether if it reaches a certain development status. Taiwan, South Korea, Singapore, and Hong Kong (known as the *four tigers*) were so graduated in 1989, and are no longer beneficiaries in the U.S. scheme. In addition, various practices of a country are examined in order to determine its eligibility for the GSP, including the extent to which it provides market access to U.S. goods and services; offers protection of U.S. intellectual property rights; refrains from unreasonable export practices; and guarantees internationally recognized rights to its workers.

The EU Scheme

Over 130 developing countries, 42 of which are classified as least developed, benefit from the EU scheme. All dutiable manufactured and semimanufactured products are accorded duty-free status. But 550 products are considered "sensitive"—namely their market in the EU may be disrupted by imports from the beneficiary countries. For each of these the EU assigns a quantitative limit for the duty-free entry. Once reached, the duty reverts to the MFN level. This constitutes a form of *tariff quota*,[24] from which the least-developed countries are exempted. For textile products, duty-free entry is granted only to the 33 beneficiaries that signed the Multifibre Arrangement, and have bilateral agreements on textiles with the EU. EU imports are sub-

---

[23] The Andean Group, which includes Bolivia, Colombia, Ecuador, Peru, and Venezuela; the ASEAN group, consisting of Indonesia, Malaysia, the Philippines, and Thailand; and the Caribbean Common Market.

[24] A tariff quota describes a situation in which a given absolute amount of imports of a certain product is subject to one tariff rate (even zero), and any imports in excess of that amount are subject to a higher rate.

ject to quantitative limitations, from which the least-developed countries are exempt. Similar limitations apply to the exports of steel products from certain beneficiary countries.

For many agricultural products the EU scheme offers duty-free entry or tariff reductions ranging between 20 and 50 percent, depending on the product. However, some products are subject to quantitative limitations.

To qualify for preferential treatment, eligible goods must be transported directly to the EU, and comply with the rules of origin criteria. The latter state that the good must be wholly produced within the beneficiary country, or if imported parts and materials are used, they must have undergone "sufficient working or processing" in that country. Processing is considered sufficient if the goods become classified under a different tariff heading than that covering the nonoriginating materials. Three regional groupings (the same as those named by the United States) are each considered as single countries for the purpose of meeting this requirement.

While the EU recognizes 42 least-developed beneficiaries to be accorded special privileges under its GSP, 33 of them are Associated States of the EU—therefore only nine least-developed countries actually use the EU scheme. In general, the 68 Associated States and 8 Mediterranean countries have special and more liberal association agreements with the EU and thus do not use the GSP.

The Japanese Scheme

Japan grants preferences to 130 developing countries, of which 38 are regarded as least developed. Most industrial products enter duty free under the scheme, while some receive 50-percent tariff reductions. However, about one-half of the eligible products are subject to quantitative ceilings, set in advance of each fiscal year. Once the ceiling is reached for any given product, the duty reverts to the MFN level. Thus, for most products of interest to the developing countries, Japan's scheme assumes the form of a tariff quota. Furthermore, preferential treatment is suspended when preferential imports to Japan from that country reach 25 percent of the quantitative ceiling. These restrictions do not apply to least-developed countries. Selected agricultural products receive various duty reductions, including zero duty. The least-developed countries receive duty-free treatment on all farm products covered by the scheme.

To qualify for preferential treatment, eligible goods must be transported directly to Japan and comply with rules of origin. These rules require that the product be wholly produced within the beneficiary country, or if imported parts and materials are used, that these be subject to "sufficient transformation" within that country. Processing is considered "sufficient" if the goods so obtained become classified under a tariff heading other than that covering any of the nonoriginating materials. Components imported from Japan by the beneficiary country are considered as originating in the beneficiary country itself. And the member states of ASEAN are considered as a single country for the purpose of acquiring origin status.

Effect of the Tokyo and Uruguay Rounds on the GSP

Tariff reductions under the Tokyo and Uruguay Rounds erode the margin of preferences accorded the developing countries. But against the loss, the developing countries are accorded the benefit of the resulting tariff reductions under the WTO. These benefits are free of (a) the restrictions on beneficiaries and on commodity coverage, (b) quantitative limitation, (c) possible removal under domestic safeguard provisions, and (d) the time limitation on the GSP program. Careful calculations have shown that these benefits outweigh the losses occasioned by the erosion in the margin of preferences.[25]

REGIONAL INTEGRATION AMONG DEVELOPING NATIONS

There is an intense desire on the part of many nonindustrial nations to form regional economic groups among themselves. Customs unions and free-trade areas have been established with varying degrees of success in Central America, South America (e.g., Mecusor), Asia (e.g., ASEAN)[26], and Africa. The main objective in most cases is to enlarge the domestic market.[27]

In the past many countries adopted an *import substitution* development strategy. One factor that has an important bearing on the success or failure of such a strategy is the size of the market. The larger the market, the better the prospect for a new import-substituting industry to someday reach an efficient size and become viable. Consequently, the developing countries often choose to expand their own markets through regional integration.

In analytical terms, there are important differences between European integration and customs unions among developing countries. While in the first case, economic researchers have been mainly concerned with the effect on world welfare, the impact of, say, a West African Common Market on international trade flows is rather insignificant. The main concern in the latter case is with the effect of integration on the integrating countries themselves. In that respect, trade creation as well as trade diversion *may* be beneficial. In Europe, trade diversion is considered harmful because it implies misallocation of fully employed resources from more efficient to less efficient pursuits. But in developing countries, the domestic labor drawn into

---

[25] See R. Baldwin and T. Murray, "MFN Tariff Reductions and LDC Benefits under the GSP," *Economic Journal*, March 1977: 30–46.

[26] Consisting of Thailand, Malaysia, Indonesia, the Philippines, Singapore, Brunei, and Vietnam, possibly to be joined by Burma, Cambodia, and Laos.

[27] A recent study showed that MFN reductions of tariff rates would yield welfare benefits to the Asian developing countries several times greater than either regional or global schemes of preferential tariff reductions among developing countries. See Dean DeRosa, "Asian Preferences and the Gains from MFN Tariff Reductions," *The World Economy*, September 1988.

trade-diverting activities may have been formerly unemployed or under-employed, so that its opportunity cost is at or near zero. There is another sense in which trade diversion in a customs union among developing countries may be welcome as "the lesser of two evils"—if the alternative to a trade-diverting, import-substituting customs union is a policy of import substitution pursued individually by the members of the union, each with a small national market. A study of the Central American Common Market[28] found the major benefits from integration to include: the savings of scarce foreign exchange as members trade more with each other and import less from the rest of the world; the utilization of low opportunity-cost labor; and the exploitation of economies of scale.

An important issue that often crops up with this approach is the distribution of the gains from integration. Because the integrating area consists of countries at different stages of development, new industries and other economic activity generated by the enlarged markets gravitate toward the most highly developed centers, much to the chagrin of those who represent the more backward regions. In East Africa, the developed center may be the Nairobi area. This tendency is often referred to as **polarization** of economic activity. The areas that were most advanced to begin with may come to dominate the entire customs union, while the less advanced areas do not share in the gain from integration. To cope with this problem, several customs unions have adopted a scheme of allocating new industries among the nations that make up the union, in the hope of ensuring equitable distribution of the gain.

Another common dilemma is the lack of adequate transportation facilities to make the enlarged market economically meaningful. It does little good to establish free-trade areas in South America if member countries find it cheaper to ship to North America and Europe than across the Andes. The natural trade orientation of many such members is toward the industrial nations, intracontinental trade constituting only a small portion of total trade. Without adequate overland transportation facilities, they cannot hope to change that.

Summary

This chapter concerns selected trade problems of the developing countries. It distinguishes between import-substitution and export-promotion development strategies, showing that the latter approach yields better results in promoting growth and employment. For that reason, many countries are

[28] See W. R. Cline and E. Delgado (eds.), *Economic Integration in Central America,* Washington, D.C.: The Brookings Institution, 1978. For a critical examination of policies designed to promote "south–south" trade, see Oli Havrylyshyn and Martin Wolf, "Promoting Trade among Developing Countries: An Assessment," *Finance and Development,* March 1982.

instituting reforms that involve less government intervention in the economy and that promote integration into the global economy.

Within the framework of UNCTAD, the developing countries are demanding schemes to stabilize the prices of primary commodities. In particular they envisage the introduction of buffer stock agreements for up to 18 commodities, under the umbrella of a common fund. The LDCs have also demanded and received preferential treatment for their exports in the form of the GSP, which is designed to promote their manufacturing exports to industrial countries. But the GSP schemes, which vary from one donor country to another, contain many restrictions that limit their usefulness to the developing countries. Finally, the LDCs have shown great interest in regional integration designed to expand the size of their market.

Important Concepts

Import substitution	Integrated Commodity Program
Export promotion	Beneficiary country
United Nations Conference on Trade and Development (UNCTAD)	Donor country
	Generalized System of Preferences (GSP)
Secular deterioration in the terms of trade	Rules of origin
Short-run commodity price fluctuations	Polarization

Review Questions

1. Compare and contrast export-promotion and import-substitution strategies of development.

2. a. Using four partial equilibrium diagrams, explain clearly how an international buffer stock functions. (Consult chapter 5 as well.)
   b. What problems arise in the operation of buffer stock agreements?
   c. Must large commodity price fluctuations result in large fluctuations in the foreign currency earnings of the exporting country?

3. a. How would the Tokyo and Uruguay Rounds affect the value of the GSP for the LDCs?
   b. Do the terms *trade diversion* and *trade creation* have a meaning in the analysis of preferences (such as the GSP)? Explain.

4.   Does the traditional analysis of customs unions apply without reservation to economic integration among LDCs? What special problems are encountered in the formation of such groupings?

5.   Describe the main features of the GSP schemes granted by the United States, the EU, and Japan.

CHAPTER 9

International Mobility of Productive Factors

Thus far the emphasis of this book has been concerned with trade in goods and services. Absent from the preceding chapters is an analysis of international factor movement. This omission is far from accidental; in fact, it is rooted in a long-standing assumption of classical economic theory. In attempting to demonstrate the gains from international trade and explain the commodity composition of trade, it is assumed that factors of production (labor, natural resources, and capital) are free to move only within each country; they cannot move between countries.

Yet observing the world around us, we notice large-scale international mobility of capital. Multinational enterprises with subsidiary companies in many countries have come to play a dominant role on the world scene. Also, despite social, cultural, and legal obstacles to mobility, people do move across national boundaries, sometimes in great numbers.

Productive factors usually move from areas of low remuneration to areas of high remuneration, lowering their supply in the first region and raising it in the latter. The workings of the market then raise the earnings of the migrating factor in the land of departure (source country) and lower it in the land of arrival (host country), thus tending to equalize factor rewards the world over. Under the Heckscher-Ohlin theory of international trade, this is what commodity trade is supposed to accomplish. Indeed, under the conditions of that model, commodity trade and factor mobility are substitutes for each other. If factors moved freely to a point where their remunerations were equalized across countries, there would be no international price differentials between commodities. In general, a labor-abundant country may import capital-intensive goods or import capital, and a capital-abundant country may import labor-intensive goods or import labor. Only lately have

| FIGURE 9.1 | *DFI Stock Among Triad Members and Their Clusters, 1993 (Billion Dollars)* |

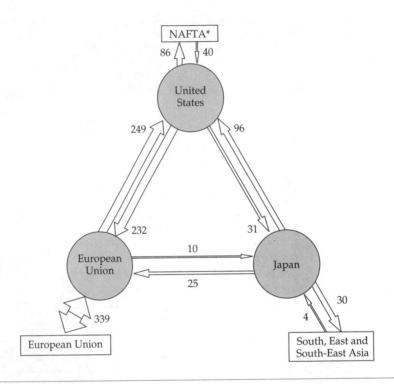

Source: UNCTAD, *World Investment Report 1995*, New York and Geneva, U.N., 1995. In addition to a wealth of empirical information, the *Report* contains an extensive review of countries' policies towards DFI.

economists begun to develop models that incorporate both commodity and factor mobility.[1]

Relaxing the assumption of immobile capital, this chapter inquires into the costs and benefits of **direct foreign investment (DFI).** DFI means investments that give the company headquarters *control* over the foreign subsidiary. Much of it is undertaken by **multinational corporations (MNC);** namely, companies with production facilities in several countries. There exist

[1] The following is an example of how the traditional results can change under such conditions. Suppose country *A* is more efficient than country *B* in the production of two products. But the degree of its advantage is identical in the two products, so that the price ratio is the same in both countries. Under the Heckscher–Ohlin model, and in the absence of factor mobility, there would be no trade. But with capital mobile, it would flow from *B* to *A* to exploit the more efficient environment, thereby raising the capital-labor ratio in *A* above that of *B*. Country *A* would then begin exporting the capital-intensive product and importing the labor-intensive one.

some 40,000 parent firms and 250,000 foreign affiliates in the world. Global sales of foreign affiliates was $5.2 trillion in 1992, while the stock of DFI is estimated at $2.6 trillion (1995). In recent years outflow of DFI grew much more rapidly than world trade. The DFI stock among triad members and their clusters (for 1993) is shown in figure 9.1.

The top ten MNCs (ranked by foreign assets) are shown below:

Company	Home country	Industry	Assets		Sales		Employment	
			Foreign	Total	Foreign	Total	Foreign	Total
			(Billions of dollars)				(Employees)	
Royal Dutch Shell	Netherlands/U.K.	Petroleum refining	69.4	100.8	45.5	95.2	85 000	117 000
Exxon	United States	Petroleum refining	47.4	84.1	87.7	111.2	57 000	91 000
IBM	United States	Computers	44.1	81.1	37.0	64.1	130 655	256 207
General Motors	United States	Motor vehicles and parts	36.9	167.4	28.6	133.6	270 000	756 000
General Electric	United States	Electronics	31.6	251.5	11.2	60.5	59 000	222 000
Toyota	Japan	Motor vehicles and parts	N.A.	97.6	41.1	94.6	23 824	110 534
Ford	United States	Motor vehicles and parts	30.9	198.9	36.0	108.5	180 904	332 700
Hitachi	Japan	Electronics	N.A.	86.7	16.5	71.8	N.A.	330 637
Sony	Japan	Electronics	N.A.	41.5	26.3	36.3	70 000	130 000
Mitsubishi	Japan	Trading	N.A.	85.2	65.3	168.4	N.A.	157 900

Source: UNCTAD, *IBID,* table 1.7: "The Top 100 MNCs"

It is estimated that the stock of U.S. direct investment abroad amounted to $600 billion at the end of 1994, while foreign investment holdings in the United States were $500 billion. This makes the United States the largest host country in the world. It is followed by the U.K. ($200 billion), France ($138 billion), and China ($130 billion). About 5 percent of U.S. private-sector workers are employed by foreign corporations. The largest investors in the United States were the British followed by the Japanese.

MOTIVES FOR DIRECT INVESTMENTS ABROAD[2]

Both economic analysis and empirical studies trace the underlying motive for investing abroad to profit expectations. American enterprises invest in

[2]Although a solid and cohesive theory of the multinational corporation has yet to emerge, there are several hypotheses attempting to explain why production is carried on by the same firm in several countries. The most popular hypothesis suggests that a firm in possession of a unique technology or some other firm-specific advantage (such as low input cost or a better distribution system) finds it best to exploit it within the firm by setting up subsidiaries (as against licensing the technology to other firms). Other hypotheses range from portfolio diversification to sales maximization, to the product cycle theory, to a desire to maintain a stake in rapidly growing markets. See R. Vernon and L. Wells, *Economic Environment of International Business,* New York: Prentice Hall, 1981; R. Caves, *Multinational Enterprise and Economic Analysis,* Cambridge: Cambridge University Press, 1982; and J. Dunning, *Essays in International Business,* 1994.

foreign countries when the prospects of profit from such investments exceed profits anticipated from the alternative uses of the funds. From the viewpoint of the national economy, the "alternative uses" consist of investments in the United States either by the same company or by others that can attain control over real resources by obtaining access to those funds. Thus, when investment funds flow to foreign countries, it may be assumed that, given the investment climate at home and abroad, expected profits (allowing for risk) from an incremental investment in foreign countries exceeded the profits expected from such activity in the United States. Factors affecting the relative investment climate include the general level of economic activity, existing and anticipated tax and tariff policies, and general institutional arrangements. Certainly the high growth rate in the United States during 1983–1989 attracted foreign investment to these shores. The subsequent decline in such investment was due partly to the slowdown in the U.S. economy in 1990–1992, with the recovery of the mid-1990s stimulating investment inflows.

Another way of viewing the motivation for direct foreign investment is to focus on international profit differentials *within* an industry. Thus if expected profit in U.K. auto manufacturing exceeds that in U.S. auto production while the reverse is true for chemicals, then there would be a flow of direct investment from the United States to the United Kingdom in the auto industry and from the United Kingdom to the United States in the chemical industry.

But while such statements lend themselves to analysis with the economists' tool kit, they are too superficial for the understanding of business behavior under diverse circumstances. Indeed, when questioned directly about their motives, business organizations may not even mention increased profits. Rather, they tend to emphasize other factors, which in turn have direct or indirect bearing on net earnings.

The factors that contribute to the increased net earnings from foreign investment are so numerous and diverse as to defy an exhaustive survey. At the risk of some oversimplification, we lump them into two broad categories. The first category comprises cost or supply considerations that lower the costs of production and distribution, while the second includes market or demand considerations that influence profits by raising total revenue. Because profit is the difference between revenue and cost, whatever factors raise revenue or lower cost also increase profit.

Cost Considerations

The desire to increase profits by reducing costs certainly plays an important role in foreign investment decisions. It is useful to distinguish between two types of cost-reducing investment. The first arises from the need to obtain raw materials from abroad. Such materials may be either unavailable at home or obtainable only at extremely high costs. But they are essential to the production and sale of final products at home or abroad. Profit opportunities would remain unexploited without them.

Indeed, the vast American foreign investment in the extractive industries are motivated by the fact that the capital must follow the resources. The product of such investment is a factor of production *complementary* to the labor and capital employed within the United States. Any diminution in the availability of this resource would directly harm the productivity and remunerations of the other two. This complementary factor includes primary materials, certain agricultural commodities (tropical products), and some semiprocessed goods brought back to the United States for further processing, with the final product marketed either here or abroad. Inclusion of the last item is dictated by the transportation costs of the primary products. When they are prohibitive or very high, the first stage of processing may have to take place at or near the extraction site, with the product brought home in a semiprocessed form. Investment in foreign transportation and communication links, which make possible or cheapen exports from the home country to otherwise isolated regions, can be regarded in the same light. Many of the American investments in developing countries are so motivated.

The second type of cost-reducing investment involves costs other than materials—primarily labor. Although to the company management it makes little difference where costs are cut, the national interest is likely to be affected differently. In the case of extractive industries, the resource whose cost is reduced is complementary to U.S. factors of production; it raises the productivity of American labor as well as capital and often leads to increased production within the United States. In some cases, such as oil, the resource is essential to the productive process in this country. On the other hand, when foreign investments are designed to lower labor costs, the savings occur in the employment of factors that are competitive with American resources. While such foreign investment raises the productivity of American capital, it tends to lower the productivity of American labor compared with similar investment in the United States.

Perhaps the most potent motive in the second category is the desire to take advantage of lower labor costs in foreign countries. The fact that wage rates in the United States are higher than in many other countries is not in itself an indication of higher labor costs. It is simply a reflection of the higher productivity of American labor. But when the wage differentials are not fully offset by productivity differentials, the result is lower labor cost in foreign countries. Industries in which the labor component is high relative to the capital component (the relatively labor-intensive industries) would be the first candidates for such cost differentials. But an unfavorable labor-cost differential may appear at times even in capital-intensive industries, when wage rates abroad lag considerably behind increases in productivity. The remarkable wage stability in Europe during the second half of the 1950s certainly contributed to that phenomenon, thereby stimulating American investment abroad. But in the late 1980s and the 1990s, U.S. labor costs were lower than their counterparts in certain European countries, motivating European and Japanese companies to establish or purchase production facilities in the United States. In the late 1980s Spain and Ireland became attractive host countries to American and Japanese investment by virtue of their low labor costs combined with accessibility to the EU market. And in the 1990s Asian countries are an attractive destination for Japanese and American investment. Labor-cost differentials can be exploited by producing abroad and selling the final product in the host country, in third countries, or even back in the source country.

Another type of saving that can be secured by manufacturing abroad is in transportation costs. When the final product is perishable or has a high weight-to-value ratio, proximity to the main markets becomes very important. It may then be advantageous to replace exports with foreign production.

Government policies often play a direct role in inducing foreign investment. The outflow of capital may be motivated by a desire to take advantage of special tax treatment. More often, tariff policies both in the United States and abroad bring about substantial relocation of plants. Successive reductions of duties by the United States can induce companies to produce abroad for sale in the United States. As American manufacturers lose their protective tariffs, they may not be able to compete against lower-cost imports, primarily those of labor-intensive products. Consequently, they may set up production facilities in low-cost areas from which to supply the American market. Likewise, the establishment of the EU provided very strong incentives for American companies to invest in Europe. Such investment enables producers to circumvent the discriminatory tariff wall they must face when exporting from the United States. And each facility in Europe can supply several national markets. Thus, the plant can be large enough to realize economies of scale and the benefits of specialization. Asian firms may invest in Mexico in order to gain duty-free access to the U.S. market. By the same token, there is little doubt that, historically, the high Canadian tariff constituted a powerful inducement for American corporations to invest in Canada. Without it, the Canadian market could easily be supplied out of stateside locations. Capital movement has become a substitute for the obstructed commodity movement. And, to the extent that U.S. investments in Mexico are motivated by the high Mexican tariff, NAFTA will remove that motivation. Fear of protectionism in the United States was a factor stimulating direct foreign investment in the United States in the 1980s. (Foreign investment in response to exchange rate fluctuations will be considered in Part Two.)

Finally, when a large company goes abroad, it sometimes becomes necessary for its suppliers at home—including banks—to establish overseas branches as well in order to provide efficient service to its foreign subsidiaries.

Marketing Considerations

On an abstract level, according to a historical pattern firms are induced to set up foreign branches as they become familiar with foreign markets through exports. The general widening of business horizons attendant upon the expansion of international trade leads businesses to increase their foreign investment. But sheer familiarity is merely an enabling condition. The desire to cater to specific market needs appears to be the real motivation. Initially, dissatisfaction with distribution techniques abroad may stimulate the establishment of a selling organization, including warehousing and service facilities, to market exports from the United States. As a second stage, the company is drawn to set up production or assembly and conversion plants so as to be close to its customers, provide better services, gear its product lines to local demands in specific markets, and, perhaps, satisfy the nationalistic feelings of its customers (or of the local government), thus increasing their acceptance of the product. But nationalistic feelings also work in the opposite direction, apparent in occasional aversion to foreign control of host-country manufacturing facilities. On balance, however, market and demand considerations constitute a potent factor in stimulating foreign investment. In addition, antitrust legislation in the United States, which often prevents firms from expanding through the acquisition of their competitors, may induce them to purchase such firms overseas.

It is an empirical question whether, on balance, DFI constitutes a substitute for trade. A 1996 Report by the WTO ("Trade and DFI") concludes that "there is *no* serious empirical support for the view that DFI has an important *negative* effect on the overall exports from the home country."

FOREIGN INVESTMENT AND ECONOMIC WELFARE (REAL INCOME)

World Welfare

It has long been an established proposition of economic theory that free movement of resources is beneficial to the world economy as a whole. When capital is attracted from one country to another by a higher rate of return, it flows from areas where it is relatively abundant and cheap to countries in which it is relatively scarce and expensive, until returns to it are equalized the world over. This flow is bound to be beneficial, because it raises total real output. The contribution of the marginal unit of capital to real output is less in the source nation than in the host nation; in other words, capital is a relatively more important productive factor where it is scarce than where it is abundant. Thus, the addition to output it brings about in the host country exceeds the diminution to output in the source country, causing a net increase in their combined real output.

Host Country

As a general rule, the **host country** benefits considerably from foreign investment. Not only does its real product rise because of the contribution of new capital, but direct foreign investment usually brings with it managerial and technological know-how as well as access to inventions and innovations and to well-developed capital markets. If the level of training of the labor force rises as a result, the foreign capital is said to generate external economies to the benefit of other firms operating in the same industry. And finally, as income in the host country rises, so do savings, and the entire economy is consequently placed on a new and higher growth path. In the case of developing countries, an important element in export and growth can be the processing of assembly and component manufactures by vertically integrated multinational companies, who use these components in their operations in other countries.

Against this background, the resentment that foreign investment sometimes generates in various host countries can be puzzling. For example, the ASEAN countries restrict foreign ownership of corporations to between 30 and 49 percent (depending on the country) of the corporate stocks, while Korea limits it to 10 percent. Foreign investment *performance standards* are common in host countries. They include a requirement that local subsidiaries of foreign companies export a minimum proportion of their output; and/or that they use in their production a minimum proportion of domestic materials and labor (local content requirements). These standards apply only to foreign investors and not to indigenous firms.[3] Performance standards are expected to be abolished as a result of the Uruguay Round, and China has already abolished its minimum export requirement.

Some charges against foreign investors may rest on economic rather than emotional foundations, and these should be sorted out. The claim that foreign-owned enterprises exploit labor in the host country and take away natural resources at less than market value is in most cases exaggerated. Exploitation can occur only when monopoly power prevails. When exploration rights for a country's natural resources are sought by many firms, exploitation is unlikely. The host country benefits in terms of taxes, royalties, wages, and salaries paid locally, and imported technology. However, when the investing company has monopoly power, exploitation is clearly possible and can undermine the terms of trade of the host country.[4] On the other hand, the producing countries can also organize a cartel and exploit the

---

[3] For an analysis of the economic effects of such requirements see C. Davidson, S. Matusz, and M. Kreinin, "Analysis of Performance Standards for Direct Foreign Investments," *Canadian Journal of Economics*, November 1985.

[4] For a more complete analysis see P. Streeten, "The Multinational Enterprise and the Theory of Development Policy," *World Development*, October 1973.

consuming countries, as was done by the OPEC nations. More serious is the complaint that foreign affiliates of American companies are governed by U.S. policies and laws that may conflict with policies of the host country. For example, a 1996 American threat to impose sanctions on foreigm companies that invest in Cuba, Libya, and Iran caused an uproar in Europe, with the EU threatening to take the dispute to the WTO.

A third allegation is that the major policy decisions of international companies and their research and development activities are centralized in the home office, leaving only routine work and less technical activities for the employees of foreign subsidiaries. This may be true in the case of some Japanese firms. But in most cases, a profit-maximizing company is likely to use local talent to the extent that it is available. Finally, certain countries object to being "dominated" by foreign firms and especially dislike having their high-technology industries controlled by foreign capital. But the concentration of American capital in the technology- and science-intensive industries is to be expected, because the United States possesses a comparative advantage in these areas. However, far from being injurious, the imported technology is highly beneficial to the host country. In sum, although there are possible losses, on balance the host country reaps a considerable gain in most cases.

Source (Investing) Country

Such a gain is not the likely outcome for the **source country,** assumed here to be the United States. In order to isolate the effect of foreign investment on American real income from its impact on other economic magnitudes, we assume that the economy is operating at full employment and that it is continuously maintained at or about that level by fiscal and monetary means. The question posed under these circumstances is how to distribute the aggregate savings generated by a fully employed economy between domestic and foreign investment so as to maximize real national product (or income). Put differently, will real national product be maximized if the distribution is left strictly to market decisions exercised by a multitude of profit-maximizing enterprises—if the location of each investment project depends on expected after-tax earnings at home and abroad?

The answer is that, particularly in the manufacturing sector, foreign investments are likely to proceed beyond what is warranted by the national interest, for several reasons. First, there are several types of risk that the firm may not fully consider before going abroad. The risk of unfavorable public regulations, such as regulations of profits, repudiation of loans, or even confiscation, affect the individual firm whether its investments are at home or abroad. But the national economy suffers only if the investments are abroad.

Second, there is a revenue loss to the U.S. government. In order to avoid double taxation, foreign investors are permitted to credit income taxes paid abroad against their domestic tax liability. Only the difference between the host country tax rate and that prevailing in the United States accrues to the U.S. government. In deciding where to invest, the private firm compares expected after-tax profit at home and abroad; it is a matter of indifference to it which government receives the tax. But this is of great concern to the national government. A foreign investment yields tax revenue mainly to the host government, while the same investment in the United States yields profits that are taxed by the U.S. government. Under present institutional arrangements, foreign investment benefits the national interest only if after-tax profits abroad exceed net earnings before taxes in the United States. To some extent this fiscal loss is offset by the need for public expenditures to service home investment, a need that is absent in the case of foreign investment.

Third, investment affects the productivity and remunerations of capital as well as labor and land. An addition to the capital stock, whether here or abroad, has the following effects: (a) total real output rises as an increasing volume of capital is combined with a relatively stable amount of other resources, mainly labor and land; (b) the productivity of the incremental unit of capital, and therefore the rate of return to existing capital, tends to decline as the capital stock rises in proportion to other factors; and (c) the productivity of labor and land, and their rate of remuneration, tends to increase as each unit of these resources is combined with an increasing volume of capital in the productive process. The private firm is concerned only with the rate of return on capital when deciding where to locate its investment. The national view, on the other hand, cannot overlook the implications to other factors of production. In the case of foreign investment, it is the productivity of foreign labor and land that would rise. If the investments are undertaken at home, these benefits accrue to domestic resources.

Furthermore, the expansion of production attendant upon the new investment usually carries with it indirect benefits. These include improvement in the quality of labor, better production methods and techniques, and superior forms of organization. In the case of foreign investment, these benefits would be lost to the domestic economy. Indeed, because foreign investment requires American technical and managerial talent, the movement of such personnel abroad deprives the U.S. economy of their services (assuming the United States is the source country).

This loss to the domestic economy may be more than offset in many instances by one important factor: The productivity of domestic capital and other resources depends in some measure on the capital endowment of the rest of the world. This phenomenon is most evident in the case of foreign investment in the extractive industries. The provision of primary materials from foreign sources (when domestic sources are not available) increases the productivity of domestic factors of production, because such materials are complementary to American capital and labor. In this case, there is a gain rather than a loss to domestic factors. Because a large share of U.S. investment in developing countries tends to concentrate in the extractive industries, the foreign policy objective of promoting investment in these areas (either as a substitute for or an addition to foreign aid) happens to coincide with the domestic economic interest.

It should be remembered that the United States is also a large host country to DFI. As such, the indirect benefits accrue to the United States, while the investment process proceeds beyond what is warranted from the foreign national point of view. The analysis does demonstrate that the assorted complaints emanating from various host countries that foreign investments are in some sense harmful to them are largely unfounded. Far from being damaging, these investments have made a tremendous contribution. The international diffusion of technological innovations and managerial know-how that takes place through the vehicle of the multinational enterprise sufficiently illustrates its contribution to the international economy. The interest of world welfare is best served by the unobstructed flow of investment capital.

Additional Insights

Taxing the Multinational Corporation   Within the United States, an immediate policy problem is the tax treatment of direct foreign investment. It is alleged that the federal tax laws discriminate against investment in the United States and in favor of foreign investment and therefore constitute an inducement to invest abroad.

Major federal tax concessions granted U.S. investment abroad are (a) the foreign tax credit; (b) tax deferral; and (c) various tax preferences given to Western Hemisphere trade corporations, investment in the developing countries, and investment in the U.S. possessions. We first consider the foreign **tax credit.**

Foreign-incorporated subsidiaries and branches of American corporations are entitled to credit against their U.S. income tax the full amount of taxes they pay to foreign governments (at all levels of government). Thus, if the subsidiary earned $1,000 and is operating in a country where profits are taxed at the rate of 20 percent, it would pay the host government $200 in taxes. Since the U.S. profit tax is 35 percent,[5] its total tax liability to the American government is $350, from which the corporation is entitled to subtract the full amount of the foreign tax. Its tax obligation to the U.S. government becomes $350 − $200 = $150. If the foreign tax rate were 35 percent, the U.S. tax obligation of the above corporation (on its foreign profit) would be zero. But the credit cannot exceed the U.S. tax of 35 percent, so a corporation operating in a foreign country where the tax exceeds 35 percent has a total foreign and U.S. tax in excess of 35 percent[6] even though it pays no U.S. taxes.[7]

---

[5] This is the highest marginal tax rate.

[6] However, U.S. corporations operating in more than one foreign country can choose to calculate this credit either on a country-by-country basis or on the overall basis of lumping together taxes paid to all foreign governments. The latter option is advantageous if one foreign country levies a tax in excess of the 35 percent U.S. tax rate and another less than that.

[7] As a result, U.S. investment in low-tax European countries (such as Belgium) increased much faster than investment in high-tax European countries (such as Germany and France).

The rationale for this tax credit derives from the (public finance) principle of *horizontal equity,* which requires equal tax treatment of persons with equal incomes. Applied to the case of foreign investment, the aim is to ensure the same total rate of taxation on domestic and foreign investment; it can be construed as horizontal equity on the international level. An alternative way of interpreting horizontal equity is to apply it to the national level. This would call for treating foreign-paid taxes in the same manner as domestically paid state and local taxes. The latter taxes are treated by the federal government as a cost of doing business. Thus, in our example, the $200 tax paid to the foreign government would be subtracted as a *business deduction* from the $1,000 profit, yielding taxable income of $800. The 35 percent U.S. federal tax would then be levied on the $800, resulting in a U.S. tax bill of $280. The total U.S. and foreign tax paid by the company on its overseas profits would then be $200 + $280 = $480, instead of the current $350.

The tax deferral provision permits the profits of foreign incorporated subsidiaries of U.S. corporations to enjoy a deferment of U.S. tax until the profit is remitted to the parent corporation.[8] At best, this implies an interest-free loan from the U.S. government to the corporation for the duration of the deferral. But because much of the earnings retained abroad are reinvested in fixed assets, this could amount to a permanent exemption from U.S. tax. Deferral clearly introduces a non-neutral incentive to invest abroad.

Apart from federal taxation, MNCs are taxed by the state. And a controversial issue that has reached the U.S. Supreme Court is the *worldwide unitary* taxing scheme used in California and six other states. Under this scheme, the state taxes the company on the basis of its worldwide income, prorated to reflect the share of the business done in California, for example. Even if the California subsidiary of the MNC lost money, it might have to pay state corporate taxes on the share of the company's worldwide profits. By contrast, the federal government and most states treat a U.S. subsidiary of an MNC as a separate corporation and tax only the income of that unit. Barclays Bank of the United Kingdom brought a suit against California, challenging its unitary tax system.

International Trade Theory and the Multinational Corporation

The emergence of the multinational corporation (MNC) as a major force on the world economic scene—with MNCs accounting for over one-fifth of all production—raises the question: Which strains of the traditional trade theory are now the most relevant?

---

[8] In contrast to the tax credit rule, tax deferral also applies to dividend income.

The Phenomenon of Transfer Pricing

International trade theory assumes that commodities are traded on world markets between independent firms, at market-determined or **arm's-length prices.** But today, about one-quarter of world trade in manufactures is conducted *within* firms. MNCs tend to be vertically integrated companies, each producing the intermediate products (for example, components) necessary for its production processes as well as an array of final goods. Various components are manufactured by affiliates or subsidiaries of the corporation located in different countries, while the final assembly plants may be located in still other countries. As components and materials move through the production processes, they are transferred from one subsidiary to another, and therefore become part of international trade. Consequently, a large proportion of international trade is actually intrafirm exchange. And the items entering such trade will be valued according to considerations other than those determining competitive market prices.

In this exchange the corporation is interested in maximizing its overall after-tax profit, rather than the profit of individual subsidiaries. The prices charged by one subsidiary on sales to another (located in a different country), known as **transfer prices,** may differ significantly from world prices. In particular, they are designed to minimize overall corporate income taxes and tariff payments. If tax rates differ between the countries in which the corporation's subsidiaries are located, the corporation will shift profits from the higher to the lower tax country. Suppose the components are sold by the Belgian to the German subsidiary of the same MNC, and corporate profit taxes in Germany are double those in Belgium. The corporation would artificially raise the price of components, so as to increase the profit of its Belgian subsidiary (where taxes are low) and reduce the profit of its German subsidiary (where taxes are high). The corporation would underprice the components if they are sold by a subsidiary domiciled in a high-tax country to a subsidiary located in a low-tax country. In this fashion it tries to minimize the profit of the subsidiaries in the high-tax country. Upon his inauguration, President Clinton suggested that the U.S. Treasury would try to recoup much of its lost revenue by vigorously auditing the transactions of MNCs, replacing their transfer prices by arm's-length prices to calculate their corporate tax liability. A mid-1995 report by the OECD contained guidelines for all member countries to follow that approach.

Second, the multinational corporation attempts to minimize its tariff payments to the country that imports components and intermediate goods. This requires underpricing of the exported components and involves shifting profits from the supplying to the importing country subsidiary. If profit tax rates are higher in the former than in the latter, the benefit to the corporation from the lower duty reinforces the gain from reduced profit taxes. In the reverse case, the two effects operate in opposite directions. In all cases, the pricing policies of the MNC on intrafirm (but international) trade would be affected by both tariff and tax considerations, and not merely by market forces of supply and demand.

The Commodity Composition of Trade

To what extent are the traditional theories (which rest on the assumption of immobile productive factors) still adequate in explaining the pattern of international trade? We can think of the MNC as a huge enclave cutting across national boundaries. It is an independent economic entity that buys and sells factors and goods, makes and receives transfers, and creates various external effects. Its linkages to a country in which it is operating include the employment of local labor and locally raised capital, the purchase of local materials and the sale of final products on the local market, the payment of taxes, and the creation of various externalities.

The corporation employs some productive factors that are immobile between countries—unskilled and skilled labor (and perhaps land)—in conjunction with two factors that move freely within the corporate empire, capital and knowledge. The return to the two **mobile factors** would be equalized between countries. But the relative factor intensities of the two **immobile factors** are still relevant in explaining the pattern of trade: Skilled-labor-intensive products would be produced in countries relatively well endowed with skilled labor, and unskilled-labor-intensive products in countries relatively well endowed with unskilled labor. This result underscores the importance of labor skills, as against the simple capital/labor ratio, in explaining the commodity composition of trade, and is consistent with empirical findings. But the skill level of countries can change over time, requiring the MNC to adjust its production configuration.

Second, the two mobile factors would be attracted to those countries that are generally more efficient because of their physical infrastructure, political stability, and similar conditions. Such countries would therefore tend to produce and export products intensive in capital and knowledge. Third, the existence of transport costs, tariffs, and other import restrictions would induce the corporation to locate close to its main markets and to produce for them. On the other hand, when increasing returns to scale are important, there would be a tendency to limit the number of locations in which any product is produced. The existence of transport costs, along with economies of scale, will confer on countries with large domestic markets a comparative advantage in economies-of-scale-intensive goods.

This rudimentary discussion demonstrates—however tentatively—that it is possible to use various strains of the traditional theory to explain location and trade in a world in which MNCs play an important role. As long as some factors are reasonably immobile and others mobile, rather familiar results may be obtained. The concern of traditional economic theory with the effect of trade and import restrictions on the welfare of a country remains valid despite the increased mobility of factors in the MNC world. This is so because certain factors—namely labor, human capital embodied in the labor force, and capital embodied in the country's infrastructure—are largely immobile. It is precisely the welfare of this immobile population that governments often seek to maximize.

INTERNATIONAL MIGRATION OF LABOR

People do not move around as freely as capital. Not only are there legal obstacles to migration, but families tend to be socially and culturally rooted in their country of birth, and such attachments are difficult to overcome. Even language is sometimes a formidable obstacle to migration. Yet there are instances of large-scale migration; in particular, the European Union has provided for free mobility of labor among the member countries. Indeed, highly industrialized areas in Europe employ migrant workers on a large scale. Movement of people around the British Commonwealth is another instance of such migration, as is the migration of Mexican workers to the United States. Such cases are rare enough that they do not negate the proposition that labor is a *relatively* immobile factor. Yet it is important to examine the welfare implications of **labor migration** when it does occur.

Under ordinary circumstances people migrate in response to economic incentives; they move from their own country to another where they can command higher remuneration. The consequences of such migration parallel those of capital movements. In most cases migration is beneficial to world welfare. The migrants' marginal productive contribution, which is reflected in the income they command, is generally higher in the new country than in the old. In other words, the loss in production to the source country from which they depart falls short of the gain in production to the host country resulting in a net gain to the world as a whole. As in the case of capital movement, the host country gains and the source country loses. But labor in the host country loses, while workers remaining behind in the source country gain.[9]

[9] See Berry and Soligo, "Welfare Aspects of International Migration," *Journal of Political Economy*, October 1969; and Thompson and Clark, "Factor Movements with Three Factors and Two Goods in the U.S. Economy," *Economic Letters*, 1983: 53–60.

So far, we have treated labor as a homogeneous factor of production. But in reality it is not, of course. Workers possess varying degrees of skills and training. International migration of highly trained scientific, technical, academic, and medical personnel, notably from the Commonwealth to Great Britain and from the developing countries to Europe and North America, has reached such proportions that it has become a cause for political and intellectual concern in many quarters. It is feared that this **brain drain** deprives developing countries, especially, of badly needed talents.

As was pointed out earlier, when migration takes place in response to economic incentives, it raises the real income of the world as a whole. The developing countries very often cannot productively absorb people who are highly trained in certain subjects, because the absorptive capacity of an economy depends on its level of development and degree of industrialization. On the other hand, there may be a crying need for these people in the industrial world. Thus, the difference between their marginal products in the two countries is very large, with migration easily resulting in a net gain to the world. In some cases, however, the country of emigration may demand compensation against the losses it incurs (even when these fall short of the gains to the receiving country), especially if it has spent resources to train the migrating specialists.

There are only two cases in which the "brain drain" may cause a loss to the world as a whole: first, if diverse taxation (or wage control) systems in the two countries distort the relationship between remuneration and marginal productivity[10] so that educated people move to countries where their marginal productivity is lower than in their native country; second, and more important, when the activity of educated people contributes to the welfare or productivity of others in the country of residence, a contribution known as *externality*, and that externality is greater in the country of origin. Such contributions as leadership capacity, originality, creativity, and inventive ability are all examples of externalities. But it is only when they are not rewarded through the market that externalities may reverse the gain to world welfare that comes from free migration. It is true that on occasion there may be a strong case for compensating the source countries for their losses. But the world as a whole nearly always benefits from unobstructed migration of trained labor. Moreover, the case against restrictions on international migration goes far beyond economics. It rests upon the cherished principles of personal freedom.

Summary

This chapter focuses upon the causes and effects of international factor movements, mainly that of direct foreign investment. The stock of U.S. investment

---

[10] Migration of a star athlete from Sweden to Monaco may be a case in point.

abroad and of foreign investment in the United States each amount to between $500 and $600 billion. The motives for a corporation to invest abroad include attempts to lower costs—for instance, the employment of cheaper labor, or the circumventing of foreign tariffs; or efforts to expand revenue by improving marketing and service facilities.

The free flow of investment capital would maximize world welfare. Capital moves from areas in which it is abundant—and hence cheap— toward areas in which it is scarce—and therefore more expensive. Its marginal contribution to output is greater in the host country than in the source country.

In the host country, the foreign capital is combined with domestic labor, increasing labor productivity. Foreign investment often introduces managerial skills and technological know-how as well, clearly benefiting the host country. But because of nationalistic and other reasons, some countries impose ownership restrictions and performance standards on direct foreign investment.

By contrast, the source country tends to lose on three counts. Some tax revenue accrues to the foreign government rather than that of the source country. The productivity of foreign labor is raised instead of the productivity of domestic labor. And technological and other innovations are introduced to the foreign country, partly at the expense of domestic industry. Since the United States operates as both a host and a source country, the costs and benefits are somewhat equalized. The United States (as well as some other countries) provides its MNCs with full credit for taxes paid abroad against U.S. corporate tax liabilities.

Many MNCs are vertically integrated. Their various subsidiaries, domiciled in different countries, produce raw materials, intermediate inputs, and final products. As a product moves through the production process, it is transferred from one subsidiary to another and thus becomes part of international trade. One-quarter of international trade consists of intracompany trade. Corporations, however, are concerned with maximizing their total after-tax profits—not the profit of any given subsidiary. Thus, when a subsidiary sells (say, an intermediate input) to another subsidiary (for further processing) domiciled in a different country, it often charges a transfer price, which is dictated largely by the differences in corporate tax rates between the two countries and by the tariff rate in the importing country. That price is designed to maximize the profit of the subsidiary operating in a low-tax country and minimize the profit of the subsidiary operating in a high-tax country.

Although the existence of MNCs affects the conduct of trade, many of the postulates of international trade theory and policy (articulated in earlier chapters) remain largely unaffected.

The international migration of labor, especially that of highly trained professionals, also affects the welfare of the source and host countries.

*Important
Concepts*

Direct foreign investment (DFI)

Multinational corporation (MNC)

Host country

Source country

Tax credit

Arm's-length prices

Transfer prices

Mobile factors

Immobile factors

Labor migration

Brain drain

*Review
Questions*

1. What is the meaning of direct foreign investment (DFI)? List some of the factors that induce companies to invest abroad.

2. Does the economic interest of a U.S. company investing abroad in manufacturing subsidiaries coincide with the interest of the United States? If not, in what ways do the interests diverge? Why does the U.S. labor movement object to foreign investment by U.S. companies?

3. How are foreign subsidiaries of U.S. companies taxed? What are transfer prices and how are they affected by differential taxation?

4. Why might the *labor skill* theory of the commodity composition of trade be appropriate in a world where production and trade are handled by *multinational corporations?* (Explain italicized terms.)

5.   Examine the effects of direct foreign investment on the welfare of (a) the source country, (b) the host country, and (c) the world as a whole.

6.   What are the effects of labor migration on (a) the world as a whole, (b) the host country, (c) the source country, and (d) labor in the two countries?

Foreign Monetary Sys

International Financial Relations

THE NATURE OF FINANCIAL RELATIONS

P art One of this book was concerned with international transactions in goods, services, and capital. But these transactions are conducted on financial markets, involving conversions from one currency to another within the framework of the international currency system. International financial matters have often captured the news headlines in recent years, for they have profound effects on the economic well-being of nations. Therefore Part Two is devoted to the monetary relations between countries.

Each nation has its own currency, issued by its central bank and used to finance transactions within the country. Among the Western countries, the five major currencies are the U.S. dollar ($), the British pound sterling (£), the Japanese yen (¥), the German mark (D.M.), and the French franc (F.F.). The U.S. dollar is the most important among them. It is widely used in *private international* transactions, and it serves as the unit by which the prices of truly international goods and services (such as oil and ocean freight rates) are priced. International trade statistics of all countries, compiled by the United Nations, are also reported in dollars.

The price of one currency in terms of another is called an *exchange rate*. For example, in a recent period $1 was worth £0.7; $1 = 1.6 D.M.; $1 = 5.6 F.F.; and $1 = ¥120. Exchange rates can fluctuate in response to market supply and demand conditions, just like any other price. Alternatively, the government can fix the exchange value of its currency by buying and selling foreign currencies out of stock (reserves) at a fixed price. This is known as a *fixed exchange rate*. Whatever the system, the exchange rate is used to convert prices quoted in one currency into another. For example, a British coat that costs £100 is worth $150 at an exchange rate of £1 = $1.5, and a German automobile costing 20,000 D.M. is worth $12,500 at an exchange rate of 1.6 D.M. = $1. Each country measures its exports and imports in its own currency. And these can be converted into dollars via the exchange rate.

A country needs to balance its international financial accounts in much the same way as a family deals with its finances. In the short run, any deficit in a family budget can be financed by depletion of previously accumulated assets (spending from savings) or by accumulation of liabilities (buying on credit or obtaining a loan). But this process cannot go on forever. Sooner or later the family must adjust its behavior: either lower its expenditures or raise its income. The inability to go on financing deficits forever acts as a constraint on the economic behavior of the family. An analogous rule applies to a country in its relations with the rest of the world. In the short run, an external deficit can be *financed* by drawing down previously accumulated assets or by accumulating debts to other countries. In time, however, an *adjustment process* must set in to eliminate the deficit.

But a country is not a family, and the analogy cannot be carried to the point of equating the adjustment processes. Family decisions concerning income and spending are made by a single decision-making unit with reasonably full information and control over its position at any given time. The action involved is both direct and prompt. By contrast, millions of individual decision makers affect a country's international accounts. They include importers and exporters who in turn must respond to the demands of consumers and producers, all individuals engaged in overseas travel, and all companies involved in the transfer of investment and other capital across national boundaries. Consequently, balancing the accounts becomes an objective of national policy, which differs considerably from family decisions.

In a free-market economy, the government has no direct control over individual decisions. Most policies subject to government jurisdiction are aggregative in nature, in the sense that they are aimed at the overall performance of the economy. They work through indirect effect on individuals and organizations who are the actual decision makers. While the individual family balances its accounts by direct action, all the government can do is press one or more policy buttons. It thereby sets in motion a sequence of internal (*endogenous,* in economists' parlance) processes as the various economic agents, individuals as well as institutions, react to the external (*exogenous*) policy push. The hope is that the series of interactions will lead the economy toward the prescribed goal.

Not only that, unlike a family, a nation has no automatically generated information about its position at any given time on which to base policy decisions. Therefore, each government must establish an elaborate reporting mechanism to compile the necessary statistics and to perform the analysis needed to guide the policymakers. Moreover, if the policies of trading nations are not to conflict with one another, those nations must act in concert to establish a framework within which their policies are to be formulated. Such a framework is known as an *international monetary or financial system.*

Thus the periodic adjustments in the system are the price that countries pay for the freedom of persons to trade and speculate coupled with the freedom of the nation-states to pursue their national objectives. The function of the monetary system is to provide a well-lubricated mechanism by means of which a multitude of traders and investors can each pursue his or her own goal and yet result in one harmonious whole. On the national level, each country compiles detailed statistics on international transactions on which to base policy decisions, and such decisions are subject to the constraints imposed by the international system. The nature of the statistical compilations involved, the policy options (along with the costs and benefits of each option) open to a country under various conditions, and consideration of the international currency system are the subjects of Part Two of this book.

Review Questions

- Define and offer examples of an exchange rate.
- Suppose that the price of a German automobile is 60,000 D.M. Determine how much it would cost the American consumer at each of the following exchange rates: (a) $1 = 2 D.M. (b) $1 = 3 D.M. (c) $1 = 4 D.M.
- Assume next that the price of an American-made aircraft is $10 million. How much would that aircraft cost the German buyer at each of the above exchange rates?
- Does the exchange rate affect the price of foreign goods sold at home and of home goods sold abroad? If so, how?

Statement of International Transactions

A statement of all the transactions between one country and the rest of the world, usually reported annually, is known as that country's **international transactions statement,** alternatively referred to as the country's *balance of payments.* The transactions included are merchandise trade, exchange of services (sometimes referred to as *invisible* items because, unlike commodities, they cannot be seen), and transfers of capital in both directions. In order to facilitate the understanding of the various items appearing in the statement, it is useful to divide them into two groups: those giving rise to **dollar inpayments** (*plus* or *credit* items) and those resulting in **dollar outpayments** (*negative* or *debit* items). This dichotomy is essential to the following discussion.

MAIN ITEMS IN THE STATEMENT OF INTERNATIONAL TRANSACTIONS

In the explanation that follows we shall make use of the U.S. International Transactions Statement for 1997, adapted from the U.S. Department of Commerce publication. A condensed version of the official statement appears in table 10.1, where all entries are divided into current account and capital account transactions. Transactions in goods and services plus unilateral transfers constitute the **current account** component of the statement. Purchases and sales of assets make up the **capital account.**

The Current Account

Merchandise trade constitutes the largest single item in U.S. current transactions. Exports of goods are an inpayments (or plus) item, whereas imports

TABLE 10.1	*U.S. International Transactions, 1997 (Billion Dollars)*	
Current Account Transactions		
1. Merchandise exports	+ 678	
2. Merchandise imports	− 877	
3. Balance on merchandise trade		− 199
4. Export of services	+ 253	
5. Import of services	− 168	
6. Balance on goods and services		− 114
(lines 3 + 4 + 5)		
7. Income receipts on U.S. assets abroad	+ 236	
8. Income payments on foreign assets in the U.S.	− 250	
9. Government grants and private remittances	− 39	
10. Balance on current account (lines 6 − 9)		**− 166**
Capital Account Transactions		
11. Change in U.S. private assets abroad, net	− 426	
(increase/capital outflow/−)[1]		
12. Change in foreign private assets in U.S., net	+ 672	
(increase/capital inflow/+)[2]		
13. Statistical discrepancy[3]	+ 97	
14. Capital account balance (lines 11 − 13)		**+ 149**
15. Official reserve transactions balance		**− 17**
(lines 10 + 14)		
16. Increase in U.S. official reserves (increase, −)	− 1	
17. Rise in foreign official assets in U.S. (increase, +)	+ 18	

Source: *Survey of Current Business*, June 1998.

[1]An increase in U.S. assets abroad means capital outflow from the U.S. and has a negative sign. A decrease means capital inflow and has a positive sign.

[2]An increase in foreign assets in the U.S. means capital inflow into the U.S. and has a positive sign. A decrease has a negative sign.

[3]What is the nature of the statistical discrepancy and how does it arise? In compiling the statistics, the U.S. Department of Commerce uses two sources of information for each transaction: the transaction itself and the means of payments for it. For example, information of a given U.S. export transaction can be obtained from the exporter who shipped the merchandise and from the bank through which the payment was made. All transactions are treated in the same manner. Theoretically, the value of all transactions should add up exactly to the value of all payments. But in fact they do not. The difference is called a statistical discrepancy.

of goods are an outpayments (or negative) item. The two are shown on lines 1 and 2 in table 10.1; the difference between them is the balance on merchandise trade or simply the **balance of trade** (line 3). In 1997, the United

States had a trade deficit of $199 billion.[1] Although it is very much a partial balance, the trade balance is reported by the Department of Commerce on a monthly and quarterly basis and is given extensive coverage by the national media. A similar balance is reported by other countries.

Line 4 shows that exports of services resulted in total inpayments of $253 billion. These include foreign tourists visiting the United States; U.S. airlines flying foreign passengers; American ships carrying foreign freight; and U.S. banks, insurance companies, and other financial institutions selling services to foreigners. All these service transactions generate dollar inpayments, and hence are considered credit items, denoted by a plus sign.

Line 5 shows that imports of services added up to outpayments of $168 billion. These include American tourists traveling abroad, foreign airlines carrying U.S. passengers, and foreign financial institutions rendering financial services to Americans.

In all, the United States had a $85 billion (253–168) surplus on service transactions. Exports minus imports of goods and services constitute the **balance on goods and services.** Shown on line 6 of table 10.1, this balance amounted to a deficit of $114 billion in 1997; and it is the primary link between the international transactions statement and the national income accounts. It is conceptually related to the net exports of goods and services (X_n) in the expenditure side of the GDP (see table 1.2 in Chapter 1), where GDP equals the sum of consumption (C), domestic investment (I), government spending (G), and net exports (X_n). However, because of two statistical differences the two figures do not match exactly.

Line 7 of table 10.1 shows repatriated earnings on U.S. investments abroad, an *inpayment* of $236 billion. Examples are the repatriated profits of American companies on their direct investments abroad (subsidiaries and branch plants); dividends realized by U.S. residents on their foreign stocks; and interest earned by Americans on foreign bonds and bank accounts. Correspondingly line 8 shows repatriated *returns* on foreign investments in the United States, an *outpayment* of $250 billion. This item includes profits made by U.S. subsidiaries of foreign companies, dividends realized by foreigners on their holdings of shares in U.S. companies, and interest earned by foreigners on their American bonds and bank accounts. It should be emphasized that investment income refers to *returns* on foreign investments accumulated over previous years; the annual investments themselves are shown in the capital account.

Unilateral transfers (line 9) are an outpayments item for the United States. They include government's foreign aid program, as well as private remittances to people living abroad.

---

[1] Although the only deficit that matters is relative to the "rest of the world" as a whole, the U.S. bilateral deficit with Japan and more recently with China have been politically troublesome.

TABLE 10.2	U.S. International Transactions in Selected Years (Billion Dollars)					
	1960	**1971**	**1980**	**1987**	**1992**	**1995**
Export of goods and services + income receipts	29	66	345	446	730	969
Import of goods and services + income payments	− 24	− 67	− 334	− 576	− 764	− 1,082
Balance on merchandise trade	5	− 2	− 25	− 160	− 96	− 173
Balance on current account	3	− 1	4	− 144	− 66	− 148
Increase (−) in U.S. official reserve assets	2	2	− 9	9	+ 4	− 10
Increase (+) in foreign official assets	1	27	15	45	40	109

Source: *Survey of Current Business,* various issues.

Adding lines 6–9 we obtain the **balance on current account** (line 10), which was in deficit of $166 billion in 1995.[2]

Throughout the 1950s and 1960s, the United States had sizable surpluses (excess of exports over imports) on merchandise trade. But from 1971 to 1981 deficits occurred in all years except for 1973 and 1975. The annual deficits grew to the $25–34 billion range beginning in 1977 (see table 10.2), partly because of the rise in price of imported oil in the 1970s. However, the trade deficit shrank between 1978 and 1980, only to rise sharply again in the years following 1982. After peaking at $160 billion in 1987, it declined to $127 billion in 1988 and $96 billion in 1992, but surged again in 1995–99.

Despite the large trade deficits in the 1970s, the **balance on goods and services and income flows** showed a surplus in all years except 1977 and 1978. Sizable earnings on U.S. investment abroad represented the main positive item responsible for offsetting the trade deficits. But since 1983 that balance registered substantial deficits.

All transactions considered thus far are current account items and do not include foreign investment or any other form of capital transfers. The resulting balances are therefore strictly partial. But they are reported regularly, as memoranda items, at the bottom of the official statement, for several reasons: The balance on goods and services is a useful link to the national income accounts; it is also a main channel through which one country's policies affect its trading partners; all three partial balances are comparable to similar balances reported by other countries and therefore make possible

[2] Because one country's deficit must equal other countries' surpluses, the current account for the world as a whole should be in balance. But the statistics do not show such a balance! Why? One reason is that interest earned abroad is credited directly to foreign bank accounts, but is *not* always reported to the government authorities in the recipient's home country (to avoid taxes). The same holds for the reporting to the home governments of reinvested foreign income of large corporations. Another reason is that goods shipped at the end of a given year may not arrive in the country of destination until the following year. They are shown as exports in year 1 and as imports only in year 2. And finally there are the problems mentioned in footnote 3 to table 10.1. For more details see S. Nawaz, "Why the World Current Account Does Not Balance," *Finance and Development,* September 1987, and *IMF Survey,* January 8, 1990.

intercountry comparisons; and the public and the press have become accustomed to monthly and quarterly reports of the trade balance. Additionally, the balance on trade and the balance on services are measures of the macroeconomic effect of international transactions. For example, whatever is exported must be produced; consequently, as exports rise so does output and hence employment. It has been estimated that every $1 billion in exports generates about 20,000 jobs in the United States. Likewise, imports often displace domestic output; so a rise in imports would cause a loss in jobs. Although international trade is a small component of the American economy, large swings in the trade balance can have significant effects on the aggregate level of economic activity. And large swings have occurred in recent years: from a surplus of $9 billion in 1975, to a deficit of $34 billion in 1978; and from a deficit of $36 billion in 1982 to deficits of $160 billion in 1987 and $199 billion in 1997. Such swings can have important effects on the economy.

Additional Insights

To better understand the current account, it is instructive to elaborate upon the main determinants of transactions in goods and services. U.S. imports depend first on U.S. output and income. As output rises, more fuel and material imports are needed to sustain production. The concomitant rise in income (remember that income equals output) makes it possible for Americans to purchase more foreign goods. Thus *U.S. imports are positively related to U.S. output or income.* Indeed this factor explains the rise in U.S. imports in 1995–99. The second determinant of imports is the U.S. competitive position. If that variable is defined as a ratio of foreign prices to U.S. domestic prices ($P_{Foreign}/P_{U.S.}$), then higher foreign prices and lower U.S. prices would result in fewer American imports. The relationship to U.S. imports is thus negative. In sum, *imports* vary positively with the country's output or income, and *negatively* with the ratio of foreign to domestic prices.

By the same token, U.S. exports depend positively on the output or income in the importing countries (the rest of the world, or Y_{RofW}). For example, U.S. merchandise exports stagnated in the mid-1990s because of poor economic conditions in Europe and Japan. On the other hand, U.S. exports to the ASEAN countries doubled between 1988 and 1993 as a result of rapid growth in the Pacific region. Secondly, exports depend on the U.S. competitive position. If the variable is defined as a ratio of foreign to U.S. prices ($P_{Foreign}/P_{U.S.}$), then higher foreign prices and lower U.S. prices would result in more U.S. exports. The relationship to U.S. exports is thus positive. In sum, exports vary *positively* with world output or income, and *positively* with the ratio of foreign to domestic prices.[3]

Canada's exports rose sharply in 1996 because of booming conditions in its major market (the U.S.) and because it became more competitive on global markets.

---

[3]The above relationship can be summarized as follows:

$$M_{U.S.} = f(\overset{+}{Y}_{U.S.},\ \overset{-}{P_{For.}/P_{U.S.}});\quad X_{U.S.} = f\ (\overset{+}{Y}_{RofW},\ \overset{+}{P_{For.}/P_{U.S.}})$$

The Capital Account

We now turn to the capital account of the statement, which records international **purchases or sales of assets.** An asset is *any* form *in which wealth is held,* such as bank accounts, bonds, stocks, buildings, or plants. Line 11 in table 10.1 shows the net change over the year in U.S. assets (other than official *reserve assets*) held abroad. This change is a result of U.S. capital outpayments (minus items) of the following varieties: (a) direct private investment abroad by American corporations, such as the establishment of foreign subsidiaries; (b) purchases of foreign securities (stocks and bonds) and deposits in foreign banks by Americans; and (c) U.S. government loans to foreign countries, less the repayment of loans by foreigners. In all cases, repatriated U.S. capital is netted out; all these net outflows increase U.S. asset holdings abroad. Therefore an increase (decrease) in U.S. assets abroad means capital outflow (inflow) and is denoted by a negative (positive) sign. In 1997, U.S. assets abroad increased by $426 billion.

Line 12 in table 10.1 shows the net change over the year in foreign assets (other than official reserves) in the United States. Such capital inpayments (positive items) include (a) direct investment in the United States by foreign corporations and (b) purchases of American securities (that is, stocks and bonds) and deposits in U.S. banks by foreigners. An increase (decrease) in foreign assets in the United States means a capital inflow (outflow) and is displayed with a positive (negative) sign. In 1997, foreign assets in the United States increased by $672 billion.

While all items reporting the transfer of capital are included in the capital account component of the balance of payments, the income on foreign investment—whether interest, dividends, or repatriated profits—is part of the goods and services section.[4] These earnings are a result of investment made in previous years.

Finally, a statistical discrepancy, amounting to $97 billion in outflow, appeared in 1997. (The nature of this discrepancy is explained in footnote 3 of table 10.1.)

The difference between a country's exports and imports of assets is the capital account balance, shown in line 14 of table 10.1. In 1997 it registered a surplus of $149 billion. This surplus, the counterpart of the current-account deficit, means a net inflow of capital into the United States. It represents an accumulation of American assets in the hands of foreigners, or an accumulation of U.S. liabilities. Because of the cumulative effect of the current-account deficits in the 1980s and 1990s, the United States had become a large net foreign debtor: In 1980, the United States was a net foreign creditor to the rest of the world to the tune of $500 billion; by the end of 1991 its

---

[4] Income on foreign investment is included in the current account because interest and dividend payments are compensation for the *services* provided by foreign investment of American companies.

net foreign debt amounted to $620 billion, and these debts continued to mount. Thus, a country's current-account imbalance equals the change in its net foreign wealth. Such imbalances redistribute wealth among countries.

All the entries covered thus far constitute a response to general economic or political factors. Trade in goods and services is mainly a result of competitive position or of relative prices in different countries, the relative purchasing power of their populations, and the geographical distribution of natural resources around the globe. Foreign investments reflect relative profit opportunities at home and abroad that in turn can be traced to a number of economic (and political) factors. Short-term capital may be attracted to the financial centers that pay the highest interest rates, although not all flows can be so explained.

Autonomous and Accommodating Items

All items considered so far are known as **autonomous** transactions. They owe their existence (and size) to general economic conditions and are not caused by the state of the balance of payments itself. When these items do not add up to zero, the balance of payments is considered out of balance or out of equilibrium. It is in *deficit* when their sum is negative and in *surplus* when it is positive. In 1997 this **official reserve transactions balance,** also known as the **overall balance,** was in deficit to the tune of $17 billion (line 15 in table 10.1). This difference between the inpayments and outpayments must somehow be settled; the means for settling it—gold, official foreign currency reserves, and official debt—are known as the *balancing* or **accommodating items** (the term *official* refers mainly to the central bank). These entries, which result from the very existence of imbalance in the autonomous transactions, are shown on lines 16 and 17 in table 10.1. Their total must equal the imbalance shown in line 15 but bear the opposite sign, so that the entire statement adds up to zero.

Changes in Official Reserves

More specifically, the accommodating or balancing items include **changes in** official liabilities to foreign official authorities—or exchange of official assets that are acceptable means of payments to all countries. These official reserve assets include widely used *foreign* currencies (mainly dollars for countries outside the United States), gold, reserve position in the International Monetary Fund (IMF) (explained in Chapter 12), and Special Drawing Rights (SDRs)—assets that the IMF created and distributed to its member countries and that the central banks of these countries accept from one another in settling debts. Most of the annual change in official reserves is composed of variations in *foreign* currency holdings of central banks.

How do central banks come to play the balancing role in the balance of payments that consists mainly of private sector transactions? The answer is that central banks buy and sell *foreign* currencies in exchange for their *own* currency in order to influence the exchange rate and macroeconomic conditions in their respective countries. Such activity is referred to as official intervention in the foreign exchange market.

Under a regime of fixed exchange rates, which was prevalent before 1973, each central bank buys and sells foreign currencies in exchange for its own currency at a *fixed price* (exchange rate). Private traders either sell their accumulated foreign currencies to the central banks (in which case the central bank's official reserves rise) or they buy foreign currencies from the central bank (in which case its official reserves decline). That is how variations in official reserves played a residual role of balancing the external accounts.

Today the exchange rates of most major currencies (including the dollar) are allowed to fluctuate. Yet central banks continue to intervene on their respective foreign exchange markets. They buy and sell their own currencies in exchange for foreign currencies for a variety of reasons, but mainly to influence the exchange rate. They purchase their own currency in exchange for foreign currency if they wish to raise the value of their currency. And they sell their currency in exchange for foreign currencies if they wish to depress its value. The Federal Reserve Bank of New York (FRB) conducts such activities on behalf of the U.S. government, buying and selling marks, pounds, yen, or francs in exchange for dollars. Each foreign central bank carries on similar transactions in its own financial center. Because of the importance of the dollar in international finance, most (but not all) of these transactions in foreign markets are conducted in dollars. Thus the Bank of England buys and sells pounds for dollars on the London market to influence the pound exchange rate, and the German Central Bank trades marks for dollars in Frankfurt to influence the mark exchange rate. Because they intervene mainly in dollars, the outcome of their activity may be an increase or a decrease in their dollar asset holdings, which is correspondingly either an increase or a decrease in U.S. liabilities (IOUs).

These activities result in a net change, over the year, in the U.S. official reserve holdings (line 16 in table 10.1) and in foreign official holdings of U.S. dollars (line 17), the latter of which are official liabilities of the United States.

Line 16 in table 10.1 shows a $1 billion increase in U.S. official reserve assets.[5] By the same token foreign central banks increased their dollar reserve holdings in the United States (line 17) by $18 billion.[6] The sum of these two items is shown in line 15 with an opposite sign. In 1997, U.S. international

---

[5] A net increase in U.S. official reserve assets is shown with a negative sign, indicating an outflow of capital (as the U.S. maintains these assets abroad); an increase in U.S. liabilities to foreign official agencies is shown with a positive sign, indicating an inflow of capital so as to agree with the method used to indicate flows of other capital transactions.

[6] A positive sign indicates an increase of foreign official holdings in the United States or inflow of such capital into the United States.

transactions totaled a $17 billion deficit. It was financed by the United States owing $18 billion to foreign central banks, as foreign official reserve assets—U.S. liabilities—rose by $18 billion; partly offset by the United States' increasing its official reserves by $1 billion. These items netted out to $17 billion. To summarize, reserve assets and official debt instruments constitute the means of financing imbalances. Thus the balance sheet for all international transactions, including those of the central banks, totals zero.

Changes in official reserves, which are noted in line 15 of table 10.1, are the only overall measures of the surplus or deficit in the balance of payments. The official reserve transactions balance arises because the central banks choose to intervene on their respective market and buy or sell foreign currencies.

In the absence of such intervention, any difference between private inpayments and outpayments would be fully reflected in variations in the value of the currency (its exchange rate), and the official reserve transactions balance would be zero. For a country with a *freely* fluctuating exchange rate (to be described in the next chapter), an external deficit would be reflected in a decline in the value of its currency relative to other currencies. Conversely, an external surplus is reflected in an increase in the value of the currency. With official intervention, part of the exchange variations are blunted by central bank sale and purchase of foreign currencies.

Because most of the imbalance on autonomous transactions results in variations of the exchange rate rather than in a change in reserves, the magnitude of the reserve changes is not fully indicative of the imbalance.

The Balance of Payments in the National Economy

We stated earlier that the balance on goods and services (or a variant of it) is one of the four expenditure channels that form the gross domestic product (GDP). The balance is labeled net exports (X_n) and equals exports minus imports of goods and services: $X_n = X - M$. In what follows we will first ignore the government sector, and then add it in a second step.

By the national-income account identities, GDP consists of consumption (C), private domestic investment (I), and net exports (X_n). The production of these goods and services generates income (Y), and in turn that income is either spent on consumption (C), or it is saved (S). This can be reduced to two equations:

$$\text{Output: GDP} = C + I + (X - M) \tag{1}$$

$$\text{Income: } Y = C + S \tag{2}$$

The value of output produced in the economy equals all income—in the form of wages and salaries paid for labor, rent paid for resources, interest paid on capital, and *profit* paid for enterprise—generated in the production process. Because output equals income, GDP = Y, the right side of the two equations is also equal:

$$C + I + (X - M) = C + S; \text{ or } I + X - M = S \qquad (3)$$

This reveals that domestic savings equal domestic investment plus the balance on goods and services (X_n). A decline (increase) in savings must be accompanied either by a decline (rise) in domestic investment or a reduction (hike) in the external surplus.

Rearranging equation (3) yields some further insights:

$$X - M = S - I \qquad \text{(Japan)} \qquad (4)$$
$$\text{or } M - X = I - S \qquad \text{(United States)}$$

An external surplus implies that domestic savings exceed domestic investment by the amount of the surplus. This represents the current economic position of Japan, with its high savings rate. Conversely, an external deficit equals the excess of domestic investment over savings. This represents the low savings rate of today's U.S. economy.

In turn, the statement of international transactions shows that under a freely floating exchange rate, the current account deficit equals the surplus on the capital account, or the net inflow of foreign funds. In other words, *to the extent that savings fall short of investment, the difference is financed by the inflow of foreign capital.*

Additional Insights

Adding the government sector (federal, state, and local) requires the inclusion of government expenditures (G) in the output equation, and taxes (T) in the income equation. Alternatively, a budgetary surplus ($T - G$) can be viewed as public savings, while a budgetary deficit ($G - T$) can be regarded as negative savings. These can be added to private savings in equations (3) or (4). Either way, equation 3 becomes:

$$I + X - M = S + (T - G) \qquad (5)$$

Rearranging the terms produces:

$$X - M = (S - I) + (T - G) \qquad (5a)$$

or

$$M - X = (I - S) + (G - T) \tag{5b}$$

External   Excess of Government
deficit   private   budgetary
investment   deficit
over savings

During the immediate postwar years, the United States was a capital-exporting country. It had an external surplus on goods and services, and correspondingly domestic savings exceeded investment. In the past 25 years the conditions have changed, as illustrated by the following table:

Savings and Investment as a Percent of GDP

	X – M	T – G	S – I
The 1970s	+ 0.2	– 0.9	+ 1.1
The 1980s	– 1.8	– 2.6	+ 0.8

In the 1970s domestic private savings exceeded investment by 1.1 percent of GDP. Because the government deficit totaled only 0.9 percent of GDP, that left a small export surplus of 0.2 percent of GDP. But in the 1980s the budget deficit grew to 2.6 percent of GDP, while $(S - I)$ declined to 0.8 percent. In other words, domestic savings were not large enough to finance both domestic investment and the budget deficit, resulting in an external deficit of 1.8 percent of GDP. The corresponding influx of foreign capital helped finance the U.S. budget deficit. This situation continued into the 1990s when the U.S. savings rate declined even further.

By contrast, Japan's large external surpluses on goods and services reflect the high savings rate of its economy.[7] Its domestic savings, after subtracting the government deficits, exceed domestic investment. Correspondingly, it experiences a current account surplus and outflow of funds (a capital-account deficit).

USES AND MISUSES OF INTERNATIONAL TRANSACTIONS STATISTICS

In attempting to simplify our exposition, we have glossed over many vexing problems embodied in the international transactions statistics. Readers who need more detailed information may refer to the U.S. statement published in

---

[7]See Y. Horioka, "Why Is Japan's Private Savings So High?" *Finance and Development*, December 1986.

the Department of Commerce monthly *Survey of Current Business*.[8] The annual *Economic Report of the President* contains data and analysis of developments in international finance and trade. Information for other countries may be found in *International Financial Statistics* and the *Balance of Payments Yearbook*, both published by the International Monetary Fund. International transactions statistics are reported annually, but quarterly data for the United States are also available.

Little or no credence should be given to news reports that draw conclusions from monthly trade returns, for these data may result from special circumstances. Even quarterly statistics can be misleading. Normally an imbalance must persist for a year or longer before it can be determined whether it is in some sense a fundamental phenomenon rather than a temporary one likely to reverse itself in due course. Economists warn against common misuses of international transactions statistics.

Long-Run Shifts in the Balance on Merchandise Trade

Because of its importance in the total payments position, the balance on merchandise trade merits special attention. Commodity trade is a large component in the balance of payments. Yet the trade balance should not in and of itself be a cause for alarm or jubilation, nor should it serve as the sole guide to policy making. In what follows, we attempt to place the balance on commodity trade in its proper perspective, particularly as it relates to the balance on capital account.

For more than twenty years following World War II, the United States mounted huge surpluses on its balance of trade, amounting to several billion dollars in practically every year. At the same time, the capital account showed substantial outflows of investment funds, often exceeding the surplus on merchandise trade.

This relationship between the two subaccounts is not accidental; it is characteristic of a capital-exporting nation. Although the causal relation is rather complex, we can say that a capital-exporting country must generate large trade surpluses in order to offset the deficit on capital account. By the same reasoning, one would expect a capital-importing country, as Australia and Canada have been in the recent past, to have a deficit on merchandise trade. Here we may say either that the deficit is financed by the import of capital or that the import of capital generates the trade deficit. Whatever the line of causation, these tend to be companion phenomena that offset each other so as to yield an overall balance.

---

[8] The *Survey of Current Business* also publishes tables showing: (a) U.S. international transactions with individual countries or regions; (b) a commodity breakdown of U.S. merchandise trade; (c) a breakdown of U.S. government transactions; (d) a breakdown of U.S. direct investment abroad and of foreign direct investment in the United States; (e) an account of capital flows other than direct investment; and (f) a detailed account of the change in foreign official assets in the United States.

What does that relation imply for the U.S. trade position—past, present, and future? It should come as no surprise that, during the historical era of large inflows of investment capital into this country, the United States experienced continuous deficits on merchandise trade. As the importation of capital subsided and gradually declined below the annual outflow of repatriated earnings as well as debt servicing and repayment to Europe, the trade deficit diminished and slowly gave way to surpluses. For it is only through trade surpluses that foreign debts can be paid and earnings can be remitted abroad. Those surpluses grew to large proportions as the United States became the world's major exporter of capital from 1944 to 1970. In subsequent years this country approached the stage of the *mature economy*—namely, a stage in which repatriated earnings exceed the net outflow of investment capital. And to accommodate large net inflows of such earnings, the trade balance must transform into a deficit position. In the years following 1982 the United States sustained sizable trade and current account deficits, and these were offset by substantial capital inflows.

It should now be realized that a trade deficit is not inherently bad, and that a surplus is not inherently good. Just to drive home the point that a trade surplus is not necessarily a favorable phenomenon, think of the country giving up more goods than it receives in return and ask yourself: "What is so favorable about that?" The term *favorable balance* as applied to a surplus is a leftover from the mercantilist period when one overriding objective of nations was to accumulate gold. Because countries that do not possess gold mines can acquire the yellow metal only through surpluses on merchandise trade, having such a surplus came to be regarded as favorable. But it is easy to realize that by giving away goods we lose the pleasure or satisfaction of consuming them, while little gain accrues to the citizenry from having stocks of gold buried in Fort Knox. However, all this should not be construed to mean the reverse—that a trade surplus is necessarily unhealthy. Each circumstance must be assessed on its own merit. For instance, the U.S. deficits of the 1980s and early 1990s are generally considered to be "too large." Japan, in the meantime, has become a major supplier of capital to the world, as it develops massive trade surpluses accompanied by annual outflow of capital. The causes and effects of the large trade imbalances in the 1980s and 1990s will be explored later in the book.

Placing Balance-of-Payments Considerations in Proper Perspective

A country as wealthy, diversified, and productive as the United States should not subject its foreign policies to the requirements of the balance of payments. Two examples will serve to illustrate the point. Decisions concerning foreign aid to underdeveloped countries and its distribution among donor nations should not be based on balance-of-payments considerations. Rather, they ought to relate to overall national priorities and to what the country can afford to spend. And it is per capita and total national income, not the balance of payments, that best indicates our ability (or any country's ability) to engage in foreign assistance. Likewise, only the income criterion can properly be used in any attempt to arrive at an equitable distribution of the aid burden. The fact that Ghana may have a balance-of-payments surplus and Great Britain a deficit does not mean that Ghana should initiate a foreign aid program to the United Kingdom. Assuming that we are able and willing to pursue a certain national objective, the balance-of-payments position should not stand in the way.

Another example concerns the U.S. commitments abroad, such as direct involvement in foreign conflicts. Any such commitments must be made in terms of the ranking of national objectives. This is not to suggest that cost considerations play no role in decisions of war and peace. They must certainly be weighed alongside any noneconomic costs and against whatever potential benefits can be expected from a given policy. The major economic burden resulting from war or foreign commitments is in the form of annual domestic budgetary expenditures. The pressure on the balance of payments resulting from any conflict is subsidiary in nature.

Limitations of Balance-of-Payments Information

Like any statistics collected from a great variety of reporting sources, the international transactions data are far from perfect. Without going into the methods of gathering the figures, we might mention that the merchandise component is allegedly the most reliable, since traders are required to make detailed reports on both volume and value when goods cross national boundaries. Probably the least dependable are accounts of private capital flows.

But even if it were thoroughly accurate, the international transactions statement does not contain all the useful information about a country's international position. Merchandise trade, which is the largest current account item, appears in an aggregative form followed by a list of selected goods in the supplementary tables. Investigators who wish to discover the commodity composition of this trade in its entirety would have to turn to sources mentioned in the introduction to Part One. More importantly, the international transactions statement only shows *changes* in a country's positions, not the positions themselves. All items in the statement refer to *flows* of goods, services, and capital over the one-year period covered. Total American holdings of overseas investment at a point of time, which are the product of flows over many previous years, are not given. Nor are the sales of foreign subsidiaries reported. Since these activities have important bearing on the strength of the dollar, information about them is collected and published separately by the U.S. Department of Commerce.[9]

---

[9]See, for example, tabulations in the annual *Economic Report of the President*.

Although the balance of payments is a global statement, it is often subdivided into the country's relations with separate continents. But the common belief that there is somehow a need to balance the external accounts vis-à-vis individual countries or groups of countries is erroneous. Such concern would be valid only if currencies were subject to government control and were not freely convertible to each other. Under the conditions of currency convertibility prevailing among the industrialized countries today, the United States can use its surplus with one country to pay for a deficit with another. It is only the overall external position that matters. And even that need not be in balance all the time. Just as a family can run into short-run deficits and cover them out of previous savings or by borrowing, so can a country finance temporary deficits out of reserves or by incurring foreign debts. It is only if the deficits persist over a period of years that they provide a cause for concern.

A Nation versus a State

Why, it may be asked, is a country the smallest unit to have an international transactions statement? Every region, state, and other subdivision conducts transactions with the world outside it: Why does one never hear of a balance-of-payments deficit of the state of West Virginia or the Rocky Mountains region? A superficial difference is that there exist no data on the economic transactions of a state with the world outside it. Only countries, with political boundaries through which goods and services must pass, collect such information.

More important is the way the problem manifests itself in the context of a state. Let us suppose that because of a technological change or a shift in consumer taste, there occurred a sharp decline in demand for the products of West Virginia. That state's exports would drop sharply, and in all probability it would develop an external deficit. Yet there would be no press reports to that effect. Instead, public discussion would emphasize the fact that workers in the export industries were thrown out of work and that production and income declined all around. If the situation persisted and nothing were done to rectify it, the state would become a depressed area, and eventually people would start migrating to other parts of the country where jobs were more plentiful—that is, to states producing the type of products for which national and world demand were booming. Such migration is much more difficult, if not impossible, between countries. In other words, whereas an independent country is said to have an external deficit or surplus, a state with a similar trade position is said to be depressed or flourishing.

But the difference does not stop here. A country has its own currency and its national government can pursue fiscal, monetary, and commercial policies aimed at curing the external imbalance. If nothing else works, it may impose import controls or exchange restrictions. By contrast, a state government can take few measures to alleviate a depression within its borders; its ability to act is much more limited. A state cannot pursue independent fiscal, monetary, or exchange-rate policies. It does not issue its own currency or control the supply of money; neither can it impose restrictions on "foreign" trade and payments. In a more general way, regions of the same country are subject to uniform economic policies affecting income and prices and, therefore, the balance of payments. Such uniformity does not exist between countries that pursue independent policies. Finally, a country can change the exchange rate of its currency; in the present system of fluctuating exchange rates such changes occur every day. In contrast, the ratio, say, of the New York to the California dollar is immutably fixed at one to one.

On the other hand, the national government of which the state is a part can take steps to help the state by direct government assistance, by a variety of transfer payments, or by encouraging the influx of private capital. For example, in the United States the federal government facilitates transfers from the northern to the southern states.[10] In general, given the proper business environment, capital is more mobile between states than between countries. Certainly, in the short run, the existence of an integrated capital market within a nation makes it easier to finance imbalances within itself than between nations. And if such financing is not adequate, the adjustment can take the form of outflow of labor from the deficit (depressed) region. The result of this comparison between a country and a political subdivision such as a state is that in the context of a state an external deficit is manifested differently; it is more likely to be offset by movement of the factors of production such as labor and capital, and it cannot be handled by policy measures which are the prerogative of the central government.

Summary

Each country's transactions with the rest of the world are summarized in its statement of international transactions. The current account component of the statement includes exports and imports of goods and services as well as unilateral transfers. The capital account records international purchases and sales of assets. In all cases the transactions that give rise to dollar inpayments (credit or plus items) are distinguished from those that result in dollar outpayments (debit or minus items). The various balances include:

Balance of trade: Exports minus imports of merchandise.

Balance on goods and services: Exports minus imports of goods and services.

Balance on current account: Balance on goods, services and income flows minus unilateral transfers.

---

[10] "The Federal Budget and the States," Kennedy School of Government, Harvard University, 1996.

Official reserve transactions balance (or *overall balance*): Private inpayments minus outpayments on goods, services, income flows, unilateral transfers, and nonofficial capital transfers. Under a freely floating exchange rate, it would be zero. Under a managed float, it is balanced by changes in U.S. and foreign official reserves.

A variant of the balance on goods and services forms the link to the national income accounts; it is one (X_n) of the four expenditure components. A country's deficit on the current account equals the excess of domestic investment over savings. The savings deficiency is offset by the inflow of foreign capital. A country's surplus on the current account equals the excess of domestic savings over investment, and that excess comprises the outflow of capital funds. The first case describes the current U.S. position, while the second case applies to Japan. However, the term *savings* needs to be expanded to include the government budgetary surplus. A budgetary deficit would be considered negative savings.

U.S. imports of goods and commercial services vary positively with U.S. output or income, and negatively with the foreign to domestic price ratio (P_F/P_D). Exports of goods and commercial services vary positively with the rest of the world output or income, and positively with the foreign to domestic price ratio. As a country moves through various stages of its development, its trade balance is expected to exhibit long-run swings.

Not all useful information on the country's external position is contained in its statement of international transactions. For the statement reports only *flows* over a one-year period. Items such as the *stock* of foreign investment are reported elsewhere.

A statement of international transactions exists only for nations and not for geographical subdivisions thereof, such as states. First of all, no statistical data are available for these regions. Secondly, instead of manifesting themselves as external deficits or surpluses, these areas are considered to be depressed or flourishing, respectively. Finally, such situations are likely to be offset by movement of productive factors out of the depressed and toward the prospering states or political subdivisions. The federal government is also likely to use policy measures to aid depressed areas.

Important Concepts

International transactions statement

Dollar inpayments

Capital account

Dollar outpayments

Current account

Autonomous items

Balance of trade

Balance on goods and services

Balance on current account

Purchases or sales of assets

Direct investment

Official reserve transactions (or overall) balance

Accommodating items

Changes in official reserves

$$X - M = S - I$$

$$M - X = I - S$$

Review Questions

1. You are given the following figures for U.S. international transactions in 1993 (in $ billions):

Merchandise imports	– $300
Merchandise exports	+ $200
Exports of services	+ $100
Imports of services	– $80
Income receipts on U.S. assets abroad	+ $60
Income payments on foreign assets in the U.S.	– $30
Foreign private assets in the United States (net increase)	+ $100
U.S. private assets abroad (net increase)	– $50
Change in U.S. or foreign official reserve holdings	0

a. *Calculate* the

- Balance of trade
- Balance of goods and services
- Balance on current account
- Official reserve transactions balance

b. Explain the relation between the current and the capital accounts.
c. Can you suggest what possible exchange standard (fixed? floating?) the U.S. dollar is on? Explain fully.
d. How do the above figures relate to the expenditure side of the U.S. income and product (GDP) accounts?

2. Based on tables 10.1 and 10.2, explain the changes in the U.S. external position between 1980 and 1987, and between 1980 and 1995.

3. Why doesn't the state of California publish annual balance of payments statistics? In what ways is it different from a country?

4. What are the main determinants of a country's imports and exports?

5. How are surpluses and deficits on goods and services related to domestic savings and investment? Explain the current situation in the United States and in Japan.

Market-Determined Exchange Rates

U nlike the situation in the period immediately following World War II, the currencies of most industrialized countries are today freely convertible to one another, at a ratio subject to daily fluctuations. This ratio—the number of units of one currency that are exchangeable for a unit of another—is known as the *exchange rate*.[1] Thus, on a certain date, the British pound sterling (£) was worth $2.00 in American currency, and the German mark (D.M.) was valued at 50 cents, which in turn means that £1 = 4 D.M. The fact that every exchange rate has a corresponding inverse is frequently a source of confusion. The dollar–mark rate can be expressed by saying that 1 mark = 50 cents or, equivalently, that $1 = 2 marks. An *increase* in the value of the mark to 60 cents is equivalent to a *decrease* in the value of the dollar to 1.7 marks. Consequently, a statement that the exchange rate has gone up (or down) requires further clarification, because its meaning depends on how the exchange rate is defined. To avoid confusion, one can use such phraseology as "the exchange value of the dollar went up" (or "down") in terms of other currencies.

Exchange rates by themselves tell us nothing about the relative strength of the currencies involved or the economies behind them. The fact that the pound sterling is set at $2 and the German mark at 50 cents is not to be construed as an indication that the first currency is four times as strong as the second. It may simply reflect the difference between the denominations into which the two countries chose to divide their respective currencies. When first decreed, the external value of each currency presumably reflected the

[1] Average monthly exchange rates are published in the Federal Reserve Bulletin. Daily exchange rates are published in major newspapers. Appendix 11–1 shows the dollar exchange rates for October 7, 1996.

country's economic conditions in general, and the purchasing power of the currency (that is, the internal costs and prices) relative to that of other currencies in particular. This relative position changes over time, and such changes may either weaken or strengthen the currency vis-à-vis other currencies. A currency is considered externally weak if it declines in value on the foreign exchange market.

Because of its strong influence on imports and exports of goods and services, the exchange rate is one of the most important prices in the economy. It is also a very sensitive price, responding rapidly to any changes, or even anticipated changes, in the economy. That is why exchange rates vary on a daily and even an hourly basis.

The market on which international currencies are traded and where exchange rates are determined is called the **foreign exchange market.** It is here that households, firms, and financial institutions, buy and sell foreign currencies to make international payments. The average daily volume of worldwide currency trading approximates $1 trillion, with London, New York, and Tokyo constituting the most important markets (in that order). Payments connected with international trade are a small part of total foreign exchange transactions. Rather, most transactions constitute exchange of one kind of assets (such as stocks, bonds, or bank accounts) for another. Many individuals and institutions maintain their wealth in the form of both domestic and foreign assets in order to minimize risk (i.e., avoid putting all their eggs in one basket). They then trade foreign for domestic assets or vice versa with the view of maximizing the return (in the forms of interest, dividends, and so on) on these assets or lowering risk. And such trades account for most of the transactions on the foreign exchange market.

Since 1973 exchange rates of several major currencies, such as the dollar, pound, and yen, have been fluctuating in response to supply and demand conditions on the foreign exchange markets. How exchange rates are determined and the causes of their fluctuations are the topics of this chapter.

Demand and Supply of Foreign Currencies

When the exchange value of a currency is permitted by the government to fluctuate freely on the foreign exchange markets (without any government intervention), it is known as a **freely fluctuating** or a **floating exchange rate.** (It is also sometimes referred to as a *clean* float.) In such a situation, market forces determine each exchange rate at the level that clears the market. A floating currency is said to **appreciate** when its exchange value increases and to **depreciate** when its exchange value decreases.

To illustrate how the exchange rate of a floating currency is determined, figure 11.1 shows the German foreign exchange market where marks are

FIGURE 11.1   *Supply and Demand Curves for Dollars in Germany*

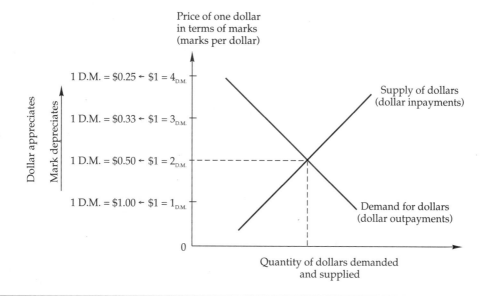

Intersection of supply and demand for foreign currencies (represented by the U.S. dollar), determines the exchange rate.

Note: The vertical axis shows the number of marks per dollar along with the corresponding inverse: the equivalent number of dollars per mark in each case.

traded for dollars. The two intersecting curves show the demand for (in color) and supply of dollars at various mark prices. They exhibit "normal" slopes: As the mark price of the dollar declines, more dollars are demanded and fewer are supplied. The equilibrium exchange rate for this particular pair of curves is 2 marks = $1; it would vary with shifts in either demand or supply. The quantity axis indicates the number of dollars changing hands. This is similar to the price determination mechanism in the market for any commodity.

But the analysis begs the more fundamental question of what gives rise to such supply and demand, because foreign currencies are not commodities. A commodity is demanded by consumers for its own sake, to enhance consumer satisfaction, and is supplied by producers through the use of productive factors. By contrast, people do not normally require foreign currencies for consumption, and foreign currencies are not manufactured in the same manner as are commodities. Rather, the demand for dollars in our illustration reflects German desire to purchase foreign goods, to travel abroad ˜nd buy other foreign services, or to transfer capital abroad for investment and other purposes. Together these items constitute the *outpayments* side of the German international transactions statement. On the other hand, the supply of foreign currencies is derived from commodity and service exports and from the inflow of foreign capital. These entries make up the *inpayments* side of the German international transactions statement. Thus, the demand curve in figure 11.1 is tantamount to a German dollar outpayments curve, and the supply curve, to a German dollar inpayments curve.[2] Since the exchange rate is determined by the intersection of the two curves, it ensures equality between inpayments and outpayments. A shift in one or both curves will also change the exchange rate to a new level, which again clears the market. In other words, a freely fluctuating rate would ensure equilibrium in the balance of payments. The official reserve settlement balance would be zero.

Additional Insights

This discussion invites an important question: If the demand and supply for foreign currencies is not the same phenomenon as the demand and supply for a product, but is instead "derived" from a desire to trade on foreign markets, how can we be sure that the curves have the usual slopes of demand and supply, as shown in figure 11.1? Consider the two curves in turn, and assume first that all international transactions consist of commodity trade.

Demand for Dollars   The German **demand for dollars** represents indirectly the German demand for American goods. If the price of $1 rises from 2 to 4 marks (moving upward along the price axis), then an American product costing $1 would double in price to the German consumer (from 2 to 4 marks), shrinking Germany's volume of imports and with it the number of dollars required to finance imports. Consider the price of a $10,000 American automobile to the German consumer at four alternative exchange rates:

Exchange Rate	Cost in Marks of a $10,000 American Automobile
$1 = 1 D.M.	10,000 D.M.
$1 = 2 D.M.	20,000 D.M.
$1 = 3 D.M.	30,000 D.M.
$1 = 4 D.M.	40,000 D.M.

As the mark price of the dollar rises (moving upward along the vertical axis), the price of American goods to German buyers (the price expressed in marks) rises:

[2]Given the German demand for dollars, one can derive the German supply of marks. This relationship is shown in Appendix 11–2.

Appreciation of the dollar (relative to the mark) makes American goods more expensive to the German consumer; U.S. exports to Germany become less competitive. As a result, Germans would purchase fewer American goods, and *at a fixed dollar price* they would demand fewer dollars to buy them. An upward movement along the vertical axis is associated with a leftward movement along the horizontal axis, giving the "demand for dollars" curve a negative slope. In other words, a rise in the mark price of a dollar is associated with a decline in dollar outpayments. Conversely, *depreciation of the dollar makes American goods less expensive to German consumers;* U.S. exports become more competitive. Germans would purchase more American goods, and *at a fixed dollar price* they would demand more dollars to pay for them. A downward movement along the vertical axis is associated with a rightward movement along the horizontal axis, producing a negatively sloping demand curve.

Supply of Dollars   By the same token, the **supply of dollars** is derived from German merchandise exports to the United States. An increase in the price of $1 from 2 to 4 marks means that American consumers of German imports would find that for $1 they can now get 4 marks' worth of German goods instead of 2 marks' worth. Consider the price of a 1,200 D.M. German camera to American consumers at four alternative exchange rates:

Exchange Rate	Cost in Dollars of a 1,200 D.M. German Camera
$1 = 1 D.M.	$1,200
$1 = 2 D.M.	$ 600
$1 = 3 D.M.	$ 400
$1 = 4 D.M.	$ 300

As the mark price of the dollar rises (moving up along the vertical axis of figure 11.1), the price of German goods to American buyers (the price expressed in dollars) declines: *Appreciation of the dollar (relative to the mark) makes German goods less expensive to the American consumer;* German exports to the United States become more competitive. As a result, Americans would purchase more German goods. But each German good (such as a camera) now sells for fewer dollars. Hence *if U.S. demand for German goods is relatively elastic*—a condition that is met in industrial countries—Americans would spend more dollars to buy them, raising German dollar inpayments. An upward movement along the vertical axis is associated with a rightward movement along the horizontal axis, explaining the positive slope of the "supply of dollars" or inpayments curve.

Conversely, *depreciation of the dollar makes German goods more expensive to the American consumer.* German exports to the United States become less competitive, and Americans would buy fewer German goods. But each good now sells for more dollars. Hence, only if U.S. demand for German goods is relatively elastic would Americans spend fewer dollars to buy them. Under elastic demand conditions, a downward movement along the vertical axis is associated with a leftward movement along the horizontal axis, yielding a positively sloping supply curve.

In sum, the supply curve has a positive slope if the U.S. demand for German goods is relatively elastic, a condition that exists in most markets.

In addition to establishing the slopes of the demand and supply curves for dollars, based on the supposition that dollars are used to finance merchandise trade, the above discussion demonstrates another important principle: *When a country's currency appreciates, its exports become more expensive to foreigners while its imports become cheaper to domestic residents.* Indeed when the U.S. dollar appreciated sharply from 1981 to 1985, American exports became noncompetitive and U.S. exporters found it exceedingly difficult to market their wares abroad, while foreign goods flooded the United States because they became cheaper for Americans. Conversely, *depreciation of a currency makes its exports cheaper to foreigners and its imports more expensive to domestic residents.* That is what happened to American exports and imports following the depreciation of the dollar from 1985 to 1988. And in 1993–95, when the dollar depreciated by 30 percent against the yen, Japanese cars in the United States came to be priced considerably higher than equivalent American-made models. Conversely, in 1996–97 the yen depreciated by 50 percent, making Japanese products more competitive. In 1996 the weakness of the Canadian dollar made Canadian products relatively inexpensive in the United States, and Canadian exports rose.

Service Transactions   Similar results are obtained for service transactions, such as tourism. Under "demand for dollars," replace the dollar price of an American automobile with, say, $100 for a night's stay in a New York hotel. Its cost to the German tourist rises from 100 D.M. to 400 D.M. as the dollar appreciates from $1 = 1 D.M. to $1 = 4 D.M. Fewer German tourists would visit the United States and they would spend fewer dollars here. Conversely, it would become relatively cheap for Germans to travel abroad if the exchange value of the mark rose (as it did for the Japanese in 1993). The demand for dollars is negatively sloped. Under "supply of dollars" replace the D.M. price of a German camera with, say, 40 D.M. for a meal at a Frankfurt restaurant. Its cost to the American tourist declines from $40 to $10 as the dollar appreciates from $1 = 1 D.M. to $1 = 4 D.M. More American tourists would visit Germany, and *assuming* that their demand for German services is *relatively elastic,* they would spend more dollars there. The supply of dollars is positively sloped.

Direct Foreign Investment (DFI)   These are investments, such as the setting up of a foreign subsidiary[3] abroad, that give the investor control over the foreign operations. If under "demand for dollars" the dollar price of an American automobile is replaced by $1 million for a U.S. plant, its cost to the German investor in the United States rises from 1 to 4 million D.M. as the dollar appreciates from $1 = 1 D.M. to $1 = 4 D.M. The outcome is again a negatively sloping demand curve. Under "supply of dollars," replacing the D.M. price of a German camera with 10 million D.M. for a German factory, and following the same procedure, yields a positively sloped supply curve.

Other Assets   Most international transactions involve the purchase or sale of foreign stocks, bonds, and bank accounts. These are known as *portfolio investments,* where the investor has no control over operations of the foreign company. To see that the slope of the demand curve for dollars is negative, replace the dollar price of an American car with $100 for a U.S. government bond and follow the same procedure. For the supply curve, replace the D.M. price of a German camera with a 400 D.M. price for a share in a German company and generate a positively sloped supply curve.

---

[3] Both a branch plant and a subsidiary qualify as DFI, the difference between them being that a subsidiary is incorporated separately in the foreign country, while a branch is not.

At any one time, the supply-and-demand forces emanating from international transactions exert their influence on the foreign exchange market to determine the exchange rate. The reason for the frequent changes in exchange rates is that the supply and demand curves shift continuously. They are never stationary. *A currency is fundamentally strong and its value may be pushed upward when the country's autonomous inpayments (exports of goods and services plus inflow of capital) exceed outpayments (imports plus outflow of capital). It is weak when this situation is reversed.* In turn, the country's inpayments and outpayments are determined by a host of domestic and foreign factors, including prices (its competitive position, for example), income, and interest rates. Anything that affects these factors at home and abroad influences the position of the supply and demand curves and therefore affects the exchange rate. The exchange rate is deeply rooted in the country's economic conditions; in no way can it be divorced from its own and other countries' general economic policies. The entire constellation of economic circumstances exerts its influence on the exchange rates through its effect on internationally traded items.

SHIFTS IN THE DEMAND AND SUPPLY CURVES

Practically all economic changes in the country shift either the demand or the supply curves for foreign currencies (or both). In the short run, variations in the rate of interest have powerful effects. A rise in the country's interest rate attracts foreign funds and increases the demand for the home currency and hence its exchange value. Any policy that affects interest rates will also affect the exchange rate. In the long run, a country's rate of inflation, relative to that prevailing abroad, determines its ability to compete on foreign and domestic markets and hence its exchange rate. Beyond these changes, a variety of psychological factors—originating in political disturbances and even rumors, economic expectations, and the like—affect the exchange rate. Unfavorable expectations about the country's economic conditions and the strength of its currency may lead to depreciation as people sell the currency, while the reverse is true in the case of favorable expectations. The above factors will be considered one at a time, in each case assuming that other factors are held constant.

Relative Interest Rates

Suppose that U.S. interest rates rose sharply relative to those prevailing abroad. Then individuals, corporations, and other economic institutions would transfer funds to the United States to be placed in high-interest-yielding securities and other financial instruments. Americans as well as foreigners would convert currencies into dollars to take advantage of high stateside interest rates. The demand for dollars would rise, and with it, their value on the foreign currency markets.

FIGURE 11.2	*Effect of a Rise in U.S. Interest Rates on the Dollar–D.M. Exchange Rate*

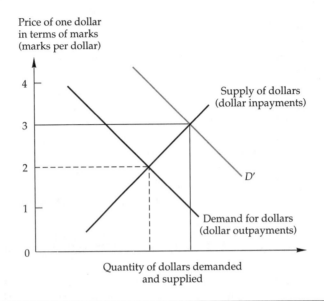

A rise in U.S. interest rates (all else remaining constant) increases demand for dollars from *D* to *D'*, and the dollar appreciates from 2 D.M. to 3 D.M. The mark depreciates from 50¢ to $33\frac{1}{3}$¢.

This is seen in figure 11.2, which describes the German foreign currency market. Demand for dollar increases from D to D': At each exchange rate, more dollars are demanded to take advantage of high U.S. interest rates. The dollar appreciates from 2 D.M. to 3 D.M.; correspondingly, the mark depreciates from 50 cents to 33⅓ cents. Conversely, a decline in U.S. interest rates or a rise in German interest rates would cause depreciation of the dollar.

Fluctuations in the exchange value of the dollar during the 1980s were often dominated by variations in interest rates. In the early years of the decade, high U.S. real interest rates (relative to those prevailing abroad) attracted foreign funds and propelled the exchange value of the dollar to a 15-year high. Between 1980 and February 1985, the dollar rose from 1.7 to 3.4 D.M. (although there were some temporary up and down fluctuations). Dollar appreciation occurred in terms of other currencies as well. Between 1985 and 1988 the dollar drifted downward with the decline in U.S. interest rates, dropping to 1.7 D.M. by 1989, and 1.5 D.M. by 1996. In October 1993 the mark depreciated as a result of interest rate cuts by Germany's central bank, while in 1996 the pound appreciated mainly as a result of climbing U.K. interest rates.

Countries sometimes adjust their interest rates in order to affect the exchange value of their currencies. In October 1989 several European central banks, led by Germany, raised interest rates in order to lift their currencies against the dollar as well as to control inflation. At the end of 1989, the Bank of Canada raised interest rates in order to control inflation. But a side effect of that action was an appreciation of the Canadian dollar, and that in turn undermined Canada's competitive position and caused a reduction in its exports. As a result, the Bank of Canada moved to lower interest rates early in 1990. Finally, in April 1990 Japan raised interest rates in an attempt to stem the decline of the yen exchange rate.

Additional Insights

Fiscal and Monetary Policies   Fiscal policy consists of changes in government expenditures and taxes, while monetary policy refers to changes in the country's money supply, and is conducted by its central bank. Both types of policy are designed to stabilize the economy. Both affect interest rates and hence the exchange rate. Expansionary monetary policy (all else unchanged) lowers interest rates both by direct action of the central bank (reducing the discount rate) and through increasing the *supply* of money. The exchange value of the currency depreciates. Conversely, contractionary monetary policy causes appreciation of the exchange rate because it raises interest rates. Even anticipation of change in the money supply would cause the exchange rate to move in the directions just indicated. By contrast, fiscal expansion (assuming no monetary change) increases aggregate expenditures, and thereby raises the *demand* for money. Interest rates rise and the exchange rate appreciates. Fiscal contraction has the opposite effects. We summarize the effect of economic policies as follows:

Policy	Effect on the Money Market	Effect on Interest Rates	Effect on the Exchange Rate
Monetary expansion	Money supply rises	Decline	Depreciates
Monetary contraction	Money supply declines	Rise	Appreciates
Fiscal expansion	Money demand rises	Rise	Appreciates
Fiscal contraction	Money demand declines	Decline	Depreciates

Two examples will serve to illustrate the effects of fiscal and monetary policies. In 1993 the United States pursued a policy of fiscal *contraction*, as President Clinton submitted a budget designed to cut the federal deficit by raising taxes and reducing expenditures. At the same time, Japan followed a policy of fiscal *expansion*; government expenditures were raised in order to cope with the domestic economic slump.

As a result, U.S. interest rates declined relative to those in Japan, and the dollar depreciated 20 percent relative to the yen. That depreciation continued into early 1994. In October 1993, the German central bank pursued expansionary *monetary* policy by lowering interest rates, resulting in a depreciation of the mark.

Both monetary and fiscal stimulation cause income to rise. But monetary expansion accomplishes this by raising the *supply* of money while fiscal expansion increases the *demand* for money. Consequently they have opposite effects on interest rates and hence on the exchange rate.

Relative Price Change

Assume next that the U.S. inflation rate far exceeded that of Germany and other major trading nations. This means that American goods and services would become more expensive relative to their German counterparts on both the U.S. and foreign markets. The American competitive position would deteriorate, and Germany would *sell more* on the U.S. market and *buy less* American goods and services.

In that case Germany would export more to the United States—increasing its supply of dollars; and it would import less from the United States—reducing its demand for dollars (figure 11.3). The dollar inpayments curve in Germany would rise or shift rightward to (the colored) S'. At each and every exchange rate more dollars would be supplied. Concurrently the dollar outpayments curve in Germany would decline or shift leftward to (the colored) D'. At each exchange rate fewer dollars would be demanded to finance purchases in the United States. Both shifts cause a reduction in the exchange value of the dollar. The dollar depreciates from 2 D.M. to 1.625 D.M., and correspondingly, the mark appreciates from 1 D.M. = 50 cents to 1 D.M. = 61.53 cents. Differential inflation rates between countries are a prime cause of currency fluctuations. All events that raise the country's price level, such as an increase in production cost brought about by a large jump in wage rates or in the price of energy, or the tightening of governmental regulations, would bring about currency depreciation. For example, in the mid-1970s, high inflation, labor unrest, and other economic dislocations reduced the competitive position of Italy and the United Kingdom, causing depreciation of their currencies. Countries suffering from hyperinflation will see their currencies depreciate precipitously. Thus the Russian ruble depreciated from 10R = $1 to 4000R = $1 between 1991 and 1994.

Because money growth is a main determinant of inflation, a sharp *expansion in a country's money supply*, which tends to stimulate inflation, would *cause its currency to depreciate*. Conversely, monetary contraction would cause the currency to appreciate. Thus monetary policy affects the exchange rate both through the interest rate and price channels. Since both effects work in the *same direction*, they are mutually reinforcing, and the

| FIGURE 11.3 | *Effect of U.S. Inflation on the Dollar–D.M. Exchange Rate* |

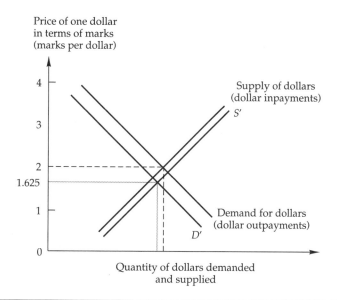

A rise in U.S. inflation reduces demand for dollars to *D'* and increases supply of dollars to *S'*. The dollar depreciates from 2 D.M. to 1.625 D.M., while the mark appreciates.

exchange rate is very sensitive to changes in monetary policy. It responds swiftly to actual and even anticipated changes in money supply. If market participants expect a sharp rise in the money stock, they also anticipate depreciation of the currency to follow. To avoid losses from holding assets denominated in a depreciated currency they sell them for assets denominated in other currencies so the depreciation occurs immediately.

Overshooting[4]   One result of this sensitivity is the tendency toward **exchange rate overshooting,** which is said to occur when the short-run response to a disturbance is greater than the long-run response. In figure 11.4, the dollar is shown to appreciate on the left panel. But its rise from level *A* to a new long-term level *B* is not a monotonous upward movement. Rather, it first overshoots to level *C*, and then drops to its new long-run level *B*. Similarly, the right panel shows overshooting in the case of dollar depreciation. It first overshoots from level *A* to *C*, and then settles at level *B*.

[4]See R. Dornbush, "Expectations and Exchange-Rate Dynamics," *Journal of Political Economy*, December 1976.

FIGURE 11.4　*Exchange Rate Overshooting*

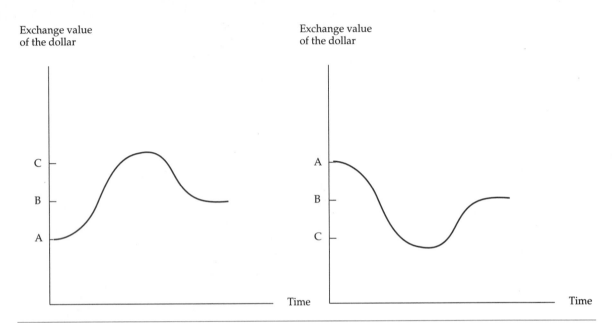

When the exchange value of the dollar rises (declines) from *A* to *B*, it first rises (declines) to *C* and then retreats to *B*.

To understand the cause of overshooting, assume that there is a permanent increase in the country's money supply (with money supply in other countries remaining unchanged). In the long run that would raise the levels of prices and wages, and the exchange rate would depreciate. But in the short run, the price level, unlike the exchange rate, is sticky: Wage contracts are negotiated only once in a few years, while prices of goods (except for raw materials) also tend to be inflexible. The price level does not immediately jump in response to changes in the money stock. It responds only with a time lag, say when wage contracts are renegotiated. Only the exchange rate adjusts immediately. It must therefore *absorb the entire impact* of a change in money supply, causing it to overshoot; it would therefore tend to depreciate excessively. Only after all prices adjust will the exchange rate recede to its long-run level. The same phenomenon occurs in the opposite direction in the case of a shrinkage of money supply. In the short run, the exchange rate bears the entire brunt of a monetary contraction; therefore it overshoots to a higher level than its new long-run equilibrium. Only after prices and wages adjust to the new conditions does the exchange rate settle back to a new permanent level. These short-term versus long-term adjustments therefore are the primary causes of exchange rate volatility. If all wages and prices were flexible in the short run, there would be no exchange rate overshooting.

Regardless of overshooting, a country with an inflation rate well above the world's average will see its currency depreciate continuously. This phenomenon is of paramount importance in the high-inflation countries like Brazil in which currencies depreciate on a monthly basis. In 1993, because of triple-digit inflation in Russia, the ruble's exchange value declined from 415R = \$1 to 1,250R = \$1. And in early 1994 it dropped further to 1,950R = \$1.[5]

Purchasing Power Parity In the long run, the relative price behavior of any two countries is a most powerful determinant of the exchange rate between their currencies. Put differently, the *exchange rate* reflects the relative *purchasing power* of the two currencies in their respective home countries. This proposition is known as the **purchasing power parity (PPP)** doctrine.

Its simplest version states that if \$1 buys the same quantity of goods and services in the United States as 2 D.M. buy in Germany, then the *long-run* equilibrium exchange rate would \$1 = 2 D.M. Thus PPP asserts that the exchange rate between two currencies, such as the dollar and the mark, equals the ratio of the price levels in the United States and Germany,[6] where the price level of each country may be measured by the consumer price index (CPI). But because the exchange rate is affected by influences other than relative price levels, the actual exchange rate can depart from purchasing power parity for extended periods. For example, over several years during the period 1981–1985, the dollar exchange rate was above 3 D.M. (driven mainly by high U.S. interest rates). Yet the purchasing power of \$1 in the United States was equivalent to that of only 2 D.M. in Germany. In other words, the dollar was *overvalued* relative to PPP. Conversely, between 1985 and 1989 the dollar depreciated, reaching 1.65 D.M. in 1990, and it was undervalued relative to PPP. In 1997 the dollar–yen exchange rate was about \$1 = ¥120, with the dollar undervalued relative to PPP. Empirical tests usually fail to confirm the PPP doctrine. One famous test, conducted by the British magazine *The Economist*, is known as the Big Mac test. In comparing the prices of Big Mac hamburgers (a homogeneous good) in various European countries, it finds that after converting the prices to one currency

---

[5] In countries suffering from hyperinflation, a foreign currency such as the dollar is often used as a means of payments instead of (or along with) the local currency. For example Argentina became highly "dollarized" in the late 1980s and early 1990s, a condition known as *currency substitution*. In 1994 Russia banned the use of foreign currencies for domestic transactions.

[6] In notational form we can write $E_{\$/D.M.} = P_{U.S.}/P_{Ger}$, where E represents the exchange rate and P the price level. Rearranging the equation we obtain $P_{U.S.} = (E_{\$/D.M.})(P_G)$. It states that all countries' price levels are equal when measured in terms of the same currency.

by the exchange rates, the prices differ a great deal. Even so, relative price changes have a powerful effect on the exchange rate in the long run.

Changes in the Balance of Trade

Continuous large U.S. deficits on goods and services increase the supply of dollars in Frankfurt, and over the years would cause the dollar to depreciate relative to the mark. Conversely, continuous sizable German deficits on current account would, in time, bring about depreciation of the mark. Consequently, an increase (or decrease) in world demand for U.S. goods would bring about appreciation (or depreciation) of the dollar. And similar results would hold for a change in world demand for the tradeable goods of any other country. Likewise, a rise in productivity in a country's tradeable-goods sector relative to other countries would lower its relative production costs and improve its competitive position. Its currency would appreciate. Additionally, because the productivity of investment would also rise, direct foreign investments may be attracted to the country, further increasing demand for its currency and accentuating the appreciation. Conversely, a decline in relative productivity in a country's tradeable-goods sector would cause its currency to depreciate. A country's international trade position is also affected by such imponderables as taste, the quality and design of its products, and accompanying services.

Examples of the above effects are not hard to find. The rise in relative Japanese productivity in tradeable goods over the past two decades has brought about a long-run appreciation of the yen. It rose from about ¥310 = $1 in 1975 to ¥120 = $1 in 1997. In the late 1970s, the United Kingdom became self-sufficient in oil, as the North Sea fields achieved full production. This reduced British outpayments for imported oil, and the pound advanced from $1.60 in 1976, to $2.33 in 1980. With the subsequent climb of the dollar between 1980 and 1985, the pound depreciated, reaching an all-time low of $1.1 in the winter of 1985, before climbing back during the remainder of the decade to $1.7. By 1996 the pound had retreated to $1.56.

Expectations

Often market participants anticipate any or all of the preceding changes based on information available to them and act before the change actually occurs. For example, a sudden spurt in the growth of the money supply leads people to expect an acceleration of the inflation rate. Anticipating that a depreciation of the currency will follow, they sell ("unload") their holdings of the currency, and as a result, its value declines even before the acceleration of inflation is evident. Similar action may be triggered by a substantial rise in wage rates throughout the country (and the attendant rise in production costs) or anything else that foreshadows future depreciation. Market agents acting on such information may sell the currency in question; it would depreciate in a manner of self-justifying expectations.

Also, the very rise (or decline) in the value of a currency may trigger expectations of further change in the same direction. Speculators would then buy (sell) the currency in the hope of realizing profits, and by that action they would push the value of the currency upward (down). Such a **speculative bubble** is said to be partly responsible for the dollar's appreciation in late 1984.

Finally, expectations about government policy can cause changes in the exchange rate. For example, in early October 1996 the dollar rose from ¥110 to ¥112 on a rumor that Japanese and American officials had privately agreed to strive for an exchange rate of ¥120 = $1.

Other Factors

Political and psychological influences can also affect the exchange rate. For example, in 1977 fears that Quebec would secede from Canada caused many Canadians to transfer their funds to the United States. To do so they had to convert Canadian dollars to American dollars, causing a depreciation of the Canadian dollar. The Canadian dollar also depreciated the day after the defeat of the Conservative party in the Canadian elections of October 1993. Likewise, the 1982 war in the Falkland Islands (between Britain and Argentina) caused a depreciation of the pound sterling. In June 1993 Japan's political crisis caused the yen to depreciate. The mark climbed in response to the democracy movement in Eastern Europe, and subsequently the dollar gained following a rumor that Gorbachev might resign as Communist party chief.

Summary

All events in the economy and all government policies influence prices (P) and the rate of interest (i). These include changes in wage rates and productivity which affect labor production costs (and the price level); changes in energy costs; fiscal and monetary policies; and a multitude of other factors. Through their impact on P and i, they influence the exchange rate. Schematically, these relationships can be shown as follows (see also appendix 11–4):

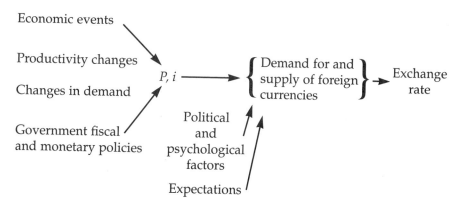

The exchange rate is deeply embedded in the economy.

It should be emphasized that in all cases what counts are the changes inside the country *relative* to changes in the rest of the world. If prices and interest rates rise commensurately on both sides of the border, the outpayments and inpayments may be similarly affected with no change in the exchange rate. By definition an exchange rate involves at least two countries.

In all cases, the effect of price, interest rate, and other changes on the exchange rate can be analyzed in terms of figure 11.1, by shifting the demand and/or the supply curve and examining the results. In each case, it is important to know which curve to shift and in what direction.

Several factors affecting the exchange rate may change simultaneously. If one of them does not dominate, and if the changes influence the exchange rate in offsetting directions, it is not possible to draw a clear-cut conclusion about the expected direction of change. A rise in interest rates (causing appreciation) accompanied by a rise in the rate of inflation (causing depreciation) is one such example; political fears accompanied by a sharp boost in the interest rate is another.

One significant conclusion of this discussion is that *depreciation is not necessarily bad, nor is appreciation necessarily good.* It all depends on the factor(s) causing the exchange rate to fluctuate. If the currency depreciates because interest rates were lowered to combat a recession, it is viewed as a favorable development. But if the depreciation is caused by a high rate of inflation, it is viewed unfavorably.

A second important conclusion is that a *freely fluctuating* exchange rate would settle at a point that clears the market; that is *with private inpayments and outpayments equated.* Both are defined to include transactions in goods and services as well as capital transfers. This takes us back to the discussion of the balance of payments in the last chapter. Had there been absolutely no government intervention in the foreign exchange market (that is, a free float), there would be no change in official reserve holdings and no overall deficit or surplus in the balance of payments. Exchange-rate fluctuations would preserve a balance in the external account, and there would be no change in official reserves (the measure of a surplus or deficit). External imbalances exist because central banks do intervene in the foreign currency markets to influence the exchange rate in a direction they consider desirable. That is how changes in international reserves occur. A regime in which the central bank intervenes in the foreign exchange market is called a **managed float** (sometimes referred to as a *dirty* float). Most currencies of the industrial countries are under a managed rather than a free float.

Under a free float the balance of payments is kept in equilibrium by exchange fluctuations. But that does not mean that each category of the international transactions is in balance. Between 1984 and 1996 the United States sustained average annual trade deficits in excess of $100 billion, and these were balanced by private capital inflows of similar amounts. A country concerned about its trade balance, because of the implications of exports and imports for domestic output and employment, would find such a situation unsatisfactory.

THE FOREIGN EXCHANGE MARKET

In the preceding discussion, references were made to the foreign exchange market. It is therefore useful to provide a short institutional description of this market.

Market Organization

International transactions call for the use of the foreign exchange market, which is composed of four main participants:

1. Commercial banks, which execute transactions for their corporate and other customers. Sometimes with the help of specialized foreign exchange brokers, they bring together buyers and sellers of foreign currencies. Banks also transact with one another for their own account; indeed interbank trading accounts for most of the activity in the foreign exchange market.
2. Corporations, which need to convert receipts or payments from one currency to another.
3. Nonbank financial institutions, such as insurance companies.
4. Central banks, which intervene in the market by buying and selling currencies to influence the exchange rate. The impact of their transactions may be great.

Although the market is highly competitive and provides traders with full information at all times, it is not to be equated with the stock exchange in terms of its organization. There is no "Big Board" on which instant price quotations (that is, exchange rates) are posted for all currencies. The foreign exchange market consists of the foreign exchange departments of the large banks as well as a number of specialized traders. They communicate instantly with each other by telephone or computers, continuously exchanging price and quantity information. It is therefore useful to think of this market as a network of telephone lines and cables. In addition, each large bank maintains correspondent banks in all major cities throughout the world, and it is through this relationship that the network of foreign exchange transactions is conducted. The foreign correspondent of a bank may be its own branch or subsidiary.[7] Thus although foreign exchange trading

---

[7] A foreign *subsidiary* of a bank is incorporated in the foreign country and subject only to host-country regulations. A branch is an office of the home bank in another country (not incorporated separately), and is subject to both host and home-country regulations.

takes place in many financial markets around the world, these markets are tightly linked.[8]

Instant communication ensures that the foreign exchange markets will be *orderly:* that the value of one currency in terms of another will be the same in all major financial centers. If the franc is worth 20 cents in Paris and 21 cents in London, financiers can purchase francs in Paris, sell them immediately in London, and realize a 1-cent profit on each franc. In doing so they demand francs in Paris, thereby exerting an upward pressure on their price, and supply them in London, with a resulting downward pressure. The process continues as long as there are profits to be realized—that is, until the price differential disappears. The transactions described here are called **arbitrage,** for they involve no risk. Profit is realized simply by taking advantage of the geographical price differential. But the arbitrager performs the useful function of ensuring that each currency has the same value on all financial markets.

While foreign exchange transactions can occur between any two currencies, most involve the exchange of a foreign currency for U.S. dollars. Suppose a Belgian company wished to trade Belgian francs for Swedish crowns, but the bank managing the transaction found it difficult to identify a corresponding agent who wished to trade crowns for francs due to the "thin" franc-crown market. The transaction would be executed first by trading the francs for dollars and then converting the dollars to crowns. Because of the dollar's widespread use, it is always possible to find parties willing to trade the dollar for any single currency. For this reason the dollar is called a **vehicle currency;** it is widely used to denominate international contracts between parties residing in countries other than the United States.

Exchange rates between nondollar currencies are called **cross rates,**[9] and the close communication between markets ensures that cross rates will be *orderly.* By this we mean that if at a given instant the franc is worth 20 cents and the pound sterling is valued at $1.80, then the pound would be worth 9 francs. We prove this by showing that no deviation from this price is sustainable. Suppose that a freak situation developed on the Swiss foreign exchange market, and the pound dropped to 8 francs in value (but with the ratios of 1 franc = 20 cents and £1 = $1.80 maintained in Paris and London, respectively). Then it would pay a financier with 8 francs to convert them into 1 British pound on the Swiss market, exchange the pound for $1.80 in London, and for that sum purchase 9 francs in Paris.

	Swiss Market	London	Paris
Schematically:	8_{FF} ⟶	£1 ⟶	$1.80 ⟶ 9_{FF}

---

[8] London, New York, and Tokyo are the three largest markets. Total international currency transactions, mainly between banks, add up to $500 trillion per year. See L. Kodres, "Foreign Exchange Markets: Structure and Systemic Risks," *Finance & Development*, December 1996.

[9] Key currency cross rates for October 7, 1996, are shown in Appendix 11–3.

Disregarding transaction costs, she makes 1 franc in profit by taking advantage of existing price differentials between geographical locations. In the process she demands pounds and supplies francs on the Swiss market, thereby pushing up the pound-franc ratio. This process, known as **triangular arbitrage,** continues as long as there is a profit to be made—that is, until the pound is pushed up to 9 francs and the profit opportunities cease to exist.

If, on the other hand, the pound were equal to 10 francs on the Swiss market, it would pay our financier to do the reverse. She would convert a pound into 10 francs, use them to buy $2.00 in Paris, and exchange this for £1.11 in London, thereby realizing a profit of one-tenth of a British pound. In the process she supplies pounds and demands francs, thereby pushing down the franc value of the pound on the Swiss market. The process will continue as long as it provides an opportunity for profit, or until the value of the pound declines to 9 francs. Simple arithmetic will show that no further profits could then be realized.

The Forward Exchange Market

Institutionally, however, the story does not end here. Partly because of the large distances involved, international transactions may not be consummated in a short time. Months elapse between the time that a London importer of automobiles places an order in Detroit and the time that the goods are delivered. Because of this and other factors, the conduct of foreign trade necessitates the use of special payment instruments not normally employed to finance domestic transactions.[10] But more important for our purposes, it

[10] Here is an example of the financing of foreign trade. Assume that exporter A in New York exports $2,000 (£1,000) worth of merchandise to importer B in London. The exporter loads the merchandise on ship and obtains the shipping documents from the ship's officer. Exporter A draws a draft for $2,000 on B, attaches the shipping documents, and sells these papers to the bank in New York. Exporter A gets paid immediately by the bank. The New York bank airmails the entire documents package to its London correspondent, who in turn notifies importer B of their arrival. B signs (*accepts*) the draft to indicate acceptance of the obligation of payment when it falls due, and in return B receives from the bank the shipping documents that will enable B to get control of the merchandise when the freighter finally arrives. Once the draft is signed, it becomes an *acceptance.* The London bank credits the account of its New York counterpart and sells (*discounts*) the acceptance on the local money market. The investor who purchases the acceptance thus actually finances the transaction while the goods are in transit. Upon its maturity, it will be presented to B for payment. Availability of funds to finance acceptance is a prerequisite for a city to become an international trade center.

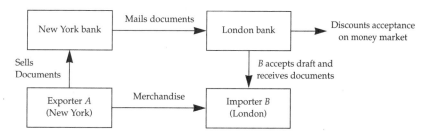

For further discussion see "Recent Developments in the Bankers Acceptance Market," *Federal Reserve Bulletin,* January 1986.

often calls for making future payments. The British importer deals in cars and assumes the normal risks involved in the automobile trade. However, inasmuch as there is a lapse of several months between the time the order is placed and the time she must make payment, additional uncertainty may arise from exchange fluctuations in the intervening period.

When the order for cars is placed, the importer undertakes to pay a certain dollar sum upon delivery. But in the meantime the dollar value of the pound sterling may change, affecting the sterling cost of the merchandise on which her calculations are based. For example, if the exchange value of the pound sterling drops from $3 to $2, then the sterling cost of a $3,000 car rises from £1,000 to £1,500. The importer would wish to insure against this contingency. Such insurance, known as **hedging,** is available to her in the *forward exchange market.* This market allows her to determine, at the time she orders the merchandise, what the sterling price of dollars will be when payment falls due. And she can therefore fully account for this price in her original calculations.

In particular, the trader would approach her bank and purchase *x* number of dollars for delivery, say, six months hence. The price of dollars in terms of sterling is agreed upon immediately, but the transaction on both sides—the exchange (or delivery) of dollars for sterling—does not take place until six months later. The price involved here is known as the **forward exchange rate,** as distinguished from the **spot exchange rate,** which applies to transactions consummated within the next two days. In a well-developed financial center there are always markets for forward dealings—and therefore market-determined forward exchange rates—for 30 and 90 days hence, as well as for other periods.[11] Again, were it not for the risk of exchange variations, the spot and forward exchange rates would be the same, as they are between California and New York dollars. In other words, with complete certainty, there would be no forward exchange market.

Under orderly market conditions, the forward and spot exchange rates are related to each other in a way that reflects the interest-rate differential in the two financial markets. As an example, let us further pursue the case of the British importer, purchasing from her bank six-month-forward dollars. The selling bank is not a speculative institution; it would normally wish to make sure not only that it is in possession of the dollars on delivery date but also that it does not lose money on the transaction from exchange fluctuations. The bank can *cover* itself by immediately purchasing spot dollars and then holding them in New York for six months, when they are scheduled for delivery to the importer in exchange for pounds. In doing so, the British

[11] There exists also a *futures* market in foreign currencies. It provides standardized contracts in predetermined amounts and with standardized delivery dates. In contrast, the forward market offers contracts in any amount, and the contract can be written for the exact date that the foreign currency is needed or is to be disposed of. See N. Fieleke, "The Rise of Foreign Currency Futures Market," *New England Review,* March 1985.

bank earns the New York interest rate instead of the London rate on these funds for the period under consideration. If the interest rate in New York is lower than that in London, the importer would have to pay the differential; forward dollars would sell at a premium compared to spot dollars, the premium being equivalent to the interest differential. On the other hand, should the New York interest rate exceed the London rate, it is actually advantageous for the bank to keep the funds there, and under competitive pressure the gain would be passed on to the importer. Forward dollars would sell at a discount compared to spot dollars, the discount equaling the interest differential between London and New York. In other words, the importer's demand for forward dollars makes it possible for the bank to enjoy a higher interest return, and under competition between banks, these extra earnings are passed on to the importer. Without this demand the bank would not shift the funds to New York for fear of exchange losses in case of revaluation of the pound sterling in terms of the dollar.

A numerical example will help to clarify this point. Suppose the British importer requires $2,000 in six months and that the spot exchange rate is £1 = $2. If the six-month interest rate is 4 percent in New York and 5 percent in London, then the British bank selling 2,000 forward dollars to the importer will charge her £1,000 (the spot rate) plus the 1 percent loss it incurs by having to keep the funds in New York at 4 percent instead of in London at 5 percent. Its total charge would be £1,000 + £10 (1 percent of £1,000) or £1,010. The six-month forward exchange rate is £1 = (2000/1010 =) $1.98: The forward pound is at a 1 percent **discount** relative to the ($2) spot pound, and correspondingly, the forward dollar is at a **premium** relative to the spot dollar. Conversely, if the six-month interest rate is 4 percent in New York and only 3 percent in London, then the British bank selling 2,000 forward dollars to the importer would charge her £1,000 *less* the 1 percent profit made by keeping the funds in New York at 4 percent instead of in London at 3 percent. Competitive pressure would force the bank to pass this differential on to the customer. The total charge for 2,000 forward dollars would be £1,000 minus £10, or £990. The six-month forward exchange rate is: £1 = (2000/990 =) $2.02: The forward pound is at a 1 percent premium relative to the ($2) spot pound, and correspondingly the forward dollar is at a discount relative to the spot dollar. While the spot and forward exchange rates are not equal, they usually tend to move together over time. Forward exchange rate quotations for October 7, 1996, are shown in appendix 11–1.

As long as orderly conditions prevail, information is complete, and fluid funds are abundantly available, the ratio of the forward exchange rate to the spot exchange rate would reflect the interest differential. Any divergence between them opens up an opportunity for riskless profit, and arbitragers would operate until the relation is restored. In this case the arbitrage equalizes prices over time, instead of between geographical centers at a given point of time, but the principle is the same.

Additional Insights

An alternative way of looking at this relationship will clarify the principle of *equalization through time*. Each currency's future value is equal to its present value plus the interest that can be earned on assets denominated in that currency over the period under consideration. (Conversely, to convert a future monetary value into its present equivalent, we *discount* it by the interest rate.) Thus, if the annual interest rate in London is labeled i_L, then the value of the pound sterling one year in the future (denoted $£_f$) is its present value ($£_p$) plus the added interest:

$$£_f = £_p \, (1 + i_L)$$

The same relation applies to the dollar with respect to the interest rate prevailing in New York:

$$\$_f = \$_p \, (1 + i_{NY})$$

Dividing the second equation by the first, we obtain the relation

$$\frac{\$_f}{£_f} = \frac{\$_p}{£_p} \times \frac{1 + i_{NY}}{1 + i_L}$$

The two currency ratios shown are the future and spot dollar-to-sterling exchange rates, respectively, and they can be denoted r_f and r_p. Thus:

$$r_f = r_p \, \frac{1 + i_{NY}}{1 + i_L}$$

This is known as the *interest rate parity* equation. It states that the forward discount or premium is equal to the interest differential.

In reality the expected relationship sometimes does not result when deposits are located in two different countries, for several reasons. First, there are market imperfections, such as transaction costs and imperfect knowledge (of the type that accounts for differences in interest rates on savings accounts paid by two banks in the same town), that can distort the relation. Secondly, because of such risks as the possible imposition of restrictions on the flow of funds by foreign governments, domestic and foreign assets *are not regarded as perfect substitutes.* A third reason is rooted in the desire of people to diversify their asset holdings in order to minimize risk. We might think of all financiers as having a portfolio of various financial assets, consisting of stocks, bonds, commercial paper, and the like. If they are risk averters (like to avoid risk), then they will choose to diversify their portfolio as much as possible to minimize the risk of default (they will not put all their eggs in one basket). Purchasing foreign assets is one way of accomplishing this. Thus, people can move in and out of foreign assets (so as to reduce risk) and thereby cause international capital flows even when no interest differentials exist.

Speculation

In contrast to arbitrage, **speculation** does not involve the taking of covered positions (as the bank did in our example). Instead, speculators sell forward dollars, hoping to deliver cheaper dollars at the future date should the value of the dollar decline in the intervening period. Specifically, speculators are said to take a **short position** when they sell foreign currency forward without at the same time owning an equivalent amount of this currency (that is, they sell what they do not have), in the expectation of buying it at a lower spot rate when the contract matures. Speculators are said to take a **long position** when they purchase foreign currency forward without incurring an obligation to make a spot payment at the time of delivery (they buy what they do not need), in the expectation that a spot sale of the foreign currency at that time will produce a profit. An example will illustrate this point: Suppose the 90 days forward exchange rate (known today) is £1 = $1.50. If you expect the spot rate 90 days from now to be £1 = $1.40, you would *sell pounds short* for $1.50 per pound, with the intention of buying pounds spot at $1.40 per pound when the contract matures. If your expectations are realized, you fulfill your contract by delivering the pounds, and in the process make 10¢ profit ($1.50 – $1.40) per pound. On the other hand, if you expect the spot rate 90 days hence to be £1 = $1.60, you would *buy pounds long* for $1.50 per pound, with the intention of selling them at $1.60 per pound when the contract matures. If your expectations are realized you fulfill your contract by buying the pounds and in the process make 10¢ profit ($1.60 – $1.50) per pound.

Because speculators do not take a covered position, the relationship between interest rates is of no concern to them. What is most important to the speculators is the relation between the forward exchange rates prevailing on the market and their personal expectation about the spot rate at some future date.[12] Indeed, speculative funds may create interest differentials that can then be covered by arbitrage funds if they are available in sufficient quantity and if market conditions are not so unsettled (such as under

---

[12]Since expectations are uncertain, the government can affect speculative activity by floating rumors and otherwise influencing expectations.

expectations of an immediate exchange-rate adjustment) that they are completely dominated by speculative activity.

Speculators demand and supply currencies in anticipation of changes in their price. If a currency is weak and the government's ability to defend it is suspect, speculators can exert additional pressure by selling the currency en masse in exchange for other currencies. Short-run capital, sometimes referred to as "hot money,"[13] would then leave the country for other financial centers that were thought to have strong and therefore desirable currencies. These currencies would be purchased by the speculators. This is the type of pressure that has often created grave disturbances on the international financial markets. For example, between 1992 and 1993, high interest rates in Germany caused massive financial flows from other European countries into Germany. This forced the depreciation of some currencies relative to the mark, and eventually fractured the exchange relationships in Europe. Speculative activities have been carried out not only by professional speculators but also by the large international corporations, which adjust their asset portfolios to accommodate anticipated changes in the exchange rates, and by the corner shopkeeper in Europe, who converts surplus cash to the currencies considered strong.

Thus, speculators, as distinguished from traders and investors, purchase foreign currencies and hold them for their own sake. Their demand is derived from a desire to profit from changes in the price of the currency itself.

Summary

This chapter explains how market exchange rates are established and what causes them to change on a daily basis. The supply-and-demand forces emanating from international transactions exert their influence on the foreign exchange market to determine the exchange rate. For instance, the demand for dollars in Germany represents dollar outpayments. Depicted in a graph, it would have a negative slope because as the foreign currency appreciates, the country's imports become more expensive in terms of the local currency. Hence, residents would import less and spend fewer dollars abroad. On the other hand, the supply of dollars in Germany represents dollar inpayments. It has a positive slope if foreign demand for German goods is relatively elastic. As the domestic currency depreciates, the country's exports become cheaper in terms of the foreign currency, and foreigners would purchase more of them. But only if their demand is relatively elastic would the rise in the volume of their purchases be more than proportional to the decline in

---

[13]Strictly speaking, the term "hot money" is capital flowing against the dictate of interest rate differentials. But the financial press often uses the term to refer to any type of speculative flow.

their dollar price, yielding a positively sloping supply curve. Similar considerations hold for service transactions and capital flows.

As a currency depreciates, the country's exports become cheaper in terms of foreign currencies, and the country's imports become more expensive in terms of the local (depreciating) currency. The country thus becomes more competitive in both the foreign and the domestic markets.

Economic changes in a country cause shifts in demand and supply curves for foreign currencies. In the short run, changes in interest rates have a powerful effect on the exchange rate. A rise (fall) in the country's interest rate relative to rates prevailing abroad causes its currency to appreciate (depreciate). Fiscal expansion increases interest rates, causing appreciation of the currency; fiscal contraction has the opposite effect. Monetary expansion lowers interest rates, causing the currency to depreciate; monetary contraction does the reverse.

In the long run, changes in relative prices have a profound effect on the exchange rate. A country experiencing sustained inflation, for example, will see its currency depreciate. The purchasing power parity (PPP) theory suggests that in the long run, the bilateral exchange rate is determined by the relative purchasing power of the two currencies in their respective countries.

When the exchange rate moves from one equilibrium point to the next it tends first to overshoot before retreating to the new long-term level. This occurs because the price level, unlike the exchange rate, responds only after a time lag. Until that happens, the exchange rate must absorb the entire impact of any policy change. A variety of other factors also affect the supply and demand for foreign currencies and hence the exchange rate.

Foreign exchange markets are both large and highly organized and therefore orderly. Triangular arbitrage ensures that cross rates are orderly as well. The forward exchange rate involves transactions to be consummated at some future time. It is related to the spot rate by the interest rate differential between the two financial markets. For a speculator the critical relationship is between the forward rate (known today) and the spot rate she expects to prevail in the future.

Important Concepts

Foreign exchange market

Freely fluctuating (or floating) exchange rate

Appreciation

Depreciation

Demand for dollars

Vehicle currency

Cross rates

Triangular arbitrage

Hedging

Forward exchange rate

Supply of dollars	Spot exchange rate
Exchange rate overshooting	Discount on forward rate
Purchasing power parity (PPP)	Speculation
Speculative bubble	Premium on forward rate
Managed float	Short position
Arbitrage	Long position

Review Questions

1. Assume that on a certain date the following exchange rates prevail: £1 = \$1.48; \$1 = 1.7 D.M.; \$1 = 5.8 F.F.; \$1 = ¥108
   a. What is the inverse of each of the above exchange rates?
   b. Calculate the bilateral exchange rates between each two of the *nondollar* currencies (cross rates), and their inverses.
   c. Suppose that \$1 = 2 D.M. and \$1 = 6 F.F. Can 1 mark equal 4 francs? Why or why not? Can 1 mark equal 2 francs?

2. In October 1996 the exchange value of the French franc was \$1 = 5.8 F.F.
   a. Show that exchange rate on a diagram similar to that of Figure 11.1.
   b. Using your diagram explain how the dollar–franc exchange rate would be affected by each of the following events:

   • A sharp rise in French interest rates
   • The appearance of double-digit inflation in France
   • A prolonged general strike in France
   • A 20 percent increase in the French money supply

   In each case assume that "all other things are constant."
   c. What is the effect of each change in the exchange rate on France's competitive position?
   d. How do you explain the slope of the demand and supply curves in your diagram?

3. Why do you suppose Canadian exporters complained bitterly when in December 1989 the Bank of Canada boosted interest rates?

4. In the early 1980s the United States pursued a policy of fiscal expansion and monetary contraction.
   a. What do you suppose was the effect of that policy mix on U.S. interest rates?

b. How did this affect the dollar exchange rate?
c. What happened to the U.S. competitive position at home and abroad? What do you suppose happened to the U.S. trade balance?
d. Did the dollar exchange rate in 1984 conform to the *purchasing power parity (PPP) doctrine?* Explain.
e. Trace the effects of the reversal in the U.S. policy mix that occurred between 1985 and 1988.

5. In 1993 the United States pursued a policy of fiscal contraction and Japan followed a policy of fiscal expansion. Assuming no change in either country's monetary policy, what do you suppose happened to the relative interest rates and the bilateral dollar-yen exchange rate?

6. Why were American exporters happy to see the dollar depreciate in the second half of the 1980s?

7. How and why do monetary and fiscal policies affect the exchange rate?

8. Explain the following terms:

a. Arbitrage	g. Short position
b. Triangular arbitrage	h. Long position
c. Speculation	i. Exchange rate overshooting
d. Spot exchange rate	j. Vehicle currency
e. Forward exchange rate	k. Portfolio investment
f. Future market	l. Direct investment

9. How do interest rates enter into the determination of the forward exchange rate? Explain the "interest rate parity."

10. Describe how each of the following developments would affect the exchange value of the (floating) Canadian dollar and Canada's competitive position in manufacturing:
a. Hydro-Quebec raises $100 million (U.S.) on the New York money market by selling bonds.
b. Foreign corporations increase direct investments in Canada by 10 percent.
c. Because of a booming Russian harvest, Canada's wheat exports decline.
d. By order of the Canadian government, Canadian natural gas exports to the United States are cut by 5 percent.

11. Explain the following statement: "Monetary policy affects the exchange rate through two channels; therefore its effect is powerful."

12. Why might monetary policy lead to exchange rate *overshooting?* Offer examples of overshooting.

Chapter 11 Appendix 11–1

Currency Trading

Exchange Rates

Monday, October 7, 1996

The New York foreign exchange selling rates below apply to trading among banks in amounts of $1 million and more, as quoted at 3 p.m. Eastern time by Dow Jones Telerate Inc. and other sources. Retail transactions provide fewer units of foreign currency per dollar.

Country	U.S. $ equiv. Mon	U.S. $ equiv. Fri	Currency per U.S. $ Mon	Currency per U.S. $ Fri
Argentina (Peso)	1.0012	1.0012	.9988	.9988
Australia (Dollar)	.7878	.7889	1.2694	1.2676
Austria (Schilling)	.09289	.09295	10.766	10.758
Bahrain (Dinar)	2.6490	2.6490	.3775	.3775
Belgium (Franc)	.03173	.03173	31.520	31.515
Brazil (Real)	.9737	.9737	1.0270	1.0270
Britain (Pound)	1.5630	1.5650	.6398	.6390
30-Day Forward	1.5623	1.5638	.6401	.6395
90-Day Forward	1.5615	1.5625	.6404	.6400
180-Day Forward	1.5604	1.5624	.6409	.6401
Canada (Dollar)	.7390	.7383	1.3532	1.3544
30-Day Forward	.7401	.7394	1.3512	1.3524
90-Day Forward	.7424	.7417	1.3470	1.3482
180-Day Forward	.7457	.7450	1.3410	1.3422
Chile (Peso)	.002419	.002420	413.45	413.20
China (Renminbi)	.1200	.1200	8.3307	8.3307
Colombia (Peso)	.0009847	.0009847	1015.50	1015.50
Czech Rep. (Koruna)	....	....	....	....
Commercial rate	.03655	.03679	27.360	27.182
Denmark (Krone)	.1706	.1706	5.8625	5.8628
Ecuador (Sucre)	....	....	....	....
Floating rate	.0003047	.0003051	3282.00	3278.00
Finland (Markka)	.2187	.2191	4.5723	4.5634
France (Franc)	.1933	.1929	5.1730	5.1840
30-Day Forward	.1937	.1932	5.1638	5.1757
90-Day Forward	.1943	.1939	5.1467	5.1580
180-Day Forward	.1952	.1948	5.1217	5.1330
Germany (Mark)	.6531	.6525	1.5311	1.5325
30-Day Forward	.6545	.6538	1.5279	1.5296
90-Day Forward	.6570	.6564	1.5220	1.5234
180-Day Forward	.6609	.6604	1.5130	1.5143
Greece (Drachma)	.004154	.004142	240.71	241.41
Hong Kong (Dollar)	.1293	.1293	7.7323	7.7326
Hungary (Forint)	.006296	.006296	158.84	158.82
India (Rupee)	.02807	.02807	35.630	35.630
Indonesia (Rupiah)	.0004306	.0004303	2322.25	2324.18
Ireland (Punt)	1.6018	1.5990	.6243	.6254
Israel (Shekel)	.3135	.3134	3.1903	3.1911
Italy (Lira)	.0006588	.0006579	1518.00	1520.00

Country	U.S. $ equiv. Mon	U.S. $ equiv. Fri	Currency per U.S. $ Mon	Currency per U.S. $ Fri
Japan (Yen)	.008993	.008945	111.20	111.80
30-Day Forward	.009034	.008982	110.69	111.33
90-Day Forward	.009110	.009060	109.78	110.37
180-Day Forward	.009225	.009175	108.40	109.00
Jordan (Dinar)	1.4065	1.4065	.7110	.7110
Kuwait (Dinar)	3.3434	3.3434	.2991	.2991
Lebanon (Pound)	.0006420	.0006418	1557.75	1558.00
Malaysia (Ringgit)	.3998	.4001	2.5010	2.4996
Malta (Lira)	2.7701	2.7778	.3610	.3600
Mexico (Peso)	....	....	....	....
Floating rate	.1329	.1329	7.5260	7.5270
Netherlands (Guilder)	.5822	.5818	1.7177	1.7189
New Zealand (Dollar)	.6912	.6977	1.4468	1.4333
Norway (Krone)	.1537	.1537	6.5065	6.5075
Pakistan (Rupee)	.02735	.02735	36.560	36.560
Peru (new Sol)	.3979	.3983	2.5134	2.5104
Philippines (Peso)	.03807	.03807	26.269	26.266
Poland (Zloty)	.3554	.3553	2.8135	2.8145
Portugal (Escudo)	.006470	.006449	154.56	155.07
Russia (Ruble) (a)	.0001846	.0001846	5418.00	5417.00
Saudi Arabia (Riyal)	.2666	.2666	3.7505	3.7505
Singapore (Dollar)	.7084	.7086	1.4116	1.4112
Slovak Rep. (Koruna)	.03263	.03263	30.650	30.650
South Africa (Rand)	.2205	.2203	4.5355	4.5385
South Korea (Won)	.001208	.001213	827.65	824.55
Spain (Peseta)	.007764	.007765	128.80	128.78
Sweden (Krona)	.1512	.1512	6.6133	6.6125
Switzerland (Franc)	.7971	.7950	1.2545	1.2578
30-Day Forward	.8000	.7977	1.2500	1.2536
90-Day Forward	.8051	.8030	1.2421	1.2453
180-Day Forward	.8131	.8110	1.2298	1.2330
Taiwan (Dollar)	.03638	.03638	27.485	27.486
Thailand (Baht)	.03929	.03932	25.453	25.433
Turkey (Lira)	.00001079	.00001084	92646.00	92257.00
United Arab (Dirham)	.2723	.2723	3.6720	3.6720
Uruguay (New Peso)	....	....	....	....
Financial	.1198	.1198	8.3500	8.3500
Venezuela (Bolivar) b..	.002148	.002146	465.62	465.88
Brady rate	.002148	.002148	465.50	465.50
SDR	1.4385	1.4385	.6952	.6952
ECU	1.2494	1.2480	....	....

Special Drawing Rights (SDR) are based on exchange rates for the U.S., German, British, French and Japanese currencies. Source: International Monetary Fund.

European Currency Unit (ECU) is based on a basket of community currencies.

a-fixing, Moscow Interbank Currency Exchange.
b-Changed to market rate effective Apr. 22.

Source: *The Wall Street Journal*, October 7, 1996.

Chapter 11 Appendix 11–2

THE RELATIONSHIP BETWEEN DEMAND FOR A FOREIGN CURRENCY (DOLLAR) AND SUPPLY OF DOMESTIC CURRENCY (MARK)

In the German foreign-exchange market the demand for dollars *implies* supply of marks. Given the demand for dollars (left panel of figure A11–2.1), one can derive the supply of marks. At 4 D.M. = $1, zero dollars are demanded; equivalently, at 1 D.M. = $¼, zero marks are supplied (point *a* on both panels).

At 3 D.M. = $1, $1 billion is demanded (left panel); equivalently, at 1 D.M. = $⅓ (right panel), 3 × 1 = 3 billion D.M. are supplied (point *b* on both panels). At 2 D.M. = $1, $2 billion are demanded; equivalently, at 1 D.M. = $½, 2 × 2 = 4 billion D.M. are supplied (point *c*). At 1 D.M. = $1, $3 billion are demanded; equivalently, at 1 D.M. = $1, 3 billion D.M. are supplied (point *d*). The quantity of marks supplied at each mark price on the right panel is equal to the area under the demand curve on the left panel. The supply curve bends backward when the demand becomes inelastic.

FIGURE A11–2.1   *Demand for Dollars and Supply of Marks*

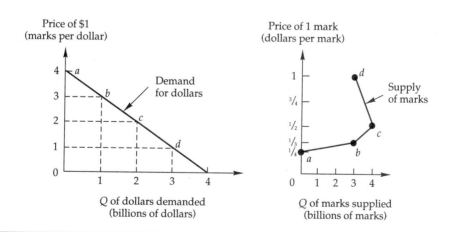

Given the demand for dollars on the left-hand panel, we can derive the supply schedule marks on the right-hand panel.

Chapter 11 Appendix 11–3

Key Currency Cross Rates Late New York Trading October 7, 1996

	Dollar	Pound	SFranc	Guilder	Peso	Yen	Lira	D-Mark	FFranc	CdnDlr
Canada................	1.3532	2.1151	1.0787	.78780	.17980	.01217	.00089	.88381	.26159	....
France	5.1730	8.0854	4.1236	3.0116	.68735	.04652	.00341	3.3786	....	3.8228
Germany	1.5311	2.3931	1.2205	.89137	.20344	.01377	.00101	....	.29598	1.1315
Italy.....................	1518.0	2372.6	1210.0	883.74	201.7	13.651	....	991.44	293.45	1121.8
Japan...................	111.2	173.81	88.641	64.738	14.775	....	.07325	72.628	21.496	82.176
Mexico................	7.5260	11.763	5.9992	4.3814	....	.06768	.00496	4.9154	1.4549	5.5616
Netherlands.......	1.7177	2.6848	1.3692	....	.22824	.01545	.00113	1.1219	.33205	1.2694
Switzerland	1.2545	1.9608	....	.73034	.16669	.01128	.00083	.81935	.24251	.92706
United Kingdom	.63980	....	.51000	.37247	.08501	.00575	.00042	.41787	.12368	.47280
United States......	....	1.5630	.79713	.58217	.13287	.00899	.00066	.65313	.19331	.73899

Source: *The Wall Street Journal,* October 8, 1996, p. A-14.

Chapter 11 Appendix 11–4

EXCHANGE RATE DETERMINATION

One way of presenting exchange-rate determination, developed by professor Martin Bronfanbrenner of Duke University, is by positioning the current and capital accounts in two adjoining diagrams. Exchange rate equilibrium on the current account, determined by Purchasing Power Parity, is Π_1. Equilibrium on the capital account, determined by relative return to capital, is Π_2. Overall exchange rate equilibrium, where the current account deficit equals the capital account surplus, is at Π_e.

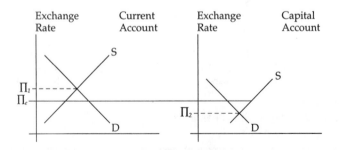

The International Currency System

For nearly thirty years following World War II, world currencies were maintained at a fixed ratio to one another (a system of fixed or *pegged* exchange rates). But this system broke down in March 1973 and was replaced by a mixture of fluctuating and fixed exchange rates. Alternative exchange-rate regimes will be explained in the following sections, leading up to the contemporary system that has prevailed since 1973.

FIXED EXCHANGE RATES

In direct contrast to freely floating exchange rates is the fixed exchange-rate system. As the name implies, **fixed exchange rates** are not permitted to fluctuate freely on the market or to respond to daily changes in demand and supply. Instead, the government fixes the exchange value of the currency. As illustrated in figure 12.1, Germany fixes its exchange rate at $1 = 2 D.M. or equivalently at 1 D.M. = $0.50; it imposes upper and lower limits to the exchange rate. Exchange variations, triggered by shifts in the demand and/or supply curves (shown in color), are permitted only within these limits. The German central bank (the Bundesbank) maintains the limits by buying and selling dollars on the Frankfurt foreign currency market. For the purpose of clarity the limits shown in figure 12.1 are drawn much wider than in actual fixed-rate systems. The difference between the upper and lower support limits is called the **spread** (or *band*). In figure 12.1 it is (2.20 D.M. − 1.80 D.M. =) 0.40 D.M. Since the *central value* (sometimes called the *par* value) of the mark is set at $1 = 2 D.M., the spread is (0.40/2.00 =) 20 percent, or 10 percent on either side of the central value.

| FIGURE 12.1 | *A Fixed Exchange-Rate System* |

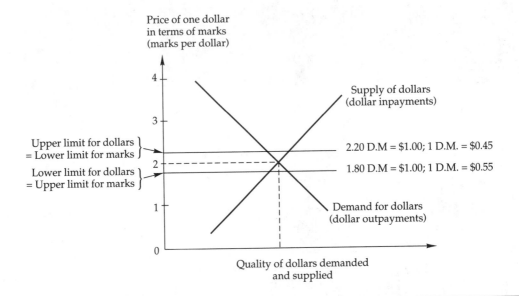

Under a fixed exchange rate, the exchange rate may fluctuate within the "band" (upper and lower limits) set by the government, but is not allowed outside the "band."

If the dollar drops to its lower support limit of 1.80 D.M. (which means that the mark rises to 55.5 cents), the central bank *buys* as many dollars, in exchange for marks, as are necessary to "defend" that limit. Conversely, if the dollar rises to 2.20 D.M. (which means that the mark declines to 45.5 cents), the central bank *sells* as many dollars for marks as are necessary to defend the limit. Recall that a country's money supply is measured by the domestic currency (marks in the case of Germany) held outside its central bank. A country's international reserves are held in the form of *foreign* currencies by its central bank; therefore, dollars are reserves for Germany, but not for the United States. Hence, when the German central bank buys dollars and sells marks, its dollar reserves rise and the domestic German money supply, measured in marks, expands. Conversely when the central bank sells dollars and buys marks, its dollar reserves decline, and the German money supply contracts.

Figure 12.2 illustrates the first case in which the supply of dollars rises to (the colored) S'. Under a freely floating exchange rate, the equilibrium would shift to e. But at the government limit set at 1.80 D.M. = $1, an excess

FIGURE 12.2   *Excess Supply of Dollars (or Excess Demand for Marks)*

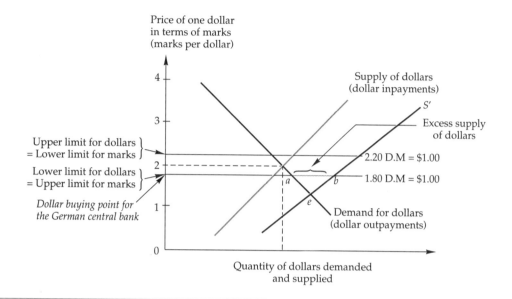

A rise in the supply of dollars to *S'* creates excess supply of dollars $\overline{ab}$. Dollars in that amount are purchased by the German central bank in exchange for marks.

supply of dollars in the amount $\overline{ab}$ emerges. The German central bank buys an amount $\overline{ab}$ of dollars in exchange for marks, and adds them to its central foreign currency reserves in order to maintain the limit. In fact, all the bank has to do is stand ready to buy an unlimited amount of dollars for marks at that price. No private trader would sell dollars for less than the 1.80 D.M. it can get from the central bank. Exchange rate of $1 = 1.80 D.M. is the **dollar buying point** for the German central bank. Note that an excess supply of dollars can also be created by a reduction in demand (leftward shift in the demand curve), such that the resulting equilibrium exchange rate moves below the lower limit.

When the German central bank buys dollars in exchange for marks, its *official dollar reserves rise*, and *German money supply (measured in marks outside the central bank) expands*. Currency intervention by the central bank that permits the country's money supply to be affected is called **unsterilized intervention.** Should the central bank wish to prevent the increase in money supply, it would sell German government bonds to "soak up" the new money so created. The two steps would then be equivalent to the central

FIGURE 12.3	*Excess Demand for Dollars (or Excess Supply of Marks)*

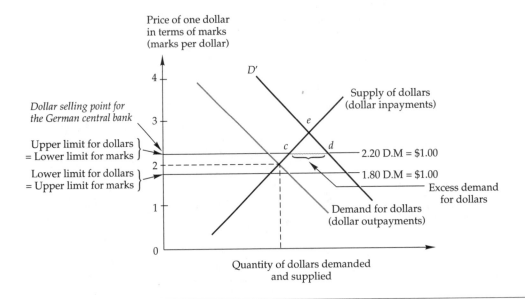

A rise in demand for dollars to *D'* creates excess demand for dollars cd. Dollars in this amount are sold by the German central bank in exchange for marks.

bank buying dollars in exchange for German government bonds. Currency intervention that does not affect the domestic money supply is known as **sterilized intervention.** Most currency interventions are sterilized.

If the central bank becomes saturated with dollar reserves and does not wish any further accumulation, it would have to permit the price of the dollar to drop below its lower limit or the price of the mark to rise. But while under a floating exchange rate regime such changes occur in frequent intervals and in small amounts, under a fixed exchange rate they take place by government decree, and they occur infrequently and in discrete amounts. An increase in the exchange value of the mark is called **revaluation** (instead of appreciation). For example, the German central bank may *revalue* the mark from $0.50 ($1 = 2 D.M.) to $1 ($1 = 1 D.M.), and move the support limits to 0.9 D.M. = $1 and 1.1 D.M. = $1.

Figure 12.3 illustrates the second case in which the demand for dollars is raised to (the solid colored) *D'*. Under a freely floating exchange rate, the equilibrium rate would shift to *e*. But at the government-set limit of 2.20 D.M. = $1, an excess demand for dollars in the amount $\overline{cd}$ is created. The

German central bank sells $\overline{cd}$ dollars (in exchange for marks) out of its central foreign currency reserves to maintain the limit. In fact, all the bank has to do is stand ready to sell an unlimited amount of dollars at that price. No private trader would purchase dollars for more than 2.20 D.M. if they can be obtained at that price from the central bank. The exchange rate of $1 = 2.20 D.M. is the **dollar selling point** for the German central bank. Note that an excess demand for dollars can also be created by a decline in supply (leftward shift in the supply curve), such that the resulting equilibrium exchange rate moves above the upper limit.

When the German central bank sells dollars in exchange for marks, its *official dollar reserves decline and the German money supply shrinks.* This is a case of *unsterilized* intervention, since it affects the German money supply. Should the central bank wish to prevent the decrease in money supply, it would buy government bonds on the open market, and thereby replenish the money supply. These two steps would then be equivalent to selling dollars in exchange for government bonds. Since the domestic money supply remains unchanged, this is called *sterilized* intervention on the foreign exchange market.

If the German central bank runs out of dollar reserves, it may have to let the value of the dollar rise above its upper limit, or equivalently, permit the value of the mark to decline. Under a fixed regime, these changes are decreed by the government, and they occur infrequently and in discrete amounts. The lowering of the exchange value of a currency is referred to as **devaluation** (instead of depreciation). In the case at hand, the central bank may wish to *devalue* the mark from $0.50 ($1 = 2 D.M.) to $0.25 ($1 = 4 D.M.), and shift the support limits to 3.60 D.M. = $1 and 4.40 D.M. = $1.

Under a fixed exchange rate, the exchange rate is set at a predetermined level. The central bank is committed to maintaining that level and therefore the upper and lower limits associated with it. Consequently, the exchange rate cannot be expected to clear the market—a function performed by the price system only if the price is allowed to vary continuously. Hence variations in official foreign currency reserves must fill the gap in cases of excess supply or excess demand for foreign currencies. Variations in official reserves are then a proper measure of a surplus or deficit in international transactions, as was noted in Chapter 10.

History of Fixed Exchange Rates

Two historical periods in which the exchange rates of all major countries were fixed were the gold standard (1870–1914) and the Bretton Woods Conference (1944–1973).

The Gold Standard (1870–1914)

Under the **gold standard** the external value of all currencies was maintained by fixing their prices in terms of gold. Each country's central bank stood ready to buy and sell unlimited quantities of gold at a fixed price in terms of its own currency. Since gold was the **common denominator** in terms of which all currencies were fixed, it also served to maintain fixed exchange ratios between the currencies themselves. For example, if one ounce of fine gold was worth £22, $44, 88 D.M., and 264 F.F., then the exchange rates would be fixed at £1 = $2 = 4 D.M. = 12 F.F. (and $1 = £0.5 = 2 D.M. = 6 F.F., while 1 D.M. = 3 F.F., and so on). Only small fluctuations around these values took place, with the size of the *spread* determined by the cost of shipping gold. To be able to redeem its currency in gold at a fixed price, each central bank had to maintain gold reserves. Thus gold was both the *common denominator* and the **official reserve asset.**

Bretton Woods (1944–1973) In the currency arrangements that emerged after World War II—initiated by an allied conference in **Bretton Woods,** New Hampshire—gold no longer reigned supreme. It was instead replaced by the U.S. dollar as the "core" of the system. All currencies were pegged to the dollar at a fixed exchange rate in the manner illustrated by figures 12.2 and 12.3. But the allowed spread between the buying and selling rates for the dollar was only 2 percent. Because the dollar was the common denominator to which all currencies were fixed, they were also pegged to each other. For example, if $1 = £0.50 = 2 D.M. = 6 F.F., then £1 = 4 D.M. = 12 F.F. and 1 D.M. = 3 F.F. Currency *intervention* by central banks in their respective foreign exchange markets was conducted in dollars.

To maintain a fixed exchange rate between its currency and the dollar, each central bank kept official dollar reserves. These were used to meet excess demand for dollars that emerged when the dollar reached its upper support limit, as shown in figure 12.3. Such support depleted the country's official reserves. Reserves were augmented when an excess supply of dollars emerged and the dollar reached the lower support limit, as in figure 12.2.

Thus, the U.S. dollar was the system's *common denominator* and *official reserve currency.* Because each central bank intervened in dollars in its own market to keep its dollar exchange rate fixed, the dollar was also the **intervention currency.** Finally, in order for the central bank to buy and sell dollars in its own national currency market, there had to be a private market for dollars in each country. And indeed, private individuals and institutions throughout the world maintain accounts denominated in U.S. dollars in their respective commercial banks so that dollar holdings outside the United States became vast.

As shown in figures 12.2 and 12.3, it was the responsibility of each nondollar central bank to maintain its currency pegged to the dollar. The United States took a *passive* stance, and the dollar's exchange rate was fixed because all other currencies were anchored to it. Thus, if the United States ran balance of payments deficits (surplus), it was up to the European and Japanese central banks to purchase (sell) dollars in order to prevent their currencies from appreciating (depreciating) relative to the dollar. And indeed during the 1960s and early 1970s, mounting U.S. external deficits resulted in large increases of their dollar reserves. As they became satiated with such reserves, their dissatisfaction with the system increased. In turn, the United States protested the system because it could not change the exchange rate of the dollar. Early in the 1970s an onslaught of market forces resulted in the breakup of Bretton Woods and the introduction of the current monetary arrangements.

The Contemporary International Currency System

Since March 19, 1973, the international currency system has been a mixture of fixed and floating exchange rates.

Fluctuating Currencies

Of the major currencies, the U.S. dollar, the British pound sterling, the Japanese yen, the Italian lira, and the Canadian dollar are allowed to float on the market, with their exchange rates determined by demand-and-supply conditions. Often the monetary authorities of each country intervene in the foreign exchange market in order to smooth out fluctuations, to maintain orderly conditions, or to prevent their currency's exchange rate from moving upward or downward to a degree that they consider excessive or undesirable.

When an excess of inpayments over outpayments pushes up the exchange value of the currency by an amount the authorities consider excessive, the central bank sells its country's currency in exchange for foreign currencies to moderate the rise. In doing so it increases its international reserves as well as its domestic money supply. As money supply rises, interest rates decline and the currency appreciation is moderated. If the central bank fears the inflationary effect of the rise in money supply, it can offset that by selling government bonds on the open market, using sterilized foreign currency intervention. In effect the central bank buys foreign currencies in exchange for domestic bonds. Conversely, when, say, an outflow of capital pushes the exchange value of the currency downward, the central bank may moderate the decline by selling foreign currencies in exchange for the country's currency. As a result, money supply declines, interest rates rise, and currency depreciation is moderated. The country's international reserves decline as well. Under sterilized intervention the central bank offsets the decline in money supply by buying government bonds on the open market. In effect the central bank sells foreign currencies in exchange for domestic bonds.

Floats subject to government intervention are known as *managed* or "dirty" floats, as distinguished from *free* or "clean" floats, which occur when no official intervention takes place.[1] But even under heavily managed floats there is no official commitment to maintain fixed limits to the fluctuations. In sum, floats can be *free* or *managed,* and under a managed float intervention can be sterilized (where the domestic money stock is shielded from intervention and held unchanged) or unsterilized. *Most floating currencies are on a managed float regime with sterilized intervention.*[2] Intervention can sometimes be massive,[3] as in the spring of 1987 when, in a coordinated action, major central banks spent nearly $80 billion in various currencies to support the dollar, or in April 1990 when central banks sold dollars for yen to support the yen. Again in 1993 the Federal Reserve sold yen in order to slow the appreciation of that currency. The frequency of U.S. intervention declined under the Clinton administration relative to the Bush years. U.S. intervention is conducted in marks and yen, while other countries primarily use dollars, along with marks and yen.

This discussion suggests that the contrast between fixed and floating exchange rates should be viewed as a continuum rather than as a two-way dichotomy. At one extreme, an exchange rate can be freely floating, while at the other extreme it can be immutably fixed. The freely floating rate can be subject to intervention by the central bank. And as the degree of intervention or management rises, we move gradually toward a fixed-rate regime. Conversely a **band** (or spread) can be added to the fixed exchange rate, within which the exchange rate may fluctuate. As the width of the spread increases, we move gradually toward a floating rate. When that width reaches infinity and government intervention is absent, the regime becomes a free float.

Two differences between free and managed floats should be noted. While under a free float the exchange rate would settle at a value that yields equilibrium in the balance of payments (that is, equalizing inpayments and outpayments), there is no such presumption in the case of managed

---

[1] See, for example, P. Wannacott, "U.S. Intervention in the Exchange Market for D.M.," Princeton, *Studies In International Finance,* December 1982.

[2] Unsterilized intervention influences the exchange rate by changing money supply and hence interest rates. Because sterilized intervention leaves the domestic money supply unchanged, it does not affect interest rates, and therefore it would appear ineffective in changing the exchange rate. But the literature identifies an alternative channel through which it might affect the exchange rate: change in the relative risk attached to domestic and foreign assets. Suppose the Federal Reserve buys foreign currency for domestic bonds. The stock of domestic-currency bonds held by the public rises and therefore the degree of riskiness attached to them rises as well. This causes portfolio diversification away from dollar-denominated assets, leading to depreciation. Conversely, if the central bank buys domestic bonds for foreign currency, their stock in the hands of the public declines, and so does their degree of riskiness. Portfolio diversification causes the currency to appreciate. Another channel through which sterilized intervention may affect the exchange rate is expectations: Market agents respond to known intervention by the central bank and move in the direction the central bank wishes. See O. Humpage, "Exchange Market Intervention: The Channels of Influence," Federal Reserve Bank of Cleveland, *Economic Review,* 1986, no. 3; "Intervention and the Dollar Decline," Federal Reserve Bank of Cleveland, *Economic Review,* 1988, no. 2; and *Economic Commentary,* March 1, 1996.

[3] Reports on exchange movements and on governments' intervention on the foreign exchange markets are published in the *Federal Reserve Bank of New York Monthly Review.*

floats: Central bank intervention may lead the exchange rate away from its equilibrium value rather than toward it. Second, no reserves are accumulated or needed when the exchange rate floats freely, for the exchange rate will always clear the foreign exchange market. By contrast, a country whose floating currency is continuously managed accumulates reserves when the central bank moderates an increase in the value of the currency and needs international reserves to moderate a decline in its value.

Under a free float, an external deficit (surplus) is reflected in depreciation (appreciation) of the currency; under a fixed exchange rate, an external imbalance causes a change in international reserves, and the accumulation or depletion of reserves constitutes a measure of the surplus or deficit respectively (see Chapter 10); under a managed float system an external imbalance results in a combination of variations in the exchange rate and a change in international reserves. Because under a managed float part of the imbalance is absorbed in exchange variations, the international transactions statement provides no clear indication of the country's external position. A major question facing the community of trading nations is the extent to which official intervention in the foreign exchange markets should be subject to certain rules and limitations, enforced by the surveillance of the IMF.

The European Monetary System (EMS)

Members of the European Union, which used to be known as the EC, except for the United Kingdom and Italy, peg their currencies to one another and float jointly against the dollar. This arrangement, known as the **European Monetary System (EMS),** was inaugurated in March of 1979. Until August 1993, the maximum band allowed by the EMS was $2\frac{1}{4}$ percent. However, following the European monetary crisis in 1992–1993, the spread was widened to 15 percent on either side, for a total band of 30 percent. The United Kingdom joined the EMS in 1989 but withdrew again in September of 1992, along with Italy. (Italy rejoined at the end of 1996.)

According to its statements, the EU (European Union) regards the rather wide range of fluctuations as temporary and intends to return to narrow bands as soon as conditions permit. In fact, the EU hopes to move further toward monetary integration, some day achieving a common currency and a common central bank. An important step in that direction might be the establishment of irrevocably fixed exchange rates. The necessary measures to achieve these goals are spelled out in an agreement negotiated by EU members in Maastricht, Holland, known as the *Maastricht treaty,* signed in December 1991. But the widening of the bands, forced upon the EU in 1993, poses a clear setback for any progress toward monetary integration.

Because the EU may return to narrow bands or to irrevocably fixed exchange rates, with all currencies anchored to the mark, it is useful to describe how that system worked and how it continues to work with wider bands. The limits to fluctuations are maintained by central banks' multiple currency intervention (mainly with marks but also with dollars) on their respective foreign exchange markets. To help facilitate intervention, short-term credit is exchanged between the central banks, and medium-term credit is available through the European Monetary Cooperation Fund. There exists a "warning system" indicating that a country, whether in a strong or a weak position, should take some action to forestall hitting the intervention limits. These warning signals take the form of *divergence indicators* from the European Unit of Account (ECU). Indeed much currency intervention takes place *within* the bands.

The ECU is a weighted average of EU currencies in which the weights are derived from each country's share in intra-European trade and in EU output. It is only a theoretical unit of account for the EMS and for EU activities, and not a circulatory currency. (In 1996 it was worth about $1.25.) The divergence indicator is calculated against the ECU at 75 percent of the allowed maximum spread for each currency. When the limit of the divergence indicator is reached, the country is under presumption to act so as to move the exchange value of its currency back toward the "center." Such action may take the form of changes in domestic fiscal and monetary policy or an adjustment of the currency's central rate. But there exists no irrevocable commitment to the central rates. In fact, 11 realignments of exchange rates within the EMS occurred during its first 13 years,[4] each requiring unanimous consent of EMS members. In this sense the EMS constitutes an **adjustable peg system** for the countries included within it.

One factor that may have helped limit the need for exchange rate realignments before 1992 was the existence of governmental controls over capital flows in several European countries. Their removal in 1992 as a part of the Unified Market program has tested the system, instigating the changes forced upon it between 1992 and 1993.

Why, then, did the EMS widen the range of currency fluctuations, and what influenced the United Kingdom and Italy to withdraw their membership? Following the unification of Germany in 1990, the German government began to pour 100 billion D.M. per year into East Germany in an attempt to build its capital stock and increase worker productivity (see Chapter 2). To raise money the government was forced to mount large budgetary deficits. Fearing the inflationary pressures that could result from such deficits, the German central bank raised interest rates sky-high in an attempt to stem the inflation. This attracted vast sums of money from other EMS countries, whose exchange rates were pegged to the mark. The only way countries like France and the United Kingdom could combat the massive outflow of funds was to raise their own interest rates and thereby reduce the relative attractiveness of German rates. However, their own economies were

---

[4] The last realignment occurred in January 1987, providing for a small revaluation of the mark, the guilder, and the Belgian franc.

stagnating, and an increase in their interest rates could plunge these countries into a serious recession—and in any event contradict their domestic needs. To cope with the initial pressure, the United Kingdom and Italy withdrew from the EMS in September 1992, and their currencies depreciated significantly against the mark. (Italy rejoined at the end of 1996 at a lower exchange value for the lira.) Sweden stopped its informal pegging to the ECU, and the krona depreciated in 1993. Spain and Portugal devalued their currencies relative to the mark, and imposed government controls on the outflow of capital.

After abating for a few months, the capital outflow resumed in 1993—this time mainly from France to Germany. But the German central bank (the Bundesbank) continued its high interest rate policy. In the end the pressure became unbearable and led to the widening of the bands in August 1993. Only by the end of 1993 did German interest rates decline sufficiently to restore calm to Europe's financial markets. By December 1993 the French franc was trading (informally) within the old, narrow band.

There is a general lesson to be learned from this episode. A system of fixed exchange rates and free capital movement between countries requires policy coordination among the governments involved—at least in monetary matters. The Bretton Woods system collapsed in part because each country followed its own domestic policy independently of other countries. It is not possible to have free capital movement and a fixed exchange rate between countries when one country pursues expansionary monetary policy with low interest rates while another engages in contractionary monetary policy with high interest rates. If narrow bands are to be restored in the EMS, policy coordination is essential. This is particularly true if a system of irrevocably fixed rates is established.

Fixed Exchange Rates

Forty-six of the world's currencies, particularly those of many developing countries (LDCs), are pegged by government action to one of the major currencies—mainly the dollar, but also the French franc. A very credible way of pegging the exchange rate is by establishing a *currency board* that issues domestic currency only when it is covered by 100 percent foreign exchange reserves. Hong Kong, Estonia, Lithuania, and Argentina have established such boards.

Additionally, 40 currencies are pegged to a weighted average value of major currencies, such as **Special Drawing Rights (SDRs)** of the IMF or to a specially designated basket of currencies.[5] Finally, in a separate group of countries the central bank adjusts the exchange rate in response to selected indicators such as inflation or official reserves. Many LDCs maintain

---

[5] See S. Takagi, "Pegging to a Currency Basket," *Finance and Development*, September 1986; and D. Burton and M. Gilman, "Exchange Rate Policy and the IMF," *Finance and Development*, September 1991.

government controls over transactions in their currencies, a system known as exchange control.

Basket-peggers peg their currencies to some weighted average of major currencies, usually the currencies of their major trading partners. Some are pegged to the SDR, which is valued as a weighted average of the dollar, yen, mark, pound, and French franc. But because a basket, such as the SDR, is not traded on the private market, intervention must be conducted in dollars to manage the peg. Since the dollar-SDR rate is published daily by the IMF, the country can adjust its dollar exchange rate to maintain a fixed rate relative to the SDR. For example, if Saudi Arabia wishes to peg the riyal to the SDR so that 1 riyal = 1 SDR, then on a day that 1 SDR = $1.40 it would peg its currency to the dollar at 1 riyal = $1.40; if on the following day 1 SDR = $1.30, it would peg to the dollar at 1 riyal = $1.30. Similar activity takes place with respect to any other basket.

Alternative Exchange Rate Regimes

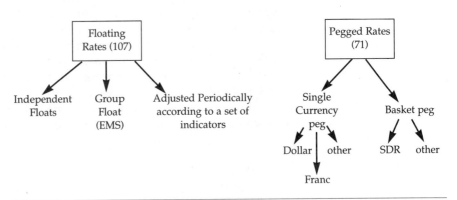

Note: The number of currencies under each category (shown in parentheses) changes periodically as countries move from one regime to another.

Summary of Exchange Regimes

Clearly, the prevailing system is a hybrid of five exchange-rate regimes: *single floats, joint floats, currencies pegged to a major currency, currencies pegged to a basket of major currencies,* and *currencies adjusted periodically according to a set of indicators.* Individual countries sometimes switch from one regime to another, as when New Zealand replaced a pegged exchange-rate regime with a free float in 1985. In general, since 1973 there has been a movement away from pegged and toward more flexible regimes, and, within the peggers, from a single currency toward composite or basket pegs. Although two-thirds of all currencies are pegged, most of world trade is conducted among countries whose exchange rates float against one another. The international currency system is summarized in the one accompanying scheme.

The Role of the U.S. Dollar

Contemporary arrangements no longer peg the European and Japanese currencies to the dollar as was the policy under Bretton Woods. As a result, the dollar is now a fluctuating currency as well. The system no longer requires a common denominator; hence neither the dollar nor any other asset performs that function. But the dollar still occupies a central role in the system, performing some functions carried over from the Bretton Woods era.

1. Although no longer a common denominator, the dollar retains a *reference* role for exchange rates, as countries measure their fluctuations in terms of the dollar.
2. The dollar is the main *intervention currency* for currencies on a managed float regime. Central banks buy and sell dollars on their respective foreign exchange markets to influence their exchange rates. To some extent even members of the EMS use dollars for intervention, although the mark has become more important within the system. Most **single-currency peggers** peg their currencies to the dollar and fluctuate along with it. Only an asset or currency that is widely used in the private sector can serve as an intervention currency for stabilizing the exchange rate, for only such a currency can be bought and sold by central banks on their respective foreign exchange markets.
3. The dollar is the main official *reserve currency,* as central banks require dollar reserves to intervene in their respective markets. To some extent this role is also played by the mark and the yen. The United States maintains its foreign currency reserves in marks and yen.
4. The dollar is the main **vehicle currency.** A trader may not be able to convert Greek drachmas to Finnish markkas because there is hardly a market between these two currencies. But she can convert the drachmas into dollars and the dollars to markkas, as there is always an active market for dollars in each country.
5. Finally, the dollar is the main international **transactions currency** for the private sector. People and institutions the world over maintain dollar accounts in banks in their own countries, known as **Eurodollars.** International transactions that do not involve the United States are

often financed with dollars. Prices of international commodities, such as oil, use dollar quotations. And United Nations trade statistics are also reported in dollars.[6] It is the existence of this vast private market for dollars in foreign countries that enables central banks to buy and sell dollars in their own markets to influence their exchange rates. In other words, it is this feature of the dollar that lets it function as an intervention currency.

Additional Insights

Eurodollars are created when an American or a foreign owner of a dollar deposit with a bank in the United States transfers these funds and deposits them in a foreign bank or a foreign branch of an American bank. Normally such transfers are prompted by higher interest rates on short-term deposits prevailing abroad, and foreign banks accept the deposits because they can in turn lend them at still higher rates. Often these funds belong to corporations that intend to use them in short order to finance international trade or investments; they are kept in dollars (rather than converted to local currencies) because of the general acceptability of the U.S. dollar in settling international transactions.

Once Eurodollars become an interest-bearing dollar deposit having a stated maturity in a foreign bank, they may be lent out and redeposited in a succession of banks before being ultimately used to finance a business transaction. Eurodollar deposits thereby multiply just as the domestic money supply does under a fractional reserve banking system. The typical Eurodollar deposit is a negotiable time deposit with a fixed term to maturity from overnight to 5 years. The interest rate is related to rates prevailing in New York.

Finally, the term Eurodollars is somewhat deceptive. It is true that most of the market consists of dollars held in Europe. But European banks also accept deposits denominated in nondollar currencies other than their own, and Japanese banks hold deposits in currencies other than the yen (mainly, but not exclusively, dollars). Total *Eurocurrency* deposits are estimated at $3 trillion, most of which is interbank deposits.

While governments heavily regulate domestic-currency deposits, banks have much greater freedom in their dealings in foreign currencies: Deposit insurance is absent; reserve requirements do not exist, as no single country can impose them; and asset restrictions and capital requirements are difficult to administer.

INDICES OF TRADE-WEIGHTED (EFFECTIVE) EXCHANGE RATES

Because the major world currencies are floating independently or in a group (EMS), it is impossible to determine by direct inspection what happens to a

---

[6] However, the IMF now uses SDRs and the EU employs the ECU in their statistical tabulations.

country's exchange rate. For example, suppose that in a simplified world there were only three currencies: the U.S. dollar, the Canadian dollar, and the mark. Assume that the U.S. dollar *depreciated 10 percent* relative to the mark and *appreciated 12 percent* relative to the Canadian dollar. Then the change in the value of the dollar is some *weighted average* of the changes in the two *bilateral* exchange rates. Since, in effect, the dollar may change in varying degrees against any number of individually floating currencies, a weighted average of all the bilateral changes is required to determine the change in the exchange value of the dollar. Such an average is called the dollar's **trade-weighted** or **effective exchange rate.** It is calculated for all major currencies. In calculating the index, a *weight* representing the comparative importance to the home economy of each foreign country is applied to the bilateral exchange rate between the foreign currency in question and the home currency. Because these calculations involve *changes* in the exchange rate over time, they are calculated relative to a base period and reported as an index.

Several possible weights can be used in calculating the average, and correspondingly, each currency can have several effective exchange rates. The weights employed depend on the purpose for which the index is developed. Thus an import-weighted index—where each partner country's share in the home country's imports is used as a weight—measures the effect of exchange-rate changes on the cost of imports into the home country. Likewise, an export-weighted index—where each partner country's share in the home country's exports is used as a weight—measures the average changes in the cost of the home currency exports to foreigners. A third alternative is to weigh each partner country by the sum of the home country's export to and import from it (namely, total bilateral trade flows), while a fourth possibility is a global trade-weighted index, where each partner country's weight is equal to its share in worldwide trade. Finally, the **International Monetary Fund (IMF)** developed weights that are designed to assess the effect of exchange rate changes on the country's trade balance. These weights incorporate both the price changes of exports and imports, and the responsiveness of trade flows to these changes, occasioned by a 1 percent movement in each bilateral exchange rate. Because of the importance of trade in constructing the weights, such indices are known as trade-weighted exchange rates.

Both the bilateral and effective exchange rates mentioned so far are known as **nominal exchange rates** because they do not account for differential inflation in the home and the foreign country or countries. For that reason they do not adequately measure the change in the country's competitive position relative to its competitors. Suppose that the dollar depreciated from 3 D.M. to 2 D.M., but over the same period the U.S. domestic inflation was one-third higher than German inflation—then the U.S. competitive position relative to Germany has not changed.

To measure the changes in a country's competitive position, we employ *real* exchange rates. The **bilateral real exchange rate** is the nominal rate

FIGURE 12.4	*U.S. Dollar Exchange Rate*

The foreign G-10 countries comprise Belgium, Canada, France, Germany, Italy, Japan, the Netherlands, Sweden, Switzerland, and the U.K.

Source: *Federal Reserve Bank of Cleveland Review,* Nov. 1996.

adjusted for the differential inflation between the two countries. For example, the real dollar/mark exchange rates equal the nominal dollar/mark exchange times the ratio of the German to the U.S. price levels.[7] The *real effective exchange rate* is the effective nominal rate adjusted for the differential between the country's inflation rate and a weighted average of foreign inflation rates.

As an example, figure 12.4 presents a trade weighted index of the U.S. dollar for the years 1992–96.

THE INTERNATIONAL MONETARY FUND (IMF)

Occupying a pivotal role in the international currency system is the IMF. In addition to its consultative functions, it coordinates and advises on central

---

[7] Real $E_{\$/D.M.} = (E_{\$/D.M.})(P_G/P_{U.S.})$

banks' intervention on their respective foreign currency markets, an activity sometimes referred to as *surveillance*. Furthermore, the IMF provides short-run credit and supplementary reserves through its regular and Special Drawing Rights (SDR) accounts.

Regular International Monetary Fund Procedures

There are 181 member countries in the IMF, of which the Group of Ten major industrial countries are the most important in terms of the volume of their international payments and their voting power within the organization. Each member country is assigned a **quota**, of which it must contribute to the IMF 25 percent in gold or convertible foreign currencies and 75 percent in its own currency. The quota is based on a rather complicated formula[8] that need not be elaborated on here. In turn the quota determines the voting power of each member country as well as the amount of loans it is eligible to receive. The initial resources of the IMF consisted of 25 percent in gold and 75 percent in holdings of a variety of currencies. Total quotas of all members add up to about $200 billion, 18 percent of which constitutes the U.S. quota.

Loans granted by the Fund to member countries require approval by the Board of Directors. The loans are given to a country in a specific foreign currency in exchange for an equivalent amount of the borrowing country's own currency. If, for example, France desires supplementary resources, it applies for a loan in the currency it needs, say German marks. If the loan is approved, the Fund provides the marks in return for an equivalent amount of French francs. Thus the Fund does not really make loans in the conventional sense of the word; it sells currencies. The French **purchase** German marks with French francs, and that is the official term used by the Fund for all borrowing activities. When the French repay the loan (in 3–5 years), they **repurchase** their own currency from the Fund for such currencies as are acceptable to the Fund at the time.

There are limits to how much a country can "borrow" from the Fund, and these are expressed in terms of how much of a given currency the Fund is permitted to accumulate. If the French continue to draw on the Fund, that means they continue to purchase foreign currencies with French francs, which in turn implies that the Fund is accumulating francs. If in the meantime other countries purchase francs from the Fund, its holdings of francs would decline. What matters is the *net* cumulative effect of all purchases on its holdings. The IMF may increase its stock of francs up to the point at which its franc holdings reach 200 percent of the French quota. Since its initial holdings of francs were 75 percent of the French quota, the total net advances that can be made to France in foreign currencies is limited to 125 percent of the French quota. The same rules apply to all countries.

---

[8] A country's national income, international reserves, imports, the variability of its exports, and the ratio of exports to national income are all part of the formula.

Cumulative purchases of a given currency (in this example, the mark) from the IMF would deplete the Fund's holdings of that currency. When these holdings fall below 75 percent of that country's quota, its currency becomes *acceptable to the Fund for repayment (repurchase) purposes.* It also makes that country eligible for large future drawings on other currencies because it increases the shortfall of the Fund's holdings from the 200 percent of the quota limit.

If the Fund runs out of currency altogether—something that has not happened thus far—that currency can be declared *scarce,* permitting other countries to discriminate against it.

Returning to the "borrowing" country of our example, France, we see that not all "loans" from the Fund are automatic. Indeed, the larger the cumulative drawings, the greater the Fund's holdings of francs, and the more difficult it becomes for the French to obtain additional loans. Specifically, the 125 percent of quota in total potential drawings is divided into 5 *tranches* (slices) of 25 percent each. The first one is known as the **reserve tranche** (previously called the *gold tranche*). The subsequent four slices are known as the **credit tranches.** Advances within the reserve tranche are automatic, as is the right to draw on any credit balance that the country may have built up by having its own currency drawn upon.

Any drawings beyond that are subject to the discretionary decision of the Fund, and the Fund may extract pledges from the borrowing country in return for the loan.[9] These pledges usually concern policies to be undertaken by the country to put its international payments situation in order. Known as the **conditionality provisions,** these consist of a set of measures designed to ensure a reduction in the country's external deficit. They are usually formulated in terms of limits on the growth of the domestic money supply or on the size of the budget deficit, perhaps coupled with currency devaluation. As such they may prove embarrassing or unacceptable to the country concerned. And countries at times avoid drawing on the IMF so as not to subject themselves to the conditions that the IMF would impose. The industrial countries that have access to the foreign exchange market hardly use the Fund's facilities. On the other hand, developing countries often must prove compliance with IMF rules before they can obtain loans from private sources. In 1982 Argentina and Mexico cut domestic budgetary spending to qualify for IMF loans. Peru, however, rejected a visit by an IMF team in 1985 and decided to bypass the IMF in negotiating with private banks.

The automatic-drawing component constitutes the country's *reserve position in the Fund.* At any given moment this equals 25 percent of its quota minus its previous drawing plus previous drawings made by other countries

---

[9]The Fund's interest charges, which are levied on any drawings beyond the reserve tranche, also increase with the rise in cumulative drawings. In addition to interest, there is a service charge on each transaction and standby commitment.

on the Fund's holdings of its currency. In other words, a country's reserve position in the IMF is the shortfall in the Fund's holdings of the currency from 100 percent of the country's quota.[10] Even the automatic drawings carry an obligation to repurchase, usually within three to five years.

Since the reserve tranche is equal to the original gold or foreign currency contribution of the member nation, the range of automatic access to the Fund's resources does not constitute a net addition to a country's reserves. Thus the net effect on global reserves of any increase in the Fund's quotas is zero. This applies to the several general increases in the Fund quotas, the latest one taking place in 1993 when the total quotas were raised to about $200 billion (145 billion SDRs). In line with the general downgrading of the role of gold at the Fund, members no longer contribute gold. They may instead contribute *freely usable currencies*—a term that applies to the currencies widely used in international transactions.

Special Drawing Rights Procedures

An increase in international reserves could be accomplished only by making advances within one or more of the credit tranches automatic. In a sense, this is the essence of its Special Drawing Rights (SDRs). The IMF created and distributed to its members 9.3 billion SDRs in 1970–72 and another 12 billion SDRs in 1979–81, in allocations proportional to their regular IMF quotas. Another allocation of between $16 and $26 billion was discussed in 1996, partly because 38 members joined the IMF after 1981, and therefore received no SDR allocations. The industrial countries combined received nearly two-thirds of the total allocation.[11]

All SDR operations are administered by a special drawing account at the IMF. Each unit of SDR was originally worth $1. But today, in the era of fluctuating exchange rates, it is valued as *a weighted average of the five most important currencies.* As of January 1996, the weights are as follows: the U.S. dollar: 39%; the German mark: 21%; the Japanese yen: 18%; the French franc: 11%; and the British pound sterling: 11%. They are subject to change every five years. The dollar value of SDRs fluctuates on a daily basis. In October 1996 one SDR was worth $1.44. Interest charges on SDR transactions are a weighted average of charges on three-month market instruments in the five major countries. Transactions in SDRs and other vital economic statistics of the IMF members are reported in the IMF's *International Financial Statistics* and in the *IMF Survey.*

---

[10] Suppose the country's quota is $200,000; its reserve tranche would then be $50,000. If its drawings on the Fund amounted to $40,000 while other countries purchased $30,000 of its currency from the Fund, its reserve position would be $40,000 ($50,000 − $40,000 + $30,000). The Fund's holding of its currency would be $160,000 (the original contribution of $150,000 plus a net addition of $10,000) or $40,000 short of 100 percent of its quota.

[11] Since the agreement required approval by countries having a total of 85 percent of the quota, it gave veto power to the EU along with the United States.

SDR allocations are executed by making credit entries for each country on the ledger of the special drawing account, but no country need make a contribution to the Fund. The attractiveness of the SDRs as a reserve asset derives from the obligation of all members to accept them. Thus, if France finds itself in need of convertible foreign currencies, it can acquire German marks (or any other currency) in exchange for SDRs. The transaction will deplete France's holdings of SDRs while increasing those of Germany. Should any other country subsequently require French francs in exchange for SDRs, the French SDR holdings would increase correspondingly. The changes in SDR holdings are merely bookkeeping changes on the ledger of the IMF.

Because of their universal acceptability in settling imbalances between countries, SDRs are part of owned international reserves. But because they are held only by central banks, they cannot be used for currency intervention purposes by central banks. Only if commercial banks and other nonofficial institutions were allowed to deal in SDRs, as they now deal in dollars, would it be possible to use SDRs as an intervention asset. On the other hand, SDRs are used as a standard to which a few currencies are pegged. Additionally, private transactions, such as bonds floated on the European markets, may be valued in SDRs.

A country generally deals in SDRs for several principal reasons:

1. To obtain foreign currencies. To meet its balance-of-payments needs, one country may transfer SDRs to another member country designated by the IMF to receive them in exchange for its currency.
2. To redeem a balance of its own currency held by another member country.
3. *To pay charges and to repurchase its own currency* from the General Account of the IMF. All IMF accounts are denominated in SDRs.

Special Facilities

In addition to the regular and SDR accounts, the IMF operates **special facilities** through which credit is extended to member countries. Examples include a compensatory finance facility designed to help countries that specialize in the export of primary commodities to deal with large fluctuations in their export earnings; an *extended fund* facility that provides assistance to members with unusually large and protracted deficits whose needs exceed their credit tranches; an *enhanced structural adjustment facility*, designed to provide balance of payments assistance to low-income developing countries; and a *systemic transformation facility* to help the former socialist states to shift to market economies. Because of these special facilities, a country's potential drawing on the Fund is 500–600 percent of its quota. The pursuit of specified domestic policies designed to improve the country's balance of payments is an IMF *condition* of any drawing on the advanced credit tranches or the enlarged facilities. Finally, the IMF charges interest on debtor countries and pays interest to creditor countries.[12]

International Reserves

A country's demand for international reserves depends on several factors, first among which is the degree to which its currency is allowed to fluctuate. A country on a fixed exchange rate requires more reserves than one on a managed float, which in turn requires more reserves than a country on a free-float regime. Also, the need for reserves is positively related to the size of the country's outpayments and to the size as well as variability of the external imbalances that the reserves must finance. That need is inversely related to the country's willingness to engage in adjustment policies (to be described in later chapters) required to restore external balance. The combined demand of all countries indicates the amount of reserves needed by the international community.

On the supply side, each country's **official reserves consist of four components: gold, SDRs, reserve position in the IMF, and convertible foreign currencies** (mainly dollars, but with the mark increasing in importance). Members of the EMS have additional reserves in their central pool to help stabilize intra-EMS exchange rates. In June 1996 the combined official reserves of all countries totaled 1,071 billion SDRs, most of which were in foreign currencies. The industrial countries owned 563 billion SDRs in reserves, and developing countries owned 508 billion SDRs.

In addition, less formal types of reserves exist. An example is the "swap"[13] network between the major central banks, under which central banks undertake to loan one another their own currencies—up to a certain limit (now 18.5 billion SDRs)—for the purpose of intervention in the foreign exchange markets.

Not only is the international currency system a hybrid of floating and fixed exchange rates, but some economists and politicians advocate a return to a general system of fixed exchange rates. Consequently, it is necessary to study the balance of payments adjustment under both exchange-rate regimes. To understand macroeconomic interactions between Germany, Japan, and the United States, we need to examine policies under fluctuating exchange rates, while interactions between Germany and France require

---

[12] For a concise summary of the IMF facilities, a list of members' quotas, the method of valuing the SDR and SDR interest calculations, as well as a review of the Fund's activities, see IMF *Survey,* October 1993, *Supplement* on the IMF. See also the monthly *International Financial Statistics* of the IMF. For a discussion of the Fund's role in centrally planned economies, see IMF *Survey,* February 5, 1990, and February 21, 1994.

[13] Known as the General Agreement to Borrow.

understanding of policies under fixed-rate regimes: The channels of inter-dependence between countries depend on their exchange-rate arrangements. In the case of fixed exchange rates, the policy problem is how to restore balance-of-payments equilibrium in times of a deficit or a surplus and how these policies affect the domestic economy. In the case of a floating exchange rate, the question is twofold: How the exchange rate is determined and how changes in the market exchange rate affect the current account and the domestic economy. These topics are addressed in the next two chapters.

Summary

At the opposite extreme from freely floating exchange rates is the fixed exchange-rate regime. In this system, a central bank—the Bundesbank, for example—pegs its currency to the dollar at a fixed price by buying and selling dollars for marks on its financial market. The fact that the dollar is a transaction currency for the private sector makes such intervention possible. The central bank must also hold dollar reserves. Intervention occurs at the upper and lower support limits, and the difference between them is called the *spread* (or band). Figures 12.2 and 12.3 show the spread at 10 percent on either side of the currency's central value, for a total of 20 percent.

Unsterilized intervention permits a country's money supply to be affected, while under sterilized intervention the effect on money supply is completely offset by the sale or purchase of government bonds. Official foreign currency reserves are always affected by currency intervention.

The official exchange rate remains at the same level until the government decides to change both it and the limits of official intervention. Such changes normally occur in discrete amounts and at infrequent intervals, as distinguished from the very small daily variations under a fluctuating exchange-rate system. A government-decreed lowering of the value of a fixed-rate currency, such as from 1 D.M. = $0.50 to 1 D.M. = $0.30, is known as *devaluation;* an increase, such as from 1 D.M. = $0.50 to 1 D.M. = $0.70, is referred to as *revaluation.* Devaluation or revaluation reflects a government decision, while depreciation or appreciation—the terms used to describe floating exchange rates—reflects the outcome of market forces.

There were two protracted periods of fixed exchange rates: the gold standard, when gold was the common denominator and official reserve asset; and Bretton Woods, when the dollar was the common denominator, intervention asset, and official reserve asset.

In the current international currency system, fixed and floating exchange rates exist side by side. Several major currencies are allowed to float under managed regimes, with sterilized currency intervention. A few European currencies, including the mark and the franc, are pegged to one another and float jointly against the dollar. Many exchange rates are pegged either to a single currency or to a basket (weighted average) of currencies. A deficit or a surplus in a country's external accounts (see Chapter 10) is reflected in exchange rate movements under free float; the official reserve settlement balance under a fixed rate; and a combination of the two under a managed float regime.

There is a general lesson to be learned from the circumstances that fractured the EMS: A system of fixed exchange rates, free capital movements, and uncoordinated domestic monetary policies is not sustainable. Bretton Woods collapsed for similar reasons.

Although not as critical as under Bretton Woods, the U.S. dollar continues to play an important role in the modern currency system. It is the intervention, reserve, vehicle, and transactions currency. The last role, exemplified by the vast Eurodollar market, is what allows the dollar to function in official currency intervention.

With exchange rates floating, changes in bilateral rates indicate neither the direction of a currency's movement, nor its extent. Instead it is necessary to calculate a weighted average of changes in the bilateral exchange rates, known as the trade-weighted or effective exchange rate. It is reported in the form of an index relative to a base period. Both bilateral and trade-weighted exchange rates can be nominal or real, where the real rate accounts for the differential inflation between the country and the foreign country (or countries). Following is a summary of some contrasting terms:

	Exchange Rate	
Nominal:	Bilateral	Trade-weighted
Real (adjusted for differential inflation):	Bilateral	Trade-weighted

	Changes in the Exchange Rate	
Floating rate:	Depreciation	Appreciation
Fixed rate:	Devaluation	Revaluation

At the center of the international currency system is the International Monetary Fund (IMF), which has several consultative and surveillance functions. It also makes resources available to member countries for up to five years, in several *facilities*. It created and distributed SDRs, which constitute a reserve asset for its members. An SDR is valued as a weighted average of the five most important currencies.

A country's official reserves consist of gold, SDRs, reserve position in the IMF (ability to draw within the reserve tranche), and convertible foreign currencies (mainly dollars).

Important Concepts

Fixed exchange rates

Spread (or band)

Dollar buying point

Unsterilized intervention

Sterilized intervention

Revaluation

Dollar selling point

Devaluation

Depreciation

Appreciation

Gold standard

Transactions currency

Eurodollars

Bilateral nominal exchange rates

Trade-weighted (effective) exchange rate (nominal and real)

International Monetary Fund (IMF)

Bilateral real exchange rate

Common denominator

Official reserve asset

Bretton Woods

Intervention currency

Band

European Monetary System (EMS)

Adjustable peg system

Special Drawing Rights (SDRs)

Basket-peggers

Single-currency pegger

Vehicle currency

IMF quotas

Purchase from the IMF

Repurchase from the IMF

Reserve tranche

Credit tranche

Conditionality provisions

IMF special facilities

Review Questions

1. Using the diagram from question 2 of Chapter 11, explain how the French central bank may maintain a fixed dollar-franc exchange rate.
   a. What happens to the French money supply in each type of intervention, first if it is unsterilized and second if it is sterilized?
   b. What happens if the French can no longer maintain that particular exchange rate?
   c. Describe two historical periods of fixed exchange rates.

2. a. What types of exchange rate regimes exist in the contemporary international currency system?
   b. How is an external deficit reflected in each one of these regimes?
   c. Does the U.S. dollar play a special role in the system? If so, what?

3. Why was the EMS forced to widen considerably the bands of exchange fluctuations, and why did the United Kingdom and Italy withdraw from the EMS in 1992? What lessons can be drawn from that experience?

4. Differentiate between:
   a. Bilateral and effective exchange rates.
   b. Nominal and real exchange rates.
   c. Basket-peggers and single-currency peggers.

5. How does the IMF make and receive payments of "loans" under the:
   a. Regular account procedure?
   b. SDR procedure?

6. How is the value of the SDR determined?

7. What are the forms of international reserves?

8. Explain the following terms:
   a. Free float
   b. Managed float
   c. European Monetary System
   d. Reserve currency
   e. Vehicle currency
   f. Intervention currency
   g. Transactions currency
   h. Reserve position in the IMF

9. The following are hypothetical U.S. international transactions (in billions of dollars) for a certain year:

a. Merchandise exports	300
b. Merchandise imports	500
c. Service transactions (imports and exports): Net	+ 100
d. Private capital flows: Net	+ 90
e. Official liabilities to foreign monetary authorities	+ 10

   Would you deduce from the previous statistics that the dollar can be a *freely floating* currency? Why or why not?

10. Explain the following statements quoted in the April 15, 1985 issue of the *New York Times* from a report released by a Senate working group:
    a. The senators were concerned that the *effective nominal and real* exchange values of the dollar were 50 percent above those of 1980.
    b. The senators recommended seeking something between "the excessive exchange rigidities of Bretton Woods and the excessive gyrations we are seeing now."
    c. The Senators recommended greater intervention in the foreign currency markets (in coordination with other countries).

11. Assume that the Saudi riyal is pegged to the SDR.
    a. What does that mean?
    b. Is currency intervention by the central bank conducted in SDRs? If not, how?

12. Distinguish between *sterilized* and *unsterilized* intervention in the foreign exchange market.

CHAPTER 13

Domestic Policies to Adjust the Balance of Payments

This chapter addresses the issue of how a country with a *fixed exchange rate* can restore balance to its international accounts if a deficit or a surplus develops in its balance of payments. This provokes the question: Why address this issue at all, since the fixed exchange rate system disappeared in 1973? The answer is that there are still dozens of countries on fixed exchange rates; fixed exchange rates prevail between the EMS countries in Europe; and because of some dissatisfaction with what is considered excessive exchange rate fluctuations, there are those who advocate a return to a fixed exchange rate system.[1] Moreover, much of the analysis in this chapter applies to *policies designed to improve the current account of a country on a floating exchange rate*, where the exchange rate itself is determined by the capital account.

SHORT-RUN IMBALANCES

If an external deficit is strictly seasonal or short-run in nature and likely to reverse itself in due course, little action need be taken. As long as there is full confidence in the ability of the government to maintain the exchange rate, private short-term capital can be relied upon to bridge the gap. Suppose that the British pound became weak in the fall because of a seasonal balance-of-payments deficit, and dropped toward the lower support limit of $2.38.

---

[1] See papers by P. Kenen, J. Williamson, and J. Frankel on "Reforming the International Monetary System," *American Economic Review*, May 1987, 184–210; and *IMF Survey*, January 25, 1988, and March 21, 1988.

$$£1 = \$2.40 \begin{cases} \$2.42 \\ \$2.38 \end{cases}$$

Individual financiers would be certain that there was only one way the pound could go: up. After all, it was only temporarily depressed and the lower support limit could not possibly be penetrated. They would act accordingly. Foreigners owing money to Britons could accelerate debt payments to take advantage of the unusually low pound price, while Britons having debts denominated in foreign currencies would postpone payments whenever possible until dollars became somewhat cheaper in terms of pounds.

In general, financiers would be induced to buy and hold pounds, expecting a profit when the "normal" price was restored. They would be certain that they could not lose by such action. Thus, a downward movement in the value of the pound generates inflow of short-term funds, which itself tends to arrest and reverse that movement. Since the expectations of people differ, one might expect the inward flow of these funds to accelerate as the pound moves gradually downward, until at some point the decline in the value of the pound is arrested.

A precisely reverse phenomenon occurs when the pound is seasonally strong and reaches toward the upper support limit. Since everyone knows that it cannot rise in value above $2.42, there is a potential gain and no risk from selling pounds for other currencies, thereby generating an outflow of funds.

These are **stabilizing** short-run capital movements. Caused by public expectations with respect to exchange-rate variations, they offset temporary deficits in the balance of payments and narrow the range of exchange fluctuations to something less than the official spread.

Variations in interest rates also bring about stabilizing capital movements. An external deficit is an excess of autonomous outpayments over inpayments. But this net excess implies that, on balance, Britons are withdrawing sterling deposits from their bank accounts to convert them into foreign currencies in order to make overseas payments. Temporarily, at least, there is a decline in the British domestic money supply and a stiffening of short-run interest rates. As interest rates rise, foreign capital is attracted to Great Britain to take advantage of higher earning opportunities. Conversely, an external surplus means an excess of inpayments over outpayments and a rise in the money supply. Interest rates are nudged downward, and short-term capital tends to leave the country.

On both counts, therefore, private short-term funds bridge temporary imbalances and stabilize the exchange rate. But it is worth repeating that all this is contingent upon confidence in the long-run value of the currency. If the government's ability to maintain the exchange rate is suspect when the pound hovers around its lower support limit, precisely the opposite movement can occur. Fearing devaluation, say to £1 = $2, the possible small gain of two or three cents from an appreciation within the official spread no longer looms important. The same may be said about small interest gains. Instead, the feared loss from a sizable devaluation may drive people away from the pound to strong currencies. Conversely, if revaluation is expected when the currency is at its upper support limit, short-term funds tend to flow inward instead of outward. These capital movements are **destabilizing** in nature and usually occur when confidence in the currency is shattered. Whether speculation is stabilizing or destabilizing depends on people's expectations with respect to future movements of the currency, which in turn depend on their confidence in the economy.

Returning to the stable case, the inflow of private capital can be reinforced by official action. The government may raise interest rates or manipulate the forward exchange market to attract short-term funds from abroad, or it can fall back on its accumulated reserves. If necessary, recourse might be sought in borrowing from other countries or from international organizations such as the International Monetary Fund. However, should the deficit last for several years and prove fundamental in nature, a deliberate course of action would have to be pursued. Even so, the more international reserves the country has, the less the pressure is on it to act. But as in the case of a family, reserves can only buy time; if they dwindle, an adjustment mechanism must be set in motion to eliminate the deficit.

The first option open to the country is the classical prescription of inducing domestic contraction by monetary and fiscal means. Indeed, some contraction in the level of economic activity (in employment, production, and income) will occur automatically in the deficit country, because external trade and domestic economic activity are intricately interrelated. Specifically, the contractionary effect will operate through both the expenditures and monetary mechanisms, leading to a curtailment in imports and perhaps an expansion of exports, thereby reducing the deficit. Since the purpose of government adjustment policy is to reinforce these tendencies, a detailed explanation of the processes involved will help clarify the mechanism through which government domestic policies affect the balance of payments. While *the analysis in the next section* is advanced in the context of a fixed exchange rate regime, it *also applies to the current account component of the balance of payments in the case of a floating exchange rate,* where the exchange rate is determined mainly by capital flows.

"Automatic" Processes

The Monetary Mechanism

Money affects the level of real production and employment through its availability and cost (the rate of interest) to producers and consumers alike. In turn, regardless of its source (whether it is the current account or the capital account), an external imbalance affects the economy indirectly through the monetary route in a manner that tends to reduce the imbalance.

A surplus or deficit in the balance of payments means that autonomous outpayments do not equal inpayments. Inpayments are received in foreign currencies either in return for exports or in the form of capital inflow. Their local recipients exchange them for domestic currency, which in turn is deposited in local banks, mainly in checking accounts, thereby creating new demand deposits. In a modern economy these deposits (that is, checking accounts) constitute the bulk of the money supply. And in a banking system that operates on the fractional reserves principle, new deposits serve as a basis for a multiple expansion of the money supply. Thus, unless *offset* (or sterilized) by deliberate action of the central bank, a net inflow of foreign exchange (currencies) results in a multiple expansion of the domestic money supply. The reverse process takes place as a result of outpayments. Buyers of foreign goods and services or exporters of capital acquire the foreign currency necessary to make payment in exchange for their domestic currency. And the latter are usually drawn out of their demand deposit, thereby causing a multiple contraction in the money supply.

In case of a surplus, inpayments exceed outpayments, resulting in a new inflow of funds and an increase in money supply. For example, suppose Germany has an external surplus of 100 million D.M. German bank deposits rise by the same amount. If the required reserve ratio of the banks is 20 percent (or one-fifth), excess reserves of 80 million D.M. are created. The money multiplier—the inverse of the required reserve ratio—is 5. Thus the banks are able to expand money supply by 400 (80 × 5) million D.M. The converse happens in a deficit country: Outpayments exceed inpayments, and the new outflow of funds reduces bank deposits and causes a multiple contraction of money supply.

Consider the case of a deficit country whose money supply shrinks. Much spending in the economy, and therefore output employment and income, depends on the availability of bank loans. As money becomes "tight," or less readily available, it is reasonable to expect certain marginal business-investment projects and consumer purchase plans to go unrealized. Also, because the rate of interest is determined by the demand and supply of credit, the effect of monetary stringency is to raise interest rates on the money markets, thereby adding to the cost of investment, home construction, and other economic activities that depend on borrowed funds. The resulting curtailment of such activity reduces employment and income in the community, and any such reduction spreads through the economy through the multiplier mechanism. And the reduction in income (or output) reduces imports (see Chapter 10). Finally, the tighter money supply curtails the rate of price increases, thereby making the country more competitive. Hence both the *income* and *price* changes have the effect of reducing imports and encouraging exports, thereby partly offsetting the balance-of-payments deficit.

In the case of the surplus country, money supply expands. This eases the supply of bank credit and lowers interest rates—both factors contributing to increased income and employment and to a higher rate of price increases. In turn, these increases raise imports and curtail the original surplus.

The Specie-Flow Mechanism   In the preceding paragraphs, the equilibrating effect of changes in the money supply was said to operate through the domestic income and price channels. Classical economic doctrine—the body of economic doctrine in vogue before the appearance in 1936 of John Maynard Keynes's *General Theory of Employment, Interest, and Money*—placed primary emphasis on the money supply—price approach. Indeed, this was an integral part of the way the classical economists viewed the aggregate level of economic activity.

One convenient way of looking at the economy is through the so-called equation of exchange:

$$MV = PO$$

M is the quantity of money in circulation, consisting of bank notes, coins, and demand deposits, and *V* is the income velocity of circulation, the number of times per year the average dollar changes hands to finance transactions in *final* goods and services (excluding goods in intermediate stages of production). Therefore, *MV* equals the aggregate annual monetary expenditures designed to finance all transactions in final goods and services.

P is the aggregate price level (index), and *O* is the real volume of final goods and services produced during the year. Thus, *PO* is the money value of goods and services produced during the year, or the gross domestic product (GDP).

This equation is in fact a truism. It is true by definition, for it states that the number of dollars spent on purchases of all goods and services equals their money value (GDP). The classical economists, however, proceeded a step further and made two important assumptions (that may or may not be true): First, that the velocity of circulation *(V)* is constant, for it depends on the payment habits of the community, which rarely change; and second, that the volume of final output is fixed at the full-employment level.[2] With *V* and *O* constant, any changes in *M* must produce proportional variations in *P*.

All this is immediately applicable to the balance-of-payments adjustment mechanism. Under the gold standard, a deficit country lost gold. And since the domestic money supply was based on fractional reserve requirements held in gold, the country experienced a multiple contraction in its money supply and a consequent reduction in prices. This improved the country's competitive standing; by encouraging exports and discouraging imports, it partly redressed the deficit. Precisely the reverse happened in a surplus country, where the expansion of the money supply raised prices, thereby impairing the country's competitive position and reducing the surplus. Under the *rules of the game* of the gold standard, central banks were supposed to *reinforce*

---

[2]Strictly speaking, the full-employment condition is not an assumption but a result of other postulates in the classical model: Complete price and wage flexibility, and savings as well as investment, are considered a function of the rate of interest.

these automatic tendencies by contracting money supply (by selling government bonds) in case of a deficit and by expanding money supply (by purchasing government bonds) in case of a surplus. This process came to be called the **specie-flow mechanism.** In short, the classical specie-flow mechanism focuses on variations in relative prices (variations in the price ratio between two countries), which under a system of fixed exchange rates must be brought about through domestic price changes.

But a number of empirical studies convinced economists that as often as not the adjustment mechanism worked too fast and too smoothly to be satisfactorily explained by the money supply–price forces. In short, when the "Keynesian revolution" came in 1936, economists were receptive and ready to apply the new ideas to the international trade field. These adaptations came after World War II.

In particular, some of the classical assumptions were questioned: Can it be assumed that gold gains and losses produce multiple changes in the money supply? The central bank can easily *neutralize* their effect by what are called *offsetting policies.* Instead of reinforcing any loss (gain) of gold by contractionary (expansionary) monetary policy, as was required under the *rules of the game* of the gold standard, the central banks could and often did precisely the reverse. In such cases, gains and losses of gold reserves would not produce the expected changes in the money supply.

Another classical assumption that came under scrutiny was the constancy of **velocity (V)**. Keynes held that money is used either for transactions or for speculative purposes. In the transactions sphere, velocity does indeed depend on the payment habits of the community and is therefore roughly constant. But speculative funds are kept idle by those who expect to benefit from an increase in the value of money in terms of other financial assets (that is, by those who expect the prices of these assets to decline). The amount so held depends on the cost of idle funds in terms of forgone earning opportunities elsewhere. This cost can be measured by the rate of interest; the higher the interest rate, the more costly it is to maintain idle balances. The velocity of these balances is zero, for they do not circulate. Total velocity is a weighted average of the zero and constant velocities in the two sectors, and thus it changes as funds are switched between speculative and transactional balances. Since the rate of interest determines the division of balances between the two sectors, it also affects the velocity of circulation. In particular, the rate of interest and velocity are positively related.[3] Hence, changes in the money supply *(M)* may affect the interest rate and produce offsetting variations in *V.* Indeed, when *M* rises (declines) there is a tendency for the interest rate to decline (rise), thereby increasing (decreasing) speculative balances and lowering (raising) *V.* Variations in *V* have an inherent tendency to offset variations in *M,* so that spending *(MV)* and, therefore, *PO* need not be affected at all.

Keynes challenged the idea that physical output is constant at the full-employment level, by questioning the constructs of the classical model that lead to this result.[4] Instead, he advanced the proposition that in industrial economies wages and prices are rigid in a downward direction. Thus, even if *MV* did vary, the impact might be on physical output *(O)* rather than on prices *(P).*

Finally, it was said, even if prices do move in the desired direction, this is not a guarantee of success. A decline in the relative prices of the deficit country means that it will sell more goods abroad. But since each unit of the commodity sold now brings a lower price, there is no assurance that total inpayments (price times quantity) will rise. That depends on whether the increase in the quantity sold is proportionately larger than the decline in price—whether the increase is large enough to offset the fact that now every unit sells for less. This would be the case only if the demand for the country's exports is relatively elastic.[5]

We summarize the challenge to the specie-flow mechanism in terms of the equation of exchange *MV = PO* as follows: (a) *M* may not vary in the expected direction;

(b) even if it did, its variations may be partly offset by changes in V; (c) changes in MV may affect O as well as P; and (d) even if P varied as predicted, the expected change in the trade flows may not materialize.

Not only did these criticisms run deep, but economists had an alternative explanation of the adjustment mechanism. Known as the expenditures income approach, it was rooted in the Keynesian ideas that became widely accepted after World War II.

Direct Effect on Private Expenditures

Income Changes   Consider the case in which a deficit appears in a country's balance of payments, and assume that the deficit is brought about by a

[3] In the following example, assume that transactions velocity is 5, and speculative velocity is zero.

Sphere	Velocity	(1) Balances	(2) Balances
Transactions	5	800	900
Speculative	0	200	100
		1,000	1,000

If the 1,000 balances are divided as in column 1, velocity is

$$\frac{(5\times800)+(0\times200)}{1,000} = 4$$

If the balances are divided as in column 2, velocity is higher:

$$\frac{(5\times900)+(0\times100)}{1,000} = 4.5$$

A rise in the rate of interest raises the cost of holding idle balances and induces a shift from column 1 to column 2. That in turn raises velocity. Hence velocity is positively related to the rate of interest: A rise (decline) in the rate of interest raises (lowers) velocity.

[4] In particular, he made savings a function of income rather than of the rate of interest and introduced rigidity into money wages in a downward direction.

[5] Economists measure the degree of response to price change in terms of *price elasticity* (η_p), which is defined as the ratio

$$\eta_p = \frac{\text{Percentage change in the quantity purchased}}{\text{Percentage change in price}} = \frac{\Delta Q/Q}{\Delta P/P} = \frac{\Delta Q}{\Delta P} \times \frac{P}{Q}$$

It is negative because price and quantity move in opposite directions. However, it is common practice to ignore the negative sign and discuss elasticity in terms of its absolute value. Thus, the necessary condition of response described in the text is such that $\eta_p > 1$, and is known as *relatively elastic demand*. Chapter 14 offers a more extensive discussion of this concept.

reduction in exports as foreign buyers shift to alternative sources of supply. The immediate consequence on the home front is a decline in production, employment, and income in the export industries. But that decline tends to spread throughout the economy in a multiple fashion. Workers and officials in the export industries, who suffer the original impact, have less money to spend on consumption of goods and services produced by other industries. To be sure, they are unlikely to reduce consumption by the full amount of the decline in their purchasing power, since it is just for such a circumstance that they have accumulated savings. But some reduction would undoubtedly occur. In turn, as income and employment decline in the "second round" of industries, their wage-earners spend less elsewhere. And so the process spreads throughout the economy in a wavelike fashion, with its force declining as it becomes further removed from the primary impact areas. At every stage at which the decline occurs, income recipients lower their consumption by something less than the cut in purchasing power, simply because it is human nature to cushion the impact of income reduction on the standard of living by drawing on one's savings. The extent of the total effect is positively related to two factors: the size of the original income reduction in the export industries and the proportion of any income reduction that is translated into reduced spending by the citizens (the **marginal propensity to consume**) at each "round." This multiplier process obviously takes time to work its way through the economy.

When the deficit is caused by an increase in imports (rather than a reduction in exports) the process is somewhat analogous. There is a direct effect on income and employment in the domestic import-competing industries only to the extent that the new imports displace the consumption of domestically produced goods (imports that are not financed out of a reduction in the rate of consumer saving). Production of such commodities declines, and the attendant reduction in income and employment spreads throughout the economy in the manner just described.

It is an integral part of economic analysis that imports vary positively and closely with variations in income. In other words, income is an important determinant of imports (though not the only one). Thus the decline in income induces a reduction in imports, and also causes a cut in the consumption of domestically produced goods, thereby leaving more of them available for exports and exercising greater pressure on producers to market abroad. The upshot of this income-expenditures mechanism is that part of the original decline in exports is offset by an induced reduction in imports and an increase in exports. These automatic tendencies narrow the balance-of-payments deficit but are unlikely to close it altogether. Also, it takes time before their full impact is felt.

Precisely the reverse process takes place in the surplus country, which experiences an increase in world demand for its exports. The primary impact occurs in the export industries, where employment and income expand to satisfy the increasing world demand. Income recipients save part of their additional earnings but spend a large share of them, which leads to an expansion of output and income in the industries producing the goods that they purchase. In turn, part of the incremental income is translated into purchases elsewhere, channeling purchasing power into a "third round" of industries. And so the process spreads in a declining sequence throughout the economy, where at each round, part of the added income is withdrawn from the spending stream. It is useful to liken this sequence to the effect of a stone dropped into a pond of water; the initial splash in the area of impact is followed by a series of waves, which spread in concentric circles throughout the pond in ever-declining intensity. This is how the expansion of income spreads throughout the economy. The total effect on income is likely to be much greater than the primary impact; the ratio between total effect and primary impact is known as the **multiplier.** Its magnitude varies inversely with the proportion of the added income withdrawn (or leaked) from the income stream at each stage.

If the surplus is brought about by a reduction in imports, then the primary impact area consists of the industries producing domestic substitutes (to the extent that domestically produced goods, rather than savings, take the place of imports). From there, successive rounds of consumer spending carry the expansion into other sectors of the economy. If the surplus is caused by the investment of foreign capital in new plants and equipment, the expansionary effect is virtually the same as when exports rise.

The income increase produced through the expenditure mechanism raises imports; it also results in an increase in the consumption of domestically produced goods, thereby leaving fewer goods available for export and reducing the pressure on producers to export. On both counts—the induced rise in imports and the decline in exports—the initial surplus would be reduced, again exhibiting an automatic tendency toward partial adjustment of the balance of payments.

To summarize, a disequilibrium in the balance of payments contains the seeds of its own partial reversal. A newly developed surplus increases income by a multiple of that surplus, and the rise in income causes an increase in imports (and a cut in exports) that partly offsets the original surplus. Conversely, a newly developed deficit results in a multiple income reduction, which in turn lowers imports (and expands exports) and offsets part of the deficit.

Additional Insights

In the years since World War II, economists have developed a body of analysis based on the ideas of John Maynard Keynes that provides a more rigorous formulation of the relationships outlined above. This is useful for two reasons: It sharpens our understanding of the processes involved; and, at a subsequent stage, allows us to measure the magnitude of each effect. In what follows we explain the multiplier formula and apply it to the problem at hand. (A geometrical presentation and proof is offered in appendix 13.1.)

The Foreign Trade Multiplier The simplest case to analyze is a small open economy without government. When output, and hence income, rises, people divide the incremental income (ΔY) between added consumption of domestic goods (ΔC), added savings (ΔS), and added imports (ΔM). Thus, $\Delta Y = \Delta C + \Delta S + \Delta M$. The share of income that is added to each component is called *marginal propensity*. In particular:

1. The **marginal propensity to consume** (MPC) is the share of *added* income devoted to *added* consumption: MPC = $\Delta C/\Delta Y$.
2. The **marginal propensity to save** (MPS) is the share of *added* income channeled into *added* savings: MPS = $\Delta S/\Delta Y$.
3. The **marginal propensity to import** (MPM) is the share of *added* income spent on *added* imports: MPM = $\Delta M/\Delta Y$.

The three marginal propensities necessarily add up to one, because additional income can be either consumed, saved, or spent on imports. These three concepts apply to both downward and upward changes in income.

Assume that the country's marginal propensities are MPC = $\frac{1}{2}$; MPS = $\frac{1}{4}$; and MPM = $\frac{1}{4}$. And suppose further that foreign demand shifts toward the country's exports, so that its annual exports rise permanently by 100. The production of the increased exports raises output, and—because output equals income—income rises by an equal amount. What would people do with the extra $100 of income? They can only divide it three ways between consumption, savings, and imports. According to the three marginal propensities, $25 is added to savings; $25 is added to imports, and $50 is added to consumption of domestic goods. While $50 of the new income leaks out of the spending stream into savings and imports, $50 is reinjected into the spending stream in the form of consumption expenditures. These consumer goods again increase production, so output, and thus income, rises further by $50.

In the next period, output and income are higher by $150: the original annual increase in exports of $100, plus the $50 in consumption expenditures. But half of the $150 is reinjected into the spending stream in the form of increased consumption, while the other half is leaked out of the spending stream into savings and imports. That raises the new output and income to $175 [100 + (150 x $\frac{1}{2}$)]. In the next period the new level of output or income will be $187.50 [100 + (175 x $\frac{1}{2}$)], followed by $193.75 [100 + (187.5 x $\frac{1}{2}$)]. And so the process continues through "rounds" of increased income and expenditures. The final level of *incremental* output or income toward which the economy converges is shown by the series: 100, 175, 187.50, 193.75 . . . 200.

In other words, an output injection of 100 in the form of increased exports raises output or income by 200. The ratio of the final rise in output to the original injection is called the **foreign trade multiplier** (k). In the above example its size is 2 (200/100). The formula for the multiplier, proven rigorously in the appendix, is

$$k = \frac{1}{1-\text{MPC}} = \frac{1}{\text{MPS} + \text{MPM}}$$

The multiplier concept applies equally to a reduction in exports; and it is applicable as well to an upward or downward change in domestic investment.

In the example above, the foreign trade multiplier is

$$k = \frac{1}{\frac{1}{4} + \frac{1}{4}} = 2$$

This means that any change in spending, be it in investment or exports—will change the income of the community in the same direction, by twice the original change. In turn, the variation in income induces a change in imports of $\Delta M = \Delta Y \times MPM$. Thus, any rise or fall in domestic expenditures must produce changes in the balance of payments. In other words, the country's internal and external positions are interrelated by the income mechanism (and others), and at no time can they be regarded as separate.

There is a difference between the effect on the balance of payments of a change in domestic spending such as investment or government expenditures on the one hand and the effect of a change in exports on the other. A $100 rise in domestic expenditures will raise income by $100\ k = \$200$ once the multiplier process has worked itself out. This will increase imports by $\$200 \times MPM = \$50$, causing a balance-of-payments deficit of like magnitude. This is an important reminder that any domestic expenditures program, governmental or private, not only raises income but also results in a current account deficit. Thus, the large U.S. trade deficits between 1983 and 1987 and again in 1993 and 1996–97 were due in part to the rapid recovery of the American economy relative to that of its trading partners.

By contrast, if the exogenous increase in expenditures is in the export sector (foreigners demanding more of the country's products), then the immediate result is a balance-of-payments surplus of $100. The rise in domestic income of $200 follows as before, but the $50 induced increase in imports will not cause a deficit. Instead it partly offsets the original surplus, lowering it to $50. Since our main interest is the second case, we shall pursue it step by step.

A $100 increase in exports *(X)*, everything else remaining the same, produces immediately a surplus of $100 in the balance of payments. Next there is a gradual effect on domestic income through the multiplier mechanism: $\Delta Y = \Delta X \times k$, or $\$100 \times 2 = \$200$. (It takes time to approach the new equilibrium.) Given the rise in income there will be an induced increase in imports[6] of $\Delta M = \Delta Y \times MPM = \$200 \times \frac{1}{2} = \$50$. The original balance-of-payments surplus, $\Delta X = \$100$, is now partially offset by $\Delta M = \$50$, so that $\Delta X - \Delta M = \$50$. In other words, the increase in imports induced through the domestic expenditures-income mechanism will reduce the balance-of-payments surplus from $100 to $50. This is a movement in the "right" direction but it is not sufficient to restore balance-of-payments equilibrium.

The above equations can be combined to describe fully the effects of income on imports:

$$\Delta M = \Delta Y \times MPM = \Delta X \times k \times MPM = \Delta X \frac{1}{MPS + MPM} \times MPM \qquad (1)$$

---

[6] Other induced effects on the increase in income will be on savings (S) and domestic consumption (C): $\Delta S = \Delta Y \times MPS = \$200 \times \frac{1}{4} = 50$. And $\Delta C = \Delta Y \times MPC = 200 \times \frac{1}{2} = 100$. Thus, the increases in imports, savings, and consumption add up to the rise in income of $200.

In our example this becomes

$$\Delta M = \$100 \times \frac{1}{\frac{1}{4} + \frac{1}{4}} \times \frac{1}{4} = \$50$$

The induced effects of a $100 increase in exports with MPM = 0.25—but with alternative values of the MPS—are tabulated below, and all are calculated in the same way as the figure of $50 we have just obtained.

ΔX	**MPM**	**MPS**	**MPC***	**k**	ΔY	ΔM	ΔS	ΔC	**ΔB of T**= $\Delta(X - M)$**
$100	0.25	0.25	0.50	2.0	$200	$50.00	$50.00	$100	50.00
100	0.25	0.05	0.70	3.3	330	82.50	16.50	231	17.50
100	0.25	0.00	0.75	4.0	400	100.00	0.00	300	0.00

*Recall that MPC = 1 – MPS + MPM.
**change in the balance of trade

As we lower the MPS, the induced increase in imports (ΔM) rises. But only at zero MPS does it completely offset the $100 original increase in exogenous exports. This is a general result, for when MPS = 0,

$$\Delta M = \Delta Y \times \text{MPM} = \Delta X \times \frac{1}{0 + \text{MPM}} \times \text{MPM} = \Delta X \qquad (2)$$

That is, $\Delta M \Delta X$. In other words, if MPS is zero, the induced change in imports equals the original change in exports. In all other cases the induced movement will stop short of restoring balance.

  If the initial change is a $100 *reduction* of exports, where a *deficit* of $100 is created, then income would *decline* by $100 × 2 = $200 and imports by $50. Again there is an automatic income mechanism that pulls the balance of payments toward equilibrium. But the induced change in imports is less than the original change in exports, leaving some imbalance in the external accounts.[7] Apart from the extreme case of zero MPS, the income mechanism induced by changes in expenditures constitutes only a partial correction of the imbalance.

  At this point it is useful to highlight the relation of trade to the national economy. Exports constitute a channel of expenditures, much the same as investment or

---

[7] The cause of the deficit can also be a $100 initial increase in imports. To the extent that these imports substitute for the consumption of domestically produced goods, there will be a primary reduction in domestic expenditures. This reduction will be short of the rise in imports to the extent that they are financed out of savings rather than substituted for domestic consumption. In terms of the example in the text, the primary impact could be, say, $80 instead of $100. It would cause a decline in income of $80 × 2 = $160 and an induced reduction in imports of MPM × $160.

consumption. A rise in exports can result from a variety of reasons: The country's prices may become more competitive; foreign taste may shift in favor of the country's products; or foreign countries may lower barriers to their imports. If exports increase, then the nation's output rises by a multiple of that increase, and with it income and employment expand. In other words, one way to move the economy from an under-employment equilibrium toward full employment is to increase exports. Conversely, a contraction in exports—for whatever reason—produces a multiple reduction in GDP and an associated cut in employment.

Imports are a function of income; therefore, as U.S. income rises so do imports of goods and services. For example, the rise in U.S. imports in 1996 was due mainly to the rise in U.S. output and income. A protracted and strong economic expansion will cause imports to increase and could bring the U.S. external balance on goods and services into deficit. Conversely, when the U.S. economy plunges into a recession, imports decline on a wide front.

Thus far we have assumed that the relationship between imports and income is stable. Although this is generally the case, there are exceptions. Many U.S. imports, such as automobiles, have close domestically produced substitutes. Suppose that concern over gasoline supplies causes the buying public to switch from domestic auto-mobiles to small, energy-efficient foreign cars. Imports rise, but not because income has increased. Rather, at every level of income, more is imported and fewer domes-tic goods are consumed. The result is a multiple reduction in U.S. GDP and an atten-dant decrease in income and employment. The same result would follow if the price of imports declined relative to that of domestically produced substitutes.

In the immediate postwar period the Keynesian expenditures approach reigned supreme. Today economists are no longer so sure. One school of thought maintains that velocity is a more stable and predictable relationship than the multiplier and that the money supply affects economic activity more than expenditures. A consensus has been reached that in the long run prices are flexible, and the economy would settle at full employment, with the level of output determined by available resources. But in the short run (which can span several years) prices are inflexible, so that the econ-omy can be at a level considerably short of full employment, and the level of output is determined by aggregate demand ($C + I + G + X - M$). Because of disagreements about the relative effectiveness of fiscal and monetary policy in influencing the course of the economy, it is necessary to take a balanced view of the adjustment mecha-nism, and to incorporate both the money and expenditure approaches as they affect income as well as prices.

We now turn to additional **automatic adjustment mechanisms.**

Price Changes In today's industrial economies, variations in the level of economic activity are usually accompanied by price movements. Thus, in the deficit country, the reduction in the level of income and employment has the side effect of curtailing the rate of price increases. When jobs are scarce, unions tend to be more restrained in their wage demands, thereby holding production costs down; and as sales decline, producers are more likely to "hold the line on prices." It is true that since World War II, industrial wages and prices have become rather rigid or sticky in a downward direction, con-siderably weakening the effectiveness of the price-adjustment mechanism under fixed exchange rates. But since our main concern is with the country's position *relative* to other countries, even a decline in the rate of price increases helps make the country more competitive, assuming that no such reduction occurs in other countries. This decline encourages exports and discourages imports, thereby contributing to automatic adjustment. The strength of this effect depends on the degree to which trade flows respond to variations in relative prices (namely, price elasticities).

Precisely the reverse happens in a surplus country, where the expansion of income and output is likely to be accompanied by an acceleration of domestic price increases. And this has the salutary effect of reducing the original surplus. In sum, these price changes reinforce the income mechanism by partially offsetting the payment imbalances caused by autonomous factors.

Summary of the "Automatic" Balance-of-Payments Adjustment

The automatic adjustment mechanism under fixed exchange rates is a function of aggregate expenditures and the money supply, both operating in the *same direction* and both affecting the economy through the income and price mechanisms. The four linkages involved may be diagrammed as:

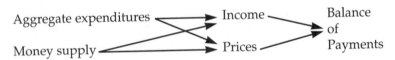

A deficit in the balance of payments automatically causes a slowdown in the country's economic activity and a slowdown of the rate of price increases through both monetary and nonmonetary (sometimes referred to as *real*) factors, while a surplus increases economic activity and accelerates the rate of price increases.

The economic slowdown resulting from a deficit contains the seeds of a mechanism that reverses the deficit in part, for it is primarily the income of the community that determines imports. A reduction in national income means that consumption of goods and services is curtailed, including the consumption of imported goods. Likewise, there is a decline in the importation of materials used in the production process. The proportion of change in national income translated into a change in imports is known as the *marginal propensity to import* (MPM). The higher the MPM, the larger the effect on imports of a given reduction in national income. Furthermore, the reduction in the level of aggregate demand in the country means that a larger portion of its productive capacity is freed to produce for export markets. The lower the level of demand is at home, the greater the pressure will be on producers to market their products overseas, for when home demand is high, producers have little incentive to seek overseas markets.

Complementing the increased availability of productive resources, and continuously interacting with it, is the improved competitive position of the country on both its own and world markets. For it is the relative behavior of prices at home and abroad that determines a country's competitive standing, and the deficit country normally experiences a slowdown in the rate of price inflation. The extent to which the improved competitive position lowers imports and raises exports depends on the degree of community response to price change (or what economists call *price elasticity*). The greater the response is, the greater will be the improvement in the balance of payments that can be expected from a given reduction in relative prices. In sum, the income-price mechanism set in motion by the deficit tends to reduce the deficit.

Accompanying the expenditure mechanism is the money supply mechanism. Unless the monetary authorities act to offset or *sterilize* it, the money supply of the deficit country is reduced. That causes a decline in the rate of inflation as well as a reduction in the level of income or at least in its rate of growth. On both counts, imports decline and exports rise, thereby reversing the external deficit at least in part.

By the same token, it has been shown that surplus countries experience expansion in income and money supply and deterioration in competitive standing caused by the acceleration of price increases. Both lead to higher imports and lower exports. Thus, a surplus as well as a deficit contains in it the seeds of its own reversal. Furthermore, if the surplus and deficit countries are important trading partners, the changes occurring in them reinforce each other. Figure 13.1 presents a schematic illustration of the processes just described. In summary, *under a fixed exchange-rate regime, income and price influence the balance of payments in the same (corrective) direction.* Under a floating exchange rate the above analysis applies to the *current account.*

GOVERNMENT POLICY

The automatic income and price mechanisms interact and reinforce each other in the direction of restoring balance. Since they may be insufficient in magnitude and slow to take effect, however, they need to be further reinforced by government policy. But in a free, private-enterprise economy, the government does not have direct control over international transactions. It can influence them only indirectly. Because income and prices (and perhaps the rate of interest) are the crucial determinants of inpayments and outpayments, the government must use measures that affect income and prices and, through them, influence the balance of payments. Thus, two links must be crossed: Government policy → Income, prices → Balance of payments.

FIGURE 13.1 Automatic Processes That Reverse External Imbalance under a Fixed Exchange Rate

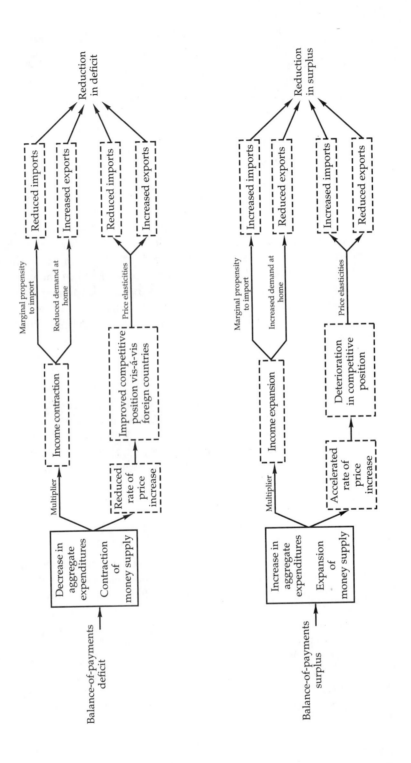

Linkages of the income-expenditures and monetary mechanisms of balance-of-payments adjustments under a fixed exchange-rate regime.

Domestic Measures and the Balance on Goods and Services

Two sets of policy instruments are available to the government to affect the level of economic activity (that is, income and prices) and through it the balance of payments. They are **monetary policies,** influencing the economy through control of the supply of money, and **fiscal policies,** influencing the economy through changes in government revenues and expenditures. Consider first the case of a deficit in the balance of payments. On the monetary side, the central bank can raise the rate of interest, thereby making borrowing more costly,[8] it can increase reserve requirements of the commercial banks, making less money available for loans; and it can sell government bonds to the public and the banks (known as open-market operations), thereby withdrawing money from the economy. These measures restrict public access to funds for spending purposes and render such funds more expensive. As spending for goods and services declines, so do production and income. And the decline spreads through the economy in a magnified fashion through the multiplier process. At the same time contractionary monetary policy reduces the rate of inflation and changes in both price and income serve to reduce the deficit on goods and services.

On the fiscal side, the treasury can raise taxes or lower government expenditures, or both, thereby withdrawing purchasing power from the public and bringing about a direct slowdown in economic activity, which spreads through the economy through the multiplier process. The decline in income is accompanied by a slowdown in the rate of price increases, and both factors work toward elimination of the deficit in the manner described in the previous sections.

This analysis explains the **conditionality** policy of the IMF. When countries experiencing external deficits wish to draw on the resources of the IMF, the Fund often insists on the adoption of contractionary monetary and/or fiscal policies (as well as other measures) by the borrowing country. This is done to ensure restoration of balance-of-payments equilibrium, so that the loan can be repaid. For example, in 1996 the IMF insisted that Russia tighten its fiscal policy, as a condition to receiving a $10 billion loan.

Precisely the opposite policies are called for in the case of a surplus. Expansion of the monetary supply and an increase in the budgetary deficit inflate the economy, with both the income and price effects leading to the removal of the surplus. Indeed, in the early 1990s Japan came under intense pressure from the United States and Europe to adopt expansionary policies in order to reduce its $100 billion annual trade surplus. And in 1993 the Japanese parliament enacted a fiscal package designed to stimulate the domestic economy and to reduce its external surpluses.

---

[8] In an open economy with international capital movements, the monetary authorities may not have full control over the rate of interest.

Such monetary and fiscal measures, designed to restore balance on the current account, are called **expenditures-changing policies,** because they remedy a deficit (surplus) by reducing (raising) aggregate expenditures. They are applicable under both a fixed *and a flexible exchange rate;* if in the latter case the government is concerned with *achieving equilibrium on the current account.*

Effect on Direct Investment Capital

There is a possibility that the equilibrating mechanism brought about by government policy may be partly offset by international movement of direct investment. Often such capital responds to relative profit opportunities at home and abroad, attracted to high-profit locations.

The expected level of profit on investment is related positively to the level of income and employment. When a surplus country experiences automatic expansion reinforced by government policy, the effect on the balance of trade is to reduce the surplus. But the expansion also attracts foreign investment, an inpayment item that increases the surplus. The converse is true of the deficit country, where domestic contraction reduces the deficit but may also encourage outflow of long-term capital (or discourage inflow), thereby aggravating the deficit. Although the strength of these influences is not known, they offset part of the equilibrating effect of domestic policies.

Effect on Other Capital Movements

Apart from direct investment, people also invest in *foreign* bonds, stock, commercial paper, bank accounts, and the like. Such funds are referred to as **portfolio capital.** A large share of it, especially the short-run variety, is sensitive to interest differentials between financial centers. If interest rates in London exceed those in New York by more than the discount on forward pounds (that is, if a covered interest differential exists), then it pays to transfer funds to London. Consequently, the British government can deal with a temporary balance-of-payments deficit by raising the rate of interest and attracting short-term capital.[9] How helpful this might be, even in the short run, depends on the sensitivity of capital movements to interest differentials. For instance, the high interest rates in the early 1980s attracted massive amounts of capital to the United States. But various empirical studies on the question have yielded mixed results, to the extent that economists have been led to reformulate their thinking on the subject. It used to be thought that barring undue disturbances in the foreign exchange markets (such as expected devaluation), the existence of a *fixed* interest differential would result in a *continuous flow* of funds until the differential was eliminated. The **portfolio approach** developed in recent years draws a different conclusion.

---

[9] This can be costly to the British government because it means higher interest payments on the internal public debt (that is, on government bonds). To avoid this cost and still achieve the same result, the government can manipulate the forward exchange market.

This approach views each financier as holding a portfolio of financial assets, the composition of which is designed to maximize the return subject to minimum risk. Foreign and domestic assets are *not* considered perfect substitutes. A major determinant of asset composition (besides the level of national income), and therefore of its distribution between domestic and foreign assets, is the constellation of interest rates prevailing on domestic and foreign money markets. This portfolio grows each year as additional assets are acquired, but these increments are very small in comparison to the total assets already in the portfolio; their distribution between foreign and domestic assets is governed by the same considerations as that of the entire portfolio and is therefore in the same proportion. For example, a New York financier may have a portfolio worth $1,000, divided equally between domestic and foreign assets, with an annual increment of $100 also equally divided between the two types of assets.

If the foreign central bank (for example, the Bank of England) raises the rate of interest, two things happen. First and foremost, the financier readjusts the portfolio to account for the fact that foreign assets now have a higher yield (assuming no increase in risk). The financier may now decide to hold $400 in domestic and $600 in foreign assets. This is the major impact, but it is a one-time rather than a continuous effect. Second, the small annual flow into new assets will also be adjusted to account for the new level of foreign interest and divided on a 40:60 percent basis. This is a continuous effect, but it is rather small. All it does is increase the annual flow into British securities by $10. These changes are summarized in the table below.

	Before Foreign-Interest Increase		After Foreign-Interest Increase	
	Domestic Assets	**Foreign Assets**	**Domestic Assets**	**Foreign Assets**
Portfolio	$500	$500	$400	$600
Annual increments	50	50	40	60

Generalizing from the behavior of this financier, we see that a rise in the interest rate has a substantial one-time effect in attracting foreign capital and only a minor continuous effect in the same direction. Empirical studies indicate that most of the portfolio adjustment occurs within one year of the change in the interest rate (or national income) that caused it, and that the annual flow effect is less than one-tenth of the one-time portfolio adjustment. Therefore, a country that wishes to continuously attract large amounts of foreign capital will have to keep raising its rate of interest to ever higher levels. A one-time increase can produce only a one-time sizable infusion of foreign capital.

But suppose a country wanted to attain just that type of infusion—for example, because its deficit was expected to be reversed within one year. How could that be accomplished with the policy tools under discussion? In other words, what are the effects of monetary and fiscal policies on the rate of interest?

Monetary contraction (assuming no fiscal change) *raises* the interest rate both because of direct action of the central bank—as it raises the discount rate and as it sells government bonds on the market, thereby depressing their price (which means higher interest)—and because of the reduction in the money *supply*. On the other hand, fiscal contraction (assuming no monetary change) brings about a reduction in aggregate expenditures (both private and public) and therefore a reduction in the *demand* for credit. Assuming that nothing is done on the monetary side to offset it, this *lowers* the price of credit—that is, the rate of interest.[10] For the country in deficit, therefore, monetary contraction helps restore balance in two ways: Exports of goods and services rise relative to imports, and there is an influx of foreign capital in response to an increase in the rate of interest. Only the first salutary effect, not the second, is present in the case of fiscal policy.

An equally important difference between them is that monetary policy does not require legislative approval, whereas under our institutional

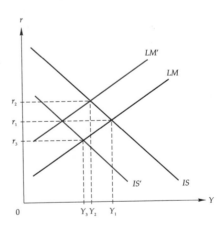

[10] This distinction can easily be understood by those readers familiar with Hicks–Hansen *IS* and *LM* functions, which determine equilibrium combinations of interest rate (*r*) and national income (*Y*). Starting from equilibrium $(Y_1 r_1)$, *monetary contraction* is shown by shifting the *LM* function to *LM'* (shown in color), leaving the *IS* curve unchanged. The effect is to lower income to Y_2, but raise the interest rate to r_2. Next we show *fiscal contraction* by shifting the *IS* function downward to *IS'* (shown in color), leaving the *LM* curve unchanged. In this case both income and interest rate are reduced, to Y_3 and r_3.

TABLE 13.1	Policies for Dealing with External Imbalance		
Economic Processes at Work		**Deficit Country**	**Surplus Country**
1.	Fiscal measures	Contraction	Expansion
2.	Monetary measures	Contraction	Expansion
3.	Implications for production, income, and employment	Contraction	Expansion
	a. Effect of 3 on trade in goods and services	Imports down, exports up	Imports up, exports down
	b. Implication of 3 for direct foreign investment	Outflow	Inflow
4.	Implication for rate of domestic price increase	Slowdown	Acceleration
	a. Effect of 4 on the country's competitive position	More competitive	Less competitive
	b. Effect of 4 on the current account balance	Imports down, exports up	Imports up, exports down
5.	Implication of 2 for interest rates	Up	Down
	a. Effect of 5 on short-term capital flows	Inflow	Outflow

arrangement fiscal measures are less flexible; on the tax side, especially, they require a long time for enactment. Consequently, many economists recommend the use of monetary policy for dealing with external imbalances while reserving fiscal measures for internal stabilization objectives.[11] Indeed, empirical investigations show that changes in the rate of interest are the measure most commonly used by industrialized countries for dealing with external imbalances.

Table 13.1 summarizes these economic processes. It is clear from lines 3a and 4b that fiscal and monetary measures bring forth an income-price mechanism that works in the direction of restoring balance to the goods-and-services account. This process is partly offset by the effect of the same mechanism on direct foreign investments, indicated by item 3b. Monetary policy has a further equilibrating effect on the balance of payments through the rate of interest and its impact on short-term capital movement, as seen in line 5a.

---

[11] Since fiscal and monetary policies are often handled by two separate government agencies (the Treasury and the Federal Reserve, respectively, in the case of the United States), each agency should be assigned a policy objective most amenable to the policy instruments under its control. The allocation of such objectives is known as the *assignment problem*.

FOREIGN REPERCUSSIONS

The analysis can be pursued further. Whenever nations are tied to each other by fixed exchange rates (such as Germany and France in the EMS), any action taken in one country affects economic conditions in the others, especially in the countries that trade heavily with the original country; and these effects reverberate back to the original country, with the changes in employment, income, and trade coming full circle (though in diminished strength).

Consider a country (country A) that for reasons of its own pursues contractionary fiscal and monetary policies. The reduction in its income lowers imports, implying reduced exports of its trading partners, countries B and C. This in turn lowers income and employment in the export industries of countries B and C, and the reduction spreads in them through the multiplier mechanism. This has the further effect of lowering their imports from A, which accentuates the reduction in its national income. Precisely the reverse process holds if country A pursues domestic expansionary measures. These effects clearly indicate that a system of fixed exchange rates links together the economic fates of countries that have close trade relations. Both depression and inflation spread from one country to the next, and no one is isolated from outside disturbances. These interrelationships hold also under a floating exchange rate system, with respect to the current account.

What are the implications of this circular mechanism? In the first place, it gives additional responsibility to the leading industrial nation, if it wishes to concern itself with the fate of others. After World War II it used to be said that when the United States sneezed, Europe caught pneumonia; in other words, Europe was so dependent on the American market for the export of goods and services that each deep recession on this side of the Atlantic brought about severe economic contraction on the other. Although this is no longer true, there are still vast areas of the world, notably Canada and Latin America, dependent on American prosperity for the maintenance of a high level of exports and therefore national income.

Between 1983 and 1989 the U.S. economy staged a robust recovery from the 1981–1982 recession. That, along with an overvalued dollar between 1982 and 1985, led to massive trade deficits in the United States. But the increased exports of other countries (the counterpart of U.S. imports) helped alleviate the recessionary conditions prevailing there. The United States served as a **locomotive country,** pulling other economies upward. Again in the mid-1990s, following a slowdown in the entire industrial world, only the United States emerged from the recession to perform the "locomotive" function.

The second implication is that, to properly calculate the foreign trade multiplier effect of any policy, one must allow for **foreign repercussions** as they complete the circuit and affect the country in which the policy originated. Recall that the foreign trade multiplier was developed by using an example of a country experiencing an autonomous expansion of exports. If it is in a *large and important* country, that increase necessarily implies a significant and autonomous rise in imports of its trading partners. The resulting decline in the income of trading partners lowers their induced imports from the home country, curtailing its exports and reducing the size of the calculated foreign trade multiplier. The foreign repercussions can be shown schematically for a two-country world, where country A experiences an autonomous increase in its exports to country B:

Country A	Country B
+ X	+ M
+ Y	– Y
+ M	– M
– X	+ X
– Y	+ Y
– M	+ M
+ X	– X
+ Y	– Y
.	.
.	.

These foreign repercussions diminish in strength as we move down the columns. Nevertheless, they dampen the effect of the original autonomous increase in exports of country A. The multiplier formula given earlier ignores these repercussions and to that extent is applicable only to small countries. For a large country, the multiplier is smaller, since a term representing the foreign repercussions is added to the denominator. Its derivation is given in appendix 13–2.

A third implication of the interdependence under fixed exchange rates is that *no country is completely free to pursue independent domestic policies;* all countries are subject to outside discipline exercised through the balance of payments. When a country gets out of line, a crisis can easily result. Thus, in 1982 French and Italian domestic expansionary policies weakened the franc and the lira within the EMS and led to their devaluation in June of that year.

Under a system of fixed exchange rates, countries are linked to each other by the exchange rates, but governments may decide to pursue policies that are independent of other countries while at the same time trying to preserve the freedom of private citizens to trade and speculate. These three features of the system are not compatible and they need not lead to one harmonious whole. It is impossible to be completely linked, yet completely independent, at the same time, all the time. To put it differently, a combination of fixed exchange rates, free capital movements, and imperfect harmonization of national economic policies that affect incomes, prices, and interest rates cannot work well. When these features clash, a crisis results, spreading from the country that triggered it to other countries. "International financial crises" are the periodic adjustments of the system to these conflicting forces. It was this kind of clash that produced recurrent crises between 1967 and 1973 and finally led to the demise of the Bretton Woods system of pegged exchange rates in March of 1973. Such a clash also led to the fracture of the EMS in August 1993.

A degree of interdependence exists even under fluctuating exchange rates. In various periods during the 1980s, the United States pursued a policy of fiscal expansion and monetary tightness. As a result, U.S. interest rates, and especially the real rates (nominal interest minus the expected rate of inflation) rose, attracting massive amounts of foreign capital to the United States (and raising the exchange value of the dollar). That forced other industrial countries to raise their interest rates in order to forestall some of the capital outflow, thus hampering their ability to reflate their economies. When U.S. interest rates declined, foreign rates followed the same downward trend. Conversely, in 1986 the European and Japanese central banks reduced their interest rates in order to enable the Federal Reserve to lower U.S. rates without fear of large-scale withdrawal of capital. This episode represented an attempt to coordinate a reduction in interest rates among the main industrial countries.

It should not be concluded from all this that an integrated capital market is a bad phenomenon. In fact, it is far superior to a system beset by an assortment of controls over international capital movements. What the foregoing examples show is that a high degree of interdependence calls for regular policy coordination among central bankers. "We are all in this together," one might say, and the economic navigators of nations, especially of small open economies, must take account of outside constraints in formulating their policies.

With this short but important digression completed, let us return to the vantage point of the individual country.

THE BALANCE OF PAYMENTS IN THE CONTEXT OF GENERAL POLICY OBJECTIVES

Since every economic measure taken by the government affects both the balance of payments and domestic conditions, economists need to concern themselves with the entire situation. If a country suffering from a balance-of-payments deficit happens to be subject to domestic inflationary pressures at the same time, it is in a relatively fortunate situation, because the domestic remedies required to cure the domestic inflation are also those needed to

TABLE 13.2   *Combinations of Economic Conditions and Policy Requirements*

Internal Conditions	Domestic Policy Response	Balance of Payments	Domestic Policy Response	Nature of Situation
Unemployment	Expansion	Surplus	Expansion	Consistent
Inflation	Contraction	Deficit	Contraction	Consistent
Unemployment	Expansion	Deficit	Contraction	Inconsistent
Inflation	Contraction	Surplus	Expansion	Inconsistent

cope with the external deficit. In both cases contractionary fiscal and monetary policies are called for, resulting in a **consistent** situation, such as that confronted by the United States in the late 1960s.

Similarly, when a country experiences simultaneously a domestic recession and a balance-of-payments surplus (as Germany and Japan did in 1977), it is in a consistent situation, because both predicaments call for expansionary policies. On the monetary side, the central bank should lower the rate of interest, lower the reserve requirements to which commercial banks are subject, and purchase government bonds on the open market. On the fiscal side, the government should curtail taxes or raise expenditures (or both), pumping purchasing power into the economy. The resulting increases in income and prices have the effect of increasing imports and lowering exports, thereby eliminating the balance-of-payments surplus. Thus, the same set of policies can be used to deal with both internal and external problems.

But a country can also find itself in an **inconsistent** combination of circumstances. It may have a balance-of-payments deficit and domestic unemployment at the same time, or a balance-of-payments surplus along with domestic inflation. In the first case the deficit calls for contractionary policies but the unemployment necessitates expansionary measures. In the second case the surplus requires internal expansion but the inflation necessitates domestic contraction. Table 13.2 clarifies the four combinations.

While the first two situations can be handled by proper domestic policies, the second two are problematical. Thus, the United States in the early 1960s was plagued by a combination of unemployment and deficit. On the other hand, in the early 1970s both West Germany and Japan confronted a combination of an external surplus and an inflationary boom.

In an open economy countries have two policy objectives: *internal balance*, which includes full employment and price stability; and *external balance*, which usually means a balance on the current account. A small external deficit is sustainable if it does not lead to an unmanageable foreign debt position, and if the associated inflow of capital is channeled into productive investment so that the debt can be repaid in the future. Likewise, a small external surplus is sustainable if it does not cause foreign countries to be in an unmanageable foreign debt position so that they can't repay their obligations (and the country would lose part of its wealth), and if policy makers are willing to allow savings to be invested abroad rather than at home. Thus the size of the current account imbalance is usually a policy target even under a floating exchange rate.

However, at no time should the balance-of-payments objective be viewed in isolation. There is no such thing as a single, isolated policy goal. At any given time, the government has several targets relating to the domestic and external performance of the economy. These goals may include full employment, high growth rate, price stability, external balance, and the like. The government also has an arsenal of policy instruments, including monetary, fiscal, exchange rate, and other policies. Application of each instrument would have different effects on each of the policy goals. Rational policy makers would view the situation in its totality and select a proper mix of instruments to deal with their set of targets. The greater the number of policy objectives (or targets) and the larger the potential conflict between them, the larger the number of instruments that must be employed to meet these objectives.

Let us return to the inconsistent positions described in table 13.2. Assume that a country is faced with unemployment and a deficit at the same time. A temporary remedy can be found in a proper combination of domestic measures. Remember that monetary contraction has a dual effect on the balance of payments: It not only improves the current account balance, but attracts short-term capital from abroad by raising the interest rate. Suppose the government combines a policy of monetary contraction and fiscal expansion. Depending on the relative size of the doses applied, the fiscal measure can more than offset its monetary counterpart in its effect on the domestic economy. We thereby obtain a net expansion, desirable for internal purposes but which increases the current account deficit. On the other hand, the increase in the rate of interest embodied in the monetary contraction attracts funds from abroad, more than offsetting the adverse impact on the current account position. This combination of measures is particularly attractive if the country has a current account surplus less than its capital outflow, yielding (under full employment) a total external deficit—a situation typical of the United States in the early 1960s. A precisely reverse combination of measures can be pursued in the case of inflation coupled with surplus, especially when the surplus is a result of a current account deficit smaller than the capital inflow.

But with the policy combinations described above, the authorities can deal only with temporary conditions of deficit and unemployment. If the causes of the inconsistent situation are deeply rooted, such domestic measures are unlikely to constitute a sufficient remedy because they do not contain a mechanism to realign the country's prices (under full employment) with those of the rest of the world. The action called for is exchange-rate adjustment, to be addressed in the next chapter.

SOME UNANSWERED QUESTIONS

Apart from the difficulty of resolving conflicts between objectives, most of what has been said so far has revolved around one main topic: the *direction* in which the economy moves as a result of the application of various policies. But the direction of change is not a sufficient guide for policy making. Two other interrelated pieces of information are essential. First, we must know how strong a force is exerted on the economy by each policy measure. This in turn determines how far in the direction of the target the economy moves in response to the policy measure—or, put differently, how great an application of each instrument is required to reach the target. Second, we need to know how long it takes for the full impact of the various instruments to be felt throughout the economy and what sort of time path the economy follows in its movement toward the target position. The second point enables public officials to know roughly what to expect at various intervals after the policy button has been pressed.

The Degree of Impact

Consider the internal measures designed to eliminate a balance-of-payments deficit. On the fiscal side the initial instrument at the disposal of the authorities is a reduction in government expenditures or an increase in taxes, or both. Such action lowers the income and the rate of inflation, which in turn lower imports and raise exports. A key concern of each of these phases is its **degree of impact.**

All that the government can control is the initial fiscal action. That step is *exogenous* to the economy in the sense that it is arbitrarily determined at a political level outside the economy. Once the action is taken the government has no further control over the final outcome, unless it wishes to take some other deliberate steps, such as a mid-course correction. The initial action sets in motion a sequence of interrelated economic processes, each depending on other economic magnitudes and therefore considered *endogenous* or internal to the economy.

In the case of a reduction in government expenditures, the following sequence of questions can be articulated:

1. By how much does gross domestic product decline for a given cut in government expenditures? The answer depends on the size of the multiplier (which is measurable), and on possible reduction in interest rates, which has the opposite effect of stimulating the economy and offsetting part of the contraction.

2. What proportion of the total reduction in gross domestic product is translated into lower imports and higher exports? Again, these have measurable magnitudes, especially the marginal propensity to import.

3. Will there be an "unfavorable" side effect to the economic contraction as long-term capital is encouraged to seek more profitable investment opportunities abroad? If so, how significant is it?
4. To what extent does the reduction in the level of economic activity force producers to curtail the rate of price increases?
5. To what extent do lower prices stimulate exports and discourage imports? This depends on various price elasticities.
6. Will the reduction in interest rates result in significant outflow of short-term capital?

Similar questions can be asked with respect to an increase in taxes or, if the country wishes to eliminate a balance-of-payments surplus, with respect to an increase in government spending and a reduction in taxes.

When it comes to monetary policy, the main instrument in the hands of the central bank is control over the money supply. In the case of an external deficit, the money supply would be contracted and interest rates would be raised. Once administered, the policy must operate through processes internal to the economy and must push the economy toward the preassigned target. Whether it will actually get there depends on the answers to the following questions:

1. To what extent does a contraction in the money supply lower the level of economic activity and slow the rate of inflation? The U.S. experience in 1981–1982 demonstrated that a combination of fiscal expansion and monetary tightness had a powerful effect both in reducing the rate of inflation and in causing a deep recession. The subsequent reversal of monetary policy produced a recovery in 1983–89.
2. By how much do a given economic contraction and price reduction discourage imports and encourage exports?
3. To what extent does an outflow of long-term investment capital occur as an unfavorable side effect to the economic contraction?
4. How sensitive is short-term capital to interest differentials between financial centers, and therefore how strongly is it attracted to the deficit country when its interest rates rise?

Answering these questions is no mean task. At any given moment a multitude of forces is operating on the economy, and it is necessary to isolate the effect of the policy under investigation. In order to find out the effect of a policy, we need to compare situations with and without the policy, all other things assumed to remain unchanged. It is the validity of this *ceteris paribus* assumption that laypeople often question when they read the writings of economists. How can it be valid if the economy is always in a state of change? The answer is that all other changes take place in the presence or in the absence of the policy under investigation. And making the assumption "other things being equal" is equivalent to comparing the situation with and without the policy. In the physical sciences this is accomplished by controlled laboratory experiments. Since this is not possible in economics, we must use theoretical abstractions and statistical techniques to achieve the same objective.

This is the role of model building in the social sciences. It is often necessary to build a simplified model of the whole economy in order to draw inferences concerning the size of the parameters being estimated. Model construction means the mathematical formulation of the relationships between various economic variables in a manner that lends itself to statistical estimation. The branch of economics concerned with such studies is econometrics. Thanks in no small measure to improved estimation techniques, policy makers today have at least a rough idea of the magnitudes of the variables involved. The following are some examples drawn from an econometric study pertaining to the two decades of floating exchange rates.[12] For U.S. trade:

- A one-percent increase in U.S. real GDP increases U.S. import volume by 1.7 percent. This income elasticity of import demand has risen from one decade to the next, indicating an *increased openness of the American economy.*
- A one-percent increase in the rest of the world's GDP raises U.S. exports by 1.3 percent. The so-called "income-asymmetry" notes that the United States has a relatively higher income elasticity of demand for imports as compared to the corresponding income elasticity of demand by foreigners for U.S. exports. Thus *similar growth rates in the United States and abroad tend to worsen the U.S. current account balance.*
- A one-percent decline in the import price index relative to the domestic wholesale price index increases imports by 1.2 percent. Most of that effect takes place two quarters following the change.
- A one-percent decline in the competitors' prices reduces U.S. exports by 0.9 percent.

Similar information is available for other industrial countries.

---

[12] D. Warner and M. Kreinin, "Determinants of International Trade Flows," *Review of Economics and Statistics,* February 1983. For a summary of other estimates see P. Hooper and J. Marquez, "Exchange Rates, Prices, and External Adjustment in the U.S. and Japan," Federal Reserve Board, *International Finance Discussion Papers,* no. 456, October 1993.

Time Lags

The second crucial question concerns the timing of policy and the time path followed by the economy as it moves toward the target position. It certainly makes a great deal of difference whether a policy instrument attains its objective in one year or five years, if for no other reason than because many things can happen in the longer time span to change the course of the economy.

There are two **time lags** common to practically all policies that are external to the economy: the lag between the need for action as reflected in the economic conditions and the recognition of that need by the policy maker, and the lag between the recognition and the point when economic action is initiated. Economists and statisticians can help reduce the recognition lag by speeding up the collection and evaluation of data about the state of the economy and the dissemination of the analytical conclusions and their policy implications. The second lag results from administrative delays and at times from the need for legislative action, as in the case of tax-rate changes.

Next in sequence come the endogenous lags—those that depend on the working process of the economic system itself. Two questions are relevant here: How long does it take for a certain fiscal or monetary action to work its way through the economy before its full impact is realized in terms of changes in gross domestic product and the price level? And how long is it before the effect of income and price changes on the balance of payments is manifested in whole or in part? These questions call for dynamic studies, based on quarterly data, that specify the time path followed by the economy as it adjusts gradually to the shock of new policy.

Summary

This chapter addresses those domestic policies designed to restore equilibrium to the balance of payments under a fixed exchange rate regime. Much of the analysis applies to the current account under a regime of flexible rates. If a seasonal or short-run disequilibrium develops, then stabilizing capital movements would redress the imbalance as long as financial markets have full confidence in the ability of the government to maintain the exchange rate. They are generated by interest-rate differentials and expectations for future movements in the exchange rate.

If the imbalance is more permanent in nature, there are two automatic processes that redress it in part: the income-expenditures mechanism and the money supply–price mechanism. An autonomous decline in exports causes an initial trade deficit. But that decline means a reduction in output and therefore income, which is magnified by the multiplier effect. That in turn reduces imports, and partly remedies the deficit. At the same time, the deficit means that outpayments exceed inpayments, so that the money supply shrinks. That reduces the rate of domestic inflation and makes the country more competitive. Again the effect is to reduce the size of the deficit. Precisely the reverse process takes place in case of a surplus caused by a rise in exports or a decline in imports. Output and income rise through the multiplier process, thereby increasing imports. Money supply expands so that inflation accelerates, making the country less competitive. Both factors serve to lower the surplus. But these effects are insufficient to eliminate the imbalance altogether unless the MPS equals zero. They rectify the imbalance only in part.

A rise in *domestic* spending—through domestic investment or government expenditures—also has a multiplied effect on output and income. But because no external surplus occurs initially, the sole external effect is to increase imports and cause a trade deficit. Indeed, the expectation of such a deficit can serve as a *disciplinary measure against excessive expansion of domestic spending*. By the same token, a reduction in domestic spending would lower output and income and hence imports, thereby producing a trade surplus.

In all cases of external imbalance the automatic mechanisms provide only partial remedies. They must be reinforced by government policies. In case of a deficit, the government needs to pursue contractionary fiscal and monetary measures. That reduces output and income and lowers imports, thereby improving the trade balance. A surplus calls for expansionary policies, which would expand output and income and increase imports. The trade balance, and hence the current account, deteriorate. Identical policy prescriptions are indicated in case of a country on a flexible exchange rate if its government is concerned with the current account (as most governments are), and wishes to maintain equilibrium on goods and services.

While the current account moves in the desired direction in response to the above policies, only monetary—not fiscal—policy induces inward flow of capital in case of a deficit and outward flow in case of a surplus. Monetary policy affects both the current and the capital accounts in a desired direction. But under the portfolio approach, its effect on capital movements is limited.

A large country needs to be concerned with foreign repercussions. If it pursues contractionary (expansionary) policies and develops a surplus (deficit) on the current account, its trading partners develop deficits (surpluses). These changes have the following implications: A major country can act as the world "locomotive," for by expanding at home it can raise output in other countries for which it is a major market. On the other hand, if a major country experiences a recession, other economies may stagnate. Also, the foreign trade multiplier of a large country is smaller than the formula in the text once foreign repercussions are taken into account. And finally, a system of fixed exchange rates and free capital movements requires coordination of domestic policies between countries. Otherwise it breaks down, as evidenced by Bretton Woods in 1973 and the EMS in 1993.

A country facing domestic unemployment and an external surplus requires expansionary policies on both counts, while a country facing inflation and a deficit needs contractionary policies on both counts. These are *consistent* situations. But a combination of domestic unemployment and an external deficit is more troublesome, as it requires expansion and contraction policies respectively. Likewise, a combination of inflation and surplus requires conflicting policies of contraction and expansion. These are called *inconsistent* situations. The only remedy in these cases involves changing the exchange rate, a policy described in the next chapter.

Apart from the direction of change, described in the foregoing analysis, a policy maker also needs to know the degree of impact of each policy on the economy and the lag between the time a policy is applied and its effects are felt throughout the economy.

Important Concepts

Stabilizing capital flows	Fiscal policy
Destabilizing capital flows	IMF conditionality
Marginal propensity to consume	Expenditures-changing policies
Marginal propensity to save	Portfolio capital
Marginal propensity to import	Portfolio approach
Multiplier	Locomotive country
Foreign trade multiplier	Foreign repercussions
Specie-flow mechanism	Consistent policy
Velocity (*V*)	Inconsistent policy
Demand elasticity	Degree of impact
Automatic adjustment mechanism	Time lags
Monetary policy	

Review Questions

1. a. Suppose that the Belgian government increased its annual domestic spending by 10 billion Belgian francs. Assuming that the MPS = $\frac{1}{4}$ and the MPM = $\frac{1}{4}$, compute the effect of that act on GDP, *C*, *S*, *M*, and the balance of trade (compute the changes in the above magnitudes).

b. What would be the effects on the above variables had Belgium experienced a rise in exports of 10 billion Belgian francs? Assume that Belgium trades only with members of the EMS where exchange rates are fixed.

c. Trace the effects of each of the above developments on the other members of the EMS combined.

2. Summarize the automatic mechanisms (expenditures and money) of the balance of payments (B. of P.) adjustment under a fixed exchange rate.

3. Prove that when the MPS = 0 the expenditure mechanism ensures full adjustment in the B. of P.

4. a. In 1983 Mexico faced a combination of external deficit and internal unemployment (under a fixed exchange rate regime). Does this represent a consistent or an inconsistent situation? Why? Can it be handled by domestic policies? Why or why not?

b. What about a combination of external surplus and inflation?

5. In 1993 the United States was urging Japan to reduce taxes and increase its budgetary deficit in an effort to reduce its external trade surplus. How would such a domestic policy affect Japan's trade position?

6. How do (a) fiscal policy and (b) monetary policy affect domestic interest rates? How do interest rates affect capital flows under the Keynesian and portfolio approaches?

7. You are given the following information:

	ΔX	MPM	MPS	k	ΔY	ΔM	ΔS	ΔC	ΔBalance of Trade
a.	-1000	0.2	0.3						
b.	-1000	0.2	0.2						
c.	-1000	0.2	0.1						
d.	-1000	0.2	0.0						

Calculate the missing columns in each row.

8. Define *expenditure changing policies.*

9. Assume that the Canadian dollar is pegged to the U.S. dollar. A Canadian news report in 1986 expressed concern over a possible future slowdown in U.S. economic activity and its impact on the Canadian economy.

a. By what mechanism would such a slowdown affect Canada, and how? In your answer incorporate graphs and formulas as necessary (see also appendix 13–1).

b. Suppose U.S. imports from Canada decline by 100. Assume that Canada's MPS = $\frac{1}{8}$ and its MPM = $\frac{1}{8}$. By how much precisely would Canada's *income* (GDP), *imports, consumption,* and *savings* be affected (and in which direction)? Show your work, and explain.

c. What would happen to Canada's balance of trade?

10. You are given the following information for a certain (private) economy: MPC = 0.5; MPS = 0.2; MPM = ? As a result of currency depreciation its exports rose by 100. Compute the effect of that increase on GDP, *C, S, M,* and the trade balance.

11. In a 1985 article, *The Wall Street Journal* suggested that the European recovery, rather than being internally generated, was largely induced by the U.S. recovery (the United States was the *locomotive*).

a. Explain how U.S. recovery can stimulate European recovery.

b. What would happen in case of a U.S. economic slowdown?

Chapter 13 Appendix 13–1

THE FOREIGN TRADE MULTIPLIER IN A SMALL COUNTRY

The National Income Accounts

It was stated in Chapter 10 that net exports of goods and services (namely, exports minus imports) constitute the link between the national income and the international transactions accounts. Net exports constitute one of the four expenditure components of GDP: $C + I + G + (X - M)$. For the sake of simplicity, our example describes an economy in which there is only a private sector and no government, so that: GDP = $C + I + (X - M)$. *If imports were netted out of consumption and investment, so that C and I refer only to domestically pro-* duced consumption and investment goods, they must also be subtracted from $(X - M)$, and the expenditures side of the accounts becomes: GDP = $C + I + X$. Over any given time period, output produced (GDP) equals income (Y) generated in the production process; and that income can be spent on domestic consumption, on imported goods and services, or it can be saved: GDP = $Y = C + S + M$. Consequently

$$C + I + X = C + S + M; \text{ or } I + X = S + M \quad (1)$$

An alternative formulation of this identity is:

$$S = I + (X - M) \quad (2)$$

	GDP (Y) (1)	Imports (M) (2)	AMP (M/Y) (3)	ΔY (4)	ΔM (5)	MPM ($\Delta M/\Delta Y$) (6)
(A)	90	0	0			
(B)	140	5	0.03	50	5	0.1
(C)	190	10	0.05	50	5	0.1
(D)	240	15	0.06	50	5	0.1

TABLE A13–1.1   *A Hypothetical Import Schedule (Billion Dollars)*

If we think of the external surplus $(X - M)$ as representing accumulation of foreign assets and label it net foreign investments (NFI), then equation (1) is the savings-investment identity, with I extended to include NFI. In other words, domestic savings can either be invested domestically or used to acquire foreign assets through capital outflow. In both cases the country uses current savings to build up its capital stock and increase its future income.

A Graphical Representation

Equation (1), $I + X = S + M$, is developed geometrically in figure A13–1.4. Recall from the principles of macroeconomics that savings varies positively with output or income. Hence the savings function, which shows real income or output on the horizontal axis and savings on the vertical axis, has a positive slope (slopes upward and to the right). Its slope equals the marginal propensity to save, which is constant along a linear savings function. The investment function, which shows domestic investment along the vertical axis and real output along the horizontal axis, is horizontal. This reflects the fact that current investment is *not* dependent on current output. The import function exhibits similar properties to the savings function, while the export function is similar to the investment function.

Total Injection and Leakage Functions

The Import Function   With prices and interest rates assumed to be constant, imports—like savings—vary positively with income: The higher the income, the more goods and services people are able and willing to import. An example of this relationship is shown in the first two columns of table A13–1.1. As income rises, so do imports. This relationship is represented graphically in the import-income space of figure A13–1.1. (The figures were deliberately selected so as to generate a straight line in the graph.) Points A, B, C, D in the graph correspond to those rows in table A13–1.1. Each level of output or income measured on the horizontal axis corresponds to a unique level of imports measured on the vertical axis. Moving up *along* the import function shows that imports increase as income rises.

Two concepts are associated with the import function: (1) The *average* propensity to import (APM) is the portion of income spent on imports: APM = M/Y. It is computed in column 3 of table A13–1.1 and is shown to increase with income for a straight-line import function. (2) The *marginal* propensity to import (MPM) is the portion of an *increase* (decrease) in income translated into an *increase* (decrease) in imports: MPM = $\Delta M/\Delta Y$, where Δ (delta) denotes change. Computed in columns 4, 5, 6 of table A13–1.1, it is constant (at 0.1) for a straight-line import

FIGURE A13–1.1   *A Hypothetical Import Function Based on Table A13–1.1*

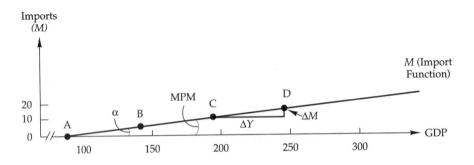

The volume of imports rises with the rise in real GDP. Slope of the function is the marginal propensity to import.

function.[1] The diagrammatic expression for the MPM is obtained by selecting the change in income between two points, such as C and D, and relating it to the corresponding change in imports. For a straight-line import function, the ratio $\Delta M/\Delta Y$ is *constant* through the function; *it is equal to the slope of the import function* in figure A13–1.1.

In an open economy, income (Y) can be spent on consumption of domestic goods (C), on imports (M), or it can be saved (S). Consequently,

$$APC + APS + APM = 1$$

Since any addition to (or deletion from) income can also be channeled in the same three ways,

$$MPC + MPS + MPM = 1$$

While moving along the import schedule shows how a change in income affects imports, there exist other influences on imports. These are represented by a shift in the entire import function. For example, suppose for some reason the price of domestic products becomes *less competitive* with imports (that is, it rises relative to foreign prices). Then at each level of income more will be imported than before, and the entire import function will shift upward. On the other hand, if consumer taste shifts away from imports and toward domestic products, then at each level of income less will be imported than before, and the entire import function will shift downward.

The Export Function U.S. exports are rest-of-the-world imports. With constant prices, their size depends on income in the rest of the world

---

[1]Another frequently used concept is the income elasticity of demand for imports, η_Y. It differs from the MPM in that it represents a ratio of *percentages*:

$$\eta_Y = \frac{\text{Percentage change in imports}}{\text{Percentage change in income}} = \frac{\Delta M/M}{\Delta Y/Y} = \frac{\Delta M/\Delta Y}{M/Y} = \frac{MPM}{APM}$$

FIGURE A13–1.2   *A Hypothetical Export Function*

Exports are not affected by changes in real GDP. But exports affect real GDP.

(that is, the importing countries); *it does not depend on U.S. income.* The export function plotted in the U.S. export-income space is shown as a straight line in figure A13–1.2: Regardless of income, exports are the same, assumed here to be 15. It is important to recognize that the statement "exports are invariant with respect to income" means that income does not affect exports. But the reverse is *not true:* As in the case of investment, a change in exports does affect income and in the same direction.

The Total Injection and Total Leakage Functions
Since exports must come out of domestic production, they constitute an injection into the income stream, along with investment. Imports, on the other hand, constitute a leakage out of the income stream, along with savings. It is now possible to combine the two injection functions (investment and exports) on the one hand and the two leakage functions (savings and imports) on the other. This is done in figure A13–1.3. The top two left panels show the investment and export functions separately. Then, in the bottom panel, exports are superimposed upon investment to obtain the $(I + X)$ or total injection function, shown in color. It shows the size of

investment plus exports at each level of GDP. The straight horizontal colored line reflects the notion that $(I + X)$ is invariant to the country's own GDP: Regardless of the GDP, the $(I + X)$ is the same. $(I + X)$ is not influenced by GDP, but the reverse is not the case: GDP is profoundly affected by $(I + X)$.

A similar procedure is followed in the three right panels with respect to the total leakage, or $(S + M)$, function. The two top panels present the savings and imports schedules separately. At each level of income, the functions show, respectively, the amount saved and the amount spent on imports. Two features are introduced for the sake of simplicity (but without loss of generality): The schedules are drawn as straight lines; and the level of GDP (or income) at which savings are zero is the same as that at which imports are zero: OY_1.

In the bottom panel, the import function is superimposed upon the savings function to obtain the total leakage or the $(S + M)$ function, drawn in color. This is done as follows: First, reproduce the savings function. Then at each level of income, add *vertically* the amount of imports (from the middle panel) *above* the amount of savings. Because the functions are

FIGURE A13–1.3   *Derivation of Total Injection and Total Leakage Functions*

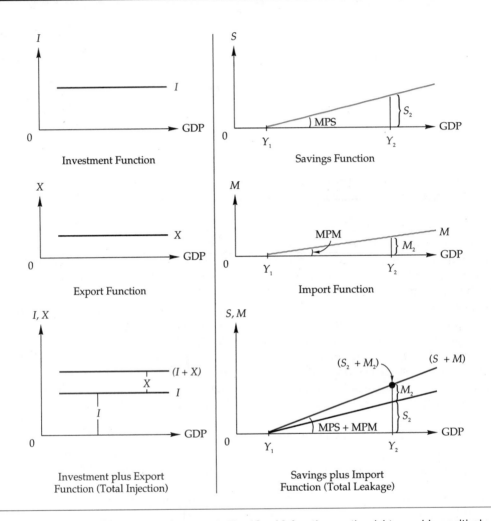

The $(I + X)$ function on the left panel is horizontal. The $(S + M)$ function on the right panel is positively sloped, and its slope equals the $(MPS + MPM)$.

Note: This analysis is restricted to the private sector. Addition of government would add government expenditures (G) to the injection side and taxes (T) to the leakage side.

linear, only two points are needed to construct the entire line. At income or output OY_1, both savings and imports are zero, so that their sum is zero. At income or output OY_2 segment S_2 represents savings and segment M_2 represents imports. Their sum is $(S_2 + M_2)$, with M_2 superimposed vertically upon S_2. Connecting the two points yields the $(S + M)$ function.

FIGURE A13–1.4   Equilibrium Output (Y_E) Occurs Where $(S + M) = (I + X)$; Capital-Exporting Country (such as Japan)

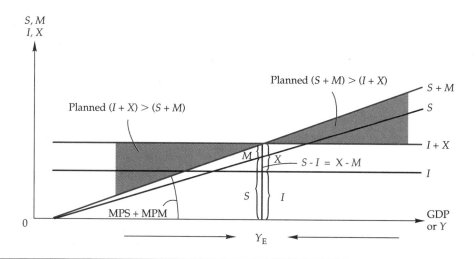

Equilibrium output is shown where $X > M$ and correspondingly where $S > I$ (by the same amount).

At each level of GDP or income, measured on the horizontal axis, the color $(S + M)$ function shows the amount of savings plus imports, measured on the vertical axis. The slopes of the savings and import functions are respectively the MPS and MPM. Consequently, *the slope of the $(S + M)$ function equals the MPS + MPM.*

Equilibrium Output As shown in equation (1), equilibrium output is the level at which $(I + X) = (S + M)$ (where all functions are in the "intended" sense). In portraying it diagrammatically, it is necessary to combine the two bottom panels—the total injection and total leakage functions—of figure A13–1.3. This is done in figure A13–1.4, where the two functions are drawn in color. Equilibrium output or income (Y_E) occurs at the intersection of $(S + M)$ and $(I + X)$. At all output levels higher than (to the right of) Y_E, $(S + M) > (I + X)$, leading to unintended accumulation of inventories; the

economy contracts. At income levels lower than (to the left of) Y_E, $(I + X) > (S + M)$, leading to unintended depletion of inventories; the economy expands. Given the four schedules, only Y_E, represents equilibrium output or income, a level which is sustainable.

There is nothing desirable or undesirable about Y_E. It is merely the level of output that is sustainable. If full employment output exceeds the equilibrium output, the difference between them is GDP gap of the inadequate aggregate demand variety and represents unused capacity and unemployment. It is often referred to as *underemployment equilibrium*. Conversely, if $Y_E > Y_{FE}$, the difference between them is a GDP gap of the excessive aggregate demand variety and represents an increase in the average price level.

The equilibrium depicted in figure A13–1.4 is characteristic of a *capital-exporting country* such as Japan; we saw in Chapter 10

FIGURE A13–1.5	*A Capital-Importing Country (such as the United States): I > S and M > X; (I – S) = (M – X)*

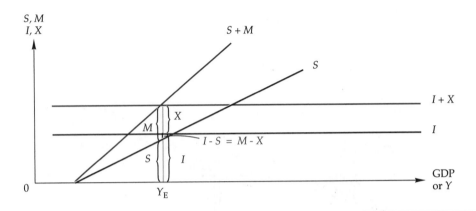

Equilibrium output is shown where $M > X$ and correspondingly where $I > S$ (by the same amount).

that such a country typically has an export surplus. It now appears that the export surplus is embedded in the domestic economy; it equals the excess of savings over domestic investment: $S - I = X - M$. Conversely, in a capital-importing country, such as the United States, imports exceed exports by the excess of domestic investment over savings. We might say that the foreign country's savings are channeled into investment projects in the capital-importing country by means of an excess of imports over exports as shown in figure A13–1.5. Finally, if $S = I$, then $X = M$, resulting in balanced goods and services.

Any of the four functions can shift in its entirety, changing the equilibrium. For analytical purposes—and based on much empirical evidence—the savings and imports functions, and therefore the $(S + M)$ function, are considered relatively stable. By contrast, the investment and/or export schedules are more volatile, subject to frequent gyrations. If either of them shifts, then the $(I + X)$ func-

tion shifts in the same direction and by the same amount.

The Multiplier Formula

To derive the formula for the foreign trade multiplier, we reproduce in figure A13–1.6 the $(S + M)$ and $(I + X)$ functions of figure A13–1.4. The initial investment and exports are presented as $(I + X)_1$ generating equilibriium output $0Y_1$. Either investment or exports increase so that the $(I + X)$ function rises to level $(I + X)_2$, drawn in color, yielding a new, higher, equilibrium output $0Y_2$. And at that new GDP higher levels of savings and imports are generated to equal the new $(I + X)_2$. Only the initial and final equilibria, and not the spending-income process in between, are shown on the diagram. Because at each of the two income levels $(I + X) = (S + M)$, it follows that the changes in the two magnitudes are equal: $\Delta(I + X) = \Delta(S + M)$. This is indicated on the diagram.

Geometrically, the ratio $\Delta(S + M)/\Delta Y$ equals the slope of the $(S + M)$ function, which

FIGURE A13–1.6   *Effect on GDP of an Increase in (I + X)*

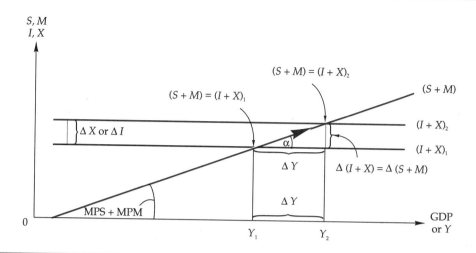

When (*I* + *X*) rises from level 1 to level 2, real GDP rises by a multiple of this amount, the multiplier being the inverse of the slope of the (*S* + *M*) function.

in turn equals (MPS + MPM). The multiplier is $\Delta Y / \Delta (I + X)$ or the inverse of that ratio. Consequently, the foreign trade multiplier, k, is:

$$k = \Delta Y / \Delta I \quad \text{or}$$

$$\Delta Y / \Delta X = \frac{1}{\text{MPS} + \text{MPM}} = \frac{1}{\text{leakage}} = \frac{1}{1 - \text{MPC}}$$

Conceptually, the formula for the multiplier is expanded to incorporate the newly added leakage into imports:

$$k = \frac{1}{\text{MPS} + \text{MPM}} \qquad (3)$$

To illustrate the use of the formula, assume that the marginal propensities prevailing in the

economy are: MPC = 0.6 and MPS = 0.3, so that MPM = 0.1, with all three adding up to 1. Then the foreign trade multiplier is:

$$k = \frac{1}{0.3 + 0.1} \quad \text{or} \quad \frac{1}{1 - 0.6} = \frac{1}{0.4} = 2.5$$

A rise (decline) in investment *or* in exports of $10 will increase (lower) output by $25 (10 × 2.5). In turn, consumption, savings, and imports will rise (decline) by:

$$\Delta C = \Delta Y \times \text{MPC} = 25 \times 0.6 = \$15$$
$$\Delta S = \Delta Y \times \text{MPS} = 25 \times 0.3 = \$ 7.5$$
$$\Delta M = \Delta Y \times \text{MPM} = 25 \times 0.1 = \$ 2.5$$
$$\text{and } \Delta C + \Delta S + \Delta M = \$25 = \Delta Y$$
$$\Delta S + \Delta M = \$10 = \Delta I \text{ or } \Delta X$$

Chapter 13 Appendix 13–2

FOREIGN-TRADE MULTIPLIER WITH FOREIGN REPERCUSSIONS

Consider a two-country world in which country A and country B trade with each other. (In all notations, then, subscripts A and B denote country.) Any change in exports or imports of one country necessarily constitutes an equivalent change in imports or exports of the other. Each country's total income or production (Y) consists of consumption (C), investment (I), government purchase (G) of goods and services, and exports (X) (all of goods and services that are produced domestically). Changes in national income, brought about by any autonomous change in expenditures, consist of changes in these four expenditure components:

$$\Delta Y = \Delta C + \Delta I + \Delta G + \Delta X \qquad (1)$$

For simplicity, assume that I and G are strictly autonomous. While a change in them generates changes in income, the reverse is not true; changes in Y do not induce changes in I or G. On the other hand, consumption and imports (that is, exports of the other country) have both autonomous and induced components. All autonomous changes in expenditures, from whatever source (investment, government expenditures, or the autonomous part of consumption) will be lumped under the term *exogenous shock* and labeled Z. They are not affected by income changes.

By contrast, changes in income do induce changes in consumption, savings, and imports, the extent of which is determined respectively by the marginal propensities to consume (denoted by c), to save (s), and to import (m). In notation form:

$$\Delta S = \text{MPS} \times \Delta Y = s\Delta Y; \Delta C = \text{MPC} \times \Delta Y = c\Delta Y;$$
$$\Delta M = \text{MPM} \times \Delta Y = m\Delta Y$$

where for each country $c + s + m = 1$. Remembering that the ΔX of each country equals the ΔM of its trading partner, we can now rewrite equation (1) for each of the two countries, incorporating the above assumptions:

$$\Delta Y_A = c_A\Delta Y_A + m_B\Delta Y_B + Z_A \qquad (2)$$

$$\Delta Y_B = c_B\Delta Y_B + m_A\Delta Y_A + Z_B \qquad (3)$$

That is, the change in income of each country is made up of the autonomous change in expenditures (Z), an induced change in consumption, and a change in exports equaling the induced change in imports in the other country. It is this last item that forms the link between the two countries and reflects the foreign repercussions.

Given equations (2) and (3), our aim is to find an expression for ΔY resulting from an exogenous shock in terms of the marginal propensities and the autonomous change. From equation (3) we obtain

$$\Delta Y_B - c_B\Delta Y_B = Z_B + m_A\Delta Y_A; \Delta Y_B(1-c_B)$$
$$= Z_B + m_A\Delta Y_A \qquad (4)$$
$$\Delta Y_B = \frac{Z_B + m_A\Delta Y_A}{1-c_B}$$

Next, we substitute equation (4) into equation (2) to obtain

$$\Delta Y_A = c_A \Delta Y_A + m_B \frac{Z_B + m_A \Delta Y_A}{1 - c_B} + Z_A$$

$$\Delta Y_A (1 - C_A) = Z_A + m_B \frac{Z_B + m_B \Delta Y_A}{1 - c_B}$$

$$(5)$$

Multiplying through by $(1 - c_B)$:

$$\Delta Y_A (1 - c_A)(1 - c_B)$$
$$= Z_A (1 - c_B) + m_B Z_B + m_B m_A \Delta Y_A$$

Then, collecting all terms in ΔY_A:

$$\Delta Y_A [(1 - c_A)(1 - c_B) - m_B m_A] = Z_A (1 - c_B) + m_B Z_B$$

Remembering that $c + s + m = 1$, we obtain

$$\Delta Y_A = \frac{Z_A (1 - c_B) + m_B Z_B}{(1 - c_A)(1 - c_B) - m_B m_A}$$
$$= \frac{Z_A (s_B + m_B) + m_B Z_B}{(s_A + m_A)(s_B + m_B) - m_B m_A}$$

$$(6)$$

By similar procedures, we can solve the equation for the second country and obtain ΔY_B. Notice that $1 - c = m + s$ is the inverse of the simple multiplier. Given an increase in autonomous expenditures (Z) in whatever form, in one or both countries, equation (6) tells us the resultant change in A's income.

Consider now the case in which the autonomous increase occurs in country A's exports to country B, arising from, say, a shift in B's taste for A's products. In other words, starting from an equilibrium position, A's exports to B (and B's imports from A) suddenly rise to a new

annual level, higher than the old one by amount Z. This produces a "shock" in A equal to Z_A. But in country B, the autonomous increase in imports may or may not produce an equivalent negative shock.

At one extreme we may assume that all the new imports into B substitute for domestically produced goods. Thus the effect of the increase in imports is to reduce the autonomous component of domestic consumption (lower the consumption function) by the same amount. This is likely to approximate reality in a large diversified economy (such as the United States) that produces close substitutes for most manufacturing imports. In terms of our notation, $Z_A = -Z_B$. Formula (6) then reduces to

$$\Delta Y_A = \frac{s_B Z_A + m_B Z_A - m_B Z_A}{s_A s_B + s_A m_B + m_A s_B + m_A m_B - m_A m_B}$$

$$(7)$$

and the foreign-trade multiplier of A is

$$k = \frac{\Delta Y_A}{Z_A} = \frac{s_B}{s_A s_B + s_A m_B + m_A s_B}$$
$$= \frac{1}{s_A + m_A + m_B (s_A / s_B)}$$

$$(8)$$

(when both the numerator and the denominator are divided by s_B).

At the other extreme, assume that country B absorbs the entire increase in imports out of savings, so that there is no autonomous reduction in the consumption of domestic goods. In that case $Z_B = 0$, and equation (6) becomes

$$\Delta Y_A = \frac{Z_A (s_B + m_B)}{(s_A + m_A)(s_B + m_B) - m_B m_A}$$

$$(9)$$

The multiplier is

$$k = \frac{\Delta Y_A}{Z_A} = \frac{s_B + m_B}{s_A s_B + s_A m_B + m_A s_B}$$

$$= \frac{1 + (m_B / s_B)}{s_A + m_A + m_B (s_A / s_B)} \qquad \textbf{(10)}$$

Between the two extremes fall any number of cases in which the impact of the increased imports in B is absorbed partly out of savings and partly out of consumption of domestic goods. Clearly, the assumptions embodied in equation (8) constitute the most dampening effect that country B can have on the multiplier of country A through foreign repercussions.

Effects of Exchange Rate Adjustments on the Current Account

Because *inconsistent* situations cannot be handled strictly by internal policies, they call for exchange rate changes. Devaluation of a pegged currency or depreciation of a flexible exchange rate is a policy of choice required in the case of an external deficit coupled with domestic unemployment. Revaluation or appreciation is a desired policy in case of an external surplus accompanied by domestic inflation. Clearly, exchange rate adjustment is an important tool of economic policy. Indeed there were numerous changes of fixed exchange rates during the Bretton Woods period, and within the EMS between 1979 and 1993. Also, substantial changes in the exchange value of floating currencies occur all the time. For example, in the two years following mid-1995 the yen depreciated by 50 percent relative to the dollar, thereby improving the competitive position of Japanese companies. After the United Kingdom withdrew from the EMS in September 1992, the pound sterling depreciated by 25 percent. Following that depreciation, the British trade balance improved *and* domestic output and employment increased. Italy experienced similar developments. Thus, the depreciation was helpful in combatting inconsistent situations.

Under a fixed-exchange-rate system, devaluations or revaluations are accomplished by government decree, and occur in discrete amounts. Floating rate systems, however, see these changes daily in small amounts as a result of market forces. Often the exchange rate is driven by the capital account of the balance of payments, and movements in the exchange rate are caused by capital flows. These small daily movements can add up to substantial adjustments of the exchange rate over a short period, as illustrated by the above Japanese and British examples. Therefore, it is instructive to ask about the effects of exchange rate changes on the balance on goods and services and on the domestic economy, while noting that governments are often concerned with improving the current account, even if the overall balance of payments is in equilibrium.

This chapter analyzes the effects of exchange rate changes upon a country, using the United Kingdom as an example. Assume, then, that the U.K. faces a combination of domestic unemployment and a current account deficit, with the pound depreciating from $3 to $2. What would be the effects of this depreciation?

RELATIVE PRICE EFFECT

The immediate impact of the depreciation is to lower the prices of goods and services produced in the United Kingdom relative to prices in other countries, making British products more competitive both at home and on foreign markets. In other words, British imports become more expensive in terms of pounds, making the home-produced substitutes relatively cheaper, while British exports become cheaper in terms of the foreign currencies in which they are sold. Thus, a $9,000 American automobile will cost the British customer £4,500 instead of £3,000 as a result of the devaluation, while the price to the American consumer of a £10 English shirt declines from $30 to $20 as the pound depreciates from $3 to $2. Likewise, an American tourist to the United Kingdom must now spend only $400 instead of $600 on a £200 package tour. Conversely, the cost to a British traveler of a $900 trip to the United States rises from £300 to £450. Indeed, when the exchange value of the dollar rose during 1981–1985, foreign vacations became cheaper for Americans whereas U.S. vacations became more expensive for Europeans and Japanese. The reverse happened in 1985–1989 with the decline in the exchange value of the dollar. Finally, a potential American investor in the United Kingdom finds the dollar cost of a given pound expenditure reduced by one-third, while the converse is true for an English company that contemplates setting up a plant in the United States. The **relative price effect** applies to all traded goods, services, and foreign investments: Relative United Kingdom–United States prices decline, even when domestic prices remain unchanged in both countries.

Becoming more competitive by lowering relative prices is not an end in itself, however. It is a means toward eliminating the external deficit, which is usually measured in terms of dollars—the internationally accepted medium for settling imbalances. In other words, the aim of British policy is to *reduce* the dollar value of *imports* (total dollar outpayments) and *raise* the dollar value of *exports* (total dollar inpayments). It is to that end that prices are reduced. The effect of the relative price change on the value of trade flows depends on the degree of quantity response to price change. But since the results in the case of inpayments and outpayments are not symmetrical, each flow will be considered separately.

Before proceeding with the analysis, we need to define more precisely the meaning of *degree of response to price change*. Consider the colored demand curve shown in figure 14.1(a). It shows the quantities (on the horizontal axis) that would be purchased at alternative prices (on the vertical axis). It slopes downward and to the right (that is, it has a negative slope) in accord with the inverse relation between prices and quantities: the lower the price, the greater the quantity purchased. In the present case, as price declines from P_1 to P_2, quantity increases from Q_1 to Q_2. This inverse relation between price and quantity is assumed to hold for most products. But the dollar value of purchases may or may not increase. Since value is price times quantity ($V = P \times Q$), and since price has fallen while quantity has risen, we cannot say, in general, whether their product ($P \times Q$) has risen or fallen. This product is represented by the rectangular area under the relevant point on the demand curve, since that area is $0P \times 0Q$, or price times quantity. In our case this area has changed from $0P_1AQ_1$ to $0P_2BQ_2$. Because the area ($P \times Q$) corresponds to dollar payments by the importer or, equivalently, to dollar receipts of the exporter, we are concerned with the manner in which it changes as a result of the price changes.

The effect of a given price change on $V = P \times Q$ depends on the size of the quantity response. Clearly, the flatter the demand curve is, the greater the quantity response that it represents. The standard measure of the degree of response is called the *price elasticity of demand* (η_p):

$$\text{elasticity coefficient} = \eta_P = \frac{\text{Percentage change in quality purchased}}{\text{Percentage change in price}} = \frac{\Delta Q / Q}{\Delta P / P} = \frac{\Delta Q \times P}{\Delta P \times Q}$$

where Q and P are used as bases to convert the absolute changes ΔQ and ΔP into percentage terms. Since price and quantity normally move in opposite directions, the elasticity will usually have a negative value. However, it is common to ignore the negative sign and measure elasticity of demand in terms of its absolute value.

Consider the value $\eta_P = 1$. By definition, this means that any given percentage change in price will exactly equal the resulting percentage change in quantity purchased. In other words, the increase in quantity is exactly sufficient to offset the reduction in the amount for which each unit now sells. This leaves dollar value $P \times Q$ (the area under the demand curve) unchanged. When the **demand elasticity** is greater than one, the percentage increase in the quantity purchased is larger than the percentage decrease in price, so that a decline in price yields an increase in the dollar value of purchases. Precisely the opposite is true when the elasticity is smaller than one. In that case a price reduction produces a less-than-proportionate increase in the quantity purchased, so that the dollar value (the area under the curve) declines. We call the first case *demand of unitary elasticity*, the second case *relatively elastic demand*, and the third case *relatively inelastic demand*.

| FIGURE 14.1(a) | *Demand Function* | FIGURE 14.1(b) | *Supply Function* |

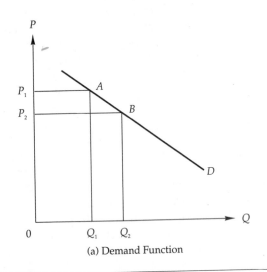

(a) Demand Function

(b) Supply Function

As price drops from P_1 to P_2, the quantity demanded rises from Q_1 to Q_2.

As prices rise from P_1 to P_2, the quantity supplied rises from Q_1 to Q_2.

The value of the elasticity changes as one moves along a straight-line demand curve. In particular, for a demand curve that stretches from the price axis to the quantity axis, the midpoint represents unitary elasticity ($\eta_p = 1$); points above it represent the relatively elastic segment of the curve, and points below it, the relatively inelastic segment. A demand curve along which $\eta_p = 1$ at all points is a rectangular hyperbola, under which the area is the same at all points. Demand is said to be infinitely elastic ($\eta_p = \infty$) when the demand curve is horizontal, because in that case the percentage change in price is zero. On the other hand, a vertical demand curve, where quantity is unchanged, portrays zero elasticity.

We are also interested in the response of suppliers to price change. The supply curve slopes upward and to the right (positive slope), indicating a direct relation between price and quantity: As price rises so does the quantity supplied, and vice versa (figure 14.1(b)). The **supply elasticity** is therefore positive; it is defined in the same manner as the demand elasticity, except that Q refers to the quantity supplied:

$$\eta_s = \frac{\Delta Q / Q}{\Delta P / P}$$

FIGURE 14.2   *Demand and Supply*

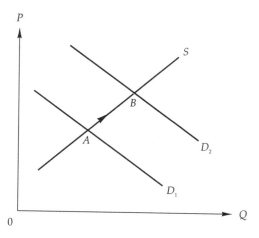

As demand increases from D_1 to D_2 equilibrium shifts from point A to point B.

Loosely speaking, the flatter the supply curve is, the higher is the elasticity that it implies. A horizontal supply curve indicates infinite elasticity of supply, while a vertical curve shows zero elasticity.

The intersection of the supply and demand curves (or schedules, as they are also called), determines the price prevailing in the market and the quantity exchanging hands. A shift in one of the curves, say a rise of the demand curve, means that at every price more of the product is demanded (for example, because of higher income). It is not to be confused with a movement along the curve. The shift from D_1 to the colored D_2 in figure 14.2 causes a movement along the supply curve from A to B and establishes a higher price as well as a greater quantity.

We are now in a position to analyze the effects of sterling depreciation upon the dollar inpayments and outpayments of the United Kingdom. Note, however, that in this discussion the *supply schedules refer to each country's supply of exports to its trading partner* and the *demand schedules refer to each country's demand for imports from its trading partner.*

Effect on Dollar Outpayments

Sterling depreciation has made British imports (an American automobile in our earlier example) more expensive in terms of pounds, with *dollar* prices remaining the *same*. Since English consumers deal in pounds, the volume[1] of imports inevitably declines, and dollar outpayments (volume of imports times the constant dollar price) must also decline. The amount by which dollar outpayments are reduced is determined only by the decline in the volume of imports, since dollar prices are unchanged. In turn, the extent of this decline depends on how responsive British consumers are to the increase in the pound price of imports, or the price elasticity of demand for imports. The more responsive they are, the greater is the reduction. One factor that invariably affects the degree of responsiveness is the availability of acceptable substitutes produced at home. The more readily available they are, the more likely it is that consumers will switch to homemade goods and thereby reduce outpayments. Thus, other things being equal, the import demand elasticity of a large country with a diversified economy is likely to be greater than that of a small country, because the large country tends to produce adequate substitutes for most of its imports.

Similar reductions in outpayments occur as British tourists are discouraged from going abroad by the fact that they must pay more pounds for the dollars they need, and as British companies contemplating overseas investments are held back by the increase in the pound cost of such ventures. In short, *dollar outpayments* in all forms *necessarily decline*, the extent of the reduction determined by the degree of responsiveness to price change.

The analytical tools of supply and demand can be used to demonstrate this point. The two panels of figure 14.3 display the usual price–quantity diagrams. They differ from each other in only one respect: Prices are expressed in dollars on the upper panel, but in pounds on the lower panel. The quantity axes are identical in all respects. We begin by observing the curves that represent the predepreciation situation. American supply to the United Kingdom ($S_{U.S.}$) is assumed, for the sake of simplicity, to be infinitely elastic (horizontal), a condition obtained if unemployment exists in the United States *or* if the British market absorbs only a small part of American output.

The U.S. supply schedule, at $3 per unit, is shown in color on the upper panel since American suppliers think in terms of dollar prices. At a predepreciation exchange rate of $3 = £1, that supply curve is transposed to the lower panel at £1 per unit (in color). British demand for imports from the United States ($D_{U.K.}$) is shown in color on the lower panel with a negative slope, because the British consumer thinks in terms of pound prices. It is transposed to the upper panel at the predepreciation exchange rate of £1 = $3, and shown in colored type, $D_{U.K.}$.

Depreciation of the pound does not affect American supply in terms of dollars or British demand in terms of pounds. This is not so for the U.S. supply expressed in terms of pounds, however, or for the British demand

---

[1] The words *volume* and *quantity* are used interchangeably to refer to the physical amount of goods measured by units or aggregated by the use of index numbers. *Value*, on the other hand, is volume times price.

FIGURE 14.3   *Effect of Depreciation of the Pound on U.K. Dollar Outpayments*

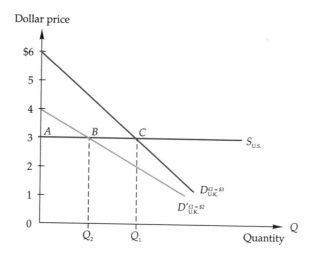

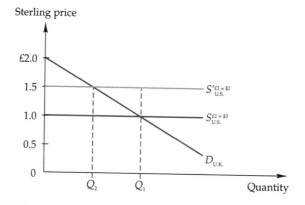

Depreciation of the pound does not affect U.S. supply with respect to dollar prices. But because it raises British import prices expressed in pounds, it reduces $D_{U.K.}$ to $D'_{U.K.}$, in the dollar panel, and lowers British dollar outpayments from the rectangular area under C to that under B.

expressed in terms of dollars. The fact that the pound now commands only $2 means that the $3 supply price translates into £1.5 instead of £1, indicated by the postdevaluation $S'_{U.S.}$ shown in shade on the lower panel. It results in reduced volume of imports—from Q_1 to Q_2. Since the dollar price remains unchanged, the reduced quantity *necessarily* translates into a reduction in *dollar* outpayments. The size of this reduction depends only on the change in quantity, which in turn is a function of the British demand elasticity; the more elastic the demand the larger the decline in dollar outpayments.[2]

Only in the extreme case of zero elasticity of British demand (when $D_{U.K.}$ is a straight vertical line) will the quantity imported, and therefore outpayments, remain unchanged. In that case sterling prices rise in exact proportion to the depreciation and dollar prices remain unchanged. In other words, there is no competitive gain for British products.

Precisely the same result can be demonstrated on the upper panel of figure 14.3. Although $S_{U.S.}$ remains at $3, $D_{U.K.}$ must change when expressed in terms of dollars. The British demand curve shows the quantities that consumers are willing to buy at various hypothetical sterling prices. These remain unchanged. But each such sterling price now translates into one-third fewer dollars than before the depreciation. Consequently, the British demand curve on the dollar price scale (upper panel) must be lowered from $D_{U.K.}$ to the shaded $D'_{U.K.}$, yielding import volume Q_2. Dollar outpayments—the volume of imports times their dollar price—is the area under the equilibrium point. It declines from $0ACQ_1$ to $0ABQ_2$. The only case in which no such reduction occurs is when the demand curve is of zero elasticity (it is vertical) and does not shift. In general, the larger the elasticity of demand, the greater will be the decline in outpayments.

Effect on Dollar Inpayments

When it comes to the inpayments side, the picture is less clear-cut. British exports become more competitive because their *dollar* prices to foreign customers are down one-third. This decline is certain to induce American consumers to purchase more English goods. But the interest of the British government is not in selling more goods in the United States per se; it lies in earning more dollars. And, as a result of the depreciation, each unit of British exports sells for fewer dollars than before. The total inflow of dollars into the United Kingdom is made up of the volume of British exports *times* the unit dollar price the exports fetch abroad. Since that price has declined by one-third, the quantity sold would have to increase by *more* than a third in order for dollar inpayments to rise. More generally, inpayments rise only if the increase in the volume of sales is more than proportional to the decline in price—more than sufficient to compensate for the fact that each unit now sells for less.

In turn, that condition depends on the degree of foreign response to the decline in prices of British goods. If foreign customers are responsive enough to offset the decline in price (if the foreign demand for British goods is *relatively elastic*), then dollar inpayments rise. The same principle holds

---

[2] Note that total outpayments expressed in sterling may increase or decrease, depending on the elasticity of $D_{U.K.}$. This is shown on the lower panel. But the main interest attaches to *dollar* outpayments.

with respect to foreign tourists visiting the United Kingdom and foreign users of all British services. It also applies to foreign corporations wishing to invest in the United Kingdom. They all find it possible to purchase each pound necessary for their transactions for fewer dollars. But whether or not they spend more dollars in the United Kingdom depends on their response to the decline in price. Only if they increase the purchases of British services more than proportionately to the decline in their dollar price will the flow of inpayments increase. (This is the qualification mentioned in the first section of Chapter 11 in connection with the slope of the German inpayments line.)

As before, this conclusion can be clarified by simple demand-and-supply analysis, except that in this case the United Kingdom is the supplier, with an infinitely elastic supply curve ($S_{U.K.}$), and the United States is the demanding country. The indigenous British supply curve, at a price of £1 per unit, is shown in color on the lower panel of figure 14.4, because British suppliers make their calculations in terms of pounds. It is transposed onto the upper panel at the predepreciation exchange rate of £1 = \$3, and shown in color as the horizontal $S_{U.K.}$ at the \$3 price. The indigenous U.S. demand is plotted on the upper panel as $D_{U.S.}$ (in color), since American consumers think in terms of dollar prices. It is mapped onto the lower panel as $D_{U.S.}$ (in color) at the predepreciation rate of £1 = \$3.

Dollar inpayments, which are our main concern, are shown on the upper panel as the area under the equilibrium point, $0ABQ_1$. They equal price times quantity ($\overline{0A} \times \overline{0Q_1}$), where $\overline{0A}$ = \$3. Depreciation does not affect the American demand relationship $D_{U.S.}$ when it is expressed in terms of dollar prices. But $S_{U.K.}$, which remains unchanged with respect to sterling prices (lower panel), is affected when expressed in terms of dollar prices (upper panel). Specifically, the £1 supply price was equivalent to \$3 before depreciation, but it is equal to \$2 after the depreciation. Correspondingly, $S_{U.K.}$ is shifted downward to the shaded $S'_{U.K.}$; that is, the depreciation has made British goods cheaper for American consumers. The new equilibrium point is D. The quantity traded rises to Q_2. Total dollar inpayments are now equal to the rectangular area $0CDQ_2$. They are larger than the predepreciation inpayments ($0ABQ_1$) if the U.S. demand elasticity is greater than one over the relevant range, and smaller if the elasticity is less than one.[3] In general, the more elastic the American demand for British imports, the greater will be the increase in dollar inpayments into the United Kingdom following depreciation.

[3]On the bottom panel in figure 14.4, where the prices are expressed in terms of pounds, British supply ($S_{U.K.}$) remains unchanged. But the American demand curve is shifted upward to the shaded curve as a result of the depreciation, reflecting the fact that a given number of dollars now buys more pounds. The quantity traded rises to Q_2, and so total sterling inpayments necessarily rise. But whether or not this rise translates into an increase in *dollar* inpayments depends on whether it is proportionately larger than the depreciation.

| FIGURE 14.4 | *Effect of Depreciation of the Pound on U.K. Dollar Inpayments* |

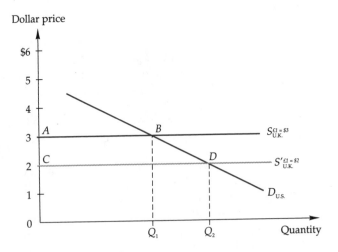

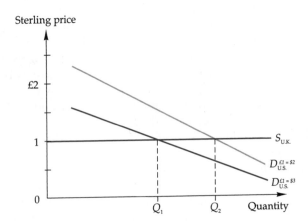

Depreciation of the pound does not affect U.S. demand with respect to dollar prices. But it raises British supply in terms of dollars from $S_{U.K.}$ to $S'_{U.K.}$. Dollar inpayments change from the rectangular area under B to that under D.

To illustrate and underscore the above principles, we turn to another example: the mid-1990s fluctuations in the $-¥ exchange rate. Figure 14.5 shows that exchange rate between 1994 and 1996. Between 1994 and 1995 the dollar declined from ¥110 to about ¥80, which means that the yen rose

| FIGURE 14.5 | *Number of Yen a Dollar Bought, Plotted Weekly* |

Number of yen a dollar bought, plotted weekly.

Its Effects on Japanese Car Prices:

	$1 = 80 yen (April 1995)	$1 = 110 yen (mid-1996)
Average cost to build and market a Japanese car		
Made entirely in Japan	$20,475	$15,600
Assembled in America with few Japanese parts, like a Toyota or Honda	$18,410	$16,980

Source: The New York Times, July 15, 1996

in value by over 30 percent. In 1995 Japanese firms complained that they were unable to compete at such a high value of the yen. Then between 1995 and 1996 the dollar climbed back to ¥110, which means that the yen dropped by about 30 percent.

Suppose we compare Japanese car prices in the last two periods. An average Japanese car built entirely in Japan could be marketed in the U.S. for $20,475 in April 1995, when the exchange rate was $1 = ¥80; but for only $15,600 in mid-1996, when the exchange rate was $1 = ¥110. For popular Japanese models which are assembled in the U.S. with some Japanese parts, the equivalent numbers are $18,410 and $16,980. By March 1997 the dollar climbed further to over ¥120, making Japanese companies very competitive across an entire spectrum of industries. Japan's exports expanded vastly while its imports sagged.

Because Japanese cars became cheaper to American consumers, more of them would be sold in the United States, but each for fewer dollars. Japan would earn more dollars ($ inpayments) from its auto sales only if sales rose proportionately more than the decline in the dollar price; namely if the U.S. demand for Japanese cars is relatively elastic ($\Sigma D_{U.S.} > |1|$).

Note that even if dollar inpayments do not rise, outpayments would decline as the yen depreciates, helping Japan's current account.

Given the sharp exchange fluctuations, a Japanese company that decided in 1995 to move its manufacturing operations abroad, on the basis of high yen value, might have made a rash decision, as the yen declined again in the subsequent year.

We return now to the main theme, concerning the depreciation of the British pound.

Outpayments and Inpayments Combined

To recapitulate, while U.K. dollar outpayments are certain to decline, the impact of the depreciation on dollar inpayments to the United Kingdom is uncertain. Here not only the size of the increase but its very occurrence depends on the responsiveness of American consumers to the reduction in the dollar prices of British goods. The reason for the difference is as follows: Because of the increase in sterling prices of British imports, the volume of these imports declines. Since their dollar prices remain unchanged, their dollar value (outpayments) is also certain to decline, the size of the reduction depending on the response of British consumers. On the inpayments side, the increase in the quantity of British exports results from a *decline* in their *dollar* prices. Their total dollar value rises only if the percentage increase in quantity is larger than the percentage decline in price. Whether or not that happens depends on the response of American consumers to the reduction in price.

Of course, the British government is interested in the net effect of devaluation on its foreign exchange position. Its target is an *increase* in *inpayments minus outpayments* (or a decrease in outpayments minus inpayments), both expressed in terms of dollars. While ideally outpayments should decline and inpayments should rise, the two components of the equation can compensate for each other. Even if the inpayments actually decline, the reduction may be more than offset by a larger cut in outpayments, thereby improving the current account.

Economists have worked out complicated formulas for the conditions that must prevail if depreciation, in its immediate impact, is to reduce the excess of outpayments over inpayments. Known as the **stability or elasticity condition,** or alternatively as the Marshall-Lerner condition (after the scholars who developed it), this condition can be seen intuitively by referring to figures 14.3 and 14.4. Assume that the elasticity of $D_{U.K.}$ is zero and that of $D_{U.S.}$ is one. Then dollar outpayments and inpayments remain unchanged when the pound depreciates. Thus, the sum of the critical values of the demand elasticities that would leave the British trade balance unaffected (when supply elasticities are infinite) equal one: $\Sigma D_E = 1$. From that point, we can raise the $D_{U.K.}$ elasticity above zero and obtain a decline in outpayments, and/or an increase in the $D_{U.S.}$ elasticity above one and obtain an increase in inpayments. In fact, the two elasticities can compensate for each other. Therefore, in the case where the two supply elasticities are infinite,[4] the condition for success is that *the sum of the demand elasticities of the two countries must exceed unity*. When supply elasticities are less than infinite, the formula becomes more complex. Also, in realistic situations, the sum of the elasticities must exceed the bare minimum to allow for reversal factors (discussed in the next sections). It bears emphasizing that this entire discussion relates to the size of the elasticities necessary to move the current account in the *desired direction,* and not to the degree of impact that a given depreciation would have or to the time lag between the depreciation and its effects.

There is abundant empirical evidence to suggest that in the case of industrial countries these conditions are indeed met. For example, numerous studies estimate the sum of the country's import-demand elasticity and the elasticity of foreign demand for the country's exports to be 2.7 for the United States, 1.7 for Japan, 1.6 for Germany, and over 2.0 for Canada.[5] The response to price change is large enough to ensure that the relative price change has the salutary effect of both raising inpayments and lowering outpayments. Depreciation of the currency is likely to decrease the country's external deficit. Whether the shift in the balance-of-payments position is sufficiently large to eliminate the deficit altogether depends on the size of the depreciation itself and on factors to be considered next.

Because the adjustment mechanism under exchange rate adjustments relies on relative price changes that induce residents to switch expenditures from imports to domestic substitutes or vice versa (while foreigners switch between local goods to imports), it is known as an *expenditure-switching* policy. This is in contrast to *expenditures-changing* policy, which relies on changes in aggregate expenditures to restore external balance (Chapter 13).[6]

Appendix 14–1 translates the upper panels of figures 14.3 and 14.4 from the commodity market to the foreign currency markets. This is done by transforming (or *mapping*) the area under the equilibrium point (price times quantity) onto the horizontal axis. Thus the vertical axis measures

---

[4]Another implicit assumption embodied in the analysis is that the devaluation occurs from an initial position of balanced trade ($X = M$).

[5]For extensive discussion, see P. Hooper and J. Marquez, *Federal Reserve Board International Finance Discussion Papers,* no. 456, October 1993.

[6]When the IMF designs an adjustment program for a country as a condition for receiving a loan, it usually recommends a combination of the two types of policies. See *IMF Survey,* November 16, 1987, 339–343.

the exchange rate, while the horizontal axis shows the quantity of inpayments and outpayments. The resulting diagram depicts the foreign exchange market.

DOMESTIC INCOME EFFECT

On the domestic front, the result just obtained implies an expansion of output, and therefore of employment and income, in the industries producing export goods and import substitutes. This expansion results from an increase in demand from foreign and domestic sources, respectively, with the initial impact on output amounting to the rise in exports plus the decline in imports ($\Delta X - \Delta M$). This expansion spreads throughout the economy through the multiplier mechanism, generating a multiple increase in gross national product. As before, the multiplier is $1/(MPS + MPM)$, so that the increase in output (or income) is

$$\Delta Y = (\Delta X - \Delta M) \times \frac{1}{MPS + MPM}$$

As income rises so do imports, reversing *part* of the relative price effect on the balance of payments. The size of this *reversal factor* depends on the ΔY and the MPM. (It may be partly offset by the attraction of foreign investments.) *In the case of exchange-rate adjustment, the relative price and income changes influence the balance of payments in opposite directions.*

Yet the domestic expansion of income and output is desirable in an economy suffering from unemployment, as the United Kingdom is assumed to be in our example. This explains why devaluation is a potent instrument for dealing with a combination of an external deficit and domestic unemployment: It lowers the deficit and increases output and employment. In fact, the 25 percent depreciation of the pound in the fall of 1992 led to an improvement in the British trade balance, and to increased domestic output and employment as predicted by this analysis.[7] Similar developments took place in Italy, which withdrew from the EMS at the same time as the United Kingdom. Appendix 14-2 offers an analysis of joint determination of equilibrium output and the exchange rate.

These advantages do not mean that it is good to "drive your currency to the ground." For depreciation has significant costs: it causes a deterioration in the term of trade as export prices decline; it can generate

---

[7]See the *Financial Times*, Sept. 24/25 1994 front page. U.K. domestic expansion was also helped by a cut in British interest rates from 10 to 6 percent. But that reduction would not have been possible had the United Kingdom remained in the EMS, with the pound anchored to the mark.

domestic inflation (see below); and it increases the local currency cost of foreign debt.

Currency appreciation has the opposite effects. For example, the Swiss franc gained 15 percent between 1993 and 1995-96, rendering many Swiss companies noncompetitive. At the same time output declined and unemployment rose from 0.5 percent in 1990 to 4.8 percent in 1996. Numerous companies were moving operations abroad, expanding employment there at the expense of jobs in Switzerland. The central bank began expansionary monetary policy to weaken the franc.

Domestic Price Effect

Once full employment of resources is approached, a likely companion to the increased level of economic activity is a rise in domestic prices. It affects the balance of payments adversely, constituting a second reversal factor. But unlike the income expansion, it is also undesirable on domestic grounds. In fact, an increase in the domestic price level can be anticipated independently of the income expansion, dissipating part of the competitive edge gained by the devaluation. The very fact of a $33\frac{1}{3}$ percent devaluation raises sterling prices of all imported commodities by 50 percent. And, since many imports enter as raw materials into the productive process, while others (like food) enter into the cost of living, which partly determines wage rates, a wage-price inflationary spiral might be triggered as producers attempt to pass on the increase in production costs to consumers in the form of higher prices.[8] The extent of inflation depends on the degree of "openness" of the devaluating country—that is, on how dependent it is on foreign imports whose prices must rise—and on the success of the government in controlling the inflationary trends by contractionary policies. Intransigent labor unions that insist on tight escalator clauses (tying wage rates to the cost of living) and other benefits can negate many of the benefits of depreciation.

Both income expansion and increases in the domestic price level have the effect of encouraging imports and discouraging exports, thereby reversing part of the relative price effect *on the balance of payments*. Therefore the elasticity conditions necessary for the success of depreciation are actually more exacting than those outlined previously, because the buyers' response

---

[8]Some economists, known as *global monetarists* (see Chapter 15) carry this point much further. They maintain that with open worldwide markets, the price of every commodity—be it a homogenous good like wheat or a differentiated product like automobiles—must be the same in all countries. This is known as the *law of one price*. Under such an assumption, the dollar price of British exports cannot be affected by the pound devaluation. Pound prices of these goods must rise in full proportion to the devaluation to ensure this result. In these conditions the analysis of U.K. dollar outpayments remains intact, for it rests solely on the rise in domestic U.K. pound prices. But what about U.K. dollar inpayments, whose rise in the foregoing analysis depended on a decline in their dollar price? Adherents to the global monetarist view suggest that an inpayments increase is still possible; the rise in the domestic pound prices of exports, in proportion to the devaluation, would increase the profitability of exports and induce exporters to draw resources from other industries and expand their overseas shipments.

to price change must be high enough to allow for the offsetting **domestic price and income effects.**

For this reason it is incumbent upon government to contain the increase in prices as much as possible. Spiraling inflation can wipe out the entire competitive gain and lead to successive but useless devaluations. There is even a danger of the development of an inflationary psychology that feeds upon itself. People begin to expect prices to rise every year, and they purchase commodities as a hedge against inflation. By that very act, they push prices up and add to the inflationary flame. In time, money may even lose its usefulness as a store of value, which harms not only the balance of payments but also the domestic growth rate, as people are induced to curtail their rate of saving. The experience of some Latin American countries and of Russia is a case in point.

This explains why the 1986 devaluation of the franc within the EMS was accompanied by a cut in French government spending, tight monetary policy, and abolition of control over currency movements. The rise in the value of the dollar between 1981 and 1985 produced a sizable trade deficit, but helped curb inflation in the United States, while the dollar depreciation of 1985–1989 reduced the trade deficit after 1988 and stimulated the U.S. economy. Sharp devaluations of the Mexican peso can exert a devastating effect on U.S. border towns: Mexicans stop shopping there, while Americans in large numbers begin shopping south of the border, where dollar prices drop significantly.

It is not possible, nor is it desirable, for a devaluating country to eliminate all income expansion. An increase in output and employment is, after all, one objective of a devaluation. In an inconsistent situation involving both an external deficit and a domestic recession, such as the United Kingdom faced in our hypothetical example, the depreciation should be large enough to allow for some offset to the relative price effect emanating from the real income sources. Only when full employment is approached and when the main impact of further expansion will fall on the price level is the policy maker obligated to slam on the brakes. Considering the possible conflict between output expansion and price stability, the policy maker is required to walk the tightrope among several objectives: achieving the necessary improvement in the external trade position, maintaining a desirable expansion in output and employment, and containing the domestic price increases.

Redistribution of Domestic Resources

While domestic price and income effects operate against the relative price effect in improving the balance of payments, depreciation also brings about domestic **redistribution of resources** favorable to its success. Recall that exporters gain a considerable competitive edge abroad, while at the same time the prices of imports increase in terms of the domestic currency. Consequently, British producers can afford to raise the sterling price of both export and import substitutes to some extent and still remain competitive.

In other words, the tendency toward domestic price increases as a result of depreciation is not evenly spread. What occurs is a differential increase because prices rise more in the foreign-trade industries (export and import substitutes) than in the purely domestic sectors (construction, services, and so on). Thus, there appears an *important change in relative prices within the economy:* the price ratio of traded to nontraded goods increases. This attracts resources to industries that produce internationally traded goods, which in most cases makes the economy more efficient and at the same time promotes the type of production that improves the current account. Many economists consider this to be a very important effect in the analysis of depreciation.

Revaluation or appreciation of the currency has the reverse effect of shifting resources away from the export- and import-competing industries to the nontraded sectors of the economy. This helps to explain the lopsided nature of the U.S. recovery between 1983 and 1985. Although generally robust, it was concentrated mainly in the nontraded industries, such as construction and services. Certain traded goods industries failed to participate because the 60 percent appreciation of the dollar between 1981 and 1985 made them noncompetitive with foreign products both at home and abroad. The subsequent depreciation of the dollar from 1985 to 1988 caused some resources to shift back to the traded-goods sector.

In the previous four sections, four effects of depreciation were traced one by one and their possible interactions were analyzed. Because of the importance of product market elasticities in the analysis, these effects are lumped into what is known as the **elasticity approach** to depreciation. Specifically, the analysis showed that depreciation is likely to help a country's external position and at the same time promote an expansion of income and employment. Although this was not explicitly stated, domestic expansion is often considered a prerequisite for improvement in the balance of payments, because the increased production of export goods and import substitutes requires the employment of new resources. Clearly the ready availability of labor and machinery to be put to productive use is of crucial importance to the success of currency depreciation.

ANOTHER VIEW OF DEPRECIATION: THE ABSORPTION APPROACH

In order to highlight the relationship between the external and internal effects of depreciation, we turn to an alternative way of analyzing depreciation: the **absorption approach.** Focusing on the relation between the current account and domestic conditions, this approach complements and sheds additional light on what has been said thus far.

Consider an economy that produces, consumes, and trades only commodities. The following equality between two pairs of magnitudes must hold for all periods: The difference between the value of goods *produced* in the economy (Y) and that of goods *absorbed*[9] domestically by all users (A) must equal the difference between exports (X) and imports (M). In other words,

$$A - Y = M - X \text{ or } Y - A = X - M$$

If absorption exceeds production, the difference between them must be made up of excess imports over exports; and when production is higher than domestic absorption, the difference must be expressed in excess exports over imports.[10] This is the fundamental identity of the absorption approach.

Additional Insights

The identity can be derived from the national income accounts. National income consists of four types of expenditure: consumption, investment, government expenditures, and net exports.

$$Y = C + I + G + (X - M) \tag{1}$$

If we omit the import component of C, I, and G, and confine these terms to spending on domestically produced goods, we must also delete M. We obtain

$$Y = C_d + I_d + G_d + X \tag{2}$$

where d denotes *domestic*. Equation (2) states that national product or income consists of what is produced and absorbed domestically ($C_d + I_d + G_d$) plus what is exported (X). The goods and services produced and absorbed domestically are called domestic absorption (A_d). That is, $A_d = C_d + I_d + G_d$. Therefore,

$$Y = A_d + X \tag{3}$$

[9] Absorption means the total of private and public consumption and capital accumulation.

[10] Think in terms of a one-good economy—one that produces cars, for example. If production is 1,000 cars each year, and domestic absorption into all uses (including inventories, whether desired or not) is 800, then exports must exceed imports by 200. Exports of 300 and imports of 100 would thus yield an appropriate balance. Alternatively, assume that production is 1,500, and imports are 500. Then the total number of cars available for disposition is 2,000. If 1,700 cars are absorbed by domestic users, then 300 are left over for exports. Hence, again:

$$\underset{(A)}{1700} - \underset{(Y)}{1500} = \underset{(M)}{500} - \underset{(X)}{300}$$

Given three of the four magnitudes, the fourth can be found by using the identity.

On the other hand, total absorption (A) consists of what is produced (and absorbed) domestically (A_d) plus imports (M). In our notation,

$$A = A_d + M \qquad (4)$$

and therefore $A_d = A - M$. We may combine this with equation (3) to obtain

$$Y = A_d + X = A - M + X = A + X - M \qquad (5)$$

Hence,

$$Y - A = X - M \text{ or } A - Y = M - X$$

Starting from a deficit position where imports (M) exceed exports (X), absorption (A) must exceed production (Y) by the same amount. This is essentially a case of *a country living beyond its means* (absorbing more than it produces), or a country investing in excess of domestic savings. When the currency depreciates, the price and income effects come into force and work their way through the economy. If the relative price effect on the balance of payments is more powerful than the interacting income effect, the final outcome is a reduction in the trade deficit ($M - X$). But that necessarily implies an equivalent reduction in $A - Y$: Either absorption (A) is reduced or domestic production (Y) is increased, or a combination of the two occurs.

When depreciation occurs under conditions of unemployment, the main impact is on Y: Production of export and import substitutes rises, and the effect spreads throughout the economy by means of the multiplier mechanism. Resources that were previously unemployed are put to work to produce the goods whose sale was made possible by the improved competitive position.[11] It is for this reason that persistent current account deficits combined with unemployed resources in the domestic economy constitute an "ideal" situation to be met by depreciation.

Under full employment, there are no free resources available for production in order to increase Y. Depreciation, which necessarily exerts

---

[11] As a result of the increase in production and income, absorption will also rise, but by less than the rise in income, because part of the increase will leak away into savings. The higher the MPS, the larger will be the difference between ΔY and ΔA, and the more successful will be the depreciation in improving the trade balance.

pressure on scarce resources, is likely to dissipate in domestic inflation. Prices rather than real output would rise. To be sure, there is reason to expect more efficient allocation of resources to follow the depreciation, so that more goods can be produced with existing resources. This is particularly pronounced when the depreciation replaces an assortment of exchange and import controls. In underdeveloped areas it is often the case that countries with overvalued currencies resort to complicated systems of control, inevitably leading to gross misallocation of resources and widespread inefficiencies. When devaluation is finally effected, economic efficiency can be expected to improve. But this is not the situation in industrial countries, where the effect of improved allocation is not likely to be great.

Thus, under full employment, the crucial question revolves around the economy's ability to reduce domestic absorption. Only a reduction in absorption can release otherwise occupied resources in order for the production of export goods and import substitutes to take advantage of the depreciation. There are reasons to expect some reduction in absorption to follow from the depreciation itself. One of them is the resource redistribution effect discussed in the previous section. Even under conditions of full employment, some resources would be drawn to the export- and import-competing industries from the nontraded sectors of the economy. Other reasons to expect a reduction in absorption follow from the alleged reaction of the public to a general increase in domestic prices following depreciation. They involve fine points of economic theory and need not detain us here.[12] In the final analysis, success depends on the ability of the government to bring about a reduction in absorption through appropriate domestic measures.

SUMMARY OF POLICY ANALYSIS

The Need for Policy Mixes

By now it should be clear why a change in the exchange rate is recommended for countries in inconsistent situations. Since *depreciation improves the balance of payments and also expands output and employment,* it is well suited for dealing with a combination of domestic unemployment and external deficits. The fact that under the Bretton Woods system the dollar was the common denominator and hence could not be devalued (when the United States experienced deficits and unemployment) made U.S. policy makers increasingly discontent with that system and was one of the factors responsible for its demise.

---

[12] Here is an example of such an effect. A general rise in the price lowers the real value of people's savings inasmuch as these are placed in fixed money-value assets such as bonds and savings accounts. To the extent that people's behavior is governed by a desire to attain some level of real saving, they would try to save more to make up for the loss by building up their monetary balances. They can do that by lowering consumption out of any given income, which in turn means that absorption is reduced.

Appreciation has the opposite effects: The deterioration in a country's competitive position lowers inpayments or increases outpayments—or both. At the same time, output and employment decline in the export- and import-competing industries, and from there the contraction spreads throughout the economy. Consequently, an upward adjustment of the exchange rate is well suited for a country experiencing persistent current account surpluses and inflationary booms (overemployment) at the same time. *Appreciation removes the surpluses and dampens the inflation.*

Attainment of the desired results on the external and internal fronts requires that exchange-rate adjustment be accompanied by appropriate domestic measures. In practice, all cases require a **policy mix** rather than one measure. The final aim of policy is to satisfy the combined external and internal objectives, including balance-of-payments equilibrium, price stability, full employment, desirable growth rate, and whatever other goals the community agrees upon. Starting from a given situation, any one policy instrument designed to attain one objective is likely to *overshoot or undershoot* the target in terms of the other objectives. Other instruments must then be brought into play to effect the necessary adjustments in these areas and put the economy on an even course. It is a rare case when one instrument can properly address more than one target. Normally, it is necessary to employ as many instruments as there are targets to attain the final objectives. For example, in 1996 Pakistan devalued the rupee, but accompanied the devaluation by a contractionary fiscal package. Partly this was done to become eligible for an IMF loan. Appendix 14–3 contains a geometric exposition of the policy mixes required to attain internal and external balances.

Effectiveness of Policy

Apart from the situation confronting a country, the optimal mix of policies depends also on the relative effectiveness of the policy itself—and that varies from country to country.

Consider, for example, the effectiveness of expenditure policies in addressing a current account deficit. A reduction of $1 billion in GDP lowers imports and stimulates exports by a fraction of that amount. The size of this fraction depends on the marginal propensity to import and on the degree of openness of the economy, or the degree to which it depends on foreign trade. In an oversimplified fashion, it might be stated that the more open the economy is, the greater will be the effectiveness of expenditure-changing policy in dealing with external imbalances, since a given change in GDP would have a greater effect on the balance of trade than in a closed economy. Conversely, in a closed economy (such as that of the United States) with a low marginal propensity to import, a given change in GDP would produce a much smaller change in the trade balance. It would take a huge reduction in GDP to bring about any noticeable improvement in the trade balance.

On the other hand, for a closed economy the cost of engaging in a switching policy, such as depreciation, is likely to be less than for an open economy. *Switching policy* is a catchall phrase for measures that rely primarily on changes in relative prices (the ratio of import prices to domestic prices) to affect the current account: Depreciation induces a switch from imports to domestic substitutes, whereas appreciation does the reverse.

In a small open economy, the cost of switching can be high. Under the trade elasticities that normally exist in the industrial countries, the commodity terms of trade deteriorate as a result of depreciation.[13] Indeed, that is a major cost of depreciation. When a large share of production and consumption is accounted for by foreign trade, a profound effect on domestic economy activity results. Foreign imports play an important role in production as well as in the cost of living, and a rise in their prices can cause many dislocations in the economy and reduce real income. The *reallocation of resources* between industries producing traded and nontraded goods following exchange rate changes may also be on a large scale. On the other hand, in a relatively closed economy all these effects are smaller in size and more minor in consequence; it is *relatively* less costly and less disruptive to adjust by switching than by means of an expenditure-changing policy. In addition, a large country may need a smaller switching dose to rectify a given imbalance than a small country would. Thus, the effectiveness of switching policies, or their cost, varies among countries.

In sum, it is not only the situation confronting a country that determines the optimal policy mix. It is also the relative cost or effectiveness of the various policies, which varies from one country to another, depending on how closed or open the economy is or on the magnitude of foreign trade relative to the gross domestic product. Both the targets and the relative effectiveness of various policies must be considered before the optimal mix can be determined.

Foreign Retaliation

This discussion cannot conclude without a reminder that depreciation, like domestic policies, has foreign repercussions. When a country depreciates its currency, it experiences an increase in output, employment, and income, because exports expand and imports contract. But, by implication, its trading partners suffer a reduction in exports and an increase in imports, with an attendant decline in output and employment. The larger and more important the depreciating country is, the greater are the effects elsewhere. If the country depreciates in order to get itself out of a domestic recession, then it merely inflicts a recession on other nations. Such a *beggar-*

---

[13]*Commodity terms of trade* are defined as the ratio of the export price index to the import price index. Their deterioration means that the country can obtain less imports for a given quantity of exports, or, equivalently, it must give up more goods by way of export to obtain a given quantity of imports.

thy-neighbor[14] policy was fairly common during the worldwide depression of the 1930s. Trading partners can easily retaliate by devaluating their own currencies competitively as they did in the 1930s. This danger is enhanced in a period of managed floats. In a system of heavily managed floats, a country can force down the exchange value of its currency by market intervention and maintain an artificially undervalued currency, thereby giving its export- and import-competing industries a competitive advantage. This is sometimes referred to as *exchange-rate protection;*[15] and there were instances of such behavior in the 1970s and 1980s. This underscores the need for international cooperation in economic policies. In a multicountry world, it is no longer possible for a country to attain internal and external balance by use of its own policy instruments. Other countries can easily frustrate the balance.[16]

What Governs Exchange Variations?

What factors determine the exchange rate when it is free to respond to market forces? In the very long run, a productivity increase in a country's traded-good industries, relative to those of other countries, is likely to cause its currency to appreciate. Thus the Japanese yen rose in value from $1 = ¥360 in 1967 to $1 = ¥120 in 1997.

Second, there are foreign developments beyond the control of the country in question that bear directly on its balance of payments. An international shift in demand that increases demand for the country's traditional exports would raise the volume and price of these exports and cause its currency to appreciate. Conversely, a shift in demand away from its traditional exports, or an economic slump in its major markets, would harm its export performance and depress the exchange value of its currency. A similar outcome would result from a sharp rise in the price of its imports, other things being equal. The quadrupling of oil prices in 1973 engineered by the OPEC cartel, and their doubling again in 1979, brought about wide fluctuations in the value of practically all important currencies. Countries possessing no energy sources of their own, and therefore depending largely

---

[14] Currency depreciation is called a beggar-thy-neighbor policy when it benefits the home country only because it worsens economic conditions abroad.

[15] See M. Corden, "Protection, the Exchange Rate, and Macroeconomic Policy," *Finance and Development,* June 1985.

[16] Another feature of policy mixes in a multicountry world is known as the *redundancy problem.* Since the balance of payments of all countries in the world combined necessarily adds up to zero (shows neither deficit nor surplus), external balance can be achieved if all countries *but one* achieve it. Thus, if each of N countries has two policy objectives—internal and external balance—except for one country, which is concerned with only one of these, the total number of objectives, and therefore the total number of policy instruments required, is $2N - 1$. There is, in a sense, a spare policy instrument in the system, giving one country some freedom for maneuverability. In the 1950s this freedom belonged to the United States, which did not have to be concerned with its balance-of-payments problem, because foreign countries were content to pile up dollar assets.

on imported petroleum, witnessed the value of their currencies decline relative to that of countries less dependent on imported petroleum. Conversely, the sharp decline in international oil prices in the 1980s resulted in depreciation of the currencies of several oil-producing countries. It was one of the factors responsible for the depreciation of the British pound and of the Mexican peso.

Under a third broad heading, we classify policies of a country's own government. Thus, the imposition of import restrictions or limitations on capital outflow raises the value of the currency. The converse of this was illustrated when, following the removal of government controls on the outflow of investment capital from the United States in January 1974, the dollar slumped on the foreign exchange markets. Other domestic economic events and government policies are likely to *depreciate* the exchange rate *if* they

1. Interfere directly with the capacity to produce and export.
2. Raise domestic prices relative to prices in other countries, thereby impeding the country's ability to compete on both the foreign and domestic markets.
3. Reduce the country's interest rate relative to those in the outside world, thus stimulating the outflow and discouraging the inflow of short-term capital.

Items 2 and 3 are the channels through which a rise in the money supply affects the exchange rate.

An interesting case of currency appreciation is worth a special note. Consider a country like the United Kingdom where the traditional exports originate in the manufacturing sector. The discovery and development of North Sea oil in the 1970s has freed the United Kingdom of dependence on imported petroleum. As a result, the exchange value of the pound sterling rose precipitously. This had the salutary effect of dampening the rate of inflation. But, on the negative side, *the competitive position of the manufacturing sector* (both at home and abroad) *deteriorated sharply.* The long-term effect may be to erode the country's industrial base to a point from which it would be difficult to recover. This so-called **Dutch disease,** named after a similar phenomenon was caused in Holland by the development of natural gas, is common in countries with a newly developed natural resource base.[17]

While the foregoing factors are fundamental in nature, short-run fluctuations may also result from speculative capital movements that can be triggered by *expectations* and rumors. Expectations may be based on underlying

[17]Another source of pressure on the manufacturing sector arises from its reduced ability to compete with the natural resource sector for productive factors when natural resources command exceptionally high prices on world markets. See Max Corden, "Booming Sector and Dutch Disease Economics: Survey and Consolidation," *Oxford Economic Papers,* 1984, 359–380.

economic trends, or they may result from sheer confidence factors in the political or sociological arena.

The Role of Fluctuating Exchange Rates

Under stable conditions, the foreign exchange market determines the exchange rate at a level that clears the market for foreign currencies. Automatic exchange fluctuations can be relied upon to ensure equilibrium in the balance of payments: A deficit would cause currency depreciation and a surplus, appreciation. These adjustments contain the mechanism that restores equilibrium to the balance of payments. The marketplace, rather than the judgment of government officials, determines the extent of exchange-rate adjustment necessary to restore external equilibrium.

Exchange fluctuations influence the domestic economy—affecting output income, prices, and resource allocation between the production of traded and nontraded goods—in a manner similar to that of a government-sponsored exchange-rate adjustment. Thus, depreciation of the currency raises domestic output and prices and shifts resources from production of nontraded goods to the export- and import-competing industries, while appreciation does the reverse. The difference between the two systems is that under fluctuating rates the adjustments occur in small, daily intervals rather than in one sizable discrete step (although many small changes in the same direction can add up to a substantial change over a relatively short period), and in response to market forces, rather than to a governmental decree.

A freely fluctuating exchange rate frees the government of direct responsibility for balance-of-payments adjustment; it can rely on the market to provide the necessary equilibrating mechanism. The government in turn can concentrate on domestic policy goals, and thus the conflict between policy objectives in inconsistent situations is removed. Also, *there is no need to accumulate and hold international reserves, for these are only required to maintain a fixed exchange rate.* By contrast, in the case of a *managed* float, the exchange rate may sometimes be nudged away from its equilibrium level, yielding deficits or surpluses in the balance of payments; for that reason, reserves are required to manage the float.

Under either type of float, overall balance-of-payments equilibrium does not mean that each subcategory of the international transactions statement is in balance. And *if the current account, or the size of the trade balance, is a policy target, the government cannot ignore the external position in its policy formulation.* That indeed is often the case. Central banks intervene in the foreign exchange markets to influence the country's competitive position, to stabilize output, and to control inflation. To do this they need reserves. And indeed global reserves quadrupled between 1972 and 1996.

Finally, inasmuch as the dollar continues to be the main intervention currency in the present-day system of managed floats, the exchange value of the dollar is partly determined by the activities of foreign central banks.

Because the exchange rate responds to market forces, a fluctuating rate regime is capable of partly shielding a country from certain disturbances *originating abroad.* For example, a decline in world demand for a country's exports, and hence its output, would cause its currency to depreciate. In turn, the depreciation lowers imports and raises exports, thereby restoring output to its original level. No such cushion exists under fixed exchange rates, where recessions and inflations spread more easily between countries. On the other hand, under a free float, *internal* economic fluctuations tend to be "bottled up" in the country in which they occur.

However, the insulation of the economy from the effects of outside fluctuations is not complete, because exchange variations produce domestic disturbances via variations in the terms of trade and shifts of resources between industries. Still, some measure of insulation is attained. Indeed this is one reason why Canada, fearing economic fluctuations imported from its giant neighbor south of the border, opted for a fluctuating exchange rate between 1951 and 1964, and again in recent years.

The discussion of the foreign trade multiplier is not fully applicable to the fluctuating exchange-rate regime. An autonomous rise in a country's exports or an autonomous decline in its imports will not necessarily expand its income, and certainly not by the amount indicated in the multiplier analysis. Rather, an increase in exports or a decrease in imports may, in due course, appreciate the exchange value of the country's currency. Depreciation can occur in the cases of an autonomous decline in exports or increase in imports. However, in the short run the exchange rate is determined mainly by capital flows and may be largely unaffected by the trade balance. To that extent the multiplier process continues to hold.

When domestic policies are not coordinated among countries, each jealously guarding its right for independent economic action, fluctuating exchange rates are more appropriate than fixed rates. However, even with fluctuating rates there is a need for some measure of consultation and coordination. At the very least, it is important to avoid competitive depreciation of currencies when the float is managed.

Additional Insights

FISCAL AND MONETARY POLICIES UNDER ALTERNATIVE EXCHANGE-RATE REGIMES

We are now in position to compare and contrast the relative effectiveness of fiscal and monetary policies, *designed to stabilize the domestic economy* (attain full employment and price stability) under fixed and freely floating exchange rates, when capital is fully mobile between countries.

Fiscal Policy

Fiscal policy is fully effective under a fixed exchange rate and ineffective under a floating rate regime. Fiscal expansion, made up of a rise in government expenditures and/or a reduction in taxes, increases aggregate demand and hence output, and raises the *demand* for money. Interest rates rise, attracting capital from abroad. Under a fixed exchange rate, the central bank prevents appreciation of the currency by buying the incoming foreign currencies (or assets) in exchange for the local currency. Domestic money supply expands until the interest rate declines to its original level, and the upward pressure on the currency stops. The rise in money supply further increases output. Similarly, fiscal contraction reduces output and causes a decline in interest rates. The resulting outflow of funds creates a downward pressure on the currency, which the central bank must meet by buying the local currency for foreign currencies. The domestic money supply shrinks, further reducing output. In either case output is affected in the desired direction first by the fiscal action and second by changes in the money supply designed to maintain the fixed exchange rate.

Contrast this outcome with that under a floating-rate regime. Fiscal expansion raises both output and interest rates. But the resulting inflow of foreign funds, attracted by higher interest rates, raises the exchange value of the currency. In this case the central bank does nothing to prevent the change in currency value. The appreciation makes the country less competitive, reduces $(X - M)$, and hence aggregate output, thereby blunting the original output expansion. Output does not change. Fiscal contraction lowers output and interest rates. But the resulting depreciation of the currency increases output, thereby offsetting the loss of output caused by the contraction.

In sum, under a fixed exchange rate the external effects of fiscal policy reinforce its effect on domestic spending, while under a floating exchange rate they offset the effect on domestic spending.

Monetary Policy

Monetary policy is fully effective under a floating exchange rate and ineffective under a fixed rate regime. Monetary expansion increases aggregate spending and output by raising the *supply* of money. Output rises and interest rates decline, causing an outflow of funds and a downward pressure on the currency. Under a fixed exchange rate, the central bank buys the domestic currency in exchange for foreign currencies to prevent depreciation. This reduces money supply, offsetting the original increase, and blunts the increase in output. Monetary contraction reduces output and raises interest rates. To prevent the incoming foreign funds from appreciating the currency, the central bank buys foreign currencies in exchange for the domestic currency. The domestic money stock rises, offsetting the original decline, and blunting the contraction in output. *Under a fixed exchange rate and with fully integrated capital markets the central bank loses control over the money supply,* and monetary policy is ineffective.

Again, contrast this outcome with the one under a floating-rate regime. Monetary expansion increases output and lowers interest rates. The lower interest rates induce an outflow of funds, causing the currency to depreciate. In this case the central bank does nothing to prevent the change in currency value. The depreciation makes the country more competitive, increasing $(X - M)$. Output rises further. Thus monetary expansion increases output through its effect on domestic consumption and investment expenditures (domestic channels), as well as through its effect on foreign spending caused by the depreciation. Monetary contraction reduces output and raises interest rates. The resulting appreciation of the currency causes a further shrinkage of output.

In sum, under a floating exchange rate the effect of monetary policy on the external current account reinforces its effect on domestic spending, while under a fixed exchange rate it offsets the effect on domestic spending.

Exchange-Rate Adjustments under a Fixed Exchange Rate

Devaluation makes domestic goods more competitive, raises $(X - M)$, and increases aggregate output. This boosts the demand for money and hence interest rates. In turn, the resulting inflow of funds puts an upward pressure on the exchange rate. To maintain that rate at the new fixed level, the central bank buys foreign currencies in exchange for the domestic currency and increases money supply, further raising output. Devaluation raises output and employment, improves the current account, and increases international reserves. Revaluation does the reverse.

Summary

When capital is fully mobile, so that interest rates are equalized across countries, the following conclusions hold: Under a fixed exchange-rate regime fiscal policy is fully effective, while monetary policy is ineffective in stabilizing the domestic economy. Conversely, under a floating exchange rate, monetary policy is fully effective while fiscal policy is ineffective. (This is demonstrated formally in appendix 14–4.) However, if the country is very large, or capital mobility is imperfect, each policy retains some effectiveness under both exchange-rate regimes, because domestic and foreign interest rates need not be fully equalized. But the *relative* effectiveness of the two policies under the respective regimes remains important.

These conclusions need to be modified in two ways. Under the dollar standard of Bretton Woods, the "center country" (the United States) could use monetary policy for macroeconomic stabilization even under a fixed exchange-rate regime (while other countries could not), because it did not need to intervene on the foreign currency market to fix its exchange rate. If the Federal Reserve increases domestic money supply, U.S. interest rates decline, causing an outflow of funds. But under the Bretton Woods system the Federal Reserve did nothing to counter the downward pressure on the dollar. Rather, in order to prevent their currencies from appreciating against the dollar, all other central banks bought dollars in exchange for their currencies, thereby expanding their own money supply and pushing their interest rates down to the level of that of the United States. Output throughout the world would expand. The ability of the Federal Reserve to influence money supply in foreign countries (but not the other way around) was one of *two asymmetries* of the Bretton Woods system, the second one being the inability of the United States, and only the United States, to change its exchange rate. Both asymmetries do not exist under the gold standard, where no country occupies a "center" position.

Second, under a managed float the central bank of any country has some autonomy in monetary policy. *But monetary policy is influenced by the exchange rate, because the exchange rate itself becomes a policy target.* The central bank faces a trade-off between domestic objectives and exchange rate stability. For example, suppose the central bank expands money supply to combat unemployment, but at the same time tries to prevent depreciation by selling foreign currencies in exchange for the local currency. Then the later act reduces the domestic money stock, and thereby hinders the central bank's ability to reduce unemployment. Conversely, in 1989 the Federal Reserve's concern about inflation called for a tight monetary policy, while its desire to hold down the exchange value of the dollar to maintain the U.S. competitive position required an expansionary posture. The Federal Reserve opted for an anti-inflationary stance, and the dollar appreciated.

SOME UNANSWERED QUESTIONS

Much economic research has been devoted to determining what combinations of policy instruments are most appropriate for moving the economy toward certain targets. But the gaps in our knowledge are still wide. They are reflected in comments that frequently emanate from high quarters to the effect that "fine tuning of the economy" is all but impossible. As in the case of the last chapter, we conclude with a discussion of some unanswered questions.

The Degree of Impact

In the case of persistent balance-of-payments deficits, perhaps coupled with unemployment and excess productive capacity, economists must determine whether the currency is overvalued and whether the overvaluation is amenable to cure by a downward adjustment in the exchange rate. If so, they must estimate the degree of devaluation required. The same principle applies to revaluation in the case of persistent surpluses.

There are two competing views of the equilibrium exchange rate.[18] One widely held principle asserts that the exchange rate should balance the external current account plus long-term private capital flows. Therefore, when a country on a fixed exchange rate devalues or revalues, it needs to pinpoint that equilibrium in advance and fix the new exchange rate at that level, or at least move the exchange rate toward it. Economists have developed elaborate models of exchange-rate changes that incorporate the price and income effects, as well as their interactions, and are able to estimate roughly, and within broad limits, the degree of adjustment required to reach equilibrium. But it is nearly impossible to determine in advance the exact equilibrium exchange rate, and in any case it is subject to frequent changes as underlying conditions change. Hence the attraction of a flexible exchange rate, where such determination is left to market forces.

A second view is that the exchange rate between two currencies must reflect their relative purchasing power or the relative price levels in the two countries. This leads to the purchasing-power parity (PPP) doctrine as a guide to exchange rate determination.

Purchasing Power Parity   Developed originally in the 1920s, the PPP doctrine has **absolute** and **relative** variants. Under the first version (discussed in Chapter 11), a comparison of the average price levels between two countries is carried out at a given point in time, and the exchange rate between the two respective currencies at that time is said to reflect that relative price level.

[18] For a detailed discussion see articles by R. McKinnon, R. Dornbusch, and J. Williamson in the *Journal of Economic Perspectives,* Winter 1988, 83–120; and *IMF Survey,* November 28, 1994.

When the two countries use the same assortment of goods, that representative basket can be priced in both currencies: If it costs £1,000 in the United Kingdom and $2,000 in the United States, then the equilibrium exchange rate is £1 = $2. One problem is that the representative basket of goods is often not the same in the two countries (different consumption habits and the like), and different commodity baskets would produce different results.

To avoid this difficulty, the *relative version* was developed. It relates the exchange rate to *changes over time* in the purchasing powers of the two currencies as measured against a prior base period when the actual exchange rate was supposedly in equilibrium. Relative PPP asserts that percentage change in the exchange rate between two currencies over some period equals the difference between the percentage changes in national price levels. If, for example, prices in the United States doubled while prices in the United Kingdom tripled, then the sterling would have to be devalued by one-third relative to its dollar exchange rate in the base period.[19] While absolute PPP implies relative PPP, the reverse is not true: Relative PPP may be valid even if the absolute version is not.

Yet either variant of the purchasing-power parity doctrine leaves many questions unanswered. Where does one find an ideal equilibrium period to serve as a base (in case of the relative version)? Which of the many price or production-cost indexes should be used for the comparison?

Most commonly used is the consumer price index. But the CPI contains many nontraded goods and services whose prices need not be equal across countries.[20] Even prices of traded goods need not be equalized, for two reasons. First, transport costs and trade restrictions create price differentials between countries. Second, oligopolistic and monopolistic practices may create price differentials. For example, the fact that the price of a Big Mac hamburger varies from one country to another may reflect the differential availability of substitute products between countries. McDonald's would charge a higher price in countries where no good substitutes were

---

[19] For a comprehensive treatment, see L. H. Officer, *Purchasing Power Parity: Theory, Evidence, Relevance*, Greenwich, Conn.: IAI Press, 1982.

[20] It is interesting to note that the prices of personal services (haircuts and dry cleaning, for example) are higher in the United States than in the less developed countries, such as Mexico. One explanation of this differential is rooted in the proposition that labor forces in poor countries are far less productive than in rich countries in tradeables, but productivity differences in nontradeables are negligible.

Prices of internationally traded goods, such as manufactured products, tend toward some degree of equality between countries because of trade flows. Since labor productivity is several times higher in the United States (because of more mechanized production, among other things), American wage rates in the foreign-trade industries are much higher than the rates in Mexican counterparts. Within each economy, mobility of labor exerts a strong pressure toward equalization of wage rates (for equal skills) in all industries. This means that wage rates in the U.S. service industries are much higher than those in Mexico. But since there is no such international productivity difference in these industries, American prices end up being several times higher than those in Mexico. And such price differences can exist in service industries because they are not traded internationally.

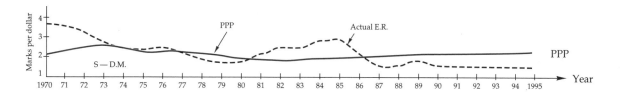

FIGURE 14.6   *Relative PPP (solid line) and Actual Dollar-Mark Exchange Rate (dashed line), 1970–1995*

The market exchange rate departs from PPP over protracted periods.

Note: relative PPP is based on unit labor cost in manufacturing in the United States and Germany.

available. Thus there are frequent departures from the so-called law of one price.[21]

Other causes for departures from PPP include differential changes of living and buying habits of the two populations being compared; differential changes in interest rates that affect capital flows and hence the exchange rate; and differential changes in incomes and employment.

Neither version of PPP is verified empirically in the short run. How about the long run? Figure 14.6 shows the actual dollar-mark exchange rate between 1970 and 1992 (dashed line) and the relative PPP (solid line) based on relative changes in unit labor costs in Germany and the United States. The figure shows prolonged departures of the exchange rate from PPP. For example, the dollar was overvalued relative to PPP over the years 1981–1986 and undervalued between 1986 and 1995. At any given point in time, the exchange rate does not reflect PPP, except at the crossing points. On the other hand, it appears to fluctuate around PPP, with the "cycles" varying in length and amplitude. Over a very long period, relative prices are certainly reflected in the exchange rate, so that they can serve as a general, albeit imprecise, guide (coupled with other considerations) for setting the exchange rate under a fixed rate regime.

In countries where inflation is rampant, price level changes tend to dominate all other factors affecting the exchange rate, and the doctrine

[21] That law states that in competitive markets, free of transport costs and barriers to trade, the price of each commodity is the same in all countries when prices are expressed in terms of the same currency. The law of one price provides the basis for the absolute version of PPP. For if the price of each commodity is equalized internationally under the appropriate exchange rate, so must the average price level.

emerges as a powerful guide to exchange-rate determination. Thus, the 1982–1985 annual inflation in Israel was in the triple-digit range. And the Israeli shekel depreciated continuously against the dollar in a manner that reflected roughly the differential inflation rates between the two countries. The same rule applies to certain Latin American countries and to Russia.

But wherever inflation differentials are small, other factors in the exchange-rate equation become important. And the inability to pinpoint the equilibrium exchange rate is one reason why many economists have been moved to advocate exchange-rate flexibility where market forces determine the exchange rate.

Despite its shortcomings, PPP is useful for conducting cross-country comparisons of output and income. Each country compiles its GDP statistics in its own currency. The figures are then converted into dollars at the market exchange rates, to facilitate intercountry comparisons of GDP and per-capita GDP, the latter figure representing the country's average standard of living. But as figure 14.6 shows, the market exchange rate does not represent the relative purchasing power of the two currencies, and is therefore not appropriate for such a conversion. To cope with this problem the IMF conducted a comparative study (released in May 1993) of countries' GDP, where the conversion to dollars was made by PPP. The study indicates that the share of industrial countries in global output is only 54 percent (and not 73 percent, as thought on the basis of exchange-rate conversion) and that of the developing countries is 34 percent (and not a mere 18 percent). China catapulted from tenth to third in the world in terms of total output (behind the United States and Japan) according to the study, while India's ranking jumped from eleventh to sixth place.[22] Among OECD countries, the highest GDP per capita is that of the United States, followed by Switzerland, Germany, and Japan.

Figure 14.6 shows that the dollar was undervalued relative to PPP from 1986 to 1995. In contrast, the mark and the yen were overvalued. That undermined the competitiveness and hence the profitability of German and Japanese companies. To counter this trend, an increasing number of these corporations have shifted production abroad in the 1990s. Japanese plants have moved to other Asian countries, as well as to the United States and Mexico. Not only is the investment itself made cheaper by the high exchange value of the yen, but subsequent production costs are cheaper than in Japan. Thus an overvalued exchange rate over a prolonged period is a factor causing companies to invest abroad, and needs to be considered along with the reasons for foreign investment discussed in Chapter 9.

Time Path

As often as not, the response of trade flows to change in the exchange rate occurs only after a considerable time lag. Between 1981 and 1985 the real,

---

[22] See IMF, *World Economic Outlook*, 1993; and *IMF Survey*, May 31, 1993.

trade-weighted, exchange value of the dollar advanced by 80 percent. Then, *after a protracted period of large overvaluation,* the dollar depreciated by 60 percent from 1985 to 1987. But that depreciation did not cause an improvement in the U.S. trade balance until 1988. In fact, its immediate effect was to *increase* the U.S. trade deficit. What factors accounted for the $2\frac{1}{2}$-year delay in the response of the trade balance to the sharp real depreciation of the dollar?

J-Curve   The term **J-curve** describes the adjustment path followed by the trade (and current account) balance in response to exchange rate adjustment. The initial impact of a depreciation is to worsen the trade balance. In the first few months after depreciation, export and import volumes reflect decisions based on the old exchange rate, because most import and export orders are placed months in advance. The only effect of the depreciation is to raise the prices and hence the value of the precontracted level of imports in terms of the domestic currency, while export prices do not change. Hence the trade balance deteriorates, represented by the declining portion of the letter J. Only after the trade volume responds to the change in relative prices does the current account improve. And that is represented by the rising portion of the letter J. The J-curve can last from 6 to 12 months.

Incomplete Pass-through   Foreign exporters attempt to preserve their share in the U.S. market by reducing their home currency prices as their currencies appreciate, thereby limiting the rise in the dollar price of their exports. There is evidence that Japanese firms absorbed about half the yen appreciation by reducing production costs and cutting into profits. Thus if the dollar depreciated by 60 percent against the yen, Japanese producers reduced the yen price of their exports by 30 percent and raised the dollar price by 30 percent. We say that the **pass-through effect** of the depreciation was (30/60) or 50 percent. The term *pass-through* refers to the proportion of the depreciation that is translated into higher import prices in the depreciating country.[23] The low pass-through certainly lengthened the lag period. By contrast to the incomplete pass-through of foreign exporters, U.S. exporters tend to pass-through 80 percent or more of an exchange rate change into their foreign import prices.

Hysteresis   A third factor contributing to the delayed response of the trade balance to the dollar depreciation is known as **hysteresis,** a situation under which the value of a variable (such as exports) depends, among other things,

---

[23] See M. Knetter, "International Comparison of Pricing-to-Market Behavior," *American Economic Review,* June 1993; R. Dornbusch, "Exchange Rate and Prices," *American Economic Review,* March 1987; and M. Kreinin, S. Martin, and E. Sheehey, "Differential Response of U.S. Import Prices and Quantities to Exchange Rate Adjustments," *Weltwirtschaftliches Archiv,* September 1987.

Because of differential pass-throughs in the United States and abroad, the competitiveness of U.S. exports in overseas markets is harmed more by dollar appreciation than that of foreign products in U.S. markets by dollar depreciation. See C. Mann, "Prospects for Sustained Improvement in the U.S. Trade Balance," Federal Reserve Board *Discussion Paper,* no. 373, January 1990.

on its own recent history. In the case at hand, if there are *significant fixed costs of entry* into a market, such as establishing a distribution network, then a protracted overvaluation (1981–1985), which leads producers to abandon foreign markets, may reduce permanently the equilibrium value of exports: *Markets once lost are not easily regained*. Likewise, *once foreign exporters gain a firm foothold in the local market, they are not easily dislodged*. Technical progress through *learning-by-doing* may have similar effects: If the level of productivity depends on past levels of output, then a *loss in competitiveness*, which leads to a fall in production today, *will lower productivity and the ability to compete in the future.*

In the United States the protracted period of large dollar overvaluation may have led to semipermanent changes in the industrial landscape, as U.S. firms transferred production facilities abroad and even went totally out of business. Likewise, there are numerous Japanese imports, such as VCRs, for which American-made substitutes no longer exist.[24] This suggests that although the dollar is now undervalued relative to PPP, its depreciation may not have gone far enough.[25]

These three factors delay the effect of exchange rate changes on trade flows.

Summary

This chapter describes the effect of exchange rate changes on the current account. Depreciation raises the price of imports in terms of the local currency and reduces the quantity imported. With an unchanged foreign currency price, outpayments denominated in the foreign currency decline. Depreciation lowers the price of a country's exports in terms of the foreign currency, and hence raises the volume of exports. But foreign demand for the country's exports must be relatively elastic for the rise in export volume to be proportionately larger than the decline in price. Only then will there be a rise in inpayments denominated in the foreign currency. Combining both inpayments and outpayments, a successful depreciation (when supply elasticities are infinite) requires that the sum of a country's import-demand elasticity and the foreign demand elasticity for the country's exports be greater than one. These conditions are generally met.

As exports rise and imports decline following depreciation, output and income rise by $\Delta(X - M) \times \frac{1}{MPS + MPM}$. That is why a depreciation is effective

---

[24] R. Baldwin presents evidence that the dollar overvaluation produced hysteresis. See his "Hysteresis in Import Prices: The Beachhead Effect" *American Economic Reviews*, September 1988.

[25] See, for example, F. Bergsten, "The G-7 Should Drive Down the Dollar," *Wall Street Journal*, May 15, 1989, editorial page; papers by P. Krugman, M. Feldstein, and J. Williamston on "Exchange Rate Policy," *American Economic Review*, May 1989, 31–45.

in addressing a combination of domestic unemployment and external deficits. Appreciation has the reverse effects of worsening the current account and dampening economic activity. It is effective in dealing with a combination of inflation and external surpluses.

Beyond the relative price and income effects, currency depreciation raises domestic prices, and causes a shift of resources from nontraded to traded-goods industries. Appreciation does the reverse. The four effects combined are known as the *elasticities approach*.

Another complementary method of analyzing depreciation is the *absorption approach*. It highlights the relation between the current account balance and the domestic economy, and emphasizes that in order for the external balance to improve, either output needs to rise or absorption must decline.

While exchange-rate adjustment is a necessary tool for resolving inconsistent situations, it alone is not sufficient. Usually it must be accompanied by some domestic measures. For the size of an exchange rate adjustment necessary for a given external imbalance is likely to overshoot or undershoot the target in curing an accompanying domestic problem. The relative effectiveness of income and exchange rate policies also varies between countries.

A variety of long-run and short-run influences at home and abroad govern exchange-rate fluctuations. In cases where a country has both an industrial base and a natural resource sector, the exchange value of the currency would rise if the global price of the natural resource increases. And that may erode the competitive position of the country's manufacturing base. In an underdeveloped country, this phenomenon—known as the *Dutch disease*—may blunt industrial development.

While a freely fluctuating exchange rate ensures equilibrium in the overall balance of payments, partial balances may still show surpluses or deficits. And often government policy is concerned with the trade or the current-account balances, because of their employment implications. As long as floats are managed, countries need to hold international reserves.

When it comes to domestic economic stabilization, fiscal policy is effective under a fixed exchange rate, while monetary policy is effective under a floating-rate regime.

The equilibrium exchange rate has been defined alternatively either as the rate that balances the current account plus long-term private capital flows, or the rate that reflects the purchasing power parity (PPP). PPP has both an absolute and a relative version, and the exchange rate is shown to fluctuate around it. It equals PPP only at the crossing points. Between 1986 and 1995 the dollar was undervalued relative to PPP. Three factors associated with exchange rate adjustment contribute to an extended time lag between depreciation and its effect on the current account balance: the J curve, incomplete pass-through, and hysteresis.

Summary of Balance-of-Payments Theories

Theory	Exchange-rate regime to which the theory applies	Essence of the adjustment mechanism
Specie-flow	Fixed	Money flows → relative prices
Income-expenditures	Mainly fixed	Income-multiplier → imports
Elasticities	Depreciation	Relative prices and other effects
Absorption	Depreciation	Changes in income (output) relative to changes in absorption
Internal-external balance	Fixed	Income effect on current account/ interest rate effect on capital account

The above table offers a summary of the various theories of the mechanism of balance-of-payments adjustment.

Important Concepts

Relative price effect

Demand elasticity

Supply elasticity

Stability or elasticity conditions

Domestic price and income effects

Resource redistribution effects

Elasticity approach

Absorption approach

Policy mix

Dutch disease

Absolute and relative PPP

J-curve

Pass-through effect

Hysteresis

Review Questions

1. a. Between 1981 and 1985 the exchange value of the dollar increased by 80 percent. Explain the effects of this advance on the U.S. trade position and the domestic economy, using charts and formulas as needed.
    b. In the year following February 1985 the dollar declined by 30 percent. Explain the effect of this depreciation on the U.S. trade position and the domestic economy. Would you expect these effects to take place in 1985–1986 or in subsequent years? Why?

2. In 1983 the Mexican government, faced with external deficits and domestic unemployment, devalued the peso by 50 percent. Explain the effects of this devaluation, using the:
   a. Elasticities approach (four effects);
   b. Absorption approach; and
   c. Internal and external balance approach. (Demonstrate why other polices must accompany devaluation to reach a certain combination of targets.)
   Repeat the analysis for the 1992 devaluation of the Spanish peseta within the EMS.

3. Why does the IMF often require both currency devaluation and domestic contractionary measures of countries seeking to draw on its resources?

4. Explain the absorption approach to depreciation. What does it say about the effectiveness of depreciation at a time of full employment? Does the existence of a large current account deficit mean that the country is "living beyond its means"? Why?

5. The 1985–1987 depreciation of the dollar had the following effects by 1988:
   a. $(X - M)$ and GDP both increased;
   b. Resources were shifted from the nontraded to the traded sectors; and
   c. Domestic inflation was precipitated.
   Would you expect depreciation to have improved the U.S. current account balance in 1985–1986 or in subsequent years? Explain.

6. Explain the following terms:
   a. J-curve   d. Pass-through
   b. Relative PPP   e. Hysteresis
   c. Absolute PPP
   How did PPP fare in empirical tests? Why? Can you think of any use for the PPP concept?

7. On June 25, 1986, the *Wall Street Journal* carried the following story:

   Japan's economic output fell 0.5% in the first quarter of 1986, the first GNP decline in 11 years. The drop was attributed to a sharply stronger yen, which caused Japanese exports to fall 4.9% during the quarter.

   Explain the above statement, showing the relation between the rise of the yen and the decline in Japan's exports; and between the change in exports and the drop in GDP. Use diagrams and formulas as needed.

8. In July 1986 China devalued its currency, the yuan, "in a bid to revive exports, tourism, and foreign investments." Explain how the 13 percent devaluation would have these effects.

9. In what ways did the following developments relate to the 20 percent appreciation of the yen in 1993?
    a. In the fall of 1993 American-made cars captured a growing share of the U.S. market relative to Japanese cars.
    b. Many Japanese companies moved production facilities out of Japan and to other Asian countries.
    c. The Japanese economy stagnated in 1993, in part because foreign markets could not replace shrinking domestic demand.

10. Did the exchange rate of the dollar in the 1980s and 1990s conform to PPP?

11. Compare the effectiveness of fiscal and monetary policies under fixed and floating exchange rates. What can you say about a managed float?

12. How does appreciation affect the trade balance, output, employment, and international reserves?

13. Under a managed-float regime, does the central bank have complete freedom to use monetary policy for domestic stabilization? Why or why not?

14. Distinguish between *expenditures-change policies* and *expenditure-switching policies*.

Chapter 14 Appendix 14–1

STABILITY OF THE FOREIGN-EXCHANGE MARKET

Chapter 14 analyzed the stability conditions of the commodity markets under the assumption of infinite supply elasticities. The first section developed the conditions under which depreciation of the home currency (the pound sterling in our example) would improve (or appreciation would worsen) the current account; that is, move it in the desired *direction*. These elasticity conditions are directly related to the stability

FIGURE A14–1.1   *Stable U.K. Foreign-Exchange Market, I*

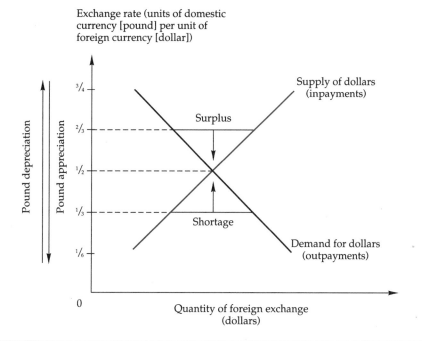

When the supply of dollars is positively sloped and the demand for dollars negatively sloped, the foreign exchange market is stable

---

of the foreign-exchange market, and here we shall move from the "commodity space" to the "foreign-exchange space" to demonstrate the relationship.

The foreign-exchange market is said to be *stable* if changes in the exchange rate induce a movement in the balance of payments in the "right" or desired direction. Depreciation is expected to improve and appreciation to worsen the country's external payments position. In other words, stability requires that depreciation of the currency increase the difference of *inpayments minus outpayments,* both

expressed in terms of dollars. It was seen in Chapter 14 that, in terms of the foreign currency, outpayments necessarily decline while inpayments may move in either direction. But even when inpayments decline, stability is achieved if the decline is outpaced by a greater reduction in outpayments.

Figures 14.3 and 14.4, which demonstrated these relationships with respect to commodity trade, can be transformed into a chart that deals directly in foreign currency flows. Consider figure A14–1.1: The horizontal axis measures the quantity of foreign exchange demanded (outpayments) or supplied (inpayments). It is equivalent to the area under the $S_{U.S.}$ or $D_{U.S.}$ curves (at the equilibrium points) in the upper panel of figures 14.3 and 14.4, respectively—that is, the quantity of merchandise traded times its dollar price. Movements along the vertical axis (the exchange rate) are equivalent to shifts in, say, the supply curves in the commodity space as the exchange rate changes. The exchange rate is defined in such a way that depreciation is portrayed as moving upward along the vertical axis; that is, as a greater number of domestic currency units per dollar.

Since depreciation always reduces outpayments, the demand-for-dollars curve is negatively sloped. It is derived from figure 14.3 by relating changes in the exchange rate to changes in the area under $S_{U.S.}$ at points of equilibrium (quantity times dollar price). The (colored) inpayments line is derived from the upper panel of figure 14.4 by relating the areas under the equilibrium points on $D_{U.S.}$ to changes in the exchange rate, as reflected in shifts of $S_{U.K.}$. The inpayments line can slope in either direction, depending on the elasticity of $D_{U.S.}$. In figure A14–1.1 it is positively sloped, showing a rise in the supply of dollars in case of depreciation and reflecting a relatively elastic $D_{U.S.}$. In other words, this case shows the outpayments line negatively sloped and the inpayments line positively sloped, so that the slope (or elasticity) of inpayments exceeds that of outpayments.

In sum, figure A14–1.1 shows the foreign exchange market when depreciation lowers outpayments and raises inpayments, and when appreciation does the reverse. On both counts depreciation improves—and appreciation worsens—the current account, and the foreign-exchange market is clearly stable. In figure A14–1.1 the dollar is undervalued and the pound is overvalued at $1 = £⅓, resulting

in excess demand for dollars (a dollar shortage). A depreciation of the pound is indicated, which would push the exchange rate toward the equilibrium point of $1 = £½ (or £1 = $2). Conversely, at an exchange rate of $1 = £⅔, the dollar is overvalued and the pound is undervalued, resulting in an excess supply of dollars (a dollar surplus). An appreciation of the pound is indicated, which would push the exchange rate toward equilibrium. In both cases the movement is in the "right" direction, indicating a stable foreign-exchange market.

While the outpayments line must be negatively sloped, the inpayments line can slope either way, depending on the U.S. import-demand elasticity.

In figure A14–1.2, the (colored) inpayment curve is negatively sloped, indicating relatively inelastic U.S. import demand, but it is steeper than the outpayment line (cuts it from above). Although both slopes are negative, the slope of the inpayment line is greater than that of the outpayment line. This is still a stable situation, for it represents the case where the adjustment in outpayments exceeds that in inpayments. As before, at $1 = £⅓ (or £1 = $3) the dollar is undervalued and the pound overvalued, creating excess demand (shortage) for dollars. Depreciation of the pound sterling reduces inpayments, but it lowers outpayments by a greater amount—so that the quantity of *inpayments minus outpayments* increases, and the market moves toward equilibrium. Conversely, at $1 = £⅔, the dollar is overvalued (and the pound is undervalued), creating excess supply of dollars. Appreciation of the pound sterling pushes the market toward the equilibrium exchange rate of £1 = $2.

Finally, consider the case in which both lines are negatively sloped, but the outpayments line is steeper than the (colored) inpay-

FIGURE A14–1.2   *Stable U.K. Foreign-Exchange Market, II*

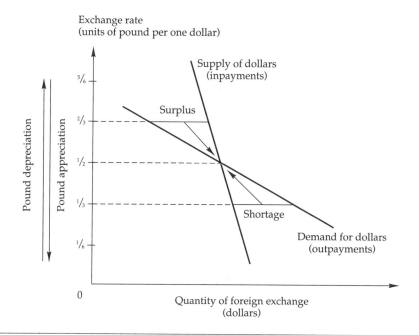

When both supply and demand for dollars are negatively sloped but supply is steeper, the foreign exchange market is stable.

---

ments line (figure A14–1.3). In other words, the slope of the inpayments line is less (has a higher negative number) than that of the outpayments line. Depreciation reduces both inpayments and outpayments, but the decline in inpayments is greater for any given depreciation, so that the difference *inpayments minus outpayments* declines rather than rises. This is the foreign-exchange equivalent of the case in which the sum of the demand elasticities is below one (in absolute value), with supply elasticities being infinite. In this case, when $1 = £⅓, there is excess

supply (surplus) of dollars and appreciation is indicated, while at $1 = £⅔ there is excess demand for dollars (a dollar shortage), which calls for depreciation of the pound. In both cases the indicated action drives the market away from, rather than toward, equilibrium. This is an unstable foreign-exchange market, and it occurs when the inpayment line has a lower slope than the outpayment line.

Cases of multiple equilibria are also possible; for example, one unstable equilibrium and two stable equilibria on either side of it.

FIGURE A14–1.3   *Unstable U.K. Foreign-Exchange Market*

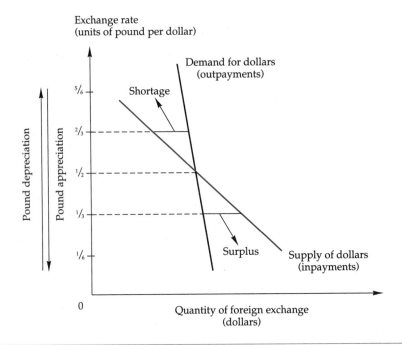

When both supply and demand for dollars are negatively sloped but demand is steeper, the foreign exchange market is unstable.

Chapter 14 Appendix 14–2

EQUILIBRIUM EXCHANGE RATE AND OUTPUT

Assume that the pound sterling is a freely fluctuating currency, and that the exchange rate is defined as the number of pounds per one dollar. An upward move along the vertical axis means pound depreciation and a downward movement—appreciation. A real depreciation of the pound can be caused either by a nominal depreciation (holding prices constant), by a fall in the British price level, or by a rise in the foreign price level. If all domestic prices are fixed, it can be caused only by nominal depreciation.

In figure A14–2.1 the exchange rate is displayed on the vertical axis and short-run output

FIGURE A14–2.1   *The DD Schedule*

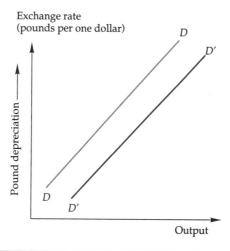

Exchange rate
(pounds per one dollar)

Pound depreciation ⟶

Output

Schedule *DD* represents points of good market equilibrium. Exchange depreciation increases ($X - M$) and therefore output. Hence *DD* is positively sloped and can shift in its entirety.

on the horizontal axis. Exchange depreciation (appreciation) increases (decreases) ($X - M$) and therefore aggregate demand and output. From that relation we obtain the (shaded) *DD* schedule that shows all combinations of output and the exchange rate under which the output market is in short-run equilibrium. Representing points of equilibrium in the commodity markets, it is positively sloped. Any rise (decline) in aggregate demand would shift the entire *DD* schedule to the right (left). In particular:

1. A rise in investment, government expenditures, or in the entire consumption function would increase aggregate demand and raise output at each exchange rate. The *DD* curve would rise (shift rightward) to (the colored) *D' D'*. A fall in the above types of expenditures would shift the *DD* curve to the left.

2. A rise (fall) in taxes would lower (raise) aggregate demand and shift the *DD* curve to the left (right).

3. A rise (fall) in the domestic price level would make domestic output less (more) competitive, reduce (raise) net exports, and shift the *DD* curve to the left (right).

4. A change in foreign prices would have the opposite effect to those mentioned under *c*.

5. A shift in global taste toward (away from) British products would raise (lower) net exports and shift the *DD* curve to the right (left).

| FIGURE A14–2.2 | *The EE Schedule* |

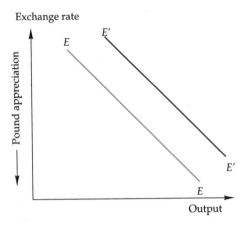

Schedule *EE* shows points of asset-market equilibrium. It is negatively sloped, because a rise in output raises the demand for money and hence interest rates. The currency appreciates.

Next, the *EE* schedule shows the combinations of exchange rates and output levels consistent with equilibrium in the foreign exchange market. A rise in output increases domestic money demand and hence boosts interest rates. The exchange rate appreciates. Thus, to maintain asset-market equilibrium a rise (fall) in domestic output must be associated with appreciation (depreciation) of the exchange rate. The *EE* curve is negatively sloped as portrayed in figure A14–2.2. Shifts in the entire *EE* function can be caused by the following factors:

1. A rise in the money supply causes depreciation of the currency at each level of output. The EE function shifts upward to (the colored) *E' E'*. A fall in money supply would move it downward.
2. A rise in foreign interest rates depreciates the currency at each level of output and shifts the EE curve upward to *EE'*. A fall in foreign interest rates shifts it downward.
3. Changes in domestic interest rates have the opposite effects to those under item 2.

Intersection of the *DD* and *EE* curves yields equilibrium output and exchange rate, as shown in figure A14–2.3. The observant reader might note that the slopes of the *DD* and *EE* curves are precisely the reverse of the slopes of the *IS* and *LM* curve in the familiar *IS-LM* model. That is because the vertical axis here measures the exchange rate rather than the interest rate, and the two are inversely related.

This model can be used to analyze the effects of various policies. An increase in money supply shifts *EE* upward without affecting *DD*; the currency depreciates and output rises. In particular the rise in money supply lowers interest

FIGURE A14–2.3 *Equilibrium Output and Exchange Rate*

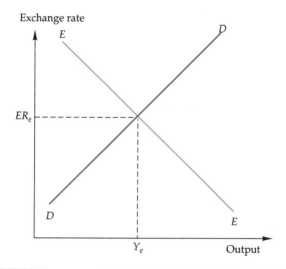

Intersection of *DD* and *EE* determines the equilibrium exchange rate and output.

rates and causes depreciation of the currency, which in turn makes home products cheaper and raises output. Fiscal expansion shifts *DD* to the right without affecting *EE*. The exchange rate appreciates and output rises. In particular, the rise in output increases money demand and raises interest rates. That causes the currency to appreciate. To sum up, monetary expansion raises output and depreciates currency, thereby improving the current account. Fiscal expansion raises output and appreciates currency, thereby worsening the current account.

Chapter 14 Appendix 14–3

POLICIES TO ATTAIN INTERNAL AND EXTERNAL BALANCE

Two convenient diagrams are often used to demonstrate the policy options open to a country attempting to attain internal and external balance. These are described below.

Expenditures-Changing and Expenditures-Switching Policies

In the first case, assume that international capital movements do not exist. External balance then implies balance on the goods and services account. With respect to domestic conditions, assume that unemployment or inflation are

FIGURE A14–3.1   *The Swan Diagram of Internal and External Balance*[1]

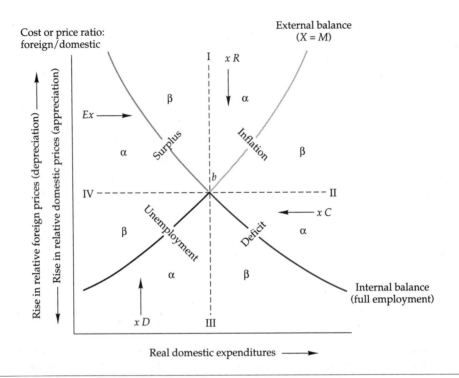

The internal balance schedule is negatively sloped: As domestic expenditures rise, the currency can appreciate (lowering *X – M*) and still maintain full employment. The external balance schedule is positively sloped: As domestic expenditures rise, increasing imports, the currency needs to depreciate to offset that effect and maintain trade equilibrium.

caused only by deficient or excessive demand, respectively. In such a case recession and inflation cannot coexist.

Figure A14–3.1 shows real expenditures on the horizontal axis and a ratio of international to domestic prices (or costs) on the vertical axis. Because the vertical axis is in a form of a ratio of foreign over domestic prices, an increase in foreign prices (domestic prices remaining unchanged) implies moving upward along the axis, while an increase in domestic prices (foreign prices remaining unchanged) implies moving downward along the axis. Thus the vertical axis can be viewed

[1] This diagram was originally presented in T. W. Swan, "Longer-Run Problems of the Balance of Payments," reprinted in R. Caves and H. Johnson, *Readings in International Economics*, Homewood, Illinois, Irwin, 1968, 455–64.

as an index of the country's competitive position. An upward movement along it means increased competitiveness leading to higher exports and lower imports. Conversely, a downward movement means lower exports and greater imports.

The internal balance or full-employment line is the locus of all combinations of real expenditures and cost ratios that yield full employment without inflation. The higher the domestic prices relative to foreign prices (limiting exports and encouraging imports), the higher real domestic expenditures must be to maintain full employment. Hence the internal balance curve slopes downward from left to right. Above the line (and to its right) are combinations of real expenditures and cost ratios that yield inflation, while below it and to the left are combinations that yield unemployment.

In contrast, the external balance line slopes upward and to the right. It represents combinations of real expenditures and cost ratios that yield equality between exports and imports of goods and services. In this case the higher the domestic expenditures, the more competitive (that is, a higher foreign-to-domestic price ratio) the country must be to maintain external balance. Below the line (and to its right) are expenditures—price ratio combinations yielding deficits in the balance on goods and services, while above it (and to the left) are combinations yielding surpluses.

The two lines divide the space into the following four regions:

Region	Domestic Condition	External Condition
I	Inflation	Surplus
II	Inflation	Deficit
III	Unemployment	Deficit
IV	Unemployment	Surplus

Regions II and IV represent consistent situations calling, respectively, for fiscal and monetary policies that contract or expand real domestic expenditures. These are known as expenditures-changing policies. The effect of such measures is shown by straight horizontal lines, such as the lines starting at points C (contractionary domestic policies) and E (expansionary domestic policies). Regions I and III represent inconsistent situations calling for policies that would change relative prices and induce people to switch expenditures between foreign and domestic goods; these are expenditures-switching policies. In region I the main therapy is appreciation, which makes the country less competitive and also combats the inflation. Conversely, in region III the main action called for is currency devaluation or depreciation, which improves the country's competitive position and expands income. The impact of these two policy measures is shown by straight vertical lines, such as those starting, respectively, from points R and D.

The objective of economic policy is to attain a combination of internal and external balance. Such a situation is obtained only at point b, the intersection of the two balance curves. Point b cannot be reached by employing only one policy measure, except in the rare cases where the straight policy lines happen to pass through it (that is, the dashed lines). All other cases call for a *combination* of expenditures-changing and expenditures-switching policies.

Consider the consistent region IV, which calls for expansionary domestic policies to combat the external surplus as well as the domestic unemployment. Only if the initial situation happens to be positioned exactly to the left of b will expansionary policies land the economy right on target. Starting from point E, for example, expansion up to the internal balance line would still leave the country with an external surplus. Getting to point b requires expansion beyond the internal balance line, accompanied by currency appreciation. Likewise, point C requires contractionary domestic policies accompanied by depreciation; point D calls for depreciation plus domestic expansion; and point R calls for appreciation and domestic contraction.

Indeed, it is possible to divide the space into four policy zones circumscribed by the straight-dashed lines and the internal and external balance lines as follows:

	Desired Policy	
Zone	**Domestic**	**External**
Iα and IIβ	Contraction	Appreciation
IIα and IIIβ	Contraction	Depreciation
IIIα and IVβ	Expansion	Depreciation
IVα and Iβ	Expansion	Appreciation

In no zone is one policy measure sufficient to attain both external and internal balance, except for situations on the dashed lines.

Chapter 14 Appendix 14–4

ON THE RELATIVE EFFECTIVENESS (FOR DOMESTIC PURPOSES) OF FISCAL AND MONETARY POLICY UNDER ALTERNATIVE EXCHANGE-RATE REGIMES

Consider a *small country*, with liquid capital *highly mobile* internationally, so that interest rates cannot diverge from world interest rates (in terms of appendix 14–3 this means a flat EE curve):

(1) With a fixed exchange rate, fiscal policy is fully effective in changing income. The accompanying diagrams show the Hicksian IS and LM curves on the income-interest rate space. The initial equilibrium is at point a, yielding Y_1 and i_1, with i_1 equal to the world interest rate. Suppose the government expands fiscally, borrowing the needed funds on the money market, without any new money being created. In figure A14–4.1, the IS curve shifts to (the colored) IS_2 and the equilibrium to point b. But the rise in interest rates attracts foreign

capital, raising the domestic money supply, with the inflow lasting until the interest rate is back to its original level, i_1, equal to the world rate. In terms of the diagram, LM shifts to (the colored) LM_2, and the final equilibrium is at point c, yielding income Y_2. The rise in income is not hampered by an increase in the domestic interest rate.

By contrast, monetary policy is ineffective in changing income. Starting from equilibrium point a in figure A14–4.2, an increase in money supply shifts the LM curve to (the colored) LM_2. But equilibrium point b involves an interest rate below the world's level (i_1). Capital flows out, reducing the domestic money supply, until the original interest level is restored, with the LM curve reverting back to LM_1. Income remains at Y_1.

(2) With a freely floating exchange rate, fiscal policy is ineffective. Starting from equilibrium point a in figure A14–4.3, fiscal expansion shifts the IS curve to (the colored) IS_2 and the equilibrium point to b. The rise in the

FIGURE A14–4.1   *Fiscal Policy under a Fixed Exchange Rate*

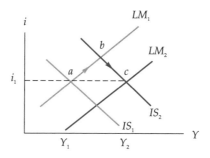

Fiscal expansion moves *IS* to *IS₂* and equilibrium from *a* to *b*. The rise in interest rate attracts foreign funds, which under a fixed exchange rate are absorbed by the central bank. The attendant rise in money supply shifts *LM* to *LM₂* and output expands further from *b* to *c*.

FIGURE A14–4.2   *Monetary Policy under a Fixed Exchange Rate*

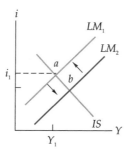

Monetary expansion shifts *LM* to *LM₂* and equilibrium from *a* to *b*. The decline in interest rate results in outflow of funds which, under a fixed exchange rate, shrinks money supply and offsets the original expansion.

interest rate above world levels would attract foreign capital. But in this case, it leads to appreciation of the currency. This lowers $(X - M)$, leading to a multiple reduction in income. *IS* reverts to its original position (IS_1), leaving income unchanged.

By contrast, monetary policy is fully effective. Starting from equilibrium point *a* in figure

FIGURE A14–4.3   *Fiscal Policy under a Freely Floating Exchange Rate*

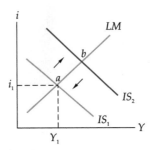

Fiscal expansion moves *IS* to *IS₂* and equilibrium from *a* to *b*. The rise in interest rate attracts funds from abroad, and the consequent appreciation of the floating currency reduces *X – M* and offsets the original expansion.

FIGURE A14–4.4   *Monetary Policy under a Freely Floating Exchange Rate*

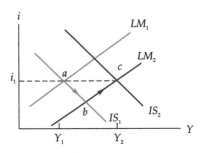

Monetary expansion shifts *LM* to *LM₂* and equilibrium from *a* to *b*. The decline in interest rate causes an outflow of funds and depreciation. In turn that raises *X – M* and shifts *IS* to *IS₂*. Output expands further to point *c*.

A14–4.4, the rise in money supply shifts LM_1 to (the colored) LM_2 and the equilibrium point moves to *b*. The decline in the interest rate below world levels would generate an outflow of capital. But in this case, the exchange rate depreciates. The resulting rise in (X – M) leads to a multiple increase in income. The *IS* curve shifts to (the colored) IS_2 until world interest rate is reached at equilibrium point *c*. Income rises from Y_1 to Y_2.

CHAPTER 15

The Monetary Approach to the Balance of Payments[1] (Optional)

C hapters 13 and 14 reviewed several mechanisms through which equilibrium in the balance of payments is maintained and restored. Although the theories involved are largely reconcilable and are certainly not mutually exclusive, they differ from one another in the economic processes each emphasizes. It has become the conventional wisdom to label them *approaches;* they are commonly referred to as the *elasticities approach*, the *income-multiplier approach,* the *absorption approach,* and the policy approach that stresses *internal and external balance.* The policy discussion in this book (except for this chapter) is based on the "traditional" approaches.

In the 1970s there emerged a new approach that highlights the role of money in the adjustment process. Labeled the *monetary approach* to the balance of payments, it is offered as an alternative to the traditional theories. Developed partly in the tradition of domestic *monetarism,* its predictions and policy implications are different from those obtained from the other approaches.

Monetarists do not use the term *balance of payments* in its conventional sense, which is the statement of international transactions. Rather, they take it to mean one of the balances or, better yet, imbalances. The most useful concept for the monetarists' formulation in the case of fixed exchange rates would be an accommodating item that shows the effect of a balance-of-payments deficit or surplus on the domestic monetary base (the latter consisting of commercial-bank reserves and currency in the hands of the nonbank public), which in turn determines money supply. The nearest approximation to this balance is the *official reserve transactions balance.*

[1] This chapter can be skipped without a loss of continuity.

This approach does not attempt to explain the behavior of individual balance-of-payments components, such as trade and service flows, long-term capital, or private short-term capital. These are all lumped together into one "above the line" category. Nor is the approach concerned with any of the "partial balances." This contrasts with other approaches that pay attention to the composition of the imbalance.

THE UNDERLYING CAUSE OF EXTERNAL IMBALANCES (UNDER FIXED EXCHANGE RATES)

As defined above, the balance of payments is viewed by the monetarists as *essentially a monetary phenomenon*. Payments imbalances are rooted in the relationship between the demand for and the supply of money. The monetary approach rests on the basic premise that over the long run—usually taken to mean a period longer than a year, but shorter than a decade—there exists a stable demand function for money as a *stock*.[2] The quantity of nominal money balances demanded is a positive function of nominal income.

Demand and Supply of Money

Recall that the equation of exchange is $MV = PO$. The terms can be rearranged to obtain $M = 1/V \, (PO)$. Labeling $I/V = k$ and substituting y for O, we obtain an equation that represents the **demand for money:** $M^d = kPy$,[3] where

M^d = Desired nominal money balances
k = Desired ratio of nominal money balances to nominal national income
y = Real output
P = Domestic price level $\Big\}$ Therefore, $yP =$ GDP

The demand for nominal money is a stable positive function of the price level and of real income. For example, if the GDP (Py) is $6 trillion and $k = 1/6$ (velocity = 6), then the desired stock of money is $1 trillion.

---

[2] A *stock* variable is distinguished from a *flow* variable in that it indicates a magnitude at a point in time. By contrast a flow shows movement of the variable per unit of time (such as a year). Thus the quantity of water in a filled tub is a stock. Inflows and outflows of water are flows that change the stock. The amount of capital in the economy is a stock, whereas annual investments are flows that add to that stock. The outstanding public debt is a stock, whereas the annual budget deficits are flows that add to that stock. Money supply at a point in time is a stock, whereas annual changes in money supply are flows that add to or subtract from the stock.

[3] In a more complete statement, it is also a function of the rate of interest, viewed as the opportunity cost of holding money.

Money supply (M^s), for which demand is a stable function, is a constant multiple (m) of the monetary base. In turn, that base has two components: domestic credit created by the monetary authorities (D), and an international component (R). The latter component can be increased or decreased by an inflow or outflow, respectively, of money from foreign countries when the balance of payments as defined previously is in a surplus or a deficit, respectively. In notational form, $M^s = m [D + R]$, where M^s is total money supply, D is the domestic credit component, R is the international reserve component, and m is the **money multiplier,** which for simplicity is viewed here as a constant.

These two equations constitute the centerpiece of the monetary approach:

(1)   Demand for money: $M^d = kPy$
(2)   Supply of money: $M^s = m[D + R]$

Demand for money can be satisfied from either domestic or international sources. Thus, if the demand for money rises—say, because of an increase in real income—while domestic supply remains unchanged, the excess demand would be satisfied by an increase in the international component—that is, by drawing foreign-source funds into the country. And that generates a balance-of-payments surplus. Conversely, a rise in domestic money supply (D), with demand for money (M^d) remaining unchanged, would produce a deficit. In general, any change in the domestic component of the money supply is ultimately offset by an equal and opposite change in the international reserve component through the balance of payments.

External Surplus

A surplus or deficit in the *balance of payments reflects stock disequilibrium between demand for and supply of money.* A surplus on the basis of official reserve transactions occurs when demand for monetary balances exceeds the money stock. If the excess demand for money is not satisfied from domestic sources, such as by an increase in domestic money supply, funds will be attracted from abroad to satisfy it. And such an inflow can be generated through a surplus on commodity trade or on the service account, direct investments by foreign companies, or an attraction of private long-term or short-term portfolio funds. The precise composition is immaterial; the important thing is that the excess demand for money stock will generate a balance-of-payments surplus. But *assuming no intervention by the monetary authorities to offset or sterilize* the resulting inflow of funds, such a surplus is necessarily *temporary and self-correcting.* It will continue only until the money stock rises to the level necessary to satisfy the demand for money balances—that is, until the excess demand for money is eliminated.

The reason for the self-correction feature is that the stable demand function for money relates to money as a stock rather than a flow. When the desired stock is reached, the inflow of foreign funds—which is the counterpart and the cause of the external surplus—ceases, and so does the balance-of-payments surplus. If starting from an equilibrium money stock of $1 trillion and GDP of $6 trillion, GDP sustains a once-and-for-all growth to $6.6 trillion, then the demand for money holdings would grow to $1.1 trillion. In the absence of any growth in the domestic money stock, the extra $100 billion will be drawn from abroad in the form of a balance-of-payments surplus (ΔR). The surplus will last until money balances are brought up to the newly desired level of $1.1 trillion. However, a surplus may be more than temporary when official sterilization of the incoming funds prevents the money stock from rising to the desired level.

Alternatively, in a *flow* formulation, continuous surpluses can occur under conditions of a *continuous* increase in demand for money over and above the rise in the domestic component of the money supply. And that can be caused by a continuous rate of increase in income in excess of the rate of growth in domestic credit creation, causing continuous excess demand for money—that is, **disequilibrium in the money market.** This was advanced as an explanation of the continuous surpluses of Germany in the 1960s and 1970s—namely, a growth rate of real income that exceeded that rate of growth in real money balances.

External Deficit

Conversely, a balance-of-payments deficit reflects excess supply of money as a stock. When the stock of money exceeds the demand for money balances, people try to get rid of the excess supply. They do that by increasing purchases of foreign goods and services, by investing abroad, or by transferring short- or long-term portfolio funds abroad to acquire foreign assets.[4] Thus, the deficit on official reserve transactions is viewed as a spillover of the excess supply of money; its composition is immaterial. The *deficit is temporary and self-correcting.* Assuming that the monetary authorities do not replace the outflowing funds by creating new domestic credit (in other words, that they do not pursue a sterilization policy), the deficit will last only until the excess supply is dissipated abroad and will stop when stock equilibrium in the money market is restored—namely, when the total money stock declines to the level of desired money balances. Starting again from an initial equilibrium money stock of $1 trillion and GDP of $6 trillion, suppose that the Federal Reserve increases money supply to $1050 billion without any

---

[4]Some critics of the monetary approach maintain that people get rid of excess money balances first by purchasing *domestic* financial assets as well as goods and services and only then buying foreign goods, services, and assets.

increase in the demand for money. This would produce external deficits ($-\Delta R$), lasting until the excess of \$50 billion is dissipated abroad. When the money supply declines to \$1 trillion, the deficits would disappear. A continuous deficit is possible if a sterilization policy is followed by the monetary authorities.

Alternatively, in a flow formulation, continuous deficits can occur if the conditions causing the excess of supply of money persist. In turn, this may be caused by a growth rate in the domestic component of the money supply in excess of the growth rate in income.

The self-correcting apparatus outlined above takes time. Except for suggesting that the period required might span between a year and a decade, the monetary approach describes neither the dynamic process that the economy must undergo to reach the new equilibrium nor the elapsed time necessary to reach it. It is concerned strictly with the *final, long-run equilibrium* position.

Role of Money

Money plays a central role in the approach. It is viewed as an *active* agent, not merely as fulfilling a passive role in transactions. In other words, people's crucial decisions concern the adequacy of their money balances. Their demand for such balances relative to supply determines the level of their expenditures on goods and services. Indeed, aggregate spending is a function of real balances. The converse view of treating purchase and investment decisions as central—and viewing money as a passive agent used to finance these transactions—is rejected by the monetarists. The self-correcting feature of the analysis derives from the focus on money as a stock. What the public demands is a stock of money balances.

As under the "traditional" approaches, a rise in the country's money supply produces an external deficit, and a decline in money supply causes an external surplus. But in the monetary approach these imbalances are arrived at by a different mechanism, and they are viewed as temporary, lasting only until (stock) equilibrium in the money market is restored. Since external imbalances are viewed as self-correcting, balance-of-payments adjustment policies are considered *unnecessary*. They are considered *ineffective*, except in the short run. The only possible long-run remedy to a deficit is a reduction in the rate of money creation.

It is often suggested that the monetary approach is the intellectual grandchild of the specie-flow mechanism developed by David Hume in the eighteenth century and described in Chapter 13. Indeed, monetary flows are central to both theories, and both regard external imbalances as self-correcting. But in the specie-flow mechanism, monetary flows rectify external disequilibria through their effect on relative commodity prices. By contrast, the monetary approach views a stable demand for money as the core of the mechanism, and relative commodity prices play no role in the adjustment process. Price elasticities are therefore considered irrelevant. Many monetarists believe in the *law of one price*: Perfect international arbitrage ensures that one price would prevail in all countries for each commodity or asset. So no changes in relative commodity prices are even possible, let alone necessary, for international adjustment.

Monetary Policy

Under fixed exchange rates a country's central bank has no control over its domestic money supply. The pursuit of any domestic objective (such as price stability) by altering the domestic component of the money supply will be frustrated by equal and offsetting changes in the international component through reserve flows. In the absence of offsetting policies (or in view of government inability to pursue them), all the government can do is control the *composition* of the money supply, not its aggregate. A *change in D will produce an equivalent and opposite change in R. And the direction of causation is from D to R*, not the other way around. Changes in the demand for money (M^d) and in the domestic component of the monetary base (D) are the active ingredients that disturb money market equilibrium. *Changes in R maintain and restore that equilibrium under fixed exchange rates.* Such changes (ΔR) constitute balance-of-payments deficits or surpluses.

There is no essential distinction between a central bank's intervention in the foreign-exchange market, which involves the direct exchange of domestic for foreign currency, and its open-market operations, which directly exchange bonds for local currency. The reason is that (in the case of expansionary open-market operations, for example) any excess supply of domestic currency will be exchanged by the public for foreign currency. For the central bank, buying bonds or buying foreign exchange has the same effect. An analogous argument applies to contractionary open-market operations.

Global Monetarism

To recapitulate, the monetary approach to the balance of payments is concerned strictly with long-run equilibrium and rests on two central assumptions: (a) The demand for money is a stable function of very few variables; and (b) countries do not pursue sterilization or offsetting policies. Although not central to the approach itself, many of its adherents also believe that (c) wage-price flexibility fixes output at the full employment level, at least in the long run, so that the Keynesian income adjustment mechanism is irrelevant; and (d) perfect substitution in consumption across countries in both the product and the capital markets ensures a single price for each commodity and a single rate of interest. In other words, the *world consists of a single integrated market* for all traded goods and for capital; the *law of one price* applies throughout the globe. Consequently, changes in relative prices are not possible and the elasticities approach is rejected. Adherents to assumptions (c) and (d), in addition to (a) and (b), are often called *global monetarists*. Thus, **global monetarism** is a subset of the general monetary approach.

POLICY IMPLICATIONS

Devaluation

It is only through possible effects on the demand for and supply of money balances that devaluation can impact the balance of payments. And any such effect must result from the increase in domestic prices caused by a downward adjustment in the exchange rate.

The direct effect of a devaluation of a country's currency is a rise in domestic currency prices of importables and exportables; and because of interproduct substitution, the prices of nontraded goods will also rise, although to a lesser degree. The general price rise increases the demand for nominal money balances, which is a stable function of money income. If that (stock) demand is not satisfied from domestic sources, an inflow of money from abroad would occur, producing a balance-of-payments surplus and therefore a gain in international reserves. Devaluation reduces real domestic money balances and forces residents to restore them through the international credit or commodity markets. However, the resulting balance-of-payments surplus will continue only until the stock monetary equilibrium is restored. In other words, the effect of devaluation will be strictly *transitory*. In the long run, devaluation has no effect on real economic variables; it merely raises the price level.

By the same reasoning, revaluation (currency appreciation) would produce a transitory balance-of-payments deficit if it lowered domestic prices, thereby reducing the demand for monetary balances and producing (stock) excess supply of money.

In sum, exchange-rate changes are incapable of bringing about a *lasting* change in the balance-of-payments position. Furthermore, since all external disequilibria are self-correcting, exchange-rate changes are viewed as unnecessary. Still, *starting from a deficit position, devaluation hastens the process of restoring balance-of-payments equilibrium by absorbing excess money balances.*

But the transitory effect of devaluation does not depend on changes in relative prices and on product-market elasticities. For the monetarists, devaluation operates through a totally different mechanism—the stock demand for and supply of money. This effect is supplemented by an increase in the domestic currency prices of traded goods (exports and import substitutes) relative to those of nontraded goods. As a result, resources shift from nontraded- to traded-goods industries, while demand shifts in the opposite direction. These changes in the production and consumption mixes help increase exports and reduce imports.

Tariffs, Quotas, and Exchange Control

A tariff increases domestic prices of imports, and through substitution, prices of domestically produced goods. This raises the demand for money. If that demand is not satisfied out of domestic sources, it will produce a transitory balance-of-payments surplus until monetary (stock) equilibrium is restored. Import quotas and exchange controls have a similar temporary effect.

Economic Growth

When the economy is growing in real terms, there is a continuous growth in the demand for real and therefore nominal money balances. The portion of this growth not supplied from domestic sources is reflected in a balance-of-payments surplus. Translated into a multicountry context, the monetarists maintain that the growth rate of a country's reserves is faster than the world's average if its real growth rate is faster than the world average.

This conclusion of a positive relation between the rate of income growth and the balance of payments, *all other things being held constant,* is diametrically opposed to the prediction of the Keynesian analysis, where imports are a function of income. However, the latter prediction applies only to the goods and services component of the balance of payments, while the monetarist prediction applies to the official reserve transactions balance. The two can be reconciled via the capital account, if economic growth attracts foreign capital in excess of the deficit on goods and services. For example, if economic growth generates a $100 rise in merchandise imports but also stimulates a capital inflow of $150, the balance on goods and services may move into deficit, while the official reserve settlement balance would show a surplus.

Change in the Rate of Interest

An increase in the domestic rate of interest raises the opportunity cost of holding money, producing a decrease in the demand for money. The resulting excess supply of money would be dissipated abroad in the form of an external deficit, lasting until stock equilibrium in the money market is restored. Conversely, a decline in the domestic interest rate lowers the opportunity cost of holding money, which produces an excess demand for money. In turn, that creates a balance-of-payments surplus, which lasts until the stock imbalance is eliminated.

As in the case of a change in real income, this prediction of the monetarist approach is diametrically opposed to that of the traditional theories. According to the latter, a rise in domestic interest rates (relative to interest rates abroad) produces an external surplus, while a decline in domestic interest rates results in a deficit.

FLUCTUATING EXCHANGE RATES

Freely floating exchange rates maintain continuous equilibrium in the balance of payments. Since reserve changes (ΔR) are held at zero, the monetary authorities maintain control over the money stock. For example, suppose the central bank increases the money supply, so that an excess supply of money is created. The resulting outflow of money depreciates the currency (in contrast to the fixed rate case where a deficit is created, and a change in R offsets the change in D). This raises the price level, thereby increasing the demand for money. M^d rises to the new level of M^s, and a new equilibrium is established in the money market with a higher money stock. Thus, floating exchange rates restore the effectiveness of domestic monetary policy.

With universally floating rates, domestic prices adjust continuously to give the existing stock of money the real value the public desires. The nature of the adjustment process is different under the fixed and fluctuating rate systems. Under fixed exchange rates, quantities of money adjust *gradually* through reserve flows to bring *equality between actual and desired money stock.* Under floating rates, changes in the valuation of the money stock occur instantaneously through domestic price changes (caused by exchange-rate adjustments), bringing full stock adjustment.

How is the exchange rate determined in a regime of freely floating rates? *It is determined by the relationship between the price levels of the two countries, which in turn depends, in each country, on the relation between the desired and actual stock of national money.* Put differently, the price of a currency is viewed as a relationship between a desire to hold *stocks* of assets denominated in that currency and the quantity of such assets in existence. Because the most stable demand function for a financial asset is that for money, the exchange rate is assessed through a comparison of the supply and demand for money in different countries. Since the demand for money depends on real income, on the price level, and on the interest rate, all these variables—along with expectations—enter into the monetarists' model of **exchange-rate determination.** The direction of their effects is as specified in the section on fixed exchange rates: Factors that were shown to cause a deficit result in currency depreciation and those shown to cause a surplus result in currency appreciation.

Additional Insights

In a more formal treatment, recall that: $M^d = kPY$. In equilibrium money supply (M^s) equals money demand (M^d), so we can write: $M^s = kPy$. Transposing we obtain: $P = M^s \times \frac{1}{ky}$. Similarly for the foreign country: $P* = M^{s*} \times \frac{1}{k*y*}$. According to the PPP doctrine, the exchange rate (E) reflects the ratio between the price levels of the two countries. Hence

$$E = \frac{P}{P*} = \frac{M^s}{M^{s*}} \times \frac{k*y*}{ky}$$

This theory of exchange rate determination rests on the twin assumptions of PPP and a stable demand for money.

Other things being equal, the exchange rate appreciates or depreciates as the country decreases or increases its money supply (in relation to its money demand); or raises or lowers its real income relative to the rest of the world.

Floating rates are not necessary for the maintenance of balance-of-payments equilibrium in the long run. Since imbalances are self-correcting even under fixed exchange rates, a preference for a fixed-rate system is indicated; why not enjoy the greater efficiency obtainable from a single worldwide currency area?

The monetary approach has serious implications for international policy coordination of *managed floating*. The traditional approaches call for surveillance and coordination of central bank direct intervention in the foreign exchange market. Under the monetary approach, this is not sufficient. A government can cause its currency to depreciate by buying domestic bonds as well as by buying foreign currencies. What is crucial is the relation between the demand and supply of money, not whether money is created by domestic or foreign assets. So policy coordination requires rules governing the compatibility of monetary policy, not just of intervention in foreign exchange markets. This implies greater restrictions on national economic sovereignty.

Finally, according to the monetary approach, the most effective way of arresting, and perhaps reversing, the depreciation of a currency is to have a preannounced permanent reduction in the rate of growth of the domestic money stock. The announcement itself would have an immediate impact on the exchange rate through the price-expectations channel. However, for this effect to be sustained beyond the initial impact period, the *actual* rate of growth in money supply must conform to the newly announced target. Only then would the public regard the target as an indicator of the future rate of money expansion.

EVALUATION

One possible method of reconciling the monetary with the traditional theories is as follows. The absorption approach highlights the fact that a balance-of-payments deficit (at least on current account) represents the fact that a country is living beyond its means. If imports exceed exports of goods and services, then absorption exceeds income (or output), and by the same amount. To remove the deficit, the country must reduce absorption or increase output until the two are equal. This proposition is pertinent to all theories. The monetary and traditional (elasticities or income) approaches differ in the mechanism by which this is accomplished. Thus, the absorption approach can be merged with either the elasticities/income or the monetary theories. But the monetary approach is distinctly different from its traditional counterparts in its analytical framework, predictions, and policy implications.

There is little doubt that highlighting the role of money in the adjustment process is a significant contribution because it counteracts the frequent tendency to ignore money and concentrate exclusively on real variables. But it is possible that the monetarists have gone too far in emphasizing monetary variables to the nearly complete exclusion of everything else and in offering their approach as a full substitute for the traditional approaches. It can also be questioned whether by ignoring the composition of imbalances the monetary approach overlooks matters that are significant to the economy. It matters for the generation of domestic output and employment (and consequently for foreign economic policies) whether the source of the disturbance is in the capital account or in the goods and services account. Also, if a deficit on goods and services is continuously financed by private short-term capital, it would cause no imbalance on official reserve transactions; yet the country's foreign indebtedness would rise over time, and that may have serious economic implications.

More fundamentally, the assumptions and predictions of the monetary approach must be tested against its alternatives. The numerous tests performed to date failed to substantiate the monetary approach. Two reasons may account for the negative results. On a conceptual level, the approach deals with the long-run nominal exchange rate and applies when the situation is dominated by monetary disturbances. But in the period over which it was tested (1970s and 1980s), the world economy experienced many real shocks as well as price rigidities, which are not modeled by this approach. On the technical level, the approach is based on the assumptions that PPP holds over the relevant period so that exchange rate changes are determined by inflation differential; and that *interest rate parity holds*—namely, that the expected returns on interest-bearing securities denominated in different currencies would be equal. Yet, as seen in figure 14.5, the exchange rate departs from PPP over protracted periods.

Summary

This chapter offers an alternative view of external surpluses and deficits (measured on the official reserve transactions balance) under a fixed exchange rate regime, and of exchange-rate determination under a floating regime. It is based on the demand for and supply of money within the economy.

In its simplest formulation, the demand for money as a stock is positively related to real income and the price level. It also relates negatively to the rate of interest. Money supply is a constant multiple of the monetary base, which in turn consists of domestically created reserves (D) and an international component (R). The latter component rises or falls with inflow and outflow of money from foreign countries through balance-of-payments surpluses or deficits.

When the supply of money exceeds demand, the excess spills over to foreign countries, creating a deficit on the official reserve transactions balance. It is a temporary phenomenon lasting until the stock of money is reduced to the level of demand—as water overflows from a full glass until the excess water disappears. An external surplus occurs when money demand exceeds money supply, attracting funds from abroad. The surplus lasts until the stock of money reaches the level of demand. Equilibrium in the money market (supply equals demand) implies equilibrium in the balance of payments.

Under this approach, devaluation or commercial policies affect the external imbalance by raising domestic prices, thereby increasing the demand for money. That brings about an external surplus, or a reduction in the deficit. But the impact is temporary, lasting only until money-market equilibrium is restored.

Under a flexible exchange-rate regime, the exchange rate is determined by the relationship between the price levels in the two countries (PPP)—which in turn depends, in each country, on the relation between the desired and actual stock of national money. The country's currency would depreciate if its money supply exceeded money demand; it would appreciate if the situation were reversed. However, empirical tests have failed to verify the theory, partly because PPP does not hold over protracted time periods.

Important Concepts

Demand for money

Money supply

Monetary base (two components)

Money multiplier

Disequilibrium in the money market

Global monetarism

Exchange-rate determination

Review Questions

1. How would each of the following developments affect the exchange value of the (floating) Japanese yen? (Assume that all other things are constant.)
   a. A sharp drop in Japan's interest rate
   b. A decline in Japan's real income
   c. A sharp drop in Japan's money supply
   d. Elimination of all tariffs and quotas on Japan's imports
   In each case explain *fully* the result and the reasons for it under the *traditional* and the *monetary* approaches. Can the two be reconciled?

2. What would be the effect of each of the above developments on Japan's balance of payments had the yen been on a fixed-rate regime?

3. Distinguish between *stock* and *flow* variables. What does this distinction have to do with the monetary approach to the balance of payments?

4. What are the implications of the monetary approach for the effectiveness of monetary policy under fixed and floating exchange rates?

5. How did the monetary approach perform in empirical tests and why?

Alternative Exchange-Rate Regimes

revious chapters reviewed the balance-of-payments adjustment mechanism under fixed and floating exchange rates, and the effects of exchange-rate changes on the domestic economy. But there are other exchange-rate regimes that deserve scrutiny. First, there are possible currency arrangements that lie between the two extremes of fixed and freely floating rates. These include wider bands within which currencies can fluctuate, and a regime where groups of currencies are pegged to one another and float jointly against other such pegged groups or against the dollar. Analytical discussion of the latter setup falls under the rubric of *optimum currency areas*. Second, many developing countries do not permit their citizens to exchange their own currency for foreign currencies without a prior government license. This arrangement, known as *exchange control,* is sometimes accompanied by multiple exchange rates and bilateral clearing arrangements.

These regimes will be considered in this chapter. It begins by reviewing the relative merits of fixed and floating exchange rates, and then proceeds to a discussion of different variations of these rate systems. Finally, situations of governmental exchange control are analyzed.

FIXED VERSUS FLOATING EXCHANGE RATES

There are several possible arrangements of globally fixed exchange rates, each with its advantages and shortcomings. They include the gold standard, in which all currencies are anchored to gold at a fixed price; and a currency standard, in which all currencies are anchored, for example, to the dollar at a fixed price. In addition, there is a proposal to convert the IMF into an international reserve-creating institution, in which all currencies would be anchored to an asset—such as the SDR—created by the IMF. The following discussion does not distinguish between these alternative arrangements; they are all considered together under a *fixed rate* regime. On the other hand, a system of *free* floats would require central bankers to abandon intervention in the foreign exchange markets. However, recall that the contemporary system is a hybrid of floating and fixed exchange rates along with point floats.

It is instructive to compare the system of free floats with a regime of fixed rates by reconstructing the original arguments in the form of an imaginary debate between a *proponent and an opponent of freely fluctuating rates*. Although such a presentation necessarily reflects a consensus of views on each side (which in fact does not exist), and is therefore, oversimplified, it at least captures the essence of the controversy.

Proponent   The main advantage of freely fluctuating exchange rates is that the values of all currencies settle at a price that clears the market for foreign currencies; that is, changes in the exchange rate equate demand and supply for foreign exchange. We can then rely on exchange fluctuations to maintain equilibrium in the balance of payments, which thereby removes one of the thorniest problems of economic policy—a problem compounded by the fact that countries are often reluctant to assign high priority to external adjustment when it conflicts with the need for domestic stabilization.

Not only does this system solve the adjustment problem, but it also eliminates the need for reserves. Only when the price is fixed is there a need for reserves. Two great issues facing the international financial community—*how to improve the balance-of-payments adjustment mechanism and how to generate adequate reserves*—would be solved by one act. Economic policy could then concentrate on the domestic objectives of full employment and price stability.

Fluctuating rates also make monetary policy an effective tool for domestic stabilization. And since monetary policy is a more flexible instrument than fiscal policy, many observers consider this an important advantage. To recapture the discussion in Chapter 14, suppose the central bank wishes to cope with a recession through monetary expansion. This stimulates domestic demand and also lowers interest rates. In turn the reduction of interest rates induces outflow of short-term capital to other countries where rates are higher. This depreciates the exchange rate and thereby encourages exports and discourages imports. The improvement in the trade balance implies a domestic expansion in employment and output. The reverse sequence takes place when the central bank combats inflation by raising interest rates.

Opponent   Fluctuating exchange rates introduce considerable risk into all international transactions and therefore lower the volume of foreign trade and investment relative to what it would be under fixed rates. Exchange rates are not like any other price, for they involve monetary values, and money is the standard by which everything else is measured. Just as it is essential to have a fixed ratio between the New York dollar and the California dollar, so it is useful to have fixed ratios between national currencies. Otherwise, commodity traders and investors cannot make advance estimates of costs and prices.

All this is particularly true in open economies, which are highly dependent on foreign trade. Constant exchange fluctuations introduce continuous variations in the domestic price level, as well as in the relative prices of traded and nontraded goods. In turn that can result in incessant reallocation of resources and perhaps even in loss of confidence in the currency as a store of value. At the very least, such fluctuations can be highly disruptive. Indeed, exchange variations have such pervasive macroeconomic effects that the central bank feels obliged to intervene in the foreign exchange market to influence the exchange rate.

While it is true that freely floating rates assure equilibrium in the overall balance of payments, *partial balances* may still show deficits or surpluses. Often the government wishes to attain equilibrium in the trade or current account balances and that calls for measures to influence the exchange rate. In sum, the exchange rate remains a policy objective that may conflict with other objectives. And the idea that floating rates give countries policy autonomy is a mere illusion.

Domestic stabilization of income and employment can be adequately handled by fiscal measures, which are fully effective under a fixed exchange rate. In fact, under fixed rates the balance of payments constitutes a restraining influence on governments, forcing them to avoid excessive inflation because it leads to balance-of-payments deficits. With fluctuating rates, all that happens in case of inflation is exchange depreciation, and the *antiinflationary discipline* exercised by the balance of payments is lost. Furthermore, to improve domestic macroeconomic conditions countries often resort to undesirable competitive exchange depreciation.

Proponent   The risk introduced by fluctuating exchange rates, and therefore its effect on the volume of transactions, is vastly exaggerated. In reality the risk depends on the size of the fluctuations: If they are small, it should be relatively cheap to ensure against fluctuations in the forward exchange market. Indeed there has been a marked increase in the role of forward currency markets since 1973.

Theoretically, fluctuating rates can be expected to be reasonably stable because exchange markets are highly competitive and the underlying demand-and-supply factors involve a high measure of response to price change. Under such conditions, it takes only a small change in price (that is, in the exchange rate) to bring forth whatever quantity response is made

FIGURE 16.1   *Elastic and Inelastic Supply and Demand Schedules*

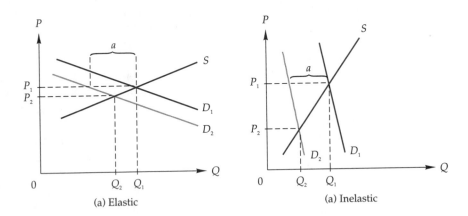

(a) Elastic

(a) Inelastic

Highly elastic supply and demand schedules lead to relative price stability.

necessary by changing circumstances on either side of the market. For example, if for some reason there is an increase in demand, it takes only a small rise in price to bring forth the needed increase in supply to clear the market. Similarly, a decline in demand would require only a small reduction in price to induce suppliers to withdraw the amounts needed from the markets.

In any market there is a positive correlation between the degree of response to price change (elasticity) and price stability. To see this, compare the effect on prices of a downward shift in the demand schedule under high and low response conditions (figure 16.1). Starting from equilibrium position at P_1, Q_1, we shift the demand curve from (the colored) D_1 to (the shaded) D_2. Clearly the price reduction resulting from the same shift in demand (the horizontal distance, a, between D_1 and D_2 is the same in both panels) is much sharper in the low-response (inelastic) case than in the high-response (elastic) case. Precisely the same result may be obtained by shifting the demand curve to the right or by shifting the supply curve in either direction while holding demand unchanged. High elasticities are associated with price stability, low elasticities with sharp price fluctuations.

Since the foreign exchange market is characterized by strong responses to price change on both the demand and supply sides, a fluctuating exchange rate would be relatively stable. Exchange fluctuations as such need not constitute an impediment to trade and investment, especially when forward exchange markets can provide insurance against them. On the other hand, fixed exchange rates often lead to the imposition of exchange and import controls as a means of coping with deficits in the balance of payments, and these limit international transactions much more than moderate exchange fluctuations.

Furthermore, the analogy to a ratio between New York and California dollars does not hold, for not only are regions of the same country subject to the same monetary and fiscal policies, but factors of production (such as capital and labor) can move between them without government restrictions and compensate for external deficits. In other words, the adjustment mechanism under fixed exchange rates works far better interregionally than internationally.

If small countries with open economies face especially severe problems under fluctuating rates, the way is always open to them to peg their currencies to the currency of a large country with which they trade a great deal. This indeed is what many countries do.

Finally, the monetary authorities can be relied upon to exercise their own anti-inflationary discipline in the management of internal economic affairs. In fact, the disciplinary effect of fixed exchange rates on the behavior of prices and wages is at best questionable. And competitive depreciation can be guarded against by policy coordination among the major countries.

Opponent   The view of quick adjustment is contradicted by the time lag in the response of trade flows to price changes in general and to exchange fluctuations in particular. Estimated price elasticities in international trade are higher in the long run than in the short run. It takes a considerable price change to induce traders to switch between domestic and foreign sources and destinations. Under these circumstances, exchange fluctuations might be more violent than the previous argument indicates. Also, if elasticities are low in the short run, then the immediate response to exchange variations falls on (stabilizing) capital movements. But depending upon expectations, capital movements may be destabilizing in nature.

Other opponents concede that the underlying factors of goods and services transactions make for reasonably stable exchange rates, but they worry about the nature of capital movements that respond to exchange fluctuations. Even small exchange fluctuations can elicit and feed upon speculative activity; as the value of a currency rises in terms of foreign currencies, speculators may expect it to rise further and may therefore *purchase* that currency in large quantities. This would indeed bring about the anticipated increase in its value (as self-fulfilling expectations). Exchange-rate overshooting exacerbates the situation. The reverse would occur in the case of a decline. Thus, speculation superimposed upon the underlying market factors would aggravate fluctuations and be destabilizing in nature. The mild variations shown on p. 434 by the solid line will be converted by the speculators to the sharper fluctuations illustrated by the dashed line. Not only can large fluctuations be costly to ensure against, but a forward hedge is not available for long-term contracts so that foreign investment commitments cannot be protected.[1]

Proponent   It is unreasonable to assume that speculation would be destabilizing over the long run. In fact, to be profitable, speculation requires its practitioners to sell when the currency's price is high (not to purchase on the basis of expectations) and to buy when it is low. On the average, therefore, speculation must be a stabilizing phenomenon that has the effect of narrowing rather than aggravating the range of fluctuations. On the other hand, speculation can be highly destabilizing under a regime of fixed rates. When a currency is weak, *speculators know with reasonable certainty that if it moves at all it can move in only one direction:* It can be devalued. They can hardly lose by selling it and buying a strong currency that can only be revalued. It is a "one-way" bet. Indeed, in a regime of fixed exchange rates, speculative activity can bring about changes in the exchange rate when it is superimposed on a certain underlying weakness or strength. Because the risk involved is very low, such speculation is often both destabilizing and excessive. Even the IMF recognizes that fact and permits the imposition of exchange control in cases of speculative attack. By contrast, fluctuating rates may dampen speculative activity by introducing more risk into it.

The Record of 1973–1996

How did floating rates actually affect national economic policies during the past two decades? Central banks regained autonomy in monetary policy, and inflation rates diverged greatly between countries. Effects of monetary and fiscal policies were transmitted across national boundaries through their impact on real exchange rates;[2] so floating rates failed to insulate countries from all disturbances originating abroad. On the other hand, the concerted disinflationary measures in industrial countries in the early 1980s demonstrated that central bank discipline can exist under floating rates. Certainly the fear that exchange-rate movements would lead to vicious circles of inflation and depreciation failed to materialize.

---

[1] To discourage speculative activity Nobel Laureate James Tobin proposed a uniform international tax payable on all spot transactions involving the conversion of one currency to another. For an assessment see articles by P. Spahn and J. Stotsky in *Finance and Development*, June 1996, pp. 24–29, and the literature cited therein.

[2] See papers by J. Frankel, A. Razin, J. Sachs, and M. Feldstein on "The International Dimensions of Fiscal Policy," *American Economic Review*, May 1986, 330–346; and M. Knight and P. Masson, "Transmission of the Effects of Fiscal Policies among Industrial Countries," *Finance and Development*, March 1987.

Central banks were not indifferent to the exchange rate. Rather, it became a policy target that at times conflicted with other objectives. Central banks intervene in exchange markets in an attempt to stabilize output, control inflation, or maintain competitive positions in the tradeable goods sector. Even U.S. intervention, dormant throughout the first term of the Reagan administration, has intensified greatly since 1985. This has produced a growing demand for international reserves.

Because central banks intervene in dollars, the system did not regain full symmetry. For if Japan and Germany intervene to prevent their currencies from appreciating (depreciating) against the dollar, their money supply rises (declines) without a correspondent decline (increase) in the U.S. money supply.

How did exchange rates behave? The amplitude of exchange fluctuations has been high and often unsettling. Exchange variability has been substantial for both nominal and real exchange rates; bilateral and effective exchange rates; and over short- or long-term time horizons. It has been greater under the floating exchange-rate system than in the Bretton Woods period. Also, variability did not decline over time. Despite the fact that the IMF conducts surveillance of the foreign currency intervention of its member nations, there have been attempts by central banks to manipulate their exchange rate to their country's advantage. Additionally there have been many significant cases of exchange rate overshooting superimposed upon changes in fundamental market conditions. Indeed, overshooting may have been experienced by the United States in the 1980s. Exchange rates diverged greatly from relative PPP over protracted periods.

But much of that volatility was a result of unsettled global economic conditions: oil shocks, droughts, stagflations, differential inflation rates between countries, and vastly different growth rates. These events could not have been accommodated by a fixed exchange-rate system. Thus the appropriate question is: Were exchange fluctuations of greater magnitude than that warranted by the economic disturbances that triggered them, so as to send improper signals to business and governments? One measure of the intensity of changing economic circumstances is fluctuation in the prices of stocks and bonds. The fact that exchange rates exhibited *less* variation than the prices of other financial assets suggests that exchange fluctuations were not excessive relative to changes in fundamental conditions.

In the 1970s there was widespread belief that floating rates were inappropriate for LDCs, partly because these countries lacked a sophisticated financial structure (such as forward markets) necessary for its functioning. In fact, LDCs objected to the introduction of floating rates. But since then the developing countries have adjusted to the system. Most peg their rates to the currency of their main trading partner, or to a basket, and fluctuate with it relative to other currencies. Either because of high inflation or inadequate reserves, some have adopted independent floats. They manage their nominal exchange rate in such a way as to keep the real rate from appreciating, thereby maintaining their competitive position.

In the 1990s the countries of the former Soviet Union and of Eastern Europe joined the IMF as a part of their transition toward market economies. Most former Soviet republics chose to issue new currencies. Countries typically introduce a separate currency first as a symbol of national independence, and second because it gives them authority over monetary and exchange-rate policies. As a prerequisite it is necessary to establish a national central bank. And success requires the maintenance of macroeconomic stability attained through conservative fiscal and monetary policies. It is desirable to maintain convertibility to other currencies, although some countries have chosen exchange control, at least for a transitory period. Beyond that, the country must choose its exchange regime. Some countries opted to peg their currency to that of a major trading partner; for example, the Estonian currency is pegged to the German mark. High-inflation countries, such as Ukraine and Romania, adopted a freely floating exchange rate.[3]

International economic relations have not been disrupted by floating exchange rates, and the system weathered well the economic crises of the 1970s.[4] As had been anticipated, the use of forward exchange markets expanded dramatically. And there is no evidence of a significant decline in the volume of trade and investment as a result of floating rates.[5] In sum, while the system is not free of problems, it is not the disaster its opponents feared.

Concern over the amplitude of exchange fluctuations is best met by improved coordination[6] among countries of their fiscal and monetary policies. So far such coordination has been far from satisfactory. While a return to fixed exchange rates, desired by some observers, is not practical as long as the underlying economic conditions vary greatly among countries, there are a number of possible currency arrangements that lie between the two extremes of fixed and floating rates.

Wider Bands and Crawling Pegs

One proposal (the **wider band** proposal) is to adopt fixed exchange rates but widen the spread within which exchange rates are permitted to fluctuate. It

---

[3]See *IMF Survey*, February 21, 1994, 52–59; P. Montiel and J. Ostry, "Targeting the Real Exchange Rates in Developing Countries," *Finance and Development*, March 1993; P. Quirk and H. Cortes-Douglas, "The Experience with Floating Rates," *Finance and Development*, June 1993; and H. Cortes-Douglas and R. Abrams, "Introducing New National Currencies," *Finance and Development*, December 1993.

[4]For further discussion, see R. Blackhurst and J. Tumlir, "Trade Relations under Flexible Exchange Rates," Geneva, *GATT Studies*, no. 8, September 1980; and M. Goldstein, "Whither the Exchange Rate System," *Finance and Development*, June 1984.

[5]See J. Gagnon, "Exchange Rate Variability and the Level of International Trade," Federal Reserve Board, *Discussion Paper*, no. 369, December 1989.

[6]See M. Feldstein (ed.), *International Economic Cooperation*, National Bureau of Economic Research Summary Report 1988; and *IMF Survey*, January 23, 1989, and February 5, 1990. Many scholars argue that the benefits from policy coordination are rather small, and suggest that exchange of information among countries is sufficient. See O. Humpage, "A Hitchhiker's Guide to International Macroeconomic Policy Coordination," Federal Reserve Bank of Cleveland, *Economic Review*, 1990, I.

would contribute to speeding up balance-of-payments adjustments and at the same time would reduce the need for reserves.

Other ideas bandied about include the so-called **crawling peg,** which would permit a country in disequilibrium to make preannounced small changes in its parity every month until equilibrium is attained. The proposal has the dual advantage over a fixed exchange rate system of permitting parity adjustments before the pressure on the country has reached a boiling point and of removing some of the political stigma attached to large, discrete exchange variations. On the other hand, preannounced exchange adjustments can stimulate speculative activity, and the country would need to manipulate its interest rates to stem destabilizing capital flows.

An automatic variant of the crawling peg has also been discussed. It would make the parity on any business day a moving average of the exchange rates (or of reserve movements) over a predetermined preceding period. Thus, if the exchange rate bounces along the lower support limit for a specified period, the official parity rate along with the entire band would gradually be nudged down. Conversely, it would move upward should the rate move along the ceiling for a time. In other words, the movements of the par value of each currency (along with its support limits) would depend on the relation between the actual exchange rate and the support limits over a certain past period. Schematically, the crawling rate proposal can be illustrated as follows:

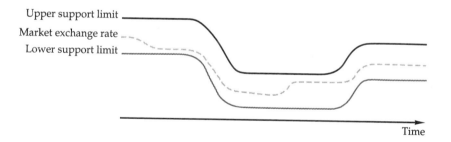

Upper support limit
Market exchange rate
Lower support limit

Time

Target Zones

Finally, it has been proposed that the IMF establish **target zones** for the major currencies and that central banks maintain their respective exchange rates within those zones through market intervention (as in the EMS). The zones, which would be subject to periodic changes, would delineate limits to sustainable exchange rates. In determining the target zones the IMF would use a variety of indicators, such as cost-price comparisons and indicators pertaining to capital flows. But given the uncertainties surrounding the future flow of international transactions, it would be difficult to determine the target zones.[7]

All these proposals involve some central bank intervention in the currency markets, and hence would call for increased demand for international reserves. Also any attempt to link the exchange rates of the major currencies would require coordination of domestic economic policies.

Optimum Currency Areas

Another proposal is to establish fixed exchange rates within a group of closely knit countries, and to permit free fluctuations between the blocs of countries, each floating jointly. Such groups of countries are often referred to as **optimum currency areas (OCAs).** While there are no specific rules that define exactly what groups of countries may qualify for inclusion in any one area, some guidelines can be articulated. It is desirable for the countries composing a currency area to have a high measure of coordination in fiscal and monetary policies, as well as a high level of factor mobility between them. These conditions help lubricate the adjustment mechanism under fixed exchange rates. Recall that when resources are highly mobile, as within a country, the adjustment process entails the movement of resources from the deficit (depressed) region to the surplus (prosperous) region.

Next, a high measure of price-wage flexibility is desirable for a country joining an OCA, because it ensures that a country can improve its competitive position (by lowering domestic prices) even under a fixed exchange rate. Also, a high level of financial integration among the countries in the region is useful for an OCA, because then capital movements between countries can finance external imbalances. Finally, a fixed exchange rate is preferred for an open economy, usually associated with a small-size country.[8]

Behind these criteria for an optimum currency area is the relative ease of the balance-of-payments adjustment process under the two alternative regimes. Under a fixed exchange rate the adjustment to an external deficit involves contraction of output, and with it income and employment, where the loss can be measured as the forgone output. With a floating exchange rate the adjustment to a deficit takes the form of currency depreciation. The cost is the loss in the terms of trade, the instability caused by movement of

---

[7]See Lars E. Svensson, "An Interpretation of Recent Research on Exchange Rate Target Zones," *Journal of Economic Perspectives*, fall 1992, 119–144; A. Dixit, "In Honor of Paul Krugman: Winner of the John Bates Clark Medal," *Journal of Economic Perspectives*, spring 1993, 183–185; John Williamson, *The Exchange Rate System*, Policy Analyses in International Economics, no. 5, Washington, Institute for International Economics, 1983; Hans Genberg, "On Choosing the Right Rules for Exchange Rate Management," *The World Economy*, vol. 7, December 1984; and papers by J. Frankel, M. Goldstein, and others summarized in the *IMF Survey*, April 6, 1987.

[8]See G. Tarlas, "The Theory of Optimum Currency Areas," *Finance and Development*, June 1993; and C. N. Wang, "On the Choice of Exchange Rate Regimes," Federal Reserve Bank of Cleveland Working Paper 9002, April 1990.

resources from the nontraded- to the traded-goods industries, and sometimes general price instability. The burden of these costs varies with the degree of openness of the economy.

Generally the adjustment costs for a large, relatively closed economy are lower under a floating than a fixed exchange rate, while the converse is true for a small, relatively open economy. This is because the terms of trade, resource shift, and price instability costs of depreciation are less burdensome when the share of foreign trade in the economy is relatively low, as is the case in a large country. On the other hand, the output shrinkage needed to deal with a given deficit is higher in a relatively closed than in a small open economy because the MPM is lower in a large country. It follows that a large country should float independently, while a small country, especially one possessing price-wage flexibility, may do well to join a currency area.

Adoption of a common currency is the most extreme form of financial integration within an optimum currency area. Money performs its functions (as a means of exchange and store of value) best if the same unit covers a wide area. Thus, a worldwide currency is the best from the viewpoint of stimulating saving and economic growth. Barring such a currency, the next best thing would be a currency common to several countries willing and able to meet the conditions for such an arrangement. In what follows we explore the issues involved in forming a currency union in the European Union.

Monetary Integration in the EU[9]   EU planners have long considered monetary unification an essential ingredient of European integration. This was expected to have two components, free mobility of capital within the EU, introduced in the Unified Market accord (EC 1992), and irrevocably fixed exchange rates within the EU, leading to a common currency, envisaged in the Maastricht Treaty of December 1991. A common currency would certainly save the cost of currency conversions inside the EU, estimated at 0.4 percent of EU GDP.

Historically, the move toward a common currency received a sharp stimulus from the adoption of the *Barre Plan* in February 1969, which set up a commission to coordinate the members' economic policies, and in particular to harmonize their monetary policies. A further step was taken in the May 1970 Werner Report, which included detailed specifics of monetary integration. Operationally, the move was reflected in the adoption of narrow exchange-rate margins for EU currencies after 1971, the joint currency float agreed upon in March 1973, and the EMS—which was introduced in 1979 but then fractured between 1992 and 1993.

Is a currency union a desirable objective for the EU? Alternatively, what type of countries can be viewed as an optimum currency area? At

---

[9] See B. Eichengreen, "European Monetary Unification," *Journal of Economic Literature*, September 1993; and C. Bean, "Economic and Monetary Union in Europe," *Journal of Economic Perspectives*, fall 1992.

one extreme, the population of a minicountry would choose to strike bargains and accumulate liquid wealth in terms of foreign currency.[10] Such a country clearly should join a monetary union with other countries, as Luxembourg does with Belgium, Liechtenstein with Switzerland, and Monaco with France. Advancing to larger states, the same reasoning does not necessarily apply to most of the small European countries. Before a country the size of Norway or the Netherlands joins a currency union, it must weigh the costs of balancing its external accounts through domestic policy, as would be required of a member of the union, and of balancing them through exchange-rate adjustment (remembering that as a member of a customs union the country has already given up its right for independent action on trade controls). The higher the country's marginal propensity to import, the lower are the costs of adjustment via domestic fiscal and monetary policy. For in case of a deficit, the higher the MPM, the more a given reduction in GDP will curtail imports and the less domestic unemployment is necessary to eliminate a given deficit. Likewise the higher the MPM, the smaller will be the increase in domestic expenditures necessary to eliminate a given external surplus. As a general rule, this implies that the smaller the country and the more open its economy, the less the cost of adjustment will be via domestic policies. The costs of adjusting to external imbalances through variations in the exchange rate include economic instability, which would arise as resources shift between the traded and nontraded goods industries in response to exchange fluctuations. Also, in the case of depreciation, there are losses in the terms of trade. These costs of adjustment tend to be larger in the case of small open economies, where foreign trade may occupy as much as one-half of GDP, than in large countries. In general, the more important trade is to a country, the greater will be the potential gain from price certainty in international trade and hence from the assurance of fixed exchange rates. Thus, the small European countries *may* do well to join a currency union.

This explains the pre-1979 arrangement where several small European countries pegged their currencies to the mark (Germany being their main trading partner) and floated jointly with it, thereby forming a German currency zone. However, the same rationale need not apply to the large members of the EU: Italy, France, Germany, or the United Kingdom. For the large countries, the cost of balancing the external accounts is less via exchange-rate adjustments than it is through domestic measures.

Are there circumstances under which even the large European countries would benefit, on balance, from a currency union—thereby justifying

[10] The chief disadvantages of floating rates for a small open region are the sheer cumbersomeness of the many foreign-exchange transactions that are necessary when most goods, and perhaps many services, are bought from and sold to other countries; the thinness of the foreign-exchange market and therefore the market's vulnerability to the machinations of individual speculators; and the sensitivity of the domestic price level to changes in import prices. Indeed, price fluctuations can be so severe that the currency would lose its store-of-value function.

the EMS and the move toward monetary unification in the EU? Two alternative sets of conditions can be so visualized: The first is a set of prerequisites which, if met, would minimize or eliminate external imbalances between members of the currency union to minimize the need to adjust. Ideally these countries should have identical growth rates in productivity and identical preferences concerning the unemployment–inflation mix that they consider desirable; their position on the Phillips curve (for example, trade union aggressiveness, industrial concentration, and structural unemployment) should be the same. A difference in any one respect can create problems, unless it is offset by a difference in another respect. Members of the EU have exhibited nonoffsetting differences in all three respects.

A second set of conditions that would (by minimizing intra-union imbalances) increase the benefits—relative to costs—of a currency union would be for members of the union to behave as though they were regions of one country. This would include a common monetary policy and a common central bank generating similar inflation rates; a high level of capital and labor mobility between members so that the depressed-flourishing area dichotomy would not be translated into unbalanced trade accounts; and an aggressive large-scale regional policy that would transfer resources to the depressed areas of the EU and stimulate economic activity in those areas by direct action of the central authorities of the union. These are not the present circumstances, and indeed the EMS has not administered a system of immutably fixed exchange rates. Eleven exchange-rate adjustments occurred within the EMS between 1979 and 1987, and the entire system was impaired during 1992–93. While fixed exchange rates within the EU *could* force members to coordinate their domestic policies and thereby attain a greater *convergence* of inflation and growth rates ("putting the cart before the horse"), the system did not weather the conditions that emerged in Europe in 1992–1993. Yet the push towards monetary unification continues unabated. It is based on the **Maastricht Treaty,** which was designed to induce members of the EU to act partly as though they were regions of one country.

The Maastricht Treaty In December 1991, leaders of the EU countries signed a treaty on monetary and political union in the Dutch village of Maastricht. It contains provisions for common social and labor policies, coordinated defense and foreign policies, and a significant transfer of power from national governments to the EU. But of special interest in the present context are the provisions for a **European Monetary Union (EMU)**[11] aimed at creating a common European currency and an independent EU central bank. Germany is by far the largest economic power in the EMU.

[11] In official publications the EC is now referred to as the EU, or European Union. For contemporary discussion see the *IMF Survey,* January 6, 1992, March 30, 1992, April 27, 1992, and June 8, 1992; and W. Hoskins, "A Market-Based View of European Monetary Union; Federal Reserve Bank of Cleveland *Economic Commentary,* April 1, 1989.

This eventual objective is to be met in stages. Initially, the policies of member countries will be closely coordinated with the idea of meeting stringent **convergence criteria** that are designed to harmonize interest rates, inflation rates, the ratio of the annual budgetary deficit to GDP, and the ratio of the country's public debt to GDP. In particular, a member state's consumer price inflation in the year before examination by the EU must not exceed the inflation rates of the three best-performing member states by more than 1-1/2 percentage points; long-term interest rates must not be more than 2 percentage points above those in the three member states with the lowest inflation; the exchange rate must have been held for two years within the narrow band of fluctuation of the Exchange Rate Mechanism of the European Monetary System (EMS) without a devaluation at the member state's own initiative; the general government deficit—that is, the consolidated deficit of the central, state, and local governments and the social security funds—must not surpass 3 percent of GDP; and the ratio of public debt to GDP should be no higher than 60 percent. The objective is to minimize the pressures of external imbalances between the EMU countries, but, as of 1996, only two member countries have met all the convergence criteria.

Once enough members achieve a sufficient degree of convergence in their fiscal stances, inflation, and interest rates, the exchange rates of the countries achieving this goal would be irrevocably fixed to the ECU (a weighted average of European currencies), and a European central bank would formulate common monetary policies. This is expected to occur before the year 2000. As currently envisaged, the overriding objective of the central bank would be to maintain price stability within the EMU area. To that end it would be prohibited from financing government deficits of member countries.

In the mid-1990s several EU members, including Germany and France, are undergoing painful belt-tightening measures to reduce their budgetary deficits to 3 percent of GDP. The EU hopes that by year 1999 a core group of member countries, centered on Germany and France but not including the U.K., will adopt irrevocably fixed exchange rates, to be followed by a common currency called the *Euro*. It is expected that budgetary discipline will continue after the adoption of the new currency. However, it is not known what monetary relations will be established between the Euro and the currencies of EU members that opted out of the common currency.

We turn next to exchange rate regimes that involve government control of currency transactions.

For updated material please see Chapter 18, "The Euro Is Coming," beginning on page 493.

EXCHANGE CONTROL

A country with a fixed exchange rate may choose to maintain an overvalued currency. Refusal to devalue in the face of persistent external deficits may be based on such reasons as the prestige accorded the exchange rate in the popular mind or the existence of large government debts denominated in

FIGURE 16.2   *China's Foreign Exchange Market*

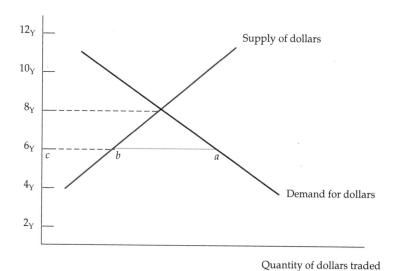

Price of foreign currency (one dollar)
in terms of Chinese yuans

While the market-clearing exchange rate is $1 = 8 yuan, the Chinese government fixes the rate at $1 = 6 yuan, yielding excess demand for dollars *ab*.

foreign currencies. Under such conditions, the government may be forced to impose **exchange control** because if foreign currencies are undervalued in price (priced below the equilibrium level) or, equivalently, if the domestic currency is overvalued, the price mechanism cannot clear the foreign exchange market. Instead, it generates excess demand for the undervalued, or "cheap," foreign currencies.

This situation can be met temporarily by using reserves or by borrowing. But if it persists over a period of years, the country may be forced to seek an alternative to the market mechanism by resorting to direct exchange control. Although comprehensive exchange control is only of historical interest for the industrial countries, it is common in the developing nations. On the other hand, the European countries were subject to such controls after World War II until late in the 1950s. Even in the 1990s Spain controls capital outflow in order to maintain a fixed exchange value of its currency within the EMS.

In figure 16.2, Chinese yuans are represented as the home currency and foreign currencies are represented by the U.S. dollar. The vertical axis shows the price of one dollar in terms of yuans; the horizontal axis indicates the number of dollars traded. Normal supply and demand curves for dollars are drawn: The equilibrium price or exchange rate is $1 = 8 yuans, or 1 yuan = $0.125. This is the price that clears the market. It performs the function of allocating available dollars among competing uses.

Suppose the Chinese government decides to fix the dollar at 6 yuans. The dollar will then be *undervalued* compared to its equilibrium price; and the yuan, at $0.167 instead of $0.125, will be correspondingly *overvalued* compared to the equilibrium price. This arbitrary exchange rate cannot be sustained for a long period of time, because it creates excess demand for dollars in the amount $\overline{ab}$ (shaded line). If the government refuses to devalue the yuan to $0.125, it will be forced to impose exchange control. This makes it possible to maintain an exchange rate that departs from its equilibrium value. Instead of the market price performing the allocative function, a government agency must now determine how to allocate the $\overline{bc}$ available dollars among the larger quantity demanded, $\overline{ac}$.

Under a system of comprehensive exchange control, all earners of foreign currencies must surrender their proceeds to the control authority (in exchange for the local currency)—the central bank or a special division set up in the treasury—while users of such currencies must obtain a government license before buying them (for the local currency), at the official exchange rate, in order to engage in international transactions.

Currency convertibility is restricted under exchange control. In fact, under this system currency is often said to be *not convertible*, because citizens cannot convert it to other currencies without a government license. Depending on the regulations, the currency can be convertible for current transactions and yet not convertible for capital transfers.

Under an exchange-control system, government officials rather than market forces determine how the available foreign exchange is to be distributed among various goods and services, among sources of supply (supplying countries), among importers and other users, and over time. Such decisions are likely to be arbitrary and at times even capricious. Furthermore, because the supply of imported commodities is restricted, their price on the domestic market rises with the imposition of controls. The importers therefore realize more profit per unit than they would have enjoyed in the absence of exchange restrictions. Thus, the foreign exchange license itself assumes a considerable market value, occasionally inviting corruption and fraud on the part of the officials issuing the licenses. On certain occasions, governments practicing exchange control have auctioned foreign currency licenses.

A corporation that is planning production or distribution activity in a country under exchange control, such as India, needs to ascertain in advance whether it would be able to repatriate the profits earned in its operations.

FIGURE 16.3   *Effect of Exchange Control*

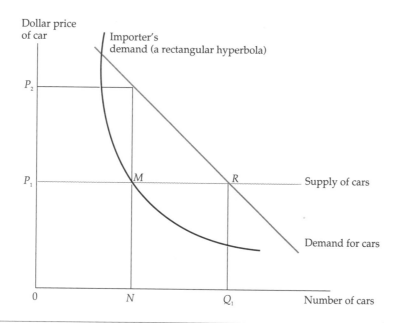

Under exchange control the importers' demand curve, governed by the fixed amount of foreign currency allocated to import the commodity, is a rectangular hyperbola. It departs from the consumers' demand curve. The price rises from P_1 to P_2, and the difference between the two prices accrues to the importer.

Additional Insights

An illustration will show the extent of price increase that results from exchange control and the consequent monopoly profit. Assume that the Indian government imposes exchange control and decides to restrict the number of dollars spent on imported automobiles to one-half the free market amount. Because India does not produce cars, the (shaded) supply-and-demand curves in figure 16.3 refers to imports. The supply curve is horizontal, reflecting the fact that India is a small importer of cars by international standards. It can import all the cars it wants at a fixed price. Free market price P_1 is established, Q_1 cars being imported at total dollar expenditures of OP_1RQ_1. This is the amount that the control authority decides to cut in half. In other words, importers would be allowed to spend only OP_1MN dollars.

While the consumer demand curve remains unchanged, the importers' demand curve now diverges from it, because it is governed by the amount of foreign exchange allocation. The new importers' demand curve is now characterized by the fact that the area under it (total dollar expenditures, or price times quantity) is fixed at OP_1MN.

Such demand conditions are represented by a (colored) *rectangular hyperbola* passing through point *M*. A rectangular hyperbola represents a unitary elasticity demand schedule, in which the price times quantity does not change as we move along the curve. This curve intersects the foreign supply function at point *M*. Thus, the quantity imported is reduced to *N* and the import price remains at P_1. Total dollar cost is OP_1MN and equals the official allocation.

But the demand of domestic consumers has not changed. Quantity *N* will command price P_2 rupees on the internal market, $P_2 - P_1$ representing the importers' monopoly rent per car.[12] The less elastic the local demand is for the product, the higher the profit per unit will be. This can be verified by drawing a steeper demand curve through point *R* and comparing the results.

Exchange control can be used as a device for limiting commodity imports in much the same way that tariffs or quotas limit imports. It makes little difference whether the authorities restrict the number of cars that may enter the country or whether they limit the quantity of foreign exchange allocated for automobile imports.

Since the government decides what shall be imported, in what quantities, and from what sources, exchange control enables the government of an LDC to guide the entire development process of the country. But it may guide it away from—rather than toward—comparative advantage configuration.

An exchange-control system is more effective than trade restriction for dealing with the balance-of-payments deficits, however, because it encompasses all transactions, including services and capital movement, while tariffs and quotas are restricted to commodity trade. Also, the usual focus and intent of exchange control is to maintain external balance, while that of tariffs is to offer protection to domestic industries from foreign competition.

A government may wish at times to place under control only capital transfers, not current transactions. This was the original intent of exchange control when it was introduced in Europe in the 1930s. The IMF charter permits the imposition of exchange control only to combat severe capital outflow, because under certain conditions, direct control may be the only way to combat the illegal flow of capital. Yet the fact that capital flight from underdeveloped countries was estimated at between $71 and $132 billion from 1976 to 1984 shows that exchange control is not wholly effective in stopping it. One way people evade the regulations and make capital transfers is under the guise of regular transactions. Exporters **underbill** the foreign importers and instruct them to deposit the difference in the

---

[12]This is a potential source of corruption for government officials. The foreign currency license is valuable to the (often wealthy) importers in terms of their profits, and it is issued by government officials with modest incomes—a clear invitation for bribery.

exporters' foreign bank accounts, while importers **overpay** the foreign exporters, with the difference deposited in the importers' foreign bank accounts. Also, like any other rationing system, exchange control generates a black market. That partial evasion by commodity traders gives rise to an undeclared supply of foreign currencies was just illustrated. On the other side of the market are potential users of foreign exchange, such as travelers, who, because they are denied an allocation by the control authority, are willing to pay a higher price than the official exchange rate. They constitute the demand side of the equation. Thus, foreign currencies are traded at a higher price, in terms of the domestic currency, than the official rate.

From an economic standpoint, exchange control and the attendant rationing of foreign exchange often result in misallocation of resources. Market prices no longer indicate priorities concerning what or how much is needed by producers and desired by consumers. Nor is there a guarantee that the arbitrary decisions of government officials will conform to these priorities.

Furthermore, in attempting to promote exports with an overvalued currency, governments resort to **multiple exchange rates** that further distort the structure of the economy (in addition to their administrative complications). If the official value of the yuan is $1 = 6$ yuans, the Chinese government may encourage certain exports and discourage other imports by placing those commodities at a lower exchange value for the yuan—say $1 = 9$ yuans. This amounts to a 50 percent depreciation of the yuan with respect to the specified commodities. Exporters obtain one-half more yuans for their foreign-currency proceeds, while importers must pay more yuans for the dollars that they need to buy the merchandise—precisely the same as under depreciation. A government may adopt a more discriminatory approach and introduce a whole array of exchange rates, with commodities classified according to the degree of encouragement or discouragement attached to their exportation and importation, respectively.

Incidentally, many types of interference with free trade and payments are tantamount to partial and disguised forms of devaluation. For example, assume that a country tries to combat an external deficit by levying import taxes and providing export subsidies, both to the extent of 10 percent. In terms of government revenue, these may roughly balance each other out to effect neutrality. But their real effect is to make imports more expensive and simultaneously to cheapen exports—precisely the effect of a 10 percent devaluation. However, whereas devaluation affects all balance-of-payments items, including service and capital transactions, the trade measures apply only to merchandise.

In general, imports can be discouraged by a whole maze of trade restrictions and exchange controls, such as a requirement that importers deposit at the central bank, for 3 to 6 months and without interest, a sum equal to a given fraction of their intended imports. This is known as an *advanced import deposit*. In turn, exports are encouraged by offering to exchange the foreign currency proceeds for domestic currency at a more favorable rate, by arranging for cheaper raw materials for the producers of export goods, offering cheap official credit to finance exports, and other measures. Indeed, the granting of official export credit at subsidized interest rates has become common among industrial countries.

Many developing countries suffer from elaborate systems of control that replace the simple market mechanism and leave a large measure of latitude to government officials in making arbitrary decisions. The result frequently is gross misallocation of resources, which radically distorts the structure of trade, investment, and production, and hampers the development process. Overt devaluation quite often replaces this disguised devaluation when the controls become so cumbersome as to be unmanageable. On occasion, a country is led to scrap its complex system of many exchange rates and substitute a dual exchange-rate regime: a fixed rate for certain specified transactions and a floating rate for all other transactions. Several Latin American countries have experimented with such a dual rate. In the 1990s, as a part of general liberalization, many LDCs have scrapped their exchange control and moved toward market-determined exchange rates. For example, Venezuela lifted exchange control in 1996. China introduced a uniform exchange rate in 1994, and plans to remove controls on current account transactions in 1997.

BILATERAL CLEARING AGREEMENTS

Countries that are devoid of foreign-currency holdings, or nearly so, and still wish to stimulate trade sometimes resort to **bilateral exchange-clearing agreements.** These were introduced on a large scale in Europe immediately following World War II. Today such agreements exist among the LDCs and between the former socialist states.

An agreement between, say, India and Russia would work as follows: Indian importers from Russia pay in rupees (India's currency) into a special account set up in India's central bank, while Indian exporters to Russia draw payments in rupees from the same account. Likewise, Russian importers from India pay in rubles (Russia's currency) into a special account set up in Russia's central bank, while Russian exporters to India draw payments in rubles from the same account. As long as the bilateral trade is balanced, the two accounts show zero balances. Trade between the two countries is reduced to its barter essentials, and no exchange of currencies is needed to finance it. To deal with cases where the bilateral trade is out of balance, the two countries agree in advance on a mutual line of credit, known as the *swing* (since it can shift directions), up to a predetermined level. Only if the cumulative deficits exceed the limit is the debtor country obligated to pay up in dollars or other hard currencies.

Because the two countries involved are usually short of hard currencies, they try to avoid such an eventuality. Suppose that Russia has a bilateral surplus, and India has a deficit. Then India would encourage its exporters to ship to Russia, and its importers to buy from non-Russian sources. The surplus country (Russia) would do the opposite, in order to avoid a bilateral surplus which obligates it to extend automatic credits to India. As a result, the volume of trade is reduced to the lowest common denominator. Equally important, the direction of trade is no longer governed by comparative advantage, as is the case if each trader sells where it is most expensive and buys where it is cheapest. Instead, trade is channeled into lines dictated by the need for bilateral balancing of the accounts. Relative prices in various sources and destinations are relegated to a secondary role, as buyer and seller alike follow government directives concerning their trading partners. Although highly disruptive, these arrangements are superior to barter trade (known as **countertrade**[13]).

Although bilateral exchange clearing agreements are now rare among the industrial countries, in the immediate postwar years Western Europe was covered by a network of over 400 such agreements. Every country had to balance its external accounts bilaterally with each of the other 17 European countries—an administrative nightmare.

To overcome this, the **European Payments Union (EPU)** was established in 1950, and it functioned in Europe until 1958. All bilateral accounts were centralized in the EPU, which provided a mechanism for multilateral clearing of balances. If in a bilateral setting country A had a surplus with country B, then B owed the money to the EPU instead of to A, while A was owed by the EPU instead of by B. In this fashion, country A's surplus with B could be applied to its deficit with country C, and the need for bilateral balancing was avoided. In addition to the clearing function, the EPU provided credit to its member countries. Having met its objective, the EPU was dismantled in 1958, as the European currencies gradually became convertible to dollars. It was replaced by another instrument of regional cooperation, the European Monetary Agreement, later followed by the EMS.

---

[13] Although trade among industrial countries is now financed by transfers of convertible currencies, transactions with the former communist or underdeveloped countries often necessitate barter arrangements. An exchange of Iranian oil for Czechoslovakian power-generating stations is a case in point, and a barter of Yugoslavian railroad cars for New Zealand butter is another. More complicated cases arise when there is nothing in the buyer's country that the seller wants. In a typical instance, an American exporter sold some used tiremaking machinery in Eastern Europe for a very attractive price but in a nonconvertible currency. Because of a surplus in a trade agreement between the buying country and Turkey, the money could be used to buy Turkish lira and, with those funds, Turkish chromium. The chromium, in turn, was sold in a fourth country for hard currency. Such transactions, known as *countertrade,* are also used by companies that find themselves holding funds blocked in a country that is under exchange control (*blocked accounts*). As they are not allowed to convert their pesos or rupees into dollars or marks, they often have to purchase local products for sale abroad. Countertrade has increased in recent years, and it now accounts for 5 percent of total world trade. See "Countertrade: Trade without Cash," *Finance and Development,* December 1983; and "Countertrade," *UNCTAD Bulletin,* March 1987. The latter article reviews the various forms of countertrade, the reasons for it, and its costs and benefits.

Summary

After considering the relative merits of fixed and floating exchange rates, this chapter reviewed alternative exchange rate arrangements, such as optimum currency areas and exchange control.

A floating exchange rate has the advantage of producing overall balance-of-payments equilibrium, and thereby obviating the need for international reserves. It also makes monetary policy an effective tool for domestic stabilization. On the other hand, it introduces risk to international transactions, and may cause a reduction in trade and foreign investment activity. This is particularly true if speculative activity magnifies the amplitude of exchange fluctuations. Additionally, a floating rate assures equilibrium only in the overall balance, and not in partial balances. Since governments are often concerned with partial balances, the exchange rate itself becomes a policy target. A fixed exchange rate does not assure overall balance-of-payments equilibrium, and requires the use of international reserves. But it reduces the risk of international transactions, except when the currency is suspected of being too weak (strong) and in danger of devaluation (revaluation). Additionally, a fixed exchange rate forces discipline in the conduct of domestic policy, because a policy that leads to inflation would produce nonsustainable external deficits.

Although the record of floating exchange-rate systems is mixed, showing rather large and prolonged exchange fluctuations, the system weathered well a number of serious disturbances in the international economy. Many LDCs opted to switch from fixed to floating exchange rates. And in the 1990s several Eastern European and former Soviet republics adopted floating rates. While some of these nations retained the Russian ruble as their currency, others chose to issue new national currencies, and established their own central banks.

Alternatives between fixed and freely floating exchange rates include proposals for wider bands, crawling pegs, target zones, and optimum currency areas (OCAs). An OCA is a group of closely knit countries that establish fixed exchange rates among themselves and float jointly against other such blocs of countries. A country would join such a bloc if the cost of eliminating an external deficit through domestic income contraction is lower than it would be through exchange depreciation. Usually that condition is met in small, open economies possessing a high measure of price-wage flexibility. It is desirable for the bloc countries to coordinate their domestic economic policies and provide for an extensive regional policy that assists depressed areas.

How does the analysis of OCAs apply to the proposed European Monetary Union (EMU)? It is likely that the small European countries do meet the criteria articulated in the previous paragraph. But Germany,

France, the United Kingdom, and Italy are unlikely candidates for an OCA. Yet if they choose to behave in such a way that external imbalances between them would be minimized, a monetary union is possible. At the very least, that requires policy coordination to ensure similar inflation and growth rates.

Indeed, this is what the Maastricht Treaty hopes to accomplish. The treaty aims at achieving a common currency in the EU, or at least immutably fixed exchange rates, by the year 2000. To approach this goal it designated convergence criteria to harmonize inflation, interest rates, and fiscal stances of member nations; countries meeting these criteria could join the EMU. Although the widening of the EMS bands in 1993 was a setback to the plan, the EU intends to proceed with monetary unification.

For a variety of reasons, a country on a fixed exchange rate may choose to maintain an overvalued currency. In that case it could be forced to impose exchange control on its citizens: All earnings of foreign currencies must be surrendered to the government (in exchange for local currency) at the official exchange rate, while people wishing to use foreign currencies must obtain a government permit before buying them for the local currency at the official exchange rate. A currency under exchange control is not convertible (at will) to foreign currencies. The government authorizes the allocation of scarce foreign currencies among competing uses. The system often leads to misallocation of resources, price increases of imported commodities, a black market in foreign currencies, and corruption of government officials.

Occasional offshoots of exchange control are multiple exchange rates and bilateral clearing agreements. Along with countertrade, these practices are more harmful to economic efficiency than mere exchange control.

Important Concepts

Wider bands

Crawling pegs

Target zones

Optimum currency area (OCA)

Maastricht Treaty

European Monetary Union (EMU)

Convergence criteria

Exchange control

Currency convertibility

Export underbilling

Import overpaying

Multiple exchange rates

Bilateral exchange-clearing agreement

Countertrade

European Payments Union (EPU)

Review
Questions

1. a. Compare and contrast a fixed and a floating exchange-rate system. What is the historical evidence concerning their relative merit?
    b. What alternative exchange-rate systems exist between the two extremes?

2. How did floating exchange rates perform in the last two decades?

3. Did the system of floating exchange rates relieve the concern of policy makers regarding exchange rates and their countries' external positions? Did it lead to national independence in the pursuit of monetary policy?

4. What currency regimes were adopted by East European countries and the states of the former Soviet Union?

5. Is the EU an ideal *optimum currency area?* Why or why not? What is an OCA?

6. Explain the Maastricht Treaty and its *convergence criteria.* Why are such criteria necessary?

7. a. Using a graph like figure 16.2, explain a system of exchange control in India. Look up the rupee-dollar exchange rate to present a realistic graph.
    b. Show (as in figure 16.3) what would happen to the price of imported computers in India.
    c. Would you expect a black market in foreign currencies to emerge? How?

8. Explain the functions of:
    a. Multiple exchange rates
    b. Bilateral clearing agreements
    c. Countertrade

9. Describe a hypothetical bilateral clearing agreement between China and Mexico.

CHAPTER
17

Historical Survey[1]

I n order to place the current international financial scene in proper perspective, it is useful to survey the past 125 years of global financial history. The era is divided into several periods, distinguished on the basis of major financial events.

The Gold Standard (1870–1914)

During these years most currencies were pegged to gold, with each central bank buying and selling gold at a fixed price in terms of its currency. London was the main financial center of the world. Although exchange-rate adjustments were not unheard of, there was a core of major European currencies whose exchange rates were kept completely fixed. This was allegedly accomplished by the central bankers adhering strictly to the **rules of the game** in their domestic monetary policies (fiscal policies of any kind were not commonly in use): They deflated in times of external deficit and inflated in times of surplus thereby reinforcing the automatic effects of imbalances on the domestic money supply. The attainment and maintenance of external balance was the paramount concern of policymakers, and domestic economic conditions were manipulated to the extent necessary to maintain external equilibrium. Even so, historical studies suggest that the rules of the game were often violated as central banks neutralized their capital flows.

Several factors helped in carrying out adjustment to external imbalances. Prices and wages were flexible in a downward as well as an upward direction. Thus, by deflating the economy in times of deficit, both the price

[1] For a comprehensive survey, see R. I. McKinnon, "The Rules of the Game: International Money in Historical Perspective," *Journal of Economic Literature*, March 1993.

and income mechanisms exerted a powerful balancing pressure. Prices in the deficit country could actually decline while those in the surplus country increased. As a consequence, large changes in relative prices in the desired direction could be attained under fixed exchange rates.

Also, wage–price flexibility took some of the sting out of contractionary policies, because a large component of the total effect of such policies was on prices rather than on income and employment. Recall that the equation of exchange, $MV = PO$, is an identity that holds at all times. If total spending on goods and services in the economy declines because of contractionary policies, the impact can be felt either on the price level or on the volume of output (and therefore employment) or on both. To the extent that prices are flexible, variations in them can absorb part of the impact, and the painful effect on output and employment is thereby mitigated. This flexibility must have made central banks more willing than they are now to accept the domestic consequences of the rules of the game.

Furthermore, Europe at that time was reasonably free of direct government controls over trade and payments in the form of import quotas and exchange controls. Even tariffs, although common, did not vary much over the years. Consequently, the price mechanism was permitted to function almost freely in the international arena and to exert its stabilizing influence.

Finally, capital movements were generally stabilizing in nature. They responded swiftly to interest differentials, making it easy for a country to bridge short-term balance-of-payments deficits by raising interest rates.

The gold standard was brought to an abrupt end by World War I. The ravages of war and the differential rates of inflation in various countries destroyed the underlying price–cost relationships on which the prewar exchange rates had been based.

Fluctuating Exchange Rates and Currency Stabilization

Under the system that emerged from World War I, major currencies were left to fluctuate. But that arrangement (1918–1923) was viewed as an interlude until conditions stabilized and countries could go back to the gold standard. The *purchasing power parity* theory was originally developed in that context. Starting from an equilibrium pre–World War I exchange rate of £1 = $5, if U.S. prices doubled during the war while the U.K. price index quadrupled, the postwar exchange rate should have been set at £1 = $2.50. Yet, despite the fact that cost and price ratios between countries changed radically during World War I, it was considered a matter of national prestige by every country to restore its prewar parity.

From 1923 to 1928, one country after another returned to the gold standard at the prewar exchange rate. The British pound, for example, was stabilized at $5. This was done by unilateral action on the part of the countries concerned; international cooperation, so vitally necessary in these matters, was totally lacking. For the now-overvalued currencies, this action contained the seeds of further disturbances. It brought a strain on the balance of payments as well as on the domestic economies that had to bear the brunt of the adjustment process.

The Devaluation Cycle (1930–1939)

Several countries yielded to pressure and went off the gold standard. The pound sterling in particular became a fluctuating currency in 1930. Since the fluctuations were at times violent, a special agency was established in 1931 to help smooth them by buying and selling foreign and domestic financial assets.

Other countries, primarily those of the **Sterling Area,**[2] pegged their currencies to the fluctuating sterling. It was through this action that the Sterling Area first assumed a formal economic status. In most cases devaluations were taken at that time either to bridge balance-of-payments deficits or to help decrease domestic unemployment by raising exports and lowering imports. Since this was done at the expense of the country's trading partners, it was subject to retaliation by competitive devaluation.

Not all countries devalued. The French led a small group of nations that remained on gold at the previous exchange rates and became known as the *gold bloc.* France chose to tackle the resulting balance-of-payments deficits by imposing import quotas. Thus, the first time an import quota was used by a major power, it was for the purpose of dealing with balance-of-payments deficits rather than for protection. Germany, on the other hand, imposed exchange control to avoid devaluation and subsequently used its control system to manipulate international power politics. The pound sterling, the franc, and the dollar became the major convertible currencies.

In 1936, France, the United Kingdom, and the United States negotiated an agreement to enable France to devalue without retaliation. The resulting *tripartite declaration,* subsequently adhered to by four additional countries, ushered in a period of informal cooperation in international finance—the only such period between the two world wars. Cooperation was short-lived, however, interrupted abruptly by World War II, during which most combatants imposed exchange control. The British operated a *dollar pool,* through which they centralized and controlled the dollar dealings of the entire Sterling Area.

Bretton Woods (July 1944)

At the end of World War II, delegates of 44 nations held a conference in **Bretton Woods,** New Hampshire, to discuss pressing economic problems. The painful lessons of the 1930s were not lost on the participants, so the aftermath of World War II was characterized by cooperation in international financial matters. While there was a widespread desire to restore

---

[2] Members of the British Commonwealth and other countries attached to the sterling.

fixed exchange rates, it was also recognized that the rules of the game would have to be modified as countries now wished to accord a relatively higher priority to domestic stabilization.

Two plans for an international monetary system were considered at the conference: the British plan authored by Keynes and the American plan of Harry White. Keynes was concerned about the excessive reliance on bilateral clearing arrangements after the war and about the deflationary bias imparted to the international economy when the responsibility of adjustment rests primarily with deficit countries. He proposed the creation of an international clearing union with unlimited opportunity for clearing balances, large automatic credit provisions, and the ability to create international reserves. Also, the code of behavior he proposed placed many of the responsibilities of adjustment on the shoulders of the surplus countries.

What emerged from Bretton Woods was a fund (the IMF) rather than a clearing union. It was akin to the White plan presented on behalf of the American delegation. In fact, the conferees agreed to set up two sister institutions: The International Bank for Reconstruction and Development, now called the World Bank,[3] which was to help in European reconstruction and later serve as an instrument for financing economic development; and the IMF, which was to become the central international financial institution. Fixed exchange rates, with all currencies anchored to the U.S. dollar, were an integral part of the Bretton Woods system.

Each central bank pegged its currency to the dollar in a manner described in figures 12.2 and 12.3 (Chapter 12). The total spread allowed under the system was 2 percent—1 percent on either side of par. When a currency became weak (as a result of a balance-of-payments deficit) and dropped to its lower support limit, the central bank bought its currency in exchange for dollars to maintain the limit. The country's dollar reserves and money supply declined. Wherever a currency became strong and rose to its upper support limit, it was up to the central bank to sell its currency in exchange for dollars to prevent it from rising above the limit. The country's dollar reserves and money supply rose. To prevent the money supply from declining or rising, the central bank could buy or sell (respectively) government bonds in the domestic market.

Because each country anchored its currency to the dollar, the dollar itself became automatically pegged to all currencies. The U.S. monetary authorities *took a passive position*, not intervening in the currency market. Thus, if the mark rose (declined) to its upper (lower) limit, it was up to the Bundesbank, and not the Federal Reserve, to sell (buy) marks for dollars. And the same held for any other currency. The dollar was the common

---

[3] Despite its name, the World Bank is in no sense an international central bank. It makes long-term loans to developing countries out of subscription capital and from funds raised on the world's capital markets.

denominator as well as the international transactions, vehicle, intervention, and reserve currency.

European Reconstruction (1945–1958)

The years 1945–1950 witnessed intense reconstruction efforts in Europe, with the outpouring of American aid first under the Anglo-American loan agreement and then under the Marshall Plan. Intra-European trade was conducted through a network of bilateral clearing agreements. The continent was starved for dollars because the United States was the only source of plant and equipment as well as consumer goods. An intense **dollar shortage** developed.

The European Payments Union was established in 1950 and functioned in Europe until convertibility was restored in 1958. The fact that the European Common Market came into being in 1958 was no coincidence; it makes little sense to set up a common market for the purpose of freeing trade among nations while foreign payments remain subject to government control.

The Dollar Glut (1959–1970)

As of the late 1950s, the United States was running balance-of-payments deficits that averaged $3 billion per year. Their counterpart was European surpluses that enabled Europe to accumulate dollar reserves. But in the 1960s European countries began to feel saturated with dollar reserves—a **dollar glut**—and demanded conversion into gold. The United States attempted to cope with the deficits through a variety of administrative measures. For example, Congress eliminated the federal gold reserve requirement for all domestic currency except notes, in order to free gold for foreign transactions.

In an attempt to discourage European companies from raising capital in New York, a tax was imposed on American purchases of European securities. Finally, the main brunt of government policy was to directly restrict American corporate investments in Europe and limit American bank loans to European borrowers. These controls were lifted in January 1974.

In the circumstances prevailing in the 1960s, it would have been far better to lower the value of the dollar relative to the continental currencies. However, because of the dollar's unique role as the international *standard of value*, it could not be devalued. Rather, it was incumbent on the surplus countries to revalue their currencies relative to the dollar. Such a step would have improved the competitive position of the United States; and at the same time it would have been in the best interest of the revaluating countries themselves. West Germany had not only been "suffering" from balance-of-payments surpluses, but was also experiencing a domestic inflationary boom. Exchange revaluation would have raised the standard of living of the West German consumers as their mark wages would have purchased more foreign goods. It also would have helped to bring German inflation under control. Moreover, since there is a limit to the amount of reserves a country is likely to need, it did no good for West Germany to go on piling up reserves indefinitely. Revaluation is merely one way of reaping and distributing the fruits of increased productivity throughout the economy.

Beyond this, placing the burden of adjustment on the surplus countries (revaluation) is beneficial to the system as a whole. Traditionally that burden has fallen on the deficit countries. But a deficit country can only apply contractionary policies, which may bring about a recession, or it can impose exchange and trade restrictions. Indeed, the whole international financial system was discredited in the interwar period because its net effect was deflationary. If surplus countries were to assume more of the responsibility for adjustment, confidence in the system would be restored.

Why did West Germany resist revaluation? The answer is that two powerful economic groups were vehemently opposed to revaluation: the big export interests, who wished to maintain their competitive position in foreign markets; and the small farmers, who feared the effects of a reduction in the import prices of foreign farm products.

By 1970 another important currency had emerged with considerable strength, namely the Japanese yen. Japan's GDP had grown at the amazing annual rate of 10 to 13 percent in real terms. At the same time Japan rolled up massive trade surpluses. Along with the mark, the Japanese yen became a major candidate for revaluation early in the 1970s. Throughout the period the United States continued to mount sizable deficits, with Japan and Europe accumulating large dollar reserves. Confidence in the dollar, the cornerstone of the Bretton Woods system, was continuously eroding.

A *two-price system* for gold was introduced in 1968, separating official from private dealings in the yellow metal. It marked the first step in downgrading the role of gold in international finance. Accompanying this decision of the world's major central bankers was a decision to introduce, beginning in 1970, the Special Drawing Rights (SDRs) of the IMF as a new form of reserve assets.

The Smithsonian Agreement

By 1971 the U.S. deficit on official reserve transactions reached $30 billion, and a trade deficit ($2.7 billion) appeared for the first time in this century. In addition, the United States was suffering from unemployment as well as an unacceptably high rate of inflation. To deal with these circumstances President Nixon (in August 1971) introduced stimulative fiscal and monetary measures, and imposed price and wage controls to curb the inflation. The controls lasted, in one form or another, until April 1974. On the international front, the president announced a series of measures designed to bring about devaluation of the dollar in terms of other major currencies.

Under the newly announced policy, dollar holdings by foreign central banks would no longer be redeemable in gold by the United States. From then on, continued pegging to the dollar by foreign central bankers would place the world on a straight dollar standard. At the same time, foreign countries were invited to revalue their currencies against the dollar. To further encourage revaluation of the yen and the continental currencies, the president imposed a 10-percentage-point tariff surcharge on imports to the United States, to last until the exchange-rate adjustments took place.

The immediate response of most major countries was to stop pegging their currencies to the dollar and to adopt a *managed float* regime. Most currencies were allowed to appreciate 5 to 8 percent in terms of the dollar, but the United States did not consider this level of currency appreciation adequate. On December 18, 1971, at the Smithsonian Institution in Washington, the major financial nations announced an agreement on the realignment of exchange rates and restabilization of currencies. Under the **Smithsonian Agreement** the price of gold was raised from $35 to $38 per fine ounce, while the major currencies were revalued against the dollar in proportions ranging from 8.5 percent (the pound and franc) to 17 percent (the yen). From that point on, IMF accounts were to be maintained in SDRs.

As a part of the package, the United States removed the import surcharge, but the dollar remained nonconvertible into gold, and the U.S. "gold window" remained closed. Subsequent legislation created the Domestic International Sales Corporations (DISC). Under DISC, companies conducting 95 percent of their business in export trade were allowed to defer one-half of their corporate profit tax obligation. Thousands of U.S. companies had set up export subsidiaries to qualify as DISC corporations. The DISC device was discontinued in 1984.

The international financial system itself was hardly changed. The dollar was maintained as the intervention currency and the standard of value to which all other currencies were pegged, although these currencies would now be pegged at new exchange rates. However, the range of permissible fluctuations for each currency vis-à-vis the dollar (that is, the *band*) was widened from 2 percent to $4\frac{1}{2}$ percent—$2\frac{1}{4}$ percent on either side of the currency's *central rate*, namely, the dollar value in which it is defined.

After several months of post-Smithsonian calm, renewed international financial jitters again affected the United States. The $7 billion U.S. trade deficit in 1972 triggered a massive flight from the dollar, mainly toward the German mark. The United States used the situation to achieve a further devaluation of the dollar in February 1973.

March 1973—The Collapse of Bretton Woods

Both the United States and Europe had reasons to be dissatisfied with the Bretton Woods system: the United States because it could not change the exchange value of the dollar and Europe (as well as Japan) because of waning confidence in the dollar, the international reserve currency. Yet the demise of the system was actually caused by the onslaught of market forces, rather than by a deliberate decision of the world's central bankers. Fresh currency jitters erupted, forcing central bankers to seek a more permanent solution.

What emerged from their deliberations was a new exchange-rate regime: a system of *generalized managed floats*. This spelled the end of Bretton Woods and resulted in its replacement by the contemporary system. In 1978 the IMF approved a revision in its charter that permitted floating exchange rates indefinitely, and called for IMF surveillance over governments' exchange rate policies.

The 1974–1975 World Recession and Its Aftermath

In late 1973 and early 1974, the world financial scene came to be dominated by cutbacks in the supply of Arab oil and by a great increase in the price of oil introduced by the oil-producing cartel (OPEC). During 1973 the price of crude oil quadrupled (from $3 to $12 per barrel), with profound effects on the economies of most countries. Globally, the price increase implied a transfer of real resources from all oil-importing to all oil-producing countries. But different groups of countries were variably affected by the increase. The developing countries can be divided into three groups: oil-producing desert countries with sparse populations, such as Saudi Arabia and Kuwait; oil-producing "high absorption" developing countries, such as Indonesia and Nigeria; and oil-importing countries. The main problem the first group faced was that of excess riches: what to do with the immense fortune amassed, and how to ensure accumulation of enough real and financial earning assets to provide a substitute for the oil revenues once the wells became dry. For the most part, the countries of the first group placed their earnings in American and European banks and contracted with the industrial countries for the establishment of new industries on their soil. For the second group of oil producers, the high prices constituted an unmitigated boon. Practically all their oil revenues were spent on imported capital equipment. Their economic development was accelerated, and the problem of investment outlets for the additional earnings did not arise. It is the third group of developing countries that was subjected to an immense burden. Not only did they lack resources to pay the added cost of oil, but they encountered increased prices of essential oil-based products such as fertilizers, which raised the specter of a cutback in farm output. Certainly there had been a setback to their economic development. To cushion the impact these LDCs borrowed heavily in financial markets. Thus petrodollars were **recycled** from OPEC to oil-importing countries through the major banks.[4] While this alleviated the immediate problem of the oil-importing LDCs, it planted the seeds for the LDCs' debt problem of the 1980s.

---

[4]A problem created by the *recycling of petrodollars* in 1974 was that Arab countries preferred to place their funds in short-term deposits, while the (Eurodollar) banks receiving these deposits were faced with demands for long-term loans. Much of this demand came from countries in balance-of-payments difficulties. Prudent banking policy dictates a limitation on such "borrowing short and lending long." Therefore intergovernmental loans were used to supplement the private capital market.

In the industrial world, the rise of petroleum prices has had three effects: (1) It contributed to the subsequent double-digit inflation experienced from 1974 to 1975, because energy inputs enter the production of practically all products.[5] (2) It contributed to a long and deep recession at the same time, because the sum of $80 billion a year was transferred—in a form similar to a tax—out of the industrial and into the OPEC countries. Combining the two effects, the increase in oil prices contributed to—but was not the sole cause of—the "stagflation" of the mid-1970s. (3) The higher import bill for petroleum caused widespread external deficits[6], with their magnitude varying from country to country according to its dependence on imported energy.

Oil prices continued to advance gradually through the 1970s, and then doubled again from 1979 to 1980, reaching over $35 per barrel. But the price increase had the expected effects on the energy sector: Oil consumption declined gradually as consumers began to use less energy and as industrial users switched in part to non-oil forms of energy. At the same time production of oil substitutes, such as coal, expanded dramatically. These factors, plus the worldwide economic slump, combined to produce an oil glut on the world market in the 1980s. Prices slumped, and OPEC annual surpluses were reduced to a fraction of their previous size. Several oil-producing countries, such as Nigeria and Mexico, ran into severe financial difficulties. OPEC was faced with an urgent need to cut production in order to prevent prices from falling further, exacerbating tensions within the cartel.

Returning to the mid-1970s, only the United States among the industrial countries adopted the necessary monetary and fiscal stimulus in 1976 and 1977. In contrast, partly because of concern over inflation and partly because of institutional constraints, the German and Japanese economies remained at a virtual standstill over the two-year period. While the growth rate of the U.S. GDP was at the 5 to 6 percent level, that of Germany and Japan remained at 2 percent or less. The inflation rate in the United States was twice that of Germany and Japan. The differential inflation and growth rates go a long way toward explaining the large U.S. trade deficit in 1977 and 1978 and the massive surpluses in Germany and Japan.

The *floating exchange rate system* weathered the oil shock well, because it *allowed each country to choose its own rate of inflation.* Indeed it is doubtful whether a fixed-rate regime would have survived the 1970s.

Together the differential inflation and growth rates led to a sharp depreciation of the dollar. Relative to the yen and the mark, the dollar declined by 28.4 and 15.7 percent respectively. Aided by resumed growth in Europe, the depreciation (after a 2–3 quarter lag) helped reverse the

---

[5] Other factors contributing to the global inflation were widespread drought, disappearance of the anchovy catch off the South American coast (anchovies are used by farmers to feed livestock), and the introduction of antipollution regulations.

[6] As people dipped into their savings to pay for the higher cost of oil, there was a reduction in $(S - I)$ corresponding to a decline in $(X - M)$.

U.S. trade performance. A turnaround occurred in 1979 and 1980 when a surge in overseas shipments increased this country's share in the manufacturing exports of all industrial countries from 14.7 to 15.6 percent. The surge in exports occurred across most commodity categories. Only autos, steel, and household appliances failed to participate. This improved U.S. trade position continued into the first half of 1981.

The Rise of the Dollar Exchange Rate, 1981–1985

Causes The situation changed dramatically during the next four years, when the international financial scene came to be dominated by the sharply rising real and nominal and exchange value of the dollar (figure 17.1). Tight monetary policy (with the Federal Reserve observing a *money supply target* between October 1979 and October 1982), followed by expansionary fiscal policy, propelled U.S. interest rates to unprecedented heights and plunged the economy into a recession. Subsequent expansion in the money supply turned the economy around, and a prolonged expansion followed in the years between 1983 and 1989.

Despite the economic recovery, **U.S. budgetary deficits** continued to grow through the 1980s, largely as a result of the Reagan tax cut early in the decade. Reaching $210 billion in 1985 (or over 5 percent of GDP, up from 2 percent in 1971–1981), the deficits caused real interest rates (nominal interest minus the expected rate of inflation) to remain high both by U.S. historical standards *and* relative to foreign rates. In contrast, tight fiscal policies in Europe helped keep European interest rates lower than U.S. rates. This attracted large sums of capital from Europe and Japan for placement in U.S. financial instruments, including treasury bonds.[7] That raised the demand for dollars and increased the dollar exchange rate. The capital influx was supplemented by a reduction in U.S. capital outflow, as U.S. banks withheld loans to the LDCs. The massive availability of foreign funds kept U.S. interest rates lower than they would have been in the absence of capital inflow.

As the demand for dollars on the foreign exchange markets rose, so did their value. Between 1980 and February 1985 the effective exchange rate of the dollar increased by over 60 percent. Its value rose from 1.71 to 3.48 D.M. and from 4 to over 10 F.F. Limited intervention in the foreign currency markets by the central banks failed to stem the tide of the rising dollar.

Effects on the United States The overvaluation of the dollar relative to PPP helped contain inflation in the United States. But, on the other hand, it discouraged exports and encouraged imports, producing **trade deficits** of

---

[7] Between 1980 and the end of 1989, foreign direct investment in the United States increased by 300 percent; private foreign holdings of U.S. government securities jumped 500 percent, and foreign holdings of U.S. equities rose by 200 percent. For analysis, see D. Danker and P. Hooper, "International Financial Markets and the U.S. External Imbalance," Federal Reserve Board *Discussion Paper*, no. 372, January 1990.

FIGURE 17.1   *U.S. Dollar Trade-Weighted Real Exchange Rate, 1979–1993 (March 1973 = 100) and the Trade Balance (in color)*

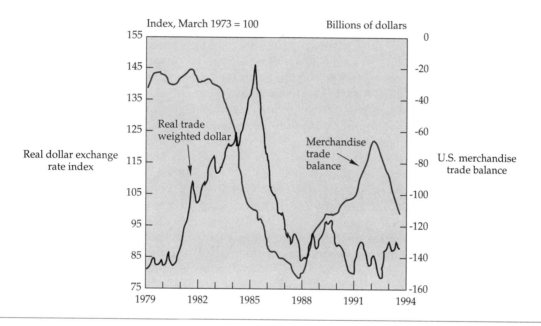

The dollar appreciated sharply in 1981–85; depreciated in 1985–88; and fluctuated since then. The merchandise trade deficit rose to a peak of $160 billion in 1987, declined during 1988–92, only to rise again in 1993 and beyond.

Source: Federal Reserve Bank of Cleveland, *Economic Trends*, December 1993.

over $100 billion per year beginning in 1983–1984. The linkages between the budget deficit and the trade deficit are as follows:

Linkages between the U.S. Budget Deficit and Trade Deficit, 1983–1985

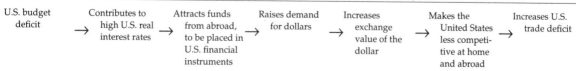

| U.S. budget deficit | → | Contributes to high U.S. real interest rates | → | Attracts funds from abroad, to be placed in U.S. financial instruments | → | Raises demand for dollars | → | Increases exchange value of the dollar | → | Makes the United States less competi- tive at home and abroad | → | Increases U.S. trade deficit |

The strong dollar explains about two-thirds of the trade deficit, while the other third is attributed to the rapid rise in U.S. real income, the reduction of Latin American imports from the United States caused by the external debt of LDCs, and the decline in U.S. farm exports as many countries became self-sufficient in food production. While the U.S. trade deficits reflected an excess of domestic investment over domestic savings (where the budgetary deficits are counted as negative savings), the sizable trade surpluses of Japan and Germany reflected an excess of domestic savings over domestic investment, and that excess flowed into the United States in the form of direct and portfolio investment. (These relationships were discussed in Chapter 10.) The United States had deficits on the current account and surpluses on the capital account, while Germany and Japan had surpluses on the current account and deficits on the capital account. The mechanism by which the United States ($I - S$) was converted to a trade-deficit country was a rise in interest rates causing an influx of foreign funds which in turn resulted in an appreciation of the dollar. In the 1980s the U.S. *current account deficits were a result of capital account surpluses* and not the other way around.

As the 1985 trade deficit approached 3.5 percent of GDP, it offset much of the stimulative effect of the budget deficit. Indeed, the overvalued dollar slowed, if not halted altogether, the recovery in the traded-goods sectors— mainly agriculture and manufacturing. These industries failed to participate in the general recovery, which was concentrated in the nontraded sectors, such as services. In the mid-1980s the United States became a net debtor nation for the first time since World War I; foreigners owned more assets in the United States (in all forms) than Americans held abroad.[8] By 1996 the net international debt position stood at $800 billion. The phrase *twin towers of debt* originated at this time, referring to the U.S. public debt caused by budgetary deficits and the related external debt caused by the trade deficits.

A serious repercussion of the sharp swings in the value of the dollar from a low in 1980 to a high in 1985 was the reallocation of domestic resources. Resources moved into the traded-goods industries between 1979 and 1980, and out of them from 1982 to 1985. For example, the low dollar signaled an expansion of U.S. agricultural capacity, supplying the export markets. The subsequent high dollar made that capacity obsolete, as U.S. farm products could not compete on world markets. This contributed to serious American farm problems in the mid-1980s.

A strong protectionist sentiment swept the Congress as a result of the overvalued dollar and the mounting trade deficits. But import restrictions in whatever form were never the proper response to what was essentially a macroeconomic phenomenon. They would invite retaliation by U.S. trading partners, raise the cost of goods to the consumer, and perhaps be partly offset by further appreciation of the dollar. Protectionism attacks the

---

[8] The United States is sometimes likened to LDCs (such as Mexico) who also mounted large external debt. Indeed in both cases it represents a *country living beyond its means*. But there the analogy ends, and two differences emerge. The U.S. debt occurred because foreigners wish to hold dollar assets; while Mexico's debt—whatever its causes—did not come about because of high world demand for pesos. Second, the American debt is denominated in dollars, of which the United States is the country of issue. LDC debt is also denominated in dollars, which these countries do not issue.

symptom of the problem rather than its root cause. Two-thirds of the deficit could be attributed to the overvalued dollar. In turn, the overvaluation of the dollar was a result of expansionary U.S. fiscal policy and tight monetary policy, whereas an opposite combination of policies prevails in other industrial countries. It is by reversing these two sets of policies that the deficits could be reduced.

In sum, the dollar appreciation had the following effects in the United States: It curbed inflation, caused large trade deficits, produced a reallocation of resources from the traded- to the nontraded-goods sectors, and induced a flurry of protectionist bills in Congress.

Effects on Foreign Countries   In foreign countries, the rising dollar stimulated the export- and import-competing sectors. In particular the German and Japanese trade surpluses were comparable to the U.S. deficits as a proportion to each country's GDP. And that had a stimulative effect on their economies and contributed to a global economic recovery. On the other hand, high U.S. real interest rates forced the European countries to maintain higher rates than they considered desirable, which had a dampening effect on economic activity.[9] This suggests that individual countries did not regain full independence in the conduct of monetary policy during the period of floating exchange rates. The widespread recognition of the effects of real exchange rate changes means that monetary policy still faces a balance-of-payments constraint: It must approximate the monetary policy being pursued abroad in order to avoid large exchange rate movements. "In the years of fixed exchange rates, the Europeans and Canadians had to follow U.S. monetary policy to avoid excessive swings in their payments balances; under flexible exchange rates, they have had to follow U.S. monetary policy to avoid excessive swings in their real exchange rates.[10]

But the European economy also suffers from structural rigidities that sharply curtail the mobility of resources (mainly labor) between sectors of the economy. In a period of rapid technological change, such rigidities produce unemployment, especially in the declining industries.[11] European unemployment was over 10 percent during 1984–87, declining to 8 percent in 1988–1990, but climbing back to double digits in the 1990s. Its high level has generated protectionist sentiment in Europe. Again protectionism is not the answer. The proper response is to address the cause of the problem which, in this case, is internal structural rigidities in Europe's labor markets and

[9] Estimates show that on balance the effect of the U.S. budget deficits on aggregate output in other industrial countries was positive. See P. Hooper, "International Repercussions of the U.S. Budget Deficits," Federal Reserve Board, *mimeographed,* January 1985.

[10] See R. M. Dunn, *The Many Disappointments of Flexible Exchange Rates*, Princeton Essay in International Finance, no. 154, December 1983.

[11] See Chap. 3 in Bela Balassa, *Change and Challenge in the World Economy*, New York, St. Martin's Press, 1985.

insufficient incentives for the unemployed to seek employment. These are the issues that EU policy makers are wrestling with in the 1990s.

The Dollar's Decline, 1985–1989

Extent of Dollar Depreciation   Although interest differentials in favor of the United States narrowed in mid-1984, the dollar continued its climb throughout the year and peaked only in February 1985.[12] In late 1984 and early 1985, its climb was rather precipitous, as was its decline in 1985 (figure 17.1). The depreciation between 1985 and 1986 was reinforced by massive and coordinated sales of dollars by the major central banks. This was a result of the **Plaza Accord,** an agreement by the finance ministers of the five main industrial nations to drive down the dollar, in a meeting held at New York's Plaza Hotel in September 1985. For the U.S. government *the intervention represented a sharp policy change from the nonintervention stance of earlier years.* The subsequent *Louvre Accord*, negotiated by the Group of Seven[13] in February 1987, set an informal (and unannounced) target zone for the dollar: between 1.7 and 1.9 D.M. and between 120 and 140 yen.

By 1987 the dollar lost half of its peak-level trade-weighted exchange value and returned to its 1980 rate. But in 1988–89 renewed interest rate differentials (reflecting the Federal Reserve's anti-inflation policy), unsettled political conditions in certain foreign countries, and the attraction of shares listed on the N.Y. Stock Exchange produced a new influx of funds into the United States. Currency intervention by the Group of Seven failed to stem the tide, and the dollar regained 10 to 15 percent of its value, only to decline again in subsequent months. In 1995 the dollar dipped to a record low of ¥80 and 1.4 D.M. but climbed back to ¥126 and 1.7 D.M. by April 1997.

Domestic Effects   The depreciation restored the U.S. competitive position, increased exports of certain industries, stimulated a measure of resource reallocation toward the traded-goods sectors, and brought about a limited resurgence in industrial production.

Because of the sizable appreciation of the yen, Japan experienced some of these effects in reverse. But mainly, Japanese companies responded by cutting production costs and moving production to other countries, mostly in the Far East, but also the United States. This movement intensified in the 1990s as the yen appreciated further. While the growing amount of Japanese investment in the United States increases American productivity

---

[12] In 1984 the attraction of high interest rates may have been supplemented by a *speculative bubble* as market actors expected to profit from further appreciation of the dollar. For review and analysis see a symposium in the *Economic Journal*, March 1987, 1–48. Another cause of the 1984 rise in the dollar may have been the removal of control on capital outflow in Japan, which possibly contributed to a surge in demand for dollar-denominated assets.

[13] The Group of Seven includes the United States, Japan, Germany, the United Kingdom, France, Italy, and Canada.

and improves management skills, it has fueled a protectionist sentiment within Congress.

Effect on the U.S. Trade Balance   The overall U.S. trade deficit failed to respond to the dollar depreciation during 1985–87. In fact the deficit continued to rise, reaching a peak of $160 billion in 1987 (figure 17.1) before receding to $127 billion in 1988 and about $119 billion in 1989.[14] Reasons for the delayed reaction include the normal J-curve effect; incomplete passthrough (foreign exporters absorbed a large share of their currency appreciation in order to limit the rise in dollar prices and maintain their share in the U.S. market); hysteresis (the prolonged overvaluation of the dollar resulted in foreign import penetration of the United States that could not be easily dislodged, and in withdrawal of American exporters from foreign markets that could not be easily reinstated); and full employment in the United States (by 1989 unemployment had dipped to 5.3 percent and capacity utilization exceeded 83 percent). Resources were not readily available for expansion of the export and import-competing industries.

The 1990s   In 1991 the U.S. trade deficit continued to decline, and because of large surpluses in service transactions, the deficits on goods and services reached a low of $30 billion in 1992. But the trade deficit rose again in 1992–95 primarily because of differential output and income growth at home and abroad. For the entire period 1990–95 the trade deficit averaged 0.9 percent of GDP, down from 1.8 percent in 1980–89. In both periods it equaled the excess of domestic investment over savings.

After eight years of uninterrupted expansion, the U.S. economy entered an eight-month recession in July 1990. Although the recession ended in March 1991, recovery was sluggish at first, with GDP growing at only one-third the rate of average postwar recoveries. Only in 1993–1997 was there a robust upswing in economic activity. Conditions in Europe and Japan were far worse, with stagnating output and rising unemployment. While the United States experienced slowly declining unemployment (to 5.2 percent by mid-1996), its trading partners had rising unemployment; in Europe its percentage reached double digits. While U.S. real GDP grew by about 2.7 percent, Europe and Japan experienced zero growth. As a result, imports into Europe and Japan stagnated, and pressure mounted on Japanese firms to seek foreign markets, mainly in the United States. At the same time U.S. imports rose because of the recovery and the 1996–7 appreciation of the dollar, accounting for the rising U.S. trade deficit in 1996.[15] The rising U.S. deficit with China is beginning to cause political friction between the two countries.

[14] See D. Howard, "Implications of the U.S. Current Account Deficit," *Journal of Economic Perspectives*, fall 1989.

[15] The dollar exchange rate declined sharply (to ¥82) in Winter 1995, only to rise again (to ¥119) in the subsequent year.

Another major event that marked the 1990s was the partial demise of the EMS in Europe, discussed in the last chapter. This was a result of large financial flows triggered by high German interest rates, along with the freeing of capital movements within the EU. But the EU appears to be pressing ahead with plans for a monetary union.

A third feature of the 1990s is the economic transformation of the transition economies in Eastern Europe and the former Soviet republics. As they move toward market economies, a few former Soviet nations issued their own national currencies, while others continued to use the Russian ruble.[16] Romania and Bulgaria adopted floating exchange rates, while some other East European countries opted for fixed rates. These countries acceded to the IMF. Finally, the 1990s witnessed the continued rapid growth of numerous LDCs, particularly in Asia. And countries as diverse as Pakistan, Argentina, and Brazil were adopting macroeconomic reforms to bolster their economies.

The LDC Debt Problem

In the early 1980s the world became painfully aware of **LDC debt.** Developing countries owed some $700 billion in external debt, constituting nearly 40 percent of their combined GDP. Their annual debt service exceeded one-fifth of their combined export earnings. The LDCs were having great difficulty in servicing (paying interest on) the debt, much less making payments on the principal. The burden of this debt was most heavily felt in Latin America. By the end of 1989 the LDC's debt approached $1.2 trillion. What caused this debt problem, and what was done about it?

Causes of the Debt Crisis   Over the years, shortage of domestic savings has forced LDCs to rely on capital inflows to finance investment. While the return to capital is potentially high (because of its relative scarcity), loans to finance consumption or unprofitable investment can easily result in bad and unrepayable debts. Over the past quarter-century, most inflows took the form of loans by private banks (attracted by high interest rates), as well as governmental and international lending institutions. Direct investment and other forms of equity financing have been low. Yet debt financing needs to be repaid regardless of whether or not profit is realized. *LDC governments usually assumed responsibility of repayment*, either because they were the borrowers, or because they guaranteed loans made to private enterprises.

LDC borrowing mushroomed in the mid-1970s and again in 1979–80 as a result of the sharp increases in oil prices. While the export earnings of the OPEC countries skyrocketed, the oil-importing countries—developed and developing alike—ran up sizable deficits. Since OPEC could not use up its surpluses fast enough, the accumulated petrodollars were placed on deposit

---

[16] See G. Spencer and A. Cheasty, "The Ruble Area: A Breaking of Old Ties?" *Finance and Development*, June 1993; and *IMF Survey*, November 14, 1994.

in the large banks of Europe and the United States. Thus, the industrial countries experienced capital inflows that offset their trade deficits. They were able to manage their balance-of-payments problem until proper adjustments could be made in the trade sector.

This was not the case for the oil-importing LDCs. To pay for their oil imports (now costing a multiple of the pre-1973 prices) they borrowed vast sums from commercial banks and other sources. Thus the petrodollars were "recycled" from OPEC to oil-importing LDCs through the large international banks.

When the time came to pay up, the LDCs were dealt a multiple blow. The worldwide recession of 1981–1982 made it harder for them to export to the industrial countries and to earn the foreign currencies needed to service the debt. Prices of primary commodities, the main export items of LDCs, plummeted. The rise in global interest rates increased the cost of servicing the debt.[17] And finally, since this debt was denominated in U.S. dollars, the sharp appreciation of the dollar raised the value of the debt in terms of all other currencies.

But these external factors explain only part of the problem. Mismanagement of their domestic economies played a central role. Overexpansionary fiscal and monetary policies, overvalued real exchange rates, and price and interest rate controls were key elements. From 1979 to 1982, for example, the public-sector deficit as a proportion of GDP rose from 7 to 15 percent in the main Latin American countries. These deficits were associated with inflationary pressures, weakening balance-of-payments positions. Overvalued real exchange rates produced a bias against the production and competitiveness of exportables while simultaneously encouraging imports. Furthermore, fears of impending depreciation, combined with high and variable inflation rates, often produced serious bouts of *capital flight*. Indeed, some estimates suggest that at the end of 1988, assets of Latin-American citizens held abroad ($300 billion) approximated their government and government-guaranteed bank debt. Finally, failure to adjust public-sector prices and interest rates weakened incentives for savings and the efficient allocation of investment.

Well-managed economies, like those of Korea and Taiwan, weathered the debt problem within a few years. But other countries, including Brazil, Argentina, and Mexico, encountered immense difficulties in meeting their debt obligations.[18] In Mexico the problem was compounded by slumping oil prices later in the decade and by the 1985 earthquake. The massive U.S. trade

---

[17]Much of this debt was contracted at "variable" interest rates tied to the London Inter Bank Offered Rate (LIBOR). Hence the cost of servicing it rises and declines with the movement of world interest rates. Between 1980 and 1983 the interest rate on the debt rose from 9.7 to 13.1 percent, raising the annual interest payments by over $20 billion. The real interest rate on Latin American debt rose from minus 10 percent in 1973–1978 to plus 8 percent in 1979–1982.

[18]Note that many of the 17 most heavily indebted countries, especially in Latin America, were *middle-income* rather than *low-income* LDCs.

deficits helped somewhat in the adjustment process, because they enabled Mexico and Brazil to mount substantial trade surpluses. But for the most part debt payments were *rescheduled* (namely, postponed for later years). In 1983 and 1984, $168 billion of external debt was rescheduled.

Although external financing available to LDCs declined significantly in the late 1980s, there were no cases of sovereign default. Because most LDC debt is government debt, default is a government decision, known as *sovereign default*. While the government is not subject to legal remedy, such default can be costly in several ways: Creditors of the sovereign defaulter may persuade their government to seize debtor assets located in their country; a defaulting country would be excluded from future borrowing on the international capital markets; and because defaulters would be unable to obtain trade credit, their ability to participate in international trade would be curtailed.[19]

Against these costs, the benefit of default is that the debtor escapes responsibility of paying interest and principal on the foreign debt.[20] This benefit rises as the country's income declines, because it becomes increasingly difficult to service and repay the debt out of lower income. But the decline in LDC incomes after 1982 did not lead to massive defaults because banks, helped by governments, acted collectively to continue loans to LDCs at a level sufficient to avert a default. The IMF often played a crucial role in this process: It coordinated the effort, assessed LDC domestic policies, and imposed stabilization programs as a condition of further loans. Continued lending has taken the forms of *rescheduling* and extension of new credits.[21]

Possible Solutions   The key to the solution of the debt problem is an overhaul of domestic economic policy in the LDCs themselves, including the introduction of fiscal and monetary discipline, realistic exchange rates, and proper economic incentives. Among other things, these policies may help restore confidence and induce repatriation of the capital that had fled abroad. Equally important is the need for robust growth in the United States, Europe, and Japan, which would increase imports from the LDCs; and

---

[19] See B. Eichengreen, "Historical Research on International Lending and Debt," *Journal of Economic Perspectives*, spring 1991, 149–170.

[20] Some scholars suggest (and others dispute) that the debt overhang is very harmful for two reasons. First, high debt-service payments require high tax rates that discourage capital formation and the repatriation of flight capital. Second, the government is the main maker of debt-service payments in most of the heavily indebted countries, and its payments figure in its budget. Hence, they can prevent a devaluation from improving the trade balance, because a devaluation raises the domestic-currency cost of servicing foreign-currency debt, thereby increasing the budget deficit, raising the growth of the money supply, and raising the inflation rate. Therefore, debtors must use less efficient methods to produce the trade surpluses required to make debt-service payments. These income-depressing effects raise the probability of default. Conversely, a debt-reduction program will raise income, reduce the probability of default, and increase the market-value of the debt.

[21] Professor S. Edwards provides an evaluation of the IMF role in "The IMF and the Developing Countries: A Critical Evaluation," *Carnegie-Rochester Conference on Public Policy*, November 18–19, 1988.

reduction of interest rates,[22] which alleviates the burden of servicing the debt. Finally, the industrial countries must keep their markets open to the exports from the LDCs, avoiding import restrictions on traditional LDC exports such as textiles and footwear. For only by mounting trade surpluses can the LDCs service their external debt. And all the while it is necessary to keep resources flowing to the LDCs to help carry out the growth enterprise, and to reduce their debt-servicing burden at the same time.[23]

Indeed, it is because many LDCs improved their domestic economic performance that the problem lost some of its urgency. It certainly disappeared from the financial headlines in the 1990s. Many of the indebted nations adopted market-oriented strategies, accompanied by fiscal and monetary disciplines,[24] and their growth rates exceeded those of the industrial countries. Their exports expanded rapidly, and private capital resumed its flow into Latin America and Asia. Creditor banks in the United States and elsewhere have considerably increased their reserves against loans to LDCs. Consequently the danger of collapse of major banks, and the attendant threat to stability of the financial system, has been removed. And finally, various devices have been employed to reduce the burden of debt servicing. They include swapping debt for equity ownership in enterprises of the debtor country and selling debt instruments for cash on a "secondary market" at a fraction of their book values.[25] Such techniques were employed in a January 1990 pact between the United States and Mexico.[26]

---

[22] However, the needs of East-European reconstruction in the 1990s raised the demand for capital around the world.

[23] For discussion of the debt problem and possible solutions, see Symposium on Developing Country Debt, with papers by K. Rogoff, P. Kenen, J. Sachs, J. Bulowa, and J. Eaton, in the *Journal of Economic Perspectives,* winter 1990, 3–56; papers by A. Krueger, S. Fisher, and R. Heller on "The International Debt Crisis," *American Economic Review,* May 1987, 159–75; *IMF Survey,* November 25, 1985, June 27, 1988, July 11, 1988, November 14, 1988, January 8, 1990, and January 20, 1990; articles by R. Cline, K. Griffin, M. Blackwell and S. Nocera, and P. Regling in *Finance and Development,* June 1988; and by B. Nowzad in *Finance and Development,* March 1990.

[24] See E. Truman, "U.S. Policy on the Problems of International Debt," *Federal Reserve Bulletin,* November 1989; and International Trade Commission, *Economic Review,* February 1990.

[25] Here are some particular methods used or proposed: In a debt buyback, the debtor country repurchases the debt at a discount, using cash. In an exit bond swap, the debtor country exchanges the currency debt for a new bond, usually carrying a lower interest rate or a lower principal repayment. In a debt-equity swap, the debtor country repurchases the debt using local currency, which is to be earmarked for an investment within the debtor country. Because it may involve the creation of new money, this method can be inflationary. Finally, in a debt-for-nature swap, a conservation group repurchases some of the country's debt and swaps it back for local currency bonds. The interest from the bonds is then designated for funding domestic conservation programs.

[26] The Mexican agreement covers $48.5 billion of medium-term and long-term government bank debt—about half the country's total foreign obligations. Banks were offered three choices: Reduce by 35 percent Mexico's debt principal outstanding by accepting discounted new Mexican government bonds; cut their interest payments by 35 percent by taking bonds with lower rates; or lend the country funds equal to 25 percent of their present holdings of Mexican government medium-term and long-term debt to be paid over the next three years. Most banks chose the first two options. Mexico also embarked on policies to reduce domestic inflation, improve the performance of the economy, and attract direct foreign investment.

But in many instances the debt problem lingers on. About 60 countries, most of them low-income but some in the middle-income category, are in arrears on debt payments.[27] In 1997 the IMF announced further measures to assist these countries.

The Mexican Currency Crisis of December 1994

One of the main debtor countries is Mexico. At the end of 1994 it experienced a financial crisis which required the assistance of the international community, led by the United States. This section explores briefly the causes of that crisis.

At the end of 1987 Mexico introduced a stabilization program consisting of tight fiscal and monetary policy, as well as liberalization of international trade and of the financial sectors and other elements. The peso-dollar exchange rate was used as a nominal anchor: it was held fixed in 1988, and subsequently allowed to depreciate slightly at preannounced rates. As a result of these measures inflation declined from triple-digit to single-digit levels, investments mushroomed, capital inflow increased, and the economy boomed during 1988–93.

But several events converged in 1994 to disrupt this progress. On the political side, an uprising in southern Mexico and the assassination of two important political figures undermined confidence in the government. On the economic side, not only did monetary policy become too lax; but because of the reasonably stable exchange rate and an inflation rate higher than that of the United States, the peso appreciated by 60 percent in real terms, undermining the country's competitive position. As a result the current account deficits grew to unsustainable levels. Confidence in the Mexican peso declined sharply, leading to massive outflow of capital. Mexican international reserves dropped precipitously from $25 billion to $6 billion.

Given Mexico's geographical proximity to the United States, the crisis drew the close attention of American policy makers. The United States organized a $50 billion rescue package, of which $20 billion were in the form of a U.S. government loan guarantee, and the remainder was standby credits from the IMF and the Bank of International Settlement. For its part, Mexico adopted tight fiscal and monetary policy and devalued the peso from $1 = 4 peso in December 94 to about $1 = 8 peso in 1996. The domestic measures threw the economy into a recession with declining output, rising unemployment, and reduced living standards. On the other hand, exports rose by 35% between 1995 and 1996 because of the depreciation coupled with the domestic contraction. The improvement in the country's external position plus the backing of the international community restored confidence in the Mexican economy. By 1996–97 Mexico was again able to borrow on the

---

[27]See UNCTAD, *World Development Report, 1993;* UNCTAD *Bulletin,* September–October 1993, 11; and *IMF Survey,* July 15, 1996.

private financial markets, it repaid the loans of the rescue package, its international reserves stabilized, and the economy began to grow again.

While this episode appears to have had a happy ending, the international community is concerned about its possible occurrence in other countries. Consequently, the IMF enhanced its financial surveillance around the globe, and created a special $28 billion credit line for emergency lending.

For updated material please see Chapter 19, "The Global Financial Crisis of 1997–99," beginning on page 500.

Summary

This chapter reviews 125 years of international financial history. That includes two periods of fixed exchange rates: the gold standard (1870–1914), when all currencies were pegged to gold; and Bretton Woods (1944–1973), when all currencies were anchored to the U.S. dollar. The interwar period was a disorderly era in international finances, reflecting the Great Depression that buffeted the world economy.

Following the breakdown of Bretton Woods, the system consisted of a mixture of floating rates, fixed rates, and jointly floating rates. It weathered well the international currency disturbances of the 1970s and 1980s. The distinguishing characteristic of the 1980s was the rise and subsequent decline in the exchange value of the dollar resulting from the monetary-fiscal policy mix in the United States. This marked the emergence of large American trade deficits that continued into the 1990s.

Another characteristic of the 1980s was the emergence of external debt crisis of the LDCs. It was partly an outgrowth of internal economic mismanagement by the LDCs themselves and partly a result of forces in the global economy over which they had no control. The issue was largely resolved by the 1990s, as many LDCs improved their economic performance, and ways were found to alleviate the debt burden. While the problem lingers in Africa and elsewhere, it certainly disappeared form the financial headlines, as the heavy burden in the international banking system was lifted. However, at the end of 1994, Mexico sustained a serious currency crisis, from which it appears to have recovered by 1997.

In the early 1990s, the U.S. trade, as well as current account, deficits continued, exacerbated in the mid-1990s by differential income growth between the United States and its trading partners. The EU has undergone a financial crisis triggered by a rise in German interest rates. Finally, the transition economies of eastern Europe are being gradually integrated into the international system.

While this volume brings the reader up to 1997 in issues of international trade and finance, the world does not remain at a standstill. But the analytical tools developed in the book will enable the student to keep up with future events as they unfold.

Important
Concepts

Gold standard

Rules of the game

Sterling area

Bretton Woods

Dollar shortage

Dollar glut

Smithsonian Agreement

Petrodollars recycling

U.S. budgetary and trade deficits

Plaza Accord

LDC debt

Review
Questions

1. Compare and contrast the functioning of the gold standard with that of Bretton Woods.

2. What was the Smithsonian Agreement, and what led to the breakdown of Bretton Woods?

3. Discuss two problems of the contemporary world financial scene.

4. In 1984 Mexico and Brazil (two principal debtor nations) experienced a resurgence in exports.
    a. How is this related to the U.S. recovery?
    b. Would a strong recovery in all OECD countries help to alleviate the debt problem? If so, how?
    c. How did the 1986 decline in world interest rates affect the LDC debt position?

5. In what sense was the U.S. trade deficit of the mid-1980s a macroeconomic phenomenon? How was it related to the fiscal and monetary policy mix in the United States and abroad? In what sense did the capital account drive the current account in the 1980s?

6. Did the system of floating exchange rates lead to national independence in the pursuit of monetary policy?

7. Stimulating the European and Japanese economies would help alleviate the U.S. trade deficits and the LDCs debt problems. Why?

8.   Define the following terms:

  • Pass-through of exchange rate changes
  • Sovereign default
  • Hysteresis
  • Debt rescheduling

  Explain how each term relates to either the U.S. trade deficit or the LDC debt.

9.   How do you explain the long lag in the response of U.S. trade flows to the depreciation of the dollar?

10.   Explain the causes of the LDC debt problem.

11.   "While the emergence of large U.S. trade deficits in the 1980s was mainly a result of relative price effects, the widening of the deficit in the mid-1990s was mainly a result of relative income effects." Explain.

12.   What major financial event occurred in Europe in the 1990s?

Bibliography

Because extensive readings are contained in footnotes throughout the book, this bibliography is limited to sources of books, supplementary readers, statistical sources, and official reports.

BOOK SOURCES

Instructors wishing to assign a book review on policy matters can consult:

1. A wide variety of titles available from the Institute for International Economics, 11 Dupont Circle, Washington, D.C. 20036, phone: (202) 329-9000, fax: (202) 328-5432.
2. OECD publications that can be secured through the OECD Publications Office, 2001 L St. N.W., Suite 700, Washington, D.C. 20036-4910, phone: 1 (800) 456-6323; fax: (202) 785-0350.
3. The Council on Foreign Relations Publications, 58 East 68th Street, New York, N.Y. 10021, phone: (212) 734-0400; fax: (212) 861-2759.

SUPPLEMENTARY READERS

Instructors wishing to supplement the text with relevant articles can consult:

King, Phillip (ed.). *International Economics and International Economic Policy: A Reader.* New York: McGraw-Hill, 1990.

Kolb, Robert (ed.). *The International Finance Reader.* Miami: Kolb Publishing Co., 1993. Covers topics in international finance.

For more advanced topics, see:

Jones, R. and P. Kenen (eds.). *Handbook of International Economics.* North-Holland, 1984. Each chapter is devoted to a comprehensive survey of a topic in international trade or finance, and contains an extensive bibliography.

Sources of Country and Regional Statistics

Following are the most widely used sources of data used in international economics.

United States

U.S. Department of Commerce. *Survey of Current Business* (monthly).

Federal Reserve Board. *Federal Reserve Bulletin* (monthly).

Council of Economic Advisors. *Economic Report of the President* (annually).

U.S. International Trade Commission. *Operation of the Trade Agreements Program* (annually), as well as reports on: the Effects of Antidumping and Countervailing Duty; Effect of Significant U.S. Import Restraints; and Impact of the Uruguay Round Agreement on the U.S. Economy and Industries.

Office of the United States Trade Representative. *Annual Reports.*

Industrial Countries

U.S. Department of Commerce. *International Economic Indicators* (quarterly).

OECD. *Quarterly National Accounts Bulletin* (quarterly); *Main Economic Indicators* (monthly and annually); *Foreign Trade.*

All Countries

IMF. *International Financial Statistics* (monthly); *World Economic Outlook* (annually).

World Bank. *World Development Report* (annually); *World Atlas* (annually).

WTO. *International Trade* (annually).

IMF, World Bank, and WTO. *Annual Reports.*

United Nations. *Monthly Bulletin of Statistics.*

United Nations Economic Commissions. *Reports about the Main Regions of the World.*

UNCTAD. *Handbook of International Trade and Development Statistics; World Investment Report* (annually).

Index

The Euro Is Coming

A NEW CURRENCY FOR EUROPE

On January 1, 1999, the European Monetary Union (EMU) was inaugurated, leading to the introduction of a European currency. And on July 1, 2002, eleven European currencies will cease to exist and be replaced by one common currency called the Euro (signed €). There will no longer be German marks, French francs, or Italian liras—just Euros, or rather "Euros and cents." During the 1999-2002 transitional period, the Euro will not be a circulating currency, but people and companies are able to write contracts and settle accounts either in Euros or in national currencies, which have a fixed conversion rate to the Euro. The 11 countries included in the Euro-zone, also known as Euroland, are Germany, France, Spain, Italy, Portugal, Belgium, Luxembourg, Holland, Ireland, Austria and Finland. By year 2002, American tourists visiting Europe will no longer have to exchange currencies at every border. And American corporations doing business in Europe will be spared the transaction costs of exchanging currencies. Introduction of the Euro will have profound effects on Europe, as well as on world finance, including the position of the U.S. dollar.

Establishing a common currency is not merely a matter of running a common printing press. Because the common money will take over throughout the zone, Europe needs one central bank to control the quantity of Euros, set interest rates for Euroland, and otherwise conduct monetary policy. Therefore, a European central bank, located in Frankfurt, Germany, began functioning on January 1, 1999, and the existing national central banks (like the Bundesbank or the Bank of France) became branches. The Bank's President—now Mr. Duisenberg of the Netherlands—and five members of the Executive Board are appointed for a one eight-year term and are supposed to be free of political pressures. Their assigned task is to stamp out inflation and keep it down. Thus, the European System of Central Banks is organizationally similar to the Federal Reserve System in the U.S.

Countries participating in the Euro-zone must give up two powerful instruments of economic policy:

1. *Monetary policy.* No longer is the central bank of each country able to adjust money supply and interest rates to deal with the country's inflation and/or unemployment rates. Rather, a uniform policy applies to the entire zone. Indeed, in December 1998, the central bank set Europe's base-line interest rate at a common level of 3 percent. And in early 1999, that base line rate was reduced to 2.5 percent in an effort to cope with the economic stagnation on the continent.

2. *Exchange rate policy.* No longer is each country able to change the exchange value of its currency relative to that of other European currencies (e.g., the franc relative to the mark) to meet its own economic objectives. Instead, one "French Euro" is worth one "German Euro," in much the same way that one New York dollar equals one California dollar. Exchange rate risk between the eleven former currencies, and hence a forward exchange market between them, will disappear.

Fiscal policy is also constrained by a "stability pact" that limits the ability of each member country to run a budgetary deficit in excess of 3 percent of its GDP. Finally, all Euro countries are also members of a customs union, the European Union, and thereby gave up the right to pursue independent commercial policy. In terms of their ability to exercise economic policy, European countries will become akin to American states or Canadian provinces.

The idea of a common currency had been bandied about in the EC over the past 30 years, until it was crystalized in the Delors Report of 1988 and the treaty for a European Monetary Union (EMU) signed in Maastricht, The Netherlands, in 1992. Much national sovereignty is relinquished with the advent of the Euro. Partly for this reason not all members of the European Union (formerly the European Community) agreed to join the EMU. In particular, the U.K. and Sweden opted to stay out at least for now and permit their currencies to fluctuate against the Euro in response to market conditions. Denmark also decided not to join. A Danish accession will require a public referendum, but the Danish Kroner will be pegged to the Euro. It is widely believed that once the British decide to join, Denmark and Sweden would follow suit. Greece may join in the year 2001. Finally, the EU will consider applications for accession to the Union from several East European countries. While they will not now adopt the Euro, they might peg their currencies to it.

Against the loss of sovereignty and the substantial transitional costs, members of the Euro-zone expect to reap substantial long run benefits from sharing one currency. Prices across the continent will be expressed in one currency, making comparisons between countries instantaneous. This transparency will increase competition at both the wholesale and retail levels and contribute to price stability. Transaction costs in international trade will be reduced, and exchange risk will be eliminated. A single monetary policy by a politically independent central bank should also deliver price stability. The huge market of Euroland would contribute to certainty for investment, promoting capital formation, and accelerating growth throughout the continent.

HURDLES CROSSED

What hurdles did each European country have to cross to become a member of the EMU? These were spelled out in the EMU treaty of 1992: A country had to keep its exchange rate stable for at least two years prior to 1998, lower its inflation rate to within 1 1/2 percentage point and its interest rate to within 2 percentage points of that of the three lowest inflation countries in the EU, bring its general government deficit to under 3 percent of its GDP and its public debt (the cumulative deficits over all years) to under 60 percent of its GDP.

Combined, these are known as the "Convergence Criteria." The last two, dealing with a country's fiscal position, placed candidate countries in a "straitjacket": they had to employ contractionary policies even when their economic conditions called for expansion. While 14 European countries brought their annual deficits to under 3 percent of GDP by 1997, several countries, notably Belgium and Italy, had a public debt well in excess of 60 percent of GDP (121 percent in the case of Belgium and Italy). So this and other criteria were fudged to require "reasonable progress" towards the stated objective. The budget criterion was largely met by eleven countries, mainly because Europe's economic growth was picking up after years of stagnation, causing a reduction in budget deficits. Only Greece was excluded from Euroland because it failed to meet all or most of the criteria. It still hopes to join by year 2001 as it moves towards the common goal. Britain, Denmark, and Sweden met the criteria but chose to stay out. Table 18.1 shows the critical dates leading to the introduction of the European Monetary Union and the Euro.

TABLE 18.1   *Countdown to EMU*

Year	Date	Event
1998	May 2–3	European summit chooses Euro members, fixes bilateral exchange rates
	May/June	European Central Bank established
	December 31	Conversion rates into Euro fixed
1999	January 1	EMU begins
2001	January 1	Greece expected to join
2002	January 1	Euro notes and coins introduced
2002	Jan. 1 – June 30	Euros circulate along with national currencies
2002	July 1	National notes and coins cease to be legal tender

Hurdles To Cross

At least in the early years, Euroland may experience rough sailing. To see why, compare the European countries with American states. Suppose a coal producing state becomes depressed because of a sharp reduction in the national and global demand for coal. Production will decline and unemployment will rise. But three features of the U.S. economy will mitigate this effect: (a) the Federal government will provide fiscal transfers to the state in the form of unemployment compensation, retraining grants, welfare benefits, and possible assistance to impacted firms and communities; (b) workers and capital will migrate to other, booming states in search of other opportunities; and (c) some workers remaining in the state will accept a cut in pay to maintain their employment.

All three mechanisms are absent in Europe: (a) Fiscal transfers within the European Union are very limited in size, and there is little enthusiasm for an expansion of EU budget to allow for large fiscal transfers. (b) Despite the removal of legal restrictions to migration within the EU, there is little labor mobility among member countries. Language and cultural barriers as well as tradition may account for that. Indeed labor mobility is limited even within countries, although it increased somewhat lately. (c) Wages in Europe are notoriously rigid.

Each European country can still use fiscal policy as a countercyclical measure. But even here the maneuvering room is limited by the EMU: its so called "stability pact" requires that a country's fiscal deficits in future years be limited to 3 percent of its GDP, or else it would be subject to a heavy fine. The thinking behind this is the notion that large deficits will necessarily weaken the currency. Instead, this would make it impossible to combat a recession with fiscal expansion, and it may even counter the effects of the built-in or "automatic stabilizers."

While the "convergence criteria" attempt to make European countries uniform in some respects, and perhaps place them on equal competitive footing, they do nothing to deal with the root causes of Europe's problem: labor and product markets rigidities. These rigidities, in part a result of government regulations, go a long way towards explaining the fact that Europe's unemployment is over 10 percent compared to 4.4 percent in the U.S. It is impossible to predict whether the EMU will help bring about the kind of structural change that would lower unemployment. But a recession in any one country would become more troublesome than in previous years because individual countries would lack the policy tools to deal with stagnant economic conditions.

In 1998, a new uncertainty was introduced by the political sea change in Europe: Most countries, and in particular Germany, elected left-of-center governments. They may apply political pressure on the new Central Bank to pursue expansionary monetary policy (namely, expand money supply and lower interest rates) in order to combat the double-digit unemployment. In doing so, they may force the Bank to compromise its exclusive focus on stable prices dictated by its charter and indeed may modify the charter itself to incorporate an employment objective as well. They may also wish to expand fiscally even in violation of the stability pact. It remains to be seen whether the politically independent central bank would yield to pressure.

First Steps (January–June 1999)

While the long-run prospects for the Euro may be bright, developments in the first half year since its introduction were somewhat disheartening to Europeans. To some extent, they reflected the loss of sovereignty alluded to above. The Euro (signed €) began at a dollar exchange rate of 1€ = $1.18. From that, it declined gradually to 1€ = $1.04 by June of 1999. In less than six months, the Euro lost 12 percent of its exchange value against the dollar, moving gradually towards the economically meaningless but politically explosive level of parity (1€ = $1). This development disappointed many European observers and strengthens the hands of Euro-skeptics in the U.K.—those who oppose giving up the sterling for the Euro.

But in and of itself, the decline of the Euro's real exchange rate is no calamity and may be a temporary phenomenon. Its positive value lies in strengthening the competitive position of European enterprises relative to their American counterparts.

What may be worrisome are the possible reasons for the decline. While no consensus has developed, most experts attribute it to the continued stagnation of Europe, especially of Germany, relative to the prolonged period of strong non-inflationary growth in the United States. Although some small European countries are growing at above 3 percent per year, German growth rate remains under 2 percent per year, while that of France is at 2 percent. In turn, this is a result of rigidities in their labor and product markets. Additionally, Italy applied for and was granted permission by the EU to increase its annual budgetary deficit from 2 to 2.4 percent of its GDP. While this is still below the magic number of 3 percent, it is said to undermine confidence in the Euro.

But to the extent that the differential U.S.–EU growth rates is a cyclical phenomenon, it may reverse itself in time, especially after the beneficial effects of the Euro manifest themselves. The long-run prospects for the Euro are much brighter, although they may appear only after a decade or two. And these have implications for the position of the dollar in the international currency system. We turn to them next.

Implications for the U.S. Dollar

For fifty years since the war the international currency system was based on the U.S. dollar: Nearly half of the foreign-held bank deposits are denominated in dollars; half of world trade is invoiced in dollars; the dollar features in nearly half of the $1 trillion per day foreign exchange transactions; and it accounts for 63 percent of official foreign currency reserves (held by central banks) in the world. The last figure compares to 14 percent of official reserves held in German marks and 7 percent in Japanese yen. For a variety of reasons the dollar is ideally suited for this central role: It is backed by a productive, strong, and non-inflationary economy—by far the largest in the world. It possesses a huge and diversified capital market, including over $5 trillion in U.S. government debt in which foreign central banks can place their reserves. Its markets are free of controls, and its government is politically stable. These conditions (combined) do not exist in any other country. Japan, the second largest economy in the world, is one-third the size of the U.S., and its government has been reluctant to create a "yen zone" in the far east where the yen would serve as the reserve currency.

A new currency arrived on the global scene, created by 11 sovereign governments rather than by one. Their combined GDP is similar to that of the U.S., although if currencies are converted to dollars by PPP rather than market exchange rate, the U.S. is considerably larger. Likewise, the two regions' share in world trade is of the same magnitude and Europe has a vast and diversified capital market making the Euro a worthy rival to the dollar as an international transactions and reserve currency. Gradually, as markets become familiar with the Euro, it will come to serve as a transaction and reserve currency alongside the dollar. But the process may take a decade or two.

At its inception on December 31, 1998, one Euro equaled in value one European Currency Unit, or ECU, which is a weighted average of the EU currencies. And, in turn, that was worth $1.18. While the Euro lost 12 percent of its dollar exchange value in its first 6 months, the question before us now relates to a period spanning a decade or two: In the long run will the Euro develop as a strong currency relative to the dollar? Assuming that the European Central Bank would conduct a tight monetary policy, that international portfolio managers would switch some of their holdings from dollars to Euros, and that European countries may sell some of their "excess" dollar reserves, the Euro should appreciate relative to the dollar. That reasoning is buttressed by the fact that the Euro-countries run surpluses while the U.S. sustains large deficits on the external current account (exports minus imports of goods and services, and earnings on foreign investment).

As an example of changing portfolios, suppose that in year 2010 Japan decides to convert a large part of its $250 billion of official reserves into Euro-denominated assets. If its reserves are now held in U.S. treasury securities, it would sell some of those, thereby lowering their price and raising U.S. interest rates. Then when the dollars are sold for Euros, the dollar would depreciate. Once placed in European bonds, their prices would rise and European interest rates would decline. Thus, interest and exchange rate variations would absorb the impact of the transfer.

TABLE 18.2	Euroland and United States Comparisons	

	Euroland	United States
Population (millions)	300	267.7
% share of world GDP (1996)	20.7%	20.4%
% share of world export (1996)	15.2%	14.7%
GDP growth	2.4%	3.8%
Budget imbalance as % of GDP	−2.8%	0

But the reflections on the future changes in the exchange value of the dollar are mere conjectures. The mix of fiscal and monetary policies on the two sides of the Atlantic will determine the relative strength of the two currencies. And that cannot be predicted.

In past years, the U.S., and only the U.S., was able to run unlimited external deficits as the rest of the world piled up dollar assets and counted them as reserves. By being able to borrow in its own currency (the dollar), the U.S. has become the world's largest debtor with equanimity. But that will become more difficult once the Euro becomes an accepted global currency. The U.S. would be forced to narrow its deficits while Europe would develop current account deficits to supply the world with Euro reserves. And that may increase protectionist pressures in Europe.

Not only a central bank, such as the Bank of Japan in the above example, can switch from dollar assets to Euro-denominated assets. Private portfolio managers can also change the composition of their portfolios. The example above shows that with two global currencies, decisions by third countries can affect monetary conditions in the two financial centers. Conversely, large swings in the dollar-Euro exchange rates can create problems for third countries depending on the pattern of their trade and the currency composition of their reserves. In short, the international currency system may become more difficult to manage with two world currencies functioning along side each other where historically there was only one.

While the original framers of the Common Market aspired to political integration, it is the 64,000 Euro question whether the introduction of the Euro will ever lead to a political union in Europe.

The Global Financial Crisis of 1997–99

THE FACTS: AFFLICTED COUNTRIES IN ASIA

In the second half of 1997 the world became painfully aware of a severe financial and economic crisis that beset five Southeast Asian countries: South Korea, Thailand, Malaysia, the Philippines, and Indonesia. The last four of these are part of the Association of Southeast Asian Nations (ASEAN) trading block that aspires to form a free trade area in the future. South Korea has advanced to a point of being admitted to the OECD group of industrial countries. Next in level of development are Thailand and Malaysia, while the least developed of the group are Indonesia and the Philippines. Indonesia is the fifth largest country in the world with a population of 200 million spread over many islands. It suffered from extreme corruption and nepotism during the many years of President Suharto's regime. Finally, it is an oil exporter and, like many countries exporting oil and materials, was buffeted by the recent decline in their prices. Its crisis runs deepest of the five countries—it is now suffering from a depression coupled with 75 percent inflation.

For thirty years prior to 1997 these economies grew at a rate of 6–10 percent per year—the highest growth rate in the world. They were dubbed "the Asian Tigers," and their performance was enshrined by the title "the Asian Miracle." They also weathered well the debt crisis of the 1980's, which profoundly affected Latin America. By contrast, their growth rate turned negative to the tune of 5–7 percent in 1998 (except in Indonesia where the decline in real GDP was in excess of 13 percent), signaling a deep recession, rising unemployment, and a sharp rise in poverty. In the case of Mexico, one year after the collapse of the peso in December 1994, the economy was growing strongly. In contrast, the afflicted Asian economies remained in a recession the year after the crisis began. The crisis has been variably termed the Asian "meltdown," "catastrophe," "cyclone," and similar adjectives. "From the Asian miracle to the Asian debacle" became a common description of the situation in Southeast Asia. This crisis is unique in several respects. It was not accurately foreseen by anybody; it has no recent precedent in terms of cause, depth, and duration; and the prospects of immediate return to high economic growth are not good.

Intensifying the crisis is the fact that the Japanese economy—the nearby giant— has been stagnant for several years and is also facing a serious banking crisis of its own. Many of its banks are burdened by bad or non-performing loans that add up to half a trillion dollars—an amount equal to the "U.S. Savings and Loan" debacle of the 1980's—for an economy that is one-third the size of the U.S. By August 1998, the yen depreciated by 30–40 percent to 140 = $1, economic growth all but ceased, and unemployment grew. In July 1998, Japan elected Mr. Obuchi, a new prime minister who promised to solve the financial problems and also inject a large fiscal stimulus package consisting of tax cuts and an increase in public spending to stimulate growth. But the effect of such steps cannot be felt in 1998. While Japan itself has sufficient international reserve to withstand a "currency crisis" (namely, speculative withdrawal of funds from the country) and is experiencing large and growing trade surpluses, the fact that it is a significant market for Asian exports and is a major source of much investments and loans flowing into the region makes the Japanese stagnation a core problem in resuscitating Southeast Asia. Although Japan's stagnation is of different origin and nature than the problems besetting the aforementioned five Asian nations, their exports to Japan and capital flows from Japan (loans and direct investments) stagnate along with the Japanese economy. Japanese banks are the most heavily exposed to Asia.

Returning to the five afflicted nations, it was not just the real economy that plunged into a recession. The financial sector was buffeted even more than real output, and many observers believe that this was the root cause of the problem. Stock markets and other asset markets (including real estate) plummeted by up to 40 percent as did the exchange rates—the most important asset in an open economy. While most Southeast Asian currencies had been pegged to the dollar at a fixed rate, the crisis forced the floatation of these currencies and caused their subsequent depreciation. Table 19.1 shows that the extent of depreciation relative to the U.S. dollar over the second half of 1997 ranged from 39 to 83 percent.

Even in Singapore, a city-state not directly involved in the crisis but affected indirectly, its dollar depreciated by 19 percent.

CAUSES OF THE ASIAN CRISIS

At the root of the crisis is an age-old problem: Full currency convertibility (including, in particular, that of the capital account), fixed or targeted exchange rates, and independent monetary policy cannot co-exist. When they collide, a crisis results. This was at the root of many a currency crisis

TABLE 19.1			

Rates of Afflicted Asian Currencies

	Exchange Rate (currency units per $1)		Exchange Rate Change (in percent)
	July 1, 1997	**Jan. 24, 1998**	
Indonesian rupiah	$2,432.00	$14,800.00	–83.6%
Malaysian ringgit	2.52	4.58	–44.9
Thai baht	24.53	54.00	–54.6
Philippine peso	26.37	43.50	–39.4
Korean won	888.00	1,744.00	–49.1

Source: Manuel F. Montes, "The Currency Crisis in Southeast Asia," Singapore, Institute of Southeast Asian Studies, 1998, Table U-1. For the American investor in Asian stocks the currency depreciation compounded the losses incurred from the drop in the stock markets.

during the Bretton Woods era, as well as of the 1992 currency crisis in Europe. The latter episode forced the U.K. and Italy off the exchange rate mechanism of the European Monetary System (of fixed exchange rates), while other European countries either re-introduced currency controls or raised interest rates sky high, thereby sacrificing domestic monetary objectives. While the 1992 crisis was triggered by a rise in German interest rates drawing capital into Germany from other European countries, it came on the heel of capital account liberalization in Europe—a part of the Unified Market Program of the European Community (EC-92). In other words, with fixed exchange rates within the EC and free capital movement within Europe, an independent move by Germany to raise interest rates (for domestic reasons) brought a flood of capital into Germany from the rest of Europe. The U.K., Italy, Spain, and other countries could not withstand the withdrawal of funds and were forced either to re-impose currency controls or to abandon fixed exchange rates.

In the same manner, the Asian crisis erupted following the removal of restrictions on the *inflow and outflow* of capital in the five countries. Indeed, countries like China[1] or India, which retain capital-account controls, were not affected directly by the crisis (although those countries as well were affected indirectly as their exports to the afflicted countries declined). This has led some leading economists to *reconsider* their position that emerging countries should abolish control on the capital account of their international transactions as soon as possible—at the least, this step *should not be taken prematurely*. The five afflicted countries also maintained a fixed (or targeted) exchange rate—pegged mainly to the U.S. dollar—and each pursued independent monetary policies.

[1] Of course, China also has $140 billion in international reserves.

But the clash between the three objectives in the Asian case ran deeper than in earlier episodes in other countries. If that is so, then it is because the proximate causes that overlay the fixed exchange rates and free capital mobility were of serious magnitude. While there is no consensus on the complete list of these causes, most observers include the following:

1. Large inflows of short-term portfolio capital that could be withdrawn on short notice in case of a decline in confidence or for other reasons. Indeed the five afflicted countries sustained a "swing" of $105 billion: from an inflow of $93 billion in 1996 to an outflow of $12 billion in 1997.

2. Sizeable current account deficits, financed in large measure by large short-term capital inflows.

3. Very high ratios (up to 210 percent in the case of Korea) of short-term foreign liabilities to international reserves. In other words, unlike Japan, foreign reserves were not sufficient to withstand massive withdrawal of capital.

4. A relatively high proportion (14 to 19 percent) of non-performing loans to total outstanding loans of the banks. Namely, a domestic banking crisis, not unlike the "U.S. Savings and Loan" crisis of the 1980's, was also at the root of the problem. It destroyed confidence in the economy and made it impossible for banks to provide adequate credit even to reputable firms and sound consumers, credit being the lubricant needed in a market economy.

5. The burst of the "bubble economy." Much capital, domestic and foreign, had been invested in the stock markets and real estate markets of the five countries, lifting asset values sky high—way above the levels justified by economic fundamentals. When domestic banks began to curtail and even call back loans and foreign investors began to withdraw their capital, these overpriced markets collapsed, causing a substantial reduction in people's wealth. Indeed, stock markets in the afflicted countries fell by up to 40 percent in less than a year.

6. In some cases *overvalued* (fixed) exchange rates contributed to the crisis, especially for countries pegged to the appreciating U.S. dollar.

Although these causes were present to varying degrees in all five countries, there was also a "contagion" effect as the crisis spread from one economy to another. It began in Thailand on July 2, 1997. Large scale withdrawal of capital forced the authorities to float the baht, and it depreciated quickly. On August 14, Indonesia floated the rupiah, and in a matter of a few months the crisis was present in all of the other three countries. Some observers attribute the contagion to a "herd instinct" of investors, coupled with expectations. As the Thai market caved in, financiers expected countries *with similar circumstances* to fall as well and started withdrawing their capital, causing self-realized expectations. This was contagion through financial markets: Once confidence in one country is undermined, investors tend to lose confidence in, and remove their capital from, other "emerging markets."

It is commonly (but not universally) believed that the real economy in at least some of the afflicted countries was solid, and that domestic fiscal and monetary policies prior to the crisis were sound. These countries avoided budget deficits, and some even ran significant surpluses, while monetary policy was neutral or even restrictive, avoiding undue expansion in money supply. This is in contrast to earlier crises episodes in other parts of the world where sizeable fiscal deficits were the rule rather than the exception.

So the crisis in Southeast Asia had its origin in the financial sector. If so, by what channels did it spread to the real economy so as to cause such a deep and prolonged recession? The real GDP of Thailand, South Korea, and Malaysia shrunk by 5–7 percent within a year after the crisis began, with Korean unemployment rising to 7 percent, while the Indonesian economy (the extreme case) contracted by 13–15 percent. The following channels suggest themselves, although others may be present:

1. A strong *negative wealth effect* on consumption as the asset bubble bursts in the financial markets following the virtual collapse of stock markets in Asia. People feel poorer as the value of their assets decline, and, therefore, they cut their consumption expenditures thereby depressing the economy.
2. A negative effect on investment due to sharply lower stock prices (where stock sale is a means of raising money to finance investment), financial collapse, uncertainty, financial tightening, and perhaps high interest rates.
3. Possible negative effect of a credit "crunch" (e.g., rationing) on production and investment where credit becomes unavailable even to sound companies because lenders become exceedingly risk averse.
4. Currency depreciation increases the burden of foreign debt on companies as well as the government because debt denominated in foreign currency (mainly dollars) now costs more to service and repay in terms of the domestic currency. That undermines the position of banks and other potential lenders, and it also undercuts the liquidity and financial strength of the corporate sector and, with it, its ability to produce. On the other hand, currency devaluation should encourage exports by making them more competitive. But that has not happened in ASEAN because export companies were beset by debt and shortage of credit. They were not able to finance purchases of materials and capital goods

needed for production, so exports of some countries actually shrunk in 1998, a clear-cut supply-side effect.

EFFECTS ON OTHER COUNTRIES—CONTAGION

A crisis of that magnitude cannot fail to affect other countries in and out of the region. The exports of Singapore and even China declined and, with it, output. But the effect has spread far beyond Asia. In August 1998, a crisis erupted in Russia, Venezuela, and South Africa. Their currencies depreciated, stock markets plummeted, and Russia was forced to reschedule payments on foreign loans involving a partial default on its debt. The central bank suspended foreign currency trading, and the ruble depreciated by 80 percent by the end of August 1998, leading President Yeltsin to replace his government. In other words, the crisis spread to the political arena. What do Russia, Venezuela, and South Africa have in common? They are big exporters of oil and/or metals and rely on these products as a major source of foreign currency earnings. Because of the deep recession in the Asian countries (plus Japan), their demand for oil and raw materials declined, producing a sharp drop in global prices. Countries that rely on such exports suffer. Will their problem spread to Argentina, Brazil, Mexico, and beyond? The stock markets of these countries plummeted at the end of August 1998 (Colombia devalued its currency in September), and that may spread to the real economy. The flip side of this is that countries like the U.S. and Europe, which import materials, benefit from lower import prices—a factor that holds down inflation.

In sum, the crisis began in the financial sectors of the five Asian countries, from there it spread to their real sectors, and from there it moved to other countries. The contagion effect on other countries occurred both through the "real" sectors as exports to the afflicted countries declined and through the financial channel as investors lost confidence and withdrew funds even from sound economies. With respect to financial contagion, it might be noted that German banks are the ones most exposed in Russia, while Japanese banks have the greatest exposure in Asia, but U.S. banks are also exposed in both areas.

At this writing (in October 1998), the main concern of the international community has shifted to Brazil, by far the largest and most important country in Latin America. As the crisis began to spread to that country, a $30 billion bailout fund is being created, and domestic policies are adjusted to deal with contagion. But serious issues require immediate attention: Should its overvalued currency (the real) be devalued and then be permitted to float despite the attendant increase in the external debt burden? Should monetary and fiscal policies be tightened, perhaps creating a domestic recession? Should capital controls be used even at the cost of scaring away some investors? These are the tough decisions facing newly re-elected President Cardoso.

Effect on the U.S.

What about the U.S. economy? Can the U.S. continue to be an island of prosperity amid global turmoil?

In the first year of the crisis only specific pockets of the economy were directly affected as their exports to the afflicted countries declined. The farm sector is certainly suffering as are certain manufacturing industries that export heavily to Asia. Indirectly, U. S. exports to its most important market—Canada—declined as the Canadian economy stagnated and its exchange rate depreciated. This occurred partly because of a cut in Canada's exports to Asia and partly because of the global decline in raw materials and oil prices that can also be traced to the Asian crisis. (Australia is similarly affected with the exchange value of its currency dropping sharply.) As exports to the region diminished, the U.S. trade deficits mushroomed, and U.S. growth slowed down. Indeed, some of the slowdown in U.S. growth—from 5.6 percent in the first quarter to 1.6 percent in the second quarter of 1998—was attributed to the Asian crisis.[2] As it were, U.S. growth rate in 1997 was probably excessive in a sense that it was unsustainable without a rise in inflation, so the slowdown was welcome. Unemployment remained at the low level of around 4.5 percent.

In the U. S. there were two offsetting factors to the drop in exports through the middle of 1998. First, American consumers continued their spending spree. Second, there has been a large influx of capital from around the world, the U.S. being regarded as a "safe haven." Much of it was directed into the bond market, raising bond prices and lowering interest rates. That stimulated housing construction, home-related purchases, and other interest-sensitive activities. Also, as people refinance their mortgages at lower interest rates, they are left with additional funds for other purchases. Finally, the European economy is at long last emerging from its stagnation, and as it revives (albeit slowly), it would absorb more U.S. exports. And *Euroland* (the 11 countries that are about to adopt the common currency, the Euro) may also get a push from the introduction of the Euro.

But as the precarious situation in Asia is prolonged and perhaps spreads to Latin America, the adverse impact on the U.S. economy could become much more significant. Already in the Fall of 1998, there were signs of diminished consumer confidence and declines in retail sales. Concern also developed about a "credit crunch." As lenders became increasingly risk averse, potential borrowers could not sell bonds to raise money on the capital market. The Federal Reserve responded by lowering interest twice in a two-week

---

[2] Also to the GM strike.

period during September–October 1998—each time by one quarter percent. It was thereby signaling the market its intention to provide sufficient liquidity and to ward off a significant slowdown in the economy.

Indeed, the U.S. is well positioned to forestall a recession or even a major slowdown provided that fiscal and monetary policies are brought to bear in a timely fashion. On the fiscal side the Federal budgetary surplus (caused by a fully-employed economy) provides a cushion for a stimulative package, while on the monetary side the near absence of inflation offers room for expansionary policy. Strong economic growth continued into 1999, stimulated by high consumer demand, which in turn was triggered by rising stock prices (wealth effect).

Probably the most important thing that the U.S. and Europe can do for the world economy is maintain a satisfactory growth rate at home and keep their markets open to imports.

REMEDY?

What has been the response of the international community to this crisis? The International Monetary Fund (IMF) has offered "bailout" packages in the billions of dollars to each of the afflicted countries. Its task is complicated by the fact that Russia is in continuous financial, banking, and economic crisis, and President Yelstin faces political resistance to restructuring in the Russian Parliament (DUMA), which is dominated by communists.

In return for IMF bailouts, the countries were required to restructure their economies in various ways. Where a banking crisis is of paramount importance (e.g., Thailand), the monetary authorities undertook to close down failing institutions, strengthen those that can be recovered, and resolve the problem of bad debts. It is absolutely essential to have a well functioning banking and credit system as corporations must have access to credit to finance production. Certain restructuring may also be necessary in other parts of the economy. In all sectors there is a need to increase transparency: The investing public—domestic as well as foreign—must have full and accurate knowledge of corporate activities. In some countries, particularly Indonesia, corruption and nepotism have run rampant and need to be brought under control.

Beyond the structural changes, the IMF often requires restrictive fiscal and monetary policy. In other words, it demands that these countries "tighten their belt" and reduce their absorption of goods and services. This is what Secretary of State Albright meant by the need to "swallow bitter medicine." Presumably, the rationale here is the need to strengthen the fiscal position and to bring about a reduction in imports so as to improve the countries' external current account. But this requirement is a subject of dispute. Distinguished economists question the need for domestic contraction. Given the deep recessions and unemployment in the afflicted countries and the soundness of their fiscal position prior to the crisis, they advocate a Keynesian expansionary (rather than contractionary) policy. This is especially true in Korea where exports have expanded recently and there are slight signs of recovery. (Recently, the IMF changed its position in this regard with respect to certain Asian countries.) One thing needed for the expansion of exports is orderly access to domestic and foreign credit by the corporate sector. Almost as important as the maintenance of growth and open markets in the U.S. and Europe is the restoration of health to the Japanese economy. Only when growth resumes can Japan play a salutary role in Asia. That was the role played by the U.S. in the Mexican crisis of 1994. In October 1998, the Japanese Parliament took an important step in this direction by approving $500 billion in public money to rescue its banking system. The money is to be used for recapitalization of weak but viable banks, government purchase of shares in failed banks, and guaranteeing deposits at failed banks. Once implemented, this step, in addition to a fiscal expansionary package, should revive the economy. Japan may also offer $30 billion in direct aid to the afflicted Asian countries.

Also in October 1998, the U.S. Congress approved an $18 billion allocation for the IMF. This step will trigger contributions from other countries, augmenting IMF resources by $90 billion and making it possible to deal with future crises. Together with the Federal Reserve monetary expansion and Japan's banking legislation, this action should go part way towards restoring confidence. Indeed, some tentative progress may be on the horizon. In October 1998, the yen appreciated significantly against the dollar, and the currencies of Korea and Thailand appear to have stabilized at 40 percent below their pre-crisis values while interest rates in the two countries declined. But no one can predict with any confidence how long the crisis will last.

This brings us back to the root cause of this crises: Full currency convertibility, fixed exchange rates, and independent monetary policies cannot co-exist for long periods of time. In the long run, many countries may have to choose which feature they wish to drop. Thus, eleven European countries gave up independent monetary policy and establish a common currency and a common central bank. Likewise, Argentina and Hong Kong gave up such policy by operating "currency boards" rather than central banks: The amount of money in circulation is governed strictly by the country's dollar reserves. Other countries may choose capital controls. These need not be draconian in nature and may rely mainly on taxing short-term capital flows.[3] Finally, some countries may opt for floating exchange rates where the exchange rate would fluctuate within a wide band. The IMF is positioning itself to take preemptive action so as to prevent crises from developing.

---

[3]Controls come in various forms. Chile and Colombia have taxed short-term borrowing from abroad. Brazil once levied a 1% tax on foreign investment in its stock market to discourage short-term trading. Mexico, for a time, restricted the foreign-currency liabilities of its banks to 10% of their total loans. The Czech Republic levied a fee on all foreign-exchange transactions with banks. Malaysia now limits the amount of cash its citizens can carry out of the country.